Portugal

3rd Edition

Marc Rigole
Claude-Victor Langlois

Travel better, enjoy more

ULYSSES
Travel Guides

Authors
Marc Rigole
Claude-Victor Langlois

Editors
Daniel Desjardins
Stephane G. Marceau

Project Director
Pascale Couture

Project Coordinator
Jacqueline Grekin

English Editing
Tara Salman
Jacqueline Grekin

Page Layout
Typesetting
Anne Joyce
Elyse Marcoux
Tara Salman
Clayton Anderson
Visuals
Anne Joyce
Raphaël Corbeil

Translation
Danielle Gauthier
Stephanie Heidenreich
Tara Salman
Tracy Kendrick
Eric Hamovich
Terry Gillett
Emmy Pahmer
Sarah Kresh

Cartographers
Patrick Thivierge
Yanik Landreville

Computer Graphics
Stépanie Routhier

Artistic Director
Patrick Farei (Atoll)

Illustrations
Lorette Pierson
Marie-Annick Viatour
Myriam Gagné

Photography
Cover Page
Phillipe Renault
Inside Pages
M. Rigole
W. Buss
G. Sioen
T. Perrin

Distributors

AUSTRALIA: Little Hills Press, 11/37-43 Alexander St., Crows Nest NSW 2065, ☎ (612) 437-6995, Fax: (612) 438-5762

CANADA: Ulysses Books & Maps, 4176 Saint-Denis, Montréal, Québec, H2W 2M5, ☎ (514) 843-9882, ext.2232, 800-748-9171, Fax: 514-843-9448, info@ulysses.ca, www.ulyssesguides.com

GERMANY and **AUSTRIA**: Brettschneider, Fernreisebedarf, Feldfirchner Strasse 2, D-85551 Heimstetten, München, ☎ 89-99 02 03 30, Fax: 89-99 02 03 31, cf@brettschneider.de

GREAT BRITAIN and **IRELAND**: World Leisure Marketing, Unit 11, Newmarket Court, Newmartket Drive, Derby DE24 8NW, ☎ 1 332 57 37 37, Fax: 1 332 57 33 99, office@wlmsales.co.uk

ITALY: Centro Cartografico del Riccio, Via di Soffiano 164/A, 50143 Firenze, ☎ (055) 71 33 33, Fax: (055) 71 63 50

PORTUGAL: Dinapress, Lg. Dr. Antonio de Sousa de Macedo, 2, Lisboa 1200, ☎ (1) 395 52 70, Fax: (1) 395 03 90

SCANDINAVIA: Scanvik, Esplanaden 8B, 1263 Copenhagen K, DK, ☎ (45) 33.12.77.66, Fax: (45) 33.91.28.82

SPAIN: Altaïr, Balmes 69, E-08007 Barcelona, ☎ 454 29 66, Fax: 451 25 59, altair@globalcom.es

SWITZERLAND: OLF, P.O. Box 1061, CH-1701 Fribourg, ☎ (026) 467.51.11, Fax: (026) 467.54.66

U.S.A.: The Globe Pequot Press, 246 Goose Lane, Guilford, CT 06437-0480, ☎ 1-800-243-0495, Fax: 800-820-2329, sales@globe-pequot.com

OTHER COUNTRIES: Ulysses Books & Maps, 4176 Saint-Denis, Montréal, Québec, H2W 2M5, ☎ (514) 843-9882, ext.2232, 800-748-9171, Fax: 514-843-9448, info@ulysses.ca, www.ulyssesguides.ca

Canadian Cataloguing in Publication Data (see page 8)
© March 2000, Ulysses Travel Publications.
All rights reserved
Printed in Canada
ISBN 2-89464-245-8

Lo! Sintra's glorious eden intervenes
In variegated maze of mount and glen...
The horrid crags, by toppling convent crowned,
The cork-trees hoar that clothe the craggy steep,
The mountain-moss by scorching skies imbrowned,
The sunken glen, whose sunless shrubs must weep,
The tender azure of the unruffled deep,
The orange tints that gild the greenest bough,
The torrents that from cliff to valley leap,
The vine on high, the willow branch below,
Mixed in one mighty scene, with varied beauty glow.

Lord Byron
Childe Harold's Pilgrimage
Canto the First

Table of Contents

Portrait **11**
 Geography 12
 Fauna and Flora 12
 History 13
 Politics 26
 Population 26
 The Economy 29
 The Arts 32

Practical Information **39**
 Entrance Formalities 39
 Embassies and Consulates 39
 Tourist Information 41
 Getting to Portugal 44
 Transportation 46
 Money and Banking 48
 Mail and Telecommuications ... 49
 Language 50
 Climate and Packing 51
 Health 52
 Insurance 52
 Safety and Security 53
 Holidays 54
 Accommodations 55
 Restaurants 59
 Entertainment 61
 Gays and Lesbians 61
 Shopping 62
 Police and Emergencies 63
 Time Zone 63
 Electricity 63
 Women Travellers 63

Lisbon **65**
 Finding Your Way Around 67
 Practical Information 74
 Exploring 78
 Accommodations 123
 Restaurants 135
 Entertainment 150
 Shopping 158

Costa de Lisboa **163**
 Finding Your Way Around 163
 Practical Information 168
 Exploring 168
 Parks and Beaches 188
 Outdoor Activities 191
 Accommodations 194
 Restaurants 201
 Entertainment 209
 Shopping 210

Costa de Prata: the South **213**
 Finding Your Way Around 213
 Practical Information 216
 Exploring 216
 Parks and Beaches 232
 Outdoor Activities 233
 Accommodations 234
 Restaurants 240
 Entertainment 246
 Shopping 246

Costa de Prata: the North **249**
 Finding Your Way Around 250
 Practical Information 252
 Exploring 252
 Outdoor Activities 269
 Accommodations 270
 Restaurants 275
 Entertainment 280
 Shopping 282

Porto **283**
 Finding Your Way Around 285
 Practical Information 288
 Exploring 290
 Outdoor Activities 302
 Accommodations 302
 Restaurants 305
 Entertainment 309
 Shopping 310

Costa Verde **313**
 Finding Your Way Around 313
 Practical Information 316
 Exploring 316
 Outdoor Activities 330
 Accommodations 331
 Restaurants 337
 Entertainment 344

Montanhas **347**
 Finding Your Way Around 347
 Practical Information 350
 Exploring 350
 Outdoor Activities 363
 Accommodations 363
 Restaurants 366
 Entertainment 371
 Shopping 371

Alentejo **373**
 Finding Your Way Around 374
 Practical Information 376
 Exploring 376
 Outdoor Activities 392
 Accommodations 393
 Restaurants 401
 Entertainment 407
 Shopping 407

Algarve **409**
 Finding Your Way Around 411
 Practical Information 412
 Exploring 414
 Parks 431
 Outdoor Activities 431
 Accommodations 435
 Restaurants 443
 Entertainment 453
 Shopping 454

Glossary **455**

Index **463**

Thanks to: **Maria Helena Mora** (ICEP-Paris), **Mme Barlier** (ICEP-Paris), **Germano de Salles** (ICEP-Toronto), **Miguel Fialho de Brito** (ICEP-Paris), **Rita Alves Machado** (ENATUR), **Luísa Correia** (Região de Turismo do Algarve), **Maria Manuel Cardo Gantes** (Região de Turismo Planície Douradas), **Cristina Pedrosa** (Região de Turismo de Leiria), **José Pereira de Carvalho** (Região de Turismo de Setúbal), **Henrique Moura** (Região de Turismo Verde Minho), **António Santos** (Região de Turismo Verde Minho), **Gaspar da Costa** (Região de Turismo Dão Lafões), **António Carneiro** (Região de Turismo do Oeste), **Vítor Marques** (Zona de Turismo Guimarães), **António Magalhães** (Câmara Municipal de Guimarães), **António Cândido Esteves de Sousa** (Região de Turismo do Alto Minho), **António José Ceia da Silva** (Região de Turismo de São Mamede), **Jorge Manuel Patrão** (Região de Turismo Serra da Estrêla), **Mário João Machado** (Turismo Sintra), **Isabel Quintas** (ICEP-Delegação no Porto), **Pedro Cardoso** (Porto Convention Bureau), **Ana Luísa Tavares** (Porto Convention Bureau), **Manuel de Lemos** (Area Metropolitana do Porto), **Ana Paula Abreu** (Area Metropolitana do Porto), **Luís Hespanha** (Região de Turismo Costa do Oeste), **Vítor Carriço** (Turismo de Lisboa), **Candida Ventura** (Turismo de Lisboa), **Kátia Peres** (Parque das Nações). Finally, special thanks to **Judith Lefebvre**, **Rosette Rigole** and **Bruno Salléras** for their precious contribution.

Map Symbols

Car Ferry		Pousada	
Passenger Ferry		Tourist Information	
Funicular		Museum	
Airport		Archeological Ruins	
Train Station		Lookout	
Bridge		Beaches	
Highway		Post Office	
Road		Hospital	
Railway		Church	
Stairs		Bus Station	

List of Maps

Administrative Divisions 10
Albufeira 415
Alentejo 375
Algarve 413
Ancient Tourist Regions 42
Aveiro 253
Beja 377
Braga 319
Cascais 167
Coimbra 261
Coimbra's Surroundings 257
Costa de Prata: the North 248
Costa de Lisboa 165
Costa de Prata: the South 212
Costa Verde 315
Division of the World in the 15th and 16th Centuries 19
Évora 387
Faro 419
Guimarães 323
La Ribeira 297
Lagos 421
Lisbon and Surroundings 185
Lisbon 64
Lisbon Metro Map 71
Location of Tours 75
Montanhas 346
New Tourist Regions 43
Portimão (Downtown) 425
Porto (Downtown) 289
Porto 287
Portugal Wine Regions 31
Railroad Network 47
Setúbal 179
Sintra (Downtown) 174
Sintra 173
Table of Distances 38
Tavira 429
The Douro Valley 355
Tomar 227
Tour A: The Rossio and the Baixa 79
Tour B: The Castelo and the Alfama 85
Tour C: Graça and East of Lisbon 89
Tour D: Chiado and Bairro Alto 93
Tour D: The Bairro Alto 97
Tour E: Rato and Amoreiras 99
Tour F: Marquês Pombal, Saldanha and North Lisbon 101
Tour F (Enlargement) 103
Tour G: Restauradores and Liberdade 105
Tour G (Enlargement) 106
Tour H: Santa Catarina and Cais do Sodré 109
Tour I: Estrêla and Lapa 111
Tour I (Enlargement A) 112
Tour I (Enlargement B) 113
Tour J: Alcântara, Santa Amaro et Belém 115
Tour J: Belém 117
Tour K: Parque das Nações 121
Villa Nova de Gaia 299
Western Point (Algarve) 417
Where is Portugal? 9

Symbols

🛶	Ulysses's Favourite
☎	Telephone Number
⇄	Fax Number
≡	Air Conditioning
⊗	Fan
≈	Pool
ℜ	Restaurant
ℝ	Refrigerator
K	Kitchenette
⌂	Sauna
⊘	Exercise Room
tv	Colour Television
pb	Private Bathroom
sb	Shared Bathroom
bkfst	Breakfast

ATTRACTION CLASSIFICATION

★	Interesting
★★	Worth a visit
★★★	Not to be missed

HOTEL CLASSIFICATION

$	less than 6,500 ESC
$$	6,500 to 10,500 ESC
$$$	10,500 to 20,500 ESC
$$$$	20,500 to 25,000 ESC
$$$$$	25,000 ESC and over

The prices in the guide are for one room,
double occupancy in high season.

RESTAURANT CLASSIFICATION

$	less than 1,600 ESC
$$	1,600 to 3,200 ESC
$$$	3,200 to 5,000 ESC
$$$$	5,000 to 7,000 ESC
$$$$$	7,000 ESC and over

The prices in the guide are for a meal for one
person, not including drinks and tip.

All prices in this guide are in escudos, unless otherwise indicated.

Write to Us

The information contained in this guide was correct at press time. However, mistakes can slip in, omissions are always possible, places can disappear, etc. The authors and publisher hereby disclaim any liability for loss or damage resulting from omissions or errors.

We value your comments, corrections and suggestions, as they allow us to keep each guide up to date. The best contributions will be rewarded with a free book from Ulysses Travel Publications. All you have to do is write us at the following address and indicate which title you would be interested in receiving (see the list at the end of guide).

Ulysses Travel Guides
4176 Rue Saint-Denis
Montréal, Québec
Canada H2W 2M5
www.ulyssesguides.com
E-mail: info@ulysses.ca

Cataoguing

Canadian Cataloguing in Publication Data

Main entry under title :

Portugal

(Ulysses travel guide)
Includes index.
ISSN   1486-357X

ISBN   2-89464-245-8

1. Portugal - Guidebooks.   I. Series

DP516.P6713   914.6904'44   C99-301657-X

We acknowledge the financial support of the Government of Canada through the Book Publishing Industry Development Program (BPIDP) for our publishing activities.

We would also like to thank SODEC (Québec) for their financial support.

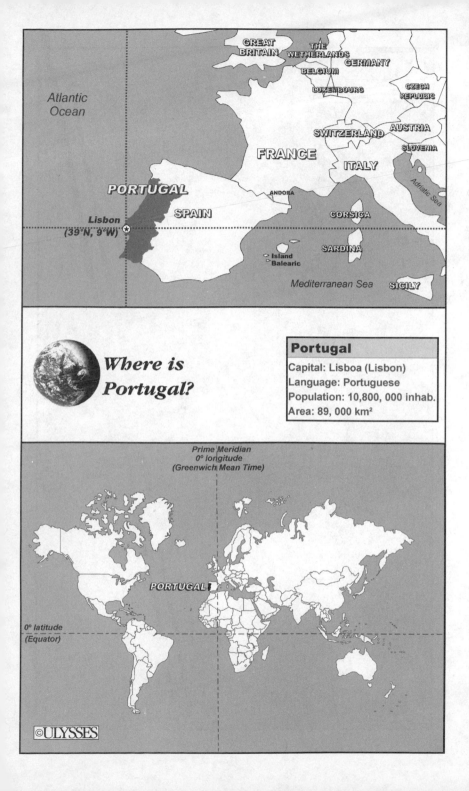

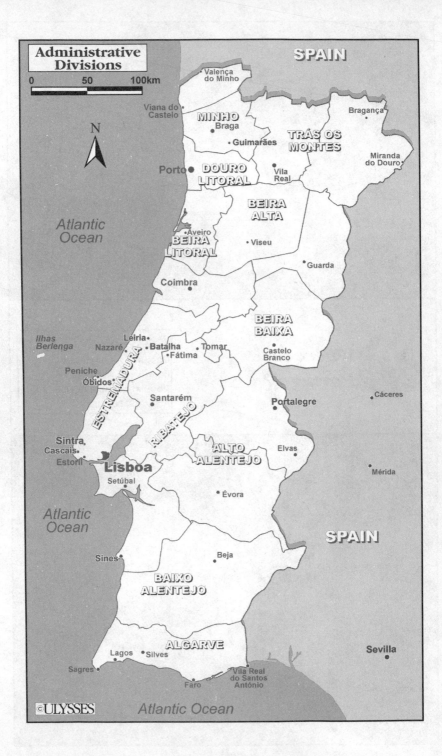

Portugal occupies a
special place in the history of the Western world.

Located at the edge of the known world for thousands of years, it contributed dramatically to the widening of that world's horizons. Sometimes it acted with the reckless zeal of a sorcerer's apprentice, like when it sent Catholic expeditions to expel demons from the Madeira archipelago, newly discovered by fishers (1420). Afterward, the country seemed to know no limits, sharing the world with Spain by papal decree and colonizing Brazil, a territory 10 times its size! Evidence of Portugal's unique role in history is found all over the country, making a trip here a veritable journey through the ages.

Broadly speaking, there are three ways to visit Portugal. The first option, increasingly popular with Europeans, is to enjoy a brief stay in Lisbon or Porto. To help make this type of trip memorable for travellers of different tastes and expectations, we have included detailed descriptions of both cities, as well as extensive lists of places to eat and stay in all price ranges. The second option, for which this guide should also prove extremely useful, is to visit the entire country, particularly those areas steeped in history, with their unique atmosphere. Since this type of trip is usually undertaken by car, we have sought out the country's loveliest roads, as well as the most charming accommodations and the best restaurants to suit every budget. Travellers who chose either of these options will find that Portugal has a lot to offer. This extraordinary country invites you on a veritable journey through Western history, back to a time when Portugal's every move had a profound effect on Europe. You will also have the chance to discover a unique art of living, perhaps even a new *movida*, in Lisbon and Porto. The third option is a seaside vacation, usually in the Algarve. We have provided descriptions of the most delightful places to visit in these mild climes, as well as a selection of the region's most charming restaurants and hotels.

Geography

Excluding the islands of Madeira and the Azores, which are not described in this guide, Portugal covers an area of 89,000km^2, and is bordered by Spain to the north and the east, and the Atlantic to the west and south. To reach the rest of Europe by land, you must pass through Spain. Portugal has always been linked to Europe, although it has often cut itself off from the continent; in World War II, for example, it was one of the few countries that remained neutral.

The only thing that sets Portugal apart geographically is its proximity to the ocean. Otherwise, it resembles the rest of the Iberian peninsula, which it shares with Spain due to a combination of historical circumstances and also, perhaps, because of the distinctive character of its inhabitants. The landscape and terrain, however, are more varied here than in Spain and change more often, even over short distances.

No part of this oblong country, which measures 560km from north to south, lies more than 220km from the sea. No peak reaches higher than 2000m; north of the Tagus river (Rio Tejo), the land is fairly hilly, made up mainly of old plateaus that shifted when the Pyrenees and the Alps were formed. There is still some seismic activity here, but nothing comparable to the earthquake that destroyed Lisbon in 1755. Generally speaking, the altitude increases from south to north, and the closer you get to Spain. The region south of the Tagus is relatively flat.

There are three major rivers in Portugal: the Tagus, which rises in Spain, (where it is known as the Tajo) and flows past Lisbon; the Douro (pronounced "*dooro*"), which runs alongside Porto; and the Minho, which marks the northern border between Portugal and Spain.

Flora and Fauna

In addition to its varied terrain, Portugal features a diverse range of soils and climates, and therefore a wide assortment of flowers. Long considered the garden of Europe, Portugal is home to more than 2,700 species of plants. It is the world's leading exporter of cork, the outer bark of the famous cork-oak, which can be found throughout the country, especially in the Alentejo, south of the Tagus. A number of species, such as the eucalyptus, have been successfully imported from Africa and South America. The maritime pine has also been widely planted as part of a major reforestation program, with the result that Portugal is much greener and boasts many more flowers than Spain (another contributing factor is the generally more humid Portuguese climate).

Portugal is often classified as a Mediterranean country, although it has no shore on that sea. As far as its climate, flora and fauna are concerned however, Portugal displays many Mediterranean characteristics.

Near Sintra, high mountains condense the rain coming in from the Atlantic, and a dense tropical and subtropical vegetation thrives in the mild, steady climate. The Algarve boasts a Mediterranean climate tempered by the Atlantic Ocean. Flowers therefore bloom longer here than in the Mediterranean – essentially from February to September. It always seems like spring in the Algarve.

Storks

There is only one national park in Portugal, Penada-Gerês, which is home to wild horses, boars, deer and golden eagles. The country also has a few nature reserves, including the Parque Natural de Ria Formosa, a stopping place for migratory birds, located in the southeast between Faro and Spain. Cabo de São Vicente, the westernmost tip of Europe, is also an important rest area for migratory birds flying between Europe and Africa. In the Alentejo, you might spot huge stork nests.

History

Early Settlement

Portugal's history is closely linked to the development of the Iberian peninsula. The Iberians were the first to settle here permanently in large groups, beginning in the fifth century BC Although their origins remain unclear, these people probably came from the Saharan region.

They spread across the Iberian Peninsula, concentrating most of their activity in Andalusia. Before long, trade in the Mediterranean basin enabled the Iberians to flourish, and they built a brilliant civilization. Around 500 BC, however, the Celts (Indo-European tribes from central Europe) invaded the Spanish territory from the northwest, and succeeded in subjugating the local inhabitants. The union of the vanquishers and the vanquished led to the birth of a new people, known as the Celtiberians.

As far as the regions that make up present-day Portugal are concerned, the first settlements were concentrated in the north. Modest traces of this period can still be found today in the ruined *castros* of the Minho region (Costa Verde). These groupings of circular stone houses, surrounded by a series of three circular ramparts, were inhabited by families who had banded together into clans. The oldest

traces of human activity found thus far in the southern part of the country are the Greek and Carthaginian trading posts along the shore.

The Origins of Lusitania

Around the third century BC, the mountainous regions between the Tagus and the Douro rivers were mainly inhabited by shepherds, whose communities resembled *castros*. According to some, this was the true cradle of the Portuguese nation. In 218 BC, the Romans attacked the Iberian Peninsula, defeating the peoples living along the Tagus by about 150 B.C. The Romans then created Lusitania, an administrative division more or less designating the region between the Tagus and the Douro, as well as part of the Spanish provinces of Extremadura and León. Confronted for the first time with an occupying force, the Lusitanians, as they were now known, banded together under the leadership of a shepherd named Viriathus and launched a ferocious war against the invaders. Despite numerous victories, however, Viriathus' assassination in 139 BC ushered in an era of Roman domination. Although the Lusitanian revolt took place too long ago to be viewed as the first sign of a Portuguese national identity, it was the first time that communities in the region joined together. The Lusitanians are thus considered the true founders of Portugal. The Portuguese view Viriathus as the nation's first hero and martyr.

Roman Colonization

It would not be an exaggeration to say that a significant part of present-day Portugal's national character can be traced back to the Romans' lengthy occupation of the country (from the second century BC to the fifth century AD). The Latin language and culture linked Portugal to Europe, while the construction of a road running from north to south, with perpendicular offshoots leading to the coast, seems to have launched the country's development towards the Atlantic. Several important cities were also founded during this period: Lisbon (then known as Felicitas Julia), Évora (Ebora), Coimbra (Conimbriga), and Portus and Cale, located on either side of the Rio Douro.

The last two are the source of the name Portucale, which later became Portugal. Starting in the fourth century, numerous barbarian invasions brought an end to the Roman occupation.

Swabians and Visigoths

Toward the fifth century, the Swabians invaded the northwest part of the peninsula and established a kingdom there, while the Visigoths, who had been driven out of Aquitaine, settled in the rest of Spain. Around 585 AD, however, the Visigoths conquered the Swabians, thus gaining almost complete control over the Iberian territory until 711. In Portugal, the major contribution of these two brilliant civilizations (particularly the Visigoths) was the rise of Christianity and the numerous monasteries in and around Braga.

Muslim Conquest

In 711, the Berber Tāriq Ibn Ziyād crossed the Strait of Gibraltar and, taking advantage of the weakened position of the Visigoth kingdom which was hobbled by internal quarrelling, succeeded in invading the

peninsula. The Muslim army was able to advance far enough to threaten such cities as Poitiers, in France. As history tells us, however, the Moors were later driven back south of the Pyrenees. In 756, Abd-Al-Rahman declared himself "independent emir" and created the caliphate of Córdoba, thus ensuring Arab domination over the peninsula for the next 300 years. In the year 1031, the caliphate splintered into 25 little kingdoms. With their power thus fragmented, the Moors became increasingly vulnerable to the Christians. Despite a certain degree of resistance and a new invasion (by the Almoravides), Muslim influence was gradually eclipsed by Christianity.

Various cultural traces of Muslim rule can still be found here and there in Portugal, although to a lesser degree than in Spain. There are some vestiges south of the Tagus (these areas were among the last to be liberated), but almost nothing remains in the north. The Muslim influence is most obviously reflected in the language, though. According to linguists, the Portuguese language contains at least 500 words of Arabic origin. As far as Moorish architecture is concerned, most large groups of buildings were unfortunately destroyed during the reconquest. As in the case of the language, however, numerous influences remain, the *azulejo* being one of the best examples (see p 34).

The Reconquest and the Creation of the Kingdom of Portugal

The northwest portion of the peninsula was the first region to be reconquered. As early as 838, Braga was recaptured, and Porto soon followed. It is true that these two cities were affected by the Arabic influence to a lesser degree than most others. Coimbra, for its part, was reconquered in 1064. As more and more territories were recaptured (Asturies, León, Castile, etc.), the land was parcelled out to counts and dukes. Thus was born the county of Portucale, which lay between the Minho River and the port of Porto; its name later came to refer to the entire country. At that point, however, there was no talk of creating a Portuguese nation. First, a kingdom had to be formed, starting with the naming of a king. This kingdom's origins resided with the Burgundian nobility. Taking into consideration the numerous military victories won by the kingdom of Castile, and by way of thanking the House of Burgundy for its assistance, King

Afonso VI, known as "the Valiant", granted the territory between the Minho and the Mondego to Henry of Burgundy in 1093. In order to understand the county's future transformation into a kingdom, it is necessary to keep two important factors in mind. First, Henry of Burgundy gradually consolidated his authority over the local population. Second, he led a great number of battles against the Muslims to defend his territory, which was in constant danger of being invaded. These two factors in combination enabled him to create a common identity among the local bourgeoisie and the people, who slowly came to consider themselves part of a nation with a sense of a unified purpose. Henry of Burgundy can thus be considered the true father of the nation, even though he remained loyal to the House of Castile, and it was his son who actually proclaimed the kingdom of Portugal.

The House of Burgundy and the Birth of Portugal

After conquering the Muslims in a vaguely defined area known as Ourique, Afonso Henriques declared himself King Afonso I of Portugal in 1139. At the time, however, his realm covered only the northern part of

modern-day Portugal. It wasn't until Afonso III seized Faro (1249) and the Moors were driven out of the Algarve once and for all (1250) that the country took its present shape. The Burgundians, having transformed Portugal into a politically independent, socially cohesive nation with defined boundaries, thus played a key role in the country's history. The following is a summary of some of their major accomplishments:

Afonso I (1143-1185) founded the kingdom of Portugal by proclaiming himself king in 1139. He seized the cities of Santarém and Lisbon in 1147 and established the Order of Aviz, an important order of knighthood.

Sancho I (1185-1211) encouraged large numbers of Britons and Germans to immigrate to work the land. He also waged several battles against the Moors.

Afonso II (1211-1223) set about reconquering the southern part of Portugal while strengthening the administrative structure of the kingdom. He established the country's first civil and penal laws and struggled to reduce the power of the clergy. He died excommunicated.

Sancho II (1223-1248), after devoting the first part of his reign to the reconquest, chose a bride who did not meet with the approval of the powers of the day and was consequently deposed by Pope Innocent IV in 1245. The queen was imprisoned by the archbishop of Braga, and Sancho II was forced to flee to Castile. He returned in 1247, at the head of a Castilian army. However, fearing excommunication, he went into exile once again, this time to Toledo, where he died.

Afonso III (1248-1279) drove the last Moors out of Portugal by liberating Faro. His royal title thus became "King of Portugal and the Algarve". He continued his father's struggle against the church, and was excommunicated as a result of his second marriage.

Dinis I (1279-1325) promoted industry and commerce and helped expand the Portuguese fleet. He restored various military orders, including the Knights Templar, later known as the "Order of Christ", and placed them in the exclusive service of the royalty. He also helped advance the arts and sciences by founding the University of Lisbon and declaring Portuguese the national language. This last measure definitively established the Portuguese identity.

Afonso IV (1325-1357) helped the Spanish drive the remaining Moors out of Spain. He ordered the execution of Inès de Castro, whom his son Pedro loved and wanted to marry.

Pedro I (1357-1367) won renown chiefly for his efforts to limit the increasing power of the Portuguese clergy. He erected a veritable sanctuary in memory of Inès de Castro.

Fernando I (1367-1383) doggedly tried to extend his power to the throne of Castile, without success. Upon his death, the Spanish laid claim to the Portuguese crown and invaded the country.

The Aviz Dynasty and Portuguese Expansion

The death of Fernando I marked an important turning point in the history of Portugal. Since the king's only heir was his daughter Beatriz, who had married the King of Castile (Juan I), the realm automatically and legally fell under the authority of the Castilian crown. However, the Cortès, an assembly representing the three orders of society (the nobility, the clergy and the bourgeoisie), wanted to preserve the Portuguese throne, mainly to protect its own interests.

In 1385, they designated João, Grand Master of Aviz and illegitimate son of Pedro I, as the only legitimate successor to the Crown; he ascended the throne as João I of Portugal. The disgruntled Castilians immediately set out to conquer the territory and take their due, but João I emerged triumphant after the battle of Aljubarrota in 1385. This victory was of great historical significance, for it not only enabled Portugal to maintain its independence, but also ushered in a new era of prosperity for the country.

The Aviz dynasty was the country's guiding light throughout this period. The family not only represented a victory for the local bourgeoisie (at the time, it was quite unusual in Europe for an assembly such as the Cortès to name a king), but also opened the doors of the world for Portugal, ensuring the country an extraordinary degree of international influence.

The main stages of the country's evolution were as follows:

João I (1385-1433), illegitimate son of Pedro I, was named king of Portugal. He was known mainly for his role in the Battle of Aljubarrota, which enabled Portugal to get out from under Spain's thumb.

Henry the Navigator (1394-1460)

Henry the Navigator (or Henrique O Navigador as he is known is Portugal), perhaps the country's most illustrious prince, would become the real driving force behind its colonial expansion. After settling in Raposeira (Algarve), he built the fortress of Sagres on a peninsula and proceeded to amass numerous documents on subjects like navigation, astrology and cartography. He thus created a veritable research facility for navigators, referred to by some as the School of Sagres. The studies conducted here prompted a craze for discovery that spread throughout Europe. Such eminent figures as Christopher Columbus, Vasco da Gama and many others obtained all sorts of information here. Although he did not actually take part in any expeditions, Henry surrounded himself with celebrated navigators and scientists in an effort to develop new methods of navigation. As a result, Gil Eanes was able to round Cape Bojador (Western Sahara) and begin exploring the coast of Africa in 1434. Thanks to the prince's exceptional administrative skills, the Portuguese were also able to set up efficient colonial trading posts, thus ensuring their country a predominant role in Africa. Later, improved shipbuilding techniques (the development of a new type of ship known as a caravel) enabled the "masters of the sea" to press on with their explorations, leading to the discovery of new riches and unprecedented territorial expansion.

Throughout his reign, he actively supported Henrique (Henry the Navigator), one of his sons (see above). In 1386, he forged an important alliance with England, ushering in a long period of bilateral relations between the two countries. He took possession of Ceuta (in Morocco) in 1415. The Madeira Islands (1419) and the Azores (1427) were discovered while he was in power.

Duarte I (1433-1438) had a short reign, during which he was known mainly for his interest in literature.

Afonso V (1438-1481) was only six years old when he ascended to the throne. His uncle Pedro (the Duke of Coimbra) served as regent until 1449, when Afonso took over and had him assassinated. Afonso spent most of his time trying to conquer Castile, which was in turmoil at the time. His obtuseness and fruitless efforts made him unpopular with his subjects. Despite several victories against the Moors in Africa, he was overshadowed historically by his uncle, Dom Pedro, who succeeded in establishing close ties with many European monarchs and men of letters, thus putting Portugal more in tune with the great changes taking place in Europe. The expeditions continued; the Cape Verde Islands were discovered in 1445, Guinea in 1446 and São Tomé e Príncipe in 1471.

João II (1481-1495) commenced his reign by

strengthening his authority and subjugating the nobility, which he believed had become too powerful and too conservative. He then concentrated on promoting the discovery of new territories, surrounding himself with eminent cartographers and navigators. Advances in navigation during this period led to the exploration of the south Atlantic coast of Africa. Other notable events during João II's reign include the signing of the Treaty of Tordesillas (see box below) and the discovery of the mouth of the Congo (1482) in present-day Zaire; the Cape of Storms (1088), renamed the Cape of Good Hope by the king, and Greenland (1492). A man of great determination, he left his successors a strengthened monarchy.

The Treaty of Tordesillas (1494)

The Spanish became increasingly irritated that Portugal had discovered the African coast and had established trading posts there, widening its sphere of influence to an alarming degree. Then, rubbing salt in the wound, the Pope granted Portugal exclusive rights to its discoveries. To assert its own influence, Spain succeeded, with the help of the papacy, in forcing Portugal to sign a treaty. The Treaty of Tordesillas (1494), endorsed by Pope Alexander VI, required Portugal and Spain to limit their power to either side of a line dividing the world into two distinct parts (see map).

Originally, Portugal was entitled to take possession of any new land discovered within 100 leagues west of the Cape Verde Islands. Dissatisfied with the limits imposed upon them, however, the Portuguese managed to extend the distance to 370 leagues, which later enabled them to discover the immense territory of Brazil. According to some, Portuguese officials were already secretly aware of the country's existence at the time of final negotiations! In any case, the treaty confirmed Portugal as a country of great explorers and gave it a disproportionate amount of influence.

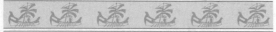

Manuel I (1495-1521), along with Henry the Navigator, is probably one of Portugal's most illustrious native sons. Aware of the enormous potential of newly discovered territories, he strongly encouraged further expeditions. His reign was marked by the country's two greatest discoveries, maritime routes to India (Vasco da Gama, 1497) and Brazil (Pedro Alvares Cabral, 1500). Spain, meanwhile, was waging a battle against its Jewish population. A shrewd diplomat anxious to humour his powerful neighbour, Manuel I was also a great patron of the Arts and Sciences, areas in which many Jews had excelled. He therefore manoeuvred skilfully in order to preserve this essential component of Portuguese society. Faced with pressure from the all-powerful Inquisition, he initiated voluntary, and then forced, conversions rather than expelling huge numbers of Jews from the country. His love of the arts inspired a rich and unique style of architecture later termed the "Manueline style" (see p 33).

João III (1521-1557) encouraged new expeditions, leading to the discovery of Japan and Macau. He also began actively colonizing Brazil. Not very receptive to new ideas and much less tolerant than his father, he introduced the Inquisition in

Great Discoveries of the 15th and 16th Centuries

Treaty of Tordesillas 1494 ▼   Treaty of Saragosse 1529 ▼

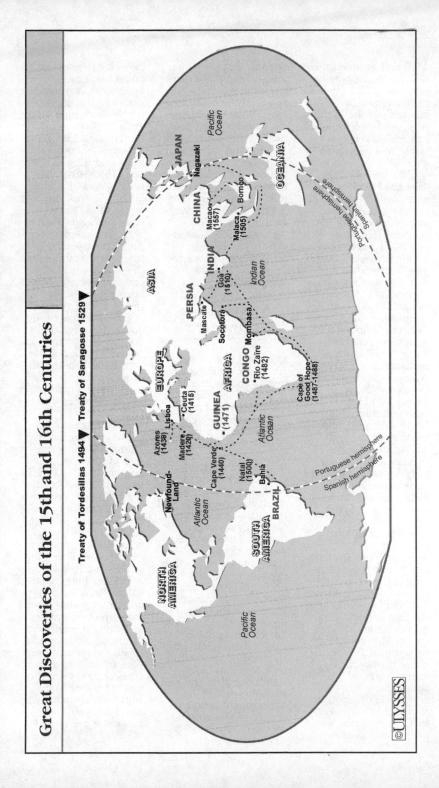

© ULYSSES

1526 and awarded the Jesuits a monopoly on education. This era was characterized by a marked decline in the Arts and Sciences, areas in which the Portuguese had previously excelled.

Sebastião I (1557-1578) ascended the throne at the age of three, and saw his great uncle, Cardinal Henrique, serve as regent. The young king's education was entrusted to a Jesuit with an excessively chivalrous nature and outdated values, which he instilled in his pupil. Concerned above all with glorifying his name for posterity, Sebastião I set out to conquer the Moors at the age of 24, with visions of being crowned ruler of a North African empire. This dream proved catastrophic for his country. In 1578, the king, accompanied by a large expeditionary force and a considerable segment of the Portuguese nobility, was slain at el-Kasr Kébir (or Alcázarquivir), in northern Morocco. Since the king had no heirs, the Cortès quickly named Cardinal Henrique king. He died in 1580, however, without having solved the problem of succession. The Portuguese royalty thus came to an end, enabling the country's powerful neighbour to step in and take over. In 1580, Portugal was integrated into the Spanish empire. The unusual circumstances surrounding Sebastião I's death in Morocco (no one actually saw his dead body) became the source of a popular legend several years later. Based on the belief that Sebastião I would miraculously return to deliver Portugal from Spanish domination, this "Sebastianism" issued mainly from the nation's deeply wounded pride and longing for independence.

The Bragança Dynasty

After 60 years of Spanish occupation, which began unobtrusively under Philip II and grew more and more oppressive during the reigns of Philip III and IV, the Portuguese began to revolt. On December 15, 1640, the Duke of Bragança was brought to power and named King João IV of Portugal. Spain, coping with a Catalan revolt at the time, was in a weakened state and faced rivalry from other great powers, such as France, England and the United Provinces. João IV, a shrewd diplomat, skilfully took advantage of these rivalries to obtain recognition of his country's regained independence. England and France both felt that supporting Portuguese sovereignty would be an effective means of diminishing Spain's power. After several failed invasions, the Spanish crown finally decided to recognize its neighbour's independence in 1668. Although the House of Bragança was one of Portugal's most enduring dynasties (1640-1910), its only historical legacy, according to some, is a series of mediocre, unambitious monarchs with little concern for their country's interests. It seems that the reign of João IV and his successors was simply a constant quest for profit, aimed at increasing the prestige of the court. Although the country lost its trading posts in India and Malaysia, the production of sugar and above all the fabulous gold mines discovered in the Brazilian colony enabled the royalty to enjoy a lavish lifestyle. During this time, the lure of gold prompted large numbers of Portuguese to emigrate, diminishing the country's already small population. The apathy of the ruling classes was so great that the country even started importing grain – the fields were no longer being cultivated! Many palaces and other architectural masterpieces now serve as beautiful reminders of the royalty's pursuit of splendour and prestige. In the mid-18th century, however, the flow of riches from Brazil began to wane, and Portugal slowly entered a period of decline.

Between João IV's accession to the throne and the birth of the republic, three major events altered the country's political and economic portrait. The first was the signing of the Treaty of Westminster and of the Treaty of Methuen; the second, the Marquês de Pombal's accession to power; and the last, the repercussions of the French Revolution and the Napoleonic Wars.

The Treaties of Westminster and Methuen

A continuation of a treaty signed shortly after Portugal regained its independence, the Treaty of Westminster, signed in 1654 under João IV, enabled the country to develop close economic ties with England. Under the treaty, Portugal guaranteed English merchants access to Portuguese markets and, more importantly, to products from Brazil. At the time, the accord seemed highly beneficial to England, which, being more industrialized, was able to flood the Portuguese market with its manufactured goods. As a result, the Portuguese, whose output was essentially limited to unfinished products, were not very inclined to update their manufacturing industries. The Treaty of Methuen, signed in 1703, was along the same lines. It allowed

for the unlimited importation of English textiles in exchange for preferential duties for Portuguese wine exported to England. These two treaties actually proved far more advantageous to Portugal than they had originally appeared. Portuguese consumers were too poor to purchase finished English products, but could easily sell the British their own inexpensive goods. In the long run, however, the treaties did cause Portugal to lag behind in the great race toward industrialization and economically bound it to its powerful partner.

The Pombal Government

The second important event was the rise to power of Sebastião José de Carvalho e Melo, commonly known as the Marquês de Pombal. When a terrible earthquake destroyed much of Lisbon on November 1, 1755, pious King José I interpreted it as a divine punishment. Not knowing how to react, he instructed the Marquês de Pombal to take whatever measures were appropriate to cope with the catastrophe. Pombal demonstrated a genuine talent for governing the state, and set about reconstructing the city almost in its entirety. He opted for an innovative style of architecture, later

known as the "Pombaline style". Taking advantage of the king's weak character, he succeeded throughout his career in setting up powerful government structures. While carrying out major reforms, he established institutions that foreshadowed modern governments. A Chamber of Commerce, a College of Nobles (a type of school for the future administrators of the state) and new faculties at the University of Coimbra were all founded during this time. Economically, he favoured the creation of factories and set the colonial economy back on track by developing the agricultural sector. Profiting from its neighbouring countries' internal and colonial conflicts, Portugal enjoyed a major renewal of economic activity. A true forerunner of liberalism to some, an enlightened despot to others, the Marquês de Pombal left his successor a strong government. By requiring the nobility and the clergy (he expelled the Jesuits in 1759) to serve the state alone, he opened the door to a wave of new ideas from beyond the Pyrenees. After the death of José I, he was removed from power and his enemies (the nobility and the Jesuits) called out for his execution. He made a narrow escape and spent the rest of his days in Coimbra, where he died in 1782.

The French Revolution

Although it was viewed favourably at first by Portuguese intellectual circles, the French Revolution marked the beginning of Portugal's decline. Portugal was actually part of the anti-French coalition, along with England and Spain, and was thus forced to make an impossible choice when the French emerged victorious. After signing a separate peace treaty with Spain, France insisted that Portugal impose a blockade against the English. The Portuguese had two options, both of them difficult: to oppose the blockade and risk a joint invasion by Spanish and Napoleonic troops or to give in and lose its trading power. In the latter instance, the English, who controlled the route to Brazil, would turn against their ally and take over its possessions. Unable to accept such a situation, Portugal had to endure being invaded, in spite of its vigorous attempts at diplomacy. The royal family and a portion of the nobility left the occupied nation and began a long period of exile in Brazil (1807-1821). Combined English and Portuguese forces regained the entire territory (aside from Olivença, which they lost to the Spanish), and the Treaty of Paris (1814) put an end to the hostilities. The country, which had practically become a British protectorate in the absence of the court, signed a new peace treaty and trade agreement with its long-standing ally in 1810. In fact, the accord enabled England to seize the main sources of profit in Brazil. Portugal, already sorely tried by the Napoleonic invasions, was consequently deprived of these tremendous colonial riches.

Although Portugal was briefly in conflict with France, the great changes taking place in that country obviously led to the emergence of new ideas among the Portuguese. Thus originated a vast movement known as the "Regeneration," which led to the creation of two parties (1815), the Conservatives, named the *Regeneradores*, and the Liberals, later referred to as the *Progressistas*. In 1820, due to the king's prolonged absence and a military uprising, the liberal-minded bourgeoisie set up a "provisional junta of the supreme government of the kingdom" and adopted the country's first liberal constitution in 1821-1822. This document includes clauses on such subjects as freedom of the press, the abolition of the Inquisition and the creation of a unicameral system. That same year, João VI accepted the situation as it stood and returned from exile upon the request of the Cortès. He left behind his oldest son Pedro IV, who not only refused to return to Portugal, but declared himself Emperor Pedro I of Brazil, thus bringing about the colony's independence.

Birth of The Republic

The death of João VI in 1826 ushered in a long period of instability, during which a power struggle erupted between the late king's two sons (Pedro IV, now Pedro I of Brazil, and Miguel), each of whom symbolized a different political trend. Pedro represented the "Chartists" (after the Charter that replaced the Constitution of 1822), who supported world-wide capitalism; Miguel, the "Septembrists" (after a group of important figures with liberal ideas), who wanted to restore the 1822 Constitution and favoured a return to protectionism and national values. While the first current reflected the interests of the international upper class, the second was backed primarily by small shopkeepers and the local nobility. After a brief return to absolutism under Miguel (1828-1834), Pedro IV managed to seize power with the help of France and England. The period that followed was a mixture of revolts and uprisings, with intervals of relative stability, during which the two great political trends continued to compete for power. Although these were fairly dark years, some important progress was made in the realm of human rights, namely the abolition of both the death penalty (1867) and slavery.

Despite this influx of new ideas, both parties wished to preserve the monarchy. In the end, it was a third party, the Portuguese Republican Party (PRP), that brought down the old regime. The PRP, founded in 1876, mainly represented the lower and middle bourgeoisie, who were seeking a more equitable distribution of wealth. The party's popularity was in some way due to a bold stroke by the English. Since losing Brazil, Portugal, like other nations, wanted above all to continue its colonial expansion. Its goal was to create a large territory stretching from Angola to Mozambique, thus uniting its two African possessions. To the great surprise of the political community, however, the English issued an ultimatum in 1890, enjoining Portugal to relinquish its plans. The Portuguese crown gave in, prompting an immediate nationalist reaction. The PRP, at the time very popular, tried to assume power by inciting

a revolt in 1891. It also demanded the overthrow of the monarchy, which was accused of having sold out the country's independence. The establishment of republican regimes in the neighbouring countries of Spain and France further strengthened the population's republican sentiments. In response, the monarchy launched a terrible campaign of repression, which, along with the monarchist parties' incessant bickering, permanently tarnished the crown's image. A clumsy armed takeover led by King Carlos I, followed by the institution of a ruthless dictatorship, sealed the fate of the monarchy once and for all. On February 1, 1908, the king and the crown prince were assassinated right in the centre of Lisbon, clearing the way for the republic. Although the king's successor, Manuel II, rapidly restored democracy, the 1910 elections brought the PRP to power. The monarchy's days were numbered; on October 5, 1910, Portugal was proclaimed a republic. The country's last king went into exile in England, where he died in 1932, leaving no descendants.

From Republic to Dictatorship

The republican period was no more than a rapid succession of

governments (45, to be exact!) characterized by political instability and violence. A large number of strikes took place, and political unity was at an all-time low. The economic decline that had begun under the old regime grew more and more pronounced. The subsequent wave of emigration led to growing discontent among the workforce in the countryside, further diminishing the already meagre production of grain. Two coups d'état, one in 1915 and the other in 1917, succeeded only in causing more unrest. By 1919, the situation had become so chaotic that it was nothing more than an infernal cycle of riots and repression. The country's entry into the war alongside the Allies in 1916 also had profound social repercussions. In spite of this dismal picture, a few positive political measures were taken, mainly between 1911 and 1915. These changes, listed below, enabled the country to free itself from the ossified spirit of the old regime.

● The secularization of the state and the nation (separation of Church and State; official registry of births, marriages and deaths; legalization of divorce, etc.).

● Significant efforts to improve public education (children aged 7 to 12 required to attend school; opening of new, diversified faculties, etc.).

• The recognition of certain civil liberties, including the right to strike.

When one considers the progressive nature of these measures, it is important to keep in mind that a large portion of the population lived in rural areas. These devoutly Catholic people, with their fundamentally traditional values, were frightened by all these changes. The government, thus out of step with the people, was soon overwhelmed by the social turmoil that ensued, clearing the way for those advocating a return to order and discipline.

The Salazar Dictatorship

On May 28, 1926, when the political situation was slowly beginning to stabilize, Maréchal Gomes da Costa, backed by the army, marched on Lisbon; within a few days, he had set up a dictatorship. After several years of political uncertainty, the authors of the putsch were gradually supplanted by General Carmona, who was even more authoritarian. As the country was still in an economic slump, the regime summoned the help of António de Oliveira Salazar, an economist

highly respected in clerical circles. Although he was named minister of finance in June of 1926 (a position assigned to him for a few days only), Salazar really began his career in 1928. After a few years of skilful manoeuvring and three orchestrated resignations, he managed little by little to gain control over the wheels of state, finally claiming the head of government on June 25, 1932.

In order to understand the dictator's effect on the country, one must understand a little about his personality. António de Oliveira Salazar was born in 1889 in the little village of Beira, in a rural area. He obtained his secondary education at the seminary of Viseu and, after completing his studies at the University of Coimbra, became a professor of political economics. He thus spent his entire youth surrounded by people whose values centred around the Catholic religion and political conservatism. Methodical, deeply religious and solitary by nature, he gradually developed a profound disgust for parliamentary government and political debates, in which he saw nothing but parasitism and disorder.

The Estado Novo

In 1933, Salazar drafted a new constitution,

marking the birth of what he called the Estado Novo, or New State. From that point on, he had absolute power over the country. Under the new constitution, he applied himself to promoting a new society geared towards "family, country, work and faith". He thus established a regime based on corporatism and a return to traditional values. The National Assembly lost all real power, becoming nothing more than a puppet government. Dismissing all criticism and adopting an extreme nationalist stance to justify his actions, he established a sinister political police force (PIDE), whose job was to silence all opposition.

Economically speaking, his reign of nearly 50 years can be summed up in a single word: backwardness. Up until the end of the Second World War, the regime's economic policy was characterized by the pursuit of self-dependence, limiting as much as possible all trade with other countries. Agriculture, the ultimate symbol of traditional values, occupied a place of honour under the regime, as did the army. Industrial development, being a potential source of disruption (unions, strikes, labour movements, etc.) was left to stagnate. During the Second World War, the country was officially neutral, but displayed a certain degree of goodwill towards its long-standing ally, Great Britain. The drastic changes that took place after the war (the creation of NATO, for example) forced Portugal to crack open its door to industrialization, and in the 1960s foreign capital began to flow into the country. Within a decade, the percentage of investment had increased 20 fold, resulting in the rapid growth of the shipbuilding, petrochemical and iron and steel industries. At the same time, the country began welcoming tourists. Its famous *pousadas*, geared exclusively toward affluent visitors, are run by the State.

Although some progress has been made, there is no denying that Portugal's economy is still far behind that of its European neighbours. The poor economic standing of the country is due not only to its isolationist policies, but also to its military effort to hold onto its colonial possessions. In the 1960s, various autonomist movements emerged in Africa, including many in the Portuguese territories (Angola, Guinea-Buissau, Mozambique, São Tome e Príncipe and the Cape Verde Islands). The ossified regime, in pursuit of a lost empire, launched a series of repressive military operations,

which not only led to considerable loss of human life, but also drained the country's finances–all in an effort to retain colonies aspiring to liberty and self-determination.

Demographically speaking, the country had to cope with waves of emigration, which were actually encouraged by the government. In fact, the 1970 census revealed an overall drop in the population, something highly unusual in Europe at that time. Despite years of political stability, therefore, the Salazar dictatorship could hardly be described as a terrific success. In order to determine just how little the country advanced under the regime, one need only consider a single statistic: in 1974, one out of three Portuguese was still illiterate!

After a long illness, Salazar died on July 27, 1970. He was replaced by Marcelo Caetano, who was more open to democratic values, but nevertheless opted for the status quo rather than making an attempt at liberalization. After a few years of this more "flexible" dictatorship, the hard-liners came into power one last time in 1972, with the arrival of a new dictator named Americo Tomas. The people, however, tired of being bled financially (in 1972, the military budget ac-

counted for about 50% of state spending) and sacrificing growing numbers of young men to protect the colonies (more than 5,000 died), were ready for a change. Consequently, when a coup d'état took place in April 1974, it was greeted with public approval.

"*O povo unido, jamais vencido*": The Return of Democracy

On April 25, 1974, a number of young officers belonging to the MFA (Armed Forces Movement), a previously unknown movement, rose up under the leadership of Ottelo Saraiva de Carvalho. Backed by the democratic wing of the army, which was in favour of change, they took over all strategic locations in the capital. The dictatorship fell within a few hours, like a ripe fruit. Immediately afterward, a junta was placed in power, with the promise that free elections would be held and all political prisoners released. Tired of so many years of stagnation, the people joyfully welcomed the soldiers of democracy in the streets of Lisbon. Thousands turned out to show their support, offering the men carnations as a symbolic gesture. A carnation in the barrel of a gun has since remained the most striking image of this day of revolution, which later came to be known as the **Flower Revolution**. By mid-May, a provisional government was set up with the participation of the two major opposition parties. The socialists and the communists, whose leaders had just returned from exile, joined forces with the centrist party (PPD) and with members of the military representing the MFA General A. de Spínola was designated President of the Republic, only to be replaced soon after. Portugal thus entered into the game of democracy, with its continual shifting of political power between the parties of the left and the right.

Politics

In 1974, Portugal emerged from the obscurantism of Salazar with the Flower Revolution. After 48 years of dictatorship, democratic politics began to be practised here. From 1974 to 1982, the Portuguese voted Soares's socialists and Cunhal's communists in and out of office. A key figure on the political scene for 20 years, Mario Soares returned to power as prime minister in 1983, then became president in 1986. Anibal Cavaco Silva, a leader of the centreright, has been prime minister since 1987. In 1991, both men were voted back into power

by an overwhelming majority (71%) in Mario Soares's case.

The local elections of December 1993 revealed that the population is polarized, with the socialists and the social-democrats each at about 35%. The latter party lost its majority in the general elections of 1995, and the presidential elections held in January 1996 brought to power the Socialist Jorge Sampaio. After enjoying three consecutive years of economic growth, electors voted the social democrats back into power in October 1999.

Portugal continues to disengage itself from the Catholic Church, a transition that was not completed by the revolution of 1974. The new president, Sampaio, is an atheist who may continue to apply pressure in this direction in spite of the presence of Prime Minister Guterres, who is a practising Catholic. The rate of participation in Sunday mass remains 25%, but the church has acquired a television station, TVI, in an effort to restore its influence. The church still has a considerable hold over a large segment of the Portuguese population, as is evidenced by the results of the 1998 national referendum on abortion. During the referendum, Prime Minister António Guterres publicly expressed his op-

position to the legalization of abortion, and his government's proposal was rejected by a vote of 50.91%. The voter abstention rate was 68%.

Population

Portugal has 10,800,000 inhabitants (excluding Madeira and the Azores), with a population density of 106 inhabitants per km², comparable to that of France, but half that of Great Britain. A total of only 3,000,000 people reside in the cities of Lisbon and Porto, which means that 70% of the country's population still live in rural areas or in small towns with fewer than 100,000 inhabitants. Almost 25% of Portuguese households do not have telephones, while over 10% do have personal computers.

A great many people emigrated, up until the end of the Salazar regime in the mid-1970s. As a result, over 3,000,000 Portuguese are now scattered all over the world, particularly in Brazil, France, the United States and Canada.

Although clearly on the decline, the illiteracy rate is still high. As a result, you might meet people who are unable to read something you show them or write down information for you.

Brief summary of the various political, social and economic changes that have taken place in the country since the Flower Revolution

From April 25 to July 15, 1974: The Flower Revolution, fall of the dictatorship and establishment of the first provisional government.

July 15, 1974: Establishment of a second provisional government, made up of members of the MFA, the two major leftist parties and the centrist party. Decolonization, still a highly contentious issue, is quickly initiated.

March 11, 1975: General A. de Spínola, one of the heros of the Revolution, leads an aborted takeover in an attempt to prevent the communists and MFA from gaining more power. As a result, elections planned for March 31 are postponed until April 25 and the Council of the Revolution is established in order to safeguard the gains made thus far. Extreme leftists manage to impose their views on the government, and in the following months, several banks and insurance companies are nationalized. The state also begins issuing compulsory purchase orders on the property of major landowners. On November 11, 1975, Angola, the last Portuguese colony (aside from Macau and East Timor), becomes independent.

March 1975 to April 1976: The political scene erupts in violence once again. Within the coalition, power struggles between radical leftist and more moderate elements intensify. In November 1975, a failed leftist uprising marks the MFA's shift back to a moderate stance. By associating with socialists and centrists, the MFA succeeds in thwarting the extreme left.

December 1975: Indonesia invades and illegally annexes East Timor. Macau is thus the only remaining Portuguese colony.

April 1976: The first real democratic elections. The socialists, although in the minority, set up the country's first democratically elected government. Mário Soares becomes head of the government, and Ramalho Eanes is elected President of the Republic shortly thereafter.

1976-1986: Promulgation of the Constitution of April 2, 1976. A series of coalitions is formed within the government. The socialists and the Democratic Alliance (a union of Social Democrats, monarchists and Centre Democrats) share the power. In 1982, the Council of the Revolution is abolished by constitutional amendment.

January 1, 1986: Portugal officially joins the European Economic Community.

1986: Mário Soares is elected President of the Republic, making him the first civilian to be elected to this position.

1987: The PSD (Social Democrat Party) comes in to power. The Azores are granted autonomous status and an accord, ceding Macau back to China in 1999, is signed.

August 1988: A terrible fire ravages the historic neighbourhood of Chiado, in Lisbon.

July 1989: Following a revision of the Constitution, state-owned companies begin to be privatized.

June 1991: Madeira becomes autonomous. The PSD is voted back into power in October.

April 1992: Introduction of the escudo into the European Monetary System.

June 1992: 64% of the Portuguese electorate abstain from voting in the European elections.

1994: Portugal celebrates the 600th anniversary of the birth of Henry the Navigator.

June 1994: following a variety of cost-cutting measures imposed by the PSD, including a 50-escudo hike in the toll for the Ponte 25 de Abril bridge, the government faces its most violent demonstration since the revolution of 1974. Chaos grips the city of Lisbon as brothers Jaime and Mario Pinto, two truck drivers at the head of the protest movement, block the bridge which is used by up to 140,000 cars on a daily basis.

October 1995: Legislative elections see the ascendancy of the socialists as Mr. António Guterres is named Prime Minister.

January 1996: For the first time since the Flower Revolution, the Portuguese elect a President for the Republic from the same political faction as the government in power. Socialist Jorge Sampaio, former mayor of Lisbon, wins 53.83% of the votes. The nomination of the son of the former President, Juan Soares, as mayor of Lisbon further places the socialists in an unprecedented position of power.

May 22 to September 30, 1998: the Portuguese capital hosts EXPO 98, the last World Exposition of the 20th century. Lisbon welcomes 12 million visitors.

April 1999: Portugal celebrates its 25th anniversary as a democracy.

October 1999: António Guterres's Social Democratic Party is voted back into power, though it fails to win a majority. Elected with 43.05% of the votes, the party forms a minority government.

October 1999: three days before the end of the election campaign, the death of Amália Rodrigues plunges the country into mourning. The "Queen of Fado" is given a state funeral.

December 20, 1999: Macau reverts back to China.

2000: Portugal presides over the European Union for the first half of the year.

In 1950, 48% of the population lived from the proceeds of agriculture; in 1990, this number had dropped to 10%. It is nevertheless important to remember that half of the Portuguese population has rural roots, although many of these people now live in cities. Agriculture, which represented 28% of the GDP in 1950, today accounts for only 8%. Life expectancy is 75 years. Infant mortality has greatly diminished in recent years, falling from 12.1 out of every 1000 births in 1989 to 7.9 per 1000 births in 1994.

The Portuguese have a few character traits that distinguish them from other Europeans. Travellers will surely appreciate knowing beforehand that most Portuguese are courteous, obliging, unaggressive and shy to the point of seeming unfriendly at first encounter. You are bound to notice the widespread *saudade*, a nostalgia that supposedly dates back to the end of the country's glorious era of exploration and colonization. Portugal's fall from power coincided with its military defeat in Morocco in 1578. King Sébastião I was killed in combat, but his body was never found. For many years, his people clung to the hope that he would return; it is said that as late as the 19th century, a significant portion of the population was still waiting for him to come back. This phenomenon is known as "Sebastianism".

Religious practice remains of central importance in Portugal, unlike other European nations. In fact, it is not uncommon to see young people in their 20s diligently attending service. This lack of curiosity about things foreign, including visitors, could be seen as a product of this conformity and of the absence of foreign influences, even at the level of cuisine – Lisbon is probably the European capital with the fewest foreign restaurants. Generally speaking, Portugal is probably the most conformist country in Western Europe.

Accordingly, ancestral traditions, such as the Festa dos Tabuleiros in Tomar, have been better preserved here than anywhere else, which can prove to be an advantage for visitors. This conformity, which contemporary Portuguese author Torga calls "the creative penury of eight hundred years of litanies", is wonderfully described in his book *Portugal*.

Another earmark of Portuguese society is that even the tiniest bar in the tiniest town has a television, which seems to be left on 24hrs a day, broadcasting sports or, more often than not, Brazilian *novelas* (soap operas). These *novelas* serve as a rare example of reverse colonization: Portugal is being invaded by Brazilian culture – be it music, television, literature or even spelling. One of the Portuguese channels, SIC, even belongs to TV Globo, the Brazilian broadcasting giant. In any case, we have made a systematic effort to seek out the few television-free restaurants, cafés and bars in the country.

The Economy

Portugal's gross domestic product (GDP) per resident is among the lowest in the European Economic Community (EEC), higher only than that of Greece. In terms of GDP per capita (purchasing power parity), $14,300, compared to $16,000 in neighbouring Spain, $22,000 in France, $22,500 in Canada, $29,000 in the United States and $21,200 in the United Kingdom.

By contrast, Portugal enjoys one of the lowest unemployment rates in the EEC: 4.4%.

While far from the total employment that existed during the second half of the 1980s, this is a perfectly respectable rate compared to 18% unemployment in Spain, 11.5% in France or 6.3% in Great Britain.

After joining the EEC in 1986, Portugal experienced a formidable period of economic growth as a result of increased trade with EEC member nations. Portugal has also benefited from EEC credit which has contributed to major infrastructure projects such as roadwork and restoration. Impressive construction sites, also funded by the EEC, are visible all over the country. These EEC grants represent between 2% and 4% percent of the country's annual GNP.

At the beginning of the 1990s, Portugal's economic growth slowed. This phenomenon has been attributed to the extreme economic rigidity imposed by leftist governments since 1976, which created a system so inflexible that the constitution had to be amended to allow privatization of state-owned companies. Since 1995, however, economic growth has regained strength and now exceeds 3%. An excellent student, Portugal will succeed in bringing its public sector deficit below the fatal threshold of 3% of GDP, the cut-off set by the Maastricht Treaty as a condition of attaining the common European monetary unit, the famous Euro-dollar.

Inflation has also been reined in, falling from more than 13% in 1990 to a rate of less than 3% in 1998.

Portugal's principal clients and suppliers are the members of the EEC, which account for three quarters of the country's dealings in both cases. Its most important clients are France, Germany and Great Britain; its suppliers, Germany, Spain and France. Astonishingly, commerce with the Portuguese-speaking countries of Africa, all former colonies, which represented up to 25% of Portugal's international trade in the late 1960s, has dwindled to a mere 2%.

The primary industries (natural resources, agriculture and fisheries) employ a quarter of the population, but generate only 10% of the GDP. This can be explained in part by the limited size of the country's farms, which has led to technological backwardness, in turn leading to low agricultural output.

The agricultural mainstays are wine, olives, wheat, corn, potatoes, tomatoes, cork and fruits of all sorts. Sheep is the most important livestock herd, with over three million head. As for energy needs, Portugal must import 20% of its electricity and all of its oil.

The manufacturing industry employs about a third of the population and generates about a third of the GDP. As this industry has never been strong in Portugal and is now undergoing profound changes world-wide, requiring more and more highly trained technical personnel, it is doubtful that the Portuguese will be able to catch up. Analysts claim that neighbouring countries create trademarks while Portugal is satisfied to manufacture products. This lack of innovation puts the country in competition with the Third World for manufacturing subcontracts. Finally, the service industries, which employ nearly half the population and generate over 50% of the GDP, are thriving due to a continued increase in tourism.

Portuguese Wines

Grape growing and wine production are ancient arts in Portugal, where they were introduced by the Phoenicians who apparently planted a variety of muscatel grape, known as the Muscat of Alexandria, in the south. Later, when the country was colonized by the Romans, other regions, particularly in the north, also discovered the potential of the vine. Despite numerous invasions (Celts, Visagoths, Arabs, etc.), wine cultivation continued to prosper, and was still practiced when the Portuguese regained control of their country. Astonishingly, Portugal managed to save one type of vine from the disastrous phylloxera epidemic that swept through Europe in the 19th century. Known as the *Ramisco* variety, this grape is cultivated in the Colares region. The sandy soil and deep roots of the vines helped it withstand this aphid-like pest.

Four methods of wine-growing are practiced in Portugal today:

The first is known as *Enforcado* (or "Hanged" method), whereby vines are planted near tree trunks that support the vines. In the second method, called *Ramada* or *Latada*, vines are planted by high stone piles arranged in rows. The branches growing up along either side ultimately meet, forming a lovely green canopy.

Although they are still in use, these two methods are no longer practiced by the majority of wine growers since they make it impossible to harvest the grapes by machine. The third method uses 1.5m T-shaped supports that provide grapes with maximum exposure to the sun. This is called the *Cruzeta* ("Cross") method. The fourth method, used by most large wine producers, is known as the "French" method and involves metal wires stretched between 1.5m-high poles. The vines grow along these wires, receiving uniform exposure to the sun. Mechanical harvesters can easily be used with this method.

Air travel has made distances much shorter, and it has become fashionable for northern Europeans to spend three or four days in Lisbon or Porto. The economic crisis of the 1980s had a negative impact on Portugal's tourist industry. The region hardest hit was the over-developed Algarve, where concrete buildings had been sprouting up unchecked for the previous two decades. Elsewhere, the *pousada* network has continued to expand, with the restoration of abandoned heritage buildings. Tourists come mainly from Spain (4.5 million), Great Britain (1.3 million), Germany (0.8 million) and France (0.6 million).

The Arts

Architecture

Until the end of the 15th century, Portugal more or less followed the same architectural movements as the rest of Europe. At the dawn of the 16th century, however, an entirely original style emerged;

it was named the **Manueline style**, after King Manuel I, who reigned from 1495 to 1521. An extension of the late Gothic style, revealing certain Muslim influences, it features complex lines and lavish ornamentation. It is worth noting that after the reconquest, many Muslims chose to stay in Portugal and adopt the Catholic religion. The artisans among them did not, however, abandon their decorative traditions.

India were being discovered. The nobility and the clergy were thus able to finance the construction of prestigious buildings, such as the Convento de Cristo in Tomar, the expansion of the Batalha monastery and the Mosteiro dos Jerónimos in Belém, which still command admiration today.

Portugal's prosperity attracted foreign artists, such as French sculptor Nicolas Chantereine.

Manueline Art

The Manueline style was also inspired by contemporary issues. It coincided with the era of discovery, when the Portuguese ruled the sea. Accordingly, the stone used in buildings is often patterned with ropes, seaweed and nautical instruments.

This style was born when the riches of America, Africa and

Bringing news of the Renaissance, with its predilection for Roman antiquity, these individuals introduced Italian-style elements into the country's architecture. No pure, fixed style emerged, however, for Portugal had become the crossroads of the world, welcoming artists from Africa and the Orient, and letting its knights, merchants and members of religious

orders draw inspiration from all they had seen elsewhere.

Next, from the late 1600s to the early 1900s, came the Portuguese baroque, examples of which can be found all over, not only in churches, but also in palaces, like the one in Queluz (a part of which has been strikingly transformed into a *pousada*), and a number of charming hotels. This style continues to gain followers to this day, as evidenced by the decor of several nightclubs in Lisbon (the Alcantara Mar, the Fragil, the Kremlin, etc.). Portuguese baroque is characterized chiefly by the fanciful, extravagantly decorated gilded wood known as *talha dourada* (see p 292). It also features portals topped by pediments and arches and other geometric lines overlapping to form intricate designs. Toward the end of the 19th century, the baroque grew more elaborate and developed into the rococo style, which is characterized by the frequent use of shells.

During the 19th century, there was a gradual shift away from the excesses of the baroque and rococo, and the neoclassical style became standard not only for official buildings, but for religious ones as well. Directly inspired by antiquity, this style is more aus-

Azulejos

These small ceramic tiles are found throughout Portugal, everywhere from historic buildings dating from the 15th century to restaurants in all different categories. Although definitely of Muslim origin, they were originally imported here from Spain; up until the 16th century, most of them came from Seville, and were only decorated with geometric or floral patterns. Then, around 1560, ceramists came from Anvers and began making *azulejos* in Lisbon. Their use of brushes to paint pictures on the tiles marked a shift away from the Moorish style, in which only non-representational decoration was permitted.

Surprisingly, it wasn't until the late 17th century that craftsmen began painting *azulejos* exclusively in cobalt blue, which then became extremely common, although multi-coloured tiles have come back into fashion from time to time. In the 19th century, *azulejos* began to appear on the exteriors of buildings, giving certain urban areas in both Portugal and Brazil a distinctive look. The *azulejo* has naturally followed the major artistic trends, such as Romanticism, Art Deco and abstractionism. Even the Lisbon metro is adorned with *azulejos*!

tere and favours the use of "noble" materials, such as marble, over stucco and wood. The English introduced the Palladian style, a particular favourite of theirs, into certain northern cities like Porto.

The Manueline style has nevertheless continued to influence Portuguese architecture to the present day. Some superb neo-Manueline palaces and villas, such as the Palace Hotel do Buçaco, have been erected in this century.

To date, over 2,500 buildings throughout the country have been classified historic monuments. A few places figure on UNESCO's list of World Heritage Sites: the monastery of Batalha, the Mosteiro dos Jerónimos in Belém, the Santa Maria monastery in Alcobaça, and the historic centres of Évora and Porto.

Literature

In the late 15th century, a period of great upheaval all over the planet and of great discoveries for Portugal, Gil Vicente pioneered the Portuguese theatre. Then, in the 16th century, Luis de Camões wrote an 8,000-verse epic poem describing the adventures of the explorers. Luis de Camões is to Portugal what Dante is to Italy or Shakespeare to England.

The 17th century sermons of Padre António Viera, an evangelist in Brazil, were masterpieces of religious oratory, and as such could not help but attract the attention of the extremely devout Portuguese.

In the 19th century, the Romantic movement emerged, led by writers like Almeida Garrett, Alexandre Herculano and Camilo Castelo Branco, who lampooned the clergy and the established order.

Azulejos

The relationship between Pessõa and his native city, which he had to leave at the age of seven when his widowed mother married the Portuguese consul to South Africa, is a veritable love story. Pessõa lived in South Africa for 10 years and was educated in English. At the age of 17 he returned alone to Lisbon and never again left. He endeavoured to make Lisbon and Portugal known the world over as he considered this culture to have been belittled by the superior attitude of its English "father-in-law". Pessõa even wrote a guide to Lisbon, in Portuguese and English, *What the Tourist Should See*, but astoundingly this work was not discovered until the end of the 1980s. It is a rather banal work of too-detailed, soulless descriptions.

To learn more about the most famous Portuguese writer of the century, visit the museum dedicated to his memory in Lisbon, **Casa-Museu Fernando Pessõa** (*Rua Coelho da Rocho no. 16, 1250 Lisboa, ☎213 96 81 90, open Mon to Fri, 1pm to 6pm; from Rua Vitor Cordon, take tram 28, or form Rossio, bus 9*).

Another important literary figure of the 20th century was **Miguel Torga**, who opposed the Salazar regime in his writing, which was repeatedly censored

The beginning of the 20th century was marked by the publication of the first and only two issues of the literary journal *Orpheu* (1915). It was founded by **Fernando Pessõa**, the most celebrated Portuguese author of the 20th century, whose name means "person". In a way, he was more than one person, for he published a number of articles and longer works under various pseudonyms. Names alone were not enough for Pessoa, however; he actually developed a biography for each "author".

Each one thus represents a different facet of his work, be it poetry, philosophy or aesthetics.

The Italian author Antonio Tabucchi describes the meeting of Pessõa with each of his pseudonymous alter egos during the course of the last three days of his life. Tabucchi also wrote, in Portuguese, *Requiem*, which is set entirely in Lisbon and which reveals captivating facets of the old city.

and seized. His book *Portugal* takes the reader on a whirlwind historical and poetic tour of the entire country.

One contemporary author who stands out is **Mario de Carvalho**, who skilfully blends the realistic and the absurd.

Although more than 200 million people across the world speak Portuguese, it was not until 1998 that Portuguese literature was honoured with the Nobel Prize, when **José Saramago** became the first Portuguese-language writer to receive this prestigious award. Born into a humble family, he dropped out of high school to earn a living and went on to ply several trades. He published his first novel, *Land of Sin*, at the age of 25. After joining the Communist party in 1959, he became involved in the fight against the Salazar dictatorship. In 1997, his book *Memorial do Convento* (or *Baltasar and Blimunda*), which has been translated into several languages, earned him international repute. In 1991, his controversial work *The Gospel According to Jesus Christ*, in which he portrays Christ as a little too "human" for some people, angered conservatives and was taken off the list of works selected in Portugal for the European Literary Prize. This prompted Saramago to

leave his native land for Spain, then for the Island of Lanzarote (Canary Islands), where he presently resides.

Painting

Vieira da Silva is without question the most celebrated contemporary painter in Portugal. Born in 1908, he left his home town of Lisbon for Paris in 1936. There is a little bit of Lisbon in all of his work, though; a number of his paintings are made up of little squares reminiscent of *azulejos*.

Cinema

At 91 years of age, **Manoel de Oliveira** is the only still-active filmmaker to have begun his career back in the silent-film era. He shot his first film, a documentary entitled *Douro, Faina Fluvial* (*Douro, River Work*), in 1931, and even acted in Portugal's first "talkie" in 1933. De Oliveira was also the first Portuguese filmmaker to shoot a film in colour, in 1959. His esoteric films are slow-paced, featuring sumptuous images and literary scripts – something that has hardly made him a household name. Indeed, only some 30,000 Portuguese have seen his films. To date, de Oliveira has a total of 35 fims to his credit, including 19 fictional features. The first of

these, made in 1941 and entitled *Aniki-Bóbó*, is a remarkable portrait of the children of Porto, de Oliveira's native city. *Viagem ao Princípio do Mundo* (*Journey to the Beginning of the World*), made in 1996-97, and *Anxiety*, released in October 1998, are among this fascinating film director's most recent films.

Music

Amália Rodrigues

On October 6, 1999, the famous *fadista* died of heart disease in her home town. Right in the midst of an election campaign and still reeling from the tragedy in Timor, the nation was hit hard by the news. Political differences were suddenly put aside, making way for national mourning. Rodrigues's state funeral was attended by a huge crowd, both young and old from all levels of society, including those with no real appreciation for *fado*. The whole country wished to pay its last respects to the "Great Lady", as she is known to the Portuguese. Amália will sing no longer, but her voice, her *saudade*, will remain in Portugal's collective memory forevermore.

Amália was born in 1920 in the Alcântara district of Lisbon. For her 75th birthday in 1995, television stations and cultural circles paid this national heroine the tribute she so richly deserved. She began her career at the age of 19 in Lisbon's Retio da Severa, a *fado* club. Her unique way of singing, powerful stage presence and radiant beauty immediately set her on the road to success. She launched her international career four years later, in 1943, first in Spain and then in Brazil. Next, she appeared in the films *Capas Negros* and *Fado, História duma Contadeira*. She "created" rituals, her songs "became" *fado,* her black clothes, an "age-old tradition". She went to New York in 1952 and 1954, but, full of *saudade* (nostalgia) for Lisbon, refused to go to Hollywood to make movies afterward. In 1955, however, she appeared in the French film *Les Amants du Tage*, in which she sang *Barco Negro*. The song was an international hit, and as a result she was invited to perform at the Olympia in 1956. From that moment on, she was no longer simply an ambassador from a far-off, little-known country, but a prominent figure on the international music scene; she sang in English, Spanish, Italian and French, always in charming Portuguese tones. She can be credited with enriching the world of *fado*, giving it new poetry, from the Middle Ages to the present day. Great mu-

sicians like Alain Oulman wrote for her, breathing new life into this form of music. In major English-speaking cities, you'll have no trouble finding the songs she recorded in English on compact disc. In Portugal, of course, you'll find her songs in Portuguese, but prices are higher than in North America. In either language, her outstanding voice and singing style will go straight to your heart, making it easy to understand why she was the first Portuguese contemporary performer to earn worldwide recognition.

She gave her last performance at the Lisbon World Exposition in the summer of 1998.

MadreDeus

MadreDeus was introduced to the world music scene in the Wim Wenders film *Lisbon Story*. The group's album *Ainda* is dedicated to Lisbon and serves, appropriately, as the soundtrack to Wenders's film.

MadreDeus' sound is a mix of traditional and modern, layered on an aural background of medieval tones. The instrumentation includes voice, guitar, cello, accordion and keyboards. With its music full of sadness and *saudade,* MadreDeus is archetypically Portuguese and has made a beautiful contribution to world music.

Tetvocal

Tetvocal got its start covering contemporary American songs. Still a cappella, the group now sings in Portuguese, drawing inspiration from all that is Portuguese.

Rio Grande

The folk sound of Rio Grande is another example of the renewal of Portuguese music through the exploration of its ancestral roots. The purity of the sound, the poetry of the lyrics and the allure of the melodies have made Rio Grande a success.

Table of distances (km)
Via the shortest Route

	Braga	Coimbra	Faro	Grenada (Spain)	Lisbon	Madrid (Spain)	Porto
Braga							
Coimbra	170						
Faro	625	460					
Grenada (Spain)	980	760	465				
Lisbon	362	200	300	660			
Madrid (Spain)	580	510	730	425	630		
Porto	50	120	570	920	310	620	
Seville (Spain)	757	578	223	166	419	519	703

Example: The distance between Lisbon and Coimbra is 200 km.

Practical Information

This chapter contains useful information for planning your stay in Portugal.

Entrance Formalities

Citizens of the EEC and Switzerland only need their national identity cards to enter Portugal. North Americans must have valid passports to enter Portugal and can stay there up to three months.

In addition, all travellers, except members of the European Union and of Switzerland, must have ongoing or return tickets. As these regulations are subject to change at any time, we recommend that you verify them with the Portuguese embassy or consulate nearest you before your departure.

Embassies and Consulates

Foreign Embassies and Consulates in Portugal

AUSTRALIA
Embassy
Rua Marques sa da Bandera 8/r/ce, 1000 Lisboa
☎213 53 25 55
⇌213 53 63 47

BELGIUM
Embassy and Consulate
Praça Marques Pombal, 14, 6th floor, 1200 Lisboa Codex
☎213 53 98 70
⇌213 53 57 23

CANADA
Embassy
Edifício MCB, Avenida Liberdade, 144/56, 2nd and 3rd floors, 1200 Lisboa
☎213 47 48 92
⇌213 47 64 66

DENMARK
Embassy
R. Castilho, 14C - 3o.
1250 Lisboa
☎213 54 50
⇌213 57 01 24

FINLAND
Embassy
R. Miguel Lupi, 12 - 5o.
1200 Lisbon
☎213 60 75 51
⇌213 60 47 58

GERMANY
Embassy
Campo dos Mártires da Pátria
38, 1100 Lisboa
☎218 81 02 10
≈218 85 38 46

GREAT BRITAIN
Embassy
Rua de S Domingos Á Lapa, 37
1200 Lisboa
☎213 96 11 91
≈213 97 67 68

ITALY
Embassy and Consulate
Largo Calçadinha Pombeiro, 6
1200 Lisboa
☎213 54 61 44
≈213 54 94 65

NETHERLANDS
Embassy
Avenida Infante Fanto, 435
1300 Lisboa
☎213 96 11 63
≈213 96 64 36

NORWAY
Embassy
Av. D. Vasco da Gama
11400 Lisboa
☎213 01 53 44
≈213 01 61 58

SPAIN
Embassy
Rua do Salitre, 1, 1250 Lisboa
☎213 47 23 81
≈213 47 53 76

SWEDEN
Embassy
R. Miguel Lupi, 12 - 2o.
1200 Lisbon
☎213 95 52 24
≈213 96 56 88

SWITZERLAND
Embassy
Travessa do Patrocinio, 1
1399 Lisboa Codex
☎213 97 31 21
≈213 97 71 87

UNITED STATES
Embassy
Avenida das Forcas Armadas
1600 Lisboa
☎217 26 66 00
≈217 26 91 09

Portuguese Embassies and Consulates Abroad

AUSTRALIA
Embassy
23 Culgoa Cct., O'Malley
ACT 2606
☎(6) 290-1733
≈(6) 290-1957

BELGIUM
Embassy
Avenue de la Toison d'Or, 55
1060 Bruxelles
☎(02) 539 38 50
≈(02) 539-0773

CANADA
Embassy
645 Island Park Drive, Ottawa
Ont., K1Y 0B8
☎(613) 729-0883/2270
≈(613) 729-2270

Consulate
2020 Rue University, Suite 1725
Montréal, QC, H3A 3A5
☎(514) 499-0359
≈(514) 499-0366

Consulate
121 Richmond St. W., 7th floor
Toronto, Ont., M5H 2K1
☎(416) 360-8260
≈(416) 360-0350

Consulate
700 West Pender St., Suite 904
Vancouver, BC, V6C 353
☎(604) 688-6514
≈(604) 685-7042

DENMARK
Embassy
Hovedvagtsgade 6
Dk-1103 Copenhagen K
☎(45) 33 12 71 17
☎(45) 33 13 13 01
≈(45) 33 14 92 14

FINLAND
Embassy
Itainen Puistotie,11 B 14
Helsinki 14-SF
☎(35) 80-171717
≈(35) 80-663550

GERMANY
Embassy
Ubierstrasse 78, 5300 Bonn 2
☎(228) 36 30 11
≈(228) 35 28 64

GREAT BRITAIN
Embassy
11 Belgrave Square, London
SWIX 8PP
☎(171) 235 5331
≈(171) 245 1287

ITALY
Embassy
Viale Liege, NR.21
00198 Rome
☎(39) 6-844801
≈(39) 6-8417404

Consulate
Via Vittor Pisani, 31
20124 Milan
☎(39) 2-66986480
≈(39) 2-66985230

NETHERLANDS
Embassy
Bazarstraat 21, 2518 Ag Den
Haag
☎(70) 363-0217
≈(70) 361-5589

SPAIN
Embassy
Calle del Pinar, 1
28006 Madrid
☎(34) 1-561-7800
≈(34) 1-411-0172

Consulate
Paseo del General Martinez
Campos, Madrid 10
☎*(34) 1-445-4600*
✆*(34) 1-445-4608*

Consulate
Ronda de S. Pedro,7-1
Barcelona 10
☎*(34) 3-318-8150*
✆*(34) 3-3185912*

Consulate
Calle Marques de Valladares
23-1, 32601 VIGO, P.O. Box 247
☎*(34) 86-436911*
✆*(34) 86-433064*

Consulate
Avenue de Francia, NR.2-1.C
P.O. Box 3115
San Sebastian (Guipuzcoa)
☎*(34) 43-276859*
✆*(34) 43-277547*

Consulate
Avenue del Cid, NR.1
41004 Seville
☎*(34) 5-4231150*
✆*(34) 5-4236013*

SWEDEN
Embassy
Narvavägen 30-32, 2tr
Box 27004
☎*(46) 8-6626028*
☎*(46) 8 6684555*
✆*(46) 8-6625329*
✆*(46) 8 6625329*

Consulate
Karl Johansg, 82, Box 12060
S-402-41
☎*(46) 31 42 1205*
✆*(46) 31 42 4320*

Consulate
St. Nygatan, 27 c
S-21-37 Malmö
☎*(46) 40 303560*
✆*(46) 40 11 8687*

SWITZERLAND
Embassy
Jungfraustrasse 1
CH 3005 Berne
☎*(41-31) 352-8329*
✆*(41-31) 351-4432*

Consulate
Zeltweg 13, Ch-8032
Zurich
☎*(41-1) 261-3366*
✆*(41-1) 251-2484*

Consulate
220, Route De Ferney
Ch 1218 Le Grand Saconnex
Geneva
☎*(41-22) 791-0511*
✆*(41-22) 788-2503*

UNITED STATES
Embassy
2125 Kalorama Rd., NW
Washington DC 20008
☎*(202) 328-9025/8610*
✆*(202) 462-3726*

Consulate
899, Boylston St., 2nd Floor
Boston, Massachusetts 02115
☎*(617) 536-8740/9408*
✆*(617) 536-2503*

Consulate
1955 N. New England Avenue
Chicago, Illinois 60707
☎*(312) 889-7405*
✆*(312) 493-2433*

Consulate
700 Louisiana St., Houston
Texas 77002
☎*(713) 759-1188*

Consulate
1801 Avenue of the Stars, 400
Los Angeles, California 90067
☎*(310) 277-1491*

Consulate
1901 Ponce de Leon Boulevard
Miami, FL 33134
☎*(305) 444-6311*

Consulate
630 Fifth Avenue, Suite 310-378
New York, NY 10111
☎*(212) 246-4580*
☎*(212) 765-2980*
✆*(212) 459-0190*

Tourist Information

In order to help readers explore the country, we have divided Portugal into several regions (see map p 10). With the exception of Costa de Prata, which we have divided in two because of its many tourist attractions, the eight regions correspond to the official groupings formerly used by the tourist bureau. The boundaries of the tourist regions were redrawn in early 1999, amalgamating them into five large zones: Lisboa and Vale do Tejo, Beiras, Porto and Norte de Portugal, Alentejo and Algarve (see map p 43). Given the many brochures that still use the old system, we decided to retain the old demarcations for practical reasons.

Additional tourist information is easy to find while in Portugal. Most towns have tourist offices (*informação turistica*). The addresses of the specific offices are listed in the "Practical Information" section of each chapter.

ICEP
(Portuguese tourist office)
www.portugal.org

Practical
Information

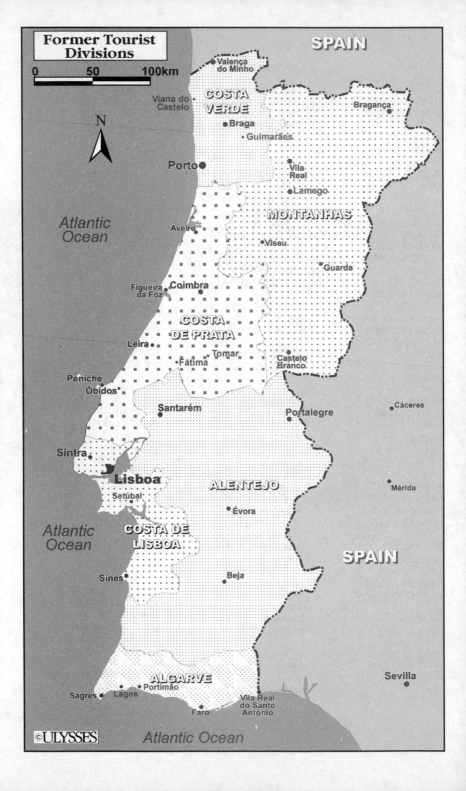

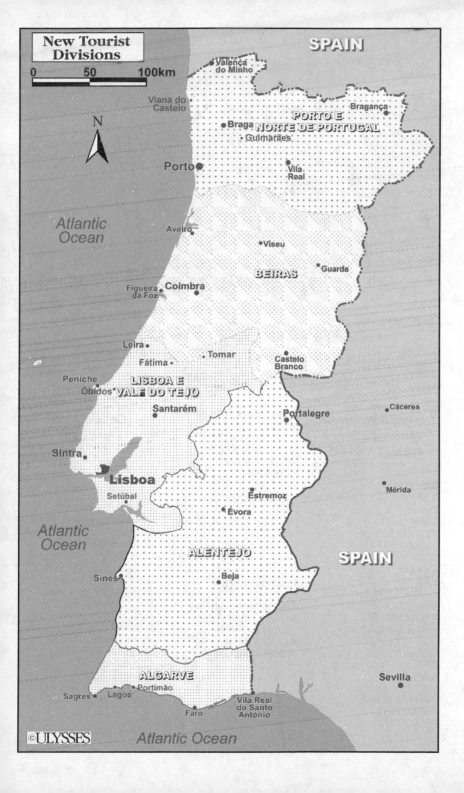

New Tourist Divisions

0   50   100km

N

SPAIN

Valença do Minho

Viana do Castelo

Bragança

Braga
Guimarães

PORTO E NORTE DE PORTUGAL

Porto

Vila Real

Atlantic Ocean

Aveiro

Viseu

Guarda

BEIRAS

Figueira da Foz

Coimbra

Leira

Tomar

Fátima

Castelo Branco

Peniche

Óbidos

LISBOA E VALE DO TEJO

Portalegre

Cáceres

Santarém

Sintra

Lisboa

Mérida

Setúbal

Estremoz

Évora

Atlantic Ocean

ALENTEJO

SPAIN

Sines

Beja

ALGARVE

Sevilla

Sagres

Lagos

Portimão

Vila Real do Santo António

Faro

©ULYSSES

Atlantic Ocean

Information About the Country

On the Internet

www.icep.pt
www.portugal-insite.pt
www.monumentos.pt
www.well.com/user/ideamen/portugal.html
www.ipmuseus.pt
www.cidadevirtual.pt
www.cusco.viatecla.pt
www.ip.pt/top5
www.sapo.pt

Telecom white pages: net118.telecom.pt/pesquisa.html
Yellow pages: www.paginasamarelas.pt

In Portugal

Telephone information line: ☎800-296-296 (toll-free)

Portuguese Tourist Information Offices Abroad

BELGIUM
ICEP
Rue Joseph II, 5, B.P. 3
1000 Bruxelles
☎(2) 230 52 50
↩(2) 231 04 47

CANADA
ICEP
60 Bloor St. West, Suite 1005,
Toronto, Ont., M4W 3B8
☎(416) 921-7376
↩(416) 921-1353

GERMANY
ICEP
Schäfergasse, 17,
60313 Frankfurt Main
☎(69) 23 40 94
☎(69) 29 05 90 34
↩(69) 23 14 33

GREAT BRITAIN
ICEP
2nd Floor 22-25A, Sackville
Street, London WIX 1DE
☎(171) 494 1441
↩494 1868

NETHERLANDS
ICEP
Paul Gabriëlstraat 70, ZH 2596
VG Den Haag
☎(70) 326 25 25
↩(70) 328 00 25

UNITED STATES
ICEP
590 Fifth Avenue, 3rd Floor
New York, NY 10036-470
☎(212) 354-4658
☎(212) 354-4404
↩(212) 575-4737

Getting to Portugal

By Plane

Charter flights from Canada aboard TAP Air Portugal are offered out of major cities. Scheduled flights to Portugal are also available with Air France through Paris, KLM via Amsterdam, Swissair via Zurich, British Airways via London, etc. The majority of visitors land in Lisbon or Porto. Faro, in the Algarve, is also served by planes from the continent and the United Kingdom.

Lisbon Airport (Portela de Sacavém)

Lisbon's international 8km airport is located about north of downtown. Besides the tourist information counter and post office, you will find exchange offices, bank branches as well as automatic teller machines (*departures and arrivals information 24hrs a day* ☎*218 41 37 00; general airport information, www.ana-aeroportos.pt*).

Several **car rental** companies have offices at the airport, these include:

Avis
☎*218 49 48 36*

Hertz
☎*218 49 08 31*

Budget
☎*218 49 16 03*

Europcar
☎*218 40 11 76*

Thrifty
☎*218 47 88 03*

Take note, however, that prices for car rentals at the airport are generally higher than downtown, except for those who have reserved in advance. An airport tax is also added to each car rental. If you plan on visiting Lisbon, rent your car in town.

Porto Airport (Francisco da Sá Carneiro)

Francisco da Sá Carneiro International Airport
(*formerly known as Pedras Rubras*)
about 11km north of Porto
flight arrival and departure information:
☎*229 48 21 41*
☎*229 48 31 41*
general airport information:
www.ana-aeroportos.pt

In addition to a tourist information counter, you will find exchange offices as well as car rental companies (Avis, Hertz, Budget) Take note, however, that prices for car rentals at the airport are generally higher than downtown, except for those who have reserved in advance.

Faro Airport

Faro Airport
6km from the capital of the Algarve
flight arrival and departure information:
☎*289 80 06 07*
general airport information:
www.ana-aeroportos.pt

Besides regularly scheduled flights from Lisbon and Porto, TAP Air Portugal offers charter flights in winter from all European capitals, from Montreal and Toronto and from the United States.

By Train

It now takes less than 24hrs to reach Lisbon from Paris by train aboard the TGV *Atlantique*. You must change trains in Irún, Spain. Fares for this train, however, are along the same lines as an airfare.

By Car

If you are already in Europe, you can drive to Portugal, though it is a long trip through France and Spain and all costs (gasoline, highway tolls, wear on your vehicle) should be factored in when determining the best mode of travel.

This trip of over 1,800km requires two to three days of driving and, unless you take the time to enjoy a bit of France and Spain along the way, will prove very taxing. If you want to have your car with you, you can always opt for the "car-train" offered by SNCF, the French railway company.

The most direct route from Paris is through Bordeaux then to Irún, Spain and into Portugal at Bragança, the more interesting option, or through Vilar Formoso. The latter border is open all night long, as are those at Elvas and Valença do Minho, though these are less practical.

Practical Information

Theft from cars is common in Portugal so be sure to take note of the safety precautions on p 53.

Transportation

By Car

Getting around Portugal by car is the best way to see all its little historic villages. While Porto and Lisbon are both easy destinations for a short stay, the other way to visit Portugal, that is to explore its countryside, can only be done with a car.

The road network is still relatively undeveloped, even though much progress has been made. There is a lot of traffic and speeds rarely go above 80 km/h. For this reason be sure to plan your excursions well.

Over the last several years, a number of freeways have been built, and the cities of Lisbon, Porto, Valença do Minho, Guimarães, Vila Real, Setúbal, Évora and Estremoz now have divided highways. Also, in Algarve, Highway E1-IP1 links Vila Real de San António and Albufeira. Nevertheless, narrow and winding sections of road are common. At press time the cost of a litre of gas was 170 ESC.

Drive with caution in Portugal: in populated regions, many of the roads have three lanes, the middle lane being a passing lane for both directions. A car with a powerful engine will be helpful. The other reason to take special care is because Portuguese drivers can be divided into two specific categories: those that seem incapable of driving faster than 50 km/h (and there are many), and those, seemingly influenced by the *movida*, who drive at least 120 km/h. Tourists generally find themselves precariously somewhere between these two extremes.

Essentially the key to driving in Portugal resides in careful, realistic planning: a lot of time for stops – to admire the countryside, to savour regional pastries or to visit a church that no guide mentions but that seems to draw you into its *talha dourada* altar. Avoid driving at night or at twilight when farmers are returning from the fields with their animals and visibility is reduced. So... *precaução e bom viagem*!

Besides the highways, there is a considerable network of national, regional and local roads that lead to the smallest most remote villages of the back country. Be careful, however, as national roads are not necessarily very wide. In fact,

they tend to be quite narrow.

Theft from cars is common in Portugal so be sure to take note of the safety precautions on p 53.

A Few Tips

Drivers License

North American and European drivers licenses are valid in Portugal.

The Highway Code

North Americans are advised that at intersections, priority is given to cars arriving on the right, regardless of which driver arrived first. However, major roads are served by roundabouts and cars within them always have priority. Therefore, wait for the way to completely clear before entering the roundabout.

The use of seat belts is mandatory in Portugal.

The maximum speed limit on highways is 130 km/h.

In certain remote areas of the country **service stations** are rare; you would be wise to fill up as soon as you come upon one.

Be sure to get a detailed **road map** of the whole country to make it easier to find your way around.

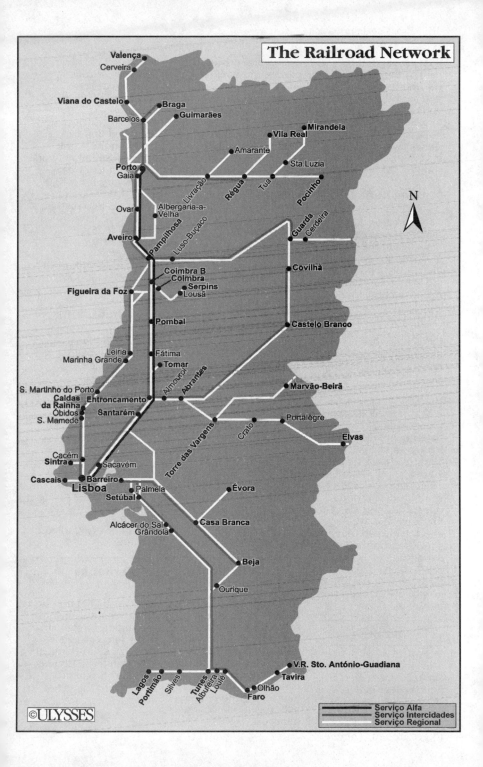

Free **parking** can be hard to find in the cities, and if you do happen to find a place, you may be expected to give 100 ESC to the homeless person or student who claims to have found you the spot.

Car Rentals

All international car rental agencies have branches in the region. Most are represented at the airports and around the main train stations. It is generally more expensive to rent a car at the airport.

Foreign driver's licenses are generally valid for renting a car in Portugal.

If you rent a car upon arrival, expect to pay around 10,000 ESC per day (unlimited mileage) for a compact car (*Ford Escort, 1,100cm³*), unless you can rent as part of a package deal. Better value deals are often offered for periods of a few days or a week; check with your travel agent or with the international reservations service before leaving. Get a written confirmation of the agreed-upon rate.

By Bus

The cities and towns of Portugal are served by an excellent network of buses. This mode of transportation is the most economical way to get around. There

are several private companies and while some specialize in a certain region, others serve all locations in the country. In each major city there is a *rodoviária* (bus station) where companies generally have their ticket offices. Below are the addresses of a few of these:

In Lisbon

Rede Nacional de Expressos
Av. Dugue D'Ávila no. 12, Terminal Arco do Cego
☎*213 54 54 39*
☎*213 10 31 11*
www.rede-expressos.pt

Renex Expressos
Campo das Cebolas
☎*218 87 48 71*
☎*218 88 28 29*
≈*218 87 49 42*
≈*218 86 45 48*

In Porto

Rede Nacional Expressos
Rodoviaria Beira/Litoral, Rua Alexandre Herculano
☎*02 31 24 59*

Renex Expressos
Rua Carmelitas
☎*222 08 28 98*

By Train

Large cities like Lisbon, Porto and Coimbra are served regularly by rapid and comfortable trains. It can be difficult, however, to reach the smaller cities and it is not feasible to imagine touring the country with this mode of transport.

The national railway company is called **Caminhos de Ferro Portugueses (CP)**. It offers passes (*bilhetes turísticos*) which permit unlimited 2nd-class travel on the whole Portuguese rail network for seven to 21 days; prices vary from 18,000 to 42,000 ESC. For more information, contact CP in Lisbon at:
☎*218 88 40 25*
☎*218 88 50 92*
www.cp.pt
There is an additional 10% discount on return tickets.

Hitchhiking

Hitchhiking is rare in Portugal and is not recommended.

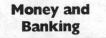

Money and Banking

The local currency is the escudo (ESC; in Portugal the $ sign is occasionally used).

For easier on-the-spot reference, all prices in this guide are quoted in escudos.

Banks

Banks usually offer the best exchange rates for converting foreign currency into escudos. Most banks in Portugal are open from Monday to Friday 8:30am to 3pm.

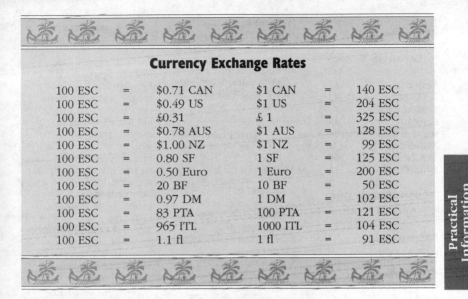

Currency Exchange Rates

100 ESC	=	$0.71 CAN	$1 CAN	=	140 ESC
100 ESC	=	$0.49 US	$1 US	=	204 ESC
100 ESC	=	£0.31	£ 1	=	325 ESC
100 ESC	=	$0.78 AUS	$1 AUS	=	128 ESC
100 ESC	=	$1.00 NZ	$1 NZ	=	99 ESC
100 ESC	=	0.80 SF	1 SF	=	125 ESC
100 ESC	=	0.50 Euro	1 Euro	=	200 ESC
100 ESC	=	20 BF	10 BF	=	50 ESC
100 ESC	=	0.97 DM	1 DM	=	102 ESC
100 ESC	=	83 PTA	100 PTA	=	121 ESC
100 ESC	=	965 ITL	1000 ITL	=	104 ESC
100 ESC	=	1.1 fl	1 fl	=	91 ESC

Practical Information

Credit Cards and Traveller's Cheques

Visa and MasterCard are the most accepted. Be sure to ask in advance, however, if you plan on paying with a credit card.

Traveller's cheques are usually not a problem.

You can use your credit card in most automatic teller machines; small service charges apply but you will generally get a better exchange rate than at the bank or exchange office. Plus you don't have to wait – these machines are open 24hrs a day.

Mail and Telecommunications

You can buy stamps at any post office, and also at the major hotels. Mail is collected on a daily basis.

Telephones

To phone Portugal from abroad dial the code for international calls in your country then Portugal's country code (*351*), then the telephone number.

Telephone numbers in Portugal recently changed to nine digits. For directory assistance dial *118*.

Remember that discount rates are available at certain times of the day.

Coin-operated public phones are easy to find in Lisbon.

Portugal Telecom
every day from 8am to 11pm
in the Rossio;
Praça Dom Pedro IV no. 68, northwest side of the square, next to the Valentim de Carvalho music store
You can place calls from here and purchase *cartões telefónicos* (telephone cards) (*1000 ESC for 50 units*).

To call abroad from Portugal, you have two options. You can direct-dial and pay local phone rates or you can use your phone company's access code to reach an operator in your country. For direct-dialled numbers you must dial 00 for the international operator, the country code, the area code and the telephone number you wish to reach

Country Codes

Australia	*61*
Belgium	*32*
Canada/U.S.	*1*
Germany	*49*
Great Britain	*44*
Netherlands	*31*
New Zealand	*64*
Switzerland	*41*

International Access Codes

International access codes connect you with your phone company's operator and you pay your phone company's rates.

Canada Direct
☎*800-800-122*

AT&T Direct
☎*0800-800-128*

MCI Direct
☎*05017-1234*
☎*0800-800-123*

Sprint Direct
☎*05017-1877*

British Telecom Direct
☎*0505-00-44*

When calling abroad from Portuguese hotels, keep in mind that hotels often charge much higher rates than the Portuguese phone company. It is much less expensive to call from a phone booth, using a Portuguese operator and even less expensive to use Canada Direct or an equivalent. In the latter case you are charged approximately the same as you

would pay to call Portugal from Canada or the United States.

In addition, most hotels offer fax and telex services, as do all post offices.

Internet

Telepac
business service:
☎*0800 251 025*
technical support:
☎*808 20 40 60*
www.telecom.pt
internet.clientes@mail.tele pac.pt
For Internet access in Portugal, contact Telepac, a subsidiary of Portugal Telecom. They offer a service (Netline) that gives access to the net for 30hrs over a two-month period for 3,315 ESC. Telepac offers the advantage of providing local access numbers in most cities of the country, which avoids long-distance charges. Normally you have to go to the head office of Portugal Telecom to get your user name and password.

Portugal Telecom
Avenida Fontes Pereira de Melo no. 38C, Edifício Forum, 1089 Lisboa
Picoas metro stop
☎*213 14 25 27*
☎*213 52 22 92*

You can always send E-mail, and sometimes receive it, from the various Internet cafés mentioned in this guide or at Portugal Telecom offices mentioned above.

Language

Latin in origin, like Italian, Spanish and French, Portuguese might seem incomprehensible to an English-speaker's ear at first, even if the person knows a bit of Italian, Spanish or French. But to see it written is perhaps another story, and you only need a few hints about pronunciation and a few of the general changes from Spanish, and before you know it someone will be telling you "*O senhor fala muito bem português*". As in most countries, knowing a few phrases in the local language will make your trip that much more enriching.

A language reveals so much about its speakers and their culture! Portuguese is often called an ancient language. Perhaps isolation and conservatism have preserved more of its Latin roots.

For example, throughout Europe, Monday is the day of the moon (Monday, *Montag, lundi, lunedi*) and all the other days refer to a different planet... except in Portugal. The church discouraged pagan references and many centuries ago imposed a way of saying the days that revolved around Sunday. Sunday is called *domingo*, while Monday is *segunda feira* (the second of the holy day), Tuesday is *terceira feira*, and so on. This custom has probably confused its share of travellers, who find themselves in front of a museum that is open from Monday to Friday, and the sign says "*seg-sexta 9h - 17h*" or even "*2o - 6o 9h - 17h*"!

A short pronunciation guide and a glossary can be found at the end of this guide. To develop your ear, pull out your Madredeus or Bévinda records, even though the Brazilian pronunciation is a bit different, or look for a Portuguese radio or television station in your area.

Climate and Packing

Generally speaking, there are advantages and disadvantages to Portugal's climate: it rains quite often, but temperatures are mild and relatively stable. Because of its latitude, days are longer than in London or New York between September 21 and March 21. Any time of year is a good time to visit Portugal, and when you go will ultimately depend on what kind of trip you are planning.

January, February and March

Above all, take note that Lisbon in January is twice a sunny as Paris or London, and 50% more than Montréal or New York. As far as temperature is concerned, newly arrived North Americans often parade around in T-shirts, taking advantage of average highs around 15°C. Lisbon nights in January are cooler, around 8°C. Both Lisbon and Porto are rainy during this month, with 11 days of rain in the capital and 13 days in Porto, which is farther north and has an Atlantic climate. Half as much rain falls in Faro, in the Algarve, than in Porto in January, but there are still seven days of rain. This, combined with average highs of 15°C, means you won't be lounging around in your swimsuit all day, not to mention that the 16°C waters of the Atlantic are not very inviting. February and March are generally the same as January.

April and May

A look at the statistics may explain a few things about history and song. The weather starts to change in April in Portugal, like during the Flower Revolution! The mercury climbs to an average of 20°C during the day in Lis-

bon and Faro, and only drops to 13°C at night. Perfect outdoor weather, especially when you consider that Faro receives only 30 millimetres of rain over five days in the month. Lisbon is less lucky and receives twice as much over eight days. In fact, it rains more in Lisbon in April than in Paris; it seems songs occasionally lead to false assumptions.

June

With only one day of rain in Lisbon and Faro (on average, of course!), and five in Porto and Miranda do Douro, this is a perfect time for a grand tour of the country – especially since the tourist masses have yet to arrive, and temperatures remain very pleasant with maximum highs around 25°C throughout the country and minimums between 10 and 20°C.

July and August

This is the big tourist season, but not necessarily the most tolerable for those who don't enjoy hot weather. Average highs hover around 28°C throughout the country, with almost no rainy days, except in Porto, where people wonder if the English didn't leave some of their weather behind.

Practical Information

September and October

Just like June – except that we are in the northern hemisphere and therefore heading towards the shortest days of the year: in October, the whole country has an average of 4hrs less daylight than in June! Nevertheless, with close to 8hrs of sunlight per day, on average, it's much more pleasant than London, New York or Montréal!

November and December

Temperatures drop everywhere, and the number of days of rain goes up. Nevertheless, the mercury does hover between 8 and 15°C in Lisbon and it only rains one out of every three days; urbanites could easily discover everything that Lisbon, Porto and their surroundings have to offer.

What to Bring

Everything depends on the kind of trip you are taking and when you are going. Remember however that shorts and jeans are not always proper dress for visiting churches and monasteries.

The Portuguese coast has some nice beaches, and southern Portugal lies at the same latitude as Sicily and the Carolinas, so sunglasses, sunscreen and a hat should always be included in your bags, no matter what time of the year it is. Lovers of the great outdoors should not forget to bring a good pair of walking shoes as the regions of Sintra and northern Portugal are especially favourable to this activity.

Health

No vaccinations are necessary before entering Portugal, and health services are generally excellent. There are a significant number of AIDS cases, and as in other places, cases of venereal diseases do occur, so be sure to take the necessary precautions.

The Sun

In spite of its benefits, the sun can cause numerous problems. Always wear sunscreen to protect yourself from the sun's harmful rays. Overexposure to the sun can cause sunstroke, symptoms of which include dizziness, vomiting and fever. Cover yourself well and avoid prolonged exposure, especially for the first few days of your trip, as it takes a while to get used to the sun. Even once you are used to the sun's intensity, moderate exposure is best. Wearing a hat and sunglasses can help shield you from the harmful effects of the sun. Lastly, don't forget that sunscreens are most effective when applied 20 to 30min before exposure to the sun.

The First-Aid Kit

A small first-aid kit can help you avoid many difficulties. It is best to prepare it carefully before setting off on your trip. Make sure you take along a sufficient supply of all prescription medications you take regularly, as well as valid prescriptions in case you lose them. Other medicines, such as Imodium or its equivalent (for intestinal disorders and diarrhoea) may be purchased before leaving but are also available in local pharmacies in the cities and even in the smaller towns.

Insurance

Cancellation Insurance

Your travel agent will usually offer you cancellation insurance when you purchase your airplane ticket or vacation package. This insurance guarantees reimbursement for the cost of the ticket or package in case the trip has to be cancelled due to serious illness or death.

Theft Insurance

Most home-owner's insurance policies in North America cover some personal possessions, even if they are stolen abroad. In order to file a claim, you must have a police report. Depending on what is covered in your policy, it is not always necessary to take out additional insurance. European travellers, on the other hand, should make sure their policies protect their property in foreign countries, as this is generally not the case.

Theft in cars is common in Portugal so be sure to take note of the safety precautions (see below).

Health Insurance

This is without question the most useful kind of insurance for travellers, and should be purchased before leaving. Look for the most complete coverage possible because health-care costs in foreign countries can add up quickly. When you buy your policy, make sure it provides adequate coverage for all types of potentially costly medical expenses, such as hospitalization, nursing services and doctor's fees. It should also include a repatriation clause in case necessary care cannot be administered on site. As

you may have to pay upon leaving the clinic, check your policy to see what provisions it includes for such cases. During your stay, always keep proof of your insurance on you, as it will save you a lot of trouble if you are unlucky enough to require health care.

Safety and Security

Though Portugal is not a dangerous country, it has its share of petty thieves, especially in resort areas and big cities. In Lisbon's busy areas (Bairro Alto, Alcântara and Santo Amaro) be particularly careful at night. As many establishments are located on dark side streets or near such places, muggings and thefts are common; one of the authors had just such an experience in the Bairro Alto. There is very little police presence in these areas and therefore we can only advise people to be extremely prudent at night. As the nightclubs open quite late, be sure to take a taxi to get there and back to your hotel, especially if you are travelling alone. If you choose to walk anyway, stick to well-lit and busy arteries and steer clear of dark side streets.

During our visit to the Baixa district, and Rua Augusta in particular, we unfortunately dis-

covered that it has become a favourite haunt for drug dealers who openly peddle their wares to passers-by (they particularly target tourists and young people), even when the police are nearby. Hopefully, this situation is only temporary. Drug possession (both "hard" and "soft") is illegal in Portugal.

If you decide to visit one of the beaches near the coast, always keep an eye on your personal objects. These places are popular with tourists and by extension with professional thieves as well. Never leave anything in your car. Leave all your valuables in the safe at your hotel.

Conceal your traveller's checks, passport and some of your cash in a money belt. Remember, the less attention you attract, the less you risk being robbed. Pack a photocopy of your passport and the serial numbers of your traveller's cheques. If the originals are lost or stolen, knowing their reference numbers will make it much easier to replace them.

Theft in Cars

It may be hard for a North American to imagine the huge risk that exists in Southern Europe of having objects stolen from your car. Portugal is unfortunately no exception, and drivers would be wise to take the following precautions:

• Never leave your luggage in an unsupervised car. Thieves need only 5min to get what they want without any trace, even in the most remote places. The authors were robbed in Portinho, south of Lisbon. Car door locks are no secret to these professional pilferers.

• Above all do not leave anything visible that might have any value: bags, jackets. The lock might be picked in hopes that the jacket contains a wallet.

• If you must keep your luggage in your car be careful when stopping for gas or for a quick bite. Place the car where you can see it constantly. In the city, pay for a parking lot, and choose a spot near the attendant.

• Always leave the glove compartment wide open, to avoid the supposition that your camera might be inside.

• Leave your bags at the hotel while you are sightseeing, even if you have checked out. The reception desk will usually keep them for you. Finally always remember that whatever precautions you've taken, you could still be robbed so avoid carrying too many valuables with you.

If, despite all these precautions, you are unlucky enough to be robbed, be sure to file a police report. You will need it to be reimbursed by your insurance company. You will, however, have to deal with the inefficient bureaucracy, but at least you'll be safe from thieves at the police station because all the officers are there!

Victims' Rights in Portugal

Note that late at night or in the wee hours of the morning, the police will not come to the scene of the crime unless the circumstances are very serious. You must go yourself to the police station downtown (*Rua Capelo no. 13*, ☎*213 46 61 41*), a station that, in theory, assists victims of theft or assault. In reality, however, no statements are taken at night, and you must wait to be taken to the central station in the Chiado. Once there, you'll have to wait while they wake up the officer on duty (!) in order to register your complaint. It goes without saying that this wake-up call is not appreciated and that the officer is therefore not very receptive to your account. Communication difficulties (officers' comprehension of English is sketchy) mean you will have to be very patient. Don't expect any sym-

pathy or support; this type of assistance is not part of the protocol and depends entirely on the officer. Finally, after enduring all of this, you have to find your own way back to your hotel. It goes without saying that some compassion and respect for victims' rights would go a long way in Portugal.

Holidays

New Year's Day
January 1

Shrove Tuesday
Variable

Good Friday
Variable

Easter
Variable

Celebration of Revolution of April 25, 1974
April 25

Labour Day
May 1

Corpus Christi
Variable

Dia de Camões e das Comunidades
June 10

Feast of the Assumption
August 15

Republic Day
October 5

All Saints Day
November 1

Celebration of Independence from Spain
December 1

Christmas
December 25

Accommodations

The hotel infrastructure differs greatly from one region to the next in Portugal. In the big cities of Lisbon and Porto, you'll find all types of lodging for all budgets, except for bed and breakfasts, which are uncommon. In regions with many historic sites there is usually a *pousada* (see below). Bed and breakfasts (*turisme de habitação*) are found throughout the countryside.

Low-budget accommodations are not always the best value. By spending just a bit more, about 10,500 to 20,500 ESC, you can find very comfortable, charming accommodations with an excellent quality-to-price ratio. **Breakfast is always included in the price of a room**, unless otherwise indicated, which is rare.

The season has a significant influence on the price. Below you'll find the low, mid- and high seasons for the *pousadas*. Keep this, as well as the climatic conditions, in mind when deciding on the best time to visit.

This guide lists what we found to be the best selections in each category. All prices, unless otherwise indicated, are for two people. We have also included the complete address of each establishment (postal address, telephone and fax number) in order to facilitate reservations before your departure.

Charges for calls made from hotel rooms in Portugal are very high. It is therefore a good idea to use the direct dialling services described on p 49, 50; you will not have to pay anything in Portugal and it will cost only slightly more than you would pay from home.

The *Pousada* Network

Pousadas (pronounced "*posadas*") are state-owned establishments run by **ENATUR**, and there are three very distinct types. First, *pousadas* in national monuments, of which there are 16, are the most spectacular as they occupy heritage buildings like those in Óbidos, Évora or Estremoz. If there are no rooms available, be sure to at least stop for a meal or a drink. Next there are *pousadas* located in historic areas. There are eight of these, and though the buildings are more recent, they lie in the immediate vicinity of heritage buildings, like the *pousada* in Batalha. Finally, there are 20 regional *pousadas*, which are generally well located, often in the countryside, and boast exceptional views. Their locations allow you to visit even the most remote parts of the country while still enjoying quality accommodations.

Unfortunately, from a budgetary point of view, the prices have risen significantly over time, and although it has its charm, the *turismo de habitação* (see p 57) type of accommodation is no longer economical. The regional *pousadas* are generally the least expensive. The *pousada* network also has two

Practical Information

Hotel-Room Rates

$	less than 6,500 ESC
$$	6,500 ESC to 10,500 ESC
$$$	10,500 ESC to 20,500 ESC
$$$$	20,500 ESC to 25,000 ESC
$$$$$	25,000 ESC and over

The *Pousada* Network

Created by the Salazar government in 1941, the *pousada* network has hardly strayed from its original mandate since it opened its first establishment: to provide travellers with lodging and restaurant facilities on a human scale while integrating regional characteristics in the architecture, decor and cuisine.

Thankfully, the network itself has expanded, rather than the individual *pousadas*. With 43 establishments, the largest only has 54 rooms, while some have only six. This formula, therefore, provides travellers with peace and quiet, enjoyment of the surroundings and human contact with the hosts. The peculiar nature of the organization does, however, show through when it comes to the staff, and it often seems like you're dealing with civil servants. Nevertheless, the personnel are polite and professional.

An interesting direction was taken at the beginning of the 1950s: the reclaiming of valuable old heritage buildings. As a result, 14 *pousadas* are set up inside old palaces, monasteries or convents. The *pousada* de Santa Mario do Bouro, which opened at the beginning of 1997 in a former Cistercian abbey, is the most spectacular example of this phenomenon. This

former monastery, which had essentially been abandoned, will now endure and serve as a witness to history for generations to come. When it comes to Castelo d'Estremoz, the jewel in the crown of the *pousadas*, it envelops visitors in such a magical ambience that it is worth coming to Portugal just to stay here. This policy of reclaiming not only preserves the old buildings but also allows visitors to relive history, surrounded by architectural and decorative elements rarely found anywhere else in the world.

Next to these very unique *pousadas* are those established in historic areas. The buildings themselves have no heritage value, but they do lie in extraordinary settings, like in Marvão or Sagres. There are eight *pousadas* in historic areas.

Finally the 21 other members of the network are known as regional *pousadas*. They were essentially created to provide most of the country with these establishments, where comfort and charm are assured. For intrepid travellers, they are virtual oases in more remote regions like Miranda do Douro or Murtosa on the Ria Aveiro.

All *pousadas* boast original decoration with local

flair, and a tour of these establishments is like an exploration of Portuguese decorative arts.

As for the cuisine, considerable effort is made to incorporate regional specialties. However, though the quality of the food is always first rate, it does get a little repetitive from one place to the next, and prices are relatively high. Finally, the service, though very professional, is a little aloof and reserved, perhaps a throwback to Salazar's times, when tourists were to have little contact with, or influence on, the population. Nevertheless, the dining rooms of *pousadas* are generally very pleasant and serve quality cuisine.

Today the *pousada* network is managed by ENATUR, a profitable state-owned organization, which, in view of the country's new constitution and globe-trotting neo-liberal politicians, may find itself privatized in the coming years. It continues to grow, nonetheless, and 10 new "historic" *pousadas*, located in heritage buildings, are due to open in the next few years. The *pousada* network is one of Portugal's riches and contributes greatly to the quality of tourist facilities. Be sure to take advantage of it!

different rates depending on the season:

Low season
from November 1 to March 31 (except the period between December 31 to January 3 and February 12-16)

High season
from April 1 to September 30

During the low season, rates for a double room with one bed vary between 12,900 and 20,300 ESC. During the high season, they vary from 16,300 to 35,700 ESC. As with most Portuguese hotels, these rates include breakfast. As for suites, like at the Lóios *pousada* in Évora, they can run up to 52,300 ESC.

In terms of meals, *pousadas* are often an excellent solution: travellers will find themselves far from large centres, arriving late at their hotels in rural areas where locals rarely head out to restaurants after 8pm. Each *pousada* may have its own unique decor with dining rooms often located in architectural wonders, but the same cannot be said of the cuisine. Regional specialties are offered everywhere; but, after a few *pousada* meals you will begin to recognize a routine, ending with the same pastry trolley filled with the same egg-and-sugar desserts. Truly original dishes are sometimes offered,

but for 5,000 ESC a plate, the quality-to-price ratio just isn't there.

For more information on the *pousadas*:

ENATUR S.A.
Avenida Santa Joana Princesa, 10A, 1749 Lisboa Codex, Portugal
☎ *218 44 20 01*
≈ *218 44 20 85*
guest@pousadas.pt
www.pousadas.pt

Marketing Ahead, Inc.
433 Fifth Avenue, New York NY 10016, U.S.A.
☎ *(212) 686-9213*
≈ *(212) 686-0271*

Keytel International
402 Edgware Road, London W2 1ED, England
☎ *(171) 402-8182*
≈ *(171) 724-9503*

Bed and Breakfasts

In Portugal, this form of touring has developed into a network of farm and country houses which generally offer incredible cachet, enchanting settings and picture-perfect furnishings and decor.

Grouped in one of several associations, these houses are listed in the quadrilingual reference book *Turismo no Espaço Rural*, sold in tourist offices (ICEP) in Portugal only.

This guide covers three categories:

Turismo de habitação: *quintas* (chateaus, manors), villas and

bourgeois residences, charmingly furnished, generally located near cities and villages, and sometimes in town.

Turismo rural: rustic country homes located in or around rural villages.

Agroturismo: farms, with or without animals, where guests can enjoy activities such as horseback riding, fishing and hunting.

It can be a bit complicated for foreign travellers to take advantage of these establishments. Most of them do not have fax numbers; the book that lists them is sold only in Portugal and they are often difficult to find. But your efforts will be richly rewarded and you will come away with memories of dreamy, magical moments!

While bed and breakfasts in other countries often allow travellers to interact with locals on a more intimate level, the natural timidity of the Portuguese generally precludes as much contact as one might hope. For some travellers, therefore, the advantage lies in the tranquillity and discretion.

Several suggestions of *turismo de habitação* are included in this guide. We wholeheartedly encourage travellers to live the experience of staying in a 17th century *quinta* (farm) for example, or in a mill or a border fortress.

For more information contact:

Privetur (*Associação Portugesa de Turismo de Habitação*)
Largo das Pereiras
4990 Ponte de Lima
℡/≈*258 74 14 93*
privetur@mail.telepac.pt
www.solares-de-portugal.com

Turihab (*Associação de Turismo de Habitação*)
Praça da República
4990 Ponte de Lima
℡*258 74 16 72*
℡*258 74 28 27*
℡*258 74 14 44*
turihab@mail.telepac.pt
www.solares-de-portugal.com

Hotels and Estalagem

Portugal has several luxury hotels, generally concentrated in the large resort areas. Some of them are exceptionally charming, like the Lapa Hotel or York House in Lisbon, or even the Palacio de Buçaco in the park of the same name, but many have nothing luxurious about them apart from the price. We have carefully avoided mentioning the huge, charmless concrete towers, except where there was no choice. Take note that some luxury establishments are called *estalagem* and are sometimes comparable to *pousadas*; they are nevertheless private establishments.

Residencial and Pensão

These two appellations refer to a variety of different establishments, from the most inexpensive to the moderately priced. In Portugal, "budget" accommodations leave a bit to be desired in terms of comfort and above all in terms of charm. For this reason, fewer of these places are recommended in this guide; *residencial* and *pensão* generally do not offer a good quality-to-price ratio. For an extra 1,000 or 2,000 ESC you can get so much more.

Camping

Fans of the great outdoors will be glad to hear that there are many private and public campgrounds throughout Portugal. These are listed in the "Accommodations" section of each chapter.

In Portugal, visitors can obtain an excellent camping guide called ***Roteiro Campista, Guia de Parques de Campismo*** (*www.roteiro-campista.pt, info@roteiro-campista.pt*), which lists most camping spots in the country. This guide is available in most large bookstores in Portugal.

Some useful addresses:

Federação Portuguesa de Campismo e Caravanismo (*Portuguese federation of camping and caravanning*)
Av. Coronel Eduardo Galhardo No. 24 r/c
1170 Lisboa
℡*218 12 69 00*
℡*218 12 68 90*
≈*218 12 69 18*

Orbitur
Rua Diogo Couto 1-8°
1100 Lisboa
℡*218 11 70 70*
℡*218 11 70 00*
≈*218 14 80 45*
www.orbitur.pt
info@orbitur.pt

Youth Hostels

Well established in Europe and North America, youth hostels (*Pousadas de Juventude*) attract a large number of young people travelling on limited budgets. This type of accommodation has certain advantages, but also, as elsewhere in Portugal, some disappointments. Some hostels are poorly maintained and have unattractive rooms, generally dormitory-style. Also, there is often a high fee for storing luggage, and the lockers provided are generally tiny. Furthermore, the staff is not always the most professional. On the up side, you are almost guaranteed to meet other travellers. However, given the high prices (*between 1,500 ESC and 2,500 ESC/2* pers. for dormitory ac commodations, and between 3,200 ESC and 5,500 ESC for a double room without breakfast), globetrotters are better off staying at a pensão or a residêncial. There are plenty of these to be found, and, for just a few escudos more, they offer more comfortable lodgings and allow guests to leave their baggage at the reception at no extra charge.

Listings for the various youth hostels are given in the "Accommodations" section of each chapter in this guide.

For more information contact:

Movijovem
Pousada de Juventude
Avenida Duque de Ávila No. 137
1050 Lisboa
☎ *213 13 88 20*
⇌ *213 52 86 21*
www.sejuventude.pt/frontoff
ice/areas/pousadas/

Restaurants

Despite the almost infinite number of dining establishments in Lisbon and Porto, the cuisine variety is limited. Outside of big cities, the situation is even more marked, with the offerings summing up to the eternal balcalhau (cod). We have made an effort to find something original, bearing in mind that after a few days of bacalhau you may be ready for a change. Another particularity is

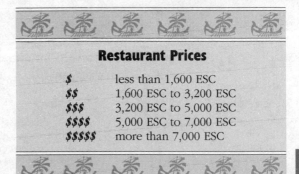

Restaurant Prices

$	less than 1,600 ESC
$$	1,600 ESC to 3,200 ESC
$$$	3,200 ESC to 5,000 ESC
$$$$	5,000 ESC to 7,000 ESC
$$$$$	more than 7,000 ESC

that, after so many discoveries, the Portuguese tend not to be very interested in exotic cuisines, and in comparison to other European countries there are very few ethnic restaurants in Portugal.

Regional Portuguese cuisine actually boasts a fair number of dishes. Three recipes are given in the boxes on pages 60 and 61 that will give you an idea of a few Portuguese specialties.

Note that it is common practice to serve appetizers (acepipes) at the beginning of a meal. **These are not free**; you will have to pay for what you have eaten.

Cheese is very expensive in Portugal, although, like queijo da serra (mountain cheese), delicious. Be aware that the actual price of your meal might differ from that listed on the menu depending on whether you are seated on the terrace or in the dining room. Generally,

posted prices are for meals served in the salão (dining room); other rates (higher ones, of course!) are applied to meals served on the esplanada or balcão (terrace).

In less expensive restaurants, half-portions (meia dose) are available. They cost about 30% less than regular servings. As the portions are very large to begin with, the meia dose is plenty.

Generally, restaurants serve food between noon and 2pm and from 7pm to 10pm. In smaller towns and villages, do not dawdle and arrive at the restaurant too late or you may have to content yourself with a sandwich and coffee. Dining later on is more feasible in larger centres.

This guide lists what we believe is the best selection of restaurants for all budgets. Each listing includes a phone number if reservations are required.

Practical Information

Carne de Porco com Amêijoas
(Pork with Clams)

(Serves four)

500 g of lean pork	4 garlic cloves
1 kg of clams	60 ml of olive oil
2 tomatoes	1 bunch of broad-leafed parsley
1 onion	juice of 1 lemon

Wash the clams thoroughly and let sit in salt water.

Cut the meat into 2cm cubes. Brown the meat in the olive oil, remove from oil after 15min. Add salt and pepper to taste. Add the chopped onion, minced garlic, peeled, seeded and chopped tomato to the oil and let cook for 15min; add the chopped parsley, stir, and add the clams. Raise the temperature so that the clams open; when they have all opened place the pork back in the pan and mix well to combine all the ingredients. Let simmer for another 15min.

Add the lemon juice just before serving.

Caldo Verde

(Serves four)

500 g of potatoes	60 ml of olive oil
200 g of finely chopped green cabbage	1 *chouriço* or beef sausage
1 large onion	2 garlic cloves
	salt

Peel and wash the potatoes. Peel the garlic and onion. In a large saucepan with 1.5l of salted water cook the potato, onion, garlic, *chouriço* and 2 tablespoons of olive oil. While this is cooking, prepare the cabbage: chop it as finely as possible, wash and drain it.

When the potatoes are cooked, take out the *chouriço* and slice it. Purée the rest of the mixture.

Keep the soup on low heat. Fifteen minutes before serving, turn up the heat, add the cabbage and let it cook.

To serve, place a slice of *chouriço* and ½ tbsp of olive oil in each bowl before adding the soup. Serve with a slice of corn bread (*broa de milho*).

Caldeirada (Fish Stew)

(serves six)

500 g of dogfish	¼ l of dry white wine
10 large sardines	4 garlic cloves
400 g of ray	2 peppers (1 green and 1 red)
500 g of small squids	2 small hot peppers
500 g of silver bream	1 bunch of broad-leafed parsley
500 g of potatoes	2 bay leaves
500 g of onion	1 tbsp paprika
90 ml of olive oil	salt and pepper

Peel and wash the potatoes. Cut them into large slices. Peel the onions and garlic. Cut them into fine slices. Wash the fish, remove the heads and fins and cut in large slices. Wash and prepare the squid. Dice the tomato and peppers.

In a large saucepan, heat the oil. Fry the onion and garlic. Add the chopped parsley, then the tomatoes, peppers, bay leaves and hot pepper. Reduce.

Place the squid over the mixture, then the different fish in layers, alternating with potato. Add the sardines last. Sprinkle with paprika. Pour equal amounts of wine and water over the mixture. Add salt and pepper. Reduce the heat. Cover and let cook without stirring.

Reprinted with the gracious permission of Éditions du Laquet

Practical Information

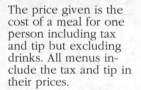

The price given is the cost of a meal for one person including tax and tip but excluding drinks. All menus include the tax and tip in their prices.

See the Gastronomic Glossary on p 461.

Tipping

The tip is included in the bill everywhere: restaurant, hotel, taxi. An extra 5 to 10% is nevertheless appreciated, especially when the service was particularly noteworthy.

Entertainment

You'll find a bit of everything in Lisbon and to a lesser extent in Porto. Weekend nights in these two big cities are endless (see also "Security", p 53). Elsewhere, however, except in resort areas, people turn in much earlier; perfect opportunity to catch up on all those books you've been meaning to read.

Gays and Lesbians

Portugal's is a profoundly conservative society where new ideas are not easily accepted, which makes life difficult for its gay community. We can at least take comfort from the fact that the lack of gay places outside the city is more a result of ignorance than intolerance, as is the case elsewhere, and there seems to be no problem of violence against gays.

In recent years, a core of militant gays has fought against discrimination and for better acceptance of openly gay people. In fact, the International Gay and Lesbian Association includes a Portuguese contingent (*www.ilgaportugal.org*). This association organizes, among other things, a gay and lesbian film festival in Lisbon in September, whose first season took place in 1997.

work or at home, in other words, to the heterosexual mould imposed by society. So night-time is just an illusion and it will take many more years for this invisible minority to be able to expose their differences to the world and to fully participate in the construction of a society without discrimination.

A few gay publications:

Trivia: monthly information newspaper
Revista Lilás: magazine for lesbians

Associação Abraço
Mon to Fri 10am to 1pm and 3pm to 8pm
Rua da Rosa 243 17th floor, 1200 Lisboa
☎ *213 42 59 29*

Shopping

Shoppers will find arts and crafts treasures throughout the country: carpets, pottery, leather, ceramics. Of course, individual *azulejos* can be found everywhere. Besides these typically Portuguese items, the best buys are shoes and leather goods. Wine is an interesting souvenir, especially a good bottle of Port. Take note, though, that prices are similar to those paid in the rest of Europe and just a bit lower than in North America.

Antique-dealers and cabinet-makers are common throughout the country but especially in Lisbon. Their shops are a delight for decorative-art fans.

Internet

International Gay and Lesbian Association:
www.ilga-portugal.org

Gay Portugal:
http://homepage.esoterica.pt/~anser
http://abraco.esoterica.pt

The first gay pride gathering in Portugal also took place in 1997, on June 28, at the Jardim do Principe Real, and brought together 3,000 people.

Of course, in Lisbon's bustling nightlife, and to a lesser degree in Porto, there are many gay or mixed nightclubs; the most prominent bars are proud to be frequented by gays. In the morning however, everyone conforms to their role at

A few organizations:

ILGA-Portugal (Centro Comunitário Gay e Lésbica de Lisboa)
Mon to Sat, 5pm to 8pm
Rua de São Lázaro, 88, 1150-333 Lisboa, Métro Socorro
☎ *218 87 39 18*
≈ *218 87 39 22*

Associação Opus Gay
Mon to Sat 4pm to 8pm
Rua da Ilha Terceira, 36 R/c 1000 Lisboa
☎ *213 15 13 96*
≈ *213 15 15 20*

A few shops are affiliated with the "Tax Free for Tourists" system which allows anyone leaving the territory of the EEC to be reimbursed for taxes paid on items they bring with them. Forms for reimbursements are available at the Lisbon airport. Remember that in order to benefit from the reimbursement you must have spent a considerable amount of money.

There is also a tax-free system for non-residents of the EEC. Information is available from:

Serviço de Administração do IVA
Avenida João XXI, 76
1000 Lisboa
☎ *21 793 66 73*

Police and Emergencies

In case of emergency dial *112*; an operator will direct your call.

Time Zone

Portugal is in the same time zone as continental Europe and 1hr ahead of the United Kingdom. It is 6hrs ahead of eastern North America, therefore when it is noon in Montréal and New York it is 6pm in Lisbon. Portugal does not advance its clocks in the spring. From April to October, therefore, there is a 1hr difference between Portugal and the rest of continental Europe, no time change between Portugal and Great Britain and 5hrs between Portugal and eastern North America.

Electricity

Electric plugs have two rounds pins and operate at 220 volts AC. Tourists from North America will need to bring along an adaptor and a converter.

Weights and Measures

Portugal uses the metric system.

Weights
1 pound (lb) = 454 grams (g)
1 kilogram (kg) = 2.2 pounds (lbs)

Linear Measure
1 inch = 2.54 centimetres (cm)
1 foot (ft) = 30 centimetres (cm)
1 mile = 1.6 kilometres (km)
1 kilometres (km) = 0.63 miles
1 metre (m) = 39.37 inches

Land Measure
1 acre = 0.4 hectares (ha)
1 hectare (ha) = 2.471 acres

Volume Measure
1 U.S. gallon (gal) = 3.79 litres
1 U.S. gallon (gal) = 0.8 imperial gallon

Temperature
To convert °F into °C: subtract 32, divide by 9, multiply by 5
To convert °C into °F: multiply by 9, divide by 5, add 32

Visitors from Great Britain will only need an adaptor with two round pins.

Women Travellers

Women travelling alone should not encounter any problems. On the whole, women are treated with respect and harassment is rela tively rare. Of course, some caution is required; for example, women should avoid walking alone through poorly lit areas late at night.

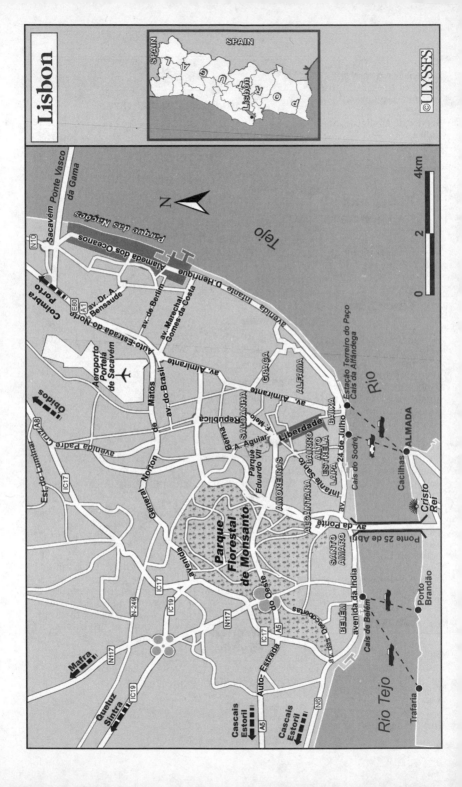

Lisbon

Situated at the mouth

of the majestic River Tagus, where it flows into the Atlantic Ocean, Lisbon (Lisboa) is home to nearly two million inhabitants.

Stretched along the steeper bank of the river, its historic section, including the Castelo and the Alfama, is concentrated on the top and side of one of the seven hills that form the core of the city.

Downtown Lisbon is divided into "upper" and "lower" sections, each made up of many different neighbourhoods. At the administrative level, the capital is divided into 53 *freguesias*, neighbourhoods: Lapa, Sé, Graça, São Mamede, etc. In the north, the suburbs sprawl all the way to the airport, 8km from downtown; on the western shore, the city stretches to the municipality of Belém, the ancient outer harbour of the city and the royal suburb. The Ponte 25 de Abril, located halfway between Belém

and Lisbon, has linked the two banks of the Tagus since 1966. To the northeast, the city opens onto a series of piers, once the site of factories and refineries. After undergoing major refurbishments in order to host the EXPO 98 world's fair, the site has now been converted into a huge recreational park known as Parque das Nações. Nearby, the Vasco da Gama bridge, a remarkable work of art with graceful curves, now allows drivers to reach the south shore of the

Tagus without having to go through downtown.

History of Lisbon

Although both the Phoenicians and the Greeks set up trading posts at the mouth of the Tagus, few traces of these two civilizations remain. To this day, historians disagree about the origin of the name *Olisipo* (sometimes spelled *Alis Ubbo* or *Alissipo*), which was apparently used to designate this area. According to some, it was an early form of the city's present name. Next came the Romans, who invaded the Iberian Peninsula and founded a number of towns here, including Felicitas Julia (named after Julius Caesar), which was built on the site now occupied by the Castelo. The residents of Lisbon thus became Roman citizens. Felicitas Julia never became an important city, however. Toward the fourth century, the barbarian invasions that swept through Europe marked the end of the powerful Roman empire, and by 458 AD, the Visigoths had taken over the city. Thanks to a relatively long period of peace, the Visigoths played an important role in Lisbon's development, most notably, perhaps, by building the city's first large-scale fortifications. Despite these defensive measures, a second invading force, the Moors, managed to take over the city in 716 AD Lisbon continued to grow and prosper under Muslim rule, and new fortifications were erected. Nevertheless, in 1147, when it already had a population of 15,000, the city was conquered one last time (not including the much later Spanish period and a brief French occupation) by Afonso I, with the help of crusaders en route to the Holy Land. The Flemish, Normans, English and many others thus participated in capturing the city. Lisbon was elevated to the rank of capital by

Afonso III in 1255, and despite an earthquake in 1344 and a thwarted Spanish attack in 1384 (whose failure can be partially attributed to the fortifications built in 1373 and still standing today), it grew rapidly and firmly established its role as a royal city.

Throughout the 15th century, the capital became more and more prosperous as new territories (Madeira, the coasts of Africa, Brazil, etc.) and the route to India were discovered. The support of the rulers of these regions and the ingeniousness of Portuguese navigators (new navigation techniques, the invention of the caravel, etc.) enabled Lisbon to become the capital of a vast kingdom. All sorts of palaces, monasteries and churches were erected here, making this one of the most envied cities in Europe, renowned for its Manueline architecture. In 1527, however, Lisbon was hit by the first of a series of catastrophes when the plague wiped out a large portion of its population. In 1531, the city was seriously damaged by an earthquake. Then, around 1569, plague swept through the region again. Finally, upon losing its last king, the country was invaded by Spain and forced to give up its autonomy.

Starting in 1640, when the country regained its

independence, and especially after gold was discovered in Brazil, Lisbon enjoyed a new era of prosperity. Many prestigious buildings, such as the Mosteiro dos Jerónimos, bear witness to this time. Once again, however, these golden days were destined to be short-lived.

November 1, 1755 marked the beginning of the city's decline. On that black day in Lisbon's history, a terrible earthquake destroyed three-quarters of the city in just a few seconds. To make matters worse, the working-class neighbourhoods in those years consisted mainly of wooden houses, so the huge fire that followed the earthquake reduced some areas to ashes, killing many Lisboans. This catastrophe created such a stir in Europe that Voltaire devoted a chapter to it in *Candide*. In spite of all its misfortune, Lisbon the Proud refused to take its fate lying down. Thanks to the brilliant Marquês de Pombal, it picked itself back up again. The ingenious reconstruction of the Baixa turned the city into one of the most modern capitals in Europe. Regardless of this achievement, however, Lisbon's era of prosperity was clearly over, and the 19th century ushered in a slow period of decline with Portugal's gradual loss of its colonies and of its international influence to the advantage of other European powers.

From the beginning of the 20th century until the establishment of the Salazar regime in 1933, the capital was the scene of numerous revolts and outbreaks of violence, which did little to further its development. The long period of dictatorship that followed ended up stifling the city's dynamic spirit and isolating it from the rest of the world. Portugal did not take part in World War II, and a large portion of its population emigrated to the United States. The enormous statue of Cristo Rei, looking out over the city from atop its ridiculous stilts and opening its arms wide in a protective gesture, is a perfect example of the mawkishness of this era. It was erected as a gesture of thanks for the city's having been spared the great upheavals of the Second World War. Despite the construction of the magnificent Ponte 25 de Abril (formerly known as Ponte Salazar) and a few horrible Stalinist-style buildings, both the city and its population continued to decline. On April 25, 1974, however, tired of the dismal atmosphere hanging over them, the people of Lisbon rediscovered their taste for new ideas and democracy, and Portugal's entry into the EEC in 1986

helped put Lisbon back on a par with the major European capitals.

Lisbon Today

Strolling through different neighbourhoods, you will notice that Lisbon is a city of many faces. Since there are seven hills in Lisbon (São Viçente, Santo André, Castelo, Santana, São Roque, Chagas and Santa Catarina), there are at least as many different faces. Whereas the Castelo immerses us in medieval imagery, the architecture of the commercial centre of Armoreiras transports us to a futuristic world, and the "village" of Alfama entices us to explore the crowded North-African medinas and the terrasse of Edouardo VII park, from which the view of the Tagus confers a "noble" look to the city.

A daytime stroll through the Bairro Alto reveals a series of charming, quiet little streets lined with artisans' shops. Come nightfall, these places metamorphose into clubs and restaurants, which are frequented by an extremely fashionable crowd. EXPO 98 also spawned a host of improvements in many of the city's other districts. For example, the warehouses on the docks of the Alcântara and Santo Amaro districts (commonly known as the *docas*)

have been converted into bars, restaurants and nightclubs, each more innovative than the last. Concurrently, with the opening of a new metro line leading to the EXPO 98 site, as well as the extension of three current lines, Lisbon experienced a long but much-needed construction boom. Finally, as part of the urban-development strategy, large, private parking lots were built on several main downtown public squares. Becoming more and more beautiful by the day, the Daughter of the Tagus is striving to recapture her former glory, to be the envy of all of Europe once again.

Finding Your Way Around

By Car

From the Airport

Take Avenida das Comunidades Portuguesas, which leads under Avenida Marechal Craveira Lopes to the Rotunda do Aeroporto. From there, take Avenida do Brasil to Campo Grande park. Turn left to go through the tunnel leading to Avenida da República, which comes to an end at the Praça Duque de Saldanha. Follow

Avenida Fontés Pereira de Melo to the Praça Marquês de Pombal. From there, Avenida da Liberdade will take you into the centre of town.

From Porto

Head south on Highway A1-E80. There are two ways of entering Lisbon, from the east or from the west. To do the former, take the second exit (for the airport) to the right after the tollbooth, then immediately after, pass under Avenida Marechal Craveiro Lopes and go around the Rotunda do Aeroporto to pick up Avenida do Brasil. Keep driving until you reach Campo Grande park, then turn left to take the tunnel leading to Avenida da República, which comes to an end at the Praça Duque de Saldanha. Follow Avenida Fontés Pereira de Melo to the Praça Marquês de Pombal. From there, Avenida da Liberdade will take you into the centre of town. To enter Lisbon from the west, take the second exit (for the airport) after the toll and immediately after, head under Avenida Marechal Craveiro Lopes and go around the Rotunda do Aeroporto to pick up Avenida Almirante Gago Coutinha, then, straight ahead, Avenida Almirante Reis and finally Rua da Palma, which will take you straight downtown.

In the City

Generally speaking, it is not very complicated to get around in Lisbon by car, the only exception being the centre of the Alfama, which is inaccessible because it has so many dead-ends and streets with staircases. Similarly, the Bairro Alto, the triangular area bounded by the Praça Luís de Camões, the Miradouro de S. Pedro de Alcântara and the Miradouro de Santa Catarina, is accessible but better avoided by motorists. The streets are not only very narrow, but many are one-way, making driving here difficult. The major problem all over the city is parking. It is easier to find parking in the evening, however, since students and people out of work stand by the side of the road and point out empty spaces. The standard tip for this service is about 100 ESC. As a general rule, though, we recommend using public transportation or exploring the city by foot.

One last note: Private **parking** lots are outrageously expensive in Portugal. Oddly enough, furthermore, the hourly rate goes up the longer you leave your car. If you have no other choice, however, the lot on Praça dos Restauradores has the advantage of being located right downtown, making it easy to

reach. Parking here will cost you about 240 ESC an hour. There is another lot next to the Praça Marquês de Pombal. Spread over five levels under Parque Eduardo VII, it has 1,454 spots and is open 24hr a day. Its hourly rate is about 240 ESC.

Fortunately, a third parking lot, below Praça do Município, has recently been added to Lisbon's urban infrastructure, and two additional underground lots (Praça da Figueira and Praça Luís Camões) were under construction at the time of our visit.

Parque das Nações

For motorists, the most direct route from downtown to the Parque das Nações (see p 120) is to head northeast on Avenida Infante Dom Henrique, which, after changing names several times, will take you straight there. If you are at the airport, take Avenida Marechal Gomes da Costa from the Rotunda do Aeroporto. This road will lead you straight to the south gate of the park, 3km away. Motorists arriving from the southern part of the country should cross the magnificent, 13km-long Ponte de Vasco da Gama to reach the site.

By Bus

From the Airport

To get downtown by **bus** if you are in a rush, take Aerobus (*one-day ticket, 450 ESC; three-day ticket, 1,050 ESC; or Passe Turístico*), an express bus that goes by every 20min. Tickets are sold on the bus (make sure to have the exact change). TAP passengers can take the Aero-Bus downtown for **free**; you must pick up your ticket at the TAP information counter, located near the customs end. Slower but less expensive (*160 ESC*), buses 44 or 45 will take you downtown by way of the Praça Marquês Pombal, Avenida da Liberdade, Praça Restauradores and the Rossio. Those wishing to go straight to the west part of the city (the Rato, Estrêla and Lapa) can take bus 22.

From Porto

Rede Nacional de Expressos and **Renex Expressos**
Rua Carmelitas, close to Torre dos Clérigos
OR
on Praça Filipa de Lencastre
OR
on Rua Alexandre Herculano
OR
on Praça Batalha (at the Garagem Atlantic)
Departure: numerous departures every day
Travel time: varies between 3hr, 50min and 5hr, 35min, depending on whether or not the bus stops in Coimbra
Fare: Between 1,900 and 2,100 ESC

These two bus lines and other transportation companies offer numerous departures every day from no less than four terminals. For Information in Porto, see p 286.

By Train

From Porto

Campanhã Station
to get there, take bus #35 or #34 from Praça da Liberdade or the commuter train from Estação São Bento
Departure: up to ten a day (the last at 7:50pm)
Travel time: approx. 3 hours, 30 min between Porto and Lisbon
Fare: Alfa 2nd class 3,150 ESC, Intercidades 2,550 ESC

Caminhos de Ferro:

Lisbon
☎218 88 40 25
☎218 88 50 92

Porto
☎225 36 41 41

Parque das Nações

The brand-new Oriente train station, a futuristic-looking building designed by Spanish architect Santiago Calatrava, offers direct service to other cities in Portugal, as well as to points outside the country.

Public Transportation

The city of Lisbon has an extensive public transportation system operated by state-owned companies. Though the bus and the subway, called the metro, are the most common modes of transportation, the most pleasant means of exploring the city is definitely the tram, or *eléctrico*.

Buses, Trams, Funiculars and *Elevadores*

Carris (☎*213 63 20 44, www.carris.pt*), a state-owned company, operates about a hundred **buses** (*autocarros*) serving the city of Lisbon and its suburbs. Besides being comfortable, they are the fastest way of getting anywhere in town (along with the subway).

Quaint little vehicles with wooden interiors and entertaining advertisements plastered outside, the **trams** (*eléctricos*) make their way up and down the streets in a slow, noisy and somewhat awkward manner. They are an essential part of life in Lisbon and add to the city's charm. It would thus be sacrilege to leave Lisbon without having taken the tram at least once.

Lisbon

The Carris company recently acquired some new, ultra-modern trams, which are considerably more comfortable than the old ones, but are not, sad to say, always in the best of taste (line 15). Only six lines remain, and let's hope that the melodious squeaking of wheels will liven up the streets of Lisbon for many years to come.

elevators. Of the city's four *elevadores*, listed below, three are actual funiculars.

The **Elevador de Santa Justa** (*every day 7am to 11:45pm*) links Rua de Santa Justa to Largo do Carmo.

The **Elevador da Glória** (*every day 7am to 12:55am*) links Praça dos Restauradores to

Eléctricos

Lisbon's four *elevadores* make it possible to go quickly from one area to another. They are not only practical, but also offer a very attractive view of the city, since they almost always lead to a *miradouro* (lookout). The fares are the same as for other means of public transportation: 160 ESC per trip. It should be noted that residents commonly use the term *elevador* for both funiculars and

the Miradouro de São Pedro de Alcântara.

The **Elevador da Lavra** (*Mon to Sat 7am to 10:45pm, Sun 9am to 10:45pm*) links Largo de Anunciação to Rua Câmara Pestana.

The **Elevador da Bica** (*Mon to Sat 7am to 10:45pm, Sun 9am to 10:45pm*) links Rua da São Paulo to Largo Calhariz.

Fares

Single ticket purchased aboard a bus, elevador or tram:
160 ESC per trip

Ticket purchased in advance at a Carris counter:
160 ESC for two trips (this kind of ticket is called a *Bilhete Único de Coroa*, or BUC 2)

Ticket good for one day of unlimited use:
450 ESC

Ticket good for three days of unlimited use:
1,050 ESC

Carris offices are found all over town; here are a few locations:

Posto de Informação e Venda Carris
Elevador de Santa Justa
Praça de Figuera
Largo do Rato
Estrêla
Alcântara
Belém

Tickets can also be purchased from many local travel agents.

Metro

The major work that was undertaken before the 1998 Lisbon World Exposition included the construction of a new metro line and the extension of two of the city's three existing lines. Once old-fashioned and only serving part of the city, the Metropolitano de Lisboa has since been transformed into a fast, efficient means of transport.

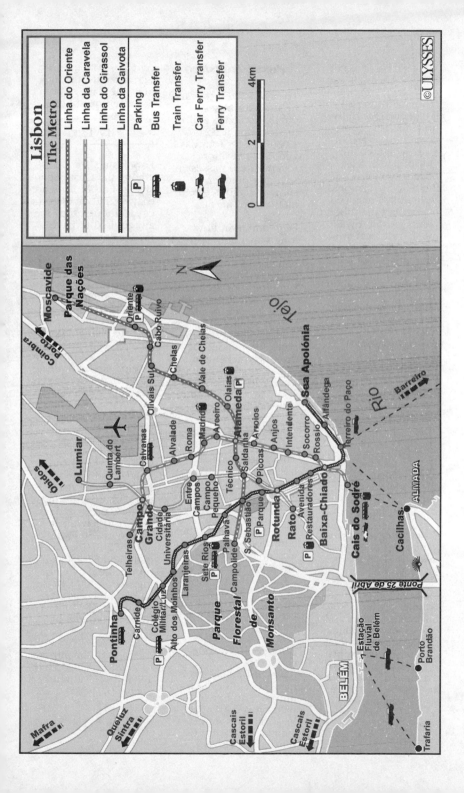

What's more, the new imposing stations can now handle three times more passengers. Even if this mode of transportation isn't your favourite, we recommend you take the *Oriente* line at least once so you can see the different stations, beautifully enhanced by *azulejos* and modern works created by a number of local artists. This guide includes a metro map (see p 71).

For more information:

Metropolitano de Lisboa
☎*217 98 06 00*
⇒*213 57 49 08*
www.metrolisboa.pt

Fares

Single ticket purchased at a subway station:
100 ESC

10 tickets:
800 ESC

Ticket good for one day of unlimited use (subway only):
260 ESC

Ticket good for one week of unlimited use (subway only):
920 ESC

Each station is equipped with ticket machines. Theoretically, these machines give change, but they are sometimes empty (especially late in the evening) and will only accept the exact fare, so it is always wise to have some change on hand.

Passe Turístico

The *Passe Turístico*, can be used for buses, trams, *elevadores* and the subway; it costs 1,680 ESC for four days and 2,380 ESC for seven. These passes are sold at a number of subway stations (see metro map, p 71)

Depending on how long you'll be staying in the capital and which types of transportation you prefer, some options are more cost-effective than others. For example, if you're staying in Lisbon for four days, you are better off purchasing a three-day ticket and a one-day ticket than a *Passe Turístico*, unless you plan on using the subway.

Lisboa Cartão

This pass entitles its holder to unlimited use of the subway, buses and most trams and funiculars, as well as free admission to 26 museums and other attractions. Pass-holders also enjoy discounts of anywhere from 10% to 50% on cultural activities (shows, exhibitions, etc.) and 5% to 10% at certain stores. As it is quite expensive (*1,900 ESC for a 24hr-card; 3,100 ESC for a 48hr-card; 4,000 ESC for a 72hr-card*), this card is most cost-effective for museum buffs who plan on spending at least six days in the capital. Beside tourist offices, the *Lisboa Cartão* is sold at most Carris stands, the airport, the Park of Nations and most hotels.

By Taxi

Lisbon's taxis are among the least expensive in Europe, and are easy to find all over the city. Although they are all required to have meters and the fares are regulated, too often, the meter is hard to read, and sometimes it is already running when you get in. Be vigilant, and always make sure that the fare you are charged corresponds with the one on the meter. Asking for a receipt can help prevent drivers from overcharging you and, if necessary, make it easier to file a complaint.

Evening (from 10pm to 6am), weekend and holiday fares are slightly higher than those charged during daytime on weekdays. Expect to pay a flat charge of 250 ESC plus about 72 ESC/km at night and 57 ESC/km during the day. Extra luggage is 300 ESC per bag and there is a surcharge of 150 ESC for taxis ordered by phone.

A taxi from the airport to Rossio costs around 1,000 ESC (without luggage)

On Foot

Lisbon is a delightful city with many different facets, and although there are all sorts of ways to visit it, its hidden beauties are best discovered on foot.

To make it easier for you to explore the city, we have divided up the local attractions by area. Furthermore, those who enjoy planned walking tours will find an itinerary for each of these areas. Visitors can thus explore each area separately or combine tours covering adjacent parts of the city.

If you plan on exploring the city on foot, it is important to remember that there are seven hills in Lisbon, and that climbing up and down them can be tiring. Visitors, like all good Lisboans, should therefore take the time to rest and sip a satisfying *bica* (espresso). To fully enjoy all Lisbon has to offer, wear comfortable shoes. Furthermore, the city is full of dead ends, passageways and streets with staircases, making it difficult to explore without a detailed map; make sure to bring one along.

Maps of the City

Unfortunately, although there are many maps of Lisbon (one of which is available free of charge at the tourist office), few of them are foolproof guides for this labyrinthine city. If your budget allows and you are spending an extended amount of time in the city, consider purchasing the *Lisboa Guia Urbano* (*2,800 ESC, available at ICEP, Praça dos Restauradores or in good bookstores*), the most complete street atlas, with a detailed index.

Lookouts

There are many lookouts in the city, some quite isolated and hard to reach. The following are close to major attractions and fairly easy to get to:

Miradouro de Santa Luzia
(see p 86)
Miradouro de São Pedro de Alcântara
(see p 96)
Miradouro de Santa Catarina
(see p 108)
Jardim do Torel
(see p 107)
Parque Eduardo VII
(see p 100)
Elevador de Santa Justa
(see p 81)
Castelo de São Jorge
(see p 84)

By Boat

Transtejo
Cais da Alfândega, Estação Fluvial Terreiro do Paço
24hr information line:
☎*213 47 92 77*
⇆*213 46 09 02*
www.transtejo.pt/princi.htm
Transtejo provides ferry service between the capital and various cities south of the Tagus.

Daily departures for:

Montijo
Fare: one-way 290 ESC

Seixal
Fare: 220 ESC

Cacilhas
Terreiro de Paço, close to the Praça do Comércio
Fare: 105 ESC

Barreiro
Fare: 320 ESC

Ferries for the cities of **Porto Brandão** and **Trafaria** also leave from Belém. Departures for **Cacilhas** are made from the Cais do Sodré.

The ferry to Cacilhas us the most interesting for tourists. In a reasonable amount of time (*15min*), you can cross the Tagus and enjoy a superb view of Lisbon. The trip is also possible from Cais do Sodré. Families or visitors out to make a day of it might be interested in package deals with several crossings. Transtejo also offers 24hr service on the **Cacilhas ferry** (*motorcycle 200 ESC, car 300 ESC*) every 30min during the day and evening and every hour at night.

Lisbon

Practical Information

Tourist Information

Portela de Sacavém Airport

The tourist office is located near the airport exit, in arrivals.

Downtown

Palácio Foz, Praça dos Restauradores
open Mon to Sat 9am to 8pm and Sun 10am to 6pm
☎*800 296 296 (toll-free)*
⇢*21 361 0359*

This building houses both the ICEP office (information on Lisbon as well as on Portugal in general) and the tourist office of the Câmara Municipal (information on Lisbon only; relatively inefficient service). You'll find maps, brochures and a few guides here.

During the summer, four small Turismo de Lisboa information booths are set up in different parts of the city: at the Rossio, on Rua Augusta, in the Bairro Alto and the Belém district.

Parque das Nações

Besides the information about the park available in tourist offices downtown, there are three information booths in the park (see map, p 121). They offer free detailed maps of the park as well as a magazine (in both Portuguese and English) about the various activities on hand.

For more information:

Parque das Nações
every day 9am to 8pm
☎*218 91 93 33*
www.parquedasnacoes.pt
info@expo98.pt

Excursions and Guided Tours

There are many options available to travellers wishing to explore the city with a guided tour.

A few are mentioned below. Considering the frequent changes, we recommend contacting each of these organizations directly for information on the tours they offer and the prices.

Bus Tours

Carris
☎*213 63 20 44*
www.carris.pt
Praça do Comércio
Departure: May to July and September, every 30min from 11am to 4pm; August, every half hour from 11am to 5pm
Fare: 2,000 ESC for adults and 1,000 ESC for children aged 4 to 10; tickets can be purchased on board

From May to September, the state-owned company Carris offers visitors a double-decker guided bus tour, available in various languages. From the upper level, with the wind blowing through your hair, you'll be led along a tour (the *Circuito Tejo*), which, after making a loop towards the north from the Praça do Comércio, follows the Tagus from Belém to downtown.

Cityrama
Avenida Praia da Vitória no. 12-B, 1096 Lisboa
Codex ☎*213 86 43 22*
☎*213 19 10 90*
⇢*213 56 06 68*
www.cityrama.pt

Some Web Sites

www.cm-lisboa.pt
www.parquedasnacoes.pt
www.eunet.pt
www.lisboafestivaldosoceanos99.viatecla.pt

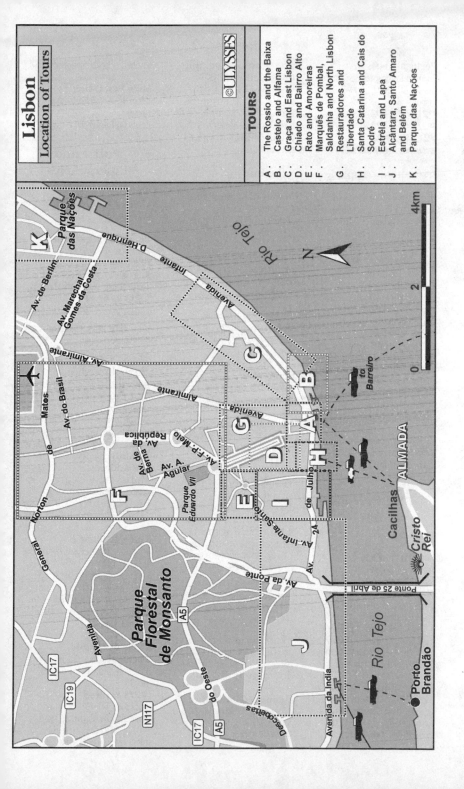

Lisbon
Location of Tours

©ULYSSES

TOURS

A. The Rossio and the Baixa
B. Castelo and Alfama
C. Graça and East Lisbon
D. Chiado and Bairro Alto
E. Rato and Amoreiras
F. Marquês de Pombal, Saldanha and North Lisbon
G. Restauradores and Liberdade
H. Santa Catarina and Cais do Sodré
I. Estrêla and Lapa
J. Alcântara, Santo Amaro and Belém
K. Parque das Nações

Portugal Tours
Avenida Defensores de Chaves
no. 15, 5th floor, 1000-109
Lisboa
☎*213 52 29 02*
☎*213 51 12 20*
⇌*213 52 29 02*
www.portugaltours.pt

Both these companies
offer guided tours of
the capital and excur-
sions to Cascais, Estoril,
Sintra, Cabo da Roca,
Óbidos and Nazaré.

Boat Tours

Transtejo
Estação Fluvial Terreiro do
Paço, close to the Praça do
Comércio
☎*218 82 03 48*
⇌*218 82 03 65*
www.transtejo.pt/turismo.btm
Departure: 11am, 1pm,
3pm and 5pm
Fare: 3,000 ESC

From April to October,
Transtejo organizes
daily 2hr *cruseiros no
Tejo* (cruises on the
Tagus) which reveal
another side of Lisbon.

Eléctrico das Colinas

Carris
Praça do Comércio
☎*213 63 20 44*
www.carris.pt
Fare: rates are fairly
expensive at 2,800 ESC
for adults and
1,500 ESC for children
aged 4 to 10; tickets
can be purchased on
board the tram.

From March 1 to Octo-
ber 15, the state-owned
company Carris offers a
guided tours in many
languages aboard a

pretty little tram called
the Eléctrico das
Colinas. As its Portu-
guese name suggests,
the *circuito colinas* (hill
tour) visits various
picturesques areas of
the city.

Schedule

March to June and
October:
*departures at 1:30pm and
3:30pm*

July:
*departures at 11:30am,
1:30pm, 2:30pm and
3:30pm*

August:
*departures at 11:30am,
1:30pm, 2:30pm, 3:30pm
and 4:30pm*

September:
*departures at 11:30am,
1:30pm and 3:30pm*

For those on a tighter
budget, a ride (un-
guided) aboard a tram
28 provides an interest-
ing look at Lisbon.
Tickets bought in ad-
vance are only
160 ESC... quite a sav-
ings compared to
2,800 ESC for the tour-
ist tram. Among the
other routes worth try-
ing are lines 25, 18
and 15.

Post Office

In addition to the one
at the airport, there are
two large post offices
downtown:

Automated Post Office
*Mon to Fri 8am to 10pm,
Sat, Sun and holidays
9am to 6pm*

Praça dos Restauradores no. 58

Main Post Office
*Mon to Fri 8:30am to
6pm*
Praça do Comércio

Police and Emergencies

Dial *112*; an operator
will instruct you.

**Polícia de Segurança
Pública**
open 24hrs
Rua Capelo no. 13, behind the
Teatro Dona Nacional Maria II
☎*213 46 61 41*

Sports Clubs

There are many sports
clubs throughout Portu-
gal, and it is no secret
that the Portuguese are
big soccer fans. Visitors
who want to stay in
shape while staying in
Lisbon might find this a
bit difficult. Below are
the addresses of a few
clubs; the fees are
unfortunately pretty
high considering the
facilities offered.

Clube de Ginásio
Rua das Portas de Santo Antão
no. 110-124
Pool, volleyball, aero-
bics and dance. Access
to the pool 800 ESC or
monthly membership
7,500 ESC.

**Clube de Ginásio
Português**
Praça do Ginásio Português
no. 1
☎*213 85 60 45*
⇌*213 85 60 49*
Aerobics, dance, yoga,
judo, aïkido, fencing
and weight training.

Below are a few suggested stops depending on how much time you have and what your interests are:

A Quick Stopover

The **Castelo** (p 84), the **Mosteiro dos Jerónimos** and **Igreja Santa Maria** (p 116), and the **Torre de Belém** (p 119).

Two to Three Days

For churches: **Igreja Santa Maria** (p 116) and **Igreja da Madre de Deus** (p 92).

For museums: **Museu Calouste Gulbenkian** (p 102).

For the outdoors: **Parque da Pena** (p 190).

For palaces: **Palácio Nacional de Sintra** (p 171).

For *azulejos*: **Museu Nacional do Azulejo** (p 91) and **Igreja e Mosteiro de São Vicente da Fora** (p 88).

For the Manueline Style: **Mosteiro dos Jerónimos** (p 116) and the **Torre de Belém** (p 119).

Three to Five Days

For churches: **Igreja Santa Maria** (p 116), **Igreja São Roque** (p 96), **Igreja da Madre de Deus** (p 92), and **Sé Patriarcal** (p 83).

For museums: **Museu Calouste Gulbenkian** (p 102), **Museu Nacional de Arte Antiga** (p 112) and **Museu Nacional dos Coches** (p 123).

For the outdoor: **Parque da Pena** (p 190), **Parque de Monserrate** (p 190), the **Castelo dos Mouros** (p 177) and **Serra da Arrábida** (p 193).

For palaces: **Palácio Nacional de Sintra** (p 171), **Palácio da Pena** (p 176) and **Palácio Nacional de Queluz** (p 170).

For *Azulejos*: **Museu Nacional do Azulejo** (p 91) and **Igreja e Mosteiro de São Vicente da Fora** (p 88), the **Pavilhão dos Desportos** (p 102) and the façade of the **Viúva Lamego** store (p 160).

For the Manueline Style: **Mosteiro dos Jerónimos** (p 116), **Igreja de la Conceição Velha** (p 82), the façade of the **Estação do Rossio** (p 80) and the **Torre de Belém** (p 119).

Lisbon

Squash Soleil
on the first floor on the Centre Commercial Amoreiras
☎213 83 29 07
☎213 83 29 08
Squash, pool, weight training, gymnastics. Access to the pool 1,700 ESC or 10 visits for 15,300 ESC.

Centro Viva em Forma
Lisboa Sheraton Hotel, Rua Latino Coelho no. 1
☎213 14 73 53
Pool, weight training, gymnastics. Use of the weight-training machines 1,200 ESC or ten visits 10,800 ESC.

O Ginásio Holiday Inn
1,500 ESC. Avenida António José de Almeida no. 28, 11th floor
☎217 93 52 22, ext. 1184
Gymnastics, pool, weight training. Access to the pool and gym.

Exploring

Tour A: The Rossio and the Baixa

(See map on p 79)

You can start off your tour of Lisbon in the heart of the city, at the **Rossio** ★, also known as Praça de Dom Pedro IV, after the first king of Brazil. This square, which dates back to the 13th century, owes its present design to the celebrated Marquês de Pombal. Today, it is lined with stores,

banks, hotels and cafés. The nonstop flow of pedestrians and motorists makes for a perpetually noisy atmosphere, but take the time to walk around the square; there are several pretty shops here. At number 21, on the west side, the narrow **Tabacaria Mónaco** has a pretty interior, with lovely frescoes on the ceiling and an elegant counter made of dark wood. Right nearby, at number 23, the quaint little Art Nouveau facade of **Café Nicolas** is also worth a look. Farther along, on the south side of the square, at numbers seven through nine, there is a **jewellery store** with a charming facade in the purest Art Nouveau style, advertising *Joias* and *Pratas* in elegant lettering. Next, walk through the arch (*Arco do Bandeira*) next to the jewellery shop to get to Rua dos Sapateiros.

Cinématografo

On the right side of the street, at number 229, you can admire the Art Nouveau ornamentation on the facade of the **Cinématografo** (now a porno theatre and peep show!).

There is a funny story behind the geometric patterns adorning the Rossio: rumour has it they were created on a whim by prisoners incarcerated in the Castelo, who had been sentenced to hard labour by the local authorities. It probably never occurred to the men who thought up the project that they were ushering in a new trend, and that these elegant patterns would one day cover many of the city's sidewalks.

On the north side of the square, you will see the neoclassical style **Teatro Nacional Dona Maria II** (*program* ☎213 47 22 46 or 213 47 22 47), built during the first half of the 19th century.

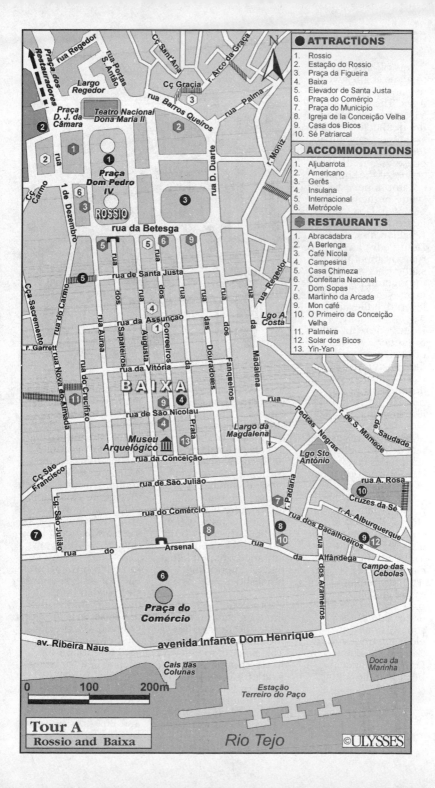

It was on this very site that auto-da-fés were declared in the Middle Ages. The statue of Gil Vicente at the top of the pediment serves as a reminder that he is the father of Portuguese theatre. In the centre of the square, set atop a pedestal, is a statue of the first king of Brazil, Dom Pedro IV, known in Brazilian history as Dom Pedro I. A strange rumour about this statue once spread throughout Lisbon. For many years, it was alleged that the statue was not actually of Dom Pedro, but rather of Emperor Maximilian of Mexico. According to the rumour, the statue had originally been destined for Mexico, but was altered to look like the king of Brazil after Emperor Maximilian was assassinated. The tale became such a subject of discussion and downright controversy that a Brazilian expert by the name of Stanislav Herstal decided to examine the statue to see if there was any truth to the rumour. He concluded that there wasn't, thus putting an end to the amusing story once and for all. On either side of the square, finally, two elegant baroque fountains, both sculpted in France, enhance the beauty of the setting.

Estação do Rossio

It is worth stopping by little **Praça João da Câmara**, located alongside the Rossio, to see the facade of the **Estação do Rossio** ★ (*to the left of the Teatro Nacional*). Erected in 1887, this neo-Manueline building looks more like a palace than a train station. Particularly noteworthy is its curious central entrance, shaped like a pair of interlocking horseshoes.

On the other side of the train station, parallel to the Rossio, lies the **Praça da Figueira** ★. This square, too, is very lively, though the north side of it is off-limits to buses and taxis, making it a quieter place to enjoy a pleasant stroll. Praça da Figueira is known above all for its many outdoor cafés, which offer lovely views of the castle. A statue of King João I, founder of Portugal's second dynasty, the Aviz line, stands in its centre. During our visit, the square was undergoing major work and an underground parking lot was being laid out.

In addition to the presence of several impressive rococo buildings, the main attraction of the **Baixa** ★ is its shops. Originally, a specific kind of merchandise could be found on each street; for example, Rua Aurea, also known as Rua do Ouro, was occupied, primarily by jewellers and Rua dos Sapateiros by cobblers.

Nowadays, however, you'll find an assortment of shops ranging from jeweller's and clothing stalls to pharmacies. There are several pedestrian streets here, the most pleasant of which is probably **Rua Augusta**. This street is not only flanked by shops with elegant window displays, but also offers an interesting view, due to its impressive triumphal arch. Unfortunately, this street seems to be turning into a favourite haunt for drug dealers who unreservedly pester passers-by (preferably young people and tourists) despite the presence of police officers nearby.

Rua de Santa Justa, which runs perpendicular to Rua Augusta, is also worth exploring to see the remarkable **Elevador de Santa Justa ★**. It was built by engineer Raul Mesnier du Ponsard, who received authorization from the city in 1899 to construct a vertical elevator that would make it easier to reach the Largo do Carmo. He was also awarded rights over the operation of the *elevador* for 99 years. It was inaugurated in 1902 and rented three years later to the state-owned Carris company, which took possession of it in 1939.

The *elevador* is a metal tower that stands about 45m high and is topped by a proportionately large platform, where the steam engines that once drove the *elevador* were located. Connected to the Largo do Carmo by a 25m bridge, the *elevador* makes it possible to reach the Chiado (see p 70 and p 92) in just a few minutes. The tower, adorned with neo-Gothic details, seems to be modelled after a belfry. On your way up to the Chiado (*150 ESC*), take the spiral staircase to the top of the platform (*not recommended for visitors subject to dizzy spells*), where you can enjoy a **magnificent view ★★** of the city, particularly of the Castelo and the Igreja do Carmo (see p 94), not to mention, of course, the majestic Tagus River. Finally, if you enjoy lounging in the open air, walk along the small streets of São Nicolau or Vitória, which are lined with attractive patios.

One of the loveliest squares in the city, the **Praça do Comércio ★★**, is of particular interest not only because it is so charming, but also because numerous historic events have taken place here. Before the earthquake of 1755, the Paço da Ribeira (Riverbank Palace) stood here. A prestigious palace erected for Dom Manuel I, it was modified and embellished

The Baixa

Located between the Rossio and the Praça do Comércio, the Baixa (lower town) is unusual in that it consists of a group of buildings forming a rectangle, in which the streets are laid out in a perfectly symmetrical grid. This remarkable example of town-planning is to some extent a result of the terrible disaster of 1755. After the lower parts of Lisbon were completely destroyed by the earthquake, the Marquês de Pombal enlisted the help of three architects to rebuild the city using methods that were not only modern, but revolutionary at the time. Exemplifying what later came to be known as the "Pombaline-style", most of the buildings stand three or four storeys high and feature uniform doors and windows, often with balconies. Lisbon thus became one of the first modern cities in Europe.

Lisbon

over and over, and housed one of the largest libraries in Europe. Today, this large square is surrounded by a series of classical buildings dating from the 18th century, which are arranged in a symmetrical manner and adorned with arcades. The pastel yellow hue ofthe buildings offsets the severity of their Pombaline-style architecture and creates an impression of great elegance. Today, as in the past, the edifices house a variety of administrative offices. The centre of the square is graced with a lovely **equestrian statue of Dom José I**, who was king at the time the buildings were reconstructed. It is the work of the celebrated sculptor Machado de Castro (see also p 83). At the foot of the statue, you will see a medallion depicting the Marquês de Pombal, a somewhat ironic reminder of that minister's key role in reconstructing the city.

On the north side of the square, an impressive baroque style **triumphal arch** ★ marks the beginning of Rua Augusta. This arch, which was not completed until 1873, features four illustrious figures (Vasco da Gama, Nuno Alvares, the mythical Viriath and the omnipresent Pombal) perched atop pedestals. They seem to be beckoning visitors to enter the heart of Lisbon in regal style. Dom

Carlos I and his heir, Luis Philipe, were assassinated nearby in 1908.

The Armillary Sphere

A symbol that appears frequently in Manueline art, the armillary sphere is a globe containing a set of rings showing the path of the stars. Dom Manuel adopted the sphere as the official emblem of the court.

It is worth making a quick stop at nearby **Praça do Municipio** ★, which was recently renovated, to see its lovely **cabled pillory** ★, topped by an **armillary sphere** (see box above). Opposite the pillory, the **neoclassical facade of city hall** (Câmara Municipal) towers over the little square. Portugal was proclaimed a republic here on October 5, 1910. Those who like rococo should head to the corner of Rua Conceição and Rua do Crucifixo, where a residential building displays an elaborate facade, painted a pretty shade of green. Finally, right nearby, between Rua de São Nicolau and Rua da Conceição, the

impressive facade of the **Banco Totta & Açores** is also sure to delight admirers of this style.

Head back toward the Praça do Comércio and take Rua do Alfândega, where you will see the **Igreja de la Conceição Velha** ★ (*tram #18; bus #39 from Praça dos Restauradores; bus #46 from the Rossio, Alfânadega stop*) on your left. Its most noteworthy features are the **two front windows** ★ and the **Manueline portal** ★: all that remains of an earlier church, which was destroyed by the earthquake.

If you walk a little farther along Rua da Alfândega, you will come to the Campo das Cebolas, and the **Casa dos Bicos** ★ (*tram #13 from Praça Figueira, Alfândega stop; bus # 39A from the Praça do Comércio; bus #46 from the Rossio, Campo das Cebolas stop*). This house has an unusual facade covered with diamond-shaped stones, hence its name (the House of Points). It once belonged to the viceroy of India, Afonso de Albuquerque. Partially destroyed during the earthquake, it was built while Pombal was in power. After being damaged again, this time by fire, it underwent a number of modifications, including the addition of the top two floors. They do not match the style of the ground floor (especially as far as their proportion and window decorations are concerned), but the building is still attractive as a whole. Immediately to the right stands an interesting (but slightly run-down) residence adorned with numerous wrought-iron balconies, a fine example of the Pombaline style.

By taking Rua dos Bacalhoeritos, turning right on Rua da Madalena and then walking to the Largo da Madalena, you can either catch tram #28 or continue on foot up to the Sé (cathedral). On the way, at Largo de Santo António da Sé, you will see the church of the same name, which houses a statue of St. Anthony of Padua. In keeping with local custom, a procession is held each year, during which the statue is carried through the Alfama.

The **Sé Patriarcal** ★★★ (*tram #28 from the Praça Luís de Camões, Sé stop; bus #37 from Praça da Figueira, Sé stop*), erected around 1147 by order of Afonso Henriques, is one of the oldest monuments in the capital. Some historians claim that it was erected on the same site as an old mosque, but this remains a subject of debate. Having been damaged by several earthquakes (1337, 1344, 1531 and 1755), the cathedral has undergone numerous

modifications. Although its exterior remains essentially Romanesque (with crenellations serving as a reminder of its defensive role and its giant, especially deep portal), a number of elements in other styles have been added, including a Gothic rose window, an ambulatory and a baroque sacristy.

Inside, to the left of the entrance, by the baptismal fonts, the walls are covered with beautiful *azulejos*. There is also an amusing panel showing St. Anthony preaching to the fish. In the neighbouring chapel, you will find an interesting **crèche**, or nativity tableau, by Machado de Castro. One of the chapels to the right of the choir (the fourth chapel in the ambulatory) shelters the 14th-century tombs of Lopo Fernandes Pacheco and his wife.

Finally, be sure to visit the 13th century **Romanesque cloister** ★ (*100 ESC; Mon to Sat 10am to 5pm; enter through the ambulatory*) to admire a group of lovely rose windows supported by elegant geminated columns, each carved in a different way. In a remarkable turn of events, while excavating the foundations of Lisbon's first cathedral (built after the Moors were driven out of Portugal) archaeologists recently discovered the foundations of a Roman temple dating from the Augustan age. A metal footbridge spans the site, enabling visitors to examine these impressive ruins. The cathedral also houses a small museum of religious art, the **Museu António** (*400 ESC; Mon to Sat 10am to 5pm; to the right of the main entrance*), which exhibits an assortment of vestments,

Lisbon

Azulejos

paintings and sacred objects. Aside from the ambulatory, nothing else that dates prior to the earthquake of 1755 has survived intact in the cathedral.

After visiting the Sé, make sure to stop in at **Espace Oikos** (*10am to noon and 2pm to 5pm; Rua Augusto Rosa no. 40*), a beautiful, extremely modern multicultural centre set up in the cloister stables. The centre is devoted to encouraging cooperation between developing countries.

Tour B: The Castelo and the Alfama

See map on p 85.

The monument best known to Lisboans is the **Castelo de São Jorge** ★★ (*tram 28 or bus #37 from Praça da Figueira, Castelo stop*) along with the Torre de Belém. When King Afonso Henriques drove out the Moors and took over the fortress in 1147, he seized the very cradle of the city. It was here, and on the hillside now occupied by the Alfama, that Lisbon first developed. The old fortifications had many occupants; first this was a Roman city, then a fortified Visigoth city and then a Moorish city (as of 716). Today, the ramparts shelter the old neighbourhood of **Santa Cruz**, whose souvenir shops and restaurants welcome tourists each

year in a somewhat artificial atmosphere. To tour the area, go through the fortified São Jorge entrance, which faces onto Rua do Chão da Feira and offers access to the former parade ground, now a pleasant lookout. An imposing statue of King Afonso Henriques stands in the centre. Climb up the shady terraces opposite the statue to see what remains of the **royal palace of Alcáçova** (on the left), itself erected on top of an old Moorish palace. This was the home of the Aviz dynasty for many years, until a new residence was built on the banks of the Tagus. The building is now mainly used for receptions. The former palace chapel (São Miguel), which is rarely open, lies right nearby, as does the commanding officer's house. The latter has been converted into a wonderful restaurant (Casa do Leão, see p 137). To tour the Castelo, walk eastward across the terraces. On the other side of the drawbridge, inside the fortress, there are two squares with staircases leading up to the rampart-walk (*not recommended for those subject to dizzy spells*), which boasts some **magnificent views** ★★ of the city and the Tagus. Each of the 11 towers connected to the castle serves as a scenic lookout. Given the historic significance of the Castelo, visitors might

be surprised to learn that the place was neglected for many years, was a neighbourhood in itself at one time and was even used as a prison. Although it was listed as a national monument in 1910, major repairs were not begun until 1938. Finally, those who want to know everything about Lisbon's foundation can visit the **Olisipónia** (*Tue to Sun 10am to 7pm*), an interpretive centre located inside the Castelo.

For a more in-depth tour of the neighbourhood, head down to pleasant **Praça Largo Contador-Mor**, which is surrounded by houses with *azulejo*-covered facades. Continuing downhill, you'll reach **Largo das Portas do Sol**, adjacent to a small esplanade that offers a **splendid view** ★★ of East Lisbon, with the pristine dome of the Igreja de Santa Engrácia standing out sharply against the sky in the distance.

On Largo das Portas do Sol itself, visit the **Museu Escola de Artes Decorativas** (*800 ESC; Sun to Fri 10am to 5pm; Largo das Portas do Sol no. 2, ☎218 86 19 21; tram #28 from Praça Luís de Camões; bus #37 from Praça da Figueira, Miradouro Santa Luzia stop*), in the former residence of the viscounts of Azurara. Ricardo do Espírito Santo Silva purchased this little palace in 1947

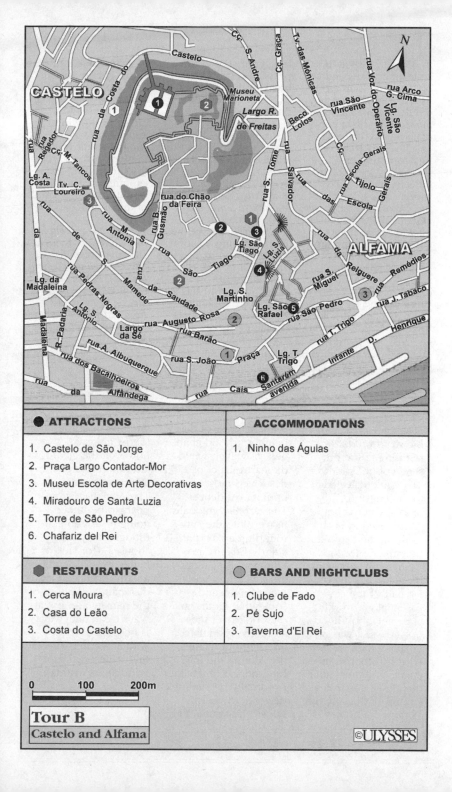

ATTRACTIONS

1. Castelo de São Jorge
2. Praça Largo Contador-Mor
3. Museu Escola de Arte Decorativas
4. Miradouro de Santa Luzia
5. Torre de São Pedro
6. Chafariz del Rei

ACCOMMODATIONS

1. Ninho das Águias

RESTAURANTS

1. Cerca Moura
2. Casa do Leão
3. Costa do Castelo

BARS AND NIGHTCLUBS

1. Clube de Fado
2. Pé Sujo
3. Taverna d'El Rei

0   100   200m

Tour B

Castelo and Alfama

©ULYSSES

in order to display his collection of decorative objects, and then established a foundation for the decorative arts. The museum boasts a particularly rich collection of 17th- and 18th-century furniture, enhanced by some magnificent curios. Make sure to take a look at the impressive *serviço de viagem*, a silver travel kit with its own special case. The splendid tapestry from Tournai, Belgium, showing a procession of giraffes and the elegant Chinese tapestry made of linen, silk and gold thread are remarkable as well. Finally, to pro-

long your stay in this pleasant setting, take a break at the museum cafeteria's pretty little patio.

Just next to the Largo das Portas do Sol is the **Miradouro de Santa Luzia** (*tram #28 from Praça Luís de Camões; bus #37 from Praça da Figueira, Miradouro Santa Luzia stop*), which offers a lovely **view ★★** of the area, enabling visitors to see how very labyrinthine it is. The place itself is graced by a little church and has a number of attractive terraces (refreshments available). This is a popular place for se-

niors to come and play cards. Finally, you'll find some beautiful *azulejos* ★ here; make sure to take a look at the ones showing a general view of the city (on the south wall of the lookout), as well as those depicting the capture of Lisbon in 1147 (on the right wall of the church).

To reach the Alfama from the Miradouro de Santa Luzia, go down the staircase immediately behind the Igreja Santa Luzia (tram #28 from Praça Luís de Camões; bus #37 from Praça da Figueira, Miradouro Santa Luzia stop).

The Alfama

Alfama: from the Arabic word *alhaman*, referring to the presence of hot springs. The name dates back to the era of the Moors, when a hot spring used to gush forth on the Largo do Chorariz de Dentro. Along with Santa Cruz, the Alfama is the oldest part of the city. Essentially a working-class neighbourhood nowadays, it was originally inhabited by wealthy Moorish merchants and then, after the Moors surrendered control of the city, by Portuguese nobles.

The character of the neighbourhood changed, however, when the earthquake of 1755 destroyed most of the opulent residences. The nobility gradually moved into the surrounding areas (particularly Belém), making way for sailors, artisans and workers, who slowly, and somewhat haphazardly, took over the area. Overpopulated, and without utilities, the Alfama slid into a long period of decline, eventually becoming a disgrace to well-heeled Lisboans. With

the growth of the tourist industry, however, the city took a renewed interest in this neighbourhood. The Alfama now appears to be undergoing restoration, although many little "houses" (for lack of a better word) are still in an advanced state of disrepair, and a tour of the narrow and not always clean alleyways is best left to those with a genuine interest in the lifestyle of the Portuguese working class.

The feeling of happenstance that prevails in the **Alfama** ★ (see map p 85) and the myriad reactions it elicits from visitors make it a delightful place to explore. There's surprise, when you head into one of countless little alleys and suddenly discover that it is only wide enough for one person to pass through at a time; pleasure, when you reach the end of an alley and find yourself in a little square surrounded by tiny houses decorated with *azulejos* and geraniums; despair, when you come to the end of a long climb uphill, only to discover another staircase that doesn't seem to lead anywhere; and finally a sense of adventure, as you stroll through unknown streets with only cooking odours and children's shouts to guide you. Although you don't need an itinerary to explore the Alfama, in fact you are better without one, make sure to visit the **Torre de São Pedro** (*Largo de São Rafael*), all that remains of the Moorish fortifications that once protected the city. At the top of the tower, in the back, is a pretty geminated window, which can be admired from Rua daJudiaria. Back on the banks of the Tagus, on Largo do Terreiro do Trigo, you'll find an elegant public fountain **Chafariz del Rei** ★ (*Rua Cais de Santarém*) built by order of Dom Dinis,

it is one of the most ancient public fountains in Lisbon. Nearby, at the corner of Rua da Regueira and Rua dos Remédios, is a beautiful **Manueline door**.

Tour C: Graça and East Lisbon

See map on p 89.

Heading east along the Tagus, you will come to the **Museu Militar** ★ (*300 ESC, free on Wed; Tue to Sun 10am to 5pm; Largo do Museu da Artilharia,* ☎/≈*218 84 25 69; bus #39A from Praça do Comércio, Estação Santa Apolónia stop; bus #46 from the Rossio, Estação Santa Apolónia stop*), a sumptuous building containing a varied assortment of weapons, which is sure to fascinate anyone with an interest in the subject. It is worth coming here just to see the **beautifully decorated rooms** in which some of the

collections are presented. They feature gilding, painted ceilings, carved woodwork and paintings by great Portuguese artists. Various artillery pieces are exhibited in a large, verdant, interior courtyard, the walls of which are decorated with lovely *azulejos*.

Of the many expressions used by Lisboans, *"obras de Santa Engrácia"* is probably one of the most colourful. It is used to designate a work in progress that seems as if it will never be completed. The origin of this expression can be traced back to the construction of the **Igreja-Panteão de Santa Engrácia** (*200 ESC; Tue to Sun 10am to 5pm; Campo de Santa Clara; tram #28 or bus #39A from Praça do Comércio, Estação Santa Apolónia stop; bus #46 from the Rossio, Estação Santa Apolónia stop,* ☎*218 88 15 29*), which was begun in the

17th century and finished in the 1960s! It now presents its virtually immaculate white dome proudly for all the city to see. Declared the **National Pantheon** in 1966, it contains cenotaphs to major Portuguese figures like Afonso de Albuquerque, Camões and Vasco de Gama.

Just uphill from the Pantheon, you'll find the **Campo de Santa Clara** (*tram #28 from Praça Luís de Camões, Rua da Voz do Operário stop*), a charming little square with a covered market at its centre. In addition to the usual vegetable stalls, you'll find all sorts of second-hand goods displayed all around the building (see "Shopping", p 159). Several handsome government buildings, including the stately military courthouse, face onto the square, and an attractive little park completes the layout. Be sure to take a look at the beautiful facade covered with *azulejos* in *trompe-l'œil* motifs at numbers 124-126.

Located, as its name indicates, outside the city walls, the **Igreja e Mosteiro de São Vicente de Fora** (*Largo de São Vicente; tram #28 from Praça Luís de Camões, Rua da Voz do Operário stop or bus #12*) is worth the detour along narrow Rua Arco Grande da Cima, with its pretty archway. Not only does the church boast a lovely **marble interior**, a

Vasco Da Gama

Vasco da Gama was born in Sines in 1469. Virtually nothing is known about his childhood, and it was as a sailor in King João II's fleet that he first distinguished himself. Under the reign of Manuel I, Vasco da Gama, then an admiral, was entrusted with four ships with which to seek out a route to India. During his two-year voyage, nearly a third of his men perished. In November 1497, after a brief stay in the Canary Islands, he reached the Cape of Good Hope (formerly known as the Cape of Storms), which had been discovered by Portuguese navigator Bartolomeu Dias in 1488. He started exploring the eastern shores of Africa, then decided to venture farther east and discovered Calicut in May 1498. The Arabs had known about this small Indian port, reputed for its spices and its calico, since the seventh century. The famous poet Luís de Camões accompanied da Gama on this voyage. His experiences inspired him to write an epic poem entitled *Os Lusíadas* (*The Lusiads*), which immortalized the era of great discoveries.

When Vasco da Gama returned to Lisbon in 1499, he received a hero's welcome and was ennobled and given a generous annuity by the king. Despite his discovery, it wasn't until his second voyage, in 1502 and 1503, that Portuguese trading posts were established in India. During this second expedition, he also founded trading posts in Mozambique. After returning to Portugal laden with riches, he was named viceroy of India. He set out on a third voyage in 1524, but died of illness a few months after arriving in Cochin.

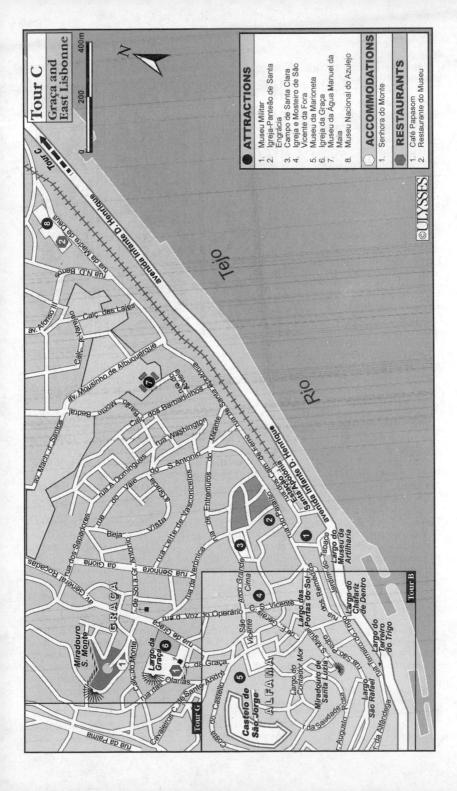

Tour C
Graça and East Lisbonne

N

0   200   400m

© ULYSSES

ATTRACTIONS

1. Museu Militar
2. Igreja-Panteão de Santa Engrácia
3. Campo de Santa Clara
4. Igreja e Mosteiro de São Vicente da Fora
5. Museu da Marioneta
6. Igreja da Graça
7. Museu da Água Manuel da Maia
8. Museu Nacional do Azulejo

ACCOMMODATIONS

1. Senhora do Monte

RESTAURANTS

1. Café Papasom
2. Restaurante do Museu

high altar topped by an impressive baldachin, and a beautiful choir floor, but the huge monastery is adorned with numerous *azulejos*. The church was built during the reign of Afonso Henriques, as a gesture of thanks to St. Vincent, the patron saint of Lisbon, after the Moors were driven out of the city. Upon entering the **cloister** ★ through the ground floor (*300 ESC; every day 9am to 12:30pm and 3pm to 8pm; to the right of the church*), take a look at the immense cistern illuminated by the skylights of the cloister. It is also interesting to see how well the vestiges of a 12th-century monastery were incorporated into the present structure. The two large cloisters on the first floor are decorated with *azulejos* ★ depicting pastoral scenes. Don't miss the remarkable *azulejos* illustrating La Fontaine's *Fables* in the south cloister. On the second floor is the the longest panel of *azulejos* in Portugal. The tiles in the caretaker's quarters depict various historic events, including the capture of Lisbon. At the far end of the cloister, the former refectory has been converted into a mausoleum for the Bragança dynasty. Here lie the remains of Portugal's last monarchs, including Queen Amélia (died in 1951) and her son, the country's last king,

Talhas Douradas

Manuel II, who died in exile in 1932. Before leaving, be sure to take in the lovely view of the city from the terrace accessible from the ground floor (*on your way back downstairs from the cloister, take the left-hand exit and then the staircase immediately to the right*).

By taking Rua de São Vicente then Rua de Santa Marinha, you'll come to Largo Rodrigues de Freitas, home of the **Museu da Marioneta** (*300 ESC; Tue to Fri 10am to noon and 2pm to 6pm, Sat and Sun 11am to 6pm; Largo Rodrigues de Freitas no. 19, ☎218 88 28 41*). On a guided tour of this museum, you can learn all there is to know about these mischief-makers.

Just steps away, on Largo da Graça, the

Miradouro da Graça commands a remarkable **panoramic view** ★★ of the city and the castle. This pleasant esplanade lies in front of the **Igreja da Graça**, whose **Manueline baptistery** ★ and numerous chapels decorated with *talhas douradas* are worth a peek.

Like *azulejos*, water is an integral part of Lisbon's history, as the Águas Livres (see p 100) aqueduct, the Mãe d'Água reservoir and the city's numerous fountains remind us. Therefore, no history buff would want to miss a visit to the remarkable **Museu da Água Manuel da Maia** (*300 ESC, guided tour of both sites mentioned above by request only; Mon and Wed to Sat 10am to 12:30pm and 2pm to 5pm; Rua do Alviela no. 12,*

☎218 13 55 22; bus #39A or 81 from Praça do Comércio, Estação Santa Apolónia stop; bus #46 from the Rossio, Estação Santa Apolónia stop; bus #12 from Marquês de Pombal, Estacão Santa Apolónia stop), located in the heart of the Xábregas neighbourhood in East Lisbon. Through documents, photographs and various kinds of machinery, visitors explore the complex history of the city's water supply system. The city's first residents drew water freely from small springs in the Alfama. The lovely Chafariz del Rei fountain (see p 87), which dates back at least to the era of Muslim rule, is a beautiful example from this period. However, as demand for water increased and supply diminished, water distribution became regulated. Originally, slaves had carried water to their masters' homes in wooden casks; now, this activity became a full-time occupation, mainly of Galician labourers. The rules were very strict, and certain people were given water before others, depending on their rank on a list: workers were first, and women were fifth! Later still, after a number of springs dried up and the demand for water continued to increase, King João V ordered the construction of the Aguas Livres aqueduct so that water could be brought in from springs outside the city. Starting

in the mid-18th century, the owners of springs located on the outskirts of the capital were obliged by royal decree to contribute to the city's water supply via a network of aqueducts. In return, a certain amount of water was distributed to their Lisbon homes at no charge. In some cases, this arrangement is still in effect today! As the demand for water continued to rise, a new aqueduct, the Aqueduto de Alviela, was built in 1871. When it became apparent that the pressure was too low in certain places, French engineers from Rouen were hired to install a **pumping station ★★**, which can be admired today at the museum. If you have a chance, go and see the machines in operation (ask the employee on duty), and make sure to climb up to the second floor to admire the huge hydraulic pistons in action; it's truly a sight to see! Today, in addition to the Alviela aqueduct, another conduit starting at the Tagus and a supply pipe connected to Castelo do Bode provide the city with water.

Portugal's inescapable *azulejos*, with their countless depictions of historic events and

social realities, are like an open book on the country's past. If you find these tiles truly fascinating, make sure to visit the Convento da Madre de Deus to see the **Museu Nacional do Azulejo ★★★** (*350 ESC; Tue 2pm to 6pm, Wed to Sun 10am to 6pm; Rua da Madre de Deus no. 4, ☎218 14 77 47 or 218 14 77 99; bus #39A from Praça do Comércio, Igreja Madre de Deus stop; tram #17 from Praça do Comércio*). Founded in the early 16th century by Queen Leonor (the widow of João II) as a place where she could retire from public life, the **Convento da Madre de Deus** was once so luxurious that it looked more like a palace than a convent. The convent and the adjacent church have undergone numerous modifications over the centuries.

Azulejos

During the reign of João III (1557-1578), the buildings were raised in order to protect them from the frequent floods of the Tagus. Then, under João V, the convent was given a major facelift, and a new sacristy was erected. The building escaped only partially damaged from the terrible earthquake of 1755. A century later, in 1867, after the convent had become government property, large sections of both the cloister and the church were destroyed by a fire while extensive renovations were being carried out. Thanks to public donations, however, the structure was quickly reconstructed and restored. In 1959, the Gulbenkian Foundation came up with the idea of opening an *azulejo* museum here, an idea that was fully realized in 1980, with the official inauguration of the Museu Nacional do Azulejo.

Inside, on the ground floor, there are two **cloisters**, the larger of which contains a great number of *azulejos* accompanied by written explanations of the various ways of making the tiles. Before going upstairs, make sure to visit the **Igreja da Madre de Deus** ★★★, adjacent to the large cloister. The remarkable interior of the church is decorated with a harmonious combination of *azulejos* and sculptures. *Talhas douradas,*

statues, Flemish and Portuguese paintings, and other baroque decorations seem to be vying for the dazzled eyes of visitors. To the left of the entrance of the church there is a remarkable group of *azulejos* depicting Moses receiving the Ten Commandments on Mount Sinai. As the church is dedicated to the Virgin Mary, a lovely representation of the *Madre de Deus* graces the high altar. After gaining access to the second floor through the **small cloister** ★, which is completely covered with beautiful *azulejos* in a rich shade of blue, you'll find yourself in a small room, where your attention will be drawn to a group of **Dutch tiles** ★★ dating from 1740, all in pretty brown hues. Each tile shows a scene from Jesus's life, with the various figures depicted in a manner reminiscent of a child's drawings. A real little wonder to behold!

Next, you'll visit the *coro-alto* ★★, at the back of the church, where the decoration of the ceiling and the walls, completely covered with big paintings with fantastically ornate gilt frames is outstanding. On your way out of the *coro-alto*, immediately to the right, is a large panel of 576 *azulejos* recreating a panoramic view of **pre-1755 Lisbon** ★. Finally, don't leave without

taking a look at the group of *azulejos* illustrating scenes from the life of **Chapeleiro António Joaquim Carneiro** ★★, known as Odito, an amazing social portrait written in Old Portuguese.

Tour D: The Chiado and the Bairro Alto

See maps on p 93 and p 97.

Though its boundaries are somewhat vague, the Chiado, with its pretty little central square called Largo do Chiado, essentially lies between Rua do Carmo and Praça Luís de Camões. From the Rossio, start off your tour by walking up **Rua do Carmo**. Along with Rua Garrett, which intersects it, this street was long home to the most elegant shops in the capital. In August of 1988, however, a terrible fire that lasted several days destroyed most of the buildings on Rua do Carmo and a number of those on Rua Garrett, reducing many luxurious, near-centenarian stores to ashes. With the help of celebrated architect Álvaro Siza Vieira, the city built as many buildings as possible, always striving to retain the spirit of the area. Strolling along Rua do Carmo, you will see many facades that escaped complete destruction and are now being preserved so that they can be

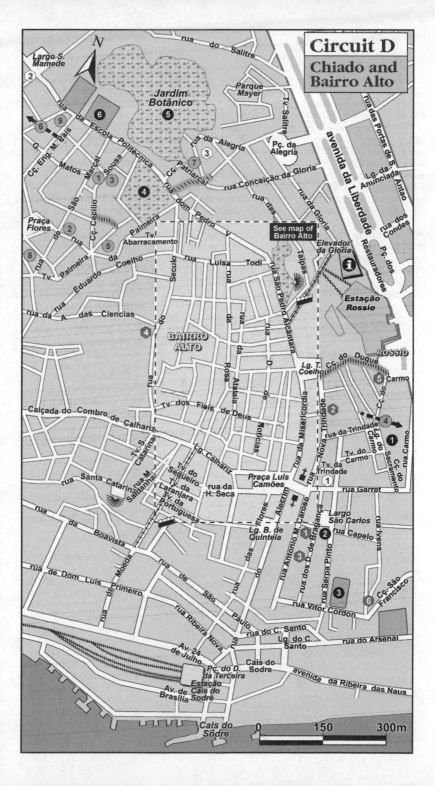

incorporated into new buildings. As a sign of new life, a large shopping centre was built at the end of 1999. When you reach number 87A (*on the right side of the street as you head uphill*), stop for a moment to admire the tiny Luvaria Ulisses, a lovely little glove shop dating from the turn of the century.

Before continuing your tour on Rua Garrett, turn right onto the Calçada do Sacremento to reach peaceful little **Largo do Carmo**.

The atmosphere was livelier back when tram #25 used to stop here. In addition to an elegant fountain, you'll find the **Igreja do Carmo ★**. Miraculously, only the church's vault collapsed during the great earthquake of 1755. Today, with arches that seem to defy the heavens, the church stands its ground proudly, as if to show that it is still keeping a close watch over the lower parts of the city.

Built in the late 14th century at the instigation of Nuno Álvares Pereira (Grand Officer of the Crown), in honour of Portugal's victory in the Battle of Aljubarrota (see p 16), it was the largest church in Lisbon for many years. The open-air **Museu Arqueológico do Carmo** (*Largo do Camo, ☎213 46 04 73; take the Elevador de Santa Justa from the Rossio*) used to display Visigoth and Roman artifacts, Arab sculptures and even a Manueline window from the Mosteiro dos Jerónimos (see p 116). However, the museum was closed for repairs at the end of 1999 and it is not sure when it will reopen.

Before heading back to Rua Garrett, *azulejo* aficionados will want to stop by numbers 28-34 on Rua da Trindade (*on the north side of the Largo*), where allegorical figures representing water, earth, commerce and industry adorn a superb ***azulejo*-covered facade ★**.

Now, take **Rua Garrett** to Largo do Chiado, the best-known square in the area. On the way, stop at numbers 50-52 for a peek inside the Ourivesaria Aliança. This goldsmith's shop is a survivor from the days when luxury shops abounded in the area. Farther along, at number 77, the window of the Paris em Lisboa shop is adorned with pretty signs and a

La Sétima Colina

While visiting the Bairro Alto or the Chiado, you might hear about the Sétima Colina, or Seventh Hill, which was one of the many projects organized by the city to celebrate its role as the "European Cultural Capital" in 1994. It was the brainchild of art historian José-Augusto França, who wanted to draw Europe's attention to his city's rich architectural heritage by creating a tour leading from the Cais do Sodré (pier) to the Largo do Rato. The route is a string of five streets, all heading in the

same direction, but running through very different types of neighbourhoods. These streets are lined with buildings of all different styles and eras, ranging from the Mudéjar style to the baroque interior of the 17th-century Igreja de São Roque and the neoclassical style of the 19th century. Thanks to this project, a large number of buildings were restored or touched up and continue to be maintained, giving Lisbon's rather dated charm a brand-new vitality.

copper-plated, Art Nouveau guardrail. Finally, make sure to go inside the Ramiro Leã notions shop (number 83) for a look at the magnificent Art Nouveau elevator and the stairwell adorned with stained glass and frescoes.

It is on **Largo do Chiado** (*tram #28 from Rua da Conceição in the Baixa; tram #24 or bus #15 from the Rato, Praça Luís de Camões stop*), once a favourite haunt of the literary crowd, that you'll find the famous café A Brasileira (see p 142). Such celebrated Portuguese poets as António Ribeiro and Fernando Pessôa used to be regular customers here. On the patio, you can have your picture taken with Pessôa (the bronze version, of course!), unless you'd prefer to be seen with that famous Renaissance poet Antonio Ribeiro, whose statue stands in the middle of the square. As a crowning touch to this beautiful spot, two churches, **Nossa Senhora de l'Encarnação** and the Italian community's **Nossa Senhora do Loreto**, stand, with freshly restored facades, across from each other on the square.

In keeping with the literary theme, **Praça Luís de Camões** (*tram #28 from Rua da Conceição in the Baixa*) has a statue of Portugal's most celebrated poet, Luís de Camões (see p 34) in its centre. This square, which is surrounded by dilapidated buildings, most certainly deserves better. At the time of our visit, major work was under way here and an underground parking lot was being laid out. Let us hope that the surrounding buildings with charming facades will also be restored in their turn.

It is worthwhile to walk farther down Rua Serpa Pinto to take a look at the **Teatro Nacional de São Carlos** (*Rua Serpa Pinto, near Rua Capelo, program ☎213 46 84 08; tickets ☎213 46 59 14; tram #28 from Rua da Conceição in the Baixa, Largo do Chiado stop*), a handsome Italian-style building from the late 18th century. The interior was modeled after La Scala in Milan.

If you like painting or modern architecture, you simply must visit the Chiado's brand-new museum. Set up inside the former Museum of Contemporary Art, the **Galeria Nacional do Chiado ★★** (*400 ESC; Tue 2pm to 6pm, Wed to Sun 10am to 6pm; Rua Serpa Pinto nos. 4-6, ☎213 43 21 48 or 213 43 21 49; tram #28 from Rua da Conceição, métro Baixa-Chiado, in the Baixa, Rua Vitor Cordon stop*) displays paintings and sculptures by major Portuguese artists like Columbano, Silvo Porto, João Voz, Soares dos Reis and Malhoa. Despite its name, the museum is devoted mainly to works from the 19th and early 20th centuries. The interior design, by the Wilmotte firm (a French architecture firm already well-known for having designed the furnishings for the Champs-Élysées in Paris), successfully combines metal and glass structures with stones and bricks, some of which date back to the 17th century. Particularly noteworthy pieces include José de Almada Negreiro's *Gato Felix*, which you'll see as you come in, and, on the second floor, the panels entitled *Bar de Marinheiro* and *Jazz*, which were part of a set of 12 Art-Deco panels that used to adorn a Spanish movie theatre. These are the only two to have survived, and they narrowly escaped destruction. Part of the museum is laid out in the former São Francisco da Cidade monastery. After being abandoned by the church then put to several other uses, the buildings served as a *bolacha* (cookie) factory from 1855 to 1898. The only noteworthy vestiges from that period are the four ovens in the José-Augusto França room, which have been perfectly integrated into the decor. Among the other works on display, Eduardo Viano's remarkable paintings are not to be missed. The museum has an attractive cafeteria with an outdoor seating area graced with a number of modern sculptures.

Lisbon

Make sure to go to the top floor, where a huge terrace offers a partial view of the Tagus. Overall, the ultra-modern decor is a bit cold, and there is far too much wasted space.

The **Bairro Alto** ★★ (see map, p 97), was originally (in the 16th and 17th centuries) made up of palatial residences, which lay stretched in front of small public squares and parks. They were later replaced by working-class houses occupied by artisans and shopkeepers. In the evening, local prostitution increased, giving the area a bad reputation. Presently undergoing yet another transformation, the Bairro Alto has become known for its nightlife (family restaurants, *fado* taverns), and more and more shops, discos and fashionable restaurants are popping up here, attracting young Lisboans in search of *movida*.

Take your time as you stroll down Rua da Rosa, located opposite the Largo, or Rua da Atalaia, a bit farther along, so that you can soak up the peaceful atmosphere that prevails in the Bairro. A sudden change comes over these streets after dark, especially on weekends, with bars, nightclubs, *fado* taverns and night-time restaurants appearing as if by magic.

Farther along, at the edge of the Chiado, the **Igreja São Roque** ★★ (*Largo Trindade Coelho; from Praça dos Restauradores, take the Funicular da Glória, beside the Palacio Foz, or bus #100*) does not look very inviting at first glance due to its nondescript facade. Its interior, however, is not to be missed. Built by the Jesuits in the 16th century, partially destroyed in the earthquake of 1755 and built shortly thereafter, this is one of the most richly decorated churches in the capital. Its nave and wood ceiling painted in *trompe-l'œil* are both very elegant, while the walls are lavishly decorated with carved woodwork and marble. There is a series of chapels, each decorated in a different manner. The **Capela de São João Baptista** ★★★ (*from the chancel, first chapel on the left*) is a veritable marvel of Italian art. Commissioned by King João V and built in Rome by numerous artisans and artists, it was transported here piece by piece by boat. Amethyst, bronze, lapis-lazuli, ivory, silver, alabaster and all sorts of other splendid materials make this chapel look like a museum of sacred art. It is almost as if everything that Italian baroque art has to offer were concentrated here. Before leaving this magical place, stop in at the

second chapel on the right (from the chancel) to see some beautiful Renaissance-era **azulejos** ★★ made in Seville.

It is also worth visiting the **Museu de Arte Sacra de São Roque** ★ (*150 ESC, free Sun; Tue to Sun 10am to 5pm; Largo Trindade Poelho, entrance from the church or from outside, immediately to the right of the church,* ☎*213 23 5000 or 213 42 08 50*) adjoining the church, which contains a rich collection of sacred objects made of silver and gold, as well as all sorts of vestments. One of the most interesting items is a 14th-century silver Virgin from Germany.

Nearby, on Rua de São Pedro de Alcântara, you can enjoy a magnificent view from the **Miradouro de São Pedro de Alcântara** ★ (*to the right when you get off the Funicular da Glória; from Praça dos Restauradores, take the Funicular da Glória, beside the Palacio Foz*). This pleasant little garden and lookout lies opposite the Castelo and offers a view of downtown Lisbon below, with the Tagus in the distance.

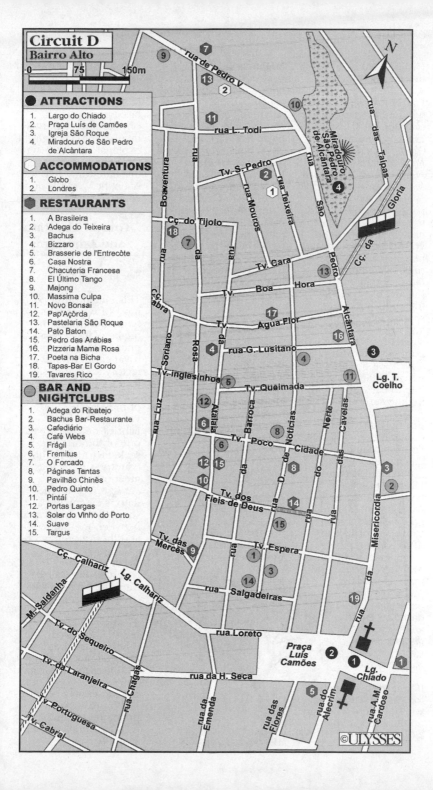

Heading back up Rua de São Pedro de Alcântara to Rua da Escola Politécnica, you will find a pretty square on your left. This is **Praça do Príncipa Real** (*from Praça dos Restauradores take the Funicular da Glória, then bus #100 or #58, Príncipe Real stop*), whose little park is a pleasant place to relax. If you come here in the afternoon, you'll find many locals playing cards on the park's little tables. In the centre, there is a remarkable cypress tree, which has been shaped into a bower and offers welcome shelter from the sun. Located right nearby is a pleasant restaurant where you can have a bite to eat while admiring the surroundings.

Just opposite, at the corner of Rua da Escola Politécnica and little Calçada da Patriarcal, stands the **Palacete Ribeiro da Cunha**, a beautiful mansion that was built in 1877 and now belongs to the University of Lisbon. After admiring the lovely facade with its Arab accents, go inside for a peek at the pretty covered patio, also influenced by Arab architecture (*take the door on the right, just past the main entrance*).

If you have a penchant for a calm setting lush with greenery, continue up the street a little farther to the

Jardim Botânico (*200 ESC; winter, Mon to Fri 9am to 6pm, Sat and Sun 10am to 6pm; summer every day until 7pm; Rua da Escola Politécnica no. 58; métro Rato or from Praça dos Restauradores take the Funicular da Glória, then bus #58, Rua da Escola Politécnica stop,* ☎213 92 18 00), laid out alongside the former Faculty of Science. A path lined with palm trees seems to beckon visitors to enter this pleasant garden. Established on a hilly site, the garden offers numerous interesting views of the city. For those wishing to go to Avenida da Liberdade, a second exit is located on Rua da Alegria.

Right near by, the **Museu da Ciência** (*free admission; Mon to Fri 10am to 1pm and 2pm to 5pm, Sat 3pm to 6pm; Rua da Escola Politécnica no. 58,* ☎213 96 18 00 or 213 96 15 21; *métro Rato or from Praça dos Restauradores, take the Funicular da Glória, then bus #58, Rua da Escola Politécnica stop*) will appeal mainly to those interested in exact sciences.

Portugal Pine

Throughout the museum, all sorts of devices are on hand so that visitors can test the basic principles of physics and chemistry themselves. Though the explanatory text is written only in Portuguese, this little foray into the scientific world is quite entertaining.

Tour E: The Rato and Amoreiras

See map on p 99.

This neighbourhood, most of which was built after the earthquake of 1755, was once known for its royal earthenware factory and large silk factory. Founded in 1767 due to the efforts of the Marquês de Pombal, the Real Fábrica de Louça was one of the first large-scale factories in the country, producing great numbers of *azulejos*. Today, the Rato is essentially a shopping area, located between the Bairro Alto and the Amoreiras.

Because it offers direct access to the Bairro Alto, the **Largo do Rato** (*from Praça dos Restauradores, take the Elevador da Glória, then bus #15, Rato stop*), the true heart of the Rato, is constantly bustling with activity. All around the square, you'll find a wide variety of shops selling reasonably priced merchandise, as well as a number of snack-bars.

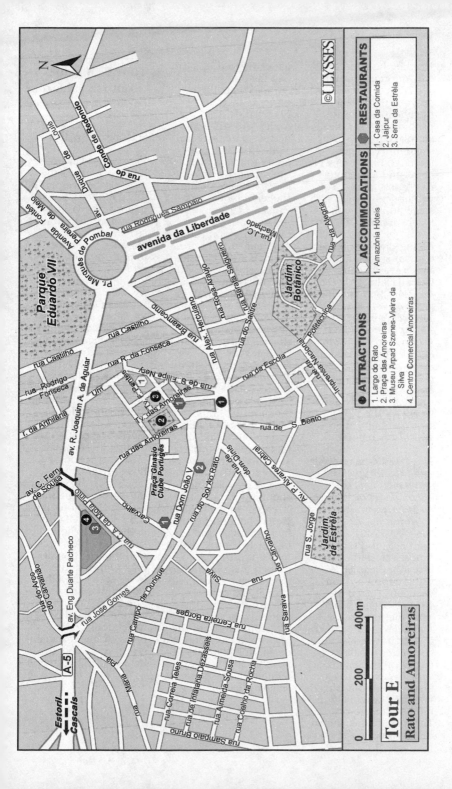

ATTRACTIONS
1. Largo do Rato
2. Praça das Amoreiras
3. Museu Arpad Szenes-Vieira da Silva
4. Centro Comercial Amoreiras

ACCOMMODATIONS
1. Amazônia Hóteis

RESTAURANTS
1. Casa da Comida
2. Jaipur
3. Serra da Estrêla

©ULYSSES

N

Tour E
Rato and Amoreiras

0   200   400m

Estoril
Cascais

A-5

Parque Eduardo VII

avenida da Liberdade

Jardim Botânico

Jardim da Estrêla

Praça Ginasio Clube Português

Pt. Marquês de Pombal

Heading back up Rua das Amoreiras, you'll see **Praça das Amoreiras** on your right. This pretty square has a park, which is a pleasant place to idle away some time. To get there, you have to walk under the Aqueduto das Águas Livres. You will notice its pillars, some adorned with lovely *azulejos*.

Facing onto the Praça das Amoreiras, the **Museu Arpad Szenes-Vieira da Silva** (*300 ESC, free Mon; Mon and Wed to Sat noon to 8pm, Sun 10am to 6pm; Praça das Amoreiras nos. 56-58, ☎213 88 00 44; métro Rato or from Praça dos Restauradores, take the Elevador da Glória, then bus #15, Jardim Amoreiras stop*) features works by the two famous painters after which it is named.

The **Mãe d'Água reservoir** (*guided tour upon request; inquire at the Museu da Água Manuel da Maia, métro Rato; Rua do Alviela no. 12,* ☎*218 13 55 22*), located right next to Praça da Amoreiras, is the last link in the capital's water supply system. It was constructed in 1834 to collect water from the impressive Águas Livres aqueduct, to which it is directly connected. With a capacity of 5,500m³, it supplied water to as many as 64 fountains via three conduits running under the city. Three fountains, including the one in the mid-dle of Largo do Carmo and the one on Largo Dr. José Figueiredo, opposite the Museu Nacional de Arte Antiga, are still connected to this system. Aside from its own pretty fountain, the site's main attraction is its vast pool of water, sheltered by elegant vaults.

Continuing north in the Amoreiras neighbourhood, you cannot help but be surprised by the futuristic **Centro Comercial Amoreiras** ★ (*from the Rossio or from the Praça dos Restauradores, bus #11, Amoreiras stop; or, from the Praça dos Restauradores, take the Elevador da Glória, then bus #15, Amoreiras stop*). This group of ultra-modern buildings, whose blend of shapes and colours is oddly reminiscent of the Art Deco style, is the work of architect Tomás Taveira. A veritable shopping mecca, it has over 350 shops (don't expect bargain prices), 50 restaurants and cafés (see p 161) and several movie theatres. Although this place is not to everyone's taste, we strongly recommend a visit to see how dramatically its architecture contrasts with the rest of the city. You can decide for yourself whether it is striking, hideous, fantastic or simply pleasant.

Tour F: Marquês De Pombal, Saldanha and North Lisbon

See map on p 101.

Vast **Parque Eduardo VII** ★ is perhaps the most distinctive part of this quarter, which might strike visitors as little more than one big crossroads (Praça Marquês de Pombal). A tour of the park starts off beautifully at the top, in the middle of Avenida Cardeal Cerejeira (*bus #2 from the Rossio, Marquês da Fronteira stop*), where a large terrace overlooking a stretch of greenery offers a lovely **view** ★★of the park, with Praça Marquês de Pombal, the Baixa and the Tagus in the distance. A formal garden graces the centre. Although it was created on the occasion of King Edward VII of England's visit to Portugal, this carpet of greenery now seems more like a tribute to the Marquês de Pombal, whose statue occupies a place of honour at the far end. Opposite the lookout, on the other side of Avenida Cardeal Cerejeira, stands a castle-like building, which looks rather pleasant but is actually a prison, so you are better off not visiting it!

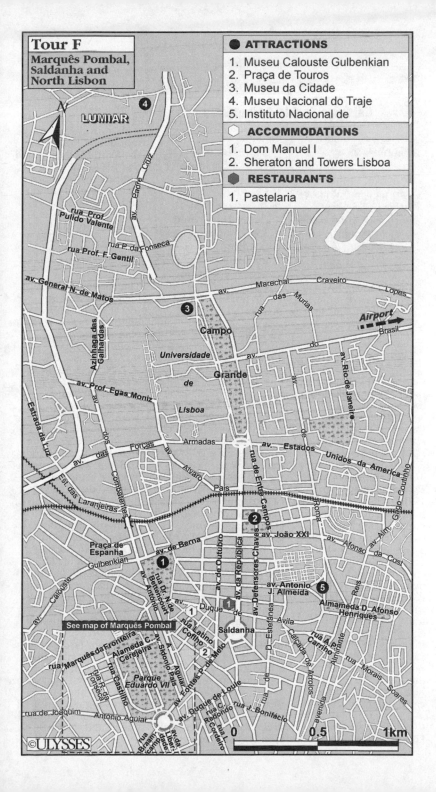

Tour F
Marquês Pombal, Saldanha and North Lisbon

ATTRACTIONS

1. Museu Calouste Gulbenkian
2. Praça de Touros
3. Museu da Cidade
4. Museu Nacional do Traje
5. Instituto Nacional de

ACCOMMODATIONS

1. Dom Manuel I
2. Sheraton and Towers Lisboa

RESTAURANTS

1. Pastelaria

LUMIAR

rua Prof. Pulido Valente

rua P. da Fonseca

rua Prof. F. Gentil

av. Padre Cruz

av. General N. de Matos

av. Marechal Craveiro Lopes

rua das Murtas

Airport Brasil

Campo

Universidade

de

Grande

Lisboa

Azinhaga das Galhardas

av. Prof. Egas Moniz

Estrada da Luz

Est. das Laranjeiras

av. dos Combatentes

Forças

Armadas

Álvaro

Pais

av. Estados

Unidos da América

av. Rio de Janeiro

av. do

Gago Coutinho

av. de Entre Campos

av. de Berna

av. Dr. N. de Bettencourt

av. António

Praça de Espanha

Gulbenkian

Caloustre

rua de Outubro

av. da República

av. de Defensores Chaves

av. João XXI

av. Roma

av. Afonso

av. Alm. Gago Coutinho

av. António J. Almeida

Almeda D. Afonso Henriques

Reis

See map of Marquês Pombal

rua Latino Coelho

Duque

de

Saldanha

rua A. Carrilho

av. de Estefânia

Ávila

Calçada de Arroios

rua Morais Soares

rua Marquês da Fronteira

Alameda C. Cerejeira

rua da Fonseca

rua Castilho

av. Sidónio Pais

Aguiar

av. Fontes P. de Melo

Parque Eduardo VII

António Aguiar

rua de Joaquim

av. Duque de Loule

rua D. Rodrigo

rua J. Bonifácio

rua L. Cordeiro

avenida

rua Braamcamp

av. da Liberdade

0   0.5   1km

©ULYSSES

Calouste Sarkis Gulbenkian

The **Calouste Gulbenkian Fundação** was created by a wealthy Armenian businessman named Calouste Sarkis Gulbenkian, who made his fortune in the oil industry. After living in London and Paris, he settled in Lisbon in 1942. A true art lover, he accumulated an impressive number of genuine works of art (6,000) over the course of his lifetime. Upon his death in 1955, a large portion of his assets went to the government and to his foundation, which now organizes many exhibits and concerts, and even has its own ballet company.

On the right side of the park as you walk down the esplanade, you'll see the **Estufa Fria e Quente** ★ (*80 ESC; open every day 9am to 5:30pm during summer, 9am to 5pm during winter, métro Marquês Pombal or Parque*), dating from 1910. Originally located in an old quarry, this greenhouse contains two gardens, one with exotic plants. Its cleverly designed bamboo roof creates a microclimate in which lush vegetation from countries as varied as Australia, Peru and China can flourish. It is extremely pleasant to stroll along the numerous pathways that wind their way through the heart of this domesticated jungle.

Closer to downtown Lisbon, but on the left this time, you'll see the dazzling baroque-style **Pavilhão dos Desportos** ★ (*Sports Stadium*). It is worth making a detour to admire its exterior, which is covered with **azulejos** ★★, most depicting historical scenes like the famous Battle of Ourique (see p 15). Particularly noteworthy is the magnificent grouping entitled *Cruzeiro do Sul*, in which five female figures, half-angel, half-fairy, seem to be showing the path of discovery to a caravel heading out to sea. Right beside the stadium, in the park, there is a picnic area where visitors can have a bite to eat and relax a while before returning to the feverish activity of the city.

Praça Marquês de Pombal (*you can take any number of buses here from Praça dos Restauradores and the Rato*), also known as the Rotunda, is a large traffic circle with a lovely central monument honouring the Marquês de Pombal and his talents as a statesman. The Praça has an elegant design and is adorned with many interesting statues. Unfortunately, however, it is difficult to get to the middle of it.

The **Museu Calouste Gulbenkian** ★★★ (*500 ESC; Tue 2pm to 6pm, Wed to Sun 10am to 6pm; Avenida de Berna no. 45, ☎217 95 02 36 or 217 93 51 31; métro São Sebastião or bus #31 or 46 from the Rossio, Gulbenkian or São Sebastião or Palhavã metro stops*) is located in the Praça de Espanha area, in a lovely park adorned with numerous modern sculptures (Parque de Palhavã). It has a large collection of decorative objects (paintings, sculptures, earthenware, curios), mostly from Europe and the Orient. All of the objects in this modern building are beautifully displayed in a series of rooms, each devoted to a different era. Almost all of these rooms are fascinating and merit a visit. In one, you can admire some lovely Egyptian pieces; in another, an interesting collection of ancient coins (mainly Greek and Roman).

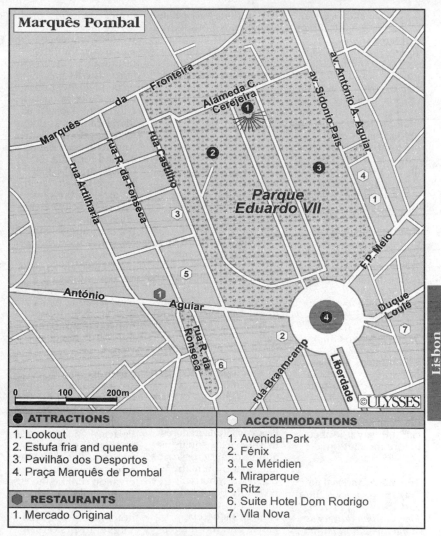

Marquês Pombal

Parque Eduardo VII

Lisbon

©ULYSSES

● ATTRACTIONS
1. Lookout
2. Estufa fria and quente
3. Pavilhão dos Desportos
4. Praça Marquês de Pombal

● RESTAURANTS
1. Mercado Original

○ ACCOMMODATIONS
1. Avenida Park
2. Fénix
3. Le Méridien
4. Miraparque
5. Ritz
6. Suite Hotel Dom Rodrigo
7. Vila Nova

Then there is a collection of articles (earthenware, carpets, books, etc.) from the Near and Middle East, as well as a room containing objects and paintings from the Far East. At the end of your tour, you will pass through a series of rooms devoted to European art, covering the Renaissance all the way through Art Nouveau, and including decorative objects from the 18th and 19th centuries. This museum, where modern technology has been put to wonderful use in the interest of art, also contains a large library and space for temporary exhibitions.

Right nearby, in the same park, the **Centro de Arte Moderna** (*same ticket used for admission to museum, same schedule; Rua Dr. Nicolau Bettencourt,* ☎*217 95 02 41*) exhibits paintings and sculptures by contemporary Portuguese artists and foreign artists working in Portugal.

If you are interested in bullfighting, go to **Praça de Touros** (*Praça de Touros; Campo Pequeno metro stop or bus #21 from the Rossio, Campo Pequeno stop*), where an unusual building houses the city's arena. Built in 1892, it has onion domes and horseshoe arches, which lend it a distinctly Moorish look. Between May and October, there are "shows" twice a week.

History buffs will enjoy the **Museu da Cidade** (*330 ESC; Tue to Sun 10am to 1pm and 2pm to 6pm; Campo Grande no. 245, ☎ 217 59 16 17; Campo Grande metro stop or bus #7 from Praça Figueira; bus #1 or #36 from the Rossio, Campo Grande-Norte stop*), which traces the history of Lisbon from prehistoric times to the birth of the Republic. The exhibit includes an interesting model of the city the way it looked before the earthquake of 1755.

The **Museu Nacional do Traje** ★ (*400 ESC; Tue to Sun 10am to 6pm; Largo Júlio Castilho-Parque do Monteiro-Mor, in Lumiar, ☎ 217 59 03 18; bus #7 from Praça Figueira; bus #36, from the Rossio, Lumiar stop*) displays a vast array of fabrics and clothing dating from the fourth century through the 15th. Artisans using various weaving techniques can be observed in the workshops surrounding the museum.

The **Instituto Nacional de Estatística** is housed in a beautiful Art-Deco building of gleaming green metalwork and golden-hued glass that blocks off the vista down Avenida António José de Almeida.

Tour G: Restauradores and Liberdade

See map on p 105.

Upon the death of Cardinal Henrique, in 1580, Portugal came under the yoke of the Spanish. About 60 years later, however, on December 15, 1640, a revolt instigated by the nobility brought the Duke of Bragança (João IV) into power, thus restoring the country's independence. In commemoration of these events, an obelisk flanked by two bronze statues was erected on **Praça dos Restauradores** in 1886. This square is an important crossroads and a stop on many bus routes, but will probably be of little interest to visitors. Numerous hotels, banks and travel agencies are located here, as is a large underground parking lot.

The most noteworthy building on the square is the **Palácio Foz** (*on the left side of the square, towards Praça Marquês de Pombal*). A former palace dating back to the 19th century, it now houses the tourist office (ICEP) (for opening hours, see p 74). Its lovely facade, the work of Francisco Fabri, is yet another testimony to the savoir-faire of Italian architects. Right next door, in the Calçada da Glória, the **Elevador da Glória** takes passengers straight into the Bairro Alto. This was Lisbon's second funicular (1885), and the first powered by an electric motor. It is the only one of the city's *elevadores* to have once been equipped with a long bench on the roof to provide extra seating. Trivia buffs might also be interested to know that the cable car used to be lit by candles at night. It now transports up to three million passengers a year.

Admirers of Art Deco are sure to notice the huge facade of the former **Teatro Eden** ★, located alongside the Palácio Foz. The top is decorated with lovely frescoes. The facade is a fine example of preservation, unlike the rest of the building, which now houses the Orion hotel (see p 130) and a Virgin music store.

The continuation of Praça dos Restauradores, the immense **Avenida da Liberdade** ★, is probably the longest and widest avenue in Portugal. Ninety metres across, it was clearly intended to serve as a showy, romantic route into the city.

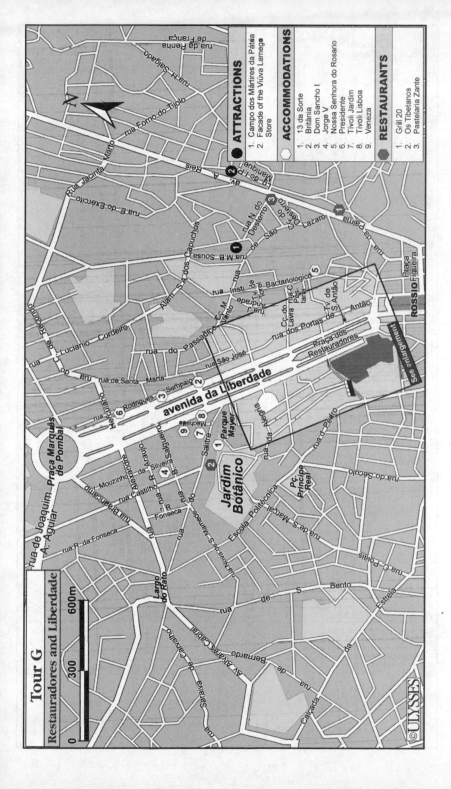

Tour G
Restauradores and Liberdade

0   300   600m

ATTRACTIONS
1. Campo dos Mártires da Pátria
2. Façade of the Viúva Lamege Store

ACCOMMODATIONS
1. 13 da Sorte
2. Britânia
3. Dom Sancho I
4. Jorge V
5. Nossa Senhora do Rosario
6. Presidente
7. Tivoli Jardim
8. Tivoli Lisboa
9. Veneza

RESTAURANTS
1. Grill 20
2. Os Tibetanos
3. Pastelaria Zante

© ULYSSES

See enlargement

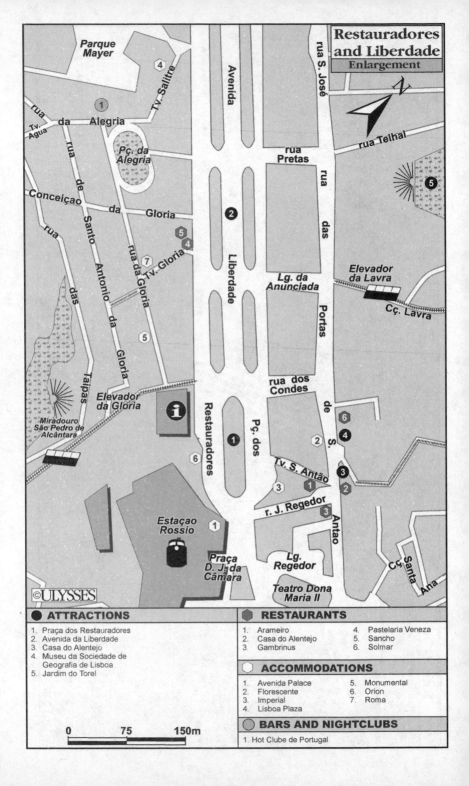

Restauradores and Liberdade
Enlargement

Parque Mayer

Tv.-Salitre

Avenida

rua da Alegria

Tv. Agua

Pç. da Alegria

Conceiçao

da Gloria

rua de Santo Antonio da Gloria

Tv.-Gloria

rua da Gloria

rua das

Taipas

Miradouro São Pedro de Alcântara

Elevador da Gloria

Restauradores

Estaçao Rossio

Praça D. J. da Câmara

©ULYSSES

rua S. José

rua Telhal

rua Pretas

rua das

Portas

Lg. da Anunciada

Elevador da Lavra

Cç. Lavra

rua dos Condes

de S.

Tv. S. Antão

r. J. Regedor

Antao

Cç. Santa Ana

Pç. dos

Lg. Regedor

Teatro Dona Maria II

● ATTRACTIONS
1. Praça dos Restauradores
2. Avenida da Liberdade
3. Casa do Alentejo
4. Museu da Sociedade de Geografia de Lisboa
5. Jardim do Torel

⬡ RESTAURANTS
1. Arameiro
2. Casa do Alentejo
3. Gambrinus
4. Pastelaria Veneza
5. Sancho
6. Solmar

⬡ ACCOMMODATIONS
1. Avenida Palace
2. Florescente
3. Imperial
4. Lisboa Plaza
5. Monumental
6. Orion
7. Roma

● BARS AND NIGHTCLUBS
1. Hot Clube de Portugal

0   75   150m

Those who designed it, however, probably never imagined that it would one day become a noisy, major artery. In any case, it is still an impressive tree-lined avenue with several stately buildings facing onto it. Among them stand the elegant facade of the building at numbers 206-216, whose ground floor, now occupied by a Fiat dealership, has been atrociously disfigured, and the charming Moorish facade of the building at numbers 226-228, adorned with splendid stained-glass windows. Lisboans come here for the movie theatres and travel agencies; tourists, for the hotels. Beneath the trees along the side roads, you can still find some outdoor cafés bordered with grass. Despite the noise of the traffic, these are pleasant places to relax and quench your thirst (see p 144). The Liberdade's mosaic sidewalks with maritime motifs are an indication of just how sophisticated the city was at the time the avenue was laid.

If you walk across the middle of the Praça dos Restauradores, you will come to the Travessa Santo Antão, which leads to the **Rua das Portas de Santo Antão**, a pleasant pedestrian street lined with restaurants. Here, you will find a social club called the **Casa do Alentejo** ★ (*Rua das Portas de Santo Antãono. 58*), an opu-

lent 19th century building, part of which is open to the public. The interior is decorated in the Mudéjar style, which was very much in fashion at the time of the building's construction. As you enter through the front door, you will find yourself in a lavish inner courtyard that will set your mind wandering to exotic Arabian locales. A majestic staircase embellished with *azulejos* leads up to the second floor. When you reach the top, go into the large room to your left, whose rococo decor, featuring stucco, gilding, crystal chandeliers and a lovely floor, is fit for a palace. Alongside this room, you'll find a restaurant (see p 144), whose beautiful *azulejos* merit a visit all on their own, while at the far end, to the right, is a smaller, less interesting room, which serves as a cafeteria.

Farther north on the same street is the **Coliseu dos Recreios** (*located between Travessa Santo Antão and Rua dos Condes, on the right side as you head north up the street*), an immense auditorium often used for concerts, among other events. It also houses the **Museu da Sociedade de Geografia de Lisboa** (*free admission; Mon, Wed and Fri 11am to 1pm and 3pm to 6pm; Rua das Portas de Santo Antão no. 100, ☎213 42 50 68*), a most outdated-looking ethnographical museum

displaying all sorts of objects accumulated by the Portuguese during their great era of exploration.

Still farther north, you will end up at the Largo da Anunciado, where you will find the Elevador da Lavra (*Calçada da Lavra*). This funicular, the first to be built in Lisbon, was a huge success right from the start. On its first day, April 19, 1884, it was in operation for 16 hours straight and transported 3,000 passengers. To avoid accidents, the operator had to alert people that the *elevador* was coming by blowing repeatedly into a horn. Thanks to this funicular, Lisboans (and tourists, of course) can reach the **Jardim do Torel** (*when you get off the elevador, turn left onto Rua Câmara Pestana, then left again onto Travessa do Torel, to reach Rua de Júlio de Andrade, on the right*). This pleasant garden, laid out in the centre of a charming old neighbourhood (best avoided at night), offers some **lovely views** of the northern part of the city. However, before going there, shutterbugs should be sure to stop off on **Calçada do Lavra** (*take the funicular halfway up*), where they can capture some especially romantic views.

Afterward, you can walk a short distance farther down Rua de Julio de Andrade to the **Campo dos Mártires da**

Patria, an immense square with a park and a statue honouring a celebrated Portuguese doctor, Dot Sousa Martins. Many women come here to lay pictures of ill or deceased relatives all around the statue and kneel to pray, hoping to benefit from the good graces of the doctor.

If you have a passion for *azulejos* and don't mind a good walk, continue your tour by taking Rua Manuel Bento Sousa, then Rua de São Lazaro, where quaint little Calçado do Desterro will lead you straight to bustling Avenida Almirante Reis. There, at the corner of Largo do Intendente Pina Manique, a handsome building proudly displays its Art-Nouveau-inspired *azulejos* and its whimsical **ironwork accents**, shaped like dragonflies, scarabs and swans. On Largo do Intendente Pina Manique itself you can admire the **facade ★★** of the Viúva Lamego store (see p 160), a real little gem that is a wonderful reward for the effort of your long excursion. You can catch a train straight downtown at the Intendente subway station, right nearby, thus winding up this lengthy tour.

Tour H: Santa Catarina and Cais Do Sodré

See map on p 109.

As with most parts of Lisbon, there are a number of itineraries to choose from when touring the Bairro Alto. The one below is a continuation of the tour of the Chiado and includes an enjoyable ride on the Elevador da Bica.

From Largo do Chiado, head south on bustling Rua do Alecrim. On the way downhill, make a brief literary stop at **Largo Barão de Quintela**, where novelist José Maria Eça de Queirós is immortalized by a **sculpture entitled** *Truth*. Farther downhill, you'll cross a small bridge with typical Lisbon trams running both across and under it, the perfect spot for some lovely snapshots. You'll notice many wrought-iron fences, just before the bridge, protecting nearby houses.

By continuing downhill toward Praça Duque da Terceira, you'll end up at **Cais do Sodré** (*Cais do Sodré metro stop, tram #15 from Praça da Figueira, tram #18 from Praça do Comércio, Cais do Sodré stop*), one of the nerve centres of the capital. In addition to a railway station (*Estaçao Cais do Sodré*) that offers frequent service to the seaside resorts of Setúbal and Cascais, there is a ferry terminal

where passengers can board boats heading across the Tagus to Cacilhas (see p 73). There are several bars and restaurants along the wharves, and you can have a drink or a good meal on one of their pleasant terraces.

Retrace your steps back to Rua da Ribeira Nova, then continue on to Rua da Moeda. The latter leads straight to the **Elevador da Bica**, which provides a fun ride up to Largo Calhariz. Once there, go to the **Biblioteca Camões** (*Tue to Sat 10am to 6pm; Largo do Calhariz no.17, entrance opposite the tram stop; tram #28 from Rua da Conceição or bus #100 from Praça da Figueira, Calhariz stop*), where a lovely **stairwell ★** with a ceiling made entirely of carved wood and walls adorned with *azulejos* is sure to send fans of this type of ornamentation into raptures.

Continue your tour on Rua Marechal Saldanha. The little lanes that intersect this street are among the most picturesque in town. Make sure to pause for a moment in front of the **Travessa da Laranjeira** and **Travessa da Portuguesa**, both genuine postcard material. Farther along, at the **Miradouro de Santa Catarina ★** (*tram #28*), which is closely watched by Adamastor, the sea monster so vividly described in Camões' *Lusiads*, you

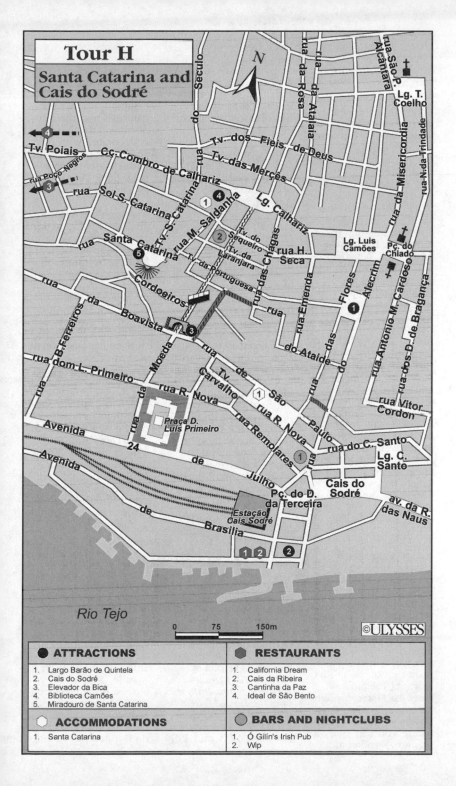

can wind up your tour with a pleasant view of the Tagus and Ponte 25 de Abril.

Tour I: Estrêla and Lapa

See map on p 111.

If you walk down **Rua São** Bento from Largo do Rato, heading towards the Palácio da Assembleia Nacional, you will pass by many **antique dealers** and **second-hand shops**. This street is known by residents as an excellent place to find all sorts of treasures from the past, and is thus sure to please anyone with an interest in antiques. The **Palácio da Assembleia Nacional** (*bus #6 or 49 from the Rato, São Bento stop; tram #28 from Rua da Conceição in the Baixa, Rua São Bento stop*), the former Mosteiro de São Bento, lies all the way at the bottom of the street, on the right side. Its monumental neoclassical facade, set back from the square onto which it faces, seems to dwarf its surroundings. The prime minister's residence is located behind the Palácio, on an adjoining property.

It is worth making a short detour along Rua Nova da Piedade to **Praça das Flores**, a pretty little tree-lined square. This is a charming area, where you can enjoy a pleasant stroll at any time of day. What's more, the square is surrounded by excellent restaurants, so you can please your palate here as well.

Retrace your steps and turn onto Calçada da Estrêla, located to the left of the Palácio da Assembleia Nacional.

Despite being a centre of political activity, Estrêla is known for its quiet atmosphere and green spaces. If you like beautiful gardens, make sure to visit the **Jardim da Estrêla ★** (*every day, 7am to midnight; tram #28 from Rua da Conceição in the Baixa, Estrêla stop; various buses from the Rato*). Not only is it one of the oldest parks in the city, but its pretty sculptures, pools, poplar-lined paths, plane-trees and cedars make it one of the most romantic as well. The crowning touch is a small bandstand decorated with lacy ironwork.

Opposite the garden, the baroque style **Basílica da Estrêla ★** (*8am to 12:30pm and 3pm to 7:30pm; tram #28 from the Baixa, Estrêla stop; various buses from the Rato*) was erected between 1779 and 1790 by Dona Maria I to give thanks for the birth of an heir to the throne. Unlike the rather elegant exterior, the interior has little charm and is decorated with pink and blue marble, which make it seem somewhat cold. Dona Maria I's tomb is located here.

Although the **Lapa ★** area has few attractions as such, it is fascinating to stroll about here and look at the numerous *hôtels particuliers*, known as *palacetes* (little palaces), many of which are surrounded by lovely gardens. Most of these buildings are now embassies, consulates or offices.

For an interesting walking tour, start at number 37 on Rua de São Domingos, a lovely old palace by the name of **Porto Covo**. Built in the 17th century, it is now the British Embassy. Farther along, at Rua do Pau da Bandeira 4, you'll find the former **Palácio dos Valenças** dating from 1870. Although it has been converted into a luxurious hotel (the Hotel da Lapa, see p 133) its owners wisely preserved its facade. On the second floor, furthermore, there is a banquet hall sumptuously decorated with gilding, stucco and imitation marble, which is bathed in light filtered through antique stained-glass windows. Now take Rua do Pau da Bandeira to Rua do

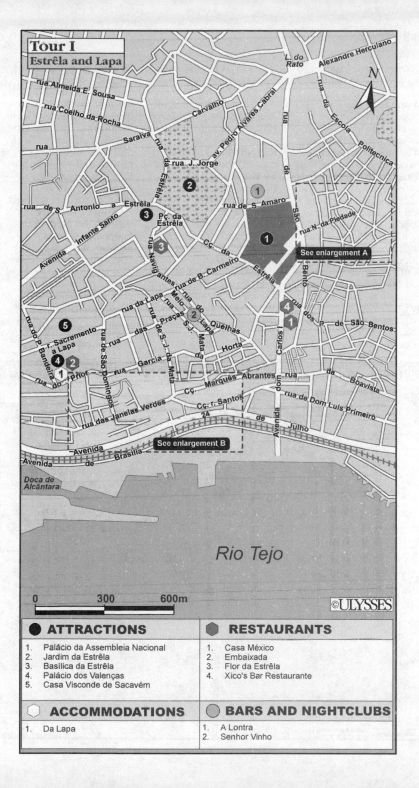

Sacremento a Lapa and turn right. At number 27, the elegant Fundação Luso-Americana boasts a pretty garden. Just opposite stands the **Casa Visconde de Sacavém ★**, worth a trip in itself. Its doors and windows are adorned with a unique mixture of *azulejos* and other ceramic decorations. To complete your whirlwind tour of the neighbourhood, walk along Rua Garcia da Orta and Rua S. João da Mata, then Rua das Janelas Verdas. You will end up near the wharves and the Museu Nacional de Arte · Antiga.

If you don't feel like walking, take tram #25 across the neighbourhood; from the Baixa, go to the terminus of tram #25, on Largo do Corpo Santo.

Partially housed in a palace once occupied by the Marquês de Pombal, the **Museu Nacional de Arte Antiga ★★** (*500 ESC; Tue 2pm to 6pm, Wed to Sun 10am to 6pm; Rua das Janelas Verdas no. 9, ☎213 67 60 01 or 213 96 41 51; bus #40 from Praça Figueira, Rua Presidente Arriaga stop; from Praça do Comércio, tram #15, Cais da Rocha stop*) boasts a rich collection (the largest of its kind in Portugal) of art and other articles dating from the 14th century all the way through the 19th. These include sculptures, tapestries, furniture, silver and gold objects, ceramics and most importantly, a large number of paintings from the great European schools. Highlights include a triptych entitled *The Temptation of Saint Anthony ★* by Hieronymus Bosch and, in the collection of gold and silver, a magnificent **monstrance from Nossa Dama de Belém ★**, a true Manueline masterpiece. Most of the pieces displayed in the

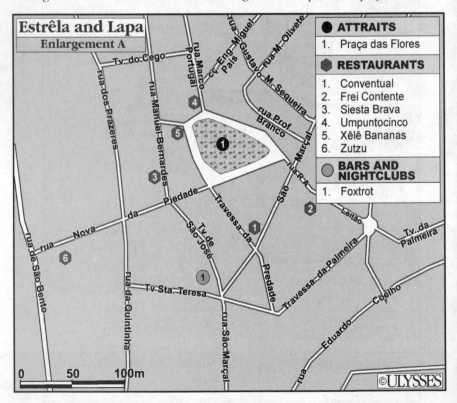

Estrêla and Lapa
Enlargement A

ATTRAITS
1. Praça das Flores

RESTAURANTS
1. Conventual
2. Frei Contente
3. Siesta Brava
4. Umpuntocinco
5. Xêlê Bananas
6. Zutzu

BARS AND NIGHTCLUBS
1. Foxtrot

0   50   100m

©ULYSSES

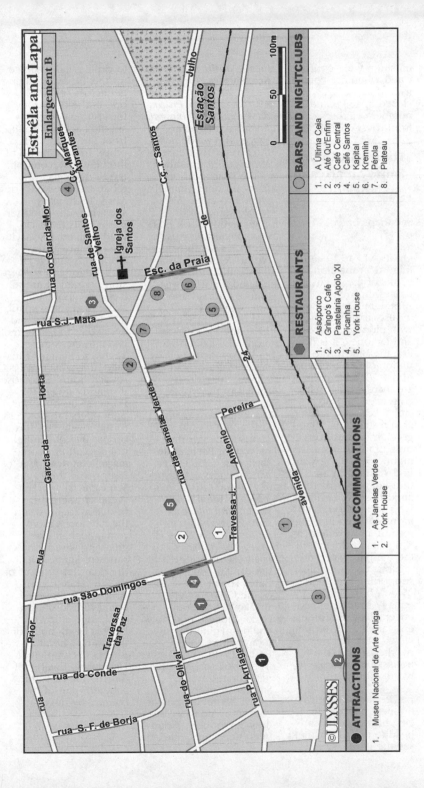

Estrêla and Lapa
Enlargement B

BARS AND NIGHTCLUBS

1. A Última Ceia
2. Até Qu'Enfim
3. Café Central
4. Café Santos
5. Kapital
6. Kremlin
7. Pérola
8. Plateau

RESTAURANTS

1. Assóporco
2. Gringo's Café
3. Pastelaria Apolo XI
4. Picanha
5. York House

ACCOMMODATIONS

1. As Janelas Verdes
2. York House

ATTRACTIONS

1. Museu Nacional de Arte Antiga

© ULYSSES

0   50   100m

Cc. Marques Abrantes
rua de Santos-o-Velho
rua do Guarda-Mor
Igreja dos Santos
Esc. da Praia
rua S.J. Mata
Horta
Garcia-da
rua
rua das Janelas Verdes
Pereira
Antonio
Travessa-J.
avenida
Prior
rua do Conde
rua S. F. de Borja
Traverssa da Paz
rua São Domingos
rua do Olival
rua P. Arriaga
24
de
Cç. r. Santos
Julho
Estação Santos

museum were confiscated when the country's monasteries were closed in 1834, and a number of others came from royal collections.

Tour J: Alcântara, Santo Amaro and Belém

See maps on p 115 and p 117.

On its way to Belém, tram #15 runs along the banks of the Tagus and passes through Alcântara. Once an industrial area crowded with old warehouses and factories, it is now, like the Bairro Alto, undergoing a metamorphosis. Local buildings are increasingly being converted into nightclubs, bars and fashionable restaurants. If you go club- or bar-hopping in Alcântara at night (see p 156), you'll find yourself in an unusual atmosphere amidst trendy Lisboans, who stroll through this industrial area looking for fun and excitement. A daytime ride aboard the tram, between the gigantic concrete pillars supporting the Ponte 25 de Abril, is an equally strange experience, albeit of a different variety. The striking view of the bridge overhead, with the houses below it, is worth a brief stop.

Before moving on to the next part of the city, history buffs can head to the Alcântara to see the impressive facade of the **Palácio das Necessidades** (*Largo das Necessidades; bus #27 or 49 from the Rato, Praça da Armada stop; bus #40 from Praça Figueira, Praça da Armada stop*), the former residence of almost every member of the Bragança dynasty up until Manuel II went into exile. A whole series of dramatic events took place here, including Pedro V's death from typhus, Queen Maria II's death at the age of 27, and the assassination of Carlos I and his son. When Manuel II fled the country in 1910, the Portuguese monarchy came to an end. Now occupied by the Ministry of Foreign Affairs, the palace is closed to the public.

If a king were visiting Lisbon, he would surely choose to enter the city by way of **Ponte 25 de Abril** ★★ (*250 ESC per car; from Praça Marquês de Pombal, take Avenida Joaquim António de Aguiar and follow the signs for Alcântara or Setúbal, or take bus #53 and get off at the tollbooth*). This bridge is to the capital what the Eiffel Tower is to Paris or the Golden Gate Bridge to San Francisco. Indeed, no one could imagine the city today without the Ponte 25 de Abril. Built from 1962 to 1966 and inaugurated under Salazar (it used to be called Ponte Salazar), it was an immediate success. Previously, it had been necessary either to drive a fair distance up the Tagus in order get across or to take one of the numerous ferries that constantly shuttle back and forth from one shore to the other. In celebration of the Flower Revolution, the bridge was rebaptized Ponte 25 de Abril. Technically speaking, it is a masterpiece of its time. Up until January 1995, with the opening of the Normandy Bridge, it was the longest suspension bridge in Europe. It is 70m above the water, its central span measures 1,013m, and every day 140,000 cars use it to cross the Tagus, sometimes causing traffic jams that last several hours. For those visiting Portugal, the Ponte 25 de Abril not only offers rapid access to the lovely beaches on the Bay of Setúbal, but also affords some **magnificent views** ★★ of Lisbon and the Tagus. We especially recommend crossing the bridge at night, when the city looks more romantic than ever, glittering with thousands of lights. With the financial support of the EEC, major construction is presently being carried out on the bridge; a lower level is being built for the train. When this project is completed, Lisbon will finally be directly linked to the southern part of the country by rail.

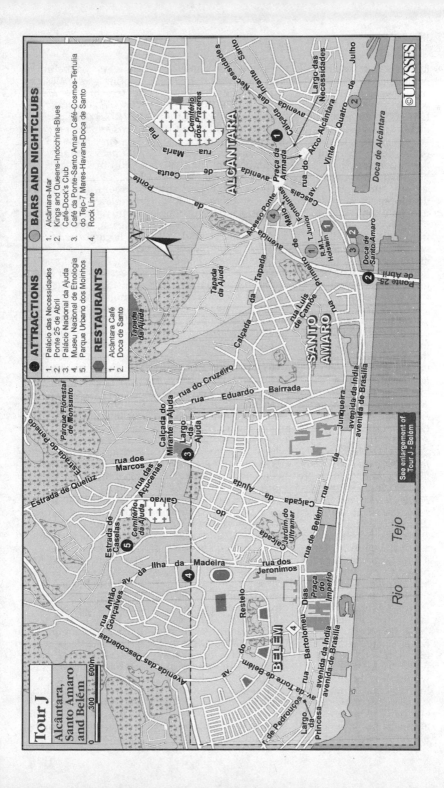

Tour J

Alcântara, Santo Amaro and Belém

0 300 600m

● ATTRACTIONS

1. Palácio das Necessidades
2. Ponte 25 de Abril
3. Palácio Nacional da Ajuda
4. Museu Nacional de Etnologia
5. Parque Urbano dos Moinhos

● RESTAURANTS

1. Alcântara Café
2. Doca de Santo

● BARS AND NIGHTCLUBS

1. Alcântara-Mar
   Kings and Queens-Indochina-Blues
2. Café-Dock's Club
3. Café da Ponte-Santo Amaro Café-Cosmos-Tertulia
   do Tejo-7 Mares-Havana-Doca de Santo
4. Rock Line

© ULYSSES

See enlargement of
Tour J - Belém

Belém ★★★, whose name is a contraction of the word Bethlehem, was once a suburb of Lisbon. As far as monuments and museums are concerned, it is one of the richest parts of the city. It was from here that the caravels set out, and the area's development was financed mainly by the riches brought back from the Indies. Flush with money, the nobility built opulent palaces here, most of which miraculously survived the earthquake of 1755.

Those with a taste for opulent decors should make a detour through the Ajuda area to visit the **Museu do Palácio Nacional da Ajuda ★** (*500 ESC; Thu to Tue 10am to 5pm, closed during official receptions; Calçada da Ajuda, ☎213 63 70 95 or 213 62 02 64; tram #18 from Praça da Comércio, Calçada da Ajuda stop; bus #60 from Praça da Figueira, Largo da Ajuda stop*), the royal residence from 1862 to 1910. The present palace was begun in 1802; it was originally supposed to be twice as big, but remained unfinished for financial reasons. When Dom Luís moved in here in 1862, he probably never suspected that his spendthrift Italian wife, Dona Maria Pia, would turn the place into a veritable museum of decorative arts. She had little interest in antiques, but adored modern design, and

furnished the palace with pieces by Europe's finest artisans. The rooms thus feature a diverse sampling of the continent's 19th century decorative output. Make sure to visit the winter garden, a gift from the viceroy of Egypt, which is perhaps the most remarkable and most modern room of all. The massive-looking neoclassical exterior of the palace is of little interest. Since the palace is often closed for official receptions for foreign heads of state, be sure to check whether it is open to the public before visiting it.

Before visiting the Mosteiro dos Jerónimos, make a short detour down **Rua Viera-Portuense** to see a pretty row of old working-class houses, which once lined the docks, and which have been fixed up and transformed into cafés, restaurants and shops. Along the way, take a look at those between numbers 52 and 40, whose projecting second floors are supported by small columns, forming a covered passageway. Next, cross Rua de Belém and go to the back of the restaurant Pão Pão Queijo Queijo, where you'll see the *pelourinho de Belém* (the pillory of Belém), curiously tucked away on a tiny street.

If there is one place that you simply must

see while you're in Lisbon, it's the **Mosteiro dos Jerónimos ★★★** (*Praça do Império, ☎213 62 00 34; tram #15 or bus #43 from Praça da Fiegueira, Mosteiro Jerónimos stop*). It was begun by Boytac in 1502, by order of Dom Manuel I, and was not completed for nearly a century. Thanks to the riches accumulated by the Portuguese after the discovery of a route to India, Manuel I and his successors were able to invest huge sums of money in the project, hiring the best artisans and architects of their time. These included João de Castilho (the Spanish architect of the Monastery of Christ in Tomar) and French sculptor Nicolas Chantereine, who, according to some historians, first introduced the Renaissance style into Portugal. The Mosteiro dos Jerónimos, made up of the monastery itself, its adjoining cloister and the Igreja Santa Maria, is a true architectural masterpiece featuring a nearly perfect fusion of Manueline art and Renaissance style. It has been listed as a UNESCO World Cultural Heritage Site.

Before entering the **Igreja Santa Maria ★★★** (*free admission; Tue to Sun 10am to 5pm*), take a good look at its two portals. The enchanting **south portal ★★**, adorned with statuettes and carved with maritime motifs, is a work

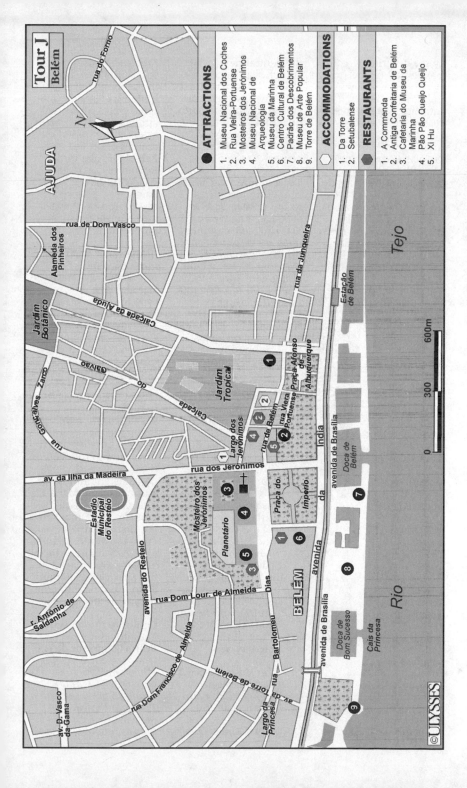

Tour J
Belém

ATTRACTIONS

1. Museu Nacional dos Coches
2. Rua Vieira-Portuense
3. Mosteiros dos Jerónimos
4. Museu Nacional de Arqueologia
5. Museu da Marinha
6. Centro Cultural de Belém
7. Padrão dos Descobrimentos
8. Museu de Arte Popular
9. Torre de Belém

ACCOMMODATIONS

1. Da Torre
2. Setubalense

RESTAURANTS

1. A Commenda
2. Antiga Confeitaria de Belém
3. Cafetaria do Museu da Marinha
4. Pão Pão Queijo Queijo
5. Xi Hu

© ULYSSES

of great intricacy, complemented by the richly decorated windows on either side. The equally intricate **west portal ★★** features two lovely statues of King Manuel and Queen Maria (by Nicolas Chantereine), as well as numerous religious scenes. Inside, the lofty vault is adorned with a complex network of ribs and supported by finely worked columns (by João de Castilho). Its construction was a true feat of engineering; considering how wide it is, it is amazing that it survived the earthquake. In the choir and the transepts, you'll find a number of tombs supported by elephants and containing the remains of several kings. On either side of the entrance, under the *coro-alto*, are the beautifully carved tombs of the celebrated poet Camões and of explorer Vasco da Gama. From the *coro-alto*, which can only be reached through the cloister, you can admire the lovely series of ribs covering the vaults of

the central nave. The church was once topped by a pyramidal bell tower, which collapsed during the earthquake of 1755; the dome you see now dates from the 19th century.

To continue your tour of the premises, head to the **cloister ★★★** (*400 ESC; Tue to Sun 10am to 5pm; entrance adjacent to the west entrance of the church,* ☎*213 62 00 34*), which, along with Batalha's, is one of the most beautiful in the country. Upon entering the building, you'll feel as if you've just stepped into a magical place. There are two levels of deep, richly carved bays adorned with just as finely worked columns. The Gothic-style first floor was designed by Boytac, the less elaborate upper floor by João de Castilho. It is particularly interesting to visit the cloister in the late afternoon, when the soft natural light gives the stone an ochre hue. Make sure to take a look at the *azulejos* and beautifully decorated vault of the **refectory ★**.

The **Museu Nacional de Arqueologia** (*350 ESC, free Sun 10am to 2pm; Tue 2pm to 6pm, Wed to Sun 10am to 6pm;*

Praça do Império, ☎*213 62 00 00*), housed in the long 19th-century building adjacent to the Igreja Santa Maria, will appeal to visitors interested in the period extending from the Paleolithic age to the Roman era. A large collection of objects (statuettes, pottery, etc.) discovered on Portuguese territory is displayed here.

In the same building, in the west wing of the monastery, the **Museu de Marinha ★★★** (*400 ESC; winter, Tue to Sun 10am to 5pm, summer open until 6pm; Praça do Império,* ☎*213 62 00 19*) is one of the most comprehensive maritime museums in the world. Model boats, navigational instruments and sea-charts are exhibited in an interesting and original manner. Don't miss the room devoted to royal barges, which contains an impressive barge used by Maria I. The same room also contains the Santa Cruz, the first airplane to cross the South Atlantic (1922). A replica of the airplane was placed in the park opposite the Torre de Belém to commemorate this event.

Opposite the Museu de Marinha, the new **Centro Cultural de Belém** (*Praça do Império, information in Portuguese only,* ☎*213 61 24 00; tram #15 or bus #43 from Praça da Figueira, Mosteiro dos Jerónimos stop*) is remarkable both for its size and its futuristic lines. This cubic colossus, built in 1993 by architects Vittorio Gregotti and Manuel Salgedo, clashes a bit with its immediate surroundings. It contains a number of theatres and exhibition spaces, as well as several shops and restaurants. It is a challenge not to get lost in this place, which is a veritable labyrinth.

On the pier opposite the monastery's museum stands a huge, stately monument, the **Padrão dos Descobrimentos ★★** (*Avenida de Brasília*), erected in 1960 on the occasion of the 500th anniversary of the death of Henry the Navigator. It shows Henry with a little caravel in his hand, standing in front of a number of famous Portuguese figures (explorers, kings, cartographers, writers, etc.) who participated either directly or indirectly in the country's great discoveries. You can take a short elevator ride (*Tue to Sun 9:30am to 6:30pm*) to the top of the monument to enjoy a **lovely view** of the Mosteiro dos Jerónimos and better appreciate the interesting **mosaic** (*at the foot of the monument*) depicting a map of the world in two hemispheres, which shows the major steps in Portugal's age of discovery and the names of the men who led the voyages.

Farther along the pier, right before the Torre de Belém, lies the **Museu de Arte Popular** (*400 ESC; Tue to Sun 10am to noon and 2pm to 5pm; Avenida de Brasília, ☎213 01 12 82*), which displays clothing, furniture, pottery and other articles from different parts of the country, all related to Portuguese folklore.

Listed as a UNESCO World Heritage Site, the **Torre de Belém ★★★** (*400 ESC; Tue to Sun 10am to 5pm; Praça do Império, ☎213 62 00 34; tram #15 or bus #43 from Praça da Figueira, Largo da Princesa stop*) is definitely one of the capital's landmarks. This handsome Manueline tower was built between 1515 and 1521 by order of Manuel I to defend the mouth of the Tagus. It was originally located in the middle of the river, but the tidal wave that followed the earthquake of 1755 shifted large amounts of sand, thus altering the course of the water.

Architecturally speaking, it is a marvellous blend of styles, combining the Moorish (architect Francisco Arruda's little domes on the turrets) with the Romanesque (the geminated windows) and the Italian Renaissance style (the second-story windows with little balconies, which are adorned with Christian crosses). To top off all this ornamentation, which is quite elaborate for an old prison (convicts were kept here until 1828), the entire tower is adorned with the rope motifs so characteristic of the Manueline style, as well as coats of arms of the Order of Christ. Particularly noteworthy inside is a lovely carved niche sheltering the Virgin with Christ in her arms, which is topped by an armillary sphere (see p 82). It is patterned with bunches of grapes, an unusual touch that gives it an exotic look.

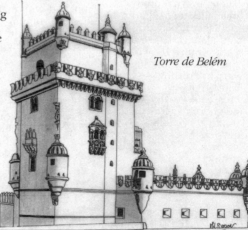

Torre de Belém

Continuing your tour farther north, in the Restelo neighbourhood, where new apartment buildings seem to pop up every day, you'll reach the **Museu Nacional de Etnologia** (*price of admission varies depending on the exhibition; Tue 2pm to 6pm, Wed to Sun 10am to 6pm; Avenida da Ilha da Madeira, ☎213 01 52 64; bus #32 from the Rossio, Avenida da Ilha da Madeira stop*), which presents temporary exhibitions. To find out what's on while you're in Lisbon, check the *Agenda Cultural* (see p 157).

Finally, if you like the great outdoors, head to the new **Parque Urbano dos Moinhos** (*winter 9am to 5:30pm, summer to 8pm; Estrada de Caselas, tram #18 from Praça do Comércio, Cemitério da Ajuda stop*), a lovely hilltop garden with some **beautiful views** ★ of the Tagus and even, in clear weather, of the sea off in the distance. There are two pretty **windmills**, a small artificial lake, a playground and a snack bar in the park. Tram #18, which runs to the park, has a very interesting route that crosses several neighbourhoods, each with its own distinct social make-up.

Tour K: Parque das Nações

See map on p 121.

At Portugal's suggestion, the General Assembly of the United Nations officially declared 1998 the "International Year of the Oceans". On the same occasion, Lisbon was chosen to host the last world's fair of the 20th century. An organizing committee thus selected a 60ha site, once occupied by a refinery around the Cais dos Olivais. In addition to the construction of a train station and a metro station, eight pavilions and a 10ha stretch of water with a waterside stage were planned for the event. And to top it all off, the imposing 100m-high Torre Vasco da Gama observation tower, at the top of which is a restaurant, was also built. On May 22, 1998, after more than a year's work, EXPO 98 was launched with many different cultural events and activities; the fair lasted until September 30, 1998.

After the euphoria of this great event, which welcomed up to 12 million visitors, the city now faces new challenges. In order to revitalize the EXPO 98 site, the city is planning an extensive urban-devel-opment project on nearly 330ha, which will include residential buildings and stores, by 2010. Several commercial spaces have already seen the light of day on the site of the defunct Expo park, and work is currently under way to transform the grounds into a vast recreational space, henceforth known as **Parque das Nações** (Park of Nations). The project was in full swing during our visit and a brochure already boasted 10 million visitors. This success is owed in part to the "**Festival dos Oceanos 99**", an event featuring scores of exhibits, concerts and night-time shows, some of which took place in the park itself. Another such festival will be held in 2000. Among other things, the establishment of a huge shopping complex on site has certainly had a lot to do with the success of the project.

A **40-car cableway** (*500 ESC; Mon to Fri 11am to 9:30pm, Sat and Sun 10am to 9:30pm*), which runs 20m above the ground, was built along the docks, giving visitors a unique perspective of Parque das Nações. A delightful experience for children of all ages, it also offers wonderful aerial views of the Tagus and its banks.

Below is a brief description of the park's main public attractions.

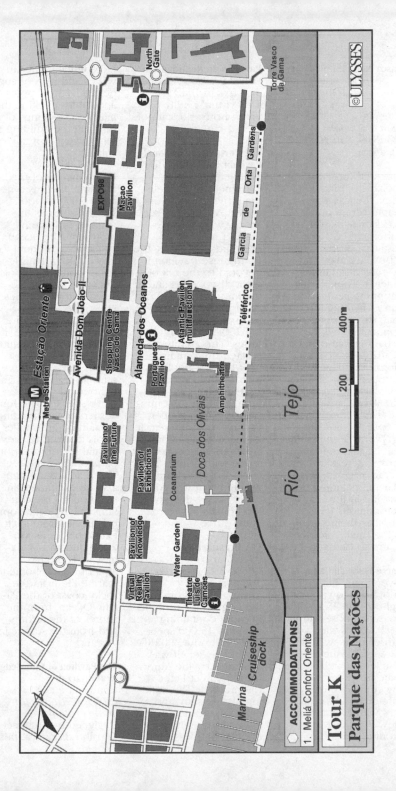

Tour K
Parque das Nações

Vasco da Gama
Stores and restaurants:
Mon to Sat 10am to mid-night
Cinema:
Mon to Sat noon to 12:45am, Sun 10am to 12:45am

First and foremost a mega-shopping complex, the Vasco da Gama centre houses 162 stores, as well as a supermarket, some 30 restaurants, many bars, a bowling alley and a 10-screen multiplex cinema. Though this shopping centre doesn't carry anything too original, shoppers will, of course, find all the usual big-name brands available in major North American and European cities.

The Macau Pavilion
(*400 ESC; Tue to Fri noon to 6pm, Sat and Sun 3pm to 8pm*) is a multimedia exhibit that introduces those interested in Asia to the many facets of Macau, including every-day life in the semi-autonomous territory. Another theme featured is the small colony's return to China in 1999.

Torre Vasco da Gama
Over 100m tall, this enormous tower built right by the Tagus River boasts an observation deck from which you can enjoy a sweeping view of Parque das Nações, as well as the majestic Tagus. The tower also houses a cafeteria and a restaurant with panoramic view 80m above ground level.

Pavilhão da Realidade Virtual (*1,200 ESC; Tue to Sun 1pm to 7pm*)
This virtual-reality pavilion houses a state-of-the-art cinema.

The Portuguese National Pavilion (Pavilhão de Portugal)
Designed by the celebrated Portuguese architect Alvaro de Siza Vieira, who has executed a number of prestigious projects, the Portuguese pavilion is devoted to the era of great discoveries and to the important role Portugal played in European expansion during the 15th and 16th centuries. The architect erected the building near the big pool, so that it would be reflected in the water, thus evoking the omnipresent link between Portugal and the sea. It includes a Ceremonial Square, a vast covered space with a huge concrete roof that is unusual in that it is concave. Today the pavilion houses a government office.

The Oceanarium
(Oceanário)
(*1,500 ESC; every day 10am to 7pm*)
This pavilion houses the largest aquarium in Europe, containing as many as 15,000 specimens of about 300 different species. It was designed by the American architect Peter Chermayeff. The building also has an adjoining space for temporary exhibitions. With its undulating glass sur-

faces imitating ocean waves and its roof supported by steel poles and cables evoking the masts and riggings of a sailboat, the building is reminiscent of a tall ship.

In the middle of the building, there is a huge 5,000m^3 pool, which serves as the main aquarium and represents the ocean. Its capacity is equal to that of four Olympic-sized swimming pools. This pool can be observed on two stories; you can walk all around it and admire the teeming marine life within through its thick, transparent walls – sharks, rays, tuna, schools of sardines and a thousand and one other species. The four corners of the building contain other, smaller pools devoted to the animal life from various parts of the world. These aquariums can also be examined on two floors. One contains magnificent tropical species from such exotic places as Mozambique and Madagascar. The other aquariums are home to marine life from the rocky coast of the Pacific Ocean, from the shores of the Azores and from the Antarctic Ocean.

The Pavilion of Knowledge
(Pavilhão do Conhecimento)
(*800 ESC; Tue to Sun 10am to 5pm*)
Designed by architect Carrilho da Graça, this

pavilion has a central section that looks like the deck of a ship. Now the property of the Department of Science and Technology, the former Knowledge of the Seas Pavilion hosts temporary exhibitions, both Portuguese and foreign, with the world's scientific and technological advances as their theme.

The Water Gardens
(Jardins da Água)
As indicated by their name, these purely ornamental gardens are dedicated to water. All sorts of fountains can be admired here.

The Garcia de Orta Gardens
Laid out in front of the former pavilions in the Northern International Zone, the Garcia de Orta Gardens feature luxuriant vegetation and beautiful landscaping. The purpose of these gardens is to display the wide variety of plants brought back over the centuries by Portuguese navigators, species that are now found all over Europe.

The Nautical Exhibition
The Nautical Exhibition not only has room for up to 600 boats, but is also a pleasant spot where all sorts of bars and restaurants with outdoor seating beckon visitors to kick back and relax.

The **Museu Nacional dos Coches** ★★ (*450 ESC; every day except Tuesday 10am to 5:30pm; Parque das Nações, Oriente metro stop,* ☎*218 95 59 94*) is devoted chiefly to royal coaches. As the Portuguese royalty had accumulated quite a few state-coaches, Queen Amelia decided to put them all in the former riding school of the Palácio de Belém and open a museum in 1905. The museum boasted one of the richest and most complete collections of its kind in the world. Because the original building is currently being restored, only part of its prestigious collection is on display. Among the pieces to be admired are coaches dating from the 17th to the 19th century. Some are so lavishly decorated that it is hard to believe that they were used for transportation.

Accommodations

Camping

Campismo de Lisboa
Monsanto, Câmara Municipal de Lisboa, Estrada da Circunvalação, 1500-171 Lisboa
☎*217 62 31 00*
☎*217 60 96 20*
⇄*217 62 31 05*
⇄*217 60 96 33*

Tour A: The Rossio and the Baixa

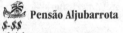 **Pensão Aljubarrota**
$-$$
sb/pb
Rua da Assunção no. 53
4th floor, 1100 Lisboa
☎/⇄*213 46 01 12*
On the 4th floor of a building, the small Pensão Aljubarrota is a most charming place, more like a bed & breakfast than a simple boarding house; the boss, of Italian origin, spares no effort to put you at ease. The friendliness and courtesy here recall the warmth of the Mediterranean. Though comfort proves limited (badly soundproofed rooms, four floors to climb and no elevator), the charm of the place quickly compensates for the few inconveniences. Lovely antique reproductions grace the little rooms, most of which have balconies. Breakfast is taken in this cordial and relaxed atmo-

Lisbon

sphere, surrounded by pretty decorative items and with a view out over the balcony (with large open windows, weather permitting). Ah! sweet Italy, but... are we truly in Lisbon? What is more, a "special" price can be negotiated for extended stays. The entrance, which is hard to find, is between the Rua Augusta and Correiros, between the two show windows of the big *sapatos lisbonense* store (shoe store). Those who like the B&B formula should definitely consider this place!

Hotel Americano
$$
pb
Rua 1° Dezembro no. 73
1200 Lisboa
☎*213 47 49 76*
⇒*213 47 49 79*
An uninviting lobby and prices a bit too high for the quality of the surroundings, but a convenient location in the heart of the neighbourhood. Relatively comfortable, decent-looking rooms.

Pensão-Residencial Gerês
$$
sb/pb, tv
Calçada do Garcia no. 6, 1st and 2nd floors, 1100 Lisboa
☎*218 81 04 97*
⇒*218 88 20 06*
Slightly set back from the Rossio on a quiet little street, the Pensão-Residencial Gerês has 24 modestly furnished rooms. The pleasant family atmosphere combined with the cleanliness of the estab-

lishment makes it a good choice.

Residencial-Albergaria Insulana
$$
pb, tv
Rua da Assunção no. 52
1100 Lisboa
☎*213 42 76 25*
Not only does this comfortable 32-room hotel have the advantage of being centrally located, it is also situated on a quiet street.

Hotel Internacional
$$
pb, tv
Rua da Betesga no. 3, 2nd floor
1100 Lisboa
☎*213 46 64 01*
⇒*213 47 86 35*
The Hotel Internacional has old-fashioned furnishings but a prime location. In an old building at the corner of Rua Augusta, a pedestrian street, it lies a short distance from the local shopping streets and major tourist attractions. Ask for one of the rooms facing the back, which are a bit dark, but sheltered from the noise of the square. Good value for your money.

Hotel Metrópole
$$$$
pb, tv
Praça Dom Pedro IV, Rossio
1100 Lisboa
☎*213 46 91 64*
☎*213 46 91 65*
⇒*213 46 91 66*
Hotel Metrópole belongs to the Almeida chain of beautiful hotels. An old establishment restored in 1993, it has character. The limited number of

rooms (36), all of which are tastefully decorated, makes for a warm, personal atmosphere. Get a room overlooking the Rossio for a pleasant view. Though the latter have small balconies, these are unfortunately of limited enjoyment due to the noise pollution caused by the heavy, never-ending traffic around the square. Other minor drawbacks include its lobby, located on the second floor and therefore inconvenient for those loaded down with luggage, and its hard-to-locate entrance, hidden between a series of unattractive terraces.

Tour B: The Castelo and the Alfama

Pensão Ninho das Águias
$$ no bkfst
sb/pb
Costa do Castelo no. 74
1100 Lisboa
☎*218 86 70 08*
Connected to the walls of the Castelo, the Pensão Ninho das Águias is most noteworthy for its romantic setting and lovely, verdant terrace, which offers a view of Lisbon (only a few rooms have a view of the city). This place is somewhat inconvenient, due to its distance from the downtown area and the steep spiral staircase leading to the reception area. Very average level of comfort and inhospitable service. Expensive but enchanting.

Ulysses's Favourites

For business travellers:
Hotel Orion (p 130), Suite Hotel Dom Rodrigo (p 128).

For luxury:
Hotel da Lapa (p 133), the Ritz (p 128), Hotel York House (p 132), As Janelas Verdes (p 132), Lisboa Plaza (p 131), Hotel Avenida Palace (p 131).

For a warm welcome:
Pensão Aljubarrota (p 123), Pensão Londres (p 126), Pensão-Residencial Gerês (p 124), Residencial Dom Sancho I (p 129).

For the best value:
Pensão Aljubarrota (p 123), Pensão Nossa Senhora do Rosario (p 129)

For the best nightlife:
Casa de São Mamede (p 126).

For the best views:
Pensão Ninho das Águias (p 124), Albergaria Senhora do Monte (p 126), Hotel da Lapa (p 133).

For romantic atmosphere:
Hotel York House (p 132).

For the best swimming pools:
Hotel Orion (p 130), Hotel da Lapa (p 13:

For the most beautiful gardens:
Hotel da Lapa (p 133).

For *azulejo* admirers:
Casa de São Mamede (p 126).

Lisbon

Tour C: Graça and East Lisbon

Albergaria Senhora do Monte
$$$ with terrace
pb, tv
Calçada do Monte no. 39
1100 Lisboa
☎218 86 60 02
≈218 87 77 83
Despite its somewhat depressing exterior and impersonal entrance hall, the Albergaria Senhora do Monte has 24 pleasant, modern rooms. If you can fit it into your budget, ask for a room with a terrace so you can savour the pleasure of sitting outside at night when the Castelo is illuminated and the city is all aglitter, offering a real feast for the eyes. This magnificent panorama can also be enjoyed from the outdoor bar (*every day 4pm to 1am*) on the top floor. The only drawback is that the place is far from downtown, so guests have to get about by car, taxi or public transportation (*tram #28, about a 10min walk away*).

Tour D: The Chiado and the Bairro Alto

Pensão Globo
$ no bkfst
Rua do Teixeira no. 37
1200 Lisboa
☎213 46 22 79
With its lovely little recently repainted facade, this modest guesthouse is perfect for those with limited budgets. Very basic level of comfort (shared shower facilities), but located on one of the few quiet streets in the area. Well-kept rooms and very hospitable service.

Pensão Londres
$-$$
sb/pb
Rua Dom Pedro V no. 53
2nd floor, 1200 Lisboa
☎213 46 22 03
☎213 46 55 23
≈213 46 56 82
Set up in a former residence, this guesthouse offers very simply furnished but well-kept rooms with private or shared baths. Pleasant decor. Considering its favourable location, in the very heart of Bairro Alto, this place offers good value for your money.

Residencial Casa de São Mamede
$$$
pb, tv
Rua da Escola Politécnica no. 159, 1200 Lisboa
☎213 96 31 66
☎213 96 27 57
≈213 95 18 96
The friendly, attentive staff at the charming Residencial Casa de São Mamede make this a very pleasant place to stay. Breakfast is served in a lovely room decorated with *azulejos*. The furnishings are a bit outdated, but nothing is lacking. There is only one minor drawback: you must reserve a long time in advance, due to the limited number of rooms. Furthermore, it is imperative that you request a room at the back, since the place faces onto a very noisy street.

Hotel Borges
$$
pb
Rua Garrett no. 108
1200 Lisboa
☎213 46 19 51
≈213 42 66 17
Facing onto a pedestrian street, the Hotel Borges offers quiet rooms. The furnishings and the facilities in general are beginning to look a bit dated, however. Central location.

Príncipe Real
$$$
pb, tv, ℜ
Rua da Alegria no. 53
1200 Lisboa
☎213 46 01 16
≈213 42 21 04
A good choice for visitors seeking a homey atmosphere and some peace and quiet. Its pretty, inviting little rooms are each decorated in a different way. The top-floor dining room offers a lovely view. The warm welcome and quality service make this a good place to keep in mind.

Tour E: The Rato and Amoreiras

Amazónia Hotéis
$$$
pb, ℝ, ≈, tv
Travessa Fábrica dos Pentes nos. 12-20, 1200 Lisboa
☎213 87 70 06
☎213 87 83 21
≈213 87 90 90
Despite its impersonal looking exterior, this large hotel will be

particularly appreciated by those seeking peace and quiet. Outside the town centre, in a relatively quiet neighbourhood, the establishment offers comfortable, modern rooms. The decor of the rooms and common areas is pleasing though nondescript. Assets include small balconies gracing certain rooms as well as an outdoor swimming pool.

Tour F: Marquês De Pombal, Saldanha and North Lisbon

Pousada de Juventude
Rua Andrade Corvo no. 46
1050 Lisboa
☎*213 53 26 96*
≈*213 53 75 41*
Picoas metro stop of bus #91 to the Picoas stop
Unfortunately, Lisbon's youth hostel is not very clean and the rooms are not very attractive either. Furthermore, the constant noise of travellers walking in and out makes sleeping difficult in the dormitory. Besides the high prices for baggage check, the reception is cold. The only good thing is that it doesn't cost much to stay here.

Residencial Vila Nova
$ no bkfst
pb/sb, tv
Avenida Duque de Loulé
no. 111, 3rd floor, 1050 Lisboa
☎*213 53 48 60*
☎*213 54 08 38*
For inexpensive accommodation, head to the Residencial Vila Nova, situated right above the

offices of the Portuguese Communist Party. This simple *residencial* is in no way connected to the party, however, except for being on neighbourly terms. The few rooms are rather badly soundproofed but always clean. Those at the rear of the building are relatively quiet. Rudimentary but economical.

Residencial Avenida Park
$$
pb, tv
Avenida Sidónio Pais no. 6
1050-214 Lisboa
☎*213 53 21 81*
≈*213 53 21 85*
Of the many hotels on this street, the Residencial Avenida Park proves to be the best bet. In a quiet setting, opposite the park, this *residencial* offers large, simply equipped rooms. Though the reception, the breakfast room and a few guestrooms have been completely renovated, several rooms still have old-fashioned, shabby furnishings. These few annoyances are soon forgiven, however, given the affordable prices for such a place. While here, be sure to check out the beautiful facade of the Order of Engineers' manor house, set back from the avenue and concealed behind a strange metal structure.

Residencial Avenida Alameda
$$$
pb, tv
Avenida Sidónio Pais no. 4
1000 Lisboa
☎*213 53 21 86*
≈*213 52 67 03*
Member of the Arcantis chain, the Residencial Avenida Alameda has square-shaped rooms that are painted white with a simple decor. The property is right next to the metro and the park.

Hotel Miraparque
$$$
pb, tv, ℜ, ℝ
Avenida Sidónio Pais no. 12
1050 Lisboa
☎*213 52 42 86*
≈*213 57 89 20*
This rather conventional-looking hotel has about 100 rooms, with a decor that is austere and devoid of any particular style. The choicest rooms are those located on the fourth and fifth floors in the front of the building, overlooking Parque Eduardo VII and the elegant Pavilhão dos Desportos.

Hotel Dom Manuel I
$$$
pb, tv
Avenida Duque de Avila no. 189
1050 Lisboa
☎*213 57 61 60*
≈*213 57 69 85*
Though a little far from downtown, near the Gulbenkian Foundation, the Hotel Dom Manuel I offers good service in a pleasant and quiet environment. The decor of the rooms and common areas is

Lisbon

polished and tasteful. Good value.

Hotel Fénix
$$$
pb, tv, ℜ
Praça Marquês de Pombal no. 8
1200 Lisboa
☎*213 86 21 21*
⇌*213 86 01 31*
Despite its unappealing exterior, Hotel Fénix has attractively renovated rooms. The windows in the rooms facing the street are double-glazed so that guests can enjoy an interesting view of bustling Praça Marquês de Pombal without having to put up with the noise. Good service but on the expensive side.

Suite Hotel Dom Rodrigo
$$$$
pb, K, ℜ*, tv,* ≈
Rua Rodrigo da Fonseca nos. 44-50, 1200 Lisboa
☎*213 86 38 00*
⇌*213 86 30 00*
An integral part of the Hotéis Tivoli, the Suite Hotel Dom Rodrigo is, along with the Orion (see p 130), one of the few hotels in the capital to offer the apartment-hotel option. The Portuguese chain offers three kinds of accommodation here, that is nine studios, 39 suites (with separate bedrooms) and nine penthouses, all equipped with modern, tasteful furniture. The suites and studios located on the seventh floor and in the front of the building each have a little terrace that is pleasant, yet it offers no particular view. For those who so desire, room service

is provided every day at no extra charge. A further advantage is the swimming pool that, though small, is quite delightful.

The Méridien
$$$$$ no bkfst
pb, ℜ*,* ℝ*,* ⌂*, tv*
Rua Castilho no. 149
1070 Lisboa
☎*213 83 09 00*
☎*213 83 04 00*
⇌*213 83 32 31*
With its futuristic lines, The Méridien ranks as one of the most modern hotels in Lisbon in terms of exterior architecture. The renowned chain's Lisbon link offers comfortable, cubic rooms, with standard, rather unoriginal decor. Though the rooms have no balconies, some offer a pleasant view of Parque Eduardo VII. On the whole, the design of the common areas, with the exception of the lobby furnishings, is not always in the best of taste. In fact it is quite tacky, especially in the restaurant, La Brasserie des Amis. Moreover, the lack of facilities (no exercise room or swimming pool) is regrettable. To its credit, the hotel boasts non-smoking floors and a fine location, opposite Parque Eduardo VII.

Four Seasons Hotel The Ritz
$$$$$
pb, ℜ*,* ℝ*,* ⊘*, tv*
Rua Rodrigo da Fonseca no. 88
1093 Lisboa
☎*213 81 14 00*
⇌*213 83 17 83*
www.fourseasons.com
True to its international reputation, the Four Seasons Hotel The Ritz offers luxury and quality – to those who can afford it, of course. Though it occupies a huge, ugly concrete building its interior is in keeping with what one would expect from such a hotel. Be sure to note the very beautiful tapestries in the ground floor lounge – true marvels of purest Art-Deco style. The suites, for their part, boast opulent and refined furnishings, and some are decorated with superb antique reproductions. To experience such luxury fully, request a room on an upper floors that overlooks the park and offers a lovely view of the city. A bar, restaurants, a conference room, lounges and exercise room (on the small side) are but a few of the amenities offered. Moreover, an entire floor is reserved for non-smokers. In such an epicurean establishment, the absence of a swimming pool, always useful in a major capital city, is unfortunate, however.

Card game at the *miradouro* of São Pedro de Alcântara.
- *W. Buss*

A beautiful example of the Manueline style at the Palácio da Pena in Sintra.
- G. Sioen

Sheraton and Towers Lisboa
$$$$$
pb, ≈, ℜ, *tv*, ☻, ⌂
Rua Latino Coelho no. 1
1069 Lisboa
☎*213 57 57 57*
≈*213 54 71 64*

You'd have to be very picky not to like this place, given all its amenities. The swimming pool and gym are particularly popular with guests (and are open to the general public), although both are a bit too small. The rooms on the upper floors (the Towers) are more luxuriously decorated and offer views of Parque Eduardo VII in the distance (of course, the prices are higher as well). The hotel also has a very pleasant terrace with a bar and a panoramic view.

Tour G: Restauradores and Liberdade

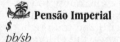 **Pensão Imperial**
$
pb/sb
Praça dos Restauradores no. 78
1200 Lisboa, enter through the optometrist's shop
☎*213 42 01 66*

On the fourth floor of a building with no elevator, the Pensão Imperial is modest, but well-kept and well-located. A few rooms offer views of the noisy square, but most are at the back, where it is much quieter. Guests receive a warm welcome. Given the limited number of rooms, it is best to make reser-

vations. An excellent choice in this category.

Pensão Nossa Senharo do Rosario
$ *no bkfst*
pb/sb, *tv*
Calçada de Sant'Ana no. 198
1st floor, 1100 Lisboa
☎*218 85 36 50*

Facing the Nossa Senhora da Pena church, the Pensão Nossa Senharo do Rosario used to welcome penniless young girls. Today, the very convivial proprietor welcomes visitors the same way – for a fee, of course. Simply decorated but particularly well-kept, this guesthouse provides decent accommodation for a relatively low price. Those who live for the true urban experience can opt for one of the front rooms, where they will be awakened by the din of the busy street below. The rooms at the rear of the building, for their part, offer pleasant views of the Graça district. Breakfast is served for the modest sum of 350 ESC. A bargain for travellers on tight budgets!

Residencial Florescente
$-$$ *no bkfst*
sb/pb
Rua Portas de Santo Antão no. 99, 1150 Lisboa
☎*213 46 35 17*
☎*213 42 66 09*
≈*213 42 77 33*

The best thing about this place is its large number of rooms at low to moderate prices. Well-kept and comfort-

able, it offers decent value for the price.

Pensão Residencial 13 da Sorte
$$ *no bkfst*
pb
Rua do Salitre no. 13
1200 Lisboa
☎*213 53 97 46*
☎/≈*213 53 18 51*

The Pensão Residencial boasts 24 clean and modestly but pleasantly decorated rooms. This guesthouse's central location and affordable rates make it a good choice in the capital.

Pensão Residencial Monumental
$$ *no bkfst*
pb, *tv*
Rua da Glória no. 21
1250 Lisboa
☎*213 46 98 07*
≈*213 43 02 13*

Small guesthouse with modest, sombre rooms lacking any charm, but well-kept and rented out at very affordable rates. A good choice for travellers on tight budgets.

Residencial Dom Sancho I
$$ *no bkfst*
pb, *tv*
Avenida da Liberdade no. 202
3rd floor, 1200 Lisboa
☎*213 54 86 48*

Set up on the 3rd floor of a stylish building on the elegant Avenida da Liberdade, the Residencial Dom Sancho I offers a few pleasantly decorated and immaculate rooms with Portuguese-style furniture. For a pleasant view, request a room with a balcony overlooking the avenue. Hospitable reception.

Lisbon

Residência Roma
$$
pb, tv
Travessa da Glória no. 22A
1200 Lisboa
☎/⇄*213 46 05 57*
Clean and comfortable,
but somewhat plain.
Twenty-four-hour bar
service.

Hotel Jorge V
$$$
pb, tv
Rua Mouzinho da Silveira no. 3
1250 Lisboa
☎*213 56 25 25*
⇄*213 15 03 19*
Though its exterior
lacks charm and its
interior appears rather
antiquated, the Hotel
Jorge V is pleasantly
situated on a quiet,
tree-lined street. Re-
quest one of the front
rooms – for they have
little balconies, a wel-
come treat in warm
weather. Rooms on the
top floor offer an inter-
esting view of the city.

Hotel President
$$$
pb, tv
Rua Alexandre Herculano
no. 13, 1150 Lisboa
☎*213 53 95 01*
⇄*213 52 02 72*
Occupying a building
with a rather imper-
sonal facade on the
corner of two noisy
streets, the Hotel Presi-
dent has an original
lobby. From the sitting
room in a corner on
the mezzanine, you'll
gaze down upon a
snack bar with designer
furniture, while a huge
modern painting adds a
cheerful note to the
place, otherwise de-
voted to studied spar-
sity. A flight of stairs,

flanked by a large geo-
metric, streamlined wall
in polished stone, leads
to the bar. Unfortu-
nately, the spirit of
creativity is sadly lack-
ing in the rooms,
where the simple decor
is bereft of any style or
interesting views. De-
spite this, the hotel
does boast a comfort-
able setting and better
value for your money
than that offered by its
close competitors.

Hotel Veneza
$$$
pb, tv
Avenida da Liberdade no. 189
1250 Lisboa
☎*213 52 26 18*
☎*213 52 67 00*
⇄*213 52 66 78*
The Hotel Veneza is
located in a very beau-
tiful bourgeois resi-
dence (*palecete*) with a
Neo-Moorish facade, an
excellent choice for this
category of hotel. An
elegant staircase with
attractive ironwork,
surmounted by a mag-
nificent glass cupola as
well as elaborate
mouldings here and
there are worth a visit
in and of themselves.
The only false note in
this beautiful setting is
the decor of the en-
trance hall, the recep-
tion hall and bar. In
truth, the large brightly
coloured paintings by
Pedro Luiz-Gomes,
hanging in the stairs of
the lobby, though
pleasing, seem some-
what out of place here.
Moreover, not only is
the cold, modern ar-
rangement in the bar
and reception hall of
questionable taste, it

constitutes another
unfortunate clash of
styles. The furnishings
and decor of the
rooms, also modern,
prove attractive and
tasteful. Hospitable
service.

🏅 **Orion**
$$$ no bkfst
$$$$/4 ppl. no bkfst
pb, ≈, ℜ, ℝ, K, tv
Praça dos Restauradores
nos. 18-24, 1250 Lisboa
☎*213 21 66 00*
⇄*213 21 66 66*
Housed in what was
formerly the Teatro
Eden, whose lovely
Art-Deco facade has
been skilfully pre-
served, the Orion
apartment-hotel is a
particularly interesting
choice. The apartment-
hotel formula proves
ideal for business trav-
ellers, for families with
young children or for
those planning an ex-
tended stay. In addition
to its ideal location,
facing lovely Praça dos
Restauradores and in
close proximity to vari-
ous means of transport
(metro and train right
nearby), the Orion of-
fers charmingly fur-
nished studios and
apartments. While the
studios are each
equipped with a com-
fortable sofa bed, the
apartments have sepa-
rate bedrooms. A
child-size bed (for
those under 10 years of
age) is also available
upon request, free of
charge. A work corner
is arranged near the
window, and a table
and chairs means you
can eat comfortably in
the studio. All studios

and apartments have fully equipped kitchenettes, including microwave ovens and dishwashers. The lovely marbled bathrooms, for their part, are all supplied with hair dryers. Housekeeping service is provided once a week. For those who so desire, room service is available on a daily basis; breakfast service is also available.

Though all rooms are accessible to the physically handicapped, three of them (studios) have been especially fitted out for such guests. Another advantage is the pleasant terrace on the top floor, offering a panoramic view of the *Castelo*, the Baixa and Avenida Restauradores. Finally, as an added treat, guests will find a superb swimming pool and a snack bar surrounded by a magnificent panorama. Whether for a business stay or a holiday, this establishment offers excellent value.

🏨 Hotel Britânia
$$$$
pb, tv
Rua Rodrigues Sampaio no. 17
(near Rua Barata Salgueiro)
1150-278 Lisboa
☎*213 15 50 16*
⇌*213 15 50 21*
www.heritage.pt
britania.hotel@heritage.pt
Lovers of Art Deco should definitely check out this hotel or, better yet, check in. During the renovations carried out in the 1970s, the owners restored this

old 1942 hotel to its original splendour, guided by the many period photographs that are still preciously preserved. You can thus admire its distinguished marbled lobby adorned with a lovely sphere, its wood-panelled bar and elegant lounge graced with Art-Deco curios and furnishings. As for the rooms, though they have been adapted to today's standards of comfort (fully equipped marbled bathroom, double-paned windows, air conditioning, etc.), some have retained their original furnishings, perfectly restored. The only flaw is the building's unattractive concrete facade, which hardly does justice to this veritable little 1940s palace.

Hotel Avenida Palace
$$$$
pb, ℝ, tv
Rua 1° Dezembro no. 123
1200 Lisboa
☎*213 46 01 51*
⇌*213 42 28 84*
Dating from the Edwardian era, this comfortable hotel has retained much of its charm and refined atmosphere; it will appeal to particularly discerning travellers. The elaborate decor includes stucco, crystal chandeliers and a beautiful marble stairwell. Ask for one of the rooms on the fourth or fifth floor, overlooking the train station, for these offer an interesting view of the Castelo and the lovely station.

Attentive service. Beautiful, but expensive.

Tívoli Jardim
$$$$-$$$$$
pb, ≈, ℜ, ℝ, tv
Rua Júlio César Machado no. 7
1200 Lisboa
☎*213 53 99 71*
⇌*213 55 65 66*
More modest in size than its "big sister" next door (see Tívoli Lisboa below), the Tívoli Jardim offers all the advantages of a world-class hotel. A large rooftop terrace, free access to the swimming pool (small, but located in a pleasant garden) and its neighbour's tennis court, constitute only a few of the amenities offered to the clientele. The rooms' decor and furnishings are modern and rather nondescript. Renting a room at the rear of the building is preferable, since the front looks out on a large parking lot.

🏨 Lisboa Plaza Hotel
$$$$$
pb, ℜ, ℝ, tv
Travessa do Salitre, 1200 Lisboa
☎*213 46 39 22*
⇌*213 47 16 30*
The Lisboa Plaza Hotel, with its ugly concrete facade, doesn't look like much from the outside. But make no mistake, for besides its singularly elegant lobby, the hotel offers some 100 medium-sized rooms with all modern conveniences. During our visit, some of the rooms were under renovation. Some of which featured elegant new fabrics as

Lisbon

well as a fully marbled bathroom. The hotel's 12 suites are even more tastefully appointed and luxurious. They come with a cozy, opulently decorated bedroom and a living room where antique furnishings, paintings and curios create a refined environment. The only things missing are a swimming pool and an exercise room, a drawback, however, compensated by the hotel's central location and varied breakfast buffet, which includes real fruit juices.

Tívoli Lisboa
$$$$$
pb, ≈, ℜ, ℝ, tv
Avenida da Liberdade no. 185
1250 Lisboa
☎ *213 53 01 81*
☎ *213 14 11 01*
⇌ *213 57 94 61*
Facing elegant Avenida da Liberdade, the Tívoli Lisboa hotel has 329 small but nicely appointed rooms. Those on the top floors, overlooking the *Avenida*, offer an interesting view. In addition to its proximity to downtown, the hotel has various amenities, such as a tennis court and a small swimming pool in a lovely garden. What is more, a terrace restaurant has been set up on the building's top floor, affording a lovely panoramic view of the city.

Tour H: Santa Catarina and Cais Do Sodré

Pensão Residencial Santa Catarina
$$
pb
Rua Dr. Luís de Almeida e Albuquerque no. 6, 1200 Lisboa
☎ *213 46 61 06*
⇌ *213 47 72 27*
The Pensão Residencial Santa Catarina is noteworthy chiefly for its peaceful location. Pleasant surroundings, but rather expensive considering the lack of services.

Tour I: Estrêla and Lapa

Hotel York House
$$$$-$$$$$
pb, ℜ, tv
Rua das Janelas Verdes no. 32
1200 Lisboa
☎ *213 96 24 35*
☎ *213 96 27 85*
⇌ *213 97 27 93*
A former monastery, the Hotel York House, like its neighbour (see As Janelas Verdas below), is one of those rare hotels that has successfully managed to combine charm with comfort. It is worth describing how to get into the hotel: after passing through the entrance, which is decorated with scores of *azulejos*, you have to climb a long flight of stairs flanked by massive pink walls covered with luxuriant greenery;

at the top, you will find yourself on a beautiful patio adorned with plants. In fine weather, you can enjoy a meal or simply sip a refreshment beneath the tall palm trees (see p 148). Next door, the luxurious and more intimate hotel bar, with its wood panelling, is also a pleasant place to have a coffee or a drink, although the prices are quite high. The rooms, for their part, are tastefully decorated with Portuguese furniture, fabrics in warm colours, gleaming wood floors and antique *azulejos*, many featuring naive motifs. Unfortunately, the rooms facing the street are somewhat noisy despite the double-glazed windows. The only other drawback is that the employees at the reception seem a little stiff. A charming place nonetheless. Good value for the price.

As Janelas Verdes
$$$$-$$$$$
pb, tv
Rua das Janelas Verdas no. 47
1200 Lisboa
☎ *213 96 81 43*
⇌ *213 96 81 44*
The beautifully furnished As Janelas Verdes occupies a sumptuous former residence whose charm has been artfully preserved. Its 17 rooms are extremely comfortable, and breakfast is served on a romantic, verdant patio.

🛥 Hotel da Lapa
$$$$$ no bkfst
pb, ≈, ℜ, *tv*
Rua do Pau da Bandeira no. 4
1200 Lisboa
☎*213 95 00 05*
☎*213 95 00 06*
≈*213 95 06 05*
The Hotel da Lapa, set in a pretty and open part of town with embassies and the like for neighbours, is probably Lisbon's loveliest hotel in this category. The building is a former palace to which a wing has been added, and architects have wisely preserved some of the original features. These include a splendid banquet hall (on the second floor) richly adorned with stucco and imitation marble and bathed in light filtered through antique stained-glass windows. The luxurious ground floor, all decorated with marble, opens onto a vast inner garden with a big swimming pool and an adjacent bar. The landscaping, complemented by a magnificent fountain decorated with *azulejos*, makes this place a true haven of peace. Each of the charming rooms is decorated differently and equipped with all the conveniences. From your balcony, you can enjoy a direct view of the verdant inner garden. If you're looking for real luxury, opt for one of the suites, from which you can see the Tagus and the Ponte 25 de Abril in the distance. And finally, if you'll only settle for the peak of perfection, there's

room #701, a presidential suite with access to a little turret offering a 360° view of Lisbon. Of course, the suites are all equipped with whirlpools and other such sophisticated amenities! To top it all off, the place has shops, conference rooms, a private underground parking lot and an elegant restaurant (see p 148). Expensive but oh, how elegant! Very good value for the price.

Tour J: Alcântara, Santo Amaro and Belém

Pensão Residencial Setubalense
$
pb, *tv*
Rua de Belém no. 28
1300 Lisboa
☎*213 63 66 39*
☎*213 64 87 60*
≈*213 62 13 72*
Located steps away from the Mosteiro dos Jerónimos, the Pensão Residencial Setubalense rents out clean rooms at moderate prices. Although the common areas are pleasant, the decor of the rooms is a bit depressing. Very good value for your money.

Hotel da Torre
$$$
pb, *tv*
Rua dos Jerónimos no. 8
1400 Lisboa
☎*213 63 62 62*
☎*213 63 73 32*
≈*213 64 59 95*
The Hotel da Torre, also near the monas-

tery, has 50 comfortable rooms. Tasteful decor, hospitable staff. A good choice.

Tour K: Parque das Nações

Meliá Confort Oriente
$$$-$$$$
pb, *tv*, ℜ
Ave. Dom João II-Parque das Nações, 1800 Lisboa
☎*218 93 00 00*
≈*218 93 00 99*
www.solmelia.es
Surprisingly, only one hotel has opened in Parque das Nações to date, namely the Meliá Confort Oriente. Like other hotels of this Spanish chain, comfort and convenience, rather than originality, are the establishment's trademarks. The hotel offers 116 somewhat mundane rooms decorated with utilitarian furnishings as well as modern curios and fabrics. The only advantage in staying here is the hotel's location within Parque das Nações and immediate proximity to the very lovely Vasco da Gama bridge, which provides fast access to the highways leading to the southern part of the country.

Lisbon

Restaurants by Type of Cuisine

Portuguese
Adega do Teixeira, p 140
Bachus, p 141
Bizzaro, p 141
Casa do Leão, p 137
Casa do Alentejo, p 144
Cervejaria da Trindade, p 139
Chez Degroote, p 138
Conventual, p 148
Flor da Estrêla, p 147
Gambrinus, p 145
Martinho da Arcada, p 137
Palmeira, p 136
Pap'Açorda, p 141
Pato Baton, p 141
Sancho, p 145
Serra da Estrêla, p 143
Tagide, p 142
Tavares Rico, p 142

Mexican
Casa México, p 147
Gringo's Café, p 146

Middle Eastern
Pedro das Arábias, p 139

Japanese
Novo Bonsai, p 141

Italian
Casa Nostra, p 141
Massima Culpa, p 141
Pizzeria Mama Rosa, p 140

Indian
Jaipur, p 143

Asian
Majong, p 139

Chinese
Xi Hu, p 149

African
Cantinha da Paz, p 146
Costa do Castelo, p 137
Ideal de São Bento, p 145

French
Frei Contente, p 147

Fast Food
Palmeira, p 136
Pão Pão Queijo Queijo, p 148
Tavares Self Service, p 142

Spanish
Siesta Brava, p 147
Tapas-Bar El Gordo, p 140

Fish and Seafood
Cervejaria A Berlenga, p 136
Solar dos Bicos, p 137
Solmar, p 144
Xico's Bar Restaurante, p 147

Steak and Ribs
Assóporco, p 146
Brasserie de l'Entrecôte, p 139
El Último Tango, p 140
Grill 20, p 144
Picanha, p 146

Vegetarian
O Sol, p 139
Os Tibetanos, p 144
Yin-Yan, p 136

Hamburgers
Abracadabra, p 136

Eclectic
A Commenda, p 149
Alcântara Café, p 149
Arameiro, p 144
Café no Chiado, p 138
Cais da Ribeira, p 146
California Dream, p 145
Casa da Comida, p 143
Charcuteria Francesa, p 138
Consenso, p 140
Doca do Santo, p 149
Dom Sopas, p 136
Embaixada, p 148
Mercado Original, p 143
O Primeiro da Conceição Velha, p 136
Pastelaria Apolo XI, p 146
Poeta na Bicha, p 139
Restaurante do Museu, p 138
Umpuntocinco, p 148
Xêlê Bananas, p 147
York House, p 148
Zutzu, p 148

Ulysses's Favourites

For Romantic Atmosphere:
Casa do Leão, p 137
Tagide, p 142
York House, p 148

For Refinement:
Casa da Comida, p 143
Casa Nostra, p 141
Consenso, p 140
Dom Sopas, p 136
Pato Baton, p 141

For True Value:
Bachus, p 141
Casa do Leão, p 137
Conventual, p 148
Embaixada, p 148
Frei Contente, p 147
Gambrinus, p 145
Sancho, p 145

For Originality:
Os Tibetanos, p 144

For Trendiness:
Alcântara Café, p 149
Café no Chiado – Ciber-Café, p 138

California Dream, p 145
Doca do Santo, p 149
Gringo's Café, p 146
Majong, p 139
Massima Culpa, p 141
Pap'Açorda, p 141

For Traditional Lisbon:
Confeitaria de Belém, p 149
Palmeira, p 136

For Decor:
A Brasileira, p 142
Casa de Leão, p 137
Casa do Alentejo, p 144
Cervejaria da Trindade, p 139
Consenso, p 140
Pastelaria São Roque, p 143
Pastelaria Versailles, p 144
Restaurante do Museu, p 138
Tavares Rico, p 142

For the Exotic:
Cantinha da Paz, p 146
Novo Bonsai, p 141
Xêlê Bananas, p 147

Lisbon

Restaurants

Tour A: The Rossio and the Baixa

Strolling along Baixa's main pedestrian mall, Rua Augusta, you will cross Rua de Santa, Rua Justa and Rua de São Nicolau, which are also reserved for pedestrians. On these streets are rows of small snack bars with patios right on the street. They all serve essentially the same food, mostly simple sandwiches at reasonable prices. Among them, **Campesina** (*Rua de São Nicolau*) offers a few daily specials, like *feijoada* and *leitão* (suckling pig). Located right across the street, the pleasant "restaurant/snack-bar" of the little **Mon Café** chain (*Rua de São Nicolau*) offers daily soups for as little as 180 ESC, sandwiches at 500 ESC, as well as a daily special for 750 ESC. A real bargain right downtown! If, however, you're looking for a designer decor without the ubiquitous television set, head to its counterpart on Rua Betesga (*at Rua das Douradores*), a popular haunt with young locals. These areas are perpetually crowded tourist spots.

Abracadabra
$
every day 9am to 2am
Praça Rossio no. 65, beside Telecom, or Rua 1º Dezembro nos. 102-108
If you crave a hamburger, head to Abracadabra for a traditional hamburger-fries-pop combo at unbeatable prices, or the MacDonalds located across the plaza. Abracadabra offers much more pleasant surroundings and the opportunity to contribute to the development of an independent local business. They also serve quiche, slices of home-made pizza and traditional pastries. There's a non-smoking room on the main floor of the building. A good place to grab a quick bite.

O Primeiro da Conceição Velha
$
Tue to Sat 8:30am to 5:45pm
Rua da Alfândega no. 108 2nd floor
☎218 86 60 36
With its pretty entranceway, a harmonious blend of *azulejos* and stone arches, the O Primeiro da Conceição Velha restaurant-cafeteria deserves a visit. The attractive little dining room is richly decorated with flower mo-

tifs. A number of different dishes are offered, such as *vol-au-vent* (900 ESC) and spinach pie served with a refreshing salad, and there are daily specials at 800 ESC and up. A pleasant change from the other restaurants in the area.

Palmeira
$
Mon to Fri 11am to 8pm
Rua do Crucifixo no. 69
☎213 42 83 72
Whether to quench your thirst, eat a *petisco*, or enjoy a typical Portuguese dish, the Palmeira restaurant hits the spot. As you enter you'll notice many large wine casks behind a big counter, which is particularly busy in the late afternoon. For a modest 40 ESC, you can enjoy a glass of red or white wine, or a mix the two, in the company of local workers. If you get a little hungry during your wine-tasting session you can always have a *pastéi de bacalhau* (100 ESC) or a fish sandwich for as little as 170 ESC. For the comfort of a table go to the arched room at the back, where simple but tasty Portuguese meals are served for 950 ESC. Tourist menu for 1,500 ESC.

Yin-Yan
$
Mon to Fri 10am to 8:30pm
Rua dos Correeiros no. 14 2nd floor
☎213 42 65 51
Located above a large grocery store, the buffet-style vegetarian

restaurant Yin-Yan offers macrobiotic meals in the sparest of environments. Unfortunately, the chilly atmosphere is not very inviting, which is all the more regrettable since opposite the restaurant is an interesting little grocery store. Nevertheless, don't hesitate to drop by for one of their delicious daily specials (*about 1,500 ESC*).

Cervejaria A Berlenga
$$
Rua Barros Queiros nos. 29-35
☎213 42 27 03
The Cervejaria A Berlenga is an authentic Portuguese tavern-restaurant, whose specialty is fish and seafood (*açorda de Marisco, arroz de Marisco*). Simple but pleasant decor. Good game dishes during the hunting season.

Dom Sopas
$$
Mon to Fri noon to 2am, Sat 7pm to 2am
Rua da Madalena no. 48
☎218 86 62 53
As you may have already guessed, this restaurant's trademarks are high-quality, rich, creamy soups: *sopa de cacão* (cocoa soup), *sopa de peixe a Dom Sopas* (fish soup), and *sopa de alho a moda de Évora* (garlic soup) among others. Soups cost around 1,000 to 1,500 ESC. Of course, the great classic Portuguese dishes are also on the menu, and a tourist menu is available for 3,000 ESC. The owner is none other than painter Eduardo

Alves, so it goes without saying that the decor is meticulous and makes maximum use of this modest semi-basement's potential.

Martinho da Arcada
$$$
Mon to Sat noon to 3pm and 7pm to 10pm
Praça do Comércio no. 3
☎*218 87 92 59*
Eating at Martinho da Arcada is a bit like following in Fernando Pessõa's footsteps. According to some people, the famous Portuguese writer composed some of his poems here. From the lovely covered terrace, the view of elegant Praça do Comercio could definitely be a source of poetic inspiration. It's the food, however, that is most important: don't miss the savoury suckling pig or the *cabrito a padeira*. Tourist menu for 1,600 ESC.

Solar dos Bicos
$$$$
Tue to Sun noon to 10:30pm
Rua dos Bacalhoeiros no. 8A
☎*218 86 94 47*
At the end of a row of fish and seafood restaurants, Solar dos Bicos, two steps from the Casa dos Bicos, offers essentially the same fare as its competitors but deserves special mention for its lush, leafy terrace. Fast and friendly service.

Cafés and Tearooms

Confeitaria Nacional
at the corner of Praça da Figueira and Rua dos Correiros
If you're looking for an authentic Lisbon pastry shop, head to the Confeitaria Nacional, where the Portuguese like to go after a tiring day of shopping. Sparsely decorated, with only a few mirrors on its cream-coloured walls, this place attracts a mature clientele, who come here for a *bica* and one of a large assortment of home-made desserts. Old-fashioned, but positively charming. Friendly service.

Café Niçola
Mon to Sat
Praça Dom Pedro IV or the Rossio
☎*213 42 91 72*
Known throughout Lisbon, Café Nicola is not only a famous café once frequented by the Portuguese poet Bocage, it is also now a brand of coffee distributed to every region of Portugal. Next to its main dining room, this restaurant has recently opened a bistro called **Nicola Gourmet** (*Rua 1° Dezembro nos. 10-14*), where you can buy coffee beans from all over the world, or, like in the original café, simply sip a *bica* and nibble a *pastéi*.

Casa Chineza
Mon to Fri 9am to 8pm
Sat 9am to 4pm
Rua Aurea nos. 274-278
also known as Rua do Ouro, or "Gold Street"
As indicated on the shop, the Casa Chineza has been serving delicious pastries since 1866. The main draw here is the large selection and reasonable prices, since the uninspiring decor does not do justice to the pretty facade. Those who would like to bring home an edible souvenir of Portugal can buy excellent coffee here.

Tour B: The Castelo and the Alfama

Costa do Castelo
$$
Tue to Sun 3pm to 2am
at the corner of Costa do Castelo and Travessa de Chão do Loureiro
☎*218 88 46 36*
The bar-restaurant Costa do Castelo serves Mozambican dishes (*the kitchen opens at 8pm*) and has a terrace with a pretty view of the city. This is a pleasant place to come in the afternoon; stop by and quench your thirst after visiting the Castelo (see p 84).

 Casa do Leão
$$$$$
every day 12:30pm to 3:30pm and 7:30pm to 8:30pm
Castelo de São Jorge
☎*218 87 59 62*
The Casa do Leão boasts a prestigious location within the

walls of the Castelo, in a magnificent vaulted room in what was once the commanding officer's residence. Impeccably laid tables and mouthwatering Portuguese dishes with a slight French influence make for an extremely pleasant meal. The restaurant is run by the ENATUR, which manages the country-wide network of *pousadas*.

Cafés and Tearooms

Bar Cerca Moura
every day 10am to 2pm
Largo das Portas do Sol no. 4
☎*218 87 48 59*
Located right beside the decorative arts museum, Bar Cerca Moura has a large terrace from which the view includes the periodic passing of tram #28 and, in the distance, the radiant dome of Igreja-Panteão de Santa Engrácia. The interior is interesting too: the decor highlights the small room perfectly and is enhanced by a tastefully lit part of the old city wall. There are also a few Art-Deco-style tables and chairs. A place that is definitely worth stopping at for a *bica* or a *cerveja*. Snacks available.

Tour C: Graça and East Lisbon

Restaurante do Museu
$
Tue 2pm to 5:30pm, Wed to Sun 10am to 5:30pm
Rua da Madre de Deus no. 4
☎*218 14 77 90*
During your visit to the Museu Nacional do Azulejo, stop for lunch at the Restaurante do Museu, in the museum building. In the unique setting of the old convent's kitchen, covered with extraordinary *azulejos* with images of rabbits, hams, pheasants, pig-heads, fish, etc., you can sample delicious stuffed savoury crepes and refreshing salads. There's also a large, elegant terrace. The only disappointment in this enchanting setting is the slow service, but it's quickly forgotten since the people are so friendly. Daily specials for 1,200 ESC and 1,400 ESC.

Cafés and Tearooms

Café Papasom
Largo da Graça
The Café Papasom, frequented mostly by young locals, is a pleasant, but loud, place to have a coffee with a *pastéi* or a simple sandwich. Except for the attractive little tablecloths, the furnishings are vaguely Scandinavian in style.

Tour D: The Chiado and the Bairro Alto

Café no Chiado
$
every day 11am to 2pm
Largo do Picadeiro nos. 10-12
Away from the very touristy Largo do Chiado area, in the centre of a theatre district, Café no Chiado is a place worth investigating. If you are seeking a bit of peace and quiet, its lovely terrace is ideal, or you can sit in the old dining room surrounded by vaulted ceilings and modern furniture. The menu consists of various good, but fairly predictable, Portuguese dishes. You can escape the confines of Europe and connect with the rest of the world at a **cyber café** upstairs from the restaurant (see p 142).

Charcuteria Francesa
$
Mon to Sat 8am to 7pm
Rua Dom Pedro V nos. 52-54
Located in an old delicatessen, the Charcuteria Francesa restaurant offers daily specials to take out or eat in (*half-portions available for 550 ESC*) and an agreeable setting. You can eat at one of the winsome tables in the main room and observe the activity at the counter or watch the world go by on the street through the large window. There is also a more intimate back room decorated with rich woodwork. This is a pleasant, unpreten-

tious spot frequented by business people at lunch and students in the afternoon.

Chez Degroote
$
Mon to Sat
Rua Duques de Bragança no. 5
☎*213 47 28 39*
In a pleasant room with vaulted ceilings, the Belgian owner of Chez Degroote invites you to discover classic local dishes, in honour of his friendly Portuguese wife, rather than the pleasures of his native cuisine. *Meia dosa* (half-portions) are available for 600 ESC and up. A great deal!

O Sol
$
closed Sat for lunch and all-day Sun
Calçada do Duque 21-23
☎*213 47 35 44*
Although it doesn't look very inviting, the macrobiotic restaurant O Sol serves good vegetarian cuisine. It lies halfway up Calçada do Duque, which leads up to the Chiado like a giant staircase. Its small terrace, located in the middle of the pedestrian mall, offers a pleasant view of the lower part of the city.

L'Entrecôte
$$
Mon to Sat 12:30pm to 3pm and 8pm to midnight, Sun to 11pm
Rua do Alecrim nos. 117-121
☎*213 42 83 43*
The menu at the Brasserie de L'Entrecôte lists salads, steaks and fries (all you can eat). The place is modeled after a Parisian brasserie, but the decor is somewhat stark. Elegant clientele, including many businesspeople. Extremely popular; reservations recommended. Tourist menu at 2,550 ESC.

🦐 Cervejaria da Trindade
$$
every day until 2am
Rua da Trindade 20C
☎*213 42 35 06*
If you like lively places, make sure to go to the Cervejaria da Trindade, where you can enjoy good Portuguese cuisine in a congenial atmosphere, surrounded by both tourists and locals. The restaurant has three rooms, which are all connected but decorated in different ways. In the first one, you'll find lovely *azulejos* painted with Masonic symbols. In the second, you can dine beneath beautifully restored vaults, which serve as reminders that this was once a monastery. The last, with its numerous candlesticks, will appeal to those seeking a cozy atmosphere. The menu consists mainly of fish and meat dishes, and there is a daily special starting at 680 ESC.

Majong
$$
every day 7pm to 11pm
Rua da Atalaia no. 3
☎*213 42 10 39*
Chinese food with an innovative touch isn't the only thing out of the ordinary at Majong. The decor, or lack of one, also draws your attention. Actually, they have chosen to go completely minimalist: modern wood tables of no particular style stand next to bare walls of roughly applied plaster. As if to reinforce this "unfinished" look, concrete-coloured flooring was installed. Despite all this, subtle lighting exudes a certain warmth and exotic plants brighten the atmosphere, making for a very comfortable evening.

🦐 Pedro das Arábias
$$
every day until 11pm
Rua da Atalaia no. 70
☎*213 46 84 94*
Pedro das Arábias is steeped in the warm atmosphere and aromatic spices of the Middle East. Dressed in a *jellaba*, the young owner serves savoury couscous or *tajines* on attractive regional dishware. Try lamb with prunes and almonds, *tagine de borrego com ameixas e amendoas*, an absolute delight! As for the decor, it will transport you to exotic lands on a musical wave of Arab rhythms. A great spot!

Poeta na Bicha
$$
every day 7:30pm to midnight
Travessa do Água da Flor no. 36
☎*213 42 59 24*
In a small, arched dining room, warmly decorated in earthy colours, with Portuguese music in the

Lisbon

background, the owner of the Poeta na Bicha restaurant greets you with a smile. There are various Portuguese specialties on the menu, including delicious *açorda* which is worth the trip in itself. Combining culinary pleasure with art, there are a number of paintings on the walls and a brief presentation of the works on display is inserted in the menu. Although there are some original ideas on the menu, some dishes combine incongruous ingredients. The copious portion of mustard turkey is served with French fries (alas, frozen) and rice.

Pizzeria Mama Rosa
$$
Mon to Fri 12:30pm to 3pm and 7:30pm to 1am, Sat 7:30pm to midnight
Rua Grémio Lusitano no. 14
☎*213 46 53 50*
Oh how we love our pizza! Two steps from Largo Trindade Coelho, Pizzeria Mama Rosa offers a wide variety of pizza made with love in a genuine Italian setting. Small tables with checkered tablecloths, terracotta dishes, rows of wine bottles and ... the smiling *mama*, all evoke Italy's *joie de vivre*.

Restaurante Adega do Teixeira
$$
Rua do Teixeira 39
If you're looking for a quiet spot in the bustling Bairro Alto, head to the Restaurante Adega do Teixeira for

some traditional Portuguese cuisine. The place has an attractive terrace as well.

Tapas-Bar El Gordo
$$
closed Sun
Rua São Boaventura nos. 16-18
☎*213 42 42 66*
As its name suggests, the Tapas-Bar El Gordo offers an assortment of little snacks. It also has an excellent wine list. Decorated with warm colours and frequented by a trendy clientele, this is an altogether pleasant place to be.

🌴 Marquês de Pombal, Consenso
$$$
Mon to Fri 12:30pm to 3pm and 8pm to 11:30pm, Sat 8pm to 12:30am
Rua da Academia das Ciências nos. 1-1A
☎*213 43 13 13*
☎*213 46 86 11*
☎*213 43 13 11*
Established in the heart of the house that is the birthplace of the Marquês de Pombal, Consenso offers three successive dining rooms with earth, fire and water as their respective themes. The small entrance room, nicely fixed up as a bar, represents the theme of air with its futuristic and spare furnishings. Parts of the old walls and stone archways have been uncovered in each of the dining rooms. The room dedicated to water is of particular interest because of its stucco walls on which rococo-style medallions

mimic the movement of waves. There is no direct lighting: light shoots up from the floor, rebounds a few times on the stone edges of the walls, then lands lightly on the frescoes and the stucco ceilings. The floors are particularly well conceived: perimeters in frosted glass for lighting, and a combination of three kinds of wood and marble tiles. As for the food, although the menu is simple, it demonstrates no lack of imagination: tarragon and oregano monkfish, *linguado com bananas fritas*, Portuguese şteak with Roquefort sauce, etc. Each dish is presented as a work of art decorated with a few leaves and sometimes even flowers – all edible, we've been assured. The service is efficient and friendly, and the ambient music is pleasant. This spot is not to be missed! The only drawback is the limited selection on the affordable tourist menu (*2,500 ESC*). Reservations are recommended.

El Ultimo Tango
$$$
Mon to Sat 7:30pm to 11pm
Rua Diário de Noticias no. 62
☎*213 42 03 41*
For meat lovers hungry for steaks grilled or rare, what could be better than an Argentinian restaurant? El Ultimo Tango has a lively atmosphere and an inviting decor under

attractive stone arches. Busy on weekends.

Massima Culpa
$$$
every day until 11pm
Rua da Atalaia nos. 35-37
☎ *213 42 01 21*
Imagine a large dining room in velvety colours, the floor covered in little cobblestones like a street, and modern furniture: this is Massima Culpa, unfortunately called a "spaghetti house". Pasta in all its forms, served with various sauces, is the specialty here. This restaurant is enchanting if you appreciate modern decor and "high society". The relatively high prices and the cold ambiance are the only shortcomings in this posh establishment.

Pap'Açorda
$$$
closed Sun
Rua da Atalaia os. 57-59, ring bell to enter
☎ *213 46 48 11*
Fashionable Lisboans get together at Pap'Açorda, whose two adjoining rooms have been decorated with great care. The first room is spacious, with soft colours and lovely crystal chandeliers, while the second will appeal to those with a taste for contemporary design. Make sure to try the *açorda*, the house specialty, a mixture of bread, oil, coriander and various other ingredients, such as seafood, all generously seasoned with garlic; it's truly delicious. The menu also includes a

good selection of traditional dishes. Very pleasant but a bit noisy. Reservations a must.

Pato Baton
$$$
Tue to Sun
Travessa Fiéis dos Deus no. 28
☎ *213 42 63 72*
The Pato Baton restaurant, with its plush decor of pastel colours and modern furniture, provides a calm contrast to nearby, lively Rua da Atalaia. With Brazilian or jazz music in the background, this is the perfect spot for a pleasant, intimate evening. The cuisine is excellent, although unoriginal; it includes many typical Portuguese dishes, enhanced by more elaborate presentations.

Restaurante Bizzaro
$$$
every day
Rua da Atalaia nos. 131-133
☎ *213 47 18 99*
The Restaurante Bizzaro offers the usual meat and fish dishes. Make sure to try the *peixe espada* (swordfish), which is served in generous portions. For dessert, the *doce de amêndoa* is an interesting treat for almond-lovers. Friendly service.

Restaurante Novo Bonsai
$$$
closed all-day Sun and Mon for lunch
Rua da Rosa nos. 244-248
☎ *213 46 25 15*
At the Restaurante Novo Bonsai, you can dine on Japanese cuisine in an authentic Japanese setting.

Casa Nostra
$$$$
Tue to Fri 12:30pm to 3pm and 8pm to 11pm, Sat 8pm to 11pm
Travessa do Poço da Cidade no. 60
☎ *213 42 59 31*
Trout salteboco alla romania and fettucine al vongole are just two of the dishes that conjure up images of warmhearted Italy at the Casa Nostra restaurant, where, in a predominantly pistachio-green decor, you can enjoy the finest of Italian meals, accompanied by a bottle of excellent *Chianti* or *orvieto*. Chic, expensive and very popular. Reservations recommended.

 Restaurante Bachus
$$$$
closed Sat lunch and Sun
Largo da Trindade no. 9
☎ *213 42 28 28*
☎ *213 42 12 60*
The Restaurante Bachus specializes in fish and seafood. This two-floor temple of gastronomy will appeal to those who appreciate top-notch classic cuisine. To pique your appetite, start off with an appetizer of little eels seasoned with garlic. For the main course, try the *calmar a Chiado*, served with shrimp (a house specialty) or the succulent sea perch with *cataplana*, both treats for the palate. As far as dessert is concerned, the orange and coconut pie takes the prize. Before heading upstairs into the 1950s decor, take the time to have a

Lisbon

liqueur (a glass of port, of course!) on the cozy ground floor, which is amply adorned with woodwork (see p 152). You can have a light meal at the bar for about 5,000 ESC.

Restaurante Tagide
$$$$$
closed Sat noon and Sun
Largo da Academia Nacional de Belas Artes nos. 18-20
☎*213 42 07 20*
☎*213 46 05 70*
As well as a beautiful view of the old city and the Tagus, Restaurante Tagide offers diners an elegant setting. In the richly coloured dining room decorated with *azulejos*, various fish and seafood dishes are served. The menu, however, is not terribly original and the price of the tourist menu (*7,000 ESC*) isn't worth the price. Reservations recommended.

Restaurante Tavares Rico
$$$$$
closed all-day Sat and Sun for lunch
Rua da Misericórdia 37
☎*213 42 11 12*
☎*213 47 09 05*
The Restaurante Tavares Rico is decorated with stucco, mirrors and crystal chandeliers, all set off by gilding fit for a palace. In these extremely "rich" surroundings, you can dine on dishes as varied as stuffed octopus and delicious steak *tartare* with whiskey. Carefully prepared international cuisine. The prices are high, but so is the quality. Reservations recommended. If

you're on a tighter budget or in a hurry, there is also fast food service upstairs at **Tavares Self Service** (*$-$$; same hours, 2nd floor, entrance at the right side of the building,* ☎*213 42 89 42*). The lack of decoration and cold neon lights are uninviting. The contrast is particularly striking to those who have had the opportunity to admire the decor of Tavares Rico. The only advantages are the moderate prices and the interesting formula of assorted "mini-dishes" (*four choices for 700 ESC or seven for 1,000 ESC*).

Cafés and Tearooms

A Brasileira
every day until 2am
Rua Garrett no. 120, at Largo do Chiado
Known throughout the Chiado, the café A Brasileira is one of those places that has become a "victim of its success". Its turn-of-the-century decor features stucco, woodwork, mirrors and paintings by Portuguese artists. In front of the café stands a statue of the celebrated writer Fernando Pessôa, a reminder that once upon a time he and other noted intellectuals used to frequent the place. Nowadays, A Brasileira attracts a lot of tourists, and, unfortunately, its prices tend to exceed its reputation. Foreign visitors are bound to be disappointed by the

small selection of pastries. Slow, apathetic and not very courteous service.

Céu de Lisboa
every day until 11pm
As its name suggests, the Céu de Lisboa will transport you into the skies of Lisbon. No, it's not a potent drink, but rather a terrace at the very top of the famous Elevador Santa Justa. If you're in town during the weekend, don't miss the excellent recitals given here (*Sat and Sun 5pm to 10pm*). The soft music and magnificent view of the hills of Lisbon bathed in late-afternoon light can make even the most blasé tourist fall in love with this city. Be careful, though: climbing up the narrow spiral staircase to the terrace is not recommended if you're subject to dizzy spells. Come early for the concerts, as both seats and space are limited. Light snacks available.

Ciber-Chiado
Mon 11am to 7pm, Tue to Fri 11am to 1pm, Sat 7pm to 1am
Largo do Picadeiro nos. 10-12
Ciber-Chiado, upstairs from Café no Chiado (see p 138), is the place to connect with the world and "surf" to your heart's delight. In addition to comfortable chairs, there is a small library set up like an opulent living room. The only unfortunate aspect of this very pleasant setting is the high cost of "web crawl-

ing": 600 ESC for a mandatory six-month subscription fee and 900 ESC per hour of internet use (*30 min, 500 ESC; 15 min, 300 ESC*).

Pastelaria São Roque
every day 7am to 7pm
Rua Dom Pedro V, at Rua da Rosa
Sudden hunger pangs in Bairro Alto provide an excellent opportunity to visit the majestically decorated Pastelaria São Roque. In a small, oval room with stuccoed ceiling and walls, pink marble columns, a large gold chandelier and Art-Nouveau-motif *azulejos*, you can sample delicious egg pastries or the daily special, served between noon and 3pm.

Tour E: The Rato and Amoreiras

Jaipur
$
Tue to Sun noon to 3pm and 7pm to 10:30pm
Rua do Sol ao Rato no. 52
☎213 88 06 30
In 1497, Vasco da Gama discovered the passage to India and brought the riches and flavours of a 1000-year-old civilization back to the western world. These same flavours emanate from the Jaipur restaurant, and the delicious dish *cabrito com coco e amêndoas* is just one example. Budget for between 950 and 1,250 ESC per dish.

Restaurante Serra da Estrêla
$$
closed Sun
located on the upper floor of the Amoreiras shopping centre
☎213 83 37 39
The Restaurante Serra da Estrêla is a great place to have a bite to eat after browsing through the shops. It specializes in cuisine from the Beíras region, in the northern part of the country, and has excellent deli products and a good selection of fine cheeses. The *tapas* platter, made up of an assortment of specialties and served with a glass of house wine, is a real feast. The little tables, laid out in a rustic fashion with handcrafted dishes, make for an unusual setting that breaks out of the monotonous shopping centre mold.

Casa da Comida
$$$$$
closed Sat for lunch and all day Sun
Travessas da Amoreiras no. 1
☎213 88 53 76
The Casa da Comida is one of those places where connoisseurs of fine cuisine simply have to go during their stay in the capital. After piquing your appetite with a glass of port and some unusual little snacks, you will be guided into a pleasant dining room that wraps its way around a garden. As its menu indicates, the Casa da Comida is eager to introduce guests to its culinary "works of art". *Piballes* (young eels),

shrimp cocktail with kiwis and Portuguese-style *escargots* are just a few of the appetizers available. You can also share the excellent *Mariscada Casa da Comida* (seafood soup with shrimp and rock lobster). The main dishes are attractively presented and served in copious portions. You can opt for meat, seafood (rock lobster *gratinée* with champagne), or one of a good selection of fish dishes. During pheasant season, make sure to try the pheasant *Convento de Alcântara*, served with a fairly sweet port sauce and chicken-liver pâté on warm toast. What a treat! The excellent desserts are very much in the Portuguese tradition, and thus egg-based. Opulent surroundings and impeccable service make for an extremely pleasant evening. Reservations recommended.

Tour F: Marquês De Pombal, Saldanha and North Lisbon

Mercado Original
$
Mon to Fri 9am to 6:30pm
Rua Joaquim António Aguiar no. 62
☎213 85 23 53
After visiting Parque Eduardo VII, drop by Mercado Original for refreshing salads, the house specialty, served in an agreeable spring-like atmosphere. There are various sandwiches

on the menu for be-
tween 400 and
500 ESC.

Cafés and Tearooms

 Pastelaria Versailles
*every day 7:30am to
10pm; tables reserved for
meals between noon and
3pm during the week*
Avenida da República no. 15A,
at the Saldanha subway exit
☎*213 55 53 44*
Steps away from the
Saldanha subway sta-
tion, the Pastelaria Ver-
sailles offers excellent
pastries in an attractive,
turn-of-the-century
decor, which, unfortu-
nately, is a bit spoiled
by the orange table-
cloths and cold neon
lighting under crystal
chandeliers. Try a
bagaço, a *bolo de chila*
or a *toucinho do céu*. At
lunchtime they serve
some interesting items
in their daily specials
such as prawn salad
and cream of garlic. A
distinguished clientele
dines amid *trompe-l'oeil*
porphyry columns un-
der a stucco ceiling.

Tour G: Restauradores and Liberdade

Restaurante Arameiro
$
closed Sat and Sun
Travessa de Santo Antão
nos. 19-21
A little restaurant lo-
cated on a little street,
the Restaurante
Arameiro serves a wide
assortment of light
dishes (salads, soups,

etc.). The perfect place
for a snack. A
2,200 ESC full menu is
also available.

Os Tibetanos
$
*Mon to Fri noon to 2pm
and 7:30pm to 9:30pm*
Rua do Salitre no. 117
☎*213 14 20 38*
Os Tibetanos, a Tibetan
vegetarian restaurant
with a very creative
menu, is a must for
health-food enthusiasts.
Dine in the pleasant
garden or in the pretty
dining room decorated
with various Tibetan
objects. Try the deli-
cious crepes stuffed
with cabbage, carrots
and tofu, the amazing
ginger cauliflower, or
the curry seitan with
aromatic basmati rice.
Although excellent
wines are available for
traditionalists, why not
discover the unusual
flavour of Tibetan *chá*,
a type of tea with a
milky, slightly salty
taste. For the grand
finale, try the heavenly
chocolate pie, the light
cheesecake or a re-
freshing cup of man-
goes and cream. For
further exploration of
Tibetan culture, there's
a small bookstore in
the entrance to the
restaurant and a Bud-
dhist teaching centre
on the second floor.

Casa do Alentejo
$$
closed Mon
Rua das Portas de Santo Antão
no. 58
☎*213 46 92 31*
The Casa do Alentejo, a
private club, is a sump-
tuous residence with a

Moorish-style decor
(see p 107); part of it is
open to the public. If
you walk up the majes-
tic staircase to the sec-
ond floor, you will find
a pleasant restaurant set
up in a large room
decorated with lovely
azulejos. You can dine
with club members on
the daily special or on
one of an assortment of
traditional Portuguese
dishes. Simple, nourish-
ing food.

Grill 20
$$
Rua da Palma no. 208B
☎*218 888 49 88*
☎*218 88 01 41*
Despite its location in
an unappealing neigh-
bourhood, the Grill 20
restaurant deserves a
visit for its delicious
veal steaks and copious
fondues. Indeed, meat
is highlighted here as
the house specialty.
Excellent dishes are
served on a small ter-
race, away from the
noise of Rua da Palma,
and in a lovely dining
room, where modern
woodwork and matte
chrome elements com-
bine to create attractive
results.

Restaurante Solmar
$$
Rua das Portas de Santo Antão
nos. 106-108
☎*213 42 33 71*
☎*213 46 00 10*
The Restaurante Solmar
specializes in fish and
seafood. This place will
appeal especially to
visitors with a taste for
the 1950s. The decor,
which looks a bit like a
stage set, is worth see-
ing: a large glassed-in

room where a giant grouping of *azulejos* is displayed like a movie screen, a high ceiling supported by massive columns and a mezzanine with curvy lines. Somewhat touristy.

Sancho
$$$
Mon to Sat
Travessa da Glória nos. 8-16
☎*213 46 97 80*
For an intimate evening or a business luncheon, Sancho is a sure bet. Dark woodwork, pewter dishes on the walls, an imposing fireplace with *talha dourada* candlesticks on its mantle, and heavy velvet curtains covering multipaned windows are all evocative of an old-time inn. The only drawback is the annoying neon lighting behind some of the windows. In this rather sombre decor the great classics of Portuguese cuisine are served in a formal manner, much to the satisfaction of a bourgeois clientele.

Gambrinus
$$$$$
every day until 2am
Rua das Portas de Santo Antão no. 25
☎*213 42 14 66*
Portuguese cuisine with top billing going to fish and seafood. Highly reputed for its excellent wine list, it is expensive, but a favourite with gourmets. A classic.

Cafés and Tearooms

Os Tibetanos
$
Mon to Sat noon to 2:30pm and 7:30pm to 10pm
Rua do Salitre no. 117
☎*213 14 20 38*
Health food enthusiasts will not want to miss the Os Tibetanos restaurant-tearoom. Light cheesecake and heavenly chocolate pie are some of the sheer delights served in the pretty dining room decorated with various Tibetan objects and in the pleasant garden. Of course classic *bica* is on the menu, as well as aromatic teas and coffees. If you're feeling adventurous, come back and try the restaurant's savoury vegetarian dishes (see p 144). There is a small bookstore at the entrance and, for your spiritual nourishment, a Buddhist teaching centre upstairs.

Pastelaria Snack-Bar Veneza
$
every day 7:30 am to 10pm
Avenida da Liberdade no. 63
At Pastelaria Snack-Bar Veneza, on long Avenida da Liberdade, enticing pastries await in a large, attractively decorated dining room. Daily specials (*around 700 ESC*) and a tourist menu (*1,500 ESC*) are offered. Agreeable and unpretentious.

Café Snack-Bar Pastelaria Zante
$
Rua da Palma no. 265
Coffees, pastries, salads, hamburgers and even omelettes can be found on the menu of the Café Snack-Bar Pastelaria Zante, all at very reasonable prices. The only interesting thing in terms of the building's decor is the Art Deco facade.

Tour H: Santa Catarina and Cais Do Sodré

Ideal de São Bento
$
Rua dos Poiais de São Bento no. 108
☎*213 95 77 51*
For a Cape Verdean meal accompanied by island music, the small Ideal de São Bento restaurant-café is a pleasant spot. You must be attentive, however, because there is neither a menu outside nor a sign indicating the establishment. It is much frequented by the Cape Verdean community and, from time to time, musicians play informally. The daily special costs between 700 to 900 ESC.

California Dream
$$
Tue to Fri noon to 11pm, Sun 7pm to 11pm
Cais do Sodré no. 42
☎*213 46 79 54*
☎*213 46 52 27*
The Santa Fé-style California Dream restaurant-bar is sure to

Lisbon

please those looking for an atmosphere that is both relaxed and refined. Under big ceiling fans, they offer California-style food, accompanied by jazz music. There is a nightclub in the basement of the building if you want to stretch out a weekend evening.

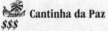

Cantinha da Paz
$$$
Tue to Thu 8pm to 11pm, Fri to Sun 7pm to midnight with live music
Rua do Poço dos Negros no. 64
Do you feel an intense *saudade* for the islands? Don't miss weekends at the Cantinha da Paz restaurant, where various singers improvise languorous Cape Verde melodies in the style of Cesaria Evora. Cape Verde cuisine is a pleasure to discover. *Feijoada de pedra*, with sweet potatoes, *bife de atum com cebol*a or *caril de gamas* – everything is delicious. For dessert, ask for the *bedinca*, a rich coconut pudding with cinnamon. Ah, what a lovely trip to the islands of "the barefoot diva"!

Cais da Ribeira
$$$$
Wed to Fri noon to 3pm and 7pm to 10:30pm, Tue and Sat 7pm to 10:30pm
Cais do Sodré, behind the train station for Cascais
☎*213 42 36 11*
☎*213 42 37 40*
The Cais da Ribeira, not to be confused with its next-door neighbour (the Cais do Sodré restaurant), deserves mention for its generous

fish dishes and its romantic view of the Tagus. Here, shrimp from Mozambique, oysters, salmon and, of course, *bacalhau* will entice seafood lovers, while wild boar with clams, calf liver with bacon and *tournedos* with raisins are other interesting choices. Tourist menu for 4,500 ESC. For a fascinating view, choose the upstairs dining room, decorated with exposed ceiling beams.

Tour I: Estrêla and Lapa

Gringo's Café
$
every day until 1am
Avenida 24 de Julho no. 116
☎*213 96 09 11*
Corona beer and *chili con carne* in a friendly, U.S.-southwest setting. Mainly for fans of Tex-Mex cuisine. Young clientele.

Pastelaria Apolo XI
$
open until 7pm; closed Sun
at the corner of Rua de Santos-o-Velho and Rua das Janelas Verdes
The pink and green Pastelaria Apolo XI serves excellent daily specials at unbeatable prices. You can have *bifinho* (a small filet of pork) with rice and salad for 500 ESC – 800 ESC if you have a beer, coffee and dessert as well. What a bargain! Friendly service and a neighbourhood atmosphere. The best place

in the area for a quick bite to eat.

Picanha
$$
Mon to Sat until 1am, closed Sun
Rua das Janelas Verdes no. 96
☎*213 97 54 01*
The Picanha, located opposite the Museu de Arte Antigua, serves one-dish meals made up of *picanha* (marinated, grilled meat) with mango sauce, *farofa* or *chimichurr*i, plus potatoes, rice, salad and beans. There is enough food to satisfy even the heartiest of appetites. If your stomach is a bottomless pit, however, you can top off your meal with a piece of cheesecake or apple pie for dessert. A pretty stone portal leads into the dining room, which is decorated with *azulejos*.

Restaurante Assóporco
$$
Mon to Sat until midnight
Rua das Janelas Verdes no. 102
☎*213 95 18 00*
If you like ribs, the Restaurante Assóporco is a must. This is an inviting place with a contemporary decor, where you can eat an unlimited quantity of ribs (the only item on the menu), along with a variety of sauces and a salad. If meat does not tempt you, you can create a vegetarian meal by combining some of the tasty appetizers. Simple, but positively delicious. For dessert, there's cheesecake and *tiramisú*. The clientele is young and

the staff friendly and enthusiastic.

Restaurante Flor da Estrêla
$$

Rua João de Deus no. 60
☎*213 96 98 69*
Located alongside the Basilica da Estrêla, the Restaurante Flor da Estrêla serves home-style Portuguese cuisine. Pleasant dining room decorated with *azulejos*. Very popular with Lisboans.

Casa México
$$$

Tue to Sun 12:30pm to 3pm and 8pm to 11:30pm
Avenida Dom Carlos I no. 140, small and poorly indicated entrance, to the right of Café Republica
☎*213 96 55 00*
In the basement of this building, located on the major artery Avenida Dom Carlos, inundated with bright colours, Casa México will make your palate zing with its spicy dishes. After a giant *margarita*, don't hesitate to tackle the excellent *fajitas*, as only Mexicans know how to make! Colonial decor, ceiling fan, colourful furniture, tropical music and staff dressed in Mexican fashion – every aspect of this place is reminiscent of the warmth of that faraway country, but... are we really still in Lisbon? The prices and excessively fast service remind us that indeed we are!

🌴 Frei Contente
$$$

Mon to Fri noon to 3pm and 7pm to 10:30pm, Sat 3pm to 10:30pm
Rua de São Marçal no. 94
☎*213 47 59 22*
French cuisine is always a pleasure, and the affable head waiter at the restaurant can be proud to be one of its worthy representatives. Agen prune rabbit, champagne duck and Alsatian sauerkraut are only a few samples from the menu. There are two or three traditional Portuguese dishes offered and some exotic creations, such as shrimp curry. The rustic decor is complemented by pretty, summery 50s-style dishware. A particularly likeable place!

Siesta Brava
$$$

Tue to Sun 12:30pm to 1am
Rua Manuel Bernardos no. 5A
☎*213 96 11 68*
At Siesta Brava, Spanish-Portuguese collaboration produces wonderful results. *Cabrito e leitão assado* and pork kebabs go well with *gaspacho andaluza, paella valenciana* and *tortilla*. Portuguese or Spanish cuisine? It's up to you to choose! Classic cooking in a very plain environment.

🌴 Xêlê Bananas
$$$

closed Sat for lunch and all day Sun
Praça das Flores no. 29, ring bell to enter
☎*213 95 25 14*
☎*213 95 25 15*
There are several good restaurants around Praça das Flores, a quiet square shaded by trees and located just a short distance from the busy Bairro Alto. One of these is Xêlê Bananas, just the place for visitors looking for a change from the usual *bacalhau*. This place strives to be innovative, an effort that is to be applauded here in Portugal, where tradition can become tiring. The menu lists original dishes made up of a tasty blend of fruit, meat and fish and served in generous portions. The chef seems to be particularly fond of sauces, some of which are a bit too sweet. Guests dine in a slightly kitschy tropical setting featuring banana trees and walls painted to look like the jungle. Friendly staff and cosmopolitan clientele. A good place to keep in mind.

Xico's Bar Restaurante
$$$

Mon to Fri until 1am, closed Sat for lunch and all day Sun
Calçada da Estrêla no. 3
Xico's Bar Restaurante, located opposite the Palácio da Assembleia Nacional, has an inviting Santa Fe-style decor and serves delicious dishes like fettucine

Lisbon

with shrimp sauce. Very popular with the political set.

Restaurante Conventual
$$$$
closed Sat lunch and Sun
Praça das Flores no. 45
☎213 90 92 46
Being close to parliament, the Restaurante Conventual is regularly frequented by Portuguese politicians. This refined setting, whose decor is mainly comprised of wood sculptures from an ancient convent and religious objects, is the site of one of the most renowned restaurants in Portugal. Don't expect revolutionary cuisine here; they serve the Portuguese classics, elaborately prepared, such as *pato com champagne e pimenta rosa*. In this temple of gastronomy, only the limited choice of the tourist menu is a disappointment: the ubiquitous *bacalhau a bras* or *carne de porco alentejana* for no less than 5,000 ESC! Reservations recommended.

Restaurante Embaixada
$$$$$
every day
Rua do Pau da Bandeira no. 4
☎213 95 00 05
☎213 95 00 06
Restaurante Embaixada, in the prestigious Hotel da Lapa (see p 133), will appeal to visitors seeking a sophisticated ambiance, as well as those looking for good international cuisine. The buffet-style brunch is particularly worthwhile as it enables you

to sample a variety of dishes for a reasonable sum. Good assortment of desserts.

Restaurante York House
$$$$
every day
Rua das Janelas Verdes no. 32
☎213 96 25 44
☎213 96 24 35
High-quality, traditional cuisine served in sophisticated surroundings. The menu lists vegetarian fettucine, duck cutlet pan-fried with grapes, roast chicken with rosemary, pig's feet with coriander sauce, etc. Simply reading it will make your mouth water. When the weather is fine, you can enjoy your meal on the hotel patio (see p 132). Expensive, but what a setting! Reservations recommended.

Restaurante Zutzu
$$$$
closed Sat for lunch and all day Sun
Rua Nova da Peidade no. 99
☎213 97 94 46
The Restaurante Zutzu serves *nouvelle cuisine* – fish carpaccio with colourful lettuce, game with coriander and lamb with mustard, to name just a few of the dishes on the menu. The main dining room, shaped like a half-moon, makes for an unusual setting. The greyish hues are a bit cold, but give the place a contemporary feel. A good place to keep in mind.

Umpuntocinco
$$$$
Mon to Fri 12:30pm to 3pm and 7:30pm to 10:30pm
Rua Marcos Portugal no. 5
For the perfect intimate evening, Umpuntocinco offers tables illuminated by candlelight, comfortable cushioned chairs, subdued lighting and warm woodwork decor, all of it two steps away from lovely Praça das Flores. A very fine trout stuffed with shrimp and ham and an excellent chicken with Roquefort sauce are two specialties. Ideal for an elegant evening.

Tour J: Alcântara, Santo Amaro and Belém

Rua Vieira Portuense, near the Mosteiro dos Jerónimos, has become extremely popular with tourists. It is crowded with all kinds of restaurants and bistros, and although none of these places are particularly noteworthy, you won't have any trouble finding somewhere to eat.

Pão Pão Queijo Queijo
$
every day 7am to 11pm
Rua de Belém no. 124-126
The Pão Pão Queijo Queijo, located right near Mosteiro dos Jerónimos, is a good place to get an inexpensive meal. The menu is primarily comprised of sandwiches for 400 ESC (including vegetarian), pita *shoarma* and salads (unfortunately served in

plastic containers with plastic utensils!). Whether on the terrace or inside, be patient since this is a popular place with tourists and is always crowded. Simple, unpretentious and economical!

Doca do Santo
$$

Tue to Sun noon to 3am
Doca de Santo Amaro
☎*213 93 04 91*
Established right on the Santo Amaro wharf, next to old warehouses now serving as discotheques, restaurants and night clubs, the Doca do Santo restaurant features a large terrace dappled with parasols. While heavy ropes are a pleasant reminder of life on the sea, the presence of palm trees contrasts unpleasantly with the environment. Inside there is a large, glass-enclosed dining room with an elegant metal V-shaped counter. The menu mainly consists of quiches, salads, sandwiches and *petiscos* served until the wee hours of the morning.

Restaurante Xi Hu
$$

every day 10am to 10:30pm
Rua de Belém nos. 95-99
☎*213 62 33 22*
For a nice change, the Restaurante Xi Hu serves most classic Chinese dishes in a setting that is... Chinese, of course! An excellent, very friendly spot. Tourist menu for 1,800 ESC.

A Commenda
$$$$

Mon to Sat 12:30pm to 3pm and 7:30pm to 10:30pm, Sun 11am to 3:30pm
in the Centro Cultural de Belém, Praça do Império
For those most interested in designer decor, the A Commenda restaurant is perfect. It is located in the brand-new Centro Cultural de Belém, a veritable labyrinth built with the support of the European Economic Community. Despite the acceptable quality of the food and service that aspires to sophistication, there is a total lack of originality and creativity in the choice of dishes. Brunch every Sunday. Mostly a place to see and be seen.

Alcântara Café
$$$$$

every day 8pm to 1am
Rua Maria Luísa Holstein no. 15, formerly Rua Primeira Particular
☎*213 63 71 76*
Already a veritable institution in Lisbon, the Alcântara Café is a must for visitors seeking out Lisbon's trendiest spots. It's a restaurant, bar, discotheque and art gallery, all in one giant space which Antonio Pinto has transformed into a temple of contemporary design. After spending many years in Belgium, where he designed two beautiful restaurants, La Quincaillerie (Brussels) and the Parkus (Ghent), Pinto returned to his native country and made the most of

this old building, which was once a printing-house and a garage. The decor? Well, in the main room, you'll find immense painted steel beams (although partly false, you can't tell), cleverly decorated columns, hanging fans to emphasize the height of the place, and to top it all off, a copy of the *Winged Victory of Samothrace* perched in the centre of a metal bar. At the back of the room, right beside a metal footbridge leading to the discotheque, is a boudoir lit with crystal chandeliers and decorated with red velvet furniture, forming a striking but attractive contrast with the rest of the decor. The cuisine is original, too, although somewhat expensive. This is actually one of the rare places in Lisbon that serves steak *tartare*. This place is an absolute must if you're looking to see and be seen!

Cafés and Tearooms

🌴 Antiga Confeitaria de Belém
every day until 11pm
Rua de Belém nos. 84-88
☎*213 63 74 23*
During your visit to the Mosteiro dos Jerónimos, make sure to stop in at the Antiga Confeitaria de Belém, the best-known pastry shop in the area. This worthy establishment was founded in 1837. The entrance hall is

furnished with nothing but a large counter and glass-doored cabinets, which completely cover the walls and are filled with old bottles of port. The only decoration is some stucco on the ceiling. The whole place is cream-coloured, and has taken on a patina with time (and with the help of cigarette smoke). It definitely has a certain charm about it. Next, there is a series of little rooms decorated with – you guessed it – *azulejos*, and filled with a motley crowd of students, neighbourhood residents and tourists awaiting their turn to sample the famous *Pastel de Belém*, a type of flan sprinkled with your choice of cinnamon or powdered sugar. A specialty of Belém, the *pastel* is supposedly served nowhere else in Lisbon. Whether that's true or not, these particular *pastels* are well worth the trip, and the house *bica* tops off this small indulgence splendidly. Sandwiches are also sold.

Cafetaria do Museu da Marinha
Tue to Sun 10am to 5pm
Praça do Império
As its name indicates, the Cafetaria do Museu da Marinha is the marine museum's cafeteria. What makes this place interesting is not so much its menu, which is fairly limited (*a few sandwiches at 400 ESC, beer for 200 ESC or coffee*), but its terrace,

which is very pleasant for lounging and admiring the marvellous west entrance of Mosteiro dos Jerónimos (see p 116).

Entertainment

This chapter presents an overview of the variety of nocturnal experiences that is available in Lisbon. For more information on shows and concerts see the section entitled "Cultural Activities", on p 157.

Tour B: The Castelo and the Alfama

Fado

Taverna d'El Red
$$$
open until 3:30am
Largo de Chafariz de Dentro no. 14/5, at the corner of Rua São Pedro
☎218 87 67 54
At the Taverna d'El Red, you can dine on traditional Portuguese dishes while listening to authentic *fado*.

Clube de Fado
$$$$
Rua São João de Praça nos. 92-94
☎218 85 27 04
Expensive and touristy certainly, but an evening spent listening to *fado* while comfortably seated at a table laden with Portuguese dishes is worth at least as much as an evening

spent at a nightclub with its pricey cover charge and exorbitantly priced drinks.

Bars and Nightclubs

Pé Sujo
Tue to Sun 10pm to 2am
Largo de São Martinho nos. 6-7
Nostalgic for Brazil? Gather round the bar at the small unpretentious Pé Sujo, where you can enjoy *musica ao vivo brasileira* every weekend.

Tour D: The Chiado and the Bairro Alto

Fado

Restaurante O Forcado
$$$$
Thu to Tue until 3:30am, closed Wed
Rua da Rosa no. 219
☎213 46 85 79
The Restaurante O Forcado serves up Portuguese cuisine and *fado* until the wee hours of the morning.

Adega do Ribatejo
every day 7pm to midnight
Rua do Diário de Notícias no. 230
Though the decor and horrible neon lighting are particularly uninspired here, visitors can nonetheless enjoy authentic *fado* in a lively ambiance.

Bars and Nightclubs

Fremitus
every day 8pm to 2am
Rua da Atalaia no. 78
Fremitus bar is just the place for fans of techno music who want to be able to hear themselves talk. The stunning decor features a giant propeller incorporated into the bar, large valves on the walls, imposing metal beams and amusing bar stools mounted on springs (those prone to seasickness or who've had one too many should abstain from using these!); this bar will give you something to write home about. Not to mention, the young and "well-behaved" clientele that seems somewhat out of place in this modern and industrial setting. Relaxed ambiance and reasonable prices.

Portas Largas
Rua da Atalaia nos. 101-105
As its Portuguese name suggests, the Portas Largas is distinguished by its large doors, making it hard to miss despite the fact that it lacks a sign. Located just opposite the very popular Frágil nightclub (see p 152), this establishment is the ideal early evening meeting place. A mixed gay and straight crowd flocks here, and on weekends, the throng of people is so great that revellers spill out onto the sidewalk. The decor is simple and cozy, with small, plain wooden tables and a few benches scattered throughout. This delightful place is a must for those who wish to discover the Lisbon of Lisboans.

Café Suave
every day 9:30pm to 2am
Rua do Diário de Notícias no. 6
With its modern and colourful decor harmoniously contrasting with the antiquity of the building, Café Suave is a particularly delightful place in which to quench your thirst and share your latest secrets, to the sounds of modern hits.

Cafediário
every day 9pm to 2am
Rua do Diário do Notícias no. 3
The Cafediário is another great spot for an evening of chatting among friends. Latin-American tunes, jazz and Brazilian songs from the 1950s set the mood. The excellent tropical cocktails here will certainly help loosen your tongue...

Café Targus
every day 9pm to 2am
Rua do Diário de Notícias no. 40
After having walked the old streets of the Bairro Alto, you might be surprised to come upon the very modern Café Targus. In a refined decor where the accent is on designer furniture, you can take a load off in one of the lovely (but uncomfortable!) chairs while sipping your choice of the many cocktails offered here. A gilded youth frequents the place, so expect to pay dearly for libations (*beer at 500 ESC, spirits at 1,400 ESC*).

Páginas Tantas
every day 9pm to 2pm
Rua do Diário de Notícias no. 85
Páginas Tantas is another good place to start off an evening to the sounds of retro music. Lengthy "happy hours", lasting from 9pm to midnight, and a refined and relaxed ambiance are particularly appreciated on this bar-lined street.

Café Webs
Rua de Diário de Notícias no. 126
In need of a little escape? Internet surfers, head to Café Webs, where you can "surf" all around the world while sipping a *bica*.

Pedro Quinto Bar-Restaurant
Mon to Sat noon to 3am
Rua Pedro V no. 14
If you like pub-style bars, you can have a drink or a light meal (*menu starting at 2,800 ESC*) at the Pedro Quinto Bar-Restaurant, which is warmly decorated with wine-red wallpaper and softly lit woodwork.

Solar do Vinho do Porto
Mon to Fri 10am to 11:45pm, Sat 11am to 10:45pm
Rua de S. Pedro de Alcântara no. 45, entrance to the right once you pass through the portal
Located inside a former private home with a somewhat dated setting, the Solar do Vinho

Lisbon

do Porto is a port-tasting salon financed and run by the Instituto do Vinho do Porto. Its purpose is to serve as a showcase for the country's port wines, of which it has an impressive selection. The quiet atmosphere is a haven in this busy neighbourhood. Unfortunately, however, there is no one to offer advice or information about the products, and the service is slow and even discourteous at times. Furthermore, although the list of ports is exhaustive, it would seem that some of the wines, especially the moderately priced ones, are not always available.

Pavilhão Chines
Mon to Sat 2pm to 2am, Sat 6pm to 2am, Sun 9pm to 2am
Rua Dom Pedro V nos. 89-91
What could be more pleasant than sipping a drink in an antique-shop setting? That's what you can do at the Pavilhão Chines, where glass-doored cabinets full of lead figurines and oriental vases serve as a reminder that the place was once a general store. There is a series of rooms, one of which has a billiard table. The illustrated drink list includes a wide assortment of whiskies and cocktails, though the prices are rather high. The entrance, with its 1920s decor, is perhaps the most interesting room, but it has unfortunately been marred by an

unattractive video system. A more varied selection of music would be an improvement as well.

Frágil
Mon to Sat 10:30pm to 3:30am
Rua da Atalaia nos. 126-128
The name Mantel Reis automatically conjures up images of the Bairro Alto for Lisboans. He is now unanimously considered to have ushered in the Portuguese movida that became all the rage in this area. About 10 years ago, he opened the truly avant-garde discotheque Frágil in what was then a quiet area, thus transforming the local nightlife. Since that time, the Bairro Alto has become a mecca for night-time fun-seekers, who still flock to the Frágil. After battling your way inside (arrive early; the doormen can be very selective), you'll find yourself surrounded by a motley crowd (the very young, the very fashionable, gays, etc.). The decor is modified regularly by local artists. The only constant is the big gilded mirror, in which Narcissus himself would never tire of watching himself dance. Guaranteed atmosphere and trendy music.

Bar-Restaurante Bachus
Mon to Fri noon to 2am, Sat 6pm to 2am
Largo da Trindade no. 9
☎213 42 28 28
☎213 42 12 60
A lovely bar surrounded by woodwork

and cabinets full of old bottles, make for a cozy atmosphere. Popular with politicians and artists. People also come here for drinks before heading upstairs to eat (see p 141).

Bar Pintáí
Tue to Sun 10pm to 3:30am
Largo Trindade de Coelho nos. 22-23
Bar Pintáí is a large, lovely and well-lit bar popular with Lisbon's gilded youth. Live music (usually Brazilian) from 11:30am on, and exotic cocktails like *doce de mais* and *caipirinha*.

Gay Bars and Nightclubs

Bar 106
every day 9pm to 2am
Rua de São Marçal no. 106, ring bell to enter
Bar 106 is one of the most popular places for gay Portuguese men to get together. It attracts a fashionable clientele and gets packed on weekends once midnight strikes. The "happy hour", from 9pm to 11:30pm, is a pleasant way to start off an evening.

Bricabar
every day 10pm to 4am
Rua Cecilio de Sousa no. 82
ring bell to enter
The Bricabar is a two-level gay bar decorated with a certain degree of elegance: royal blue curtains, contemporary furnishings, strategic lighting. Although popular with Lisbon's young and beautiful

people, this big place seems to have a hard time filling up. The music is not only original and interesting, but also not too loud, which is a plus.

Tattoo
Mon to Sat 8pm to 2am
Rua de São Marçal no. 15, ring bell to enter
Tattoo appeals to those who prefer a more mature clientele.

Trumps
1,000 ESC cover charge, one drink included
Tue to Sun 11pm to 4am
Rua da Imprensa Nacional no. 104-B
Trumps is a large gay discotheque that is also popular with straights. This place is frequented above all by serious clubbers, especially as the night wears on. Friendly ambiance, with some extravagant behaviour here and there, like the Sunday and Wednesday night shows at 2:30am.

Agua no Bico
every day 9pm to 2am
Rua de São Marçal no. 170, ring bell to enter
Set up on the ground floor of a handsome building, the small Agua no Bico, with brightly coloured walls, is a very pleasant place where you can meet your soul mate or simply have a drink at the large marbled bar. Unfortunately, like many other establishments, this one is equipped with a giant screen, monopolizing clients' attention and thus impeding conversation.

Finalmente
every day 11pm to 6am
Rua da Palmeira no. 38, ring bell to enter
On the outskirts of Bairro Alto, the nightclub Finalmente welcomes a gay and lesbian clientele in a simple room with kitschy decor and a small stage. Every night at 2:30am, there is a transvestite show, a performance that is faithfully attended by a large, enthusiastic audience. Not to be missed!

Satyros
every day 10pm to 6am
Calçada da Patriarcal nos. 6-8 corner Rua da Alegria, ring to enter
Located a few steps from the pretty park in the Praça do Príncipe Real, Satyros is a small gathering place for gay men, young and old. The decor is a bit on the kitschy side and the music is an enjoyable mix of French, Brazilian, English, American and even Spanish. Drag queens perfrom on weekends (*Fri and Sat as of 2:30am*). This is a simple and unpretentious spot worth remembering.

Memorial
cover charge
Tue to Sat 10pm to 3:30am, Sun 4:30pm to 8:30pm
Rua Gustavo de Matos Sequeira no. 42, ring bell to enter
Set in the basement of a small building, the Memorial caters mainly to a lesbian clientele. In a vaulted cave decor, a young clientele (20-35 years old) lets loose to the beat of an assortment of music: Brazilian sounds, Portuguese disco and dance beats.

Tour E: The Rato and Amoreiras

Bars and Nightclubs

Enclave
cover charge
Wed to Sun 11pm to 4am
Rua do Sol ao Rato no. 71-A
Located in the basement of a Cape Verde restaurant, the Enclave restaurant plays African music, notably from Cape Verde. In a decor bordering on kitsch, a variety of musicians appear while "a most respectable" audience dances with abandon to these frenetic rhythms. Proper dress required.

Lisbon

Tour G: Restauradores and Liberdade

Bars and Nightclubs

Hot Clube de Portugal
cover charge
Tue to Sat 10pm to 2am
Praça da Alegria no. 39
☎*213 46 73 69*
*www.isa.utl.pt/HCP/informat
ions.html*
Jazz-o-philes should head to the Hot Clube de Portugal. Various concerts are staged Thursday to Saturday, from 11pm to 12:30am in a small room with Spartan decor, located in the basement of an office building. Jam sessions are organized on Tuesday and Wednesday nights, with no cover charge.

Tour H: Santa Catarina and Cais Do Sodré

Bars and Nightclubs

Ó Gilín's Irish Pub
every day 11am to 2am
Rua dos Remolares nos. 8-10
You guessed it, this is the place where Lisbon's English-speaking, beer-guzzling crowd gathers. On weekends, you can listen to *música ao vivo* in a particularly boisterous ambiance, for the beer flows like water here. The establishment serves various Irish specialties and gets particularly

crowded on weekends, so be sure to get here early if you want a table. An Irish brunch is also offered on Sundays as of 11am. Friendly and unpretentious.

WIP
Wed to Sun 2pm to 2am
Rua da Bica de Duarte Belo nos. 47-49
On the very street where the delightful elevador da bica runs, you will find WIP (Work In Progress), a most original concept. Indeed, here is an establishment that is at once a bar, a hair salon and clothing boutique, no less! In a "futuristic" decor, you can quench your thirst while getting your hair done or picking up a new outfit. Friendly and unpretentious.

Tour I: Estrêla and Lapa

Fado

Senhor Vinho
Mon to Sat 8:30pm to 3:30am
Rua do Meio in Lapa no. 18
☎*213 97 26 81*
The owner of the Senhor Vinho restaurant sings *fado* in the purest Portuguese tradition. Somewhat expensive, but unforgettable. Reservations recommended.

Bars and Nightclubs

Café Santos
every day 9:30pm to 2am
Rua de Santos-o-Velho nos. 2-4
Café Santos is a very pleasant place in which to start off the evening. On weekends, between 10pm and midnight, a young clientele meets up here for the first drink of the night. Spilling out onto the sidewalk, patrons, with drinks in hand, engage in animated discussions. Functional Scandinavian designer furniture, marble floors and small candle-lit tables make up the greater part of the decor.

Foxtrot
every day 6pm to 2am
Travessa de Santa Teresa 28
☎*213 95 26 97*
The Foxtrot, with its indoor terrace and sumptuous decor, is a delightful place to start off or wind down an evening out. The place has several rooms, one of which contains a variety of games, including pinball, snooker, etc. You can eat here as well.

Pérola
Tue to Sun 10pm to 2am
Calçada Ribeiro Santos no. 25
Another good rendezvous to kick off your evening (starting at 10pm here) is the Pérola, with a great location, close to two renowned discos, the Kremlin and the Plateau. Before hitting the livelier nightclubs, a young crowd gathers here amidst the kitsch.

A small back room, decorated with comic strips and a few tables, welcomes those craving a little sustenance. Various *petiscos* as well as a daily special are offered as early as 10pm, that is if the cook shows up on time (which is not always a given here, it seems!).

Até Qu'Enfim
every day 10pm to 2am
Rua des Janelas Verdes no. 8
Até Qu'Enfim bar is the place for *música ao vivo* on weekends. Quench your thirst as you relax on a sofa or at the bar, while listening to somewhat retro rock music.

A Lontra
cover charge 2,000 ESC including 4 drinks
every day 11pm to 4am
Rua de São Bento no. 157
You can dance the night away to African rhythms at A Lontra, one of the best-known African discos in Lisbon. A chic and well-off clientele frequents the place; showing up in "proper" attire – preferably with a well-padded wallet – is therefore a must.

A Última Ceia
Tue to Sun 8:30pm to 4am
Avenida 24 de Julho no. 96
Whether you're starting off or winding down your evening, stop in at A Última Ceia, a lovely place nestled at the far end of a verdant courtyard. On the ground floor, you can sample all sorts of cocktails (clearly an activity very much in fashion in

Lisbon); simple snacks (*pesticos* or salad for 600 ESC) are served on the second floor. This is a cosy place, although the music is a bit loud. Friendly staff.

Café Central
every day 10pm to 4am
Avenida 24 de Julho nos. 110-112
If you're looking to party until the wee hours of the morning, head to the Café Central, where you can warm up with a cocktail (large selection, but relatively high prices), then head next door to **Metalúrgica**, a discotheque. Both the bar and the disco have been beautifully decorated by architect Mantel Graça Dias, who designed the Portuguese pavilion for the World Fair in Seville. Student clientele.

Kapital
every day 10:30pm to 4am, Fri and Sat until 6am
Avenida 24 de Julho no. 68
Spread out over two floors, this large disco attracts a crowd of rock and techno fans. The decor is cold and sterile; upstairs patrons enjoy drinks at the bar, while on the ground floor, a young and wild crowd lets it all out to unbelievably loud music. Expect selective admission and a particularly expensive evening – all drinks cost 1,000 ESC (and they do not accept credit cards!). A place for those who like being at "the place to be."

Kremlin
Tue to Thu midnight to 6am, Fri and Sat midnight to 8am
Escadinhas da Praia no. 5
Along with the Alcântara Mar, the Kremlin was one of the first nightclubs in the capital to remain open into the wee hours of the morning. Large arches make up the bulk of the basement decor of this place, where you can groove to techno, dance and house music, provided of course you made it past the severely guarded entrance – this is the Kremlin after all!

Le Plateau
Tue to Sat midnight to 6am
Escadinhas da Praia no. 7
Le Plateau is definitely one of the most fashionable discotheques in the capital. Once again, it is worth coming here just to see the decor, which features columns shaped like upside-down cones and adorned with burning candles, mirrors, gilding and candelabra. Lisbon's decorators seem to draw a lot of inspiration from the splendour of the baroque era. A large map of the Old World makes the place seem even more like a lounge. The well-off clientele includes middle-aged business people and young cruisers: appropriate dress recommended! Varied music on the weekend and rock on Thursdays.

Lisbon

Tour J: Alcântara, Santo Amaro and Belém

Bars and Nightclubs

Alcântara

Alcântara-Mar
Wed to Sun 11:30 until you drop
Rua Maria Luísa Holstein no. 15, formerly Rua Primeira Particular
☎*213 63 71 76*
The Alcântara-Mar is part of a complex including a restaurant, a bar and an art gallery (see p 149). Oddly enough, the discotheque has three entrances, one by way of the footbridge in the Alcântara-Café (mainly for patrons of the restaurant), another on Rua Maria Luísa Holstein (for "guests" and "friends") and the last, for mere mortals, on Rua Cozinha Económica (*1,000 ESC cover charge*). As the place is very popular, and those permitted to enter are selected very quickly, you are better off arriving fairly early. The decor is surprising and imaginative. It might feature anything from crystal chandeliers to big mirrors and gilded columns. The music is mostly techno, except on Wednesdays (retro night), while the crowd is a fashionable mix of affluent, urbane, and trendy types, both gays and heterosexuals, who come here with the sole intention of letting loose until breakfast time.

Discoteca Rock Line
every day until 6am
Rua das Fontainhas no. 86
The Discoteca Rock, located in the same area, caters to a much younger and less fashionable crowd (in Portugal, you only have to be 16 to get into discotheques). As far as the music is concerned, the name says it all: rock.

The following four nightclubs (*Mon to Sat 8:30pm to 6am*) stand side by side in old warehouses at the port, just southeast of the Avenida Infante Santo viaduct, which transects Avenida Vinte Quatro de Julho in front of the Doca de Alcântara. They are all good examples of successful efforts to restore the urban heritage and allow visitors to take advantage of the romantic Tagus so close by, in the heart of downtown.

Since its very opening, **Kings and Queens** has attracted, perhaps due to its name, a young, modern clientele of all sexual orientations. Despite its large space, the candelabras, mirrors, rose windows and other elements borrowed from the Baroque give it a rich and warm atmosphere. A magnificent Art-Deco chandelier disrupts these historical references, as does the techno music, the half-naked dancers atop loudspeakers and the occasional transvestite shows. The place also boasts a terrace.

Things are much more low-key next door at the smaller **Indochina**, featuring a very lovely Asian decor of red-lacquered walls, Chinese lamps, wood panels and Buddhas, and a *bacalhau* clientele. This place is not for posers, but rather for those who just feel like having a fun time, letting loose to the exotic sounds of the Flamenco version of *All of My Love* or to a medley of Spanish hits. You can take in the scene from the mezzanine or from a table while seated on comfortable stools. For a little variety, Thursdays are "vintage music" nights, when classic, soul, jungle, salsa and hip hop follow one after the other in an almost-perfect mix.

Each bar has its own crowd, and the **Blues Café**'s is young, professional and conventional-minded. A large pub with big picture windows giving out on the Tagus, it is an attractive place with brick walls, floors and ceilings of dark wood as well as a billiard table. The clientele and decor go hand in hand with the top-40 commercial music played here, and strobe lighting pulsates throughout the bar on occasion.

Lest you forget that you are at the port, you can

take to the open sea at **Dock's Club**, with its maritime decor of bulwarks, metal, pale wood and old colonial-style ceiling fans. Upstairs, there are delightful couches with Angolan leopard patterns and Cape Verdean palm trees. Little lamps on each table shed subdued lighting, but the house music will soon bring you back to the reality of the docks!

Santo Amaro

Much like those of the Doca de Alcântara, the old warehouses of the Doca de Santo Amaro (*before the Doca de Alcântara, southeast of the Rua de Cascais viaduct which crosses Avenida da India and spans over the railway and Avenida Brasilia*) have also been the objects of clever restoration. In fact, bars, discotheques, restaurants and boutiques succeed one another along the pier and the marina. Unlike its counterpart (the Doca de Alcântara), however, the long succession of establishments here starts to get repetitive and confers a very commercial and rather artificial quality to the place. The fact of the matter is that competition is fierce here, and every bar, restaurant and nightclub seems to want to play the originality card at any cost (not always very successfully) in order to attract as many clients as possible. Moreover,

the music, playing at ear-shattering volume and spilling out of the various establishments, generates such a racket that this stretch seems more like a permanent fair than it does a strip of nightclubs. By walking the pier from west to east, you will see: the **Café da Ponte**, a bar equipped with a large terrace; the **Santo Amaro Café**, a bar-restaurant where 18 television screens make up most of the decor and where latino music is worshipped; the **Cosmos** discotheque; the very chic (and over-priced) **Tertulia do Tejo** restaurant, featuring regional Portuguese cuisine, for those who like to be seen; the **7 Mares** bar, where several screens broadcast sports programmes and where, on weekends, patrons can listen to *música ao vivo*; the **Havana** bar-restaurant-discotheque, where *salsa*, *cumbia* and *merengue* are played, and finally, housed in a building slightly set back from the pier, the **Doca de Santo** bar-restaurant (the fist bar in the area) closes out this long list. Of all the establishments mentioned above, the last is the most original by far. Huge windows and small tables line either side of this long, narrow space, while a very modern, V-shaped bar monopolizes the entire middle section. Two terraces, one of which is covered, pleasantly complement

this architecture with refined lines and an airy appearance. The only problem is those palm trees, which just don't fit.

Cultural Activities

The century's last world's fair in 1998 generated a flurry of cultural activities and art events of all kinds in the capital. Furthermore, the summer of 1999 featured the Festival dos Oceanos (Oceans Festival), which was such a success with its daily and nightly exhibitions and shows that organizers have decided to repeat the event in the summer of 2000.

Bearing in mind the great number of activities offered in the capital, we invite you to consult the various publications listed below. These will give you detailed information on current events and schedules as well as rates. Addresses and phone numbers of a few facilities and venues as well as other sources of information are also listed below.

Publications

Agenda Cultural: Cultural monthly issued by the City of Lisbon. Available free of charge at most tourist or cultural facilities (bookshops, hotels, bistros) or at the head office: Rua de São Pedro de Alcântara 3 (*www.bpv.pt/lisboa/agenda*)

Lisbon

City: Monthly Portuguese-language leisure magazine (*480 ESC*) detailing all upcoming concerts and exhibitions as well as the latest restaurants and entertainment venues in the capital and the rest of the country.

Sete: Weekly information guide to all the goings-on about town (film, theatre, opera, concerts, bars). Available at newsstands.

Diário de Notícias: This widely circulated daily paper publishes a special section every Friday entitled "Programas", detailing all cultural activities taking place in the city (*www.dn.pt*).

Público: Another national daily, in which you will find "Zap," a section published every Friday dedicated to cultural activities in Lisbon (*www.publico.pt*).

JL Jornal de Letras, Artes e Ideias: A particularly interesting newspaper devoted to art and literature (*320 ESC, published every two weeks*).

Follow Me Lisboa: Official information guide published by Turismo de Lisboa in Portuguese, English, Spanish and French. Available for free at tourist offices and many hotels. Strangely enough, though the guide is a multilingual publication, its title is in English rather than Portuguese.

Film

Most films are presented in the original language with Portuguese subtitles. A few places worth checking out are:

Cinemateca Portuguesa
Rua Barata Salgueiro no. 39
☎ *213 54 65 29*
Film museum; retrospectives, sometimes featuring English-language films.

Cinema São Jorge
Avenida da Liberdade no. 175

Cinema Tivoli
Avenida da Liberdade no. 188

Most shopping centres in the city, including those of **Amoreiras** and **Vasco da Gama**, have cinemas.

Theatres, Concerts and Shows

One hub of cultural activity in the capital is the **Coliseu dos Recreios** (*between the Travessa Santo Antão and Rua dos Condes, on the right side as you head north up the street,* ☎ *213 46 19 97*). Numerous concerts (classical and modern), operas, plays and more are presented on a regular basis in its huge hall.

For those who prefer the great classics of the theatre and opera, the **Teatro Nacional Dona Maria II** (*Praça Dom Pedro IV,* ☎ *213 42 22 10*) and the **Teatro Nacional São Carlos** (*Rua Serpa Pinto 7,* ☎ *213 46 59 14,*

217 95 02 36 or 217 93 51 31) are just the places, as long as you speak Portuguese. As for the **Grande Auditório Gulbenkian** (*Avenida de Berna no. 45,* ☎ *217 93 51 31*), its reputation is firmly established when it comes to concerts. Visitors can also take full advantage of the numerous free concerts presented in churches such as the Sé, the Igreja São Roque and others, all year round.

Finally, the latest among great cultural complexes is the **Centro Cultural de Belém** (*Praça do Império no. 1,* ☎ *213 61 24 00*), a huge, modern building, constructed thanks to the generous support of the European Economic Community. Conferences, shows, concerts and temporary exhibitions are organized here on a regular basis.

Shopping

Tour A: The Rossio and the Baixa

The Baixa has become a shopping mecca. You will find all sorts of shops within the rectangle bordered on either side of Rua Aurea (also known as Rua do Ouro) and Rua dos Fanqueiros. Of the many streets in this area, the most pleasant by far is Rua Augusta.

A pedestrian mall with fashionable boutiques (selling clothing and leather goods, for the most part), it offers a lovely view of the triumphal arch. Since the street is so popular with tourists, however, the prices are significantly higher here than elsewhere (for less expensive shopping, head to Restauradores, the Bairro Alto or the Rato).

Groceries

Celeiro Dieta (*Mon to Fri 8:30am to 8pm, Sat 8:30am to 7pm; Rua 1° Dezembro no. 65*) sells macrobiotic food and books on the subject. Not to be confused with the "classic" **Super Celeiro** (*Mon to Fri 8:30am to 8pm, Sat 9am to 6pm; corner of Rua 1° Dezembro and Calçada do Carmo*) located on the same street, which offers a wide choice of food: from pasta and assorted prepared meats to cheese and vegetables.

If you like specialty food shops, make sure to stop by Lisbon's version of Harrod's food court, **Tavares** (*Rua da Betesga nos. 1A-1B*). Dried fruit, home-made preserves, deli products, wine, port and all sorts of other treats. Expensive, but how could anyone resist?

The **Manteigaria Silva** (*Mon to Fri 9am to 7pm, Sat 9am to 1pm; Rua Dom Antão de Almada nos. 1C-1D*) is a real

find! Your mouth will begin to water as soon as you enter this modest deli-style cheese and prepared-meat shop, which is sure to whet your appetite with its many delicacies! It is all you can do to resist the plump and glistening black and green olives or the sumptuous spread of fine cheeses. What more can we say about this place, teeming with temptations for the palate, except to head there as soon as possible! Excellent and inexpensive.

Music

Valentim de Carvalho (*Mon to Fri 10am to 8:30pm, Sat 10am to 8pm, Sun 10am to 7pm; Praça Dom Pedro IV no. 58*) is a pleasant shop that offers everything you're looking for, whether a CD, a magazine or even the latest best-selling novel. Customers are always served with a smile. Many works are also available in English.

Discoteca Amália (*Sat until 7:30pm, Rua Aurea/Rua do Ouro no. 272*) offers a good selection of Portuguese and Brazilian music.

Santos Ofícios (*Mon to Sat 10am to 8pm; Rua da Madalena no. 87; ☎218 87 20 31*) sells figurines, carpets, blankets, crockery and many other handicrafts from all over the country, to the greatest delight of those in search of a

typical little Portuguese souvenir. A good choice for its reasonable prices and wide selection.

Tour B: The Castelo and the Alfama

Crafts

At **Espace Oikos** (*10am to noon and 2pm to 5pm; Rua Augusto Rosa no. 40*), a wonderful multicultural centre set up inside some old stables, you can purchase lovely objects (jewellery, masks, fabrics, records, etc.) produced in developing countries. Reasonable prices.

Tour C: Graça and East Lisbon

Second Hand Shops

If you have a fondness for antique objects and curios, make sure to go to the Campo Santa Clara during your visit to the Panteão de Santa Engrácia.

Held right in the middle of the square every Tuesday and Saturday, the **Feira da Ladra** is a flea market where, with a little perseverance, you may well find the deal of the century!

Lisbon

Azulejos

Fans of antique *azulejos* should head to the **Museu Nacional do Azulejo**'s boutique (*Tue 2pm to 6pm, Wed to Sun 10am to 6pm; Rua da Madre de Deus no. 4, ☎218 14 77 47*), where you can purchase reproductions of various works exhibited at the museum, and at very affordable prices (*azulejos at 2,000 ESC and more*). Magazines and books about *azulejos* are also available.

Flea Markets

The **Feira da Ladra** (*Wed and Sat 7am to 6pm; Campo de Santa Clara; bus #39A from Praça do Comércio, Estação Santa Apolónia stop; bus #46 from the Rossio, Estação Santa Apolónia stop; bus #12 from Marquês de Pombal, Campo Santa Clara stop*) is a big flea market.

Tour D: The Chiado and the Bairro Alto

Before a terrible fire ravaged the neighbourhood in 1988, the Chiado was a shopping mecca, whose major arteries were Rua do Carmo and Rua Garrett. Although the area is still under reconstruction, it is pleasant to stroll about here and admire the few surviving shops, most of which are chic and expensive. Local curiosities include the tiny and elegant **Luvaria Ulisses** (*Rua do Carmo 87A*), which is probably the smallest glove shop in Europe, but nevertheless boasts a vast selection. The goldsmith's shop **Aliança** (*Rua Garret 50-52*) is also noteworthy for its richly decorated interior.

Art

Visitors will find a good choice of watercolours depicting the city of Lisbon at the **Livraria & Galeria Stuart** (*Rua Nova do Almada nos. 20-22, ☎213 43 21 31*), and for all budgets, too. As its Portuguese name suggests, books are also available, though most are secondhand.

Azulejos

Azulejos of all shapes and colours can be found at the **Fabrica Sant'Anna** (*Rua do Alecrim no. 95*), a 200-year-old Lisbon institution.

If you have a taste for antique *azulejos*, make sure to go to **Solar** (*Rua Dom Pedro V nos. 68-70*). Vast selection.

Shoppers will find every conceivable pattern at the **Viúva Lamego** boutique (*Mon to Fri 9am to 1pm and 3pm to 7pm, Sat 9am to 1pm; Calçada do Sacremento no. 29, ☎213 46 96 92*), where the vast choice of styles and colours, which have made its *azulejo* factory in the Sintra region famous, are available. Very pricey, but truly beautiful!

Bookstores and Stationer's

Livraria Bertrand (*Rua Garrett no. 73*) carries international newspapers and a good selection of books. There is another one in the Amoreiras shopping centre.

A Bibliófila (*Rua da Misericórdia no. 102*) is a slightly old-fashioned, but interesting Portuguese bookstore with many books on art and history, as well as old prints, which can be framed on the premises.

Livraria Britânica (*Mon to Fri 9:30am to 7pm, Sat 9:30am to 1pm; Rua de São Marcal no. 168A*) is an English-language bookstore with a very wide selection.

Crafts

If you appreciate quality handicrafts, make sure to visit the simple **País em Lisboa** boutique (*Mon to Fri noon to 7pm, Sat 2:30pm to 7pm; Rua do Teixeira no. 25, ☎213 42 09 11*). In lovely surroundings cooled by stone walls and arches, visitors can feast their eyes on jewellery, curios, paintings and clothing from various regions of Portugal. The selected artifacts are of high quality, and the charming proprietor will be glad to show them to you.

Decorative Items and Knick-Knacks

For beautiful (but somewhat costly) fabric, head to **Soleiado** (*Largo do Carmo no. 2*), on pretty Praça do Carmo. The location alone is worth the trip.

If you're yearning for the exotic, stop by **De Natura** (*Rua da Rosa no. 162-A,* ☎*213 46 60 81*), a lovely shop that sells decorative objects from Africa, Asia and other parts of the world. Both the merchandise and the setting in which it is displayed will take you to far-off places. Prices are a bit steep, however.

Groceries

Mercado do Bairro Alto (*Mon and Sat 7am to 2pm; corner of Rua da Atalaia and Rua Boa Hora*) is a local market carrying fruit, vegetables, etc..

Music

Discoteca do Carmo (*Rua do Carmo no. 63*) has a good record selection (same owner as the Discoteca Amália, in the Baixa).

Tour E: The Rato and Amoreiras

Decorative Items and Knick-Knacks

The **Loja Conceição Vasco Costa** (*Rua de Escola Politécnica no. 237*), a lovely shop located in a restored palace, specializes in fine fabrics. The furniture shop next door (same owner) is also very interesting.

Shopping Centres

Those who enjoy wandering through the malls and department stores of Paris, London, Montréal or New York will appreciate the **Amoreiras Shopping Center de Lisboa** (*from Rossio or Praça dos Restauradores bus # 11, Amoreiras stop, or, from Praça dos Restauradores, take the Elevador da Glória then bus #15, Amoreiras stop*) and its futuristic architecture. With its 200 shops, 10 cinemas, 47 restaurants, supermarket, gym and several banks, visitors could spend days on end here.

Tour F: Marquês de Pombal, Saldanha and North Lisbon

Bookstores and Stationer's

From novels and travel guides to books on the city's architecture and history, you will find everything you've always wanted to know about Lisbon at **Livraria**. **Municipal** (*Mon to Fri 10am to 7pm, Sat 10am to 1pm; Avenida da República no. 21-A,* ☎*213 53 05 22*), the Câmara Municipal's official bookstore. Aficionados of Lisbon, do not miss out!

Tour G: Restauradores and Liberdade

Azulejos

Be sure to stop by the marvellous **Viúva Lamego** boutique (*Mon to Fri 9am to 1pm and 3pm to 7pm, Sat 9am to 1pm; Largo do Intendente Pina Manique no. 25,* ☎*218 85 24 08*) while exploring the Graça district. In addition to a wide choice of *azulejos* available in numerous styles and colours, you can also admire the storefront's extraordinary facade, a real work of art, also entirely covered in *azulejos*. Oriental characters and landscapes are depicted and, to the right of the balcony, an amusing little monkey can be seen. Founded in 1849, the establishment owes its reputation to the parent company, the Fábrica Cerâmica Viúva Lamego, set up in the Sintra region. The only small disappointment in the face of such refinement is the high prices. Count on spending between 42,400 and

46,400 ESC for a panel of 12 *azulejos*!

Bookstores and Stationer's

Ipsilon (*corner of Avenida da Liberdade no. 9 and Calçada da Glória, next to the Borges bank, facing the Restauradores metro*) carries a wide range of foreign magazines and newspapers.

Groceries

Located in the Centro Commercial Libercil, the **Super Nobrescolha** (*Avenida da Liberdade no. 20*), while not the most pleasant grocer's, offers a vast choice and a relatively late closing time.

Souvenirs

The **Mercearia Liberdade** (*until 9pm in summer; Avenida da Liberdade no. 202, near Rua Barata Salgueiro*) is a beautiful craft shop selling everything from *azulejos* and pottery to excellent port wine. Good selection, reasonable prices and friendly service.

Tour H: Santa Catarina and Cais do Sodré

Bookstores and Stationer's

Livraria Centro Cultural Brasileiro (*Largo do Dr. António de Sousa Macedo no. 5,* ☎*213 60 87 60*). You guessed it, Brazilian literature holds a place of honour here, in lovely wood-panelled surroundings.

Tour I: Estrêla and Lapa

Azulejos

Ratton (*Mon to Fri 10am to 1pm and 3pm to 7:30pm; Rua Academia das Ciêncas no. 2C,* ☎*213 46 09 48*) certainly carries *azulejos*, but not just any *azulejos*! Indeed, here, modernism complements an age-old art form, offering original patterns and new compositions. In addition to the works exhibited in this little gallery, visitors can consult a thick catalogue containing numerous creations. As artists cannot live on inspiration and fresh air alone, expect to pay the modest sum of 82,000 ESC per *azulejo*! Who says you can't put a price on art?

Costa de Lisboa

I magine your dream world: a verdant land with an abundance of vegetation from the four corners of the earth, with a baroque palace, a romantic *quinta*, fashionable beaches, fine golf courses and Lisbon, all close at hand.

W ell, your dream world is a reality in Costa de Lisboa. In this veritable playground for Lisboans, you can escape the city for a few days of relaxation, or perhaps stay in one of the nearby *pousadas*, in Queluz or Palmela, or at the beach resorts of Cascais or Estoril. And don't miss Sintra and the surrounding area, where hikers can head off on spectacular trails lined with exotic, twisting vegetation. Once in Sintra, why not make the pilgrimage to the end of Europe and head for Cabo de Roca, if only to say you have tread upon at least one of the continent's extremities! Finally, in this history-laden region,

the treasures of Santiago do Cacém, with its gripping Roman ruins and its proud castle are must-sees. And you thought you could pass through this area quickly!

Finding Your Way Around

By Car from Lisbon

Cascais and Estoril

Quick Route

From the centre of Lisbon, take Avenida da Liberdade to the Praça Marquês de Pombal and turn left on Avenida Joaquim António Aguiar, which will lead you directly to Highway A5 towards Estoril and Cascais.

Scenic Route

From the Praça do Comércio, head west past the piers along Avenida 24 de Julho and then continue along Avenida da Índia. The latter goes to the N6, which runs along the coast, leading directly to Estoril and Cascais.

Mafra

Quick Route

Take Highway A1-E80 north to the junction with the N8, which you must take in the direction of Torres Vedras. Once on the N8, travel 4km to the intersection with the N116 (Malveira exit), which leads directly to Mafra, 11km from the intersection.

Scenic Route

From the centre of Lisbon, take Avenida da Liberdade to Praça Marquês de Pombal and then turn left onto Avenida Joaquim António Aguiar, which leads directly to Highway A5. A few kilometres past the point where you get on the A5, take the N117 toward Mafra.

Palmela

After reaching the Ponte de 25 de Abril, head south on Highway A2-E1-E90. About 37km farther along, at the turn-off for Setúbal, take the exit located immediately to your right to reach the N252

heading south. Just a few hundred metres farther, take the N379 west. Palmela is 1km farther along that road.

Santiago do Cacém

Take Highway A2-E1-E90 heading south past Setúbal, and then continue south by the N5-E1 to the junction with the N120. Once there, head 29km toward Sines, where you will find the N261, which leads to Santiago do Cacém.

Setúbal

After reaching the Ponte de 25 de Abril, continue south along Highway A2-E1-E90. About 35km farther, an interchange leads to the centre of Setúbal.

Sesimbra

Scenic Route

Upon arriving in Setúbal via Highway A2 (with tolls), and after crossing Avenida Luísa Todi (heading east), take Estrada da Figueirinha, continuing in the same direction, to the N10-4, a little farther on. This road runs along the ocean and affords spectacular views. Turn off at the junction with the N379-1 to reach the N379, heading west. This road leads to an intersection with N378. Turn left here to reach Sesimbra.

Queluz, Sintra and Cabo da Roca

From the centre of Lisbon, head along Avenida da Liberdade to the Praça Marquês de Pombal and turn left on Avenida Joaquim António Aguiar, which leads directly to Highway A5. After several kilometres along this road, take the N117 toward Queluz and Sintra to reach the IC19, which goes first to Queluz and then to Sintra. To get to Cabo da Roca from Sintra, take the N247 past Colares and then the N247-4 toward Cabo da Roca.

By Train from Lisbon

Cascais and Estoril

Cais do Sodré station
on the pier to the west of the Praça do Comércio
Departure: several times a day at 30min intervals
Travel time: about 30min for Estoril and 40min for Cascais
Fare: 200 ESC

Setúbal

Although this town can be reached by train, this means of transport is not really practical because there is no direct line from the centre of town. You must first take the river ferry (*board at the Estacão Fluvial Sul e Sureste*) at the Praça do Comércio to reach

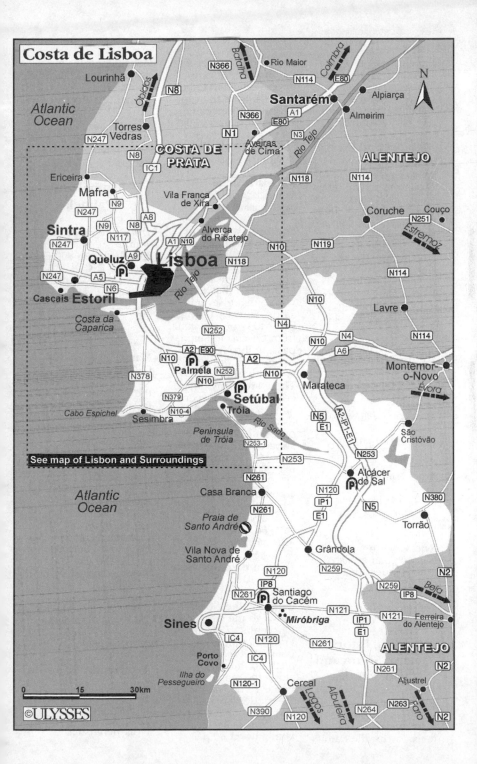

Barreiro station on the other side of the river, in a suburb of the capital, from where trains leave for the southern part of the country.

Queluz and Sintra

Rossio station
Departure: several times a day, every 20min
Travel time: about 30min for Queluz and 45min for Sintra
Fare: 170 ESC for Queluz and 200 ESC for Sintra

For Caminhos de Ferro departures and information in Lisbon, see p 69.

By Bus from Lisbon

Rede Nacional de Expressos
terminal at no. 18B Avenida Casal Ribeiro
Departure: many per day

Renex Expressos
Cais das Cebolas,
near Casa dos Bicos
Departure: many per day

Note: Other transportation companies also offer frequent daily departures.

For information in Lisbon, see p 69.

Cascais, Estoril, Queluz, Sintra and Cabo da Roca

Because of the very good railway service between the capital and these towns, the train is

faster and cheaper than the bus. There is no direct service to Cabo da Roca from the capital, but a connecting service operates eight times a day between Sintra and Cabo da Roca:

Rodoviária Sintra
59 Avenida Miguel Bombarda, near the railway station.

For those wishing to explore this magnificent region, the bus company Stagecoach offers a day ticket (*1,250 ESC*) that allows you to make several stops. Thus by taking bus #403 you can get from Cascais to Sintra, passing through Cabo da Roca, in one day and with one ticket. There are many other connections between Sintra, Cascais and Estoril. Stagecoach also offers a similar trip aboard a double-decker bus with an open roof fro 1,500 ESC.

Stagecoach Portugal
Rua Capitão Rey Vilar no. 383, Alvide, 2750 Cascais
☎ *214 86 76 81*
⇌ *214 86 81 68*

Costa da Caparica

To get to Costa da Caparica, the closest beach to the city, take Carris bus #75 from the Praça Marquês de Pombal. It leads directly to the beach along the magnificent Ponte 25 de Abril for the modest sum of 500 ESC (ask for a *1-Dia-Praia* ticket). A family ticket *4 PAX*

(four people) is also available for 1,500 ESC.

Santiago do Cacém

Travel time: approx. 2hrs and 25min
Fare: between 1,150 ESC and 1,350 ESC

Setúbal and Palmela

Travel time: approx. 40min
Fare: between 800 ESC and 950 ESC

By Boat

Cacilhas

Many Ferries go to Cacilhas from the Terreiro do Paço near the Praça do Comércio in Lisbon. The trip is also possible from Cais do Sodré for 105 ESC and takes 30min.

Transtejo
Cais da Alfândega, Estação Fluvial Terreiro do Paço
information 24hrs:
☎ *213 47 92 77*
⇌ *21 346 09 02*
www.transtejo.pt/princi.htm
Departure: every 30min during the day and evening and every hour at night
Cost: motorcycle 200 ESC, car 300 ESC
This company provides 24hr service on the Cacilhas ferry.

Península de Tróia

A passenger ferry and a car ferry link downtown Setúbal with the Tróia peninsula.

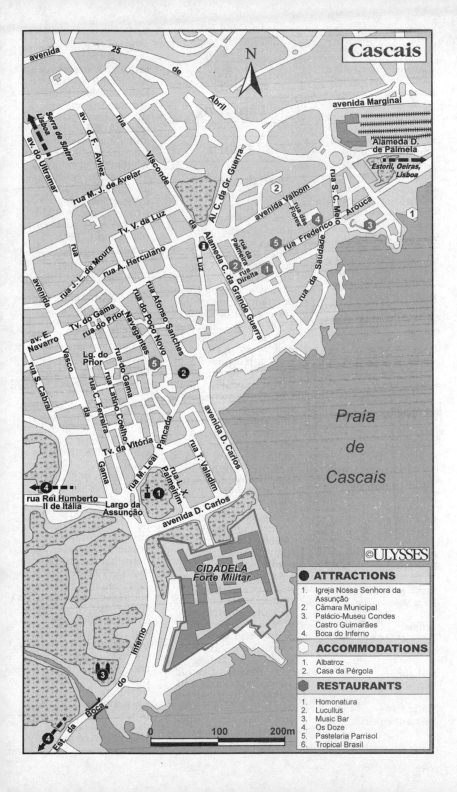

Passenger ferry schedules vary considerably according to the season (*summer; every 1.5hrs until 10pm*), and departures are from the Doca de Recreio (*Avenida Jaime Rebelo*). The car ferry makes numerous daily crossings year-round and runs 24hrs a day (*from 10pm to 7:15am every hour; from 7:30am to 9:15pm every 30 to 40min*). The car ferry leaves from the Doca do Comércio (*860 ESC/2ppl.; Rua Barão do Vale, at the eastern end of Avenida Luísa Todi*). The crossing takes approximately 20min.

Practical Information

Tourist Information Offices

Estoril
Arcadas do Parque

Cascais
Rua Visconde da Luz 14-A

Santiago do Cacém
Praça Mercado

Setúbal
Travessa Frei Gaspar and Largo do Corpo Santo

Sesimbra
Largo da Marinho

Sintra Vila
3 Praça da República

Exploring

Estoril

Once visited for the benefits of its curative waters, Estoril really took off in the 1950s when several famous figures took up residence here, among them deposed kings such as King Humberto of Italy and King Juan of Spain (father of the current Spanish king). Though the construction of an impressive casino, preceded by an elegant park lined with luxury hotels, has drawn a wealthy clientele, its renowned sporting competitions (the Tennis Open, Formula One grand prix auto racing, and sailing regattas) have conferred upon it an international reputation.

All these attractions, combined with an intense cultural life (theatres, concerts, festivals and so on) and a mild winter climate, have long attracted a sophisticated public, composed in large measure of artists, politicians, business people and sports stars. Estoril's star, however, seems to be fading these days, and its old prestigious hotels and mansions bear witness to a bygone decadent era. There are no special attractions for tourists, apart from the casino and its park as well as the many luxurious mansions lining its avenues. Estoril will suit people who appreciate a comfortable and traditional holiday in a sophisticated but somewhat artificial setting. Prices at this resort, as a general rule, are exaggeratedly high for what you get. See also "Parks" and "Beaches", p 188 and p 190.

Cascais

Few traces remain of the prosperous little fishing village that Cascais once was. A victim of its strategic location and twice ransacked by foreign troops (in 1580 by the French occupiers and in 1589 by the English), the city also had to endure the terrible earthquake of 1755, which obliterated it once again. Despite this succession of setbacks, Cascais has always boasted a consistently mild climate, and thus benefited more than any other from the vogue for seaside vacations that flourished in the late 19th century. Each autumn the royal court, seeking eternal spring, moved to this spot, bringing in its wake the Portuguese nobility and a crowd of courtiers. Between 1930 and 1950, many secondary residences were built here, bringing the town a certain degree of wealth and a renown that spread far and wide. Toward the

1970s, when mass tourism began its crusade, Cascais once again fell victim to its geographic location and was among the first resorts to suffer from this devastating assault. Less than 30km from the capital and easy to reach, Cascais is besieged by day-trippers year-round, turning it into one of the country's busiest resorts. For those who enjoy a lively scene and constant crowds, Cascais is a dream come true. Even if prices here are more reasonable than in Estoril, Cascais remains a rather expensive beach resort. See "Parks" and "Beaches", p 188 and p 190.

In terms of tourist attractions, besides its prettily cobbled **pedestrian streets**, which are good for strolling, Cascais has few interesting monuments. Listed below are some that justify a brief visit, nonetheless.

Igreja Nossa Senhora da Assunção (*Largo do Assunção, just near the citadel of Cascais*) is worth a look for its fine *azulejos* and its beautiful *talha dourada* altar.

The **Câmara Municipal** boasts an elegant *azulejo*-adorned **facade**.

The **Palácio-Museu Condes de Castro Guimarães** (*210 ESC for a guided tour, free Sun 10am to 12:30pm; Tue to Sun 10am to 5pm;*

Avenida Humberto II de Itália, west of town, off the N247-8, along the coast, Estrada da Boca do Inferno). Hidden within a small bay topped by a picturesque stone bridge, this curious dwelling unfailingly conjures up images of a fairy-tale castle. Dating from the beginning of the 20th century, this noble residence was transformed by the municipality into a museum and library, and it now houses Portuguese furniture and knick-knacks mostly dating from the 18th and 19th centuries and, of course, an important collection of very old books.

Heading west, the **Boca do Inferno** is located at the edge of Cascais, just past the Palácio Condes de Castro Guimarães. As its name suggests, this oddity is an impressive chasm where the ocean waves crash with noisy commotion. These "forces of nature" can be more closely observed from a platform reached by a small bridge. Unfortunately, there is quite a lot of littler left by previous visitors, leading one to conclude that the municipality is not taking very good care of the site. Also, the kitschy souvenir shops and unappealing snackbars detract from the natural beauty of the spot, which is especially regrettable since Caicas itself has a limited number of attractions. Despite all this,

be sure to make a quick stop if only to enjoy the ocean spray!

Mafra

Situated about 30km from Lisbon, the town of Mafra is above all renowned in Portugal for its famous **monastery-palace** ★, one of the most imposing in the country. Although Mafra does have a pleasant historic area (*Vila Velha*), the newer part of the town (*Vila Nova*), where the monastery is located, attracts more tourists. Built between 1717 and 1730, this gigantic building was erected on orders from Dom João V in acknowledgement – to have a child with his wife, Mary Ann of Austria. The German architect (Frederick Ludwig) chosen by the king to direct the project, along with his Italian and Portuguese colleagues, produced a particularly imposing work that bears witness to an era during which the Portuguese court spent freely the riches accumulated in its colonies. So, with its 220m-long facade, its area of 40,000m², its 4,500 doors and windows, and an enclosing wall that is almost 20km long, the designers of the building seem to have had one goal: to rival El Escorial, a monastery-palace in Spain.

Costa de Lisboa

As for the building itself, which is laid out in a square, it encloses at its centre a **basilica** ★ of impressive dimensions. During our visit, the basilica was closed for renovations, but you can still admire its elegant Italianate facade. If the basilica is open, once inside, visitors will be struck by the preponderance of multicoloured marble, which is the principal decorative feature here. At the transept crossing, a huge, awe-inspiring **dome** entirely made of pink and white marble rises almost 70m. In addition to the **high altar** and a rich collection of **organs** dating from 1807, sculpture fans will not want to miss the many **statues** and **bas-reliefs** in the side chapels. The latter are beautiful examples of the **Mafra school**, a sculpture school created by João V that gathered and instructed a large number of renowned artisans such as Alessandro Giusti and Machado de Castro for the purpose of glorifying the monastery-palace.

After leaving the cathedral, if you are up to an hour of walking through a maze of corridors and a succession of rooms, you can explore more of this site by visiting the **monastery** and the **national palace** ★ (*guided tours only; 400 ESC, free Sun am; Wed to Mon 10am to 5:30pm; entrance on the left side of the main facade*).

Laid out on either side of the cathedral, the monastery is especially interesting to aficionados of religious art and, in addition to a little museum that exhibits sacerdotal robes and sacred objects, its kitchens, a pharmacy and a room that once served as an infirmary may be visited. The more interesting *Palácio Nacional*, upstairs from the monastery, displays an impressive succession of rooms richly decorated in period furniture, evidence of generous royal contributions. Finally the **library** ★ ★ is worth the visit in itself; in fact it is an absolute must. It dates from 1717, and it stores, in an exuberant baroque rococo decor, over 38,000 books.

The long, narrow room with a vaulted ceiling that contains this rich library is also one of the few rooms that directly links the king's apartments with those of the queen. Were the ends of love served by culture in this marvellous place, or vice-versa?

Queluz

Located halfway between the capital and Sintra, the **Palácio Nacional de Queluz** ★ ★ (*400 ESC, free Sun 10am to 1pm, 50 ESC admission to garden only; Wed to Mon 10am to 1pm and 2pm to 5pm; access by the IC9, Largo do Palácio Nacional*) is considered by many to be Portugal's Versailles, and with reason.

Palácio Nacional de Queluz

Its gracious rocaille-accented baroque facade, softened by soothing Portuguese colours, makes it one of the most elegant baroque palaces in the country. Also, as at Versailles, the palace is fronted by perfectly ordered gardens, worthy of the purest French tradition. It was at the initiative of Dom Pedro, the second son of João V, that work began in 1747. Portuguese architect Mateus Vicente de Oliveira is responsible for the facade as well as the wing in which the throne room is located.

After a brief interruption because of the 1755 earthquake, the work was turned over to the French architect Jean-Baptiste Robillon who, with the help of his Portuguese colleague, completed the main buildings. From 1786 to 1807, Dona Maria I brought several additions to the interior decoration and had another section built, thereby completing the building as we see it today. The Queluz palace became a royal residence with the accession to the throne of Dom Pedro III and was inhabited until 1807, when Napoleonic troops invaded and the royal family fled to Brazil. The Queluz palace was the last great prestigious undertaking of the royal family. Despite the opulence of its decoration and the freshness of its

gardens, Queluz bears memory to the sad end of Queen Dona Maria I, struck with madness toward the end of her reign. Nowadays, the building belongs to the government and serves as a residence for foreign dignitaries on official visits. An excellent restaurant (see p 204) is now housed in the same wing as the palace's former kitchens.

A tour of the **palace apartments ★★** will appeal mainly to those with a taste for period furniture and objects. Among the many rooms that may be admired, make sure to visit the **throne room ★★★**. Oval-shaped and adorned with numerous mirrors, it is reminiscent of the Galerie des Glaces in Versailles. Imposing Venetian crystal chandeliers hang from the attractively decorated ceiling, which seems to be held up by four Atlases. From May to October, concerts are held here on weekends (*usually around 6pm*), making the place that much more enchanting (*concert information ☎214 35 00 39 or 214 36 38 61, ≈214 35 25 75*). Among the other rooms open to the public, the **Queen's dressing room ★** and the **Don Quixote room ★**, both graced with superb parquet floors, are lovely as well. Finally, in the little oratory next to the Don Quixote room, the magnificent Indo-Portuguese ivory

calvary ★★ is a real little masterpiece.

A tour of the premises wouldn't be complete without a stroll through the magnificent **gardens ★★**. In addition to the **Neptune pool ★**, designed by the architect Robillon, visitors can admire numerous alabaster statues, ceramic vases and a whimsical fountain adorned with hydras and statuettes of clothed monkeys. In the background, an elegant **ceremonial facade ★★** completes this majestic, fairy-tale setting. Below the gardens is a canal with a small stream flowing through it. The low walls running along its banks and the little bridge over the Jamor river are covered with beautiful *azulejos ★*.

Sintra

Along with Buçaco and the Serra de Monchique, the Serra de Sintra constitutes one of those magical places of wonderfully dense and varied vegetation. Besides tropical flora, you can find one of the most charming palaces in Portugal, the **Palácio Nacional de Sintra**, as well as another building, the **Palácio da Pena**, notable for its whimsical architecture. Though these two national monuments are often mentioned as must-see tourist attrac-

Costa de Lisboa

tions, Sintra Vila has much more to recommend it, including courtly dwellings, *quintas*, convents and gardens, that also deserve a visit and that make this area among the most interesting in the general region of the capital. Sintra is also a veritable Eden; its beauty has been praised by numerous noblemen, writers and artists, including Lord Byron and William Beckford, English writers famous for *Childe Harold's Pilgrimage* and the *Sketches of Spain and Portugal*, respectively. Sintra today is made up of three distinct areas. Visitors arriving from Lisbon by train will disembark in Estefânia, the modern part of town. Those arriving from the capital by road will pass through the São Pedro area, famous for its antique shops (prices are out of sight, however) and for its bi-weekly market. Finally, the historic district, called Sintra Vila or Vila Velha, is where you will discover the pearl in the oyster that is the Sintra area. If damp weather is enough to ruin your day, avoid visiting when it is cloudy, for the Serra da Sintra is often shrouded in a heavy fog and is the first area to "welcome" the rain. On a brighter note, however, Sintra's delicious little locally made pastries, called *queijadas*, are the perfect consolation on a rainy day. These sweet,

cheese-based cakes, made since the 13th century, are the pride of local inhabitants.

If you are pressed for time, start off at the **Palácio Nacional ★ ★ ★** (*400 ESC, 30mim guided tour without narration, free Sun 10am to 1pm; 10am to 1pm and 2pm to 5pm, closed Wed; in the centre of Sintra, Terreiro da Rainha Dona Amélia*), a wonderful summer residence formerly inhabited by the kings of Portugal. Although some visitors may rightly detect a certain lack of architectural unity, this is a unique palace. Its mixture of styles, ranging from the Gothic to the Mudéjar to the Manueline, gives it a certain character, enhanced by two enormous chimneys that are as surprising as they are elegant. Currently, some rooms in the palace are reserved for the president of Portugal for protocol purposes.

Before going in, take the time to examine the exterior, where the evolution of styles in Portuguese history is revealed. The central buildings, set on the site of a Moorish palace of which scarcely any traces remain, are the oldest parts. Dating from the end of the 14th century, they were built by order of João I. By expanding the existing buildings, he wanted to make them a summer residence for the Avis dynasty. You

can still make out a few Gothic-style elements, even if the whole group underwent substantial modifications later on. An interesting aside: the building had not yet been completed when important royal decisions were already being taken here, for example the order to launch an expedition to capture Ceuta, on the Moroccan coast. Next, observe the right wing, added in the 16th century during the reign of King Dom Manuel I. These Mudéjar-influenced geminated windows show the attraction that the Hispano-Moorish style, very fashionable at the time, held for the bourgeoisie. The two gigantic conical chimneys, located in back, are fine examples of this. Finally, in a purely Portuguese touch, the Manueline windows have ship's rigging as motifs, recalling the influence of the great expeditions on architecture. Thus, unlike the Palácio da Pena, whose exterior architecture seems inappropriate in the Portuguese context, Sintra's national palace is a page of history, and one can easily imagine the dramas and joyful events that went on here: joy when Dom Sébastião was proclaimed king here and when Camões read *The Luisiads* here for the first time, and drama as the feeble-minded King Dom Afonso VI was held

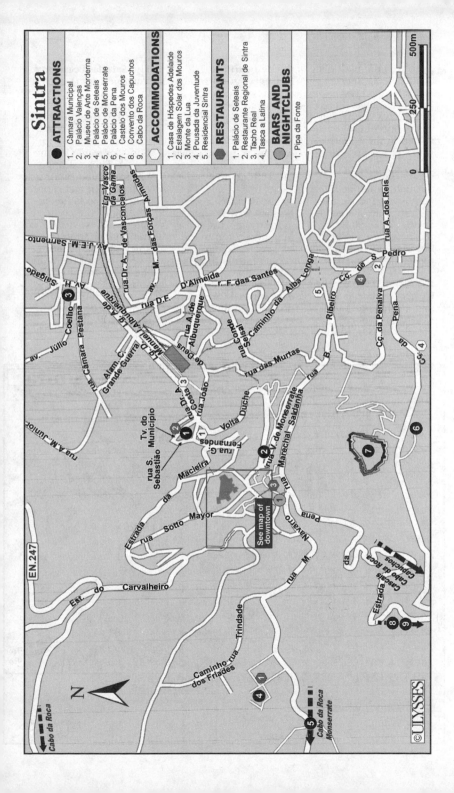

prisoner here until his death.

Inside, amongst the ample crowd (this palace is one of the most visited in the country, although groups are limited to 30 persons), you can wander through an impressive number of rooms, each with its own character. Several Moorish-looking patios are also visible. Here are a few rooms not to miss:

● The impressive **kitchen**, especially to admire the interior of its hearths whose breadth is astonishing.

● The **Quarto de Hôspedes** (guest room), where you can see what may be the world's first sofa-bed.

● The wonderful *azulejos* ★ in the **Capela-Mor**, some dating from the 15th century.

● The **Sala dos Brasões** ★★★ (heraldry room), the most beautiful room in the palace, to admire its 74 coats of arms representing the Portuguese nobility. Magnificent *azulejo* panels ★★ representing hunting scenes may also be viewed.

The **Sala das Pegas** ★★ (magpie room), including an interesting ceiling painting that portrays 136 magpies holding in their beaks a rose with the inscription "*por bem*" (for the good). These strange birds, painted by order of João I, in fact represent the 136 ladies-in-waiting of the court. These ladies, victims of rumours relating to a spicy adventure between one of them and the king, are thus besought to speak only the truth: the king's acts were "*por bem*" of the kingdom!

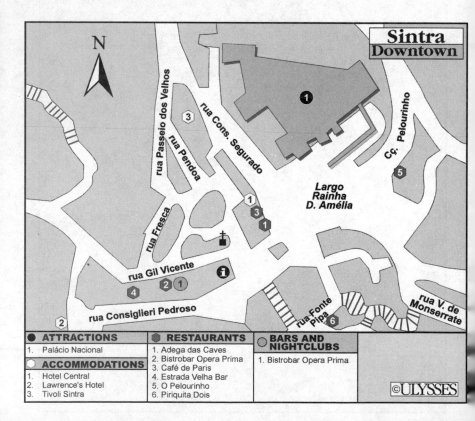

Sintra Downtown

N

rua Passeio dos Velhos

rua Cons. Segurado

rua Pendoa

C.ç. Pelourinho

rua Fresca

Largo Rainha D. Amélia

rua Gil Vicente

rua Consiglieri Pedroso

rua Fonte Pipa

rua V. de Monserrate

● ATTRACTIONS	🔶 RESTAURANTS	○ BARS AND NIGHTCLUBS
1. Palácio Nacional	1. Adega das Caves	1. Bistrobar Opera Prima
○ ACCOMMODATIONS	2. Bistrobar Opera Prima	
1. Hotel Central	3. Café de Paris	
2. Lawrence's Hotel	4. Estrada Velha Bar	
3. Tivoli Sintra	5. O Pelourinho	
	6. Piriquita Dois	

©ULYSSES

The **Sala dos Cisnes** ★ (swan room), the biggest in the palace, with portraits of 27 crown-bearing swans, each in a different position. These paintings honour the coat of arms of the de Lencastre family, whose members included the wife of João I. Also on view are a superb sideboard as well as fine Chinese vases.

Head now to the Camâra Municipal.

The **Câmara Municipal** (*Largo Dr. Virgilio Horta*) is worth a short stop to admire its very pretty **Manueline facade**.

The **Palácio Valenças** (*Rua Visconde da Monserrate*), now housing the town library, also has a pretty facade decorated with an imposing coat of arms. The town archives are kept here.

Just a few steps away from the station lies the brand-new **Museu de Arte Moderna** ★★ (*600 ESC; Wed to Sun 10am to 6pm; Avenida Heliodoro Salgado, Estefânia, ☎219 24 81 70*), formerly the Sintra casino. Completely remodelled, this neo-baroque building dating from 1920 proudly displays its pretty facade, which is painted white and pastel yellow and strangely topped by a bull's-eye window that serves as a niche for a statue. Displayed inside are no fewer than 400 works of modern art (paintings, sculptures, photographs and video installations) dating from the post-war period to the 1980s. Visitors can admire pieces by such renowned artists as Vieira da Silva, Bissière, Riopelle, Michaux. A portion of the museum is devoted to pop art, highlighting the work of several masters of that movement, including Roy Lichtenstein and Tom Wesselman. For anyone who appreciates modern art, this place is worth a visit.

★

Seteais

(2km from Sintra)

Located in the Serra de Sintra, less than 2km from the village of Sintra, the **Palácio de Seteais** ★ (*along the N375; Rua Barbosa Bocage no. 10*) is a very elegant palace formed by two buildings connected by an imposing arch. The buildings now house a luxurious hotel (see p 197) which is well worth a visit. In the 18th century, each wing formed a distinct property. While the right wing housed the elegant Quinta da Alegria, the more recent left wing was built by the Dutch consul as a residence. It was he who laid out the grand esplanade facing the two buildings. The two properties became one at the beginning of the 19th century when the marquis of Marialva acquired all the lands and had the imposing central arch built to link the two wings. Besides a remarkable **interior decoration** ★ where frescoes, ancient tapestries and period furniture incite admiration, we suggest a little stroll on the **terrace**, with its beautiful French-style gardens and its **panoramic view**, romantic to perfection. Some say the origin of the palace's name may be explained as follows: the word *seteais* is the contraction of "sete aïes", in other words seven repetitions of the exclamation "aïe" created by echoes from the valleys facing the terrace. Sceptics can decide for themselves!

Returning from the Palácio de Seteais toward Sintra, on the right side of the N375 (*Rua Barboasa Bocage no. 9*), notice the fine residence called the **Quinta da Regaleira** ★★, a stunning, sumptuous neo-Manueline residence dating back to the turn of the century. Unfortunately, visitors are not allowed inside this extravagant palace. However, its **gardens** ★★ (*2,000 ESC; guided tours by apt.; www.regaleira.pt; Jun to Sep 10am to 7:30pm, Oct to May 10am to 5:30pm; ☎219 10 66 50, ≈219 24 47 25*) have recently been opened to the public, which may view them by taking a 1.5hr guided tour. During the tour, a surprising mysti-

Costa de Lisboa

cal-romantic universe dreamed up by its owner and an Italian architect unfolds. The Chapel of the Trinity, a heavenly terrace, the ritual fountain of the Temple Knights – these are the fantasies of the bourgeoisie in search of a spiritual grandeur, and are enough to transport you to another universe. Rest assured, however, that the exorbitant price of the visit will quickly bring you back down to earth!

Monserrate

(4km from Sintra)

Set on vast grounds, the **Palácio de Monserrate** *(along the N375; during our visit, work was in progress for an indeterminate period and only the garden was accessible to the public)* was built for Francis Cook, a wealthy English businessman who held the noble title of First Viscount of Monserrate. The name may have come from a little church of the same name, now gone, that may have been built to commemorate a pilgrimage to Monserrate, in Catalonia, made by a monk in the 16th century. Throughout the 17th and 18th centuries, many buildings occupied this site, among them a neo-Gothic building inhabited by the famous writer

William Beckford. The last important modification took place in 1856 when Francis Cooke decided to have a Mongolian-influenced oriental palace built and to turn the garden into a park, the **Parque de Monserrate** ★★ (see "Parks", p 190).

Palácio da Pena

(4km from Sintra)

Perched 500m high, on one of the hilltops in the Serra da Sintra, the **Palácio da Pena** ★ *(400 ESC, free Sun 10am to 1pm; Tue to Sun 10am to 1pm and 2pm to 5pm; from the centre of Sintra, take the Estrada da Pena)* cannot fail to draw attention with its lively, provocative colours.

Before continuing with a brief description of this spot, keep in mind two pieces of advice for a pleasant visit.

First, go early in the morning, for the site is quickly overrun by hordes of tourists and Portuguese families all year long. Second, if you are driving, park your vehicle in the Castelo dos Mouros parking area, the first one you come to on your way up the Estrada da Pena (on the left). If you are the sort who hates walking, you can always try to find space in the second parking area, located farther up near the entrance to the grounds. The entrance to the actual castle is then less than 500 metres away. If you truly hate walking, there is another spot (fee for parking) just next to the castle, but you will really need the blessing of the gods to find a space here! Whatever solution you choose, be prepared for a memorable crowd scene.

Palácio da Pena

For a pleasant stroll, walk to the palace across its magnificent **garden** ★★★ located below it (see "Parks" p 190), where extraordinary flora awaits.

We cannot say for sure whether it is the whimsical shapes or the appearance of a Bavarian castle that attracts so many people, but this is among the most extravagant examples of what "Prusso-Portuguese" architecture could produce. It was in 1839 that Ferdinand II of Bavaria's house of Saxe-Cobourg-Gotha, the husband of Dona Maria II, bought the ruins of a monastery with the aim of turning it into a summer residence. A Prussian engineer, Baron Ludwig Von Eschwege, was put in charge of the project. Starting with the former Manueline monastery dating from 1503, the engineer erected a genuine castle with a happy mixture of a great number of styles: Moorish, Gothic, Manueline and Renaissance, all combined with a Germanic flair. Although they may look like something out of Hollywood, the bright colours that now grace the palace do tone down its rather severe countenance.

After a careful look at its extravagant exterior architecture, it is no surprise to discover just as extravagant an interior, where furnishings and rococo knick-knacks mix with stucco carvings and other Moorish-inspired sculptures. A visit here will be of particular interest to those who enjoy a rich interior, with the exception of Dom Manuel II's bedroom, practically empty in comparison with the other rooms in the palace. All that remains of the primitive convent is its Manueline cloister, in which beautiful *azulejos* may be seen; also, its chapel contains an elegant **retable**, a work by Nicolas Chantereine.

Located right near the Palácio da Pena, the **Castelo dos Mouros** ★ (*free admission; every day 10am to 4:30pm in the winter, until 5:30pm in the summer*) is an ancient Moorish castle built during the eighth and ninth centuries, whose walls have been saved almost intact. Conquered by Afonso I in 1147, the castle was abandoned and later fell into oblivion. It was only toward 1860 that Ferdinand of Saxe-Cobourg-Gotha decided to restore its walls and to reforest the surroundings of the castle. Walking across the site today, you can see the ruins of a pretty Roman chapel and reach the castle's spectacular **circular road**. The road is literally attached to the sides of steep hills, making this a photographer's delight

with its many **panoramic views** ★ of Sintra and of the Palácio da Pena.

Capuchos

(9km from Sintra)

The **Convento dos Capuchos** (*every day 10am to 5pm in the winter, until 6pm in the summer; from the Palácio da Pena, go 8km along the N273-1, then go right and follow the signs for about 1km*) is a curious monastery founded in 1560 where you can admire the monks' minuscule cells carved out of the rock and covered with cork to protect them from the cold. During your visit, leave nothing in your vehicle, for the parking area is unguarded and the spot is rather isolated. This excursion will allow you to explore the thick, lush forest covering the Serra da Sintra. Also, for those wanting to see the site of Cabo da Roca, the route along here makes for a pleasant little jaunt.

Costa de Lisboa

Cabo da Roca

(19km from Sintra)

Although someone may actually offer you a certificate (*costing 400 to 600 ESC, no doubt!*) testifying to your presence at this, the most westerly point in continental Europe, the site of **Cabo da Roca** (Rock Cape) is nothing special. Overlooking the sea from 140m above, this promontory offers fine **viewpoints** of the coast, with an often violent sea smashing against jagged cliffs. This vista will invigorate lovers of dramatic scenery. A lighthouse has been built here, along with a tourism office. This is an ideal excursion for those who appreciate the sea air.

★

Costa da Caparica

A 30min boat or bus ride from the capital, the Costa da Caparica is best known for its vast beaches (see p 189), its nature reserve with interestingly shaped cliffs (see p 190) and **Lago de Albufeira**, an immense lake well suited to windsurfing. The resort itself has no historic attractions and is choked with buildings, as well as numerous restaurants and all kinds of shops. However, away from the coast, on top of some cliffs, the **Convento dos Capuchos** (*in Capuchos,*

exit to the left from the N10-1, towards Praia da Costa da Caparica) is worth mentioning for its lovely gardens and *azulejo* panels depicting scenes from monastic life. Built in the 16th century, the monastery was damaged in the 1755 earthquake and has now been remodelled into a cultural centre offering various activities.

Cacilhas

This little "suburb" is often confused with Almada, and has little to offer visitors, with the exception of a multitude of fish and seafood restaurants. Worth mentioning, however, is the **Cais do Ginjal**, where visitors can enjoy a stroll and take in the **beautiful views** ★ of the city of Lisbon. The place is especially lovely in the late afternoon, when the sun sets over the capital – a truly magnificent sight. The short ferry crossing from Terreiro do Paço or Cais do Sodré (approx. 30min) is an enjoyable excursion, and very refreshing on a hot day.

Setúbal

Little is known to this day about the pre-Roman period, but it has now been proven that this area was inhabited by humans back in prehistoric times. In the coastal region, however, the oldest traces still visible today go back to the Roman period, falling between the first and fourth centuries AD. At that time, Romans settled both shores of the Rio Sado and founded Cetóbriga, a major port and fishing centre. Toward the fifth century, however, a powerful landslide destroyed the town and actually transformed the configuration of the Sado's mouth. This, combined with frequent barbarian invasions, left the area long bereft of human activity, as people preferred to seek refuge inland. It was not until the consolidation of the reconquest and the full confirmation of Portuguese sovereignty that a fortified village was developed in the 14th century, this time, only on the right bank of the Sado. Later, the era of great discoveries led to the enrichment and progressive growth of the village, with its port serving as the embarkation point for several expeditions. Among the great achievements to follow, the Igreja de Jésus, built in the 15th century, and the

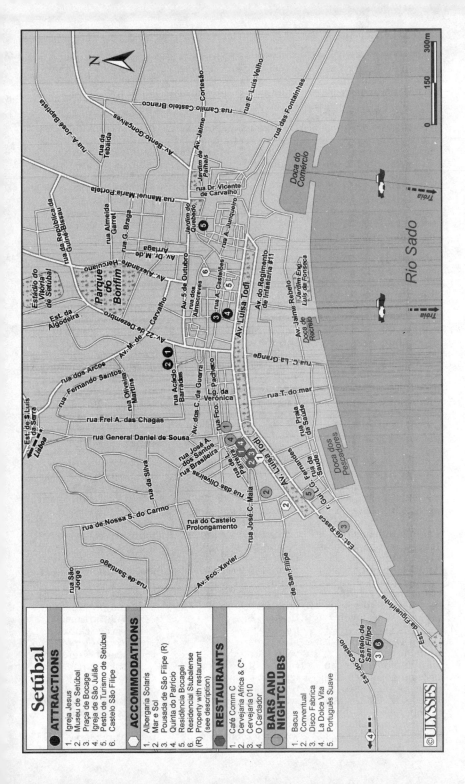

Castelo de São Felipe, dating from the 16th century are worthy of mention.

Today, Setúbal is the country's third most important seaport and has become home to many factories, including cement works, chemical plants, fish processing plants and automobile assembly operations. Moreover, the construction of an expressway running straight to the capital has spurred a considerable population increase, and Setúbal, located less than 50km from Lisbon, is slowly becoming a bedroom community. Across from the port, on the other side of the Sado, the Tróia peninsula and the mouth of the river together create a vast interior sea; great expanses of saltwater marsh as well as a wildlife reserve form its estuary. Besides salt production, many oyster shoals are cultivated here, with nearly all production exported to other European countries. West of Setúbal is the beautiful Serra da Arrábida, part of which has been turned into a nature park, offering magnificent hilly scenery as well as lovely beaches in hidden coves. During your visit to the town and its surroundings, you can taste an absolutely delicious local cheese, Queijo de Azeitão. And do not miss sampling the area's excellent wines, not the least of

which is a delicious, very sweet muscatel wine called "Moscatel de Setúbal".

Despite its respectable size, the country's third biggest city, ranked by population, has rather little to offer tourists. The number of tourist attractions in the centre of town is rather limited, although it could be interesting to stay at the beautiful *pousada*. Two hours are more than sufficient to explore the heart of the city. The many shopping streets, some of them for pedestrians only, will delight avid shoppers. You will probably enter the city along Avenida Luísa Todi, named after a famous Portuguese singer who came from Setúbal.

Go first along Avenida 22 de Dezembro to the jewel of the city, **Igreja Jésus ★** (*at press time the church and museum were closed for renovations; Rua Acácio Barradas*). Dating from 1491, this church is worth visiting especially for its remarkable **interior**, where Boytac, one of the master architects who worked on the Belém monastery, first achieved a type of decor that would later be called the Manueline style. You can see impressive **wreathed columns ★** as

well as fine ribbing surrounding vaults and windows. Outside, take a glance at the fine Gothic portal made of marble from the Serra da Arrábida. Just adjacent, in the cloister attached to the church, the **Museu de Setúbal** exhibits a series of **primitive works** by an unknown artist, commonly referred to today as the Master of Setúbal.

Continuing along Avenida 5 de Outubro, facing the Praça Miguel Bombarda and taking the second street on your right, you will come to the **Praça de Bocage**, named after the well-known Portuguese poet Manuel Barbosa de Bocage, who was born in Setúbal. Built in the centre of this charming square, the **Igreja de São Julião** is worth a brief stop to contemplate its two **Manueline portals**. Walking by the church toward the east, you can explore a series of little alleyways which are pleasant for a stroll. They make up the town's historic district. People interested in the town's Roman past should not miss the **Posto de Turismo da Região de Setúbal** (*Largo Corpo Santo*), near the Igreja de Santa Maria da Graça, to look through a cleverly designed glass floor at the foundations of a Roman building which was used to preserve fish.

Located away from the centre of town, the **Castelo de São Filipe** ★★ (*Estrada de São Filipe*) is one of the few must-see attractions here. To reach it, go to the western end of Avenida Luísa Todi and, once there, take the last street on your right, then Rua de São Filipe immediately on the left. Continue climbing and follow the signs to the *pousada*. Built in 1590 on orders from King Filipe I, better known as King Felipe II of Spain, this castle and fortress were built not to protect the town but rather to keep watch over the coast. The king of Spain greatly feared the English navy, a power with which Portugal had built long-standing alliances. The inhabitants of Setúbal, for their part, had little appreciation for the Spanish seizure of the country. Today, the fortress houses a *pousada* (see p 200) with an impressive entrance. After passing through its imposing fortified gate, you reach the central part of the building by a long vaulted passageway. One of the arches is decorated with beautiful *azulejos* showing baroque motifs. On the top floor, a big terrace offers a spectacular **panoramic view** ★ of the city and the Tróia peninsula. The buildings which now house the *pousada* used to provide lodgings for the guards and also for the region's governor.

On the side, is a little **chapel** (*unfortunately, opening hours are very irregular*) dating from the 18th century and displaying a remarkable **interior** ★ entirely covered with *azulejos* simulating a three-dimensional baroque decor. In the centre of the vault, you can see the emblem of João V, seemingly placed there to exorcise the memory of an affront that remains unforgotten.

★

Palmela

(*8km from Setúbal*)

Although the discovery of prehistoric grottos in the area (near Quinta do Anjo) has shown that the human presence here goes back to about 5000 BC, the village of Palmela owes its place in Portuguese history mainly to its fortress and its sinister dungeon, in which the bishop of Évora lay dying.

Built by the Moors on the foundations of Roman buildings, the castle was conquered by Dom Afonso I in 1148, recaptured by the Moors in 1165, and then captured for good by Dom Sancho I in 1166. Expanded, modified, destroyed and then rebuilt, the castle and fortress would undergo many modifications over the centuries, with the result that the vestiges now go back to a period stretching between the 14th and 18th centuries. Before beginning your climb toward the fortress, take a moment, while at the top of the village, to admire the very elegant façade of the **Câmara Municipal**, adorned with a fine colonnaded gallery, as well as the **pillory** in front dating from 1645.

Costa de Lisboa

Once at the top of the hill, you enter the fortress by an imposingly large fortified gate. After a hairpin turn, visitors face the ruins of the former **Igreja Santa Maria do Castelo**, destroyed by the 1755 catastrophe. By looking carefully, it is still possible to see a few yellow and blue *azulejos*. Just beside the church, a stairway leads to the ancient dungeon of the fortress, which still has the "tank" in which the bishop of Évora was imprisoned for having conspired against the king. Some say it was on the orders of João II himself that the bishop's mysterious elimination was carried out, by poisoning, it seems. Whatever one makes of this, going to the top of the dungeon, you can enjoy a breathtaking **view ★**. For those who suffer from vertigo or who shun long climbs, an esplanade located in front of the dungeon also allows for the enjoyment of the absolutely magnificent view. Also on the esplanade, beyond the ruins of various buildings, a corridor leads to a souvenir shop and an art gallery.

Retracing your steps, now stand in front of the former Santiago monastery, transformed in 1979 into a wonderful *pousada* **★**. It is well worth a look; having a drink or a meal there (see p 207) is certainly an excellent pretext for exploring this spot (or

vice versa!). Lovers of the baroque will not want to miss the church attached to the monastery (*unfortunately, it is often closed*), where beautiful *azulejos* may be seen.

Serra da Arrábida

Covering an area of some 10,000ha and encompassing the Parque Natural da Arrábida, the Serra da Arrábida is definitely worth a visit for its beautiful landscapes. Comprising a chain of mountains, which have a rugged topography but are not very high, the scenery creates a dramatic effect between the horizon and the sea. The scenic roads that wind through the mountains boast sheer cliffs that plunge into the ocean, lovely little beaches with fine golden sand (see p 189), a fortified convent, as well as places to stop and enjoy delicious sheep cheese and liqueur-like wine, both typical of the region.

An excellent way to explore this idyllic region, barely 50km from the capital, is to take the N10-4 west from Setúbal, then backtrack along the N379-1 before following Route 528 to Vila Nogueira de Azeitão, which boasts a number of local specialties and superb gardens. We have described some of

the curiosities found along this route below so that visitors will get the most out of the tour.

Portinho da Arrábida

(*12km from Lisbon*)

After driving down a steep hill, you will come to the **Museu Oceanográfico** (*200 ESC; Tue to Fri 10am to 4pm, Sat and Sun 3pm to 6pm*) on the right, in a particularly impressive bend of the road. This museum displays various marine species in the Santa Maria da Arrábida fortress, which dates back to the 17th century and served as an outpost to defend against frequent pirate attacks.

The first floor of the museum contains the collection of Luís Gonzaga do Nascimento, a naturalist from the early 1900s. The display comprises marine animals captured in the area: most of them can no longer be found in the region. A series of aquariums housing a large number fish are also located on this floor. Unlike the animals in the do Nascimento collection, these are very much alive and can still be found in the region.

The second floor is devoted to flora and fauna that can still be admired in the Serra da

Arrábida and the Rio Sado estuary. Before leaving this charming site, be sure to visit the lovely terrace on the top floor to take in the **superb panorama ★**. T-shirts and other souvenirs are sold on site, and brochures (in English and Portuguese) are available for those interested in learning more about the park's natural riches.

esting thing about the chapel may well be its setting: it is full of stalactites and is illuminated only by light reflected from the water. The sound of waves can be heard in the cave, and a large bay partly extends into its opening. The combination of natural and mystical elements makes the place enchanting.

Continuing down to the bay, the road comes to a dead end in front of a lovely **beach** (see p 190) with a few services and facilities. Unfortunately, thieves are known to prowl the area, so don't leave ANYTHING in your car.

However, before descending towards this exotic *praia*, be sure to visit the **Gruta Lapa Santa Margarida ★**, a marine cave that houses a little chapel with unusual decorations.

Unfortunatley, the place has been much vandalized in recent years. The most inter-

To reach the cave, visitors must descend a long flight of steps overgrown with vegetation which leads through relatively pristine land, adding to the sense of magic and discovery, and offers some beautiful views of the ocean. The path begins on the right-hand side of the street, just before the museum, 3km from the junction with the N10-4, by a building with a sign that reads: "Lar de Ferias da Casa do Gelato". Take the path opposite this building. The stairs begin beside a metal gate overgrown with

brush. The path is not recommended for people who are afraid of heights or suffer from vertigo since the steps are steep and there is no hand-rail.

Perched on the mountainside, the **Convento da Arrábida** (*Route N379-1*) and its sun-faded edifices, surrounded by lush green vegetation, create a picturesque ensemble. The best view of the convent is from the intersection of the N10-4 and the road leading to the Praia Portinho da Arrábida. This fairytale convent and the landscape that surrounds it are picture-perfect, presided over by an azure sky. The estate was founded in 1542 by a Franciscan order with the Duke of Aveiro as their patron. It was expanded in the 17th century, and comprises no fewer than two monasteries, several chapels, a retreat for the Duke, and accommodations for pilgrims. The stations of the Cross, with interesting turret-shaped chapels along the way, were added in the 18th century and lead to the sanctuary of Bom Jesus.

The monastery was used until 1834, when the Franciscan order was expelled from the country. The property is now in the hands of a private foundation, the Fundação Oriente, which has turned it into a cultural centre that also serves as a convention centre. Unfortu-

Costa de Lisboa

nately, access is restricted to guests; the public is rarely allowed inside except during the annual festival of Capuchos music, which is held in July and August. Among other things, visitors can purchase honey produced right on the estate.

After trekking across the Serra, be sure to stop in the small village of Vila Nogueira de Azeitão where you can visit the **José Maria de Fonseca winery** (*free visits by appointment; Mon to Fri 9am to noon and 2:30pm to 4pm; ☎212 19 89 40 or 212 18 02 27, ≈212 19 89 42 or 212 19 03 73, www.jmf.pt*) known for its *moscatel* which has been produced here for several generations. Apart from local wines (*moscatel* and *periquita*), the shops in town sell Queijo de Azeitão, a delicious sheep cheese called. Locals claim the cheese derives its unique flavour from the thistle used in the production process.

Sesimbra

Sesimbra has few historic attractions for visitors, except for its **Castelo**, which is located several kilometres from the centre of town. Although it has been almost too well restored, it offers some good views of the city. Once a small fishing village, Sesimbra has become a modern city filled with new, soul-

less buildings. Only the little streets near the beach have been spared this unfortunate transformation. Meanwhile, the beach is invaded every weekend by residents from the capital, who come to bathe in the warm waters and enjoy the fine-sand beach. The city is packed with restaurants, and fish lovers will find plenty of places to choose from. More than anything else, Sesimbra is an excellent place to stop for a meal before heading off to Cabo Espichel.

Cabo Espichel

Cabo Espichel is a truly magical place. The encounter between land and ocean is even more dramatic here than at Sagres or Cabo da Roca, and the waves crash against the cliffs with magnificent abandon. This majestic promontory, where the strong ocean winds sweep across the sparse vegetation that grows on its flat, plateau-like summit, is topped by the **Igreja de Nossa Senhora da Cabo**. Bordered by two long rows of dwellings that were once used to house pilgrims, this church also has perfectly aligned arcades, creating a picturesque setting that looks like a theatrical backdrop. This site is most impressive when it is

deserted. Although the abandoned houses are in poor condition, the church's interior has been well preserved and is worth a quick visit to see the high altar. The altar is crowned with astonishing twisted columns and adorned with elegant Baroque paintings dating back to the 18th century, when the church was built. On the second floor, to the right, is the royal gallery.

The small road that leads past the lighthouse and continues on to the west coast of the peninsula leads to the 15th-century **Capela de Memória**. The small chapel's white walls contrast with the blue decor and will delight those who enjoy picturesque scenes.

Península de Tróia

(*98km from Setúbal*)

Facing the city of Setúbal, the 17km-long **Península de Tróia** is a spit of sand at the end of which is the village or, rather, the tourist complex of Tróia. In fact, the complex mainly comprises a group of high-rise apartments that can be rented on a weekly or monthly basis. They are linked to a nearby golf club, Tróia Golf. Despite the Bica, Lilas and Costa da Galé beaches, this spot is not likely to appeal to travellers as it is a private estate designed with its perma-

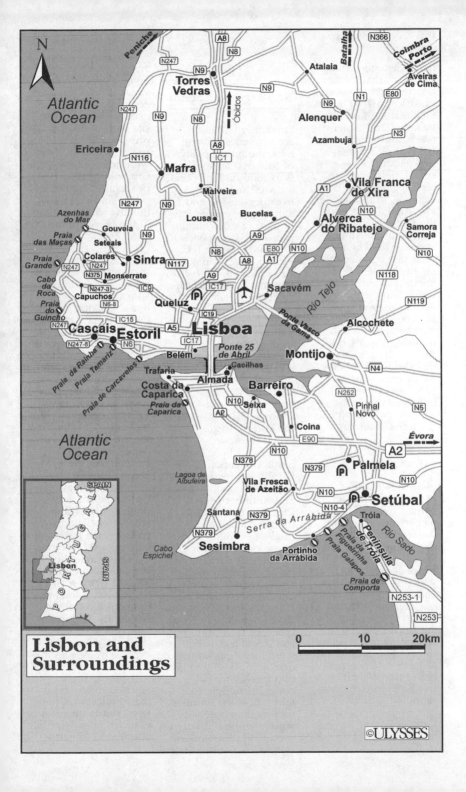

Lisbon and Surroundings

nent residents in mind. There are many other beaches (see Costa da Caparica, p 189) in the area that are just as beautiful and easier to reach, and which are not marred by such unpleasantries as smoke-belching factories far off on the coast, or the sight of countless abandoned towers on the peninsula. The only attractions worthy of attention are the few **ruins** that have been uncovered. There are a few modest vestiges of Cetóbriga, the ancient Roman seaport built between the first and fourth centuries and destroyed by a landslide in the fifth century. You can observe what remains of the baths and of several buildings used for fish preservation, as well as the ruins of a temple.

The road (N253-1) that crosses the peninsula does not offer any good views of the ocean, and the litter left behind by careless picnickers detracts from the scenery. Leaving the peninsula, be sure to visit the charming **Museo do Arroz** (*N261*, ☎*265 49 75 55*) at the entrance to the village of Comporta. In addition to discovering all the steps involved in cultivating rice, visitors can enjoy a meal at the restaurant-bar. A number of rice plantations can be seen in the surrounding area.

Santiago do Cacém

Stretching within an area covering several hills, the municipality of Santiago do Cacém is located on lands that are well suited for livestock-raising and agriculture, explaining in part an early human presence dating back to the third century B.C. Although Celts inhabited this area, almost no important traces of this civilization remain. Only Miróbriga, the Celtic name of an important Roman site located 1km from the present-day village, recalls these distant origins. The Moors occupied the area and built a series of fortifications on the site of the current castle. They called the spot "Cacém", whose origin is still not certain. During the reconquest, the site passed back and forth between Christian troops and then the Muslims, finally becoming Portuguese once and for all in 1217. Its current name comes from the Order of Santiago (St. James), to which King Dom Sancho I conferred the site in recognition of its recapture in 1185. If a traveller were to define Santiago do Cacém briefly today, two images would come unfailingly to mind: first, the wonderful ramparts perched atop a gentle hill where proud cypresses reign

and pretty little houses lie nestled in a white streak amidst the greenery; and, second, the extraordinary Roman site surrounded by cypresses and hills that recede to the horizon with bell-clad sheep gambolling about peacefully, adding a gentle and melodious tinkling to the rustling of the leaves in the wind.

Besides a romantic stroll though its peaceful alleyways, lined with charming little houses, Santiago de Cacém's main attraction remains, of course, the impressive **ramparts ★** of its castle. Built under Muslim occupation, the fortifications were extended and strengthened by the Knights Templar soon after the reconquest of this area toward 1157. Heavily damaged in the 1755 earthquake, the site was abandoned for a long time. Today all that remains are its double row of four-sided crenellated ramparts, which have been marvellously restored. You can circle the entire site and enjoy magnificent **views ★** of the nearby hills, dominated by picturesque little windmills. Within the ramparts, a cemetery shaded by majestic cypress trees is an inviting spot for meditation.

Situated right next to the fortifications, the **Igreja Matriz** (the parish church), entirely rebuilt after the 1755 earthquake, still has (on the left side of the building) an interesting Romano-Gothic portal dating from the 13th century, the era of its founding. An interesting **Gothic bas-relief**, dating from the 14th century and portraying São Tiago fighting the Moors, can also be seen inside.

During your climb toward the *castelo*, stop at the **Praça do Conde de Bracial**, a wonderful, peaceful little square where, besides the fine **bourgeois dwellings**, you can observe a very elegant **pillory** dating from 1845.

Miróbriga

(1km from Santiago do Cacém)

This is the largest Roman site discovered south of the Tagus. Little is known to this day about the origins of this spot. Some say it has been firmly established that this site was first inhabited by groups of Celtic origin, as its name suggests. Taking over from them, the Romans built an important post whose role (pilgrimage site, advanced military post, thermal source?) has not yet been determined with any degree of certainty. Moreover, the reasons for its abandonment remain an object of research. In this open-air museum, you can observe

extraordinary **ruins** (*100 ESC; Tue to Sun 9am to noon and 1:30pm to 5pm*) in a truly enchanting setting. The map, provided free of charge at the museum entrance, leads to the remains of numerous houses and commercial establishments and also to a chapel, thermal baths (especially interesting), and a bridge, as well as an inn still containing several bits of fresco. The temple still has three of its granite columns, one of them adorned with a Corinthian cornice. Visiting this spot is made all the more impressive by the Roman streets, which retain their original paving-stones, and provide access to the various attractions. Returning to the entrance, do not miss the little museum located near the ticket stall. Even if the descriptions are given only in Portuguese, the panels and diagrams attached to the displays are worth lingering over for the insight they provide. Finally, 1km away, lies something quite exceptional: the ruins of a grand horse-racing track were discovered in 1984, the only such discovery to this day in Portugal; unless you are a true archaeology buff, however, you will find nothing really spectacular in it since the vestiges are as yet scarcely visible.

Porto Covo

A peaceful town nestled at the top of cliffs that plunge into the crashing waves of the ocean, Porto Covo is the stereotypical image of Portugal's past, which seems to have been almost forgotten in Europe over the past century. If it weren't for the presence of constantly multiplying businesses crowding the main street, visitors might believe they had entered a different era. At the entrance to the town, the **Largo do Marquês de Pombal** ★ forms a picturesque scene with its little church and houses with striking white façades. The Vasco da Gama, a paved street with numerous fish and seafood restaurants, runs through the entire town, ending at a rocky promontory. The view of the jagged coastline here resembles the coast of Brittany, and the mysterious Ilha do Pessegueiro is visible in the distance. In good weather, you can even see the city of Sines and the ominous chimney stacks of its industrial park.

Ilha do Pessegueiro

The well-preserved ruins of the **Ilha de Dentro** fortress are located right on the

Costa de Lisboa

coast, and are visible at the end of a road that runs through the bucolic countryside. Meanwhile, the **Ilha do Pessegueiro** fort was built in the early 16th century, but little of the structure remains as it was destroyed during the same century by pirates who infested the European coast. Since the island is difficult to reach and there is little to be seen, a visit is not really worthwhile. Roman salt-works found on the island (no longer visible today) prove that the island has been inhabited by humans since the first century.

Beaches

Estoril

Today, Estoril is a slightly out-of-fashion resort with old prestigious hotels and mansions that bear witness to a rather wild era. Its beach, **Tamariz**, separated from the village by railroad tracks that run along the coast, is rather small but there is a large swimming pool (*closed Sep to Apr*).

Here you will find numerous restaurants with terraces, as well as several bars. There are two ways of getting to the beach: use the pedestrian passage beside the old train station to cross the train

tracks and continue to Rua Olivença, or take the underpass located across from the Estoril tourist office.

Praia da Carcavelos

This modest, medium-sized beach 8km from Estoril is known for its surfing. There are many shops specializing in surfing equipment, as well as a number of bars and cafés.

Cascais

Less than 30km from the capital and easy to reach, Cascais is besieged by day-trippers year-round, turning it into one of the country's busiest resorts. Today, restaurants, shops, discotheques and game parlours reverberate day and night, attracting many young people in search of weekend fun. For those who enjoy a lively scene and constant crowds, Cascais is a dream come true. As for its rather small beach, show up early to claim your spot and be prepared to elbow your way in! Even if prices here are more reasonable than in Estoril, Cascais remains a rather expensive beach resort.

★

Praia do Guincho and Praia da Galé

Once outside the town of Cascais, a beautiful **scenic highway**, the N247, follows the coast toward Praia do Guincho. This section of the Costa do Estoril is the most interesting part, because it is still fairly wild and unspoiled. Two beaches where it is pleasant to linger are the **Praia do Guincho ★** and, right next to it, **Praia da Galé**. Praia do Guincho is the more popular, famous for sailboarding and surfing. Moreover, it has a broad stretch of white sand lined on one side by dramatic, jagged cliffs and on the other by green hills. The relative lack of crowds at this spot is explained by a rough sea that makes bathing more dangerous than elsewhere. Casual swimmers will prefer the beach beside it, the Praia da Galé, which is less impressive but is washed by much calmer waters.

Praia Grande, Praia das Maçãs and Azenhas do Mar

These three neighbouring seaside resorts are located only a few kilometres from the marvellous town of Sintra, so getting there makes for a wonderful day-trip. Each beach has its own unique character, and visitors who love lingering by the sea are sure to find one of them ideal. **Sintra Atlântico** (*500 ESC; irregular schedule; Stagecoach Sintra, Ribeira de Sintra, ☎/≈219 29 11 66*) has linked Sintra and Praia das Maçãs for several years with a charming old tram that makes the trip in 40min, running along the verdant Serra de Sintra to Colares and Praia das Maçãs. This mode of transportation is a pleasant way to reach these destinations.

Although **Praia das Maçãs** is the region's longest beach, it is not the most charming. Some of the many buildings along it are of dubious taste, and the place looks like a seaside resort that is past its prime. Nevertheless, families looking for vacations in the sun descend on this beach on weekends and summer holidays. If you like these types of crowds, this is the resort for you.

On the other hand, those who wish to escape the crowds should head to nearby **Praia Grande** ★. Minimal development (there are only two hotels and a few restaurants) has been carried out on this beach surrounded by high cliffs. The place is ideal for solitary walks as well as surfing. Expert surfers have been coming here for a long

time, and visitors can admire their exploits in the waves.

The final resort, **Azenhas do Mar** ★, can be said to have the most character. This charming little village with small white-washed houses, some of which are built right into the cliff, is located at the crux of a bay with steep shores, at the curve of a sharp bend in the road. At the lower end of town, by the little river, is a swimming pool with stepped terraces that allows visitors to swim in fresh water while still enjoying the sea breezes. Still farther down, on the beach, is a curved jetty that forms a basin that fills with sea water at high tide and traps the water when the tide goes out. Thus, less experienced swimmers can safely bathe in natural sea water. Unfortunately, these unique installations were in a state of abandon, and debris was beginning to accumulate around them.

Costa da Caparica

Like Cascais, **Costa da Caparica** (*from Marquês Pombal or Metro Palhavã bus 75; single ticket 1 Dia-Praia 480 ESC or family ticket for four passengers 1,440 ESC*) is a popular tourist spot on weekends. Because it's close and easy to reach, this area is regularly invaded by people from Lisbon in search of a beach and a suntanning

session. However, unlike the other beaches, the Costa da Caparica has **beaches** ★ which stretch out over many kilometres, and most of the coastline has been left in its natural state because part of it has been classified as a protected zone. In the summer, a little train takes passengers along almost 10km of the coast. Whereas many families go to the beaches close to the village of Caparica, nudists and gays (17th, 18th and 19th stops) often frequent the beaches that are farther away. The bus trip from the capital is all the more enjoyable because the bus crosses the impressive Ponte 25 de Abril (bridge) from which you can get a superb view of the Tagus and Lisbon.

Praia da Figueirinha and Praia de Galápos

Located 7km from downtown Setúbal, Praia de Figueirinha is the first of a number of beaches that line the Serra da Arrábida if you are heading east. This is not the most peaceful beach to be found in the Serra, since it is located close to the road and has a large parking lot. Nevertheless, the beautiful fine sand and proximity of the more isolated Praia de Galápos, make this a relatively pleasant place to stop.

Costa de Lisboa

Praia do Portinho da Arrábida

A beautiful **scenic highway** ★ and an abrupt descent ending in a cul-de-sac lead to **Praia do Portinho da Arrábida** ★ (*18km from Setúbal*), a beautiful **beach** nestled in a bay where you can swim to your heart's content. Some services are available here, including a restaurant at the edge of the beach. Before heading for the water, remember theft is an unfortunate reality in this region and that you should exercise caution and leave NOTHING in your vehicle.

Porto Covo

After following Vasco da Gama street with its numerous restaurants and terraces, it is a true pleasure to discover, a jagged coastline, riddled with coves and bays at this end of the promontory. Unfortunately, the coast is difficult to reach. The most accessible cove is the one containing the pretty **Praia dos Buizinhos**, which can be reached by a series of stairs built into the rock. It is recommended

to bathe only at low tide and to exercise a high degree of caution, since the sea is especially treacherous here.

Parks

Sintra

Located within the bounds of the Serra de Sintra (see p 171), the **Parque da Pena** ★★★ (*Tue to Sun 10am to 4:30pm, closed Mon*) has many hiking trails which will enable you to explore some extraordinarily rich and diversified flora. From the temperate to the subtropical, the park has no fewer than 3,000 different species of trees, including firs, palms, cork oaks and arbutus. Moreover, the many exuberantly designed palaces surrounding the park have transformed the region into a veritable fairyland. Those who enjoy romantic walks will be especially receptive to the charm of this area. Even in rainy weather, nature reveals its many wonders. The mists that waft from the neighbouring forests form a landscape imbued with an almost hallucinatory mystery.

Monserrate

Stretched over a vast manor, **Parque de Monserrate** ★★ (*200 ESC; 10am to 4:45pm in the winter, until 5:45pm in the summer*) is worth a visit to admire its especially diverse flora. Everything here is an object of wonder, whether it be tree ferns from New Zealand, the powerfully scented eucalyptus, the African palms, the giant cedars, or simply the generous cork oaks. This wonder is well described by Lord Byron in his tale *Childe Harold's Pilgrimage*, in which he places his cherished Eden in this spot.

Paisagem Protegida da Arriba Fóssil da Costa da Caparica

Created in 1984, this protected area includes the dunes that cover part of the Costa da Caparica, as well as the Reserva Botânico Mata dos Medos, comprising a total area of 1,570ha. Part of the terrain is covered by pines, myrtles and other Mediterranean trees, while a series of cliffs, called **Arriba Fóssil** ★, make up another. These cliffs, which are now separated from the sea by vast sand dunes, are unique in that they contain innumerable fossils of marine animals that were deposited there over time as the sea receded. Specimens dating back as far as 15 million years have been discovered here. The cliffs are also distinguished by their unique shapes, which were sculpted by centuries of erosion by wind and water and resemble those found in some canyons in the American west. Despite the proximity of the popular Costa da Caparica seaside resort, it is easy to find peace and quiet here, since there are no fewer than 13 beaches to accommodate visitors.

Reserva Natural do Estuário do Sado

Already inhabited in Roman times, as attested by the salt-works on the Tróia peninsula, the Sado estuary boasts a flourishing underwater environment, as indicated by the many waders that populate it. In addition to fishing opportunities, the area has huge salt-works that still employ a significant number of people, while several rice plantations occupy the banks of the Rio Sado, at the head waters of the estuary. This large zone of 23,000ha has been a protected area since 1980, and provides ample opportunities for bird-watching. Storks and pink flamingos come here to feed in the fall and winter, while herons, water hens, ducks and many other species can be observed year-round. A small colony of some 30 dolphins, known locally as *roaz*, also live here. With a little patience, you might catch a glimpse of them playing in the waves if you make an excursion around the Tróia peninsula, across from Praia da Costa da Galé. You may also see a *Galeão do Sado*, a boat with elegant sails which was used until the mid-20th century to transport passengers and goods from Rio Sado to the Tróia peninsula.

Outdoor Activities

Hiking

In the Serra de Sintra, the **Parque da Pena ★★** (*Tue to Sun 10am to 4:30pm, closed Mon*) has many hiking trails which will enable you to explore some extraordinarily rich and diversified flora. Among the easily accessible hikes, we suggest the one going to the Palácio da Pena by the "gate to the lakes", one of the most magical. To do this, take the Estrada da Pena leaving Sintra Vila, following the signs to the palace.

You will find the **Portão dos Lagos** about halfway up, on the right of the highway, near a parking area. This is where the trail begins so park your vehicle here. After entering through the gate, take the trail running alongside the water on the left. Three small lakes follow, each lined with flourishing vegetation. You can contemplate magnificent tree ferns originating in Australia and New Zealand. Continue your walk along the main road until you come to the first intersection, where you turn left; at the next crossroads, go left again. The entrance to the castle is at the end. Allow one to two hours to reach it. Those who enjoy **panoramic views ★** should take the trail on the right, located at the second intersection after the lakes. This leads to the **Cruz Alta**, at an altitude of 530m, from where you can observe the Serra da Sintra as well as the Pena palace, perched on its rock and standing out from distant plains. It takes about 2hrs to get there.

If you are interested in longer walks with many viewpoints, take the trail leading to the Palácio da Pena, passing through the beautiful site of the **Castelo dos Mouros ★** (*free admission; every day 10am to 4:30pm, see p 177*).

see p 177

Costa de Lisboa

Golf Courses

Name	Number of Holes	Par	Length (in metres)	Address
Golf do Estoril	18	69	5,240	Av. da República 2765 Estoril ☎214 68 01 76 ⇌214 68 27 96
Estoril Sol	9	31	1,800	Estrada da Lagoa Sul, Linhó 2710 Sintra ☎/⇌219 23 24 61
Quinta da Marinha Golf Club	18	71	6,100	Casa 36 2750 Cascais ☎214 86 98 31 ⇌214 86 90 32
Quinta da Beloura Golf Club	18	73	5,814	Estrada da Albarraque 2710 Sintra ☎219 10 60 35 ⇌219 10 63 59
Penha Longa	18	72	6,290	Estrada da Lagoa Azul, Linhó 2710 Sintra ☎219 24 00 14 ⇌219 24 90 24
Belas Clube de Campo	18	72	6,380	Casal da Carregueira 2745 Belas ☎214 31 00 77 ⇌214 31 24 82
Lisbon Sports Club	18	69	5,275	Casal da Carregueira 2715 Queluz ☎214 31 00 77 ⇌214 31 24 82
Mosteiro	9	35	2,590	Caesar Park Penha Longa Estrada da Lagoa Azul, Linhó 2710 Sintra ☎219 24 00 11 ⇌219 24 90 24
Termas do Vimeiro Golf Club	9	34	2,350	Porto Novo 2650 Torres Vedras ☎261 98 41 57 ⇌261 98 46 21

The Baroque
exuberance of
Bom Jesus do
Monte.
- *G. Sioen*

A visit to the
Mosteiro dos
Jerónimos in
Belém is a must!
- *Marc Rigole*

The beach of
Nazaré and its
typical fishing
boats.
- *W. Buss*

Woman drying
fish the
traditional way
on the beach.
- *W. Buss*

Montado Golf Club	18	72	6,010	Apartado 4o, Algeruz 2950 Palmela ☎265 70 66 48 ⇌265 70 67 75
Clube Quinta do Peru	18	72	6,036	2830 Quinta do Conde Azeitão ☎212 13 43 22 ⇌212 13 43 21
Tróia Golf Club	18	72	6,335	Complexo Turístico de Tróia 7570 Grândola ☎265 49 41 12 ⇌265 49 43 15
Aroeira Golf	18	72	6,045	Herdade da Aroeira Fonte da Telha 2825 Monte da Caparica ☎212 97 13 14 ⇌212 97 12 38

To get there, from the centre of Sintra Vila take Rua Visconde de Monserrate, which later becomes Rua Bernardim Ribeiro. After passing a curve in the street, a stairway located on your right leads directly to the Igreja da Santa Maria, which faces the forest administration buildings of the Serra da Sintra. From there, just next to the buildings, a long, winding trail leads to the ruins of the dos Mouros castle, from where you can enjoy several **panoramic views** ★ of the village of Sintra. Continue climbing; the path joins the main road, the Estrada da Pena, leading to the Pena palace. You then have two choices: left on the Estrada da Pena leads directly to the palace, or to the right leads to the Portão dos Lagos below, from where you

can reach the Pena palace by way of narrow trails (see the previous tour). If you opt for the second route, allow for a complete afternoon leaving from Sintra Vila.

Located between Setúbal and Sesimbra, the **Serra da Arrábida** ★ is an immense nature park covering nearly 10,800ha (more than 26,000 acres). Besides superb beaches, the park has several trails allowing you to observe magnificently verdant and hilly scenery set against an azure blue sea. Four paths have been cleared by the management of the Parque Natural da Arrábida to allow visitors to explore the beauty of the local flora. The length of the proposed tours varies between 5 and 15km, each presenting a different level of difficulty.

An excellent little guide (*free; Guia de Percursos Pedestres Arrábida / Sado; at press time this was available in Portuguese only*) that gives precise details of the various hikes in the region and the **Reserva Natural do Estuário do Sado** is available at the Posto de Turismo da Região de Setúbal (*Largo Corpo Santo*), in the centre of Setúbal.

Golf

Just like in the Algarve, golf has become a much appreciated sporting specialty here, and the Costa de Lisboa ranks second among the regions in terms of the number of golf courses. There are no fewer than nine courses on the Costa de Estoril and around Sintra, four

Costa de Lisboa

of which are south of the capital near Setúbal.

Accommodations

Estoril

Pensão Smart
$$
pb
Rua Maestro Lacerda no. 6 2765 Estoril
☎*214 68 21 64*
Graced with a charming garden, the Pensão Smart is a good hotel with reasonable rates. Its few rooms are impeccably kept, and a few of these afford a pleasant views.

Hotel Inglaterra
$$$
pb, tv, ≈
Rua do Porto no. 1, 2765 Estoril
☎*214 68 44 61*
⇌*214 68 21 08*
Situated right next to the park and close to the casino, this former bourgeois residence converted into a hotel has 50 comfortably and tastefully arranged rooms. Opt for one of the upstairs rooms, as these offer a beautiful view. Like most establishments in Estoril, however, this one is rather pricey considering the few services offered.

Hotel Palácio Estoril
$$$$$
pb, tv, ≈, ○, ☉
Rua do Parque, 2765 Estoril
☎*214 68 04 00*
⇌*214 68 48 67*
Many of the hotels that stretch along the coast look modern, impersonal and uninteresting. Among the few remaining buildings that predate World War I, the Hotel Palácio Estoril is worthy of mention for its pleasant setting, both inside and outside. Its 162 rooms have classic furnishings, all in good taste, and the interesting lighting brings out the warm decor. The bathrooms are especially big, decked out in fine marble and well equipped. On the ground floor, the hotel has several lounges, most of them tastefully appointed. The Austrian-style lounge with its piano, as well as the games room adorned with oriental rugs and exotic wood panelling, are worth a visit. The elegant breakfast room, with fine antique marble, is also worthy of mention. A plentiful breakfast buffet is served there. Finally, a big pool, open year-round and surrounded by a perfectly manicured English lawn, renders this spot very pleasant. A bit expensive.

Carcavelos

(8km from Estoril)

Hotel Praia Mar
$$$$
pb, tv, ⊗, ℜ, ≈
Rua do Gurué No. 16
2776-997 Carcavelos
☎*214 57 31 31*
⇌*214 57 31 30*
An integral part of the Almeida chain, this hotel has some 100 rooms in a building just off Carcavelos beach. Although the hotel's exterior lacks in charm, the interior is agreeable. Despite the dated look of the furniture and the bathrooms, the rooms are comfortable and pleasant. For a good view, choose a room facing the sea. These have balconies from which the beautiful sunsets can be enjoyed. Breakfast consists of a copious buffet served in the vast dining room of the hotel's restaurant. Located on the top floor, this room has a view of the entire coast. The hotel also has a large swimming pool, which is ideal for those who do not like to bathe in the sea.

Oeiras

(8km from Estoril)

Pousada de Juventude Catalazete
$ dormitory, no bkfst
4,100 ESC double, bkfst incl
Estrada Marginal, next to the INATEL building
2780 Peiras
☎/⇌*214 43 06 38*

Cascais

 Casa da Pérgola
$$* or *$$$
sb/pb
closed Oct to mid-Mar
Avenida Valbom no. 13, 2750
Cascais
☎*214 84 00 40*
⇌*214 83 47 91*
Located in the centre of
town, this little six-
room hotel is worth
considering both for its
relatively affordable
prices and for its
slightly old-fashioned
charm. Its *azulejos*,
flower garden, and old
knick-knacks and furni-
ture will please the
most romantic visitors.
Friendly and profes-
sional service.

Hotel Albatroz
$$$$$
pb, tv, ≈, ℜ
Rua Frederico Arouca no. 100
2750 Cascais
☎*214 83 28 21*
⇌*214 84 48 27*
Set by the seaside, the
Hotel Albatroz has two
distinct buildings, now
set around a single
terrace overlooking the
cliffs. The older part,
formerly a resort for the
nobility, still has some
rooms decorated in the
old style, as well as a
restaurant and a bar
with panoramic views.
Most of the rooms and
a small luxury shop-
ping gallery are located
in the new building.
Rooms are appointed
with modern furniture,
and most have balco-
nies with sea views. On
the broad terrace, a
small saltwater pool as
well as many lounge
chairs will delight

sunbathers and idlers.
The only regret is the
singular lack of green-
ery.

Praia do Guincho

(8km from Cascais)

**Campismo do
Guincho/Orbitur**
at Areia, 2750 Cascais
☎*214 87 21 67*
☎*214 87 04 50*
⇌*214 87 21 67*

Hotel do Guincho
$$$$$
pb, tv, ℜ
9km west of Cascais, Estrada do
Guincho, 2750 Cascais
☎*214 87 04 91*
⇌*214 87 04 31*
The designers of the
Hotel do Guincho did a
good job of blending
the crudeness of a
former military building
with the elegance and
comfort required today
for any quality hotel
establishment. Although
it looks modern from
the outside, this hotel
was built from the ruins
of a fortress. While
some elements in the
common areas recall its
distant past (doors with
semi-circular arches, a
stairway and walls in
crudely cut stone), the
atmosphere has been
rendered warmer by
luxurious carpets and
classy furniture. The
guest rooms are set in
the former vaulted
cells, linked around a
central courtyard still
equipped with its well.
Some of them have
small enclosed galleries
with views of the coast.
The decor of both the
magnificent meeting
room, with its fully

medieval appearance,
and the congenial res-
taurant, with its pan-
oramic view of the sea,
are worth a glance.

Queluz

 **Pousada Dona
Maria I**
$$$$$
pb, tv, ℜ
facing the Palácio de Queluz
2745 Queluz
☎*214 35 61 58*
☎*214 35 61 72*
⇌*214 35 61 89*
The latest in a presti-
gious line, the Pousada
Dona Maria I is just as
spectacular as its cous-
ins. Facing the splendid
Palácio de Queluz (see
p 170), the *pousada* is
set up in a building that
was to have been part
of a vast grouping of
buildings next to the
palace. French inva-
sions and the flight of
the Court to Brazil
were, however, to
change the course of
things. As such, besides
the lack of an identical
building to complete
the central square, the
original blueprints do
not indicate a tower.
The present clock
tower was added to the
existing building after
the fact. To this day,
historians still ponder
the reason for the
addition; what is
known is that the clock
started running on the
very day Dona Maria II
was born, that is July
28th, 1819. Designed as
an outbuilding to the
palace, the present
building served mainly
to accommodate the
great number of ser-

vants assigned to the Court. Today, it consists of 24 rooms and two suites, all comfortably and luxuriously furnished. The clever arrangement of the premises as well as the preservation of various period elements, such as the small theatre's balcony and the impressive clock mechanism, add still more cachet to the place. Its ideal location, close to all the sights (Lisbon, Sintra, Cascais, Estoril, etc.) as well as the magnificent palace gardens make this *pousada* a perfect place to combine the pleasures of discovery with those of luxury and comfort.

Almornos

(*12km from Queluz*)

Clube de Campismo de Lisboa
in Almornos, near the N117
1675 Caneças
☎*219 62 39 60*
⇌*219 62 37 60*

Sintra

Pousada da Juventude
$ double room, no bkfst
Santa Eufémia
2710 Sintra
☎/⇌*219 24 12 10*

Casa de Hóspedes Adelaide
$
sb, pb
Avenida Guilherme Gomes
Fernandes no. 11, 1st floor,
2710 Sintra
☎*219 23 08 73*
Two hundred metres from the Sintra train station, the Casa de Hóspedes Adelaide will

especially appeal to travellers seeking low-priced accommodation. In this guesthouse, there are several rather austerely furnished, but always clean, rooms. Only a few among them have private showers, however. The friendly reception will further your appreciation of this place's simple charm.

Residencial Monte da Lua
$$ no bkfst
pb
Avenida Miguel Bombarda
2710 Sintra
☎/⇌*219 24 10 29*
Located just across from the Sintra train station, the small Residencial Monte da Lua has only seven rooms, each pleasantly but simply decorated and above all very well kept. The mood here is distinctly family oriented. A few rooms have lovely views of the surrounding mountains, with the ocean in the distance. Bearing in mind the few low-priced accommodations in Sintra, this establishment offers good value.

Pensão-Residêncial Sintra
$$$
pb, ≈
Travessa dos Avelares 12,
Calçada de São Pedro, 2710 São
Pedro de Sintra
☎*219 23 07 38*
In a beautiful large residence, rather sparingly decorated, lies the Pensão-Residêncial Sintra. Despite its respectable size, this guesthouse has only 10 rooms, and this makes

it preferable to reserve far in advance. Its pretty terrace, with views of verdant hills, as well as its garden and pool, will delight those who seek space and open air.

Hotel Central
$$$
pb, tv
Praça da República no. 35
☎*219 23 09 63*
☎*219 23 00 63*
The best reason to stay at the Hotel Central, which looks rather antiquated but has a great deal of cachet, is its location right in the middle of the village next to the Palácio Nacional da Sintra. Its lovely breakfast room is certainly worth a look even if you aren't staying here. In fact the staff is so aloof to guests that it is quite easy to roam about this hotel. You may well have to wait a while at the reception before someone appears to serve you! Fairly expensive, but central.

Estalagem Solar dos Mouros
$$$
pb, tv
Calçada São Pedro no. 64, São
Pedro da Sintra, 2710 Sintra
☎*219 23 02 64*
☎/⇌*219 23 32 16*
A 10min walk from downtown Sintra, in the quaint little village of São Pedro de Sintra, is the Estalagem Solar dos Mouros, a modest hotel with a family atmosphere. Its seven rooms are exceptionally well-kept but very plainly decorated, and

a pleasant veranda acts as a breakfast room. Given the services offered, the rates are a bit high, a disadvantage compensated for partly by the warm welcome.

Tívoli Sintra
$$$-$$$$
pb, ≈, ℜ
Praça da República, behind the Palácio Nacional
2710 Sintra
☎219 23 35 05
⇄219 23 15 72
Though this hotel boasts a decent interior decor, the presence of such a modern building so close to the magnificent Palácio Nacional is indeed regrettable – a mistake that is all the more unfortunate as it is the only such building in the area. Indeed, this is a truly deplorable example of tourist development showing little concern for the setting, an example of an administration with little respect for the city's heritage. If this clash of the centuries does not bother you, however, you will find 75 comfortably equipped rooms, most benefitting from small terraces with pleasant views.

Lawrence's Hotel
$$$$$
pb, tv, ≈, ℜ
Rua Consiglieri Pedroso
No. 38-40
2710-550 Sintra
☎219 10 55 00
⇄219 10 55 05
www.portugalvirtual.pt/lawr
ences
When the owners built Lawrence's Hotel during the second half of

the 18th century, they no doubt anticipated that it would welcome some illustrious personalities, like writer Lord George Byron who stayed here in 1809. After a number of modifications carried out in a haphazard manner, the Dutch Willem-Bos family bought the property in 1989 and reopened the establishment under its original name. The building has an elegant pastel-coloured façade and contains 16 guest rooms arranged to ensure the utmost in comfort. Each room has its own unique character, and the furniture bespeaks the greatest refinement in taste. The lucky guests staying in the best rooms are treated to an almost paradisiac view of the plain that stretches out below the hotel, or of the fairytale Palácio da Pena nestled in its Serra. A completely remodelled library fitted with luxurious wooden panelling and a bar with a terrace complete the amenities. Of course, to enjoy such luxuries, one must be prepared to pay a handsome sum. After all, wasn't Sintra the preferred city of a certain nobility?

Seteais

(2km from Sintra)

Hotel Palácio de Seteais
$$$$$
pb, ℜ, ≈
Rua Barbosa Bocage nos. 8-10
Seteais, 2710 Sintra
☎219 23 32 00
☎219 23 42 77
⇄219 23 42 77
Less than 2km from Sintra, the Hotel Palácio de Seteais is set in a magnificent palace (see p 175) dating from the 19th century. Its 30 rooms are appointed with beautiful period furniture and offer a level of comfort worthy of the best hotels. Walking through its common areas, you can observe elegant frescoes as well as a great number of knick-knacks and antique tapestries. In front of the buildings is a majestic esplanade which is enticing for a walk, while behind them, a terrace looks out over a beautiful French-style garden, and offers a truly romantic and panoramic view of the surrounding countryside. For those seeking refinement and luxury, this is an unforgettable experience.

Costa de Lisboa

Várzea de Sintra

(*4km from Sintra*)

Pátio do Saloio
$$
pb, tv, ℜ
Rua Padre Amaro Teixeira de
Azevedo no. 14, Várzea de Sintra
☎*219 24 15 20*
☎/⇌*219 24 15 12*
Four kilometres from
Sintra, the Pátio do
Saloio is a small guest-
house run by a friendly
Belgian couple. This
quaint country house
has nine simply but
very tastefully deco-
rated rooms. The pro-
prietors are, in fact,
seasoned decorators:
the living room as well
as the very beautiful
Bistrobar Opera Prima
(see p 204), located in
downtown Sintra, are
two beautiful examples
of their work. Finally,
why not give into
temptation and try the
fine cuisine offered at
the restaurant of the
same name? Excellent
value.

Monserrate

(*4km from Sintra*)

🏅 **Quinta da Capela**
$$$$
pb, ≈, △, ☉
along the N375, to the right of
the old road going from Sintra
to Colares, shortly before the
Palácio de Monserrate
2710 Sintra
☎*219 29 01 70*
⇌*219 29 34 25*
Built in 1773 on the site
of the former residence
of the Duke of Cadaval,
the Quinta da Capela is
one of those spots that
leaves you with a cer-
tain sense of nostalgia.

Set within the Serra da
Sintra (see p 171), this
property is humble and
noble at the same time,
and is literally over-
grown with exuberant
vegetation. As you de-
scend the little cobbled
road leading to the
quinta, you are sur-
rounded by a silence
that is disturbed only
by the rustling of the
leaves in the wind and
by the songs of birds.
The powerfully aro-
matic flora bespeaks its
African and South
American origins. In
rainy weather, mists
spread from the neigh-
bouring forests and
form scenery that is
even more beautiful
and hallucinatory. Will
visitors find the Eden
so splendidly described
by Lord Byron?

The main building,
rather modest-looking
from the outside, has
seven rooms decorated
with exceptionally re-
fined furniture and
ornaments. Whether it
be the elegant lounge,
the breakfast room or
simply the corridors,
good taste is evident
throughout. Facing the
building, a superb
French-style garden
entices the visitor to
stroll, as two white
swans in a little pond
keep jealous watch
over their surroundings.
Going to the end of the
garden, you can admire
a pretty little Manueline
chapel (Nossa Senhora
da Piedade), the only
survivor of the 1755
earthquake, which de-
stroyed the rest of the
property. Located just

below the main build-
ing is an annex con-
taining three fully ap-
pointed cottage apart-
ments with a terrace
bathed in greenery.
Here also, meticulous
decoration turns rooms,
lounges and kitchens
into objects of wonder.
Finally, to fully enjoy
this dream place, a
sauna and a pool as
well as an exercise
room have been pro-
vided for the pleasure
of guests. One of the
best quality-to-price
ratios in the area.

Praia Grande

(*11km from Sintra*)

Campismo Amistad
Praia Grande, 2710 Colares
☎*219 29 05 81*
☎*219 29 18 34*

Setúbal

A Toca do Pai Lopes
Câmara Municipal de Setúbal
2900 Setúbal
☎*265-52 24 75*
⇌*265-53 35 96*

Residência Bocage
$$
pb
Rua de São Cristóvão no. 14
2900 Setúbal
☎*265 22 15 98*
⇌*265 22 18 09*
Located on a pedestrian
street, the Residência
Bocage has 39 rooms
that, though well-kept,
have no particular
charm. A good place
for those with limited
budgets.

Residencial Setubalense
$-$$
pb, tv
Rua Major Afonso Pala No. 17
2900 Setúbal
☎*265 52 57 90*
☎*265 52 59 63*
≈*265 52 57 89*
Located on one of the charming little pedestrian streets that run through the heart of the historic city centre, Residencial Setubalense has 24 impeccably maintained rooms. Unfortunately, the furniture is strictly functional and has no particular charm, unlike the lovely façade with its little wrought iron balconies. The sparse decor is made to look even more so by the vast expanse of white walls and floors. The television drones on even early in the morning in the small breakfast room with uninviting cafeteria-style tables. The small selection of dishes offered here (white bread, mass produced jams, tasteless cheese and artificially flavoured orange juice) are far from tempting.

Despite its faults, this is a good place to stay because of its central location and friendly welcome. As an aside, there is a lovely chapel, in a state of complete disrepair, right near the hotel at the corner of Rua Major Afonso Pala. The chapel houses São Francisco Xavier, the city's patron saint.

Residencial Mar e Sol
$$
pb, tv
Avenida Luísa Todi No. 606-608
2900 Setúbal
☎*265 53 48 68*
≈*265 53 20 36*
At the western edge of the city, close to numerous restaurants and bars, Residencial Mare e Sol has 71 spacious and comfortable rooms in a modern building without much character. The rooms facing Avenida Luísa Todi all have lovely little balconies, and those on the upper floors have views of the Rio Sado. However, if peace and quiet is more important to you, ask for a room at the back of the building: though they don't have balconies, they are less noisy. Although the building is not brand new, it has a welcoming atmosphere and a pleasing décor. Considering its competitive rates, this is one of the best values for hotels in this category.

Albergaria Solaris
$$$
pb, tv
Praça Marquês de Pombal no. 12, 2900 Setúbal
☎*265 52 21 89*
≈*265 52 20 70*
Attractive because of its facade and its location in the heart of town on a pretty little tree-shaded square, the Albergaria Solaris will suit those for whom comfort and the purely functional take precedence over everything else. Sparkingly clean and adorned with mod-

ern furniture, this hotel has a bar, a conference room, a TV room, etc. – in short just about everything. This is not, however, a spot for romantics or lovers of squeaky doors!

Quinta do Patrício
$$-$$$
pb, ps, K, ≈
at the western end of Avenida Luísa Todi; follow at first the signs on the left for the Pousada de São Filipe, Estrada do Castelo de São Filipe, 2900 Setúbal
☎/≈*265 23 38 17*
Hidden in the Serra da Arrábida, near the Castelo de São Felipe, the Quinta do Patrício is a rural property established in a beautiful setting. It includes a charming main residence with rooms equipped with various modern conveniences. Close by, a secondary residence as well as a charming windmill have been turned into well-appointed apartments. Whichever you choose, all rooms are carefully decorated with delicate rural taste. Besides a particularly warm welcome, you can enjoy a natural setting that is perfect for walking.

Costa de Lisboa

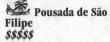 **Pousada de São Filipe**

$$$$$

pb, tv

go west along Avenida Luísa Todi and, at the end, turn right and then immediately left to reach Rua de São Filipe, which will lead you directly to the fortress, Rua de São Filipe 2900 Setúbal

☎*265 52 38 44*

⇆*265 53 25 38*

Overlooking the town of Setúbal, the Pousada de São Filipe is set in the central building of a former fortress dating from 1590 (see p 181), built by order of Felipe II of Spain to keep watch over the coast and the town below. You can take a room in the very building that served as a residence for the governor of that period. The entrance to the *pousada* lies through a long vaulted corridor with several fortified gates, and it is sure to impress. Atop the stairway, a magnificent terrace with a panoramic view of the Tróia peninsula awaits you. The comfortably appointed rooms are tastefully decorated and offer sea views. You can also keep watch over the coast, which these days has been overwhelmed by tall buildings. Some of the rooms are set in the former dungeon of the fortress, a dungeon whose comfort today would surprise the former governor!

Palmela

(8km from Setúbal)

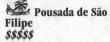 **Pousada de Palmela**

$$$$$

pb, tv, ℜ

atop the village of Palmela 2950 Palmela

☎*212 35 12 26*

☎*212 35 13 95*

⇆*212 33 04 40*

Opened in 1979 in an ancient 15th-century monastery, the Pousada de Palmela was the saving grace of this beautiful but long abandoned historic site (see p 182). At the entrance, your attention will be drawn to the imposing dimensions of the vaulted halls and of the galleries surrounding the cloister. Several comfortable lounges as well as a particularly convivial bar have been set up here. After walking along a series of broad corridors where the coolness of the stone contrasts pleasantly with the thick carpeting covering the floor, you will reach one of the 26 rooms. It is through a small door that you enter your cell, which has been transformed into a cosy room. Besides the knick-knacks and beautiful Portuguese-style furniture, from the southwest wing you can enjoy a grandiose view of the surrounding valleys and the distant sea. In the morning, breakfast awaits you in one of the galleries facing the cloister; the atmosphere is completely monastic.

Alcácer do Sal

(53km from Setúbal)

Pousada Dom Afonso II

$$$$$

pb, tv, ℜ, ≈

7580 Alcácer do Sal

☎*265 61 30 70*

☎*265 61 30 71*

⇆*265 81 30 74*

On the banks of Rio Sado, at the summit of a hill, Pousada Dom Afonso II benefits from a prestigious setting in the ancient fortified castle of the little village of Alcácer do Sal. Built during the Moorish era, enlarged after the expulsion of the Moors and later abandoned, this imposing edifice was recently the object of major restoration work in an effort to ready it for membership in the Enatur network. Set in a beautiful landscape of lovely green valleys which surround the castle, the *pousada* is a perfect stopover for travellers headed to the south of the country.

Santiago do Cacém

Residencial Gabriel

$$

pb, tv

Rua Professor Egas Moniz 24 7540 Santiago do Cacém

☎*269 82 22 45*

⇆*269 82 61 02*

With its modern look, the Residencial Gabriel has 23 modestly appointed rooms, far from luxurious but quite comfortable all the same.

Pousada de São Tiago
$$$
pb, ℜ, ≈
Rua de Lisboa, 7540 Santiago do Cacém
☎ *269 82 28 71*
☎ *269 82 28 74*
⇄ *269 82 20 73*
Located along the road leading to the Roman ruins of Miróbriga, the little Pousada de São Tiago is one of the oldest *pousadas* still in operation today. Set in a villa dating from 1947, it offers four rooms, two of them with superb views of the village and its castle. Its old-fashioned furniture, as well as its quaint plumbing, give this spot plenty of charm and a particularly rustic atmosphere. Behind the main building, a recent annex houses four other rooms, equipped with markedly more modern furniture and plumbing. A romantic flower garden, lovingly cared for, as well as a pool and a terrace, render this spot undeniably delightful. The friendly staff will great you with a smile.

Lagoa de Santo André

(*10km from Santiago do Cacém*)

Campismo Municipal da Lagoa de Santo André
7500 Santo André
☎ *269 70 85 50*
☎ *269 70 91 50*

Porto Covo

Miramar
$$
pb, *tv*
Rua Cândido da Silva No. 57
☎ *269 90 54 49*
The Miramar restaurant-bar rents out several rooms in its modern and slightly faded edifice. The simple rooms are not particularly luxurious; like the building, they are somewhat dreary. On the other hand, some rooms have balconies with a pleasant view of the ocean. Very friendly welcome.

Ilha do Pessegueiro

Parque de Campismo Ilha do Pessegueiro
$ camping
$$ studio/4pers.
pb, K
Estrada Ilha do Pessegueiro
7520 Porto Covo
☎ *269 90 51 78*
⇄ *269 90 50 67*
In addition to campsites, the Parque de Campismo Ilha do Pessegueiro has recently opened a dozen motel-style studios that can accommodate up to four people each and come with fully equipped kitchenettes and even a fireplace. The modern furniture is not particularly charming, but good enough for family vacations. Each unit has a parking space and a small terrace. The complex is surrounded by large, well-kept gardens filled with flowering plants.

There is also a restaurant, a bar and a small supermarket on site. The grounds are near the sea and the lovely Ilha de Pessegueiro, located 3km away. The peaceful countryside surrounding the Parque de Campismo is ideal for nature-lovers. Good quality for the price, and a friendly welcome.

Restaurants

Estoril

Restaurante-Bar Frolic
$$
Av. Clotilde, near Av. Marginal
With its slightly faded decor and cloying music, Restaurante-Bar Frolic is not the most happening place in the country, although it is representative of another era. If the weather permits, make use of the terrace, which gets full sun in the afternoons and has a vantage of the park across the way. Meanwhile the menu, which is eclectic to say the least, includes pizza and salads, as well as dishes derived from French cuisine, in addition to traditional Portuguese food. This place also has several vegetarian choices, such as cheese soufflé with spinach and asparagus. The reasonable prices are another of this establishment's delightful surprises.

Costa de Lisboa

Four Season Grill
$$$$
Rua do Parque
☎214 68 04 00
Traditionalists will not want to miss the Four Season Grill, the opulent restaurant attached to the Hotel Palácio Estoril. Comfortably set around a small dance floor, you will be lulled by music from another era, performed live; customers sometimes waltz a few steps. The 1970s-style curtains and carpets form an outmoded decor that could use some serious freshening-up. Classic cuisine is served here, with few surprises but good quality. Among the dishes worthy of mention, the venison with chestnuts and the *suprême* of hake with saffron are recommended. The veal liver with avocado and the chicken with shrimp are also excellent. Despite a worn setting and disturbingly slow service, this restaurant will be appreciated by lovers of good traditional cuisine. Meals starting at 3,500 ESC.

La Villa
$$$$$
every day 10am to midnight
Avenida Marginal, Praia Tamariz, right beside the Tamariz swimming pool
☎214 68 00 33
La Villa restaurant is housed in an old bourgeois villa built right on the seaside, with a beautiful yellow façade that has recently been fixed up. In addition to the lovely view of the sea through its large windows, guests can enjoy the highly original interior décor. The room in the rotunda has a sparse, modern style enhanced by a few Baroque-style pieces. This unusual combination of styles is not the least of the surprises, however, since the menu is equally inventive. A vichysoisse accompanied by toast and smoked ham might be followed by risotto with mushrooms and wild asparagus, or *sushi* and *sashimi*. Those preferring to stick to the classics might commence with an appetizer of oysters before indulging in cod baked in *mille-feuille*, accompanied by an olive-and-coriander purée. The only drawbacks to this unique establishment are the high prices and restrictive business hours.

Carcavelos

(8km from Estoril)

🌴 Restaurante Praia Mar
$$$
Hotel Praia Mar, Rua do Gueré No. 16
Praia Carcavelos
☎214 57 31 31
Located in a high-rise near Carcavelos beach, the restaurant at the Hotel Praia Mar is worth mentioning for its menu as well as its location. Although the edifice is not particularly charming, the dining room is on the top floor and has a lovely panoramic view of the surroundings. Meanwhile, the menu offers a variety of dishes. Both the appetizers (pears *au gratin*, vegetable terrine with shrimp) and main courses (chicken brochettes with dates, minced ostrich in mustard sauce, duck with olives) are pleasant alternatives to traditional Portuguese dishes. Tourist menus available for 3,200 ESC and up.

Cascais

Restaurante Music Bar
$-$$
every day 11am to 2am
Largo da Rainha
Situated on the coast, relatively secluded from the main tourist thoroughfares, this restaurant is notable for its pleasant terrace and its dining room with a direct view of the sea. In addition to the mainstays of traditional Portuguese cuisine, this place serves sandwiches, for as little as 600 ESC. The perfect place to fill up without breaking the bank!

🌴 Homonatura
$$
every day noon to 10pm
Rua Direita No. 24
☎214 83 73 82
Literally hidden away on the second floor of an unassuming building located behind a small homeopathic pharmacy (the entrance is between the Real Estate agency and the Militária Curiosidades e

Velharias souvenir shop), Homonatura serves good vegetarian food in a friendly environment. Quiche and vegetable pie, sweet and savoury crêpes and simmered tofu or seitan dishes are the healthy and nutritious offerings on the menu. On sunny days, guests can enjoy their meals on the large rooftop terrace. Whether you come here to dine or simply to savour a delicious natural fruit juice (beer and wine are also available), Isabel Alexandre, the charming owner of the establishment, will offer a friendly welcome with her characteristic warmth.

Os Doze
$$
Thu to Mon noon to 10:30pm, closed Tue evening and Wed
Rua Frederico Arouca no. 71 opposite Rua da Saudade
For good classic Portuguese cuisine, head to Os Doze, where whitewashed walls and stone arches form a warm decor. Very popular with a Portuguese clientele.

Restaurante Tropical Brasil
$$
take the Beco dos Inválidos located just left the town "câmara", then turn left at the first small street to reach the small square where the restaurant is located
If a Brazilian evening tempts you, Restaurante Tropical Brasil will satisfy you with its *feijoada* or its *tutu à mineria*. Count on

spending between 900 and 1,450 ESC for the daily special. Atmosphere guaranteed.

Lucullus Restaurante
$$$$
Rua da Palmeira no. 6
☎214 84 47 09
Lucullus Restaurante offers an excellent choice of Italian dishes (*fettucine Alfredo, osso buco all Fiorentino*, etc.) in a very congenial setting. If you have the chance, choose the rear terrace, for its setting is especially pleasing.

Cafés and Tearooms

Pasteleria Panisol
Rua Frederico Arouca 21-23
A pretty pastry shop offering a vast selection.

Praia do Guincho

(*8km from Estoril*)

Hotel do Guincho
$$$$$
8km west of Cascais Estrada do Guincho
☎214 87 04 91
The designers of the Hotel do Guincho have done a great job of blending the crudeness of a former military building with the elegance and comfort required today for a hotel of this calibre. Although it looks modern on the outside, this hotel and restaurant were actually designed starting from the ruins of a fortress. While some elements, including the entrance, recall its distant past (doors

with semi-circular arches, a stairway and walls in crudely cut stone), the atmosphere has been warmed by luxurious carpets and classy furniture. The dining room offers a panoramic view of the sea and has a pleasant foyer. During your visit, be sure to take a peek at the beautiful conference room, as medieval-looking as can be. Specializing in seafood and fish at outrageous prices.

Mafra

Escondidinho
$
Travessa da Quinta No. 17
Shrimp omelettes for 800 ESC, roasted chicken for 1,200 ESC or *dobrada feijoada* (literally "double-fat with beans"!) for 1,100 ESC, all of it available in *meia-dose* (half-portions), as well. Excellent value in a decor that also seems to be "*meia-dose*", but for these prices, who can complain?

Frederico Restaurante-Bar
$$
Wed to Mon
Terreiro Dom João V
☎261 81 42 90
Despite its aging décor, Frederico is still a pleasant place to stop after an interminable visit to the Mafra monastery. Guests are seated at small tables with tablecloths, and can enjoy a *sopa de nabiça* (soup made from the leaves of young turnips) fol-

Costa de Lisboa

lowed by fried sticklebacks accompanied by rice. Of course, those who prefer cod can always order the *bacalhau a casa*. A good, unpretentious place to eat – and with a monastery right across the way!

Queluz

🌴 Retiro da Mina
$$
Wed to Mon
Avenida da República no. 10
☎214 35 29 78
The Retiro da Mina restaurant has a faithful following of Portuguese families who flock to it in great numbers for traditional Portuguese fare at very reasonable prices. For 1,900 ESC diners are served good home-made soup, a savoury *açorda de marisco* or *pato ao forno com arroz*, accompanied by a *vinho da casa* (in general an excellent *vinho verde*). To finish in fine style, dessert and coffee are also served. A real deal! Amiable and unpretentious.

Restaurante Palácio del Rei
$$
Mon to Sat
Largo Mousinho de Albuquerque nos. 1-4
☎214 35 06 74
In its county-style decor replete with exposed beams and *azulejos*, the Restaurante Palácio del Rei offers a meat, fish or fowl tourist menu for 2,750 ESC. *Arroz de mariscos* and *pato no forno* are just a couple

of the Portuguese specialities on the menu.

🌴 Cozinha Velha
$$$-$$$$
in the west wing of the Palácio de Queluz
☎214 35 02 32
Occupying the west wing of the old Palácio de Queluz, right in the palace's former kitchens, the Cozinha Velha is faithful to the reputation of the Pousadas de Portugal chain. In addition to the fine cuisine included in the regular menu, the restaurant offers of a three-course meal ($$$$) of more elaborate dishes such as *cataplana de lombinhos de porco com amêijoas e camarão* (fried pork loin with shrimp and clams) and *cabrito frito com migas de grelos* (goat meat served with fried bread and broccoli), which proves rather expensive. As for the setting, there is a pleasant, modern little terrace, and on impressive, enormous old central fireplace, supported by eight columns and an adjoining marble table.

Cafés and Tearooms

Pitada Daqui Pitada Dali
Wed to Mon 9:30am to 6pm
Palácio Nacional de Queluz
In the prestigious palace of Queluz, the *cafetaria-bar* Pitada Daqui Pitada Dali is a good spot for coffee before your visit. Various daily specials are served for 1,200 ESC.

Sintra

🌴 Bistrobar Opera Prima
$
every day 9am to midnight
Rua Consiglieri Pedroso no. 2A
☎219 24 45 18
The friendly Belgian owners of Bistrobar Opera greet guests with the smile and kindness characteristic of their culture. Decorators, they have made the most of the two basement rooms, one of which is equipped with a bar, that make up the restaurant. Stone walls and warm colours in the first room create the perfect setting for an intimate evening, while the second room, with its highly original, bright decor, is ideal for lunch. In addition to large mirrors adorned with Art-Nouveau designs, you will discover amusing twisted metal decorations here and there and an attractive painting, under a vault, recalling Moorish Portugal. As for the cuisine, Nele Duportail prepares a tasty *prato económico* (about 750 ESC) with the rich aromas of Belgium, accompanied by delicious whole-wheat bread (a rare treat in Portugal). A tourist menu is also available for 1,350 ESC. A wonderful place, not to be missed!

Estrada Velha Bar

$

every day, 11am to midnight

Rua Consiglieri Pedroso no. 16

This friendly little bar, very popular with young people, offers meals including soup, sandwich and beer starting at 1,200 ESC. Ideal for coping with bouts of hunger. Service with a smile.

O Pelourinho

$

next to the palace

Calçada do Pelourinho no. 4

The little O Pelourinho café and bar offers very good light meals and tasteful decor. The absence of television and of fluorescent lighting renders this spot, with its stone arches, all the more pleasant. Friendly, smiling staff.

Adega das Caves

$$

Rua da Pendora no. 2

☎219 23 08 48

The little Adega das Caves, located below the Café de Paris, prepares simple Portuguese dishes such as salads, plates of sardines and pork chops. Simple and unpretentious.

Restaurante Regional de Sintra

$$

Mon to Fri 9am to 10:30pm, Sat and Sun noon to 10:30pm

next to the town hall

Adjoining the pretty Câmara Municipal, Restaurante Regional de Sintra, though modest on the outside, has a pretty dining room

upstairs where you can enjoy deliciously prepared salmon or rabbit dishes.

Café de Paris

$$$

every day until midnight

Praça da República no. 32

☎219 23 23 75

In the heart of Sintra, in a building with a beautiful facade of blue *azulejos*, the Café de Paris is decorated in the style of a Paris bistro (of course!). It offers some dishes that are unusual in Portugal, such as a melon and port appetizer, vichyssoise, coriander clams, and grilled halves of rock lobster. This is a busy, lively place, with a view of the palace from an abundantly flowered, covered terrace.

Tacho Real

$$$

closed Wed

Rua da Ferreira no. 4

☎219 23 52 77

Set in the upper part of town, the Tacho Real has a particularly refined and elegant decor and very friendly service. You will find Portuguese food, somewhat more elaborate than usual, although without surprises.

Cafés and Tearooms

Piriquita Dois

Rua das Padarias No. 18

A tranquil terrace, a *bica* and a delicious little Portuguese pastry, all within a stone's throw of a lovely pal-

ace – and paradise seems within reach.

Seteais

(2km from Sintra)

Hotel Palácio de Seteais

$$$$$

every day 12:30pm to 2:30pm and 7:30pm to 9:30pm

Rua Barbosa Bocage no. 10

Seteais

☎219 23 32 00

Located less than 2km from Sintra, in Seteais, the restaurant of the Hotel Palácio de Seteais offers an excellent four-course meal starting at 6,500 ESC in a truly beautiful setting (see p 175). The chicken braised in Madeira is a delight, as is the pork medallion with dates. The dining room decor, worthy of a palace, includes magnificent frescoes and fine period furniture. Before starting your gourmet evening, however take a little stroll on the terrace with its splendid views of the French-style gardens and of the surrounding countryside.

Cacilhas

Atira-te ao Rio

$$

Tue to Fri 7pm to midnight, Sat and Sun 4pm to midnight

Cais do Ginjal 69/70

☎212 75 13 80

About 1km along the Cais do Ginjal, in an out-of-the-way spot, is the Brazilian restaurant Atira-te ao Rio, where diners savour *feijoada* and other typical Brazilian dishes. Friendly and unpretentious. Given its distance from downtown, reservations are recommended.

On the banks of the Tagus, beside the Atirate ao Rio Brazilian restaurant, the) serves typical Portuguese fare of no particular interest. Nonetheless, the view from the restaurant's terrace, right on the docks, is simply magnificent. With the Tagus flowing at your feet, you can admire the rolling hills of Lisbon in the distance, lighting up, at nightfall, with fabulous colours. The sunset alone is worth the long walk along the quay (*about 1km*).

Setúbal

O Cardador
$$
every day 12:30pm to 3pm and 7:30pm to 10:30pm
near the Praça Marquês de Pombal, behind the Albergaria Solaris
Fish and seafood top the menu in this charming restaurant with a pleasant little terrace. Friendly, smiling staff.

Cervejaria Africa & Cᵃ
$$
every day 11:30am to midnight
Avenida Luísa Todi No. 448/A
Contrary to what its name might suggest, Cervejaria Africa & Cᵃ serves Argentinian steak, not African cuisine. This restaurant-brewery has a warm and tasteful décor, and offers an extensive selection of tapas (*from 450 to 800 ESC*), or, if you are really hungry, South American meat dishes for 2,000 to 2,500 ESC. Several daily specials are offered on weekdays, including the popular *bacalhau*, prepared in various ways. Small tables with tablecloths are set up under elegant parasols on the terrace in the front.

Cervejaria O 10
$$$
Avenida Luísa Todi nos
☎265 52 52 12
Although meals are prepared without great originality, Cervejaria O 10, unlike many of its competitors, serves meals all day long, without interruption. This is an unpretentious and convenient spot.

Pousada de São Filipe
$$$
go west along Avenida Luísa Todi to the end, turn right and then immediately left to reach Rua de São Filipe, which will lead you directly to the fortress, Rua de São Filipe
☎265 52 38 44
Overlooking the town of Setúbal, the restaurant at the Pousada de

Moscatel de Setúbal

This very sweet wine received its DOC appellation in 1908, and can be served as an apéritif or as a dessert wine. It is one of the first wines to have been produced in Portugal. The Phoenicians are believed to have introduced winegrowing to the country's southern region some 2,000 years ago by importing a grape variety known as "Muscat of Alexandria". This wine was especially popular with the nobility, and several European rulers kept it in their wine cellars, most notably King Louis XIV of France. Produced primarily in the Serra da Arrábida, near Setúbal, *moscatel* is made by fermenting grapes, with their skins, in a mixture of sugar and alcohol for several months. Visitors can tour the wine cellar of the José Maria da Fonseca winery (see p 184) in the small town of Vila Nogueira de Azeitão, where the process of making *moscatel* is explained in greater detail.

São Filipe is one of the most pleasant spots in Setúbal for a meal. Opening onto a former fortress dating from 1590 (see p 181), its impressive entrance leads through a series of vaulted corridors with several fortified gates. At the top of the stairway, a magnificent terrace with panoramic views of the Tróia peninsula and the sea entices you to linger for a pre-dinner drink. The dining room, although warmly decorated, lacks originality for such an exceptional spot. It is relaxing nonetheless, and fish lovers can enjoy an excellent *caldeirada à Setubalense* as well as excellent *moscatel* wine, both regional specialties.

Cafés and Tearooms

Café Comm C
every day 10am to 2am
Avenida Luísa Todi no. 184
Jute coffee bags adorn the walls at this friendly little bar: the ideal surroundings in which to sip a coffee or perhaps a delicious *Moscatel* wine, a specialty of the region.

Palmela

(*8km from Setúbal*)

Pousada de Palmela
$$$
atop the village of Palmela
☎212 35 12 26
Set in the little village of Palmela, the restaurant of the Pousada de Palmela enjoys the

exceptional setting of a former monastery dating from the 15th century (see p 182) teetering atop a steep rock formation. Upon entering, the eye is drawn to the imposing dimensions of the numerous vaulted halls and galleries that surround the cloister. You may have an apéritif in the friendly, comfortable bar before taking your meal in the former refectory of the monastery or, if you prefer, on the elegant terrace around which the cloister stands. Besides the regional specialties, do not miss the excellent local wine, *moscatel*.

Sesimbra

Padaria Bar Restaurante
$$$
summer every day to 1:30am, winter Tue to Sun
Rua da Paz Nos. 5-11
☎228 03 81
Located in a building with rounded corners, perched halfway up a flight of stairs, the Padaria Bar Restaurante will appeal to visitors looking for unique establishments, which are hard to come by in Sesimbra. Inside, a pleasant room awaits, with the lower half of the walls decorated with tiles, while a temporary exhibit of contemporary paintings hangs above. The absence of a television, as well as the subdued lighting from a candelabrum, creates a relaxed atmosphere. As another

special touch: each table has its own candlestick. Guests are seated in old, rustic wooden chairs and are served Portuguese specialties such as rice with seafood (*3,300 ESC/2pers.*), *feijoada do Mar* (1,650 ESC) or fish and seafood *au gratin* (2,300 ESC). There is also an open-air terrace on the steps of the street. Unfortunately, the establishment's otherwise perfect record is marred by the banal furniture on the terrace, which stands in stark contrast to the tasteful decor found inside.

Felicidade
Rua Cândido do Reis No. 78
☎212 28 17 63
Those who could stand a change from fish and seafood will be happy to discover that Felicidade specializes in traditional Chinese cuisine. Dishes comprise noodles or fried rice with chicken or pork, and are served in cluttered but agreeable surroundings.

Barca Delta
$$
Wed to Mon
Rua Serpa Pinto No. 8, near the public market
☎212 23 36 81
Upon entering the small Barca Delta restaurant, it quickly becomes clear that fish and seafood are the house specialties. The prow of a boat is mounted on a wall near the entrance, and various objects used for fishing hang as decora-

Costa de Lisboa

tion throughout the restaurant. In addition to the ever-popular *bacalhau*, dishes such as *faijoada de gambas* (1,700 ESC) and *cataplano de tamboril* (for two; 3,500 ESC) are served. Less gourmet diners may opt for the grilled sardines, priced at 900 ESC. The tables have pretty checkered tablecloths, but the lighting is hardly atmospheric, and the ever-present *televisão*, the scourge of Portugal, detracts from the ambiance. Nevertheless, this place is worth a detour for its pleasant decor and good location on a lovely pedestrian street some distance away from the noisy Avenida 25 de Abril.

Cafés and Tearooms

Café de Manhá
Tue to Sun 7am to 7pm
corner of Avenida da Liberdade and Rua da República
The Café de Manhá is characterized by a spare, modern decor and impeccable cleanliness. Here, guests can enjoy a *bica* accompanied by a pastry, or a light lunch at very reasonable prices. The soup of the day costs a mere 180 ESC, and a chicken and tuna salad costs less than 600 ESC. For those who insist on traditional Portuguese cuisine, the *bacalhau* comes recommended, at 900 ESC.

O Caseiro
Avenida da Liberdade No. 15
Right across from the Café de Manhá, O Caseiro is a coffee and pastry shop that offers a number of Portuguese desserts, each more alluring than the last. These treats can be savoured in warm surroundings, decorated with traditional *azulejos*.

Santiago do Cacém

Restaurante O Retiro
$
Mon to Sat noon to 3pm and 7pm to 10pm
Rua Machado dos Santos 8
☎269 82 26 59
This little restaurant serves good-quality Portuguese cuisine at very reasonable prices. Besides a full menu starting at 1,850 ESC, you can enjoy an excellent *arroz de pato à Alentejana* (rice with duck prepared Alentejo style) for two people for as little as 2,600 ESC. Wine lovers should taste the excellent house wine, Terras del Rei (at 250 ESC for a half-bottle, this is a true bargain!). As for the decor, numerous agricultural implements are part of the very warm setting. Service is family-style and friendly.

Pousada de São Tiago
$$$
Rua de Lisboa
☎269 82 24 59
☎269 82 28 74
On the road leading to the Roman ruins of Miróbriga, the restaurant at the little

Pousada de São Tiago is set in a former villa dating from 1947, fully surrounded by greenery. Its slightly old-fashioned regional furniture makes for a particularly charming, rustic atmosphere. A terrace with views of a romantic garden enables you to take your drinks in the open air before starting in on regional dishes such as *açorda à Alentejana*, a delicious garlic-bread stew. Friendly staff welcome you with a smile.

Miróbriga
(*1km from Santiago do Cacém*)

Restaurante O Refugio do Mirante
$
Mon to Sat
along the road leading to the ruins, Estrada das Ruinas de Miróbriga
☎269 22 37 32
Restaurante O Refugio do Mirante, which has the special advantage of being situated near the Roman ruins, serves unpretentious Portuguese food in a pretty, rustic setting. Meals starting at 1,300 ESC.

Porto Covo

Miramar
$$
Rua Cândido da Silva No. 57
☎269 90 54 49
Located at the edge of town, right across from the rugged coastline, the Miramar restaurant-bar is a pleasant place to dine, even if the menu does not list

any particularly delectable offerings. Like its competitors, the restaurant serves mainly fish and seafood. However, this place distinguishes itself with its large, pleasant terrace that has a view of the ocean in the distance. Also, the welcome is very warm and friendly.

Cafés and Tearooms

Cafetéria & Pasteleria
Largo Marqês de Pombal
What better way to top off a visit to the romantic Largo Marquês de Pombal than with a delicious Portuguese pastry? Head to the Cafetéria & Pasteleria for a *pastel* or *bolo*, or another of the tempting array of homemade sweets.

Ilha de Pessegueiro

 A Ilha
$$
Estrada Ilha do Pessegueiro
☎ 269 90 51 13
A Ilha is worth a visit for its superb location right on the beach, across from Pessegueiro island and near the ruins of an ancient fortress. The interior is not the most elegant, but has a warm ambiance. The tables in the front room enjoy views of Ilha do Pessegueiro in the distance. Unfortunately, the abundance of cars parked all around the building, a symptom of our affluent times, mars the otherwise idyllic

views of the surroundings. As for the food: those who wish to deviate from the standard fare of seafood and fish should try the *coelho a pessegueiro*, rabbit prepared in the local fashion, or *carne a alentejano*, both of which are very satisfying. A good place to stop for a meal after a long walk along the coast.

Entertainment

Bars and Nightclubs

Estoril

Danse Pub Alô Alô
every day 10pm to 4am
Beco Esconso
Pool tables, a dance floor and *música ao vivo* every Friday aim to satisfy night owls. In case a hunger pang hits, light meals are also served.

Queluz

Património Bar
cover charge 1,000 ESC
Avenida da República nos. 4-8
The best thing about this modest, unpretentious bar is its proximity to the magnificent Pousada Dona Maria I. *Música ao vivo* on weekends, with Brazilian rhythms in the background.

Sintra

Bar Fonte da Pipa
4pm to midnight
Rua Fonte da Pipa nos. 11-13
Situated next to a superb fountain in a lovely part of town, the Bar Fonte da Pipa is a pleasant spot for a drink. The old-fashioned decor with a preponderance of wood panelling and cushioned booths, lends itself well to the enjoyment of a nice cold beer.

Bistrobar Opera Prima
$
9am to midnight
Rua Consiglieri Pedroso no. 2A
The stone walls and warm tones of the Bistrobar Opera Prima are conducive to intimate conversation. The staff is very friendly, making this pleasant and refined place worth checking out.

Setúbal

Bar Iguana
Rua Pereira Cão no. 44
A friendly little bar. Musicians every Friday starting at 10pm.

Disco Fabrica
along the N10-4 toward the west, 300 m after the end of Avenida Luísa Todi
This big nightclub set in a former factory will delight nocturnal people who can get down and dance into the wee hours of the morning.

La Dolce Vita
Praça Marquês de Pombal
Whether you want a late-night glass of wine or simply a *bica*, head

Costa de Lisboa

to La Dolce Vita, a pleasant, laid-back little bar on a small square set away from the traffic. An array of sandwiches and appetizers is also offered here to satisfy those little cravings.

Bacus
Praça Marquês de Pombal
Right across the street is Bacus, a similar establishment with little tables and rustic wooden chairs that create a convivial atmosphere in this small space.

Português Suave
Rua Joachim dos Santos Fernandes No. 2-4-6
Português Suave is a typical Portuguese pool bar where patrons gather in a large, rustic hall to quench their thirst and check out the action. And if the game happens to appeal to you, there is nothing stopping you from joining in!

Conventual
6pm to 2am
Travessa da Anunciada no. 2
A vaulted brick hall, decorated only with a few wrought-iron lamp fixtures and walls of bare stone, is what awaits at the Conventual. This bar, located inside an old convent, is definitely one of the most elegant in Setúbal and also tries to be one of the most original by regularly hosting art exhibitions and concerts.

Sesimbra

Central Coffee
corner of Rua Dr. Anibal Esmeriz and Largo José Antonio Pereira
Young people from the Sesimbra area gather at Central Coffee to sip a cold *cerveja* or a glass of *moscatel*, a liqueur-like white wine from the region, in a large, antiquated room which still has that certain Old World charm.

Santiago do Cacém

Bru Bar
Rua de Lisboa 5
This charming village of only 7,000 inhabitants has a little bar, the rustically decorated Bru Bar, that is something of a hangout for young people from the area. Drinks are served in a lively and friendly atmosphere that proves the general exodus from the countryside is not the norm here.

Shopping

Cascais

Shopping Centres

On par with the Amoreiras shopping centre in Lisbon, as well as with all of those in the great European capitals, the **Cascais Shopping** (*Alcabideche, 6.8km from the centre of Cascais via the EN9*) has no less than 130 shops

and seven cinemas – bring your credit card!

Sintra

Azulejos

In the charming **Azul Cobalto** studio-boutique (*Calçada de São Pedro no. 38, São Pedro da Sintra*), you can purchase *azulejos* with imaginative patterns and even, if you so desire, have your own made-to-order design reproduced. It's worth a look!

Decorative Items and Knick-Knacks

In search of beautiful fabric or original curios? Stop by **Ikat Interiores** (*corner of Calçada de São Pedro and Rua Dr. Higínio de Sousa, São Pedro da Sintra*), where a friendly woman will show you various little marvels.

The magnificent artifacts exhibited at the **A Janela de São Pedro** boutique (*Mon to Sat; Calçada de São Pedro no. 32, São Pedro da Sintra, ☎219 24 43 97*) clearly attest to the proprietors' passion for Africa. Wood and stone knick-knacks, masks and fabrics, there is nothing commonplace here, particularly not the sculptures, for their original forms and use of materials. Surely the most exceptional boutique in Sintra!

Bookstores and Stationer's

Walking into the little **Livraria Alfarrabista** bookshop (*Wed to Sun 10am to 7:30pm; Volta do Duche no. 16, Sintra,* ☎ *219 23 19 98*) is like entering an old library, with that peculiar bookish smell that seems to herald the discovery of precious documents or a rare tome. Great piles of books fill the shelves here, from the book on the history of the Sintra region to the obscure novel, forgotten by the general public.

Those looking for the latest best-seller or simply a map of the region can rest assured, however, for the friendly staff here will help you find anything you're looking for – with a smile at no extra charge.

Setúbal

Those who like contemporary art should stop in at the **Arte & Imaginação** gallery (*Tue to Sun; Travessa do Garim No. 8, beside Largo de Santo António*), which exhibits modern paintings and sculpture.

It also sells various little souvenirs, including pretty handpainted *azulejos.*

Grocery Store (*Rua António Girão, across from the Internacional House language school*). Whether you are heading out for an excursion into the beautiful Serra da Arrábida or simply looking for a culinary souvenir, this small grocery store on Rua António Girão will delight fine-food lovers. Fruit, olives, nuts, cheese and Portuguese wines are only some of the ingredients for a sensational locally flavoured picnic available here.

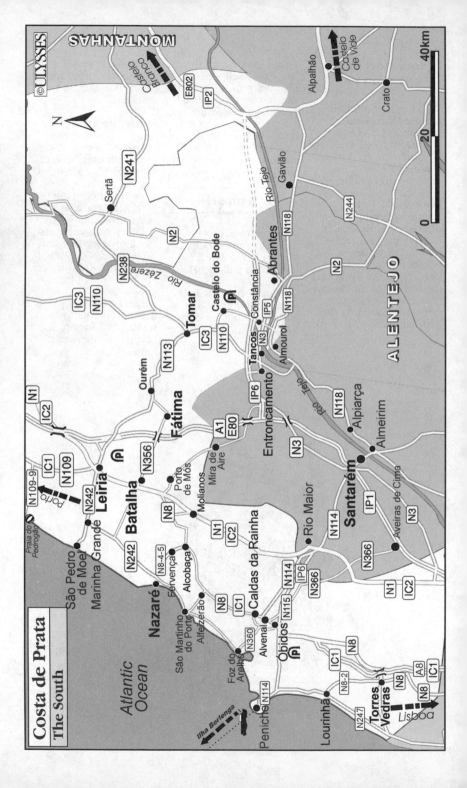

Costa de Prata: the South

I f you can only spend a few days outside of Lisbon, the nearby southern part of the Costa de Prata is your best option.

This is especially true for anyone interested in history – the epic history of the Knights Templar, who became so powerful that their order was disbanded, only to be re-established in Portugal as the Order of Christ, or as the Order of the Dead Queen, posthumous sovereign of the Alcobaça. Architecture buffs will also enjoy visiting this region, with its medieval keeps, like the one in Óbidos (where you can actually stay), and its Manueline buildings, whose style is unique to Portugal and best exemplified by the chapter window of the Convento de Cristo in Tomar. If you have a taste for magnificent settings, furthermore, you won't want to miss the castle of Almourol, that impressive sentinel

rising up out of the middle of the Tagus, surrounded by cacti. Óbidos, with its charming village and medieval fortifications, is equally remarkable. Finally, if lively beaches are what you're looking for, you can head to Nazaré, which has been extensively developed but has nevertheless managed to retain its unique character.

Finding Your Way Around

By Car from Lisbon

Alcobaça

Quick Route

Take Highway A1-E80 north to Aveiras de Cima. From there, pick up the N366, and then the N1, heading towards Rio Maior. Continue past Rio Maior to Molianos (23km). Just after the village, take your first left and keep going until you reach Alcobaça (7km).

Scenic Route

Head north on Highway A8-IC1, which turns into the N8-IC1. This road leads to Óbidos and then on to Alcobaça.

From Tomar to Almourol

Quick Route

Take the N110-IC3 south to Entroncamento, then head towards Abrantes on the N3-IP6. Head right at the junction for Lisbon, then right again 300m farther, at the sign for Almourol. This road leads to the banks of the Tagus, opposite the castle.

Scenic Route

Take the N110-IC3 south, then head towards Constância on the N358-2. After passing the impressive Castelo do Bode dam, the highway leads into a deep and lovely valley, then runs alongside the Rio Zêzere. The road is quite narrow, so be extremely cautious. Continue past Constância in the direction of Entroncamento. You will reach Almouril after about 6km.

Batalha

Quick Route

Take the A1-E80 north to the exit for Fátima, then turn left on the N356, which leads to Batalha.

Scenic Route

Head north on the A8-IC1, which turns into the N8-IC1. After Alcobaça, the road intersects with the N1-IC2. Keep heading north to Batalha.

Fátima

Head north on the A1-E80 and take the exit for Fátima.

Leiria

Quick Route

Head north on the A1-E80 and take the exit for Leiria.

Scenic Route

Head north on the A8-IC1, which turns into the N8-IC1. After Alcobaça, the road intersects the N1-IC2. Continue north to Batalha and then on to Leiria.

Nazaré

Quick Route

Head north on the A1-E80. At the Fátima exit, take the N356 towards Batalha. Continue past Batalha on the N356, then turn left on the N242, which leads

south to Nazaré, about 15km away.

Scenic Route

Head north on Highway A8-IC1, which turns into the N8-IC1. Continue past Óbidos to Alcobaça. From there, take the N8-5 and then the N8-4 to Nazaré.

Óbidos

Quick Route

Follow the A1-E80 north to Aveiras. From there, take the N366 and the N116 to Avenal, then bear left to get to Óbidos, 5km farther.

Scenic Route

Head northward to Óbidos on Highway A8-IC1, which turns into the N8-IC1.

From Leiria to Ourém

Take the N113-IC9 to Tomar. When you get to Vila Nova de Ourém, 25km farther, turn right at the sign for the Castelo and Torres Novas. About 1 kilometre farther, take the road on the left and continue for 2km. Turn right onto the paved road at the sign for Santo Amaro, then left when you get to Beltroa.

Peniche

Quick Route

Take Highway A8-IC1, which later turns into the N8-IC1, heading north until you reach São Mamede, just before Óbidos. From there, take the N114, which will lead you straight to Peniche.

Scenic Route

Take the N117 toward Queluz, then the IC19, which will lead you directly to Sintra. From there, follow the N247 north to reach the N114, which leads right to Peniche.

Tomar

Quick Route

Head north on the A1-E80, then pick up the N357, to the left of the exit for Fátima. Four kilometres farther, take the N113-IC9 west to Tomar.

Scenic Route

Head north on Highway AB-IC1, which turns into the N8-IC1. After Óbidos and Alcobaça, the road intersects with the N1-IC2. Continue straight ahead to Leiria, then take the N113-IC9 west to Tomar.

By Train from Lisbon

Though some of the towns described below are accessible by train, using this means of transportation is not entirely practical. In fact, excluding such destinations as Abrantes, Leiria and Caldas da Rainha, timetables prove irregular and connections difficult. For Caminhos de Ferro departures and information see p 69.

Abrantes

Departure: several trains per day
Fare: Interregional 980 ESC

Leiria

Departure: several trains per day
Fare: Interregional 1,250 ESC
The Leiria train station is in the village of Sesmarias, 3km from downtown; several buses also stop here.

Caldas da Rainha

Departure: several trains per day
Fare: Interregional 720 ESC
The Caldas da Rainha train station is close to downtown, on Rua da Estação.

By Bus from Lisbon

The Rede Nacional de Expressos and Renex Expressos bus companies offer frequent departures every day as do several other transportation companies. Most departures are from the terminal located at 18B Avenida Casal Ribeiro. Renex Expressos departures are from Cais das Cebolas, close to Casa dos Bicos. For information in Lisbon see p 69.

Alcobaça

Travel time: approx. 2hrs
Fare: between 1,050 and 1,250 ESC

Almourol

There is no direct bus service from Lisbon to Almoural. You can transfer in Tomar or Entroncamento.

Batalha

Travel time: approx. 2hrs
Fare: between 1,000 and 1,200 ESC

Fátima

Travel time: approx. 1hr, 30min
Fare: between 1,000 and 1,200 ESC

Leiria

Travel time: approx. 2hrs, 15min
Fare: between 1,000 and 1,200 ESC

Nazaré

Travel time: approx. 2hrs, 10min
Fare: between 1,000 and 1,200 ESC

Óbidos

There is no direct bus service from Lisbon;

travellers must first take the bus to Caldas da Rainha (*up to seven departures a day, average travel time: 1hr, 25min, count on spending about 950 ESC*), and, from there, the bus to Óbidos (*frequent departures, average travel time: 20min*).

Ourém

Travel time: approx. 2hrs, 40min
Fare: between 1,150 and 1,350 ESC

Peniche

Travel time: approx. 1hr, 45min
Fare: between 800 and 1,000 ESC

Tomar

Travel time: approx. 2hrs, 30min
Fare: between 850 and 1,050 ESC

Practical Information

Tourist Information Offices

Alcobaça

Praça 25 de Abril

Batalha

Largo Paulo VI

Fátima

Avenida D. José Alves Correia da Silva

Leiria

Jardim Lúis de Camões

Nazaré

At the corner of Avenida da República and Rua Gomes Freire

Óbidos

Rua Direita

Ourém

Praça do Minicipio

Peniche

Rua Alexandre Herculano

Tomar

Rua Dr. Cândido Madureira near Praça do Infante Henriques

Exploring

Alcobaça

Alcobaça lies in a fertile valley where fruit farming is still the main activity. It was named after the two rivers that meet at this point, the Alcõa and the Baça. Afonso I drove the Moors out of this area in 1153 and granted the newly conquered land to Dom Bernard, abbot of the Clairveaux monastery in France. This was a logical choice, as the Cistercians were reputed for their building and farming skills. The Mosteiro de Santa Maria d'Alcobaça was begun in 1178, but all work came to a halt when the Muslims invaded the area again in 1195. The project was abandoned until the early 13th century, and the church was finally consecrated in 1252. As more buildings were erected and more land cleared, Santa Maria became one of the principal abbeys in the kingdom, and held that rank until the mid-14th century. In those years, the abbot of Alcobaça was a highly influential person, with authority over at least 14 important villages. In 1475, however, the king began appointing abbots himself, thus combining their interests with those of the nobility and the royalty.

The new abbots cared little about the Cistercian community, and the abbey slid into decline until the early 17th century. Then, around 1642, after the pope granted their order greater autonomy, Alcobaça became the Cistercians' headquarters, and the king decided to restore the abbots' privileges. The abbey thus enjoyed a period of revitalization until the early 19th century, when the entire country began facing troubled times. In 1834, when all religious orders were abolished, the abbey became state property. After being neglected for many years, it was restored in the 20th century and is now Alcobaça's main attraction, drawing large numbers of tourists each year. In addition to its many souvenir shops and pretty, bustling public squares, the town is also known for its beautiful blue and white earthenware.

After strolling around Praça República, an extremely pleasant, well-designed square, you can start off your tour at the **church of the Mosteiro de Santa Maria de Alcobaça** ★★★ (*free admission; same hours as the abbey, see below*). Before going inside, take a look at the facade, which is topped by pinnacles. The Gothic portal and its rose window are the only original elements. The two bell towers and the rest of the facade, which is baroque in style, were modified during the 18th century. The interior of the church, a true Gothic masterpiece, is one of the finest examples of Cistercian architecture in existence. Once decorated with all sorts of baroque eye-teasers, it was stripped down to its austere original state during the Salazar era. Because it is so narrow, the nave looks even higher than it is (20m).

In the transepts, you can admire the lavish **royal tombs** ★★★ of Dom Pedro I and his beloved Inês de Castro (see box). Dating from around 1360, they are by far the loveliest reclining statues in Portugal, and their flawless stonework makes them true jewels of Gothic art. Inês de Castro's tomb includes a panel showing the Last Judgement, which was unfortunately damaged by Napoleon's troops during their retreat. She is surrounded by six graceful angels and a greyhound sleeps at her feet as a symbol of fidelity. Pedro I is also surrounded by six angels, but the dog lying on his tomb seems to be waiting for his master to awaken. The magnificent rose window in front of the tomb is sure to capture your attention. According to legend, the tombs are placed opposite one another so that the couple will come face to face as soon as they rise on Judgement Day.

Continue your tour at the monastery, also known as the **Mosteiro de Santa Maria d'Alcobaça** ★★★ (*400 ESC; every day 9am to 7pm during summer, 9am to 5pm during winter; enter the cloister through the left transept*). The Dom Dinis cloister, also known as the **Claustro do Silencio** (Cloister of Silence), is one of the largest in Europe.

A magnificent example of Gothic architecture, it was built between 1308 and 1311 and originally had only one level. The combination of lovely geminated columns and rose windows over the arcades is exquisite. The Manueline upper floor was added in the 15th century.

If you take the passage to the right to the other side of the cloister, you will come to the **monastery kitchen** ★★. Modified in 1752, this room is remarkable for a number of reasons. The hood of the fireplace is at least 18m high. Along with those of the Palácio Nacional, its chimneys are probably the most impressive in Portugal. Supposedly, the monks used to cook up six or seven steers here at once; surely to feed the up to 140 monks that might be staying in the abbey at one time! Equally remarkable is the pool at the back of the kitchen, which is fed by a branch of the Rio Alcôa, diverted for that purpose. Running water in an 18th century kitchen! Talk about ingenuity!

Among the many other rooms you can visit, don't miss the **refectory**, with its lovely staircase, built right into the wall, leading to the pulpit, and the **monks' room**, whose floor compensates for the uneven ground.

The Dead Queen or the Love of a Wronged King

When Constanza of Castile was presented to Pedro I before they were to be married, Pedro noticed a beautiful woman among the ladies-in-waiting, one Inês de Castro. Despite his marriage to Constanza, a marriage of convenience demanded by his father, Afonso IV, to strengthen relations with powerful Castile, Pedro I fell helplessly in love with the beautiful Inês. Before long they became lovers. Seeing the liaison as a threat to his designs on Castile, Afonso had Inês exiled from the Court. When Constanza died in 1345 while giving birth to a third son, Pedro finally believed he was free to pursue his true love, and secretly wed Inês de Coimbra. Afonso IV was furious and, taking advantage of his son's absence in 1355, he had the supposed usurper assassinated. Pedro returned and, in a fit of sorrow, swore revenge. Three years later, immediately following his father's death, Pedro I ascended the throne. These three years of silence had only heightened his sorrow and desire for vengeance. So much so that in 1357, shortly after his coronation, he ordered the arrest of the murderers. Before being condemned to the stake their hearts were cut out under Pedro's orders. Some say Pedro even witnessed the scene, whence his nickname, the "Cruel King". It was not until 1361, however, that he finally achieved the ultimate revenge. He ordered the exhumation of Inês's body and called the whole Court to come and pay homage to the new queen. Inês's decomposing body was thus placed on the throne and each noble was ordered to kiss her hand as a sign of submission. The body was then transported to Alcobaça and placed in a stone tomb that can still be seen today.

In addition to its many cafés, pleasant **Praça Dom Afonso Henriques** boasts two lovely **archways** ★, which are incorporated into 18th century houses. They are located in the passageway leading to Praça da República, which lies in an attractive area well worth exploring on foot.

Outside of town, the **Museu Nacional do Vinho** (*10am to 12:30pm and 2pm to 5:30pm; Olival Fechado, on Highway IC-1-N8, 1.4km from Alcobaça on the way to Batalha*, ☎*262 58 22 22*) will appeal mainly those interested in the divine nectar of Bacchus.

Although the museum displays an impressive number of objects (including wine-making equipment), and a line on the floor shows you which way to go, the museum is not very educational. Explanations would do much to improve this attractive place.

Batalha

The little town of Batalha lies hidden in the valley of the Rio Léna. It owes its existence to the Battle of Aljubarrota, which took place nearby. When Fernando I died in 1385, the Spanish reclaimed control over Portugal (see p 16). The Portuguese nobility, afraid of losing its privileges, quickly put João I on the throne in order to preserve the country's monarchy. That same year, the disgruntled Spanish invaded Portugal and found themselves confronted by João I's army. The king promised the Virgin that if his forces emerged victorious, he would show his gratitude by building a great church, and that is exactly what came to pass in 1388, here in this valley strewn with vines and orchards. First, the Mosteiro de Batalha was erected, and then the town grew up around it. Batalha has some pretty squares, a handful of restaurants and souvenir shops and a little parish church, but the monastery is still the main attraction. An architectural jewel featuring a harmonious blend of Gothic and Manueline styles, it is the ultimate symbol of the Portuguese people's pride in their country, and thus merits a lengthy visit. Various members of the Aviz dynasty are entombed here, including Henrique o Navegador (Henry the Navigator). You can start off your tour by taking a quick look at the equestrian statue of Nuno Alvares Pereira on Largo Mestre Afonso Domingues.

It was erected as a tribute to the commander's courage during the Battle of Aljubarrota. Right nearby, the **Mosteiro de Batalha ★★★** (*400 ESC; Oct to Mar, 9am to 5pm; Apr to Sep, 9am to 6pm*), otherwise known as the Mosteira da Santa Maria da Vitória, lies stretched in all its glory along a large esplanade. If you walk over to it and stand in front of the main entrance, you will be able to appreciate its beauty even better. The most striking thing about the monastery is its unusual proportions. The general plan for the building was drawn up by Portuguese architect Afonso Domingues in 1388. With no towers at the front to draw the eye upward, the structure has a particularly massive look about it, but its numerous pinnacles, rich ornamentation and elegant flying buttresses make it very aesthetically pleasing.

The **main portal ★★** is decorated with an impressive number of sculptures of apostles, angels and other Biblical figures, with the coats of arms of João I and his wife at the top.

Upon entering the church, you may be surprised by its stark decor. The imposing pillars create an impression of great austerity, which is fortunately offset to a certain degree by the lighting in the three naves. Immediately to the right of the entrance is the **Capela do Fundador ★★** (Founder's Chapel), built around 1426 to house the tomb of João

I and his wife. An architect by the name of Huguet (sometimes referred to as Ouguete) is credited with the design. Aside from the lovely tomb of the royal couple in the middle and the even more remarkable tombs of their sons along the walls, the chapel's most striking feature is its star-spangled dome, which has eight ribs. Along with the dome in the chapter-house, it is the only one of its kind in Portugal. Also noteworthy are the lovely Gothic stained-glass windows.

The Gothic **Claustro Real ★★★** (*enter through the left transept, just before the choir*), or Royal Cloister, was begun during the reign of João I. It was designed by Afonso Domingues, who supervised part of its construction and was then succeeded by Huguet. The lavish Manueline decorations were added around 1510 by Mateus Fernandes and Boytac. The latter also executed a number of projects at the Mosteiro dos Jerónimos in Lisbon. Most of the ornamentation was thus added between 1495 and 1521, under the reign of Manuel I. The archways, once bare, were carved with an incredible jumble of thistles and armillary spheres, fleurs-de-lys and Christian crosses. They are also supported by elegant little cabled columns. This fusion of

Gothic architecture and opulent ornamentation based largely on plant motifs creates an impression of great harmony. There is no denying that this cloister, like the one at the Mosteiro dos Jerónimos, is among the most beautiful in the world.

The **chapter-house ★** lies on the same side as the entrance to the cloister. In it, you will find a tomb of the Unknown Soldier, honouring the Portuguese who fought in the First World War. The most striking thing about this room is its vault, a marvel of engineering, which has an incredibly wide span and no structural reinforcement in the middle. Standing here in the semi-darkness, you can enjoy an interesting view of the cloister.

Now go to the other side of the cloister, where you will find the refectory. Before going inside, take a look at the pretty fountain encased in stone. Upon entering the **refectory**, you will discover a small World War I museum, which is of little interest in itself. It is nevertheless worth visiting the room to admire the beautiful **pulpit** (*access forbidden*), which can only be reached by way of a narrow staircase hidden in the wall. On your way to the second cloister, you will see a former dormitory on

your right, which is now used for temporary exhibitions.

The **Dom Afonso V Cloister ★**, named after the king who commissioned it, was designed by Fernão, an architect from the city of Évora. It was built between 1448 and 1477, and is a fine example of the spare style of architecture that became popular during that period and that can also be seen at the Convento de Cristo in Tomar.

Now exit the building through the Dom Afonso Cloister and walk along the right side of the buildings to reach the **Capela Imperfeitas ★★★**, or Unfinished Chapels. Aside from the famous chapter window in Tomar (see p 229), there is no finer example of the Manueline style. Even the portal leading to the chapels is incredible. Notched like the mouth of a cave, this masterpiece was created by Mateus Fernandes, who completed it in 1509. It is graced with thousands of sculptures, and it would take an equal number of hours to fully appreciate the exquisite workmanship that went into carving it. If you walk to the centre of the octagonal rotunda, you will see the chapels commissioned by King Duarte I, who wanted to build himself a pantheon of even greater beauty than those of his predecessors. Although the project was begun in 1434, it was interrupted on several occasions, and the building was never completed. The eight pillars, which bear Dom Manuel's initials (R.M.) and were probably intended to support a dome, date back to the reign of Manuel I. Today, they are topped only by the lovely blue dome of the Estremadura sky. As far as the eight chapels are concerned, visitors are sure to be fascinated by their rich ornamentation.

It is worth making a trip to the **parish church** (*near the Largo da Misericórdia*) to see its **Manueline portal** ★, built in 1512 by Mateus Fernandes.

Fans of baroque architecture will enjoy a quick tour of the **Igreja da Misericórdia** (*on the square of the same name*).

Porto de Mós

(*7km from Batalha*)

In 1147, pushing southward with his army, Dom Afonso Henriques captured Porto de Mós and its castle from the Moors. The **castle** ★, which had been seriously damaged, was built under Sancho I (12th century) and later underwent numerous modifications. Those carried out in the 15th century, during the reign of Afonso V, were the most enduring.

Despite massive damage caused by the earthquake of 1755, the castle still looks magnificent, having been largely restored in 1956. The odd-looking cones topping some of its towers seem like reminders of its Moorish past. Its overall appearance is characteristic of the 15th century, a time when Portuguese nobles attempted to make their homes more elegant and comfortable. Palace-like features were added to the castle's purely military architecture, with curious but nonetheless attractive results. With its lovely loggia overlooking the Léna valley, the castle is bound to remind visitors of its big brother in Leiria (see below). Short and sweet, a trip to Porto de Mós is a must.

Mira de Aire

(*21km from Batalha*)

Many underground caves lie hidden in the region between Fátima and Porto de Mós. The most impressive caves are the Grutas da Modeda, de Alvados, de Santo António and **Mira de Aire** ★ (*600 ESC; take the N243 from Porto de Mós to Mira de Aire, then follow the signs, www.virtual-net.pt/GrutasMiradeAire*), not only because of their size and shape, but also because of their lovely colours. They are the largest caves to have been discovered in Portugal

to date. A guided tour takes about 50min.

Leiria

Renowned for its locally made furniture and handicrafts (pottery, glassware and tinware), Leiria is also an important administrative centre. Located in the lush valley of the Rio Liz, it is a peaceful town abounding in flowers, that has been home to many poets, including Rodrigues Lobo and Afonso Lopes Vieira. Aside from its picturesque little alleyways and public squares with outdoor cafés, its main attraction is the handsome castle overlooking the town.

Occupied by the Moors for many years, Leiria was recaptured by Henriques I around 1135. Soon after, the king built the **Castelo de Leiria** ★ (*135 ESC; every day 9am to 6:30pm*) on a steep hill overlooking the Liz valley. Seized twice by the Moors, once in 1140 and then again in 1190, the castle underwent numerous modifications. Although almost nothing remains of the original structure, there are still some sections dating back to the 14th century reign of Dom Dinis I. Start your tour at the **keep** (*take the staircase to the left of the main entrance of the castle*), erected under Dinis I in 1324.

If you climb to the top (*not recommended for those subject to dizzy spells*), you can enjoy an **interesting panoramic view ★** of the castle and the surrounding countryside.

If you climb back down the stairs and walk to the left of the keep, you will enter the **Alcazar**, or fortified palace. Few of its many rooms are of interest, with the exception of its magnificent **gallery ★**, whose eight ribbed vaults, supported by lovely geminated columns, combine beautifully with the **view** of the town and surrounding countryside below.

Before concluding your tour, take a walk in front of the Alcazar to see the ruins of Leira's oldest church, the Gothic **Igreja de Nossa Senhora da Pena**, whose choir is decorated with Manueline motifs.

It is worth stopping by the **Romanesque church of São Pedro** (*near the entrance of the castle*) to see its capitals, which are adorned with plant motifs.

Praça Rodrigues Lobo has some pleasant outdoor cafés where you can kick back and relax. Finally, a pretty loggia serves as a footbridge over picturesque **Rua Afonso Albuquerque**.

★

Ourém

(25km from Leiria)

Don't confuse the lower village of Ourém, known as Vila Nova de Ourém, with the one inside the ramparts. To avoid disrupting the tranquil atmosphere of this charming place, visitors are strongly advised to park their cars near the gates of the fortress.

Like Porto de Mós, Tomar and many other fortified towns, Ourém was once occupied by the Moors. Recaptured by the Portuguese in 1136, it was later established as an earldom and then granted to Count Afonso, an illegitimate descendant of João I, in the 15th century. Most of the monuments you see today were erected during João I's reign. Today, Ourém seems almost unreal. The impressive ramparts shelter an adorable little **village ★**, which seems to have retained more of its medieval flavour than other Portuguese towns of the same era. Furthermore, unlike other towns in this region, Ourém has not been invaded by cars, shops, bars and restaurants, so it is extraordinarily peaceful. During our visit, a *pousada* was under construction.

After entering the walled village, walk across the Tabuleiro da Misericórdia, a small public square, and take a look at the pretty **fountain** adorned with Count Afonso's coat of arms. The magic will start to work, and before you know it, you'll find yourself several centuries in the past. Welcome to the Middle Ages! For a pleasant tour of the area, turn right, in silence, onto Rua São João, an absolutely charming little street that winds alongside the ramparts to the gates of the castle, offering **magnificent views ★★** along the way.

The **Castelo de Ourém ★★** is similar in some ways to the castle in Porto de Mós. Here, too, the numerous modifications executed in the 15th century were intended to transform the castle into a comfortable palace. Ourém, however, has retained more of its original military appearance, a case in point being its imposing machicolations.

If you follow the rampart walk, you will end up back in the village. On your way past the **collegiate church of Nossa Senhora da Misericórdia**, which was completely rebuilt in the second half of the 18th century, make sure to visit the **crypt ★**. All that remains of the original 15th century church, it has columns with lovely capitals and contains the tomb of Count

Alonso, adorned with his crest.

Fátima

(24km from Leiria)

Fátima's fame dates back to 1917, when the Virgin supposedly appeared here. Now a shrine, it attracts thousands of Catholic pilgrims every year from May 13 to October 13 (the same time the Virgin is said to have appeared). In addition to a basilica and a chapel, there are all sorts of souvenir shops and places to eat here.

Nazaré

Keep in mind that Nazaré refers to three distinct areas, the Praia, the Sítio and, less directly, Pederneira. Originally, Nazaré only covered the area known as the Sítio. There is a legend behind its name: sometime in the past (no one knows exactly when), a monk supposedly brought back a statuette of the Virgin from Nazareth. After a miracle occurred in 1182 (see p 223), a chapel was built here, and the place soon became a pilgrimage site. Over the years, Nazaré became a renowned sea resort, and is now overrun with tourists every summer. In spite of the crowds, the town has managed to retain the character

of a charming little fishing village. Its beauty and its excellent location near the major historic towns make it one of the most popular resorts in the region.

The area known as the **Praia** ★ essentially covers the lower part of town along the beach (*"praia"* literally means "beach"). It really only dates back to the second half of the 19th century; in fact, up until the 17th century, the sea stretched all the way to the foot of **Pedernaira**, about 700m from the present beach. Two important factors led to the development of this area, the first being the dramatic changes brought about by the sea, which resulted in the Bay of Serra filling up with sand. This in turn led to a decrease in the risk of piracy. Since they no longer had to fear constant pirate raids, local fishers began settling nearer to the beach.

Today, the village is made up of scores of narrow, parallel alleyways sloping down toward the sea and flanked by charming little houses that are almost perfectly aligned. To avoid parking headaches, don't drive your car to the beach. Start your tour at the top of the village, where you can enjoy a pretty **view** of the unevenly paved lanes with their tiny white houses. In the distance, the azure sea frames

little roofs of earth-coloured tiles. As you head down towards the beach, you will see an increasing number of shops, restaurants, bars and discotheques bustling with lively activity. The waterfront is lined with a big, beautiful **beach** of fine white sand, whose waters are perfect for swimming (p 232). If you're looking for a quaint and picturesque scene, keep in mind that the traditional dress of this region – a black felt hat and layers of coloured skirts for women and a long black cap and long pants worn tight around the ankles for men – is only worn during local festivities. As for the traditional image of colourful little fishing boats hauled up onto the beach by hand, that, too, disappeared when an artificial harbour was created to the south of the beach. Fishing itself, however, is still an important activity in Nazaré, so visitors can feast on a variety of fish-based dishes. Local specialties include grilled sardines and the famous *caldeirada*, a type of bouillabaisse.

Perched at an altitude of 110m, and thus easy to defend, the **Sítio** ★, literally "the Seat", was inhabited at a very early date. By 1182, it had already become a pilgrimage site, due to a miracle that supposedly took place here. According to legend, a commanding officer, who was fond of hunting, was chasing a deer on his horse one day in 1182. It was a particularly foggy day, and the man, swept up by the thrill of the chase, raced straight for the cliff, doomed to fall to his death. At the last moment, he realized how close he was to the precipice and called upon the Virgin to save him. At that exact moment, right at the edge of the cliff, the horse miraculously stopped short. To show his gratitude, the officer erected the **Capela da Memória** (*facing Largo de Nossa Senhora de Nazaré, near the lookout*), which is still adorned with lovely *azulejos* depicting the event.

The Sítio's major attraction is its **magnificent view ★★** of the lower part of town and its surroundings. The lookout (*miradouro*) overhanging the cliff commands an unimpeded view of the coast and the Serra da Pederneira. Make sure to come here in the evening, too, when the soft light casts a golden hue over the town. Adding to the pleasure of a visit to the Sítio is the ride up in the **funicular** (*10 ESC*), a classic model that is an attraction all on its own. Visitors fleeing the crowded beaches will be enchanted by this peaceful village, which, as in the past, is protected from invasions – tourist invasions these days.

It is worth stopping by the **Igreja de Nossa Senhora da Nazaré**, near the lookout, to see its lovely 13th-century Dutch *azulejos* and beautiful choir decorated with *talhas douradas*. If you go behind the choir from the left side, you will find a series of corridors, also covered with *azulejos*, which lead to the sacristy.

Pederneira (*take the EN8-4 towards Alcobaça*), located in the Serra da Pederneira, has a peaceful atmosphere and old alleyways, where you can enjoy a pleasant stroll. The **lookout** (*Largo da Misericórdia*) at the south end of the village offers a **beautiful view** of the coast and the Praia.

★★★

Óbidos

In 308 BC, when the Celts founded the village now known as Óbidos, the coast was still right nearby, and most of the local activity was centred around the sea. Over the following centuries, the mouth of the Arelho gradually silted up, and Óbidos became more and more isolated from the shore, which is now 10km from the village. Aside from the Hagoa (lagoon) de Óbidos, located a few kilometres away, Óbidos is now surrounded by verdant countryside. Although

the village was occupied by the Romans, the Visigoths and finally the Moors before being recaptured by the Portuguese in 1148, it wasn't until Dom Dinis I ascended the throne that Óbidos finally attained a certain level of renown. In 1282, when Dom Dinis I was married, he gave the village to his bride, Dona Santa Isabel, as a wedding gift. This became a tradition, and the village was passed on to each subsequent queen until 1834. Óbidos was thus doted on by the queens of Portugal, who maintained its pretty little white houses and peaceful alleyways over the centuries. The town's beauty attracted two celebrated painters here as well, Baltazar Gomes Figueira and Josefa de Ayala, also known as Josefa d'Óbidos, a native of Seville.

The charming village of Óbidos is still surrounded by magnificent ramparts and crowned by a castle that looks as if it came straight out of a fairy tale. Each year, it attracts large numbers of visitors, both foreign and Portuguese. Thanks to a strict historic preservation policy put into effect during the Salazar era, Óbidos has retained its old-world character and is still a very pleasant place to visit. On weekends, when Portuguese visitors mingle with the tourists, the place is literally mobbed. If you're looking to enjoy a romantic outing, therefore, it is much better to come here on a weekday.

Aside from its castle, Óbidos doesn't really have any important monuments. Its main attraction, as you have probably already gathered, is its flower-decked alleyways and gleaming white houses, which are occasionally adorned with a dash or two of ochre. The pretty tiled roofs, set against the towering wall that encircles the town, are a feast for the eyes. To help you make the most of your visit, we have described a few local curiosities below.

Before entering the walled village, take a look at the long aqueduct that ends near the Porta da Vila. Built in 1573 during the reign of Queen Catarina, it stretches 3km. On your way through the **Porta da Vila**, take the time to admire the beautiful 18th century *azulejos* with which it is decorated.

You will also see a niche containing a statuette of Nossa Senhora da Piedade, which is easier to see from the rampart walk.

As you stroll along Rua Direita, which is lined with charming houses and a handful of souvenir shops, you will pass by the **Pelhourino** (*on the right side of the street*), the Pillory, featuring the crest of Queen Leonor. You will also see a reproduction of a fishing net, a reference to the tragic death of the queen's son, whose body was found in the Tagus and brought back in a fishing net. The **Igreja de Santa Maria**, which stands below, on the site of a former mosque, is decorated with lovely 17th-century *azulejos* and paintings by **Josefa d'Óbidos**. If you keep walking along Rua Direita, you will end up in front of the **Igreja São Tiago**. Partially destroyed by the earthquake of 1755, it was reconstructed and converted into a handsome public auditorium.

Óbidos Castle

Right beside it, you'll see the entrance to the **Castelo ★ ★ ★**. Seized by Afonso I in 1140, this fortress subsequently underwent several modifications, the most important being the addition of a keep in 1375 and the conversion of its main buildings into a palace in the 16th century. The palace, which was also partly destroyed in the earthquake, still has lovely **Manueline windows ★** and an elegant **door** in the same style. The last major changes were made in 1951, when the castle became the first historic building in Portugal to be transformed into a *pousada*. The perfectly restored **rampart walk ★** (*narrow and somewhat awkward; not recommended for visitors subject to dizzy spells*) and the **parade ground ★** both offer an **idyllic view ★ ★ ★** of the village and its surrounding countryside. The scene is particularly romantic at sunset.

★

Foz de Arelho to São Martinho do Porto

For those who have the time and want to make the trip to Nazaré from Óbidos, the little road that runs along the coast is definitely worth a detour. The section linking Foz de Arelho and São do Porto is particularly

Costa de Prata: the South

noteworthy for its beautiful **ocean views** ★. For a picture-perfect panorama, take a walk along one of the many sea-bound trails by an old derelict mill on the left side of the road. The trails cross the fields, treating you to views of seemingly never-ending expanses of ocean and beaches. A perfect spot for a country picnic!

Peniche

The peninsula on which the town of Peniche now lies was once an island and was later joined to the mainland as deposits gradually accumulated in the formation of the port of Atouguia, causing land-bridges. This port was then located on the mainland, facing the island. Though traces of former inhabitants were discovered on the site of the present fortress (*castrum*), the population here only really swelled as of the 12th century, when Dom Alfonso Henriques I entrusted this town to the French crusader Guillaume de Corni for his help in the Reconquest of Lisbon.

As Portugal's second largest port, this peninsula, graced with sheer cliffs, has become a very popular tourist destination over the last few years. Indeed, every year, a great number of tourists flock here to enjoy scuba

diving off the Berlengas archipelago and surfing along the beaches of Alfarroba and Baleal, though these are sadly polluted by all kinds of household waste. To this day, however, the major tourist attraction remains the island of Berlenga, located about 10km off the coast and safeguarded as a nature reserve.

By crossing Peniche, visitors will discover a port city whose ominous past sometimes gives it a somewhat severe and dour appearance. Around dinner time, the odour of smoked fish permeates very busy Avenida do Mar as restaurants lining the avenue attempt to lure diners to their tables. At the end of this very avenue stands a monument in memory of fishers and, to the south, stands the Peniche fortress, which is now a museum.

Built on the order of King Dom João III, the **Fortaleza de Peniche** underwent major changes and extensions throughout history, the last of which was the transformation of part of it into a museum (see below) in 1984. Work began in 1557 with the construction of the *baluarte redondo*, the oldest part still standing, was interrupted on numerous occasions and remained unfinished until 1645. Though originally built solely for purposes of defence, the f*ortaleza*

was soon perceived as an ideal internment camp by those in power; in 1758, the Marquis of Pombal sentenced one of his political enemies to life imprisonment here. After having served as a prison, a barracks and even a visitor's centre for Boer refugees from South Africa, in 1934 the structure became one of Portugal's most sinister places: a prison in General Salazar's dictatorial regime. Ironically listed as a "national monument" by the regime, this place housed thousands of prisoners, namely Portuguese citizens in political and artistic circles, some of whom were tortured simply for failing to toe the party line. It was only in 1974, with the so-called Flower Revolution, that the Peniche Fortaleza reverted to the role of a simple historic building and unfortunate witness to a terrible past.

Museu de Peniche
(*120 ESC; Tue to Sun 10am to noon and 2pm to 6pm, summer until 7pm; in the fortress, at the south end of Avenida do Mar*). In addition to several rooms where regional handicrafts are displayed, the museum boasts a section dedicated to the region's history as well as several documents recounting its sordid past. A few cells are also open to the public and, from the *baluarte*

redondo, visitors can enjoy a beautiful view.

Escolas de Rendas de Bilros (*Mon to Fri 10am to noon and 2pm to 5pm; Rua Alexandre Herculano, in the same building as the tourist office, in the middle of a small park*). Thanks to its artisans, Peniche has acquired a solid reputation as a "city of embroidery"; this craft has been practised here since the late 16th century. At Peniche's lacemaking school, embroidery lovers can enjoy observing young apprentices at work, supervised by older teachers whose capable hands are truly marvels to behold.

Igreja de São Pedro (*Rua José Estêvão, at Largo Castilho*). Erected in 1698, this modest church is worth a visit if only for its beautiful *talha dourada* **choir** and lovely paintings, all attributed to Josefa de Óbidos' father (see p 224).

At the entrance to town, Avenida Marginal (EN114) runs west along the coast, circling the peninsula before ending in the heart of Peniche. By taking this avenue, you can enjoy lovely views of Berlenga Island and watch the ocean waves crashing violently against the jagged coast.

Continuing to Cabo Carvoeiro, you can admire the oddly shaped **cliffs** ★, so formed by intensive erosion, as well as the **lighthouse** of the same name (*closed to the public*). A little farther along, at the end of the cape, stands a restaurant. Here you'll find directions to **Laje dos Pargos** ★, a large observation deck surrounded by cliffs and accessible from a stairway carved out of the very rock (not recommended for those afraid of heights). Once there, you can witness a stunning phenomenon: down below, powerful waves come crashing into cavities hollowed out

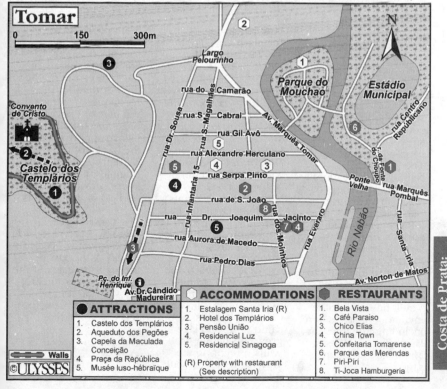

Tomar

0   150   300m

N

Parque do Mouchao

Estádio Municipal

Largo Pelourinho

Convento de Cristo

Castelo dos Templários

rua do Camarão
rua S. Magalhães
rua S. Cabral
rua Gil Avô
rua Alexandre Herculano
rua Serpa Pinto
rua de S. João
rua Dr. Joaquim Jacinto
rua Aurora de Macedo
rua Pedro Dias

Av. Marquês Tomar
rua Centro Republicano
rua da Fonte do Choupo
Ponte Velha
rua Marquês Pombal
Rio Nabão
rua Santa Irita
rua dos Moinhos
rua Everardo

Av. Norton de Matos

Pç. do Inf. Henrique
Av. Dr. Cândido Madureira

Walls

©ULYSSES

Costa de Prata: the South

beneath the cliffs, causing a dull, thunder-like rumbling every time. A not-to-be-missed spectacle!

Berlenga Island ★ (see "Parks and Beaches", p 232, 233 and "Outdoor Activities", p 232, 233)

Tomar

The little town of Tomar, which lies on either side of the Rio Nabão, is renowned for two attractions: its castle, built by the Order of Christ, and its Festa dos Tabuleiros (see box), which takes place every second July.

Its enchanting old centre is crisscrossed with picturesque, narrow alleyways paved with cobblestones of various colours. The scores of flowers adorning some of these streets make the place even more charming. The peaceful Rio Nabão fits in beautifully with the landscape of this lush valley. An island in the middle of it has been laid out as a park. If you're pressed for time, head straight for the castle; it is worth making a trip to Tomar simply to see the treasures it holds. You'll find a veritable inventory of styles here, including Romanesque, Byzantine, Gothic, Manueline and Renaissance.

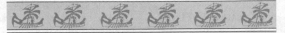

La Festa dos Tabuleiros

Dating back to the 14th century, La Festa dos Tabuleiros is highly representative of Portuguese culture, as well as being one of the most colourful festivals in the country. At the beginning of every other July (in odd-numbered years), young girls parade through the streets wearing traditional dress. They walk two by two, carrying on their heads a column as tall as they are, which is made of loaves of bread adorned with colourful paper flowers and topped by a crown. This ceremony is reminiscent of the festivities once held by the Brotherhood of Espírito Santo and is believed by some to be an ancient pagan fertility ritual.

The **Castelo dos Templários** ★ (*Jun to Sep 300 ESC, Oct to May 200 ESC; May to Jun 9:15am to 12:15pm and 2pm to 5:15pm, Jul to Sep 9:15am to 12:15pm and 2pm to 5:45pm, Oct to Apr 9:15am to 12:15pm and 2pm to 4:45pm; follow the signs on Avenida Dr. Cândido Madureira*) was begun in 1160 by order of the Grand Master of the Knights Templar, Gualdim Pais. Christened Tomar, from the Arabic word *Tamar* meaning "fresh water" (probably a reference to the Rio Nabão), the fortress was erected near the border between the Muslim and Christian worlds. At the same time, a village grew up within its walls, preparing the way for renewed settlement of the area. Around 1190, the town fought off a final Muslim attack, and, as of the 13th century, when the Portuguese reconquered the southern part of the country once and for all, a new village sprang up on the banks of the river. All that remains of the original castle is the keep, surrounded by a portion of its ramparts.

The **Convento de Cristo** ★★★ (*see Castelo dos Templários, above, for hours*). After passing through the gates of the fortress, you will enter a lovely garden, which is a pleasant place to relax.

If you walk to the far end, you will discover an esplanade (*take the staircase at the far end of the garden*), with the church facing onto it. Before entering the church, take a good look at its exterior, whose octagonal shape is reminiscent of Jerusalem's Holy Sepulchre. The splendid **portal** ★★★, with its blend of Manueline and flamboyant Gothic styles, contrasts sharply with the primitive appearance of the rest of the building. Upon entering the building, you will find yourself in a two-storey **Manueline nave** ★ with beautiful stained-glass windows. The nave and the numerous decorations surrounding it were added between 1512 and 1520, during the Manueline era. Some of these are the work of celebrated poet Gil Vicente. To the left of the entrance, you will see the Byzantine **Charola** ★★★ (*under restoration during our visit*). Its interior was completely redone during the reign of Manuel I, and almost nothing remains of its original decoration, save an odd-looking picture of St. Christopher with the head of a dog, painted right onto one of the walls (hidden from view during the renovations). Built in the 12th century, this rotunda was originally used as an oratory, but became the choir of the present church when the nave was added.

Two cloisters, the **Claustro do Cemitério** (Cemetery Cloister) and the **Claustro da Lavagens** (Ablutions Cloister), are connected to the rotunda (*closed to the public when this guide went to press*). They were added in 1433, when Henry the Navigator was commanding officer of the Order of Christ (having initially refused the title of Grand Master). With their austere Gothic architecture, they resemble the cloister of Dom Afonso V in Batalha (see p 220).

If you take the staircase (*to the right of the Manueline portal*) up to the *coro alto*, you can visit the second floor of the **Claustro dos Felipes** ★, the main cloister. Drawing inspiration from the Renaissance, of which Dom João III was a devotee, Diogo de Torralva erected a new cloister here around 1558. A great admirer of the Palladian style, the architect had no qualms about placing the new building right alongside the church, thereby concealing the latter's Manueline windows and eliminating some of its ornamentation. You can still see the decorations of one of the two windows near the staircase at the entrance. The cloister, considered by some to be the finest example of the Renaissance style in Portugal, has a noble quality about it, but its austere architecture is

not altogether compatible with the exuberant Manueline style of the church. Unlike the Gothic style, the Renaissance style does not seem to blend harmoniously with the Manueline style. This cloister is also the least favourite of the Portuguese, although their lack of appreciation probably has less to do with the style of the building and more to do with the fact that Felipe II of Spain was crowned here.

Last but not least is the **window of Tomar** ★★★ (*only visible from outside*), sculpted between 1510 and 1513. Visitors can enjoy a full view of it from two places, the terrace of the main cloister (*take one of the spiral staircases on the gallery of the cloister*) and the terrace of the Claustro da Santa Barbara (*take the passageway on the right, on the north side of the gallery*). The window, which could use a cleaning, is Portugal's most eloquent testimony to its great age of exploration. It is fancifully adorned with a variety of motifs, including seaweed, coral and shells, ropes, chains and – oddly enough – trees and roots held up by a sailor.

Other Attractions

Aqueduto dos Pegões ★★ (*adjacent to the Tomar Monastery*). Built on the order of King Filipe I to

The Order of Christ

The Order of Christ is a direct descendant of the Order of the Knights Templar, which was founded in Palestine in 1118 after the crusade of Godefroy de Bouillon. Several offshoots of the Order were then established in Europe. The Portuguese branch was originally based in Coimbra. Highly regimented, the Order was divided into several categories: knights (made up only of nobles), esquires, or men-at-arms, and chaplains. The purpose of the Order was to introduce the virtues of Christianity to "barbarians" (usually with the help of swords!). By backing Afonso Henriques in his quest for a kingdom and then helping him reconquer the country, the Portuguese Knights Templar acquired major privileges and were granted numerous pieces of land. By the 12th century, they owned a large portion of the middle of the kingdom. Accumulating wealth left and right, and even becoming the Pope's banker and providing loans to kings and princes, the Order eventually began to arouse the envy of the rich and powerful. In 1307, the French king Philippe le Bel, finding himself penniless, decided to ban the Order and confiscate its possessions on the pretext that its members were heretics. In Portugal, however, the Knights Templar continued to enjoy their privileges, due to their unflagging support of the monarchy. In 1312, when the pope issued a bull disbanding the Order, a reluctant Dom Dinis I began to enforce the decree. In 1319, however, he was granted permission to create a new order known as the Order of Christ (Ordem de Cristo). The new order was given the property confiscated from the old one and its members' rights were restored. The Order of Christ, even more dependent on the Portuguese monarchy than the Knights Templar had been, thus became one of the court's most faithful servants and played an active role in conquering the New World. Even Henry the Navigator was a member. In 1359, Tomar found its place in Portuguese history when it was chosen as the headquarters of the Order of Christ. In keeping with its new status, it was endowed with a magnificent monastery. After a period of ever-increasing prosperity, João III obtained authorization from the pope to appropriate the title of Grand Master of the Cross, the supreme leader of the Order. Only kings could bear the title from that point on, thus reducing the power of the Order, which grew weaker and weaker in relation to the monarchy.

supply the Knights of the Order of Christ with water, this elegant aqueduct, spanning almost 6km, is particularly impressive due to its double row of no fewer than 180 arches. Construction began in 1593, but was not completed until 1613, the year in which Pedro Fernandes Torres finished this marvellous masterpiece of engineering. Photography buffs in search of beautiful subjects, take note!

It is worth stopping by the **Capela da Imaculada Conceição** ★ (*Jul to Sep 11am to 12:15pm and 4pm to 5pm, Oct to Jun 11am to noon; located halfway along the road to the castle, to the right*), mainly to admire its attractive Renaissance architecture. Although it was built to house the tomb of João III, the king was never laid to rest here.

The **Praça da República** ★ is a pleasant, black and white, checkered square. Facing onto it are the Câmara Municipal and the Igreja de São João Baptista, which has a pretty **Manueline door**. Inside the church, you will find a beautifully carved **pulpit**, also in the Manueline style. While exploring Tomar, you will notice that the streets follow a grid pattern. Henry the Navigator designed the layout, which was quite innovative for the time.

Make sure to include the **old town** ★★ in your tour. Abounding with flowers, its pretty streets are delightfully picturesque. Stroll along Rua Dr. Joaquim Jacinto, probably the most verdant street in the area, to the **Museu Luso-Hebreu** ★ (*closed Wed; 9:30am to 12:30pm and 2pm to 5pm during winter, until 6pm during summer; Rua Dr. Joaquim Jacinto 73*), which houses a collection of sacred objects. The building itself, a 15th-century synagogue, is of considerable interest, especially its recently excavated baths. During your visit, take a look at the cavities in the upper corners of the rooms, which have pitchers inside of them. The sound of prayers would reverberate off these vessels and thus be amplified.

The **Igreja de Santa Maria do Olival** (*go all the way up Rua Santa Iria*), which stands on a hilltop outside of town, houses the tombs of several members of the Order of Christ. It boasts a lovely **view** ★ of the Nabão valley and the castle, as well as a handsome Gothic portal (which has unfortunately been damaged), topped by an elegant rose window. Also of interest is the burial site of Gualdim Pais (see p 228).

Castelo do Bode

(*13km from Tomar*)

This area is known mainly for its large dam, the Barragem de Castelo do Bode. It is worth making a quick stop here to take in the **beautiful view** of the Zêzere valley. If you like scenic highways, take the N358-2 to Constância. This is a particularly impressive stretch of road that runs along the Zêzere valley.

Tancos

(*28km from Tomar*)

Though devoid of any major historic attractions, the little village of Tancos, on the banks of the Tagus, is worth a stop on your way to Almoural. In fact, from the town, not only can you enjoy a most romantic **view** ★ of the *castelo* of Almourol, which stands on an islet in the middle of the Tagus, but also of the delightful village of Arripiado and its lovely church.

Come nighfall, the setting becomes all the more enchanting as the castle ruins and Arripiado are lit up, creating a fairy-tale scene in the distance. Finally, leaving from the main dock on weekends are wonderful excursions aboard one of the pleasure crafts (*500 ESC; Sat and Sun 10am to 7pm*) that cruise along the river to the castle.

★★★

Almourol

(29km from Tomar)

Erected in 1171 by the Knights Templar, the **castle of Almourol ★★** *(every day 9am to 7:30pm; boat ride to the island 100 ESC return)* stands on a rocky promontory in the middle of the Tagus, thus forming a small island. Partly surrounded by sandbanks, it has rather unusual vegetation made up essentially of bamboo and cacti. Some of the latter are as tall as trees, making for an enchanting setting. The Tagus and the Zêzere come together nearby, and the castle, which was partially restored in the 19th century, was built to monitor traffic on the two rivers. This is an extremely romantic place to visit, but certain precautions should be taken. The staircases are quite dangerous, and anyone prone to dizzy spells should definitely steer clear of the rampart walk. Furthermore, the last flight of stairs leading up to the square tower is particularly steep, so visitors should proceed with the utmost caution. If you make it to the top, you will be rewarded with a **superb view ★★** of the Tagus valley. Even if you stay on the ground, however, this charming little island is worth visiting.

Parks and Beaches

★

Berlenga Island

Located approximately 10km off the coast, Ilha de Berlenga is part of the Berlengas archipelago which comprises about 20 islands and islets: Berlenga, Farilhão Grande, Farilhão Pequeno, Estrelas and Forcados are among the largest. In the Tertiary era, the present archipelago and the Peniche peninsula formed one large island isolated from the mainland. Granitic by nature, these islands, constantly swept by winds off the Atlantic, are covered with nothing but moors and are entirely devoid of trees. Their isolation, sparse vegetation and small size have spared them from becoming intensively populated; only Berlenga is inhabited by a small community of fishers. This island has been listed as a nature reserve for several years now and, in addition to a rather considerable population of birds and a few lizards, exceptionally rich marine life can be observed here. Among the latter, the particularly extensive variety of crustaceans found in abundance here is the pride of the island's

fishers. Besides that, the few inhabitants pride themselves on showing tourists numerous **caves** with crystal-clear waters flowing through them, an ideal spot for observing marine life (see "Outdoor Activities", p 233). One cave, known as **0 Furado Grande ★**, even spans the length of the island and boasts a gigantic **arch** (*Cova do Sonho*), close to 70m high. On a clear day, you can observe the mainland as well as the other islands from its 85m-high summit. Fans of historic monuments, for their part, can head to the island's old fortress, the **Fortaleza de São João Baptista ★** while taking a pleasurable walk. Dating back to the 17th century, it is located in the cove of a small bay and is erected on a small rocky island. A charming little bridge connects the fortress to the island (photography buffs take note!). Now converted into a hotel-restaurant, it welcomes visitors seeking solitude during the summer.

Nazaré

Renowned for its big, beautiful **beach ★** of fine white sand, Nazaré is an excellent place for sun-worshippers to enjoy their favourite "sport". Its waters, furthermore, are perfectly safe for swimming, so you can splash about to your heart's content. Keep in mind, however, that this is the Atlantic, and the water can be a bit chilly. The atmosphere is always lively here during the high season.

Tomar

Located on a little island in the middle of the Rio Nabão, **Parque Mouchão** ★ (*take Rua da Fonte do Choupo or Avenida Marquês Tomar*) is a pleasant place for a stroll and offers some magnificent views of both the castle and the town. You'll find a water-wheel near the bridge leading to Avenida Marquês Tomar.

Outdoor Activities

Hiking and Bicycling

Peniche

The beauty of its jagged cliffs makes the Peniche peninsula a delightful place to roam on foot or by bicycle, even more so as the road skirting it offers many different views of the ocean. Eight kilometres long, this bracing tour will allow visitors to get a good dose of fresh air and en-

counter a few sights worth stopping at, such as the Cabo Carvoeiro lighthouse and the small Nossa Senhora dos Remedios sanctuary. On a clear day, fortunate visitors can also discern Berlenga Island in the distance. To begin your tour, take Rua de São Marcos heading west (away from the port) to the Estrada Marginal-N114 farther along on the left. After a long loop that circles the peninsula, the Estrada joins Avenida 25 de Abril at the north end of the Peniche port.

Bicycle Rentals

Before venturing out, make sure the bicycle is in good condition as rental bikes are not always in tip-top shape.

Duas Rodas
near the Ponte Velha, outside the fortifications and very close to the bus station
*800 ESC/day
(400 ESC/half a day)*

Radio Micro-Moto
Avenida do Mercado
*900 ESC/day
(500 ESC/half a day)*

Cruises and Scuba Diving

The Berlengas Archipelago

Two agencies in the heart of Peniche offer excursions to the

Berlenga nature reserve. While the first, the Viamar agency, offers its services from May 15 to September 20, the second, Berlenga Turpesca, provides year-round transportation. The latter also organizes scuba-diving and deep-sea fishing trips. Whichever you choose, be advised that the crossing takes approximately 45min and is not recommended for those subject to seasickness. Navigation conditions on the Atlantic Ocean vary greatly from day to day; whatever the season, visitors will sometimes have to arm themselves with patience as boats do not venture out when the sea proves too turbulent. Moreover, due to its status as a nature reserve, the law limits the number of people visiting the archipelago to 300 per day. Making reservations well in advance is therefore essential. Otherwise, during high tourist season, arrive as soon as the ticket office opens (see schedule below) and be patient.

Fare: between 2,500 and 3,000 ESC for the return crossing to Berlenga Island.

Schedule

● May 15 to June 30, departure from Peniche to Berlenga at 10am. Return to Peniche at 4pm.

- July 1 to August 31, departures from Peniche to Berlenga at 9am, 11am and 5pm. Returns to Peniche at 10am, 4pm and 6pm.

- September 1 to September 20, departure to Berlenga at 10am. Return to Peniche at 4pm.

- September 20 to May 15, varying schedule; contact Turpesca.

Viamar
Residencial Aviz, Rua Alexandre Herculano (near the Tourist Office), 2520 Peniche
☎*262 78 21 53*

Burlenga Turpesca
90 Rua Marechal Gomes Freire de Andrade, 2520 Peniche
☎*262 78 99 60*
↪*262 78 30 13*

Golf

The southern part of the Costa de Prata is hardly conducive to this type of sport, the many tourist attractions in the region having prevented the development of the game. Nevertheless, this region has three professional-class golf courses; below are their addresses and main features.

Accommodations

Alcobaça

Pensão Corações Unidos
$
pb
to the right of the monastery, Rua Trei Antônio Brandão 39 2460 Alcobaça
☎/↪*262 58 21 42*
Although the Pensão Corações Unidos has a very modest decor and poorly soundproofed rooms, it is located just steps away from the monastery. Friendly, but somewhat unprofessional service. For undemanding visitors on a limited budget.

Golf Courses

Name	Number of Holes	Par	Length (in metres)	Address
Golf Botado	9	36	2500	Complexo Turístico do Botado Praia da Consolação 2520 Peniche ☎*262 75 77 00* ↪*262 75 07 17*
Praia d'El Rey Golf Club	18	72	6465	Vale de Janelas 2510 Obidos ☎*262 90 96 26* ↪*262 90 96 29*
Golden Eagle Golf Club	18	72	6200	Quinta do Brinçal Arrouquelas 2040 Rio Maior ☎*043 981 48* ↪*043 981 49*

Hotel Santa Maria
$
pb, tv
Rua Dr. Francisco Zagalo
2460 Alcobaça
☎*262 59 73 95*
⇒*262 59 67 15*
The Hotel Santa Maria is probably the best value in the region. The rooms are well colour equipped and attractively decorated. Ask for one facing the front so you can enjoy the magnificent view of the monastery.

Fervença
(5km from Alcobaça)

Hotel das Termas da Piedade
$$
pb, tv, ℜ
5km from Aldobaça, on the left side of the road to Nazaré
2460 Alcobaça
☎*262 59 69 79*
⇒*262 59 69 71*
www.hoteltermaspiedade.com
Surrounded by fields at the foot of a hill, the Hotel das Termas da Piedade is conveniently located between Alcobaça and Nazaré. This is a modern establishment that will appeal to visitors seeking peace and quiet. The property is surrounded by beautiful trees, and there is a terrace where guests can sit back and enjoy the serenity of the enchanting setting. Friendly service.

Alfeizerão
(15km from Alcobaça)

Pousada da Juventude, S. Martinho do Porto
Estrada de Alcobaça 8
2465 Alfeizerão
☎*262 99 95 06*
☎*262 58 20 65*

Batalha

Residencial Gladius
$
pb
Praça Mouzinho de Albuquerque, 2440 Batalha
☎*244 76 57 60*
Situated right in the heart of Batalha, a stone's throw from its magnificent monastery, the Residencial Gladius has a few rooms that are small and modestly furnished but well maintained. A good choice for those with limited budgets.

Casa do Outeiro
$$
pb, ≈, tv
Largo Carvalho do Outeiro 4
2400 Batalha
☎*244 76 58 06*
At the Casa do Outeiro, which is located a bit out of the way, visitors can enjoy the lovely scenery of the surrounding hills. Attractive decor and reasonable rates.

Residencial Batalha
$$$
pb, tv
Largo da Misericordia
2440 Batalha
☎*244 76 75 00*
⇒*244 76 74 67*
Set alongside the pretty little Igreja da Misericórdia, the

Residencial Batalha is a sizable, modern hotel offering comfort, a tasteful decor and friendly service. Good value.

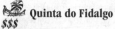 ### Quinta do Fidalgo
$$$
pb and ps
Avenida D. Nuno Alvares Pereira
2440, Batalha
☎*244 76 51 14*
⇒*244 76 74 01*
A converted 17th-century residence, the charming Quinta do Fidalgo lies in a verdant setting with a view of the monastery. It has several comfortable, tastefully decorated rooms. The only minor drawback is the proximity of the N1, which detracts somewhat from the surroundings.

Pousada do Mestre Afonso Domingues
$$$$
pb, ℜ, ℝ, tv
Largo Mestre Afonso Domingues, 2440 Batalha
☎*244 76 52 60*
☎*244 76 52 61*
⇒*244 76 52 47*
Pousada do Mestre Afonso Domingues lies on the main square, opposite the monastery church. The building is fairly modern, but already looks a bit outdated. The rooms are very comfortable, and some of them offer views of the church, which is lit up a good part of the night making the view that much more outstanding after dark. The only drawback is the sound of tourists constantly trooping through the square during the day,

which makes it difficult to contemplate the view in peace. Furthermore, the nonstop noise of people parking their cars in front of and alongside the hotel makes it necessary to keep your windows closed. In spite of these minor inconveniences, this is still a pleasant and comfortable place to stay.

Leiria

Pousada da Juventude, Largo Cândido dos Reis
7D, 2400 Leiria
☎ *244 83 18 68*

Hotel Lis
$$
pb
10 Largo Alexandre Herculano
2400 Leiria
☎ *244 81 40 17*
⇄ *244 81 50 99*
With its lovely facade adorned with *azulejos* and an old-fashioned lobby where the furniture and decor recall the 1940s, the Hotel Lis offers small, relatively clean and simply furnished rooms. The woodwork, which makes up the greater part of the decor, confers a charming, rustic atmosphere to the place; by choosing a room facing the front, visitors will benefit from a lovely view of the *castelo*, which stands proudly over the city. Unpretentious and welcoming.

Praia do Pedrogão
(32km from Leiria)

Parque de Campismo da Praia do Pedrogão
Praia do Pedrogão
2425 Coimbrão
☎ *244 69 54 03*

Nazaré

Camping Vale Paraíso
Estrada Nacional 242
2km from Nazaré
Apdo 15
2451 Nazaré
☎ *262 56 18 00*
⇄ *262 56 19 00*
Small hotels and *pensãos* abound in Nazaré. Many local residents, furthermore, will accommodate tourists in their homes, especially during the high season. Depending on the house, you can rent single, double or triple rooms, and the rates vary according to the season, as well as the location and the services offered. Expect to pay a minimum of 2,000 ESC during the low season and between 4,000 and 6,000 ESC in summer. As you walk through town, you are sure to see many signs advertising rooms for rent.

Pensão Central
$-$$
sb/pb
Rua Mousinho de Albuquerque 85, 2450 Nazaré
☎ *262 55 15 10*
A small boarding-house with an outmoded decor, the Pensão Central is slightly removed from the beach, and lies on a rather

busy street, making it best suited to people who like a lively atmosphere both day and night.

Albergaria Mar Bravo
$$
pb, tv
corner Rua da República and Praça Sousa Oliveira
2450 Nazaré
☎ *262 55 11 80*
☎ *262 55 10 92*
⇄ *262 55 39 79*
The Albergaria Mar Bravo is an old turn-of-the-century residence. Its rooms are charming and decently equipped, although a little on the small side. Only a few of them offer views of the waterfront. Good value for your money.

Pensão-Restaurante Ribamar
$$
pb
Rua Gomes Freire 3-9
2450 Nazaré
☎ *262 55 11 58*
The Pensão-Restaurante Ribamar is a small hotel with lots of charm. The old-fashioned decor and wooden floors give the rooms a 17th-century flavour. Ask for a room with a view of the beach, which lies right in front of the hotel.

Residencial Beira Mar
$$
pb and ps, ℜ
Avenida da República 40
2450 Nazaré
☎ *262 56 13 58*
The Residencial Beira Mar, located above the restaurant of the same name, has 15 modestly decorated but comfortable rooms. The place

is clean and well kept, and faces onto the beach. Only a few rooms offer views of the sea, however. Reasonable rates.

Hotel Praia
$$$
pb, tv
Avenida Vieira Guimarães
☎*262 56 14 23*
=*262 56 14 36*
The best thing about this big hotel is that some of its rooms offer attractive views of the Sítio (ask for one at the back). The rooms are comfortable, too, although their modern decor is somewhat impersonal. Most of them have balconies. Relatively expensive, considering the location.

Óbidos

Tasquinha da Moura
$ no bkfst
at Rua Josefa d'Óbidos and Rua P. Nunes Tavares
Located right by the south gateway to the village, above a grocer's, this boarding house offers budget travellers three small but appealing rooms. Despite its modest appearance (somewhat old-fashioned furnishings and shared bathroom), the rooms are comfortable, pleasantly decorated and spotless, and offer a view of the castle's fortifications. The only drawback: the owner does not accept reservations, so you'll have to take your chances like everyone else!

Óbidos o Sol - Casa de Hóspedes
$ no bkfst
Rua Direita 40, 2510 Óbidos
☎*262 95 91 88*
The Óbidos o Sol - Casa de Hóspedes only has a few rooms. Simple, with no frills, but clean. Friendly service. Mainly for visitors on tight budgets.

Albergaria Rainha Santa Isabel
$$ no bkfst
pb, tv
Rua Direita, 2510 Óbidos
☎*262 95 93 23*
=*262 95 91 16*
The Albergaria Rainha Santa Isabel boasts a prime location inside the ramparts. Modest but well kept.

Albergaria Josefa d'Óbidos
$$
pb, tv, ℜ
Rua Dom João de Ornelas
2510 Óbidos
☎*262 95 92 28*
=*262 95 95 33*
The Albergaria Josefa d'Óbidos is located in a pretty setting at the foot of the ramparts and is decorated in a traditional manner. Ask for a room at the back of the building, away from the main road.

Casa do Rochedo
$$$
pb, ≈
Rua do Jogo da Bola, against the ramparts, on the west side
2510 Óbidos
☎*262 95 91 20*
A medium-sized hotel located right next to Óbidos's fortifications, Casa de Rochedo has eight rooms whose decor, much like the building itself, has a

certain rustic though hardly opulent charm. However, besides its quiet atmosphere, it is one of the few hotels in the village that has an outdoor swimming pool, the terrace of which offers magnificent panoramic views of the castle and its ramparts as well as the village's quintessential tiled roofs. Prices are a little high, but the great location will soon banish this from your mind – at least for a little while! For those who cannot afford such accommodations, the owner also has two other establishments (Casa do Poço and Casa do Relógio) that are more affordable but, alas, have no swimming pool.

Estalagem do Convento
$$$
pb, ℜ
Rua Dom João de Ornelas
2510 Óbidos
☎*262 95 92 14*
=*262 95 91 59*
Also at the foot of the town walls, the Estalagem do Convento welcomes visitors in a lovely monastic setting. The rooms are quiet and comfortable, and there is a lovely garden.

Casa d'Óbidos
$$$
pb, ≈
Quinta São José
2510 Óbidos
☎*262 95 09 24*
=*262 95 99 70*
Those who value peace and quiet are sure to appreciate Casa d'Óbidos, a former

quinta now converted into a *turismo de habitação* guesthouse. The attractive manor house is accessible via a dirt road that runs through fields dotted with grazing sheep. Those in search of a refined setting will be delighted with the place, filled with antique objects and furnishings. The owner is passionately fond of interior decorating, and both the rooms and bathrooms are decorated with precious ornaments, all meticulously chosen and tastefully arranged. Indeed, the establishment's every nook and cranny seems to be graced a golden touch, making the lounge, library and billiard room havens of relaxation. Moreover, to the great delight of visitors, each of the rooms has its own character. Everything is unique, from the furniture to the curtains to the bouquet of flowers placed it some of the rooms. A few of the rooms even have a direct view of the Castelo de Óbidos in the distance. All rooms feature a comfortable bathroom, except for the one on the main floor, which comes with a shower.

Unfortunately, the hotel sometimes has hot-water shortages, which can make waking up somewhat brutal. A drawback to be sure, but one soon forgotten at the sight of the incredible breakfast spread: real orange juice, fresh fruit (grapes, melons, pineapples, oranges, etc.), yogurt, cereal, homemade jams, several kinds of bread (white, whole-wheat or corn), various brioches, cold cuts (ham, chorizo sausage, smoked bacon, etc.) and scrambled eggs. Finally, for those not yet sated, Portuguese biscuits and fruit cake top off this feast fit for a king or queen.

Right next to the main house is a charming self-catering **cottage** (*$$$ no bkfst*) with two bedrooms, a living room with fireplace, an equipped kitchen, a play room as well as a private garden, perfect for anyone travelling with children or in small groups. Finally, to top off this enchanting setting, a big swimming pool has been set up in a large, lovingly tended garden. Guests can thus enjoy a lovely dip against the idyllic backdrop of the ramparts of Óbidos in the distance. Excellent value for the price for this category of hotel.

Pousada do Castelo
$$$$$
pb, ℜ, ℝ, *tv*
the *pousada* is located within the town walls, inside the castle, 2510 Óbidos
☎ *262 95 91 05*
☎ *262 95 91 46*
≈ *262 95 91 48*
In 1951, this castle became the first historic monument in Portugal to be converted into a *pousada*. It would be impossible to describe the feeling of staying in a place such as this, which is absolutely steeped in history.

Imagine a prince returning to his castle after a romantic stroll in the marvellous village of Óbidos. After an excellent meal in the rustic dining room, he retires to the tower of the keep and stretches out on a canopy bed. The rough, imposing stone walls surrounding him give him a feeling of complete security. Thus cut off from the rest of the world, he can reflect on his own destiny and that of his subjects. Early the next morning, he steps out onto his terrace and watches the sun rise over the sleeping village. The mist slowly rises in the surrounding countryside. There are no enemies on the horizon. He takes a long, reassuring look at the imposing ramparts surrounding the village. Once again, from atop his castle overlooking the town, he feels that he has been charged with an important mission: to guide and protect his subjects. These days, however, the prince is you! Now you have an idea of the kind of effect this magical place will have on you. Staying in such prestigious surroundings is a unique experience that is well worth living. All of the rooms are equipped with antique furniture and are very comfortable. Most of them offer a view of the castle's inner courtyard. The ones in the towers are suites, and can accommodate several guests. Given the popularity of this *pousada*, it is wise to make reservations well in advance.

Foz do Arelho

(*15km from Óbidos*)

Parque de Campismo Municipal de Foz do Arelho
Foz do Arelho, 2500 Foz do Arelho
☎*262 97 91 97*
☎*262 97 91 01*
⇌*262 97 83 33*

Peniche

Parque de Campismo Municipal de Peniche
Avenida Monsenhor M. Bastos
2520 Peniche
☎*262 78 95 29*
⇌*262 78 01 11*

Residencial Restaurante Marítimo
$ no bkfst
pb
109 Rua José Estêvão
2520 Peniche
☎*262 78 28 50*
Located a few steps from the Peniche fortress, the modest Residencial Restaurante Marítimo will primarily suit travellers with limited budgets. Despite rudimentary bathroom facilities and lack of hot water at certain times of day, rooms are comfortable and well kept. Without charm but ideal for small budgets.

Residêncial Rimavier
$ no bkfst
pb
Rua Castilho no. 6-8
2520 Peniche
☎/⇌*262 78 94 59*
www.ciberguia.pt/rimavier
Located above a souvenir shop, this modest hotel offers a few simply furnished but comfortable, spotless rooms. For a pleasant view, opt for one of the rooms looking out on the Praça de São Pedro and its lovely church. Guests enjoy a warm welcome and awake to the tolling of the bells!

Residencial Vasco da Gama
$$
pb, tv
23 Rua José Estêvão,
2520 Peniche
☎*262 78 19 02*
⇌*262 78 98 07*
This *residencial* offers comfortable rooms, each equipped with a modern bathroom. Breakfast is served in a pleasant living room. One of the best quality/price ratios in Peniche.

Tomar

Parque de Campismo Municipal de Tomar
2300 Tomar
☎*249-32 26 07*
☎*249 32 26 08*
⇌*249 32 10 26*

Residencial Luz
$ no bkfst
pb
Rua Serpa Pinto 144
2300 Tomar
☎*249 31 23 17*
Only the basics, but clean and cheap!

Pensão Residencial União
$
sb/pb, tv
Rua Serpa Pinto 94
apartado 19, 2300 Tomar
☎*249 32 31 61*
⇌*249 32 12 99*
The *azulejos* adorning the Pensão Residencial União are worth the trip all on their own. This pleasant little boarding-house has relatively comfortable rooms decorated in a tasteful though slightly rustic manner. Some of them offer views of the castle. Attractive breakfast room. Gracious staff. Very good value for the price.

Residencial Sinagoga
$$
pb, ℜ, tv
Rua Gil de Avô 31, 2300 Tomar
☎*249 32 30 83*
⇌*249 32 21 96*
The Residencial Sinagoga is a comfortable modern hotel located in the heart of the medieval town. The decor is rather simple, but the rooms are well maintained.

Estalagem Santa Iria
$$$
pb or ps, ℜ
at the tip of the island, in Parque do Mouchão,
2300 Tomar
☎*249 31 33 26*
☎*249 32 12 38*
⇌*249 32 10 82*
The Estalagem Santa Iria is probably the most charming hotel in Tomar. Set on an island in the middle of the Rio Nabão, it offers a quiet, relaxing atmosphere. Ask for a room facing the park, so you can enjoy the marvellous

view of the main tree-lined path. The lush vegetation and pervading tranquility give the place a magical quality. The rooms with balconies at the back of the building offer interesting views of the river. Tasteful decor and congenial staff.

Hotel dos Templários
$$$
pb, tv, ≈, ℜ, ☉
1 Largo Cândido dos Reis
2300 Tomar
☎*249 32 17 30*
☎*249 31 12 41*
⇆*249 32 21 91*
Located right next to the Rio Nabão and facing a small island, the large Hotel dos Templários offers 176 recently renovated rooms, equipped with all the comforts offered by large hotel chains. Guests can benefit from an exercise room as well as a pleasant swimming pool and tennis court. In terms of decor, both the rooms and common areas have been accommodated with tasteful furnishings. For a pleasant view, request a room facing the park; some even offer panoramas of the city with the castle in the distance.

Almourol

(29km from Tomar)

Pensão Soltejo
$
ps
Estrada Novo, Highway N3 between Entroncamento and Vila Nova da Barquinha
☎*249 71 02 31*
Ask for a room with a view of the Tagus. Simple decor and basic level of comfort.

Castelo do Bode

(13km from Tomar)

Campismo de Castelo do Bode, Martinchel
2200 Abrantes
☎*241-84 92 62*
⇆*241 84 92 44*

Pousada de São Pedro
$$$$$
pb, ℜ, ℝ, tv
from Tomar, head towards Entroncamento on the N110 for 7km, then turn left on the N358-2 and continue in the direction of Constância for 6km; the *pousada* is located on the left, just past the dam, 2300 Castelo do Bode, Tomar
☎*249 38 11 59*
☎*249 38 11 75*
⇆*249 38 11 76*
Located at the edge of the Zêzere valley, right beside an impressive dam, the Pousada de São Pedro is an extremely peaceful place, in operation since 1954. The building, originally designed to accommodate the engineers working on the dam, recently underwent a complete overhaul. Like most *pousadas*, it is tastefully decorated, and the

rooms are well maintained. Some of them have small, private terraces with views of the dam and the valley. Alongside the sitting room, there is a large terrace, where you can admire the surroundings while soaking up the peaceful atmosphere. The restaurant, with its big picture window, also offers an impressive view.

Restaurants

Alcobaça

Rosata Pizzas
$
closed Wed
80-81 Praça 25 Abril
If you're in the mood for pizza, Rosata Pizzas is a good choice. It has a pleasant, spacious terrace beneath the trees on Praça Dom Afonso Henriques, where you can share a nice, big pizza. Prices start at only 850 ESC.

Restaurante Celeiro dos Frades
$
Rua Arco Cister, under the arches on Praça da República
Visitors looking for somewhere a little cozier can head to the Restaurante Celeiro dos Frades, where arches create an intriguing atmosphere. However, the noisy television in the main dining room is disruptive.

Café Restaurante Trindade
$$
Praça Dom Afonso Henriques 22
The Café Restaurante Trindade serves standard Portuguese cuisine. You can enjoy your meal on the terrace, which is shaded by trees.

Restaurante Ti Fininho
$$
Rua Frei António Brandão no. 32
☎262 59 65 06
Restaurante Ti Fininho is a small, unpretentious locale where you can sample some *corvina* (a white-fleshed fish). It has a pleasant terrace with a view of the monastery.

Cafés and Tearooms

Cafetaria Dom Pedro
closed Sun
Praça 25 Abril 57, opposite the monastery
The Cafetaria Dom Pedro, which has a little terrace with a view of the monastery, is a good place to stop for a snack. The menu consists mainly of sandwiches and pastries.

Pastelaria Saraiva
Praça Dom Afonso Henriques 4
To satisfy your sweet tooth, head to the Pastelaria Saraiva, where a wide selection of goodies awaits you.

Tancos
(28km from Tomar)

Restaurante Almourol
$$$
Wed to Mon noon to 2:30pm and 7:30pm to 10:30pm
Route N3, on the way into the village of Tancos, on the right side of the eastbound road
☎249 71 04 32
Located on the way into the small village of Tancos, Restaurante Almourol is set up inside a large house with a typical gleaming whitewashed facade. Whether you choose to eat in its elegant (though overly air-conditioned) dining room or on its terrace, you can enjoy local specialties such as the *fritada de peixe do Rio* (grilled fish from the Tagus) or the congereel stew as well as many other singular culinary selections. Moreover, the terrace offers a view of the river and the romantic village of Arripiado. All this plus fast service and a friendly staff make this place a perfect stopover in the region.

Almourol
(29km from Tomar)

Restaurante Sol Tejo
$$
Sat to Thu 8am to 2:30pm and 7pm to 9:30pm
on the N3, between Entroncamento and Vila Nova da Barquinha, right beside the Pensão Soltejo
Despite the unpleasantness of being next to a gas station, this restaurant is a good place to stop on your way to Almourol. The dining room, with its luxurious but outmoded decor, offers a lovely view of the Tagus and its valley, as well as of the little village of Vila Nova da Barquinha. The home-style cuisine is excellent, and you can enjoy dishes like *febras de porco* (grilled filet of pork) and *fígado de vaca* (beef liver), served with generous portions of home-made fries. The tables are decorated with fresh flowers, and the service is attentive. A safe bet.

Castelo do Bode
(13km from Tomar)

Pousada de São Pedro
$$$
from Tomar, head towards Entroncamento on the N110 for 7km, then turn left on the N358-2 and continue in the direction of Constância for 6km the *pousada* is located on the left, just past the dam,
2300 Castelo do Bode
☎249 38 11 59
☎249 38 11 75
Located at the edge of the Zêzere valley, right beside an impressive dam, this restaurant is set up inside the building that accommodated the engineers during the construction of the dam (1946-1952). The place was completely renovated a short time ago. Before your meal, you can enjoy a relaxing drink on the spacious terrace. It is worth coming here just for the striking view of

the dam and the valley. The tastefully decorated dining room has an immense bay window, which also offers a magnificent view of the area. You can top off a delightful evening with a pleasant after-dinner stroll on the nearby dam. Reservations required.

Batalha

Dom Duarte
$$$
Largo Papa Paulo VI
☎244 76 63 26
Dom Duarte, which specializes in seafood, is decorated in a non-descript manner, but has a pleasant terrace.

Pousada do Mestre Afonso Domingues
$$$
Largo Mestre Afonso Domingues
☎244 76 52 60
☎244 76 52 61
This restaurant lies on Batalha's main square, in a fairly modern building that already looks a bit dated. In addition to its central location, just steps away from the local attractions, it offers an outstanding view of the monastery church. In the evening, when the buildings are lit up, the scene is truly striking. The only minor drawback is the nonstop tumult of tourists looking for parking, which detracts somewhat from the view. Reservations required.

Cafés and Tearooms

Pastelaria Oliveira
Praça Dom João I
On the terrace of the Pastelaria Oliveira, you can enjoy a sweet or a small sandwich while taking in a lovely view of the main square and the monastery church.

Leiria

Esplanado de Leiria
$$
Jardim Luís de Camões
☎244 81 23 20
This self-serve restaurant offers a wide variety of Portuguese dishes in a simple and rather unoriginal setting. It is, however, located in the middle of a small park and therefore features verdant surroundings. It also has a large terrace from which you can admire the Castelo de Leiria, which dominates the city. Unpretentious and pleasant.

Cafés and Tearooms

Café Lereno
$
Praça Rodrigues Lobo
In addition to the ubiquitous *bica*, wonderfully paired with a *pastel*, this modest bistro offers sandwiches, hot dogs and toasted ham-and-cheese sandwiches. Though the place is simple, it has a terrace looking out on a pleasant, lively square named after poet Rodrigues Lobo.

Nazaré

Casa Marques
$
Rua J.B. de Sousa Lobo
For a "community-style" meal, try the Casa Marques, which has big tables and a virtually nonexistent decor. Lively, friendly atmosphere.

Pizzeria Meu Jardin
$
Rua Ma Gil Vicente 67
If you are spending a few days in Nazaré and are already on your fourth meal of seafood, try the Pizzeria Meu Jardin for a change of pace. It offers 15 different kinds of pizza in a friendly setting.

Caravela
$
Praça Sousa Oliveira no 14-16
☎262 55 23 60
Located on a touristy square, Caravela's decor and plastic tables and chairs are much like those of the other restaurants on the square.

What sets this restaurant apart from its competitors is its affordable, varied menu, which includes tuna or *feijão* salad, various pizzas and many traditional Portuguese dishes. Among the latter, the *bacalhau com natas* deserves praise for both its creamy taste and its reasonable price (*950 ESC*). Courteous welcome and efficient service. A good, affordable choice.

Casa O Bragaia
$$
8am to 1pm and 3pm to 2am
Rua Ajtónio Caravlho Laranjo 61
If you love fish and delicious seafood *açordas*, stop by the Casa O Bragaia. Simple decor.

Casa Bizzarro
$$
Rua António Caravlho Laranjo 25
On the same street, the Casa Bizzarro serves unpretentious, home-style cuisine. If you want to escape the noise of the television, which seems to be on all the time, ask for a table on the pretty little terrace.

Casa O Pescador
$$
Rua António Caravlho Laranjo 16B
Still on the same street, just a little farther along, the seafood restaurant Casa O Pescador also has an attractive little terrace. Here, too, the nonstop noise of the television detracts from the atmosphere inside.

O Casalinho
$$
Praça Sousa Oliveira 6
☎262 55 13 28
O Casalinho serves quality cuisine in a rather pleasant setting. The menu naturally features grilled fish and seafood. Personal service despite the size of the dining room.

A Lanterna
$$
Rua Mouzinho de Albuquerque 59
A Lanterna is noteworthy mainly for its pleasant decor. Traditional cuisine at reasonable prices.

A Moiteria
$$
Avenida de República 35-37
☎262 56 21 96
A Moiteria has a lovely setting and several tables with views of the sea. Make sure to try the traditional dish of Nazaré, *caldeira* (a type of bouillabaisse) or *caldeira de mariscos* (with seafood). Unfortunately, the service is slow and inattentive.

Restaurante O Navigante
$$
Rua Sub Vila
If you like lively places, try the Restaurante O Navigante, which has an attractively decorated dining room and stays open until 2am.

Restaurante San Miguel
$$
Avenida da República, at the end of the beach
The huge Restaurante San Miguel, located at the foot of the cliff, will appeal to visitors who enjoy lively, crowded places. The traditional menu includes some standard snacks. The large terrace is a pleasant place to sip a drink.

Restaurante Ribamar
$$
at the corner of Rua Gomes Freire and Avenida da República
☎262 55 11 58
Located in a pleasant waterfront hotel with a slightly old-fashioned charm about it, the Restaurante Ribamar serves regional cuisine in a cozy setting. Some tables offer views of the sea.

Óbidos

O Celta
$
Rua Direita, next to Restaurante Alcaide
Though hardly the height of luxury, this very modest bistro does offer little sandwiches as well as various snacks at very affordable prices (*200 to 350 ESC*). It is also one of the few places along this tourist-swamped alley where locals still gather.

Snack Bar Lidador
$$
Rua Direita
As its name suggests, this eatery offers various sandwiches at relatively affordable prices. However, the establishment's main asset is its pleasant terrace, one of the few set up right on touristy Rua Direita.

Restaurante Alcaide
$$$
Rua Direita
☎262 95 92 20
The Restaurante Alcaide has a wooden ceiling and a lovely tile floor. In addition to

serving good regional cuisine, it offers a beautiful panoramic view of the area. Terrace. Professional service.

Estalagem do Convento
$$$
Rua D. João d'Ornelas
☎*262 95 92 14*
The restaurant at the Estalagem do Convento serves traditional cuisine in a lovely setting where opulent tables and candlelight enhance the monastic decor (see p 237).

O Caldeirão
$$$
Largo Senhor da Pedra, opposite the Sántuario do Senhor
Jesus la Pedra, on the N8, just before Óbidos
☎*262 95 98 39*
A good place for meat eaters, this restaurant offers an extensive menu that includes the great classics of Portuguese cuisine as well as a dozen varieties of steaks. For those with a taste for original concoctions, we recommend the excellent *bife a brasileira*, a steak served with mushrooms and coffee sauce. Wide selection of regional wines and gracious, smiling service that brings needed warmth to the somewhat cold main dining room of roughcast walls and ceilings.

Dom João V
$$$
Tue to Sun
Largo Senhor da Pedra, opposite the Sántuario do Senhor
Jesus da Pedra, on the N8, just before Óbidos
☎*262 95 91 34*
If the menu at the O Caldeirão restaurant is not to your liking, head next door to Restaurante Dom João V. After walking through its modest lobby, you will be greeted by friendly, smiling servers in a large, pleasant dining room with rows of attractively set tables. Portuguese food is prominently featured on the menu, and those with heartier appetites will be delighted with the near-gargantuan portions served here. What's more, the fast service is exemplary. A place sure to please lovers of traditional Portuguese cooking.

Pousada do Castelo
$$$$
the *pousada* is located within the town walls, in the castle
☎*262 95 91 05*
☎*262 95 91 46*
At the Pousada do Castelo, you can enjoy the unforgettable experience of dining in a 16th-century castle. In 1951, this became the first historic building to be converted into a *pousada*. Making your way here through the pretty village of Óbidos is a pleasure all in itself. The decor of the dining room is a rustic re-creation of medieval times. The lovely fire-

place and beautiful pair of Manueline windows are real treats for the eyes. If you are lucky enough to be seated by one of the latter, you will also be able to admire the garden below, with its pruned shrubs. Reservations required.

A Ilustre Casa de Ramiro
$$$$
Fri to Wed
Rua Porta do Vale
☎*262 95 91 94*
After the restaurant in the *pousada*, A Ilustre Casa de Ramiro is probably the most sophisticated restaurant in Óbidos. Picture a room with a vaulted ceiling, walls painted pale pink, dark wood furniture and scores of plants, bathed in soft light. Talk about a feast for the eyes! The food is very good, but a bit on the expensive side.

Ourém

(*25km from Leiria*)

Cafés and Tearooms

Taberna Típica
just opposite the church on Praça Tabuleiro de Misericórdia, near the tourist office
The aptly named Taberna Típica, run by a kind elderly woman, is a small sweet shop and a bar in one. The interior features two tables and a large wooden counter, *azulejos*, small, antique cabinets with glass

doors, a wooden ceiling and a floor made of big paving stones. The whole place just oozes character, so make sure to stop in and take a look. While you're here, you can quench your thirst with a nice cold draft beer (*90 ESC*).

Peniche

Numerous restaurants line the very busy Avenida do Mar, most serving fish and seafood, which, it would seem, are the only specialties available here. At dinner time, the smell of smoked fish literally hangs in the air, restaurateurs going about their "grilling business" and thus competing to attract tourists to their tables. Unfortunately, the uninteresting view of the port and the constant vehicular traffic along the avenue spoil the experience somewhat.

Nau dos Corvos
$$$
Avenida Marginal, Cabo Carvoeiro
Fri to Tue noon to 3pm and 7pm to 10pm
☎262 78 90 04
Given its location, this restaurant was, of course, destined to specialize in fish and seafood. However, it stands out for its excellent locale rather than its food. Erected atop a cliff on the very tip of the peninsula, the establishment offers a magnificent view of the

sea and the dramatic cliffs, as well as Berlenga Island in the distance. The menu features the great classics of oceanic cuisine, from *açorda de mariscos* to *linguado grelhado* (sole) to grilled grouper. Traditional and nothing to write home about, but what a view!

Tomar

Ti-Joca Hamburgerie
$
49 Rua dos Moinhos
open from 8:30am to midnight
If you are on a tight budget or are simply in the mood for a burger, try the Ti-Joca Hamburgerie.

Parque das Merendas
$
alongside the river, on the left side as you head towards the island and Parque do Mouchão from Rua da Fonte do Choupo
Located in the park surrounding the local sports stadium, the Parque das Merendas, with its view of the Rio Nabão, is an enchanting place to enjoy a simple meal.

Piri-Piri
$$
noon to 3pm and 7pm to 10pm, closed Tue
at the corner of Rua dos Moinhos and Rua Dr. Joaquim Jacinto
Piri-Piri is a little grill located in an absolutely charming neighbourhood.

China Town
$$
every day noon to 3pm and 7pm to 11pm
Rua Dr. Joaquim Jacinto no. 31
☎249 31 47 43
Located in a lovely alley with an interesting view of the castle of Tomar, this restaurant serves up traditional Chinese food, from sweet-and-sour chicken to beef with Chinese mushrooms and almonds to angel-hair soup. Though the decor is hardly the most imaginative, the food is a real palate rouser!

Bela Vista
$$
Wed to Sun 10am to 3:30pm and 7pm to 9:30pm, Tue 7pm to 9:30pm
Rua da Fonte do Choupo 6
☎249 31 28 70
For the pleasure of dining alfresco, head to the Bela Vista, where you can savour roast kid beneath a ceiling of greenery. The terrace is unfortunately set a bit too close to the road.

Restaurante Estalagem Santa Iria
$$
every day 12:30pm to 3pm and 7:30pm to 9:30pm
at the tip of the island, in Parque do Mouchão
☎249 31 33 26
☎249 32 12 38
The interior and exterior of the Restaurante Estalagem Santa Iria are reason enough to stop in (see p 233). The decor features big leather chairs and candlesticks.

Traditional menu. Excellent fish soups.

Chico Elias
$$
Wed to Mon
on the EN349-3, 1km from Tomar, 70 Rua Algarvias
☎*249 31 10 67*
To enjoy authentic regional cuisine, head to the Chico Elias restaurant, where you can savour a delicious *bacalhau com carne* (a cod dish served with meat) or a generous serving of *couves à D. Prior* (cabbage à la D. Prior) in a warm ambiance. Good value for your money.

Cafés and Tearooms

Confeitaria Tomarense
Praça da República 32
The Confeitaria Tomarense is attractively decorated with *azulejos*, lovely wooden doors and an interesting counter. A cup of coffee will cost you 50 ESC.

Café Paraíso
8am to midnight
Rua Serpa Pinto 126
The Café Paraíso has a large bistro-style dining room with an inviting, old-fashioned decor. A good place to sip a drink and people-watch through the big front window.

Entertainment

Óbidos

Bar Errik Rex
Rua Direita, near the entrance of the pousada
Quench your thirst at the Bar Errik Rex, which has a busy but nonetheless tasteful decor. Warm, friendly atmosphere.

Petrarum Domus
Rua Direita, past the Travessa Bénéficão Malhão
As its Latin name suggests, the bar Petrarum Domus is located inside a pretty stone house. Its varied and amusing decor, enhanced by careful lighting, makes it a pleasant place to spend the evening. The little mezzanine is perfect for intimate conversation.

Albergaria Josefa d'Óbidos
Rua Dom João de Ornelas
Disco fans can head to the Albergaria Josefa d'Óbidos, which is hopping every Friday and Saturday night from 11pm to 4am.

Lagar da Mouraria
Rua da Mouraria
Enjoy a glass of port or a *cerveja* at Lagar da Mouraria, a former press room that was converted into a small bar. *Fado* evenings every Friday (*from 9pm*).

Tancos
(*28km from Tomar*)

Esplanada-Bar Cais del Rei
Route N3, on dock in the village of Tancos
Located right by the Tagus, this modest bar is just the place to have a drink or a light snack while visiting the castle of Almourol. Its terrace offers a particularly romantic view of the village of Arripiado, just across the river, and come nightfall, you can admire the fully illuminated Almourol fortress in the distance. A scene straight out of a fairy tale!

Shopping

Most of the towns mentioned above are very popular with tourists and therefore have a lot of shops. Although each town has its own specialty as far as handicrafts are concerned, you won't have any trouble finding articles from all over Portugal in one place. Clothing, jewellery, pottery, basketry, fabrics, carpets, souvenirs, etc. abound in the most touristy areas. Below you'll find those places that have a unique character or carry hard-to-find products.

Nazaré

Bio Natura (*Rua Dr. Jose Maira Carvalho Jimon, to the left of Avenida Veira Cuimarães on the way down to the sea*) Muesli, tea and all sorts of other food, as well as a good selection of homeopathic products.

Óbidos

Lojo do Vinho (*Rua Direita, opposite the Travessa Béneficão Malhão*). Wide selection of reasonably priced regional wines.

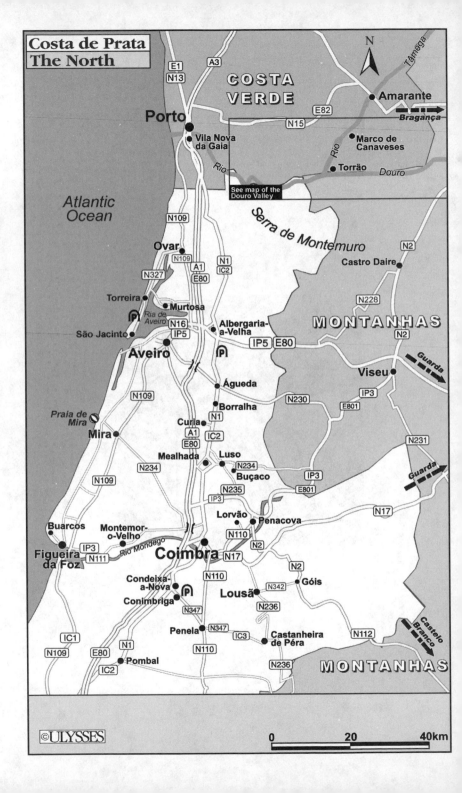

Costa de Prata: the North

T he northern part of the Costa de Prata provides for wonderful jaunts along small mountain roads that pass through sleepy little villages, where lovely baroque churches stand, surrounded by old escutcheoned palaces.

T hese are villages where you can stop at the only café, where the men of the village are gathered and will be happy to talk to you. In this region, you move through the landscape as through a kaleidoscope, each mountain hiding the one just passed and revealing another.

O f course, Coimbra will captivate you; keep reading and you will be tempted to see its churches and, most of all, its university. And then Aveiro and its canals will cast a spell on you; or you can get lost on the back roads in the hills somewhere between Condeixa and Penela for a few days, where we have unearthed great places to stay and delightful restaurants. Set aside a day to walk in Buçaco park and visit the hotel of the same name, a former royal hunting palace in neo-Manueline style. Your travels will surely take you to Conimbriga, where you will find some of the most exciting Roman ruins in Portugal.

H ere, then, is a region worth travelling through slowly; you'll regret it if you whiz through too fast for you will be depriving yourself of the joy of so many discoveries!

Finding Your Way Around

By Car

Aveiro

Quick Route

From Lisbon, take Highway A1-E80 north to the junction with the N16-IP5, and then head toward Aveiro.

From Porto, take the same road south.

Scenic Route

From Lisbon, take Highway A8-IC1 north to Leiria. After passing this town, the road crosses great monotonous expanses of dunes and marshes. At Leiria, it is therefore preferable to take Highway A1-E80 north and go directly to Aveiro.

Coimbra

Quick Route

From Lisbon, take Highway A1-E80 north. The exit for Coimbra leads directly to the centre of town.

From Porto, take Highway A1-E80 south and, shortly before the Rio Mondego, take the exit toward Coimbra. At the junction with the N1-IC2, go right. There is also another exit after passing the Mondego

river, but that route is longer.

Scenic Route

From Lisbon, head north along Highway A8-IC1 which, farther along, becomes the N8-IC1. After passing the town of Leiria, the route crosses great monotonous expanses of dunes and marshes. At Leiria, it is therefore preferable to take Highway A1-E80 north and go directly to Coimbra.

Condeixa-a-Nova, Conimbriga and Penela

To reach Condeixa **from Lisbon**, take Highway A1-E80 north; at the exit toward Condeixa-a-Nova, take the N1-IC2 south. To reach Conimbriga, once you have arrived at Condeixa-a-Nova, take the IC3-N347 toward Penela. The turn-off to the ruins is 1.5km along, on the right side of the highway. The entrance to the ruins is 700m farther. A big unguarded parking area has been set up at the entrance. Since the stretch of highway between Coimbra and Condeixa is very congested and consists alternately of two-lane and three-lane portions, it is important to be especially prudent. To reach Penela, continue along the IC3-N347.

From Porto, take the same road south.

Figueira da Foz and Montemor-o-Velho

Quick Route

From Lisbon, go north along Highway A1-E80 and take the exit toward Coimbra soon after passing Rio Mondego. Continue toward Coimbra until the junction with the N111-IP3, which leads directly to Montemor-o-Velho, and then to Figueira da Foz.

From Porto, go south along the same highway, and take the exit toward Coimbra before the Rio Mondego.

Scenic Route

From Lisbon, to get to Figueira da Foz, take Highway A8-IC1, which later becomes the N8-IC1, going north until Leiria. From there, go along the N109-IC1 as far as Figueira da Foz. To reach Montemor-o-Velho from Figueira da Foz, take the N111-IP3.

Lousã

Quick Route

From Lisbon, heading north along Highway A1-E80, take the exit toward Coimbra shortly before the Rio Mondego and continue along the N17. About 15km farther, take the N236 to Lousã.

From Porto, follow the same route, taking the exit toward Coimbra after the Rio Mondego.

Scenic Route

From Lisbon, take Highway A8-IC1 and head north until the town of Leiria. After passing this town, take the N1-IC2 north until the junction with the N347-IC3; take this road to the village of Penela and then Castanheira de Pera. From there, continue north along the N236 to Lousã.

Penacova and Buçaco

Quick Route

From Lisbon, head north along Highway A1-E80 until the exit for Coimbra, located after the Rio Mondego. To reach Penacova from there, take the IP3-E801. For Buçaco, take the exit toward Mealhada or toward Luso from Highway A1-E80, and then follow the signs for Buçaco.

From Porto, head south along Highway A1-E80. For Buçaco, take the exit toward Mealhada and continue until Luso on the N234, then follow the signs for Buçaco. To reach Penacova, take the N235 south from Luso; a faster but less pleasant option is to take the exit toward Coimbra from Highway A1-E80, situated before the Rio Mondego, and then to continue along the IP3-E801.

Scenic Route

From Lisbon, head north along Highway A8-IC1, which later becomes the N8-IC1. After passing the town of Leiria, the highway crosses great monotonous expanses of dunes and marshes. It is preferable to continue your trip along Highway A1-E80 until Coimbra. To reach Penacova, take the exit toward Coimbra, located just before the Rio Mondego and then the N110. To get to Buçaco, after arriving at Penacova, take the N235, located on the right.

By Train

Although some of the places described below are accessible by train, this mode of transport is not really practical. In fact, except for Aveiro and Coimbra, schedules are irregular and connections are difficult. For additional information contact Caminhos de Ferro, see p 69.

Aveiro

From Lisbon

Departure: up to seven trains a day. To reach the centre of Aveiro, take Avenida Dr. Lourenço Peixinho from in front of the station, leading directly to the Praça Humberto Delgado, in the very heart of the town. *Travel time*: approx. 3hrs

Fare: Alfa 2nd class 2,550 ESC, Intercidades 1,900 ESC

From Porto

Departure: up to seven trains a day
Travel time: approx. 1hr
Fare: Alfa 2nd class 950 ESC, Intercidades 900 ESC

Coimbra

From Lisbon

Departure: up to 10 trains a day. The station, Estação Velha-Coimbra B is located several kilometres from the centre of town; it is best to take one of the many buses going to Coimbra's second station, Estação Nova-Coimbra A, located right in the heart of town (*information*: ☎239 83 49 98)
Travel time: approx. 2hrs, 30min
Fare: Alfa 2nd class 2,150 ESC, Intercidades 1,650 ESC

From Porto

Departure: up to 10 trains a day
Travel time: approx. 2hrs, 30min
Fare: Alfa 2nd class 1,500 ESC, Intercidades 1,200 ESC

Figueira da Foz

From Lisbon

Departure: many trains daily. The Figueira da Foz station is around a 20min walk from the beach, on Largo da Estação

Costa de Prata: the North

Fare: Intercidades
1,400 ESC

By Bus from Lisbon

There are many departures daily with the Rede Nacional de Expressos and Renex Expressos bus companies, as well as with several other public transportation companies. Rede Nacional de Expressos departures are from the terminal at no 18B Avenida Casal Ribeiro. Renex Expressos departures are from Cais das Cebolas, near Casa dos Bicos. For information in Lisbon, see p 69.

Aveiro

Travel time: approx. 4hrs, 15min
Fare: 1,500 ESC to 1,700 ESC

Coimbra

Travel time: approx. 2hrs, 50min
Fare: 1,250 ESC to 1,450 ESC

Figueira da Foz

Travel time: approx. 3hrs
Fare: 1,250 ESC to 1,450 ESC

By Bus from Porto

The Rede Nacional de Expressos and Eva Expressos bus companies offer numerous departures every day, as do several other public transportation

companies. There are no fewer than four bus terminals in Porto: on Rua Carmelitas, near Torre dos Clérigos; on Praça Filipa de Lencastre; on Rua Alexandre Herculano; and, finally, on Praça Batalha (at Garagem Atlantic). For information in Lisbon, see p 69.

Practical Information

Tourist Information Offices

Aveiro

Rua João Mendonça 8
There is also a touch-screen computer along pretty little Rua dos Mercadores that provides information.

Buçaco

Rua António Granjo, Luso

Coimbra

Largo da Portagem; Praça da República and Praça Dom Diniz

Figueira da Foz

Avenida 25 de Abril, on the ground floor of the Edifício Marisol

Lousã

Rua João de Cáceres

Montemor-o-Velho

In the Igreja de Santa Maria dos Alcáçova, within the castle, and in the village on Rua Direita

Penacova

In the town hall building, next to the Terreiro de Penacova lookout
(*see also Coimbra, above*)

Exploring

Aveiro

When Dona Joana, the daughter of King Afonso V, retired to Aveiro toward 1472, the town was already in full development with its business activity growing, particularly because of its port. During a good part of the 15th century, Aveiro built a solid reputation for cod fishing, with its sailors going as far as Newfoundland to cast their nets. It seemed nothing would prevent the town from prospering. In 1575, however, a violent storm devastated the coast completely. By displacing immense quantities of sand, the sea literally moved the beach and formed a long sandbar parallel to the coast. By isolating the port, this sandbar deprived the town of direct access to the sea.

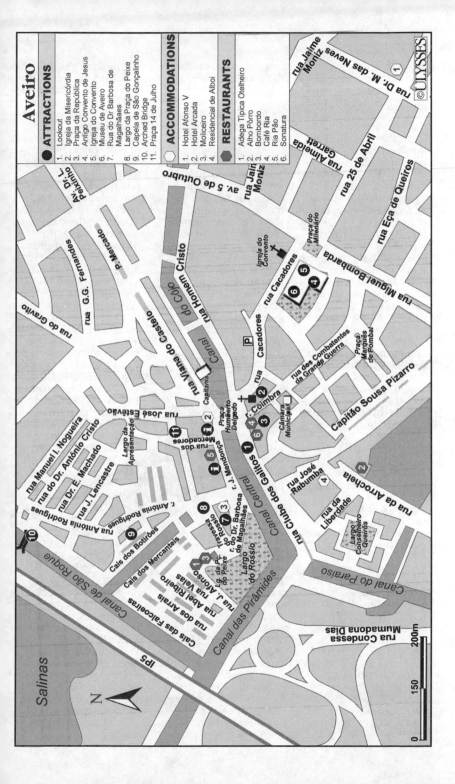

Aveiro

● ATTRACTIONS

1. Lookout
2. Igreja da Misericórdia
3. Praça da República
4. Antigo Convento de Jesus
5. Igreja do Convento
6. Museu de Aveiro
7. Rua do Dr Barbosa de Magalhães
8. Largo da Praça do Peixe
9. Capela de São Gonçalinho
10. Arched Bridge
11. Praça 14 de Julho

⬡ ACCOMMODATIONS

1. Hotel Afonso V
2. Hotel Arcada
3. Moliceiro
4. Residencial de Alboi

◆ RESTAURANTS

1. Adega Típica Otelheiro
2. Alho Pôrro
3. Bombordo
4. Café Ria
5. Ria Pão
6. Sonatura

© ULYSSES

Moreover, the three rivers that previously had emptied into the sea at this point formed an immense lagoon that flooded a large part of the coast. During the 16th and 17th centuries, the many efforts aimed at linking the port with the sea again ended in failure. At the same time, the appearance of many marshy areas favoured the development of diseases that eliminated much of the population. Aveiro seemed condemned to a slow death. Toward 1808, however, new efforts succeeded this time in digging a canal that linked the town to the sea once again. Throughout the 19th century, Aveiro took up its fishing trade with renewed vigour, adding earnings from the exploitation of the saltworks established in the lagoon. At the dawn of the 20th century, Aveiro again became a rich and prosperous town, as the presence of numerous mansions bears witness even today.

Since the industrialization of the country, the town continued to benefit from its ideal location. Many factories were located on the edge of its lagoon and, besides a major shipyard and an automobile assembly plant, a gigantic cellulose plant was built there. Today, Aveiro and the surrounding region from the third most impor-

tant industrial centre in the country, after Lisbon and Porto.

As for tourism, the town of Aveiro has been able to preserve the charm of yesteryear. Its beautiful mansions, picturesque little streets and romantic canals, in which *moliceiros* sometimes show off (see below), recall the old city of Bruges. From a culinary point of view, besides cod (alas, all too common in Portugal), you can enjoy sardines and eels (the latter are a local specialty). For dessert, don't miss *ovos moles* (literally, "soft eggs"), little egg-yolk-based pastries.

Since the town is compact and parking is limited, it is preferable to leave your car in the big parking area located next to the Canal do Côjo.

A tour of the town starts with the **Praça Humberto Delgado**, a square that overlooks the canals that dissect the town. From this spot, facing the Arcada hotel, you can admire the Canal Central on your left and the Canal do Côjo on your right. While the Canal do Côjo is of little interest, except for the pretty building at its entrance, the **Canal Central ★** is

worth an in-depth visit. Starting with the streets that border it, admirers of baroque style can spot several fine examples of elegant bourgeois dwellings. For a fine overall view, go along **Rua Clube dos Galitos**, facing the canal, where you can enjoy a particularly romantic **view ★★** of the canal. There, on the canal, the *moliceiros* show their beautiful curved prows. These flat-bottomed boats, equipped with square sails and fitted with a type of rake called an *ancinho*, were used to dredge the bottom of the lagoon to gather algae, called *molicos* in Portuguese; this was used mostly as fertilizer for the fields. The prows of the *moliceiros* are generally painted in lively colours and decorated with little paintings displaying religious motifs.

Moliceiros

Going back up Rua Coimbra, facing the Praça Humberto Delgado, stands the **Igreja da Misericórdia ★** on the left. Its interior is worth seeing: its walls are covered with beautiful *azulejos*, with yellow and blue dominating.

Continuing along the same street, a little higher and on the right this time, you will notice the **Praça da República**, which is worth a short stop to admire the elegant 18th-century **town hall**. Unfortunately, a horrible modern building has spoiled this pleasant square, which used to offer a fine view of the canals. Continue your climb along Rua Coimbra, which later becomes Rua dos Combatentes da Grande Guerra. Once you reach the intersection with Rua Miguel Bombarda, go left to reach the Praça do Milenário, where you will find the **former convent of Jesus ★**. Founded in 1458, the convent received Princess Joana, the daughter of King Afonso V, in 1472. Canonized after her death, the princess would be venerated under the name Saint Joana. During the three centuries that followed the installation of the Infante, the convent became progressively bigger and wealthier. Despite the extensive damage wreaked by Napoleonic troops during their expedition, the convent still contains many works of art gathered in a museum. After briefly admiring its early 18th-century baroque facade, proceed to the **Igreja do Convento ★★**. Besides its vault and its painted ceilings, the inside of the church is heavily laden with *talhas*

douradas, whose exuberance near the choir stall is such that one can imagine for a moment having entered a grotto. You can also admire the multicoloured marble **tomb of Saint Joana ★**, a true exploit of inlay work. After a brief visit to the Renaissance **cloister**, head to the **Museu de Aveiro** (*250 ESC, guided tours only; Tue to Sun 10am to 12:30pm and 2pm to 5pm; access through the upper gallery of the cloister*). Besides many canvases and religious objects, there is a beautiful **painting on wood** representing Princess Joana.

To continue your tour, go back down Rua Cacadores as far as the Praça Humberto Delgado and then, after passing the bridge, take Rua João Mendonça, which runs alongside part of the central canal and comes, farther along, to **Rua do Dr. Barbosa de Magalhães**. On this latter street, lovers of Art Nouveau will want to peek at the house situated at **number 6**, and above all, at the magnificent **facade ★** (unfortunately, it has been poorly preserved) located at **number 10** of the same street. Next, bypass the street to reach **number 8 of the Largo da Praça do Peixe**, where you can examine the rear of a beautiful dwelling and daydream in front of its pretty garden and its *azulejo*-covered walls.

At the end of the street, the picturesque **Praça do Peixe**, the square where the fish market is held, is worth a short stop to enjoy its many cafés, ideal spots to have lunch or to sip a coffee. After this short pause, take Rua Antónia Rodrigues, leading you to a little square where you will find the curious **Capela de São Gonçalinho** (*Rua Antónia Rodrigues*). With its hexagonal shape, baroque facade and polygonal dome curiously covered with oriental-coloured *azulejos*, it is worth the few extra steps. Continuing along this same street, you will end up at Rua Dr. António Cristo, where you go left to reach the picturesque **arched bridge** that crosses São Roque canal. While climbing it, the saltworks are visible stretching endlessly in the distance. Unfortunately, the presence of the IP5 highway now spoils the scenery. The neighbourhoods bordering the canal here formed the fishing village at the time the town was in direct contact with the sea.

To explore this former fishing area, head back toward the centre of town by retracing your steps along Rua Antónia Rodrigues and then, where it crosses Rua Jorge de Lencaster, turning left. This will lead you directly along the Largo da Apresentação, followed by the very lively **Praça**

14 de Julho. This little square and the surrounding streets are especially picturesque, and we advise you wholeheartedly to stroll here for a while. To complete this tour, pass beneath the arcades located next to the square, and return to the central canal and the Praça Humberto Delgado.

Ria de Aveiro

The main attraction around Aveiro remains, of course, its immense, fish-filled lagoon called Ria de Aveiro. There you can see many little fishing boats and, on lamentably few occasions, some *moliceiros*. Protected by the immense peninsula of sand dunes, this seems to be a dream spot for outdoor activities. On the ocean side, its great stretches of virgin beach are the delight of lovers of water sports. We have to admit, however, that the Ria has lost part of its charm in the last few years. Visitors may be disappointed by the sight of numerous smoke-belching factory chimneys in the distance. Moreover, the regular and perceptible sound of sirens announcing the beginning and end of work is not especially pleasant. And worse still, the presence of a monstrous cellulose plant occasionally creates a nauseating odour, which the wind sometimes spreads over a large part of the lagoon. As for the point of the peninsula, it offers little of interest apart from its nature reserve whose dunes are rich in flora and fauna. Powerful currents make swimming here rather dangerous. Thus this spot is best suited to those who seek long, solitary walks. The village of São Jacinto is of little interest, and the proximity of a military base does not help the situation. Despite this exhaustive description of its drawbacks, the Ria nonetheless still has attractive spots to be explored, and it would be a pity not to head out there briefly. For the fullest enjoyment, we advise you to limit your exploration to the section between the little villages of Torreira and Ovar. The scenery is verdant, and the lagoon is prettier and more romantic than anywhere else. Those wishing to extend their stay in this area should head 5km south of Torreira, where they will find a pretty *pousada* (p 271) right at the water's edge.

Buçaco

Located atop the Serra de Buçaco, the **Parque do Buçaco ★★** (*park entry 500 ESC per car*) is a vast forest area where an infinite variety of trees and plants have been growing for generations. Although it reaches an altitude of only 545m, this chain of hills receives the full force of moisture-laden winds from the Atlantic, thus allowing for the growth of species that are unusual at these latitudes, just as at Sintra. Apart from the 400 types of indigenous trees, you can also observe 300 exotic species brought from overseas territories. Besides the many creeks and rivers that cross it, the forest is also enriched with many tree ferns, camellias, rhododendrons and various other plants that grow here and there in the clearings.

This great diversity is thanks in some ways to the conservationist spirit of the Catholic Church, of which Buçaco was a private estate for nearly nine centuries. When this property passed from the Benedictines to the Carmelites in 1628, the forest still had many of its original species. The Carmelites dedicated themselves to a veritable cult of nature protection, going as far as obtaining a papal edict forbidding woodcutting on the estate. Toward 1630, walls were erected to better protect the estate, and a monastery was built. Soon afterward, the great territorial discoveries led the Carmelites to become interested in

The narrow cobblestone lanes of Óbidos make for a pleasant stroll.
- *W. Buss*

Springtime in the Alentejo.
- *T. Perrin*

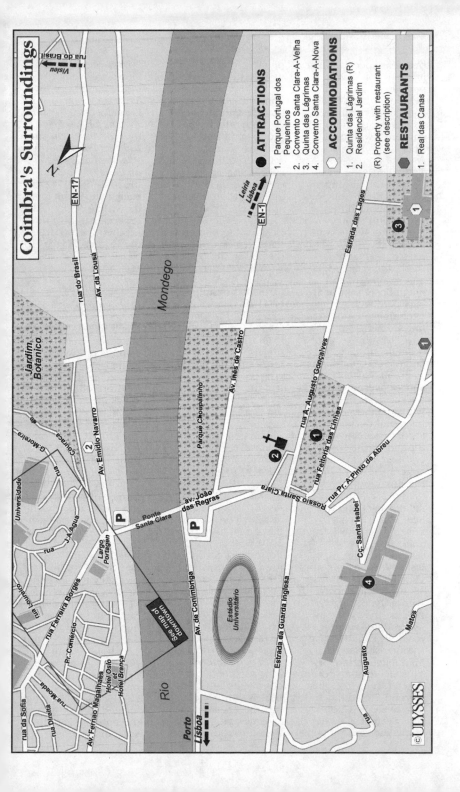

Coimbra's Surroundings

ATTRACTIONS
1. Parque Portugal dos Pequeninos
2. Convento Santa Clara-A-Velha
3. Quinta das Lágrimas
4. Convento Santa Clara-A-Nova

ACCOMMODATIONS
1. Quinta das Lágrimas (R)
2. Residencial Jardim

(R) Property with restaurant (see description)

RESTAURANTS
1. Real das Canas

© ULYSSES

overseas species. Their introduction over a period of two centuries, helped by the Serra's special microclimate, would enrich the original forest with exotic flora.

Toward 1834, a royal decision abolishing all the kingdom's religious orders allowed the royal court to take over the estate. While continuing the extraordinary conservation work, the court added an extravagant and magnificent **royal hunting palace** ★★ to the exuberance of the setting. In neo-Manueline style, it is the work of the Italian architect Luigi Manini. Built next to the monastery, and almost overpowering it, the palace is decorated with numerous sculptures and decked with a noble watchtower topped by the royal emblem, the armillery sphere. Now converted to a luxurious hotel (see p 272), this marvellous fairy-tale palace, which seems to arise miraculously from a clearing, is worth visiting. On the **inside** ★★, do not miss glancing at its impressive **stairwell**, decorated with gorgeous *azulejo* panels, and above all its beautiful **dining room** ★, enhanced by a rotunda-shaped neo-Manueline **terrace** ★. This is a dream spot for lunch (see p 272). Just beyond the entrance is a **vestibule** ★ where finely sculpted white stone and *azulejos* com-

plement each other wonderfully, creating an inviting spot for contemplation. Finally, outside and to the left of the hotel, admire the group of little **columns** ★, each sculpted differently and supporting an *azulejo*-covered gallery. You are sure to find one you like!

Besides the numerous trails that have been created in the park (see p 269), you can also visit the **Mosteiro dos Carmelitas Descalços** (*100 ESC, guided tours only; 10am to 1pm and 2pm to 6pm*). Dating from the 17th century, this former Carmelite monastery has cells covered in cork to protect the monks who were living there from the cold.

The **Museu da Guerra Peninsular** (*200 ESC, guided tour; Tue to Sun 10am to 1pm and 2pm to 5pm; to the left along the road leaving the Parque de Buçaco by the Porta da Rainha*) recounts the battle that took place in 1810 between Anglo-Portuguese troops and the Napoleonic army. Of special interest for enthusiasts of military history.

The **Monumento à Batalha do Buçaco** (*take the little road going up from in front of the museum*). This esplanade, with its commemorative obelisk, is worth the detour mostly for the impressive **view** ★ it offers of the surrounding hills.

Lovers of spectacular views will want to go to the summit of the Serra de Buçaco, at the **Cruz Alta** (*take the same road as for the obelisk, and continue climbing until the Porta da Cruz Alta, then take the road on the left*), where a lookout (545m) offers a **panoramic view** ★ over the whole region. The lookout can also be reached by foot from the Buçaco Palace Hotel.

Curia

(14km from Buçaco)

Much like its neighbour Luso, the small town of Curia is renowned for its thermal baths. But it is also notable for its plethora of restaurants specializing in *leitão* (suckling pig). Indeed, a series of such places lines the IC2-N1, offering visitors the very same dish prepared a variety of ways. Be that as it may, what makes Curia truly worth visiting are its many turn-of-the-century manor houses. Among them, the **Curia Palace Hotel** ★★ (☎*231 51 21 31*) is probably the loveliest Art-Nouveau hotel in all of Portugal. Everything here exudes the Roaring Twenties, and those with a passion for this era should make a point of lounging about in the lobby, a true period gem. After doing so, head to the lounge located to the right of the entrance, another splendid example of the 1920s. Once you've contemplated its perfectly preserved Art-Deco furnishings and graceful stained-glass windows representing the country's various cities, make your way to the former service corridor, right next to the bar. Along this corridor are a small theatre, a barber shop, a billiard room, a tobacco store as well as a doctor's office – just like a turn-of-the-century luxury liner!

The entire hotel is decorated with period furniture, dusty, but in perfect condition. Like an old ship in distress, the Curia Palace Hotel unfortunately seems to be on its last (sea) legs and several rooms are now closed off. In fact, only a few of its suites and its restaurant remain in use. If you wish to see what the palace's "glory days" were like, go up the stairs to its restaurant, where many photographs exhibit its illustrious past. Let us hope that this venerable hotel will once again know better days, and that potential property developers will give it a new lease on life while preserving its interior decor. To end your time here on a high note, be sure to tour the romantic garden with its large swimming pool, another Art-Deco gem.

★★★

Coimbra

Arriving in Coimbra for the first time after having visited Porto, one cannot help noticing a certain resemblance between the two cities. Bordering a river, like the city of Porto, Coimbra is also situated atop a small hill and also has alleyways lined with numerous stairways. Moreover, just like its big northern sister, the city is identified with a tower marking the summit. Here, it is the university tower that is the symbol of the city. However, unlike Porto, neglected by the royal court, this university city enjoyed long-time royal support. It was the capital of the kingdom until 1385. Furthermore, from 1308 onwards it was virtually the permanent seat of what was the kingdom's only university until 1911. Before achieving this, however, the city underwent a slow progression.

Already known in Roman times by the name of Aeminium, this little village underwent substantial growth starting only in the sixth century. This occurred because of the brutal decline of the town of Conimbriga and the transfer of its bishopric to Coimbra. It was also around this period, the result of a

deformation of the word Conimbriga, that the word Coimbra appeared, gradually displacing the name Aeminium. Besieged by the Moors toward the eighth century, the town continued developing and, after three centuries of Muslim presence, it achieved such a degree of prosperity that, after its reconquest in 1064, the Moors were allowed to stay. Absorbed into the county of Portucale, of which Henry of Burgundy was then master, the town quickly developed ties with the Portuguese crown. In 1140, in fact, Dom Afonso I, the first king of Portugal, chose to establish his court here. Later, in 1385, João I was proclaimed king here, thus renewing Coimbra's ties with the Portuguese monarchy. Still later, it was in its palace, adjoining the former convent of Santa Clara, that Queen Isabella, wife of Dom Dinis I, chose to retire. Then, in a final link of complicity, a tragic one this time, it was in this town that the passion of a son and the hatred of a father resulted in the incredible love story of Dom Pedro I and the beautiful Inês de Castro (see p 218).

While Porto works, Coimbra studies, goes the saying. The town has remained an important university centre since 1308, when the university was transferred from Lisbon to

Coimbra. Well known from the 15th century onwards for the excellence of its studies in Roman law and philosophy, the university trained many students who became famous. The poet Camões is one of the most illustrious examples. A town of knowledge *par excellence*, Coimbra enjoyed a renown that quickly spread abroad. Toward 1530, several French artists, including Jean de Rouen and Nicolas Chantereine, came to live in Coimbra. They became associated with Portuguese figures as famous as João and Diogo de Castilho, and the little group created the Coimbra School, a school of sculpture that later became famous.

Today, during examination period, you still have a chance to see students in traditional costume, dressed all in black and wearing a great cape on their shoulders, sometimes decorated with strange fringes. Each of these fringes is supposed to represent a disappointment in the student's love life. Students' satchels are often decorated with a coloured ribbon representing their faculty. Another curiosity of university life is a tradition under which most students belong to communities called *repúblicas*, whose only goal is the sharing of lodgings and common chores during the semester. The university still receives up to 18,000 students each year.

Besides this age-old activity, Coimbra has important industries, mostly connected with textiles and food. In terms of tourism, despite its many attractions and its great popularity with visitors, Coimbra lacks mid-range hotels and interesting restaurants. This absence of quality services detracts from a visit here, and many people merely pass through.

Like Porto, Coimbra is divided into two main areas, the lower town, called Baixa, which has many businesses, and the upper town, called Alta or Alcácova, the name of the hill on which it sits. It is in the upper town that university life is centred.

Our tour begins in Baixa in front of the **Arco de Almedina** (literally, "the Medina arch," or "the gate of the Muslim town"), located along elegant Rua Ferreira Borges. In Moorish times, this fortified gate served as the main entrance to the town, which was protected by a wall. Damaged during the reconquest, this gate was greatly modified in the 15th century. A Renaissance niche above the arch and a tower were attached to it. This tower, visible after passing through the gate, currently houses the town archives. Continue straight to reach a series of stairs forming Rua do Quebra Costas, literally meaning street of the broken hill. This very lively, shop-lined street leads directly to the Largo da Sé Velha, where Coimbra's ancient cathedral is situated.

Somewhat overpowered by the neighbouring buildings, the **Sé Velha ★★** was built in 1139 by the first king of Portugal. Its fortress-like appearance shows us how great the fear of invasion still was during this period. The Moors still occupied the areas situated south of the Rio Mondego, and their incursions were far from rare. During the following centuries, the Sé would undergo several modifications. To its marvellous original Romanesque style was added a Renaissance **portico** called Porta Especiosa. Located on the left side of the cathedral, this portico is the work of Jean de Rouen, a Frenchman who emigrated to Portugal with a group of artists toward 1530. This was one of the first examples of the Renaissance style in Portugal. Although it constitutes a beautiful work, this portico clashes with the fine Romanesque ensemble.

Entering the cathedral, in the choir stall you can observe a beautiful **retable ★** in flamboyant Gothic style by the

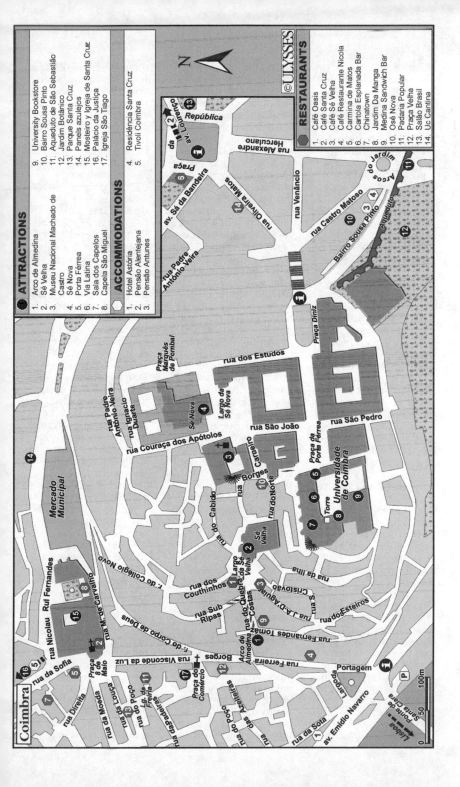

Coimbra

● ATTRACTIONS

1. Arco de Almedina
2. Sé Velha
3. Museu Nacional Machado de Castro
4. Sé Nova
5. Porta Férrea
6. Via Latina
7. Sala dos Capelos
8. Capela São Miguel
9. University Bookstore
10. Bairro Sousa Pinto
11. Aqueduto de São Sebastião
12. Jardim Botânico
13. Parque Santa Cruz
14. Painéis azulejos
15. Mosteiro y Igreja de Santa Cruz
16. Palácio da Justiça
17. Igreja São Tiago

■ ACCOMMODATIONS

1. Hotel Astória
2. Pensão Alentejana
3. Pensão Antunes
4. Residência Santa Cruz
5. Tivoli Coimbra

⬡ RESTAURANTS

1. Café Oasis
2. Café Santa Cruz
3. Café Sé Velha
4. Café Restaurante Nicola
5. Carmina de Matos
6. Cartola Esplanada Bar
7. Chinatown
8. Jardim Da Manga
9. Osé Nova
10. Medina Sandwich Bar
11. Praça Velha
12. Padaria Popular
13. Salão Brasil
14. Uc Cantina

© ULYSSES

N

0   50   100m

Lisboa
Ponte de
Santa Clara

Flemish artists Jean de Ypres and Olivier de Gand. A beautiful Renaissance **chapel**, located to the right of the choir stall, and the Manueline **baptismal fonts**, located just in front of the chapel, are also worth looking at. Be sure to stop in to the Gothic **cloister** (*200 ESC; 9:30am to 12:30pm and 4pm to 5:30pm*), apparently the oldest one of this style in Portugal.

Continue the tour by climbing Rua Borges Carneiro, which leads to the **Museu Nacional Machado de Castro** ★★ (*300 ESC, free on Sun; Tue to Sun 9:30am to 5:30pm*). Named after a famous Portuguese sculptor, this museum is set in the former episcopal palace, itself built in the 12th century on the site of an ancient Roman building. Although entirely redone in the 16th century, it still has part of its original cloister as well as certain elements dating from the Roman period. The presence of a flagstone dating from AD 305 recalls Coimbra's former name, Aeminium.

To reach the actual museum, you must enter through a fine Renaissance-style **portal** onto a patio. From there, go beneath the elegant arcades enclosing the west side of the patio to admire a magnificent **view** ★ of the lower town and the Sé Velha. Inside the mu-

seum, the room housing the **medieval sculptures** and the amazing sculpture portraying a **horseman armed with a mace** ★ are must-sees. Many works by the Coimbra School (Jean de Rouen, Nicolas Chantereine and others) are exhibited on the ground floor, while upstairs you can admire paintings (Gil Vicente, Josefa D'Óbidos), ceramics, gold and silver objects, and various other items. To end your visit in a special way, go to the basement where various objects from the Roman period are presented in the **cryptoportico** ★.

Leaving the museum, a small detour via the square of the Largo da Sé Nova provides a glimpse of the elegant **facade** of the Sé Nova. Built in two phases, it has a classical facade enriched by a baroque-style upper level. As for the inside, if you're interested in *talhas douradas* make sure to go in and see the choir, which is literally streaming with gilding and sculptures. The chapels on the side, richly decorated but, unfortunately, poorly lit, are also worth investigating.

One must not leave Coimbra, of course, without visiting its paramount attraction, the **university** ★★★. To get there from the Largo da Sé Nova, retrace your steps to the museum and then con-

tinue by taking Rua São João, which will take you directly to the Praça da Porta Férrea and the entrance to the university. All around, you will see various faculty buildings dating from the Salazar period and interspersed between far more ancient buildings. The dominant architecture, close to Stalinist in style, reflects the penchant of that period for a certain rigour.

In very early times, the university moved intermittently between Lisbon and the Santa Cruz convent in Coimbra. It was transferred permanently to Coimbra in 1537 by order of João III. Fearing hotbeds of protest more than anything else, João III installed the university in his former royal palace, far from the capital. If one is to judge by history, it seems this location suited his successors very well, for until 1911 Coimbra was the only city in the country to have a university. In 1540, after the royal palace in Coimbra was reorganized, it became the Paço dos Estudios, or palace of studies. By way of anecdote, it may be of interest that it was not until 1895 that the university admitted its first woman to write examinations. She obtained degrees in mathematics and philosophy, and she was first in her class in medicine. You may enter the university by the **Porta Férrea**, or iron gate. Above this portal reign allegories of the faculties. In the main courtyard, you can admire a series of buildings that follow one another very harmoniously despite their different styles.

Before exploring the buildings themselves, start with a little stroll through the **Via Latina**. This is a covered, column-lined alleyway that runs alongside the building located to the right of the iron gate. The building attached to it dates from the 17th century. In its right wing it houses the rectory, and in its left wing is the great Hall of Acts, or **Sala dos Capelos** ★★ (*500 ESC including a tour of the library; every day 9:30am to noon and 2pm to 5pm; the visitors' entrance, which was not marked during our visit, is located behind the second door of the Via Latina, heading toward the right from the tower*). To get there, go to the front part of the Via Latina, take the big door on the right, and climb one flight of steps. Upstairs is a beautiful **view** of the hall and its **arched ceiling** ★. Formerly the noble hall of the palace, it is used today for official ceremonies such as the opening of the academic year or the appointment of the rector. The canvases hung all around the hall portray Portuguese kings. Continuing along the long corridor next

to the Hall of Acts, you end up at the private **examination room**, with fine portraits of various rectors and a vault laden with decorative paintings. If luck is smiling upon you, continue to the end of the corridor, where a door (sometimes locked) provides access to the **panoramic terrace**, where the **view** ★ over the town and the Rio Mondego will delight photographers.

To continue your tour, return to the central courtyard to admire the elegant **Manueline portal** of the university chapel, the work of artist Diogo de Castilho. To visit the interior, enter by the door located left of the tower, then push the door located again to your left. The interior of the **Capela São Miguel** ★★ is worth a detour to discover a wall completely covered with 17th-century *azulejos* ★. The imposing baroque-style organ, whose overbearing presence seems to break the harmony of the chapel, dates from 1733. A small **museum of sacred art**, adjacent to the chapel, exhibits various religious objects.

Finally, the most spectacular marvel of this campus is the **university library** ★★★ (*200 ESC, or 500 ESC if combined with a tour of the university; every day 9:30am to noon and 2pm to 5pm; access from the central courtyard, left of the cha*

pel), bestowed by King João V in 1724. The exuberance of its baroque style makes it one of the richest libraries in Portugal. Inside, besides the copious gold leaf and decorations, you may observe the interesting optical illusions created by the artwork between one room and another, where wooden arches imitate marble admirably well. Each room, developing various colonial themes, portrays a continent. An immense table with finely worked overlapping leaves is also worthy of attention.

To continue your visit, go back to Praça da Porta Férrera and a little farther to Praça Dom Diniz. On the way, you will notice the architecturally austere and cold buildings housing the faculty of medicine on one side of the street and the faculty of

sciences on the other. These Stalinesque science buildings, built during the Salazar regime, create a striking contrast to this very baroque university.

Upon arriving at Praça Dom Diniz, which has a statue of King Diniz, take the avenue to the right of the imposing stairs facing the square. At the end of this avenue, just before Praça dos Arcos do Jardim, you will come across a small street called **Bairro Sousa Pinto**, where you will see many *repúblicas* – houses converted into communal residences, occupied and managed by students. Some are painted in whimsical colours and they are often adorned with all sorts of paraphernalia. The name *república* (republic) was chosen to reflect the autonomous spirit of their occupants.

Nearby, Praça dos Arcos do Jardim owes its name to the **Aqueduto de São Sebastião**, built in the 16th century, which, with its beautiful arches covered in greenery, passes over Avenida Júlio Henriques. When going under the aqueduct, to the right of the street, you will come across the **Jardim Botânica**, a calm haven in the heart of the city. This tiered garden will particularly delight people interested in rare and tropical plants.

Now go back to Rua Alexandro Herculano, which will lead you directly to Praça da República.

On the east side of Praça da República, **Parque Santa Cruz**, also known as Jardim da Sereia, is worth a visit for its lovely **baroque portal** ★. Offered to the church by King Dom João III, this elegant garden includes the **Fonte da Nogueira** ★, a charming fountain overgrown with moss and adorned with *azulejo* **medallions**. Before heading off for a *bica* at one of the terraces on the very lively Praça da República, notice the two marvellous little houses with beautiful **facades** on Avenida Lourenço, at numbers 2 and 4.

Now go down Avenida Sá da Bandeira, a wide street, pleasantly lined with trees and flowerbeds. Once you have reached Rua Nicolau Rui Fernandes, stop for a moment to look at the amusing *azulejo* **panels** on the right side of the street.

Each panel represents one of the city's historical monuments. Across from them is the entrance to the **Mercado Municipal** (see p 282) where you can get a feel for the spirit of local residents.

Take Rua Nicolau Rui Fernandes to Praça 8 de Maio.

Another marvel not to be missed is the **Mosteiro y Igreja de Santa Cruz** ★★★ (*Praça 8 de Maio*). Built during the reign of Dom Manuel I in the 16th century, the building replaced an ancient monastery dating from the 12th century and erected during the reign of the first king of Portugal. The beautiful **portal** ★★, now gloriously restored, dates from 1523 and is the work of three artists of the famous Coimbra School: Diogo de Castilho, Nicolas Chantereine and Jean de Rouen. Strangely, a baroque-style arch was added during the 18th century, thus disfiguring the original work. Entering the church, visitors will immediately be seduced by the **central vault** ★, supported by beautiful wreathed columns. While the walls of the building are decorated with *azulejos*, a magnificent, finely sculpted **pulpit** ★★★ (*on the left side of the nave*) displays its immaculate whiteness. In the divided opinions of some historians, it may be the work of Nicolas Chantereine or of Jean de Rouen. One thing is certain, though: this is a true masterpiece, and it indisputably deserves the title of most beautiful pulpit in Portugal.

Now go near the main altar; on each side are superb **royal tombs** ★★ containing the remains of the first two kings of Portugal, Afonso Henriques and his son. In the main nave, you may also admire the baroque **organ sideboard**, especially interesting for its rich colours and its pipes. Finally, there is the **cloister of silence** ★ (*300 ESC; every day 10am to 12:30pm and 2pm to 6pm; entry by the left side of the choir stall*). This cloister, in bare Manueline style, has fine wreathed columns topped by clover-leaf decoration. Notice the elegant but unusual colours of the *azulejos* ★ that adorn the galleries of the cloister. Climbing one floor (*closed temporarily for repairs during our visit*), you can visit the Coro Alto, with its magnificent **stalls** ★★. The splendidly sculpted human and animal figures evoke Portugal's sea-going days.

And finally, if you're interested in *azulejos* continue on Rua da Sofia, at the northwest corner of Praça 8 de Maio, to get to the **Palácio da Justiça** (*Rua da Sofia*), which is in an old religious building

once inhabited by Dominicans. All around this handsome monastery dating back to the 16th century you can see beautiful *azulejo* **panels** ★★. In addition to the scene representing the recapture of the city in 1064, don't miss the panel depicting the **reconstruction of the Sé** ★, as well as the one depicting the scene of Inês de Castro's assassins being put to death, which is particularly expressive and cruel. On the second floor of the monastery, aside from other attractive scenes on *azulejos*, you can observe the beautiful sculpted wooden ceiling. To go upstairs, you can take the large marble staircase to the right of the main entrance, which is also covered in ceramic tiles in lovely yellows and blues.

The **Praça do Comercio** is worthwhile for its pleasant terraces and for **São Tiago church**, with its fine Romanesque portal.

Parque Portugal dos Pequeninos (*500 ESC, children under 10 150 ESC; every day 9am to 5:30pm; take the bridge overlooking the Rio Mondego; the park is on the left side of the main highway*). This is an amusing park with copies of various Portuguese monuments and dwellings.

The **former Santa Clara-a-Velha convent** (*closed for repairs*), located beside

the Parque Portugal dos Pequeninos, is an attractive Gothic building that held the remains of Inês de Castro before her transfer to Alcobaça. Work is now underway to save the building, which is slowly sinking into the mud from the river.

Farther east, no one should miss the chance to wander through the extremely pleasant **Quinta das Lágrimas gardens** ★ (*Estrada das Lages, Santa Clara, 3040 Coimbra, less than 2km from downtown, ☎239 44 16 15, ≠239 44 16 95*), where Dom Pedro I and Inês de Castro (see p 218) secretly met and fostered their love. In addition to a multitude of trees from various parts of the world, many of which date back to the beginning of the 19th century, there is a small stream called the *fonte dos amores* (lovers' fountain) near some captivating church ruins. The story is told that, with the help of this stream, Dom Pedro I sent love letters to his beloved Inês, who was then residing at the Convento da Sant-Clara-a-Velha; the convent used this stream as a source of running water. Attached to a piece of wood, the letters were transported to the convent, located 500m away. Farther along, the *fonte das lágrimas* (fountain of tears), which according to legend was created by

Inês de Castro's tears, reminds us that this was the site of Inês's savage assassination. Close to the fountain, you will also see a stone engraved with a passage from *The Lusiads* recounting the tragic death of Inês. The stone as well as two redwood trees planted nearby were contributed by the Duke of Wellington during his short stay at the *quinta*.

The **convent of Santa Clara-a-Nova** *(closed for renovations)*, located atop a hill on the left side of the shore, is worth the detour for the delicate **silver shrine** ★ that houses its church and for the fine **view** ★ of Coimbra.

Góis, Lousã, Penacova and Lorvão

Góis, Lousã, Penacova and Lorvão are just a few of the many villages that are worth visiting in the region. We have selected three (Lorvão, Penacova and Lousã) that are especially charming and which can easily be explored as part of the same excursion. Count on spending an afternoon to visit all three villages.

From Coimbra, take Highway N17 toward Guarda and, farther along, the N10 toward Penacova. The highway runs alongside the Rio Mondego as far as

Rebordosa, where you turn left to reach Lorvão by a small road leading uphill.

Lorvão

(24km from Coimbra)

This peaceful village, tucked into a green valley, has a very pretty Joanian-style church attached to a former monastery which has been converted into a health centre. Dating from the 18th century, the **Igreja de Lorvão** *(every day 9am to 5pm)* has two finely worked **silver tombs** containing the remains of two daughters of Dom Sancho I, who had retired to the attached monastery. Besides a two-faced organ and a fine **grill** separating the choir from the nave, an impressive **group of stalls** ★ decorated with mask-like sculptures can be found on the lower seating level. A real little wonder!

Continue the tour by getting back onto the main road and, farther along, heading toward Cernelha, where you turn right toward Penacova.

Penacova

(22km from Coimbra)

Located at an altitude of 300m, Penacova is a beautiful little village overlooking the Rio Mondego valley. The main attraction is its lookout on the central square. Beneath a roof of greenery, you will

discover a magnificent **view** ★ of the area. There is also an excellent panoramic restaurant (see p 279), making this excursion even more pleasant.

Cross the Rio Mondego to take the N2 toward Vila Nova de Poiares. At the first big intersection after passing this village, turn right on the N17. About 7km farther, take the N236, located on the left of the highway, which leads directly to the village of Lousã.

Lousã

(30km from Coimbra)

Located in the magnificent region of the Serra da Lousã, the village of Lousã is well worth visiting. The presence of numerous **heraldry houses** with generously decorated facades is particularly striking in this peaceful little village. Mostly dating from the 18th century, the majority of them are concentrated along the main street below the Praça de São Cabral, where the town hall is. Among these houses, do not miss the **Visconde Espinhal manor** ★, one of the most elegant on this street.

After this little stroll in the centre of the village, head to the **Nossa Senhora da Piedade castle** by the twisting little road to the right of the main road, shortly before the edge of the village. Overlooking the São João river, the castle's fortified tower *(climbing the tower is not advised for those who are afraid of heights or have health problems)* offers a magnificent **view** ★ of the Serra de Lousã and more particularly of the little Nossa Senhora da Piedade church, located below a spot of greenery. This church, built atop a steep boulder, is linked to a chapel built above the church on another mound. The two buildings are connected by an amusing, twisting little stairway. Although the church offers no special attraction, visiting this spot is a pleasant excursion in itself. To reach it, you have to go to the bottom of the valley and climb back up toward the church by an interminable series of steps. Since the bottom of the valley cannot be reached by car, we advise you to park your vehicle near the castle. Before setting out, however, make sure not to leave anything of value inside.

To complete this tour, head back toward the N17 and, at the intersection, turn left toward Coimbra.

Conimbriga

The main attraction in this ancient Roman city is its extraordinary **archaeological site**, where

regular digs have been organized since 1930. A veritable open-air museum, Conimbriga also has an indoor museum with beautiful exhibition halls devoted to the prehistoric and Roman periods in Portugal.

Although the Roman presence in Conimbriga goes back to the second century BC, the spot was already inhabited by people of Celtic origin, as the Celtic suffix *briga* would indicate. Taking advantage of its ideal location for relays between Braga and Olisipo (a former name of the city of Lisbon), the town developed very quickly and grew considerably. Beginning in the third century AD, however, it suffered several barbarian attacks and, despite the construction of imposing fortifications, surrendered to the Swabians toward AD 465. With the destruction of the town, Conimbriga disappeared for nearly 14 centuries until its recent resurrection for archaeological purposes.

With an area of nearly 130,000m³, the **Roman ruins** ★★★ *(300 ESC including entry to the museum; summer Tue to Sun, 9am to 1pm and 2pm to 8pm; winter, 9am to 1pm and 2pm to 6pm)* of Conimbriga are the biggest Roman site discovered to this day in Portugal. Admirably restored, the ruins are

located in a truly enchanting setting and surrounded by verdant countryside. Among the ruins, you can explore the many **mosaics** covering the floors of the houses, an amphitheatre, baths, a forum and a Christian basilica. For a detailed exploration of the site, we recommend the excellent little map sold at the entrance to the ruins. Here are a few attractions not to be missed.

The **Roman road**, marking the entrance to the ruins, linked Lisbon with Braga and passed through the centre of Conimbriga.

The **house with the water jets** ★★ *(immediately to the right of the entrance)* dates from the first half of the second century AD It was built on the ruins of a former dwelling dating back to the first century and whose basement is still visible today. Close by, right on the ground, the admirable **mosaics** ★★★, with reproductions of many animals (horses, dolphins, dogs and others), suggest something about the refinement of the inhabitants. A coin-activated apparatus (*10 ESC*) next to this house triggers the water jets.

In the **swastika house** (*on the right, shortly past the entrance*), you can observe beautiful mosaics decorated here and there with the swastika, a Hindu religious symbol.

The well-preserved **second defensive wall** ★★ was built in the fourth century to protect the town from barbarian attacks. Its construction literally amputated part of the site.

Finally, for a fine exploration of Roman civilization in Portugal, do not miss visiting the **museum** ★★★. Statuettes, coins, mosaics, a scale model of the site and numerous explanatory pictures are exhibited in modern buildings.

Penela

(14km from Coimbra)

Penela is worth a short detour for its **fortified castle** ★ *(take Rua Prof. Correia de Seixas, turning left at the village café; continue climbing and keep right until the castle)* dating from the 12th century. Built on a rocky promontory, you can discover fine **views** ★ of the surrounding countryside from atop its crenellated walls. Inside its walls is the pretty Capela Santa Eufémia with a fine retable of the Coimbra School. Those who suffer from vertigo, however, should avoid climbing the dangerously narrow track. To enjoy just as fine a view, go outside the walls, where a pleasant esplanade has been set up.

Figueira da Foz

Originally a little fishing village, Figueira da Foz has learned over the decades to profit from the bounties of nature. Protected from the cold north winds thanks to the Serra da Boa Viagem and benefiting from a broad bay magnificently bordered with fine golden sand beaches, Figueira da Foz has become one of the most popular resorts in Portugal. Besides its tourism activities, the town still has an active fishing port as well as a shipyard.

Figueira's main attraction is still of course its 3km of **beaches** ★ which, at low tide, seem to extend forever. But, the *bairro novo* (new district), with its hotels, bars, restaurants, discotheques and shops, also attracts curiosity. Unless you go during the low season (boredom assured!), this spot will appeal mostly to those who like the company of crowds, the pleasures of bathing, and tanning all day long. As for night owls, they will find the hustle and bustle they're looking for. Although it has beautiful beaches and

flourishes non-stop in the summer, Figueira da Foz lacks charm. Its many hotels and residential buildings, weak on aesthetics and too often showing signs of age, sprawl along the edge of the beach, detracting from the beauty of the place. The old town, although more pleasant with its beautiful parks, offers few attractions apart from two museums.

The **Museu Municipal Dr. Santos Rocha** *(Tue to Sun 9am to 12:30pm and 2pm to 5:30pm; Rua Calouste Gulbenkian)* is worth a visit for its collection of items ranging from prehistoric times to the Roman period, as well as a room containing decorative items.

The **Casa do Paço** *(Rua 5 de Outubre)*, an attractive building dating from the 17th century, holds an impressive number of Delft ceramic pieces (up to 8,000 pieces).

Montemor-o-Velho

(16km from Figueira da Foz)

Midway between Figueira da Foz and Coimbra, Montemor-o-Velho makes for a pleasant stop to admire its perfectly preserved **fortress** ★ *(Tue to Sun 10am to 12:30pm and 2pm to 5pm, until 8pm in the summer)*.

Dating partly from the 11th century and embodying a double wall, it is an impressive sight. These fortifications were built to serve as an advance guard post to protect Coimbra. Later converted to a palace, some historians believe the fortress may have been the spot where Afonso IV plotted the death of the lovely Inês de Castro. From its many towers and its high walkway, visitors can enjoy magnificent views of the Rio Mondego valley and its rice fields. Within the second wall, make sure to visit the **Igreja de Santa Maria dos Alcáçova** (*same times as for the castle*). Built in the 12th century, this Romanesque church has elegant Manueline wreathed columns, a choir stall and side chapels decorated with attractive *talhas douradas* and remarkable *azulejos* with Moorish-influenced motifs (*located near the main portal*).

Outdoor Activities

Pedal-boating

Ovar
(55km from Aveiro)

Although the Ria de Aveiro offers an environment that is well suited to sports, it should be recognized that pollution from nearby factories spoils the enjoyment of this spot somewhat. Those who seek nonetheless to benefit from a bit of relaxation on the water can rent pedal-boats at the Vela Areinho restaurant (*to the right along highway N327, just a little after Torrão do Lameiro heading north*) and enjoy a verdant, quiet environment.

Hiking

Buçaco

A wonderful wooded park with exotic scents, Buçaco is a dream spot for lovely romantic walks. There are numerous trails, and visitors can easily spend a full day here. Here are a few curiosities not to be missed.

The **Fonte Fria** ★, made of a gigantic 144-step stairway with a stream flowing though the middle. Very romantic!

The **Vale dos Fetos** ★, (literally, "the valley of ferns") where you can observe impressive tree ferns.

The **Porta de Coimbra**, a lookout adorned with two beautiful portals, offers extended views of the area.

The **Cruz Alta** ★, at an altitude of 545m, leads you to the highest point in the park. Photographers will enjoy superb panoramic views of the Serra de Buçaco. Access is by Via Sacra, a pilgrimage trail where you can observe chapels and religious statues all along your climb to paradise! Be warned, however, that penance requires some effort!

Kayaking and Mountain Biking

Coimbra

O Pioneiro do Mondego (*3,000 ESC; Apr to mid-Oct, information every day 1pm to 3pm and 8pm to 10pm;* ☎/≠239 47 83 85) offers a 25km trip down the Rio Mondego by **kayak**, lasting 3 or 4hrs. Departure from Coimbra at 10am from the parking area located beside the Santa Clara bridge, near the tourism bureau. You can also rent **mountain bikes** (*3,000 ESC per day*). Reservations suggested.

Golf

To date, there are only two professional-class golf courses in the northern part of the Costa de Prata. Below are the addresses and main features of these courses.

Golf Courses

Name	Number of Holes	Par	Length (in metres)	Address
Miramar Golf Club	9	34	2570	Ave. Sacadura Cabral 4405 Valadares ☎*227 62 20 67* ⇌*227 62 78 59*
O Porto Golf Club	18	71	5600	Lugar do Sisto 4500 Espinho ☎*227 34 20 08* ⇌*227 34 68 95*

Accommodations

Aveiro

Residencial de Alboi
$$
pb
Rua da Arrochela, 6 3800 Aveiro
☎*234 38 03 90*
⇌*234 38 03 91*
www.residencial-alboi.com
This hotel has a tasteful decor and modern furniture. It offers the advantage of being located just a few steps from the very pleasant Rua José Rabumba, in front of the Rossio, Aveiro's lively neighbourhood.

 Hotel Arcada
$$
pb, tv
Rua Viana do Castelo 4
3800 Aveiro
☎*234 42 30 01*
⇌*234 42 18 86*
Set in a charming old house, this hotel is advantageously located in front of the central canal, in the centre of

Aveiro. The decor differs from one room to the next, so you should ask to see a room before deciding. Rooms located in front offer pleasant views.

Hotel Moliceiro
$$$
pb, tv, ≡
Rua Barbosa de Magalhães no. 15-17, 3800 Aveiro
☎*234 37 74 00*
⇌*234 37 74 01*
Housed in a small, modern building, Hotel Moliceiro offers medium-sized but cozy, carefully fitted-out rooms. Those who appreciate luxurious surroundings will feel perfectly at ease here, since virtually every room in the building is overrun with opulent armchairs, curios and paintings as well as Oriental carpets. A small garden with artificial plants even complements the hotel grounds.

Hotel Afonso V
$$$
pb, tv, ℜ, ℝ
Rua Dr. Manuel das Neves 65
3800 Aveiro
☎*234 42 51 91*
⇌*234 42 88 20*
Somewhat away from the centre of town, this international-class hotel is very comfortable and is well suited to those who seek calm. The hotel has many rooms for conventions.

Mira

(29km from Aveiro)

Pousada de Juventude
(Youth Hostel)
Parque de Campismo Jovens
3070 Mira
☎/⇌*231 47 12 75*

Águeda

(32km from Aveiro)

Pousada de Santo António
$$$
pb, ℜ, tv, ≈
From Hwy. A1-E80-IP1, take the IP5 toward Viseu; 5km farther, turn right on the N1-IC2; the pousada is about 3km from there, not far from Serém
3750 Águeda
☎*234 52 32 30*
⇌*234 52 31 92*
This *pousada* has a thoroughly rustic decor: hand-painted lampshades, wooden country-style furniture, a fine collection of china, tablecloths made by artisans, pretty *azulejos*, and so on. A pleasant circular dining room allows you to enjoy the surrounding countryside with your meals. The presence of a big pool in the garden, amidst scenery reminiscent of Tuscany, is another asset for this decidedly agreeable *pousada*. The only drawback is the background noise coming from the nearby N1 highway, with its heavy truck traffic.

Borralha

(34km from Aveiro)

Palácio de Águeda
$$$
pb, tv
From Águeda, head south on the N1-IC2, then take the first road on the left toward Borralha
Quinta da Borralha
3750 Águeda
☎*234 60 19 77*
⇌*234 60 19 76*
Set in a magnificent 18th-century palace, this hotel has 42 comfortably appointed rooms with period furniture. In the baroque setting inside you will see some antiques, while outside you can stroll through the big gardens and daydream of your new life in a castle.

Torreira

(65km from Aveiro)

Estalagem Riabela
$$$-$$$$ fb
pb, ≈, ℜ
via the N109 and N109-5
3870 Murtosa
☎*234 83 80 90*
⇌*234 83 81 47*
Located in a calm setting, facing the Ria de Aveiro, this hotel has a big pool and an attractive tennis court. It offers standard rooms and classic comfort. The decor is outmoded and could stand to be renewed.

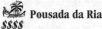 **Pousada da Ria**
$$$$
pb, tv, ℜ, ≈
about 5km south of Torreira by the N109 and N109-5
3870 Murtosa
☎*234 83 83 32*
⇌*234 83 83 33*
Built overlooking the water, the Pousada da Ria gives visitors the feeling they are aboard a ship at anchor. The decor, a tad exotic, consists mostly of bamboo furniture, green plants and jute rugs. Rooms face the Ria directly and have small terraces where superb sunsets can be enjoyed. Try to be up at dawn to see the little fishing boats going down the lagoon to cast their nets. At that hour the suffused light over the lagoon is particularly soft, and the overall sense of calm is almost miraculous. An experience not to be missed! Service and food, although adequate, seem a little less discriminating than in the other *pousadas* and should be improved. A pleasant but rather small pool adds to the setting.

São Jacinto

(63km from Aveiro)

Campismo Parque de São Jacinto
3800 Aveiro
☎/⇌*234 33 12 20*

Buçaco

Pensão A Regional
$
pb
Rua D. Lúco Abranches
3050 Luso-Mealhada
☎*231 93 92 72*
This little family-run hotel, located a few steps from the Buçaco estate, has a few simply decorated but very clean rooms. Very good quality-to-price ratio.

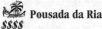 **Vila Duparchy**
$$$
pb, ≈
along the N234, 6km from Mealhada, on the left side heading toward Buçaco, Rua de José Duarte Figueiredo Luso
3050 Mealhada
☎*231 93 07 90*
⇌*231 93 03 07*
Located on a beautiful estate, the Vila

Duparchy with its six rooms, belongs to the *turismo de habitação* bed and breakfast system (see p 57). This charming dwelling from the late 19th century will delight the romantically inclined. Each room is decorated differently with furniture of a particular style. A lovely pool surrounded by a magnificent flower garden enhances this spot. Its location near the Buçaco park also makes it an ideal spot for lovers of open-air strolls. Friendly and professional service.

Buçaco Palace Hotel
$$$$$
pb, ℜ, tv
Mata do Buçaco,
3050 Mealhada
for reservations:
Rua Dr. Álvaro de Castro 73
1600 Lisboa
☎*231 93 01 01*
⇋*231 93 05 09*
Anyone looking for life in a castle will not pass up a stay at the Buçaco Palace Hotel. Part of the renowned Almeida chain, this hotel is set in a former royal hunting palace. The neo-Manueline interior is an attraction in itself (see p 258) with its fairy-tale decoration. For a royal ascent to the rooms, after passing a vestibule sculpted like a grotto, take the majestic stairway adorned with beautiful *azulejo* panels. The rooms have been astutely decorated to provide both comfort and an old-fashioned character. In the morning, breakfast may be taken on the neo-

Manueline terrace, with its view of the park, or in the magnificent dining room with its richly sculpted arched ceiling, bringing you into a world where the exuberance and opulence are in keeping with the magnificence of the surrounding park. Expensive but unforgettable.

Luso
(2km from Buçaco)

Grande Hotel de Luso
$$$
pb, tv, ≡, ≈, ℜ, ○
Rua dos Banhos, 3050 Luso
☎*231 93 04 50*
⇋*231 93 03 50*
Located in the heart of Luso's spa, the Grande Hotel de Luso will please those who appreciate comfort above all. The rooms are appointed with rather nondescript furnishings, but offer all modern conveniences. The hotel not only has two large swimming pools, one indoors and one outdoors, but also direct access to the thermal baths, graced with a lovely Art-Deco sculpture. A tennis court and a sauna round out the facilities. Finally, admirers of 1950s decors will be delighted with the in-house restaurant (see p 276), whose dining room is adorned with a magnificent painting.

Coimbra

Pousada de Juventude
Rua Henriques Seco 14; 20min walk from the centre of town
3000 Coimbra
☎/⇋*239 82 29 55*

Campismo Municipal de Coimbra
Câmara Municipal de Coimbra
Praça 25 de Abril
☎*239 70 14 97*

Residência Santa Cruz
$ with or without bkfst
Rua Castro Matoso no. 4
3000 Coimbra
☎*239 82 36 57*
Right near the Aqueduto de São Sebastião, the Residência Santa Cruz offers a few very rudimentary, old-looking rooms with ill-assorted furniture. Suitable for travellers on very restricted budgets.

Pensão Residencial Jardim
$
pb/ps
Avenida Emidio Navarro 65
3000 Coimbra
☎*239 82 52 04*
A little beyond the centre of town, Pensão Residencial Jardim is set in a former residence with old-fashioned charm. While the lobby is adorned with beautiful *azulejos*, the rooms are rather simple. This spot is clean and well maintained. Asked for a room located in back, for the front faces a very busy street.

Pensão Alentejana
$
pb
Rua Dr. António Henriques
Seco 1, 2nd floor, 3000 Coimbra
☎*239 82 59 03*
⇄*239 40 51 24*
This little guest house,
a 20min walk from the
centre of town, has 15
simply appointed
rooms that are perfectly
comfortable.

Pensão Residencial Antunes
$$
pb
Rua Castro Matoso no. 8
3000 Coimbra
☎*239 82 30 48*
☎*239 83 83 54*
⇄*239 83 83 73*
Set up in a modest
single-family house, the
Pensão Residencial
Antunes offers rooms
of average comfort with
attractive old furniture.
It's of particular interest
for its moderate prices
and its location two
steps away from the
university and right
near the old town.

Hotel Astória
$$$
pb, ℜ, tv
Avenida Emidio Navarro 21
3000 Coimbra
☎/⇄*239 82 20 55*
☎*239 82 20 56*
⇄*239 82 20 57*
Part of the De Almeida
family's hotel chain,
Hotel Astória is set in a
beautiful, early 20th-
century building, at the
edge of the Rio
Mondego. Admirers of
Art Deco will be espe-
cially pleased with the
charm of the furniture
which, for the most
part, has been perfectly
preserved. While a

pretty little interior rail-
ing decorates the
lobby, the circular din-
ing room houses an
excellent restaurant.
Rooms on the river side
are particularly pleasant
because of the views
they offer.

Hotel Tivoli Coimbra
$$$
pb, tv, ℜ, =, ⊗
Rua João Machado no. 4-5
P.O. Box 593, 300 Coimbra
☎*239 82 69 34*
⇄*239 82 68 27*
Located in an unap-
pealing modern build-
ing, Hotel Tivoli
Coimbra offers approxi-
mately 100 rooms that
are comfortably
equipped and ade-
quately furnished yet
lacking any particular
style. For a good view
of the upper city, get a
room on one of the
upper floors facing the
street. This lovely view
of the old part of town
is unfortunately marred
to some extent by a
horrible glass tower in
the distance. To make
up for it, you will find
all the comforts of a
higher-ranked hotel,
including desks in
some rooms. In the
basement there is a
small pool, which is
free for clients, as well
as an exercise room
next to it that costs
1,000 ESC per session
(*13,500 ESC for 10 visits*).

Quinta das Lágrimas
$$$-$$$$
pb, tv, ℜ, ≈
Estrada das Lages, Santa Clara
3040 Coimbra; less than 2km
from downtown, on the south
shore of Rio Mondego
☎*239 44 16 15*
⇄*239 44 16 95*
After successively be-
longing to the royal
family of Portugal, the
university and a reli-
gious order, the beauti-
ful Quinta das Lágrimas
was acquired in 1730
by the Duke of
Wellington's previous
aide-de-camp, António
Maria Osório Cabral da
Gama e Castro, whose
descendants still own
the property. Located
south of Rio Modego,
this *quinta* has been
visited by many a
prominent figure in-
cluding the Duke of
Wellington, King Dom
Miguel I of Portugal
and Emperor Dom
Pedro II of Brazil. It
was also the setting of
Portugal's most tragic
love story, that of Inês
de Castro and King
Dom Pedro I.

Over the centuries, the
quinta has undergone
several modifications;
the most important was
the reconstruction of a
large part of it follow-
ing a major fire in 1789.
The only remaining
structure from the origi-
nal building is the left
side. In recent years,
two additional wings
have been added to the
back of the main build-
ing in order to trans-
form it into a hotel. In
the oldest part, there
are now 23 rooms (in-
cluding four suites),

each of them arranged differently. In addition to having very attractive furniture, the rooms are decorated with luxurious fabrics in warm colours. The only disadvantage is that most of the rooms face the courtyard, which, although lovely, doesn't offer a view of the gardens. During your stay make sure to visit the small library where you will discover a beautiful parquet floor as well as a decor consisting entirely of richly sculpted woodwork. The main salon, with its 19th-century paintings, old curios, precious furniture and oriental rugs, recalls the building's noble past. And finally, if you get the chance to have breakfast in the old dining room (in summer only, also see p 278), you will undoubtedly be charmed by the many frescoes, mouldings and stucco pieces that adorn the room.

In the two new wings, there are 20 comfortable rooms, furnished in a less luxurious manner than those in the original building, but all nonetheless agreeably decorated. These constructions, which contrast in style to the original section, have long walkways flanked by Doric columns and are separated by a pond. Despite this incongruity, the overall result is aesthetically pleasing, and the rooms in the right wing have the additional benefit of small balconies that overlook the property's magnificent garden (see p 265).

Finally, as a crowning glory to this haven, across from the gardens, there is a pool and a tennis court, both of which open onto an area surrounded by orange trees. From here, there is a particularly picturesque view, with the university buildings and their famous steeple visible in the distance. The Quinta das Lágrimas is also home to an excellent restaurant (see p 278) that will delight gourmets.

Condeixa-a-Nova

(13km from Coimbra)

Pousada de Santa Cristina
$$$$$
from the N1-IC2, follow the signs to Condeixa-a-Nova
3150 Condeixa-a-Nova
☎*239 94 12 86*
☎*239 94 40 25*
⇌*239 94 30 97*
Built a short time ago, the Pousada de Santa Cristina is located atop a hill less than 2km from the Roman ruins of Conimbriga. While rather modern-looking, the interior common areas are admirably adorned with furniture from a former palace in Lisbon. The rooms have period furnishings as well as luxurious marble bathrooms decorated with *azulejos*. Some of them also have small terraces with views of the countryside. While a spacious garden will delight lovers of the outdoors, children (big and small alike) will have plenty of fun in the big pool located there.

Penacova

(22km from Coimbra)

Parque de Campismo de Penacova
Estrada da Carvoeira
3360 Penacova
☎/⇌*239 47 74 64*

Pensão Avenida
$
pb
Avenida Abel Rodrigues de Costa, a little before the central square, along the highway coming from Luso
3360 Penacova
☎ *239 47 71 42*
This old-fashioned guest house hides an antiquated charm with its wooden floors and its old furniture. Ask for one of the rooms on the upper floors and at the rear of the building, which offer fine views. Friendly service.

Lousã

(30km from Coimbra)

Residencial Martinho
$
sb/pb, tv
Mon to Sat
Rua Movimento das Forças Armadas, 3200 Lousã
☎*239 99 13 97*
Located very near the village's central square, in the rear of a family residence, this *residencial* offers simple but comfortable little rooms with an *azulejo* decor. Warm, friendly

service. Breakfast is not served on Sundays or holidays. Good quality-to-price ratio.

Figueira da Foz

The seasonality of tourism has a big influence on prices here, and it is not unusual to see prices drop by half in the winter. Do not hesitate to bargain at this time, when resort hotels are almost deserted and customers are few in number. Figueira's high season runs mostly from June to September, when prices are at their highest. If you are planning to stay during that period, it is essential to reserve far in advance.

Campismo Municipal da Figueira da Foz
Estrada de Tavarede 3080 Figueira da Foz
☎233 40 28 10

Residencial Aliança
$ sb, $$ pb
tv
12 Rua Miguel Bombarda, corner Rua Cândido dos Reis and Rua Miguel Bombarda 3080 Figueira da Foz
☎234 32 21 97
A small and unpretentious guest house, this spot is clean and not too expensive compared with the exorbitant prices charged elsewhere.

Hotel Ibis
$$$
pb, tv, ≡
Rua da Liberdade no. 20 3080 Figueira da Foz
☎233 42 20 51
≈233 42 07 56
www.hotelibis.com
Although the Hotel Ibis does not offer an ocean view, it does provide pleasant rooms with a modern decor. True to the hotel chain's reputation, this establishment is comfortable, though neither highly refined nor original.

Hotel Mercure
$$$-$$$$
pb, tv, ≈, ℜ
Avenida 25 de Abril 3080 Figueira da Foz
☎234 32 25 39
☎234 32 21 46
≈234 32 24 20
The main asset of this big 102-room hotel is its seafront location. Rooms with sea-views all have big balconies except for those located in the tower attached to the hotel. A pleasant pool is available to guests from June to September.

Restaurants

Aveiro

Restaurante-Bar Bombordo
$$
every day noon to 4pm and 7pm to 2am
Largo da Praça do Peixe 10 Fish, of course, in this fitting spot. Its pleasant decor, friendly welcome and terrace should be taken into account.

Sonatura
$$
8am to 8pm, until 3pm Sat and Sun
Rua Clube dos Galitos 6 In the boutique-restaurant Sonatura you can not only eat vegetarian dishes but also make some purchases at reasonable prices.

Adega Típica O Telheiro
$$
9am to 11pm, closed Sat
Largo da Praça do Peixe 20 A pleasant restaurant specializing in fish dishes. The big counter and the wooden tables give this place a warm atmosphere.

Alho Pôrro
$$
Mon to Sat 10:30am to 2pm and 7pm to 10:30pm, closed Sun
Rua da Arrochela 23 Meats, fish and seafood are on the menu in this friendly, unpretentious little restaurant.

Cafés and Tearooms

Ria Pão
7am to midnight
Rua João Mendonça 27 Popular with young people, the Ria Pão is a pleasant spot for a pastry or a quick bite. Modern setting, efficient service and friendly staff.

Café Ria
Rua Clube dos Galitos nos. 5-6 Despite its unattractive decor, this spot is pleasant because of its

terrace with views of the canal. Light meals offered until midnight (omelettes, pizzas, etc.). A mixed clientele of gays and straights.

Águeda

(32km from Aveiro)

Pousada de Santo António
$$$
from Hwy. A1-E80-IP1, take the IP5 toward Viseu; 5km farther turn right on the N1-IC2; the *pousada* is about 3km farther, not far from Serém
☎*234 52 32 30*
With its thoroughly rustic decor (wooden country-style furniture, a fine collection of porcelain dishes, pretty *azulejos*, and so on), the rotunda of the *pousada*'s pleasant dining room offers fine views of the surrounding countryside, which is particularly beautiful and reminiscent of Tuscany. The only drawbacks are the absence of a terrace for meals and the background noise caused by the proximity of the N1, with its heavy truck traffic.

Ovar

(55km from Aveiro)

 Vela Areinho
$$$
noon to 3pm and 7pm to 10pm
Prata do Areinho, along the N327 just past Torrão do Lameiro
☎*256 59 26 52*
On an island linked to the highway by a little bridge, the Vela Areinho restaurant

enjoys an enchanting setting. Its panoramic view of the canal and its wood-trim decor and plants make this spot very pleasant. Classic Portuguese cuisine on the menu.

Torreira

(65km from Aveiro)

A Varina Churrasqueria
$$
facing the port of Terreiro along the N327
Grilled dishes on an attractive terrace with a view of the little port and its boats.

A Passoeira
$$
in Torreira, along the N327
Not far from the Vela Areinho (see above), A Passoeira restaurant offers Brazilian and Portuguese dishes in a congenial setting.

Pousada da Ria
$$$
about 5km south of Torreira via the N109 and N109-5
☎*234 83 83 32*
Built overlooking the water, the Pousada da Ria gives visitors the impression of being aboard a ship at anchor. From its restaurant, you can enjoy a superb sunset over the lagoon while savouring its seafood, the house specialty. For an unforgettable experience, we advise you to come for breakfast early in the morning, for that is when fishers go down the lagoon to cast their nets. The view of the Ria and its little fishing boats, with the soft

sunlight, is especially beautiful. The service and the food, although adequate, seem a little amateurish compared to the other *pousadas* and could use some improvement.

Luso

(2km from Buçaco)

Selas
$$
Rua Emidio Navarro no. 144
☎*231 93 91 82*
Housed in the Residêncial Astória, in a small dining room where extensive woodwork and a large stone fireplace create a rustic setting, this restaurant specializes in Portuguese food. Among the dishes served, the famous regional specialty, *leitão* (suckling pig prepared a multitude of ways), is a must. Other nice perks include the attractively draped tables and the absence of a television.

Cruz Alta
$$$
12:30pm to 2:30pm and 7:30pm to 9:30pm
Rua dos Banhos
☎*231 93 04 50*
In the Grande Hotel de Luso, the Cruz Alta restaurant is sure to please admirers of 1950s decors. Patrons can thus enjoy many Portuguese dishes or a few international dishes in a large dining room enhanced with elegant period lighting and a magnificent large painting. Nothing to write home about, but sure value for the money!

The only drawback is the limited business hours.

Coimbra

UC Cantina
$

Rua Oliveira Matos, on the left side of the road going uphill
If you're on an very tight budget, you can try your luck at the university cafeteria, UC Cantina where they offer sandwiches starting at 150 ESC. However, as it is normally reserved for University of Coimbra students, it is possible in certain cases (it isn't controlled systematically) that a student card be required to take advantage of these great prices.

Padaria Popular
$

Largo da Freiria
Padaria Popular, a small bakery with a terrace, is tucked away at the far end of a small square in the business district of the lower part of the city. For a few escudos, you can enjoy a sandwich or one of their small daily specials.

Salão Brasil
$

Largo do Poço no. 3, 2nd floor
Still in the lower part of the city, inside a large hall with the decor of a run-down cafeteria, Salão Brasil offers meals for the modest sum of 650 ESC every day at lunch; they include the daily special, half a bottle of

wine, bread and coffee. Quite a deal! Part of the room has been converted into a pool hall, and on evenings and weekends you can come and listen to *musica ao vivo.*

China Town
$

Sun to Fri
Beco da Fanado; Rua da Sofia on the left side when leaving downtown, take the small street between Farmacia Figueiredo and the Infinito shop
Located in a back alley of a working-class neighbourhood, the China Town restaurant serves good Chinese dishes with no great surprises, at prices that will thrill low-budget travellers. Various meals available from 1,000 ESC.

Café Sé Velha
$

Mon to Sat 8:30am to midnight
Rua de Joaquim Antonio d'Aguiar nos. 132-134, on the right side facing the Sé
This little self-service restaurant offers light meals and, something not very common in this sort of spot, a good choice of salads and cheeses. Although the setting is warm and the decor pleasant, a noisy television spoils the atmosphere. To escape it, you can go to the little terrace located a little farther along, just next to the stairs leading to the Sé. A young clientele, made up of tourists and locals.

O Sé Nova
$

Rua Borges Carneiro 64
This little neighbourhood café-restaurant, decorated with *azulejos*, is frequented mostly by students and professors. Ordinary family-style cuisine (the ubiquitous *bacalhau* and egg-based desserts) are served here. Half-portions are available. To escape the omnipresent television, you can take refuge on the small terrace. Good and inexpensive, but rather amateurish service.

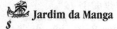 ### Jardim da Manga
$

Sun to Fri
Rua Olímpio Nicolau Rui Fernandes, in the Jardim da Manga
☎239 82 91 56
Facing a small garden, this self-serve restaurant with old-fashioned decor is worth the trip for its hearty, inexpensive food. Among the choices offered are the Portuguese-style rib steak, grilled veal with sautéed potatoes and vegetables of the day, or the fillet of fish with rice. At only 690 to 830 ESC per dish, it's a real bargain! A soup (*a transmontana* or *canja*) accompanied by a salad will satisfy those with small appetites for as little as 295 ESC. And last but not least, desserts go for less than 300 ESC. At that price, there's simply no good reason to deny yourself!

Restaurante Praça Velha
$$
every day 8am to 11pm
Praça do Comércio 69-71
Part of the attractive
setting on the pretty
Praça do Comércio, the
Restaurante Praça Velha
offers a menu of classical Portuguese cuisine.
This spot is pleasant
because of its big terrace facing the square.
A tourist menu is available for 2,000 ESC and
up.

Carmina de Matos
$$
Tue to Sun
Praça 8 de Maio no. 2
☎*239 82 35 10*
Located on pleasant
Praça 8 de Maio and
facing the lovely Igreja
de Santa Cruz, the
Carmina de Matos offers various Portuguese
specials such as excellent *chanfana* (goat
with wine casserole),
rojões a casa (homestyle
pork chops cooked in
fat and served cold)
and *bife recheada*
(stuffed meat) as well
as a tourist menu for
1,750 ESC, and oh,
miracle of miracles, no
bacalhau!

Café Restaurante Nicola
$$
Mon to Sat 7am to midnight
Rua Ferreira Borges 35
For a good and unpretentious daily special.
Pizzas starting at
600 ESC, plus a big
choice of pastries, including the Coimbra
specialty, *pastel de
Tentugal*, made with
eggs, of course.

Restaurante Real das Canas
$$$
Thu to Tue
7 Vila Mendes; from central
Coimbra, cross the Ponte de
Santa Clara and, just after
Parque dos Pequenitos, take
Rua Professor Alberto Pinto de
Abreu; the restaurant is on the
left, half-way up
☎*239 81 48 77*
Known in the area for
its regional dishes,
Restaurante Real das
Canas offers good Portuguese cuisine in a
warm rural setting.
Among the many specialties on the menu,
the roast goat with
wine casserole
(*chanfana*) is not to be
missed. If you're not
very hungry, just have
a main dish as portions
are particularly generous here. And finally,
to have a fully satisfying experience, in addition to the quality food,
the restaurant has many
tables with panoramic
views of Coimbra and
the surrounding countryside. To take advantage of this great opportunity you have to
reserve a few days in
advance (the owner
speaks many languages). Excellent
value for the price and
friendly, courteous service.

🛥 **Restaurante Quinta das Lágrimas**
$$$$
Estrada das Lages, Santa Clara
less than 1km from downtown
☎*239 44 16 15*
In the heart of a prestigious *quinta* converted
into a hotel (see p 273),
the Restaurante Quinta
das Lágrimas is definitely the most romantic place to dine in
Coimbra. Instead of
entering by the side
door leading directly to
the restaurant, try the
front entrance to see
the majestic Quinta
entrance hall and its
beautiful frescoes as
well as, farther on, the
boudoir and the salon,
both richly decorated.
As for the restaurant
itself, on the ground
floor of the building, it
is composed of two
completely modernized, fascinating rooms.
The first one, somewhat dark with opulent
decor, is more suited to
intimate meals in a
traditional setting,
whereas the second,
quite sparse but well-lit
by large bay windows
overlooking a garden,
is delightful if you are
interested in a more
contemporary environment. The food here is
considered to be
among the best in the
region. For an entrée,
don't miss the delicious
crepes stuffed with
shrimp and covered
with a rich lobster-bisque sauce. As a
main dish, the *garoupa*
(grouper) served with
pear purée, or the *filete
de vedea* (filet of venison) served with vegetables and fresh mushrooms, are only two
exquisite examples of
what you will find on
the menu. The only
disappointment is the
traditional choice of
egg-based desserts,
presented, as usual, on
a cart. Why not finish
this outing on a high
note with a walk on the

beautiful grounds of the property (see p 265) and thus return to where Portugal's most passionate love story took place?

Cafés and Tearooms

Medina Sandwich Bar
closed Sun
Rua do Quebra Costas, near Rua Fernandez Tomáz
The Medina Sandwich Bar offers sandwiches, as its name indicates, but also little sweets and other snacks, with service until 2am, all of it is a modern decor. A pleasant terrace.

Cartola Esplanada Bar
every day 7am to 2am
Praça da República no. 26
Very popular with young people, the large terrace of the Cartola Esplanada Bar invites passers-by to sit down and enjoy a coffee or one of the many pastries (sandwiches also available) at very reasonable prices. In fact, a *bica* here costs only 70 ESC, about one-tenth the price of a cup of coffee at Covent Garden in London! Take advantage of it!

Café Santa Cruz
Mon to Sat 7am to 2am
closed Sun
Praça 8 de Maio 4-6
Café Santa Cruz probably has the most beautiful decor of any café in Coimbra. Set in part of the former convent of Santa Cruz, it has an extraordinary vault in the Manueline style. With its big, solid marble counter, its

beautiful, dark woodwork and its leather chairs, this café is one of the more enjoyable spots to spend a few moments sipping a drink.

Café Oasis
Largo da Sé Velha
With its resolutely student atmosphere, Café Oasis is a friendly spot to grab a coffee on the run.

Condeixa-a-Nova

(13km from Coimbra)

Pousada de Santa Cristina
$$$
from the N1-IC2, follow the signs to Condeixa-a-Nova
3150 Condeixa-a-Nova
☎239 94 12 86
☎239 94 40 25
Located atop a hill, the Pousada de Santa Cristina has the advantage of being less than 2km from the Roman ruins of Conimbriga. Although it is set in a modern-looking building, the dining room is pleasantly adorned with antique objects, most of which come from a palace in Lisbon. Its spacious garden constitutes an ideal spot for a pre-dinner drink. Excellent wines and cuisine that is even more meticulous than at its counterparts. One of the best choices in the area.

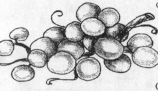

Penacova

(22km from Coimbra)

Restaurante O Parque
$
Sun to Fri noon to 3pm and 7pm to 9pm
next to the Parque Municipal 50m from the central square
Simple Portuguese cuisine. Meals starting at 1,200 ESC.

Restaurante Pensão Avenida
$
every day noon to 2pm and 7pm to 9pm
Avenida Abel Rodrigues de Costa, a little before the central square coming from Luso
☎239 47 71 42
This restaurant is part of the guest house of the same name. Old-fashioned furnishings and unpretentious cooking.

O Panorâmico
$$
every day noon to 3pm and 7pm to 9pm
on the main square, entrance to the right of the Câmara Municipal
☎239 47 73 33
This restaurant serves quality cuisine with greater variety than most restaurants in the area. The tuna and tomato salad and excellent pineapple pie are surprisingly good. Look for tables with a view... far from the television. Located high up, the dining room offers magnificent views of the surrounding mountains and Rio Mondego, which flows lazily from the hollow of the valley. Clouds of swallows that

seem to have moved to this spot enjoy pirouetting over the valley, passing in front of the restaurant and adding an amusing little show to this idyllic view. Not be missed.

Cafés and Tearooms

Café Turismo
upstairs from the O Panorâmico restaurant entrance on the left of the building
A pleasant terrace with a panoramic view of the Rio Mondego.

Lousã

(30km from Coimbra)

Churrasqueiria Borges
$$
Rua Dr. João Santos no. 2
☎239 99 34 89
A pleasant place in which to savour all kinds of grilled meats, salmon or pork chops. The economy menu starts at 1,500 ESC while a litre of house wine goes for 600 ESC, all of which can be enjoyed in an unpretentious yet appealing setting.

Conimbriga

A **self-service restaurant** (*$$*) is located next to the museum and very near the Roman ruins. Several rather ordinary hot dishes are available each day, as are items to take out. Prices are obviously higher than elsewhere, but the view from the terrace com-

pensates somewhat for this drawback.

Figueira da Foz

Aliança
$
Rua Miguel Bombarda 12
connected to the small hotel of the same name
The advantage of this spot lies mostly in its surroundings (located on a pedestrian street) and its rather pleasant decor. Half-portions are available.

Astrolábio
$$$
Avenida 25 de Abril
☎233 42 21 46
☎233 42 25 39
The restaurant of the Hotel Mercure, the Astrolábio offers a classical Portuguese menu and an excellent selection of wines. The big dining room, recently renovated, offers seafront views. On Sundays, a copious Brazilian buffest brunch is served for 2,000 ESC.

Restaurante Foz de Mondego
$$
28 Rua Eng. Silva
This restaurant has a classic menu and a warm setting, away from the tourist zone and the crowds.

Teimoso
$$$
Estrada do Cabo Mondego head toward Buarcos and continue for 5km along the main road next to the sea
Facing the sea, the Teimoso restaurant prepares ordinary classical Portuguese

cuisine. The advantage of this restaurant, well away from the centre of town, is that it offers interesting views overlooking the sea.

Entertainment

Aveiro

Plaza Bar
9am to 2am
Travessa do Rossio no. 14
A pleasant, modern bar frequented by local people. The moderate volume of the music allows for conversation.

Coimbra

Fado

O Trovador
$$
Mon to Sat
Largo da Sé Velha no. 15-17
☎239 82 54 75
Located just across from the impressive Sé Velha, the O Trovador restaurant has *fado* on weekends in a sparse and somewhat cold setting, which is warmed up by a few *azulejos* and coloured tablecloths. A tourist menu is available for 2,500 ESC with a choice of either an appetizing white wine pork stew or Trovador-style calamari. On the menu, you will find many regional specialties such as *caldo verde* and an amazing almond vichyssoise.

Bars and Nightclubs

Piano Negro

Rua Borges Carneiro 19

A bar, a venue for musicians, an art gallery: all of these descriptions fit the Piano Negro. Besides an interesting setting, a pleasant little terrace allows you to sit side by side with some of Coimbra's hip youth.

Bohémia Bar

Rua do Cabido 6

Located very close to the Sé, Bohémia Bar welcomes a group of musicians each weekend (*500 ESC cover*) in a room where *azulejos* and woodwork create a country atmosphere. Mixed clientele. Ideal for a drink or a snack (eggs, sandwiches and fries served day and night!)

Gadobravo

Mon to Sat

corner of Largo da Sé Velha and Rua dos Coutinhos

On weekends, the Gadobravo dance club plays host to a mostly young, diverse clientele. You can let off some steam on one of the two dance floors until the wee hours of the morning in an "airy" setting. You shouldn't miss the house special, the famous cinnamon-flavoured Gadobravo cocktail, and if by chance you commit a few sins during the evening, you can always go confess at the Sé, just across the street, before heading home.

Academico and Tropical

corner of Praça da República and Rue Alexandre Herculano

Hot spots for university students, the terraces of the Academico and Tropical bars which are located next to each other, start filling up at 10pm. In this very lively atmosphere you can have a drink (sandwiches also available) while observing the nocturnal wildlife of Coimbra which seems to come alive here.

Varadero

500 ESC Sat and Sun

open Fri to Sat from midnight on

Quinta da Insua-Azinhaga, Rua Parreiras

from downtown, after the Ponte de Santa Clara, turn left at Avenida Inês de Castro, then, after the first gas station, take the first street on the right; the bar is on the right side of this street, at the end of the parking lot, down from the gas station

Located some distance from downtown Coimbra, the Varadero dance club is the most popular meeting place for young people in Coimbra. On the large dance floor on the first floor you can dance to a variety of rhythms, and, on weekends, they have bands upstairs. If you're looking for something a little calmer, a small pub decorated in woodwork with subdued lighting can be found there. Also, during the summer, they serve light meals on the terrace to appease those late-night cravings.

Café Galeria Almedina

every day 8am to 4am

Arco de Almedina

Located next to the town's ancient fortified gate, the Arco de Almedina (see p 260), the Café Galeria Almedina is a modern bar with original decor. At the entrance, the wall has been stripped bare to offer a glimpse of the ancient fortification. Besides admiring temporary exhibitions of paintings, you can hear groups of musicians on certain days and sometimes even catch a play (*starting at 11pm*). A clientele of tourists and students.

Theatre

Teatro Académico de Gil Vicente

Praça da República

reservations and tickets: ☎239 82 94 74

If the Portuguese language is no longer a mystery to you, the Teatro Académico de Gil Vicente in the University of Coimbra's cultural centre, offers a particularly rich program with theatre and repertory cinema. Also, if you don't speak Portuguese, you can still appreciate the top-notch ballet and other dance performances that are presented.

Shopping

Coimbra

Coimbra has many shops that can satisfy the most demanding of shoppers. **Rua Ferreira Borges,** the big pedestrian street, remains the most important shopping street. You can do some shopping or merely window shop in the fashionable, and expensive, boutiques.

Crafts

Those looking for handicrafts should go to the **Casa de Artesano Sé Velha** (*Rua do Quebra Costas 61*), where a big choice of terracotta dishes awaits.

Food

Wine, fruit, vegetables, pasta, even shampoo, soap, tissues and more – you'll find it all at **Pingo Doce supermarket** (*Rua João de Ruão*).

Vinho verde, port wine, *licor Beirão* and *aguardente velha* are only a few examples of what you can buy at **Merceria A Camponesa** (*Rua da Louça*), a shop that specializes in alcoholic beverages. Excellent sparkling wines are also available starting at 250 ESC. A great find!

Market

Fruits, vegetables, flowers, clothing and even a few stalls selling takeout food: the very lively **Mercado Municipal** (*Rua Nicolau Rui Fernandes*) offers a pleasant shopping experience. It is located behind Igreja e Mosteiro de Santa Cruz and across from the post office. During your visit to the market, don't miss the amusing *azulejo* panels on Rua Nicolau Rui Fernandes (see p 264).

Porto the hard-working:

this is how the city's inhabitants define their home town. According to the popular saying, while Lisbon has fun, Coimbra studies and Braga prays, Porto works.

Portugal's second-biggest city in terms of population, it remains today, as in the past, a city of business and a major port. Despite its worldwide fame, Porto is relatively poor when it comes to monuments. Scarcely had the conquest of Portugal ended than the movers and shakers of the day showed a preference for Lisbon. Visitors should thus not expect to be wowed by a great number of attractions, but they will be surprised without fail by the spell-binding and mysterious atmosphere this city radiates. Porto, for reasons that seem irrational, practically seduces those that pass through it. After a short stroll through the heart of the city, visitors cannot help succumbing to its charm.

Imagine, for a moment, working-class districts with decrepit houses just a few steps away from sumptuous mansions with baroque ornamentation. Imagine a city where granite churches come across as so austere that it just seemed right to decorate their interiors to excess, with gold leaf streaming everywhere. Imagine broad, orderly avenues skirting alleys, passageways and stairways that criss-cross in an outrageous disorder and complexity. Finally,

imagine the whole ensemble clinging to steep hillsides looking into a harsh river whose banks are tempered by the presence of romantic boats and piers brought to life by a perpetual animation. Is it the telescoping of these various pictures that creates the charm of this great lady? It is up to you to find out.

Even if it is true that Porto, contrary to popular belief, cannot claim to be the place where that marvellous liquid bearing its name is actually produced, the city can pride itself nonetheless on having given the country its name. The names Portus and Cale (also spelled Calle) have been around since 138 BC when these two cities on opposite sides of the Douro were under Roman domination. During the many periods of foreign occupation (Swabian, Visigoth and Muslim), the city of Portus, which meanwhile had become O Porto ("The Port"), developed rapidly and soon overtook its neighbour, Cale, which had originally been the bigger of the two. Toward 1093, as a gesture of thanks for the help provided by the House of Burgundy in its struggle for reconquest, the Castilian Crown entrusted the lands situated between the Minho and the Mondego to Henry of Burgundy. Thus was born the county of Portucale. Although Braga was the capital of this county, O Porto remained an important city.

In 1146, the crusaders of reconquest stopped in its port; influenced by the bishop, they rallied to support the army of King Afonso Henriques and its quest to conquer Lisbon. In this way O Porto confirmed its role as an important seaport and the departure point of many vessels bound for the reconquest. In 1415, under the aegis of Henry the Navigator (one of the city's illustrious sons), a major expedition was mounted to capture Ceuta. The city of O Porto, faced with the task of provisioning the royal fleet, was heavily imposed upon and forced to relinquish most of its food supplies. After the soldiers' departure, the inhabitants had to content themselves with what remained, mostly tripe and offal, which are difficult to conserve during military campaigns. Following this, the inhabitants of Porto were unjustly scorned as *tripeiros* (tripe-eaters). During the 15th and 16th centuries, the port of Porto continued to be a very active spot, occupied mainly with shipbuilding and trade. Despite these activities, the city was forsaken by the Crown to the benefit of Lisbon, its southern rival, and it drew little gain from the great riches brought back from the newly discovered territories, and few prestigious monuments were built there. Later on, the el-Kasr el-Kebir (Alcázarquivir) disaster and the Spanish occupation that followed from 1580 to 1640 plunged Porto into a period of depression punctuated by numerous revolts.

The signing of the Treaty of Methuen (see p 21) in 1703 and the accession of João V marked a period of renewal for the city. While wine production in the Douro Valley grew steadily, its trading and storage in Vila Nova de Gaia (across the shore from Porto) attracted an almost entirely English bourgeois class. Despite the English near-monopoly, Porto benefited from this new manna, and many traders built lavish mansions and enriched their city. Around the same period, King João V, prospering from the discovery of gold mines in Brazil, decided to beautify the city by hiring the era's finest European artists and architects, mostly Italians. Porto became a city where the baroque aesthetic was expressed with such exuberance that some saw it as a sign of pagan perversion.

The 1755 earthquake spared the region, and the city continued to prosper until that Portugal joined the anti-French coalition. In March 1809, Porto was invaded by Napoleonic troops and, while a tragic drowning (see p 296) marked the end of resistance to the invaders, part of the nobility fled into exile in Brazil. Despite its liberation soon afterward, the city and the entire country failed to overcome certain difficulties: the throne was exiled and weakened, and the riches of Brazil had fallen more or less into English hands.

Except for the construction of two major bridges crossing the Douro and the improvement of communications and trade with the rest of the country, Porto's golden years had ended. Throughout the 19th century, the city was shaken by numerous revolts. First there was the liberal revolution of 1820, then the republican uprising of 1891. Moreover, there were disturbances preceding the proclamation of the republic in 1910 and, later, disorders caused by open war between landowners and the working class contributed to a general economic decline. This situation lasted until the dictatorship was established. In 1974, Porto, which had managed rather well under the long years of stability during the Salazar regime, took an active role in the Flower Revolution.

Today, with its half-million inhabitants, Porto is the second biggest city in Portugal. With the artificial port of Leixões, located downstream to the north, the city continues to enjoy great importance as a port city. While exports of wood and its derivatives are significant, fishing still represents an important part of the local economy. Porto continues today as in the past to be an important centre for the distribution and export of wines whose renown is well established.

Several of Porto's historic districts as well as its Dom Luís I bridge (or Ponte Luís I) have been listed as UNESCO World Heritage Sites. The houses of the Ribeira are consequently being restored, and this most popular district is now slowly but surely being overrun with chic restaurants and hip bars. The intrepid city was also selected as 2001's "European Capital of Culture". A great start to the new millennium!

Finding Your Way Around

By Car

From the Airport

To reach the city centre, take the N107 toward Porto. This highway becomes Via Marechal Carmona once it reaches Porto. Continue along this same road and, after passing the large interchange leading to the Cintura Interna, keep right heading toward the Estação da Boavista and the Praça Mouzinho de Albuquerque. After reaching the *praça*, take Rua de Júlio Dinis to the end, then turn left on Rua de Dom Manuel II. At the end, turn right, then left, and head toward the Praça de Lisboa, where the Torre dos Clérigos is situated. It is better to look for parking here and continue on foot. There is a private parking lot along the square.

To reach the airport from the city centre, the most direct route is to go to Rua da Boavista and then to the Praça Mouzinho de Albuquerque. Then follow the same roads mentioned above.

From Lisbon

Take Highway A1-E80 northbound until it enters the city at the Ponte da Arrábida, then take the first exit on the right and continue until the first big intersection, with Rua do Campo Alegre. There, turn right and head to the Praça da Galiza. Then turn right on Rua de Júlio Dinis and, at the end of this street, go left on Rua Dom Manuel II, also taking this street to the end. After that, turn right and then left, and head to the Praça de Lisboa, where the Torre de Clérigos is situated. It is better to look for parking here and continue on foot. There is a private parking lot along the square.

To reach Lisbon from the Praça de Lisboa, head toward the Praça de Gomes Teixeira, situated right next to it, and from there take Rua Dom Manuel II. Then follow the same roads described above.

In the City

The centre of Porto is a difficult place to get around by car. We recommend visiting the city on foot. Besides orientation problems, even more serious here than in Lisbon, parking is a major headache. If you are determined to reach the city centre by car, we advise you to park your vehicle in a guarded parking area, even if it is more expensive. Apart from the time you save, this will protect you from the misfortune of theft which, lamentably, is becoming more frequent in Portugal. The parking lot located next to the Praça de Lisboa, near the Torre dos Clérigos is the most practical for its very central location. Count on spending 560 ESC for 4hrs or 2,500 ESC for 24hrs.

By Bus

From the Airport

STCP (*Sociedade de Transportes Colectivos de Porto*) buses #56 and #87 run regularly between the airport and downtown. Their terminus is right in the heart of the city, at the Praça de Lisboa, near the Campo dos Mártires da Pátria. *Travel time*: approx. 1hr *Fare*: 170 ESC

From Lisbon

Rede Nacional de Expressos and **Renex Expressos** (as well as various other transportation lines) terminal at Avenida Casal Ribeiro, no. 18B *Departure*: many times daily *Travel time*: from 3hrs and 50min to 5hrs and 35min, depending whether the bus stops at Coimbra *Fare*: between 1,900 ESC and 2,100 ESC For information in Lisbon, see p 69.

Leaving Porto

Northbound

Terminal Rodoviária Nacional Praça Filipa de Lencastre Information in Porto: ☏ *222 00 31 52*

Southbound

Terminal Rodoviária Beira Litoral, Rua Alexandre Herculano Information in Porto: ☏ *222 31 24 59*

In the City

The centre of Porto is small enough, and the attractions close enough to each other, that the use of public transport is not really practical.

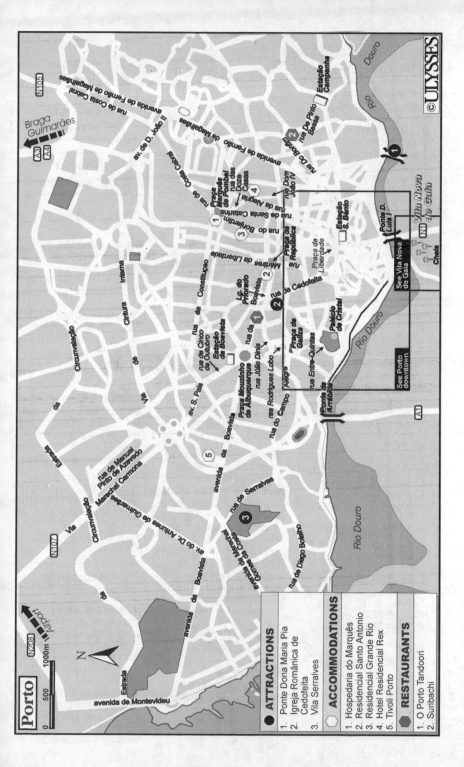

Porto

1000m 500 0
N208 Airport

N

ATTRACTIONS
1. Ponte Dona Maria Pia
2. Igreja Românica de Cedofeita
3. Vila Serralves

ACCOMMODATIONS
1. Hospedaria do Marquês
2. Residencial Santo Antonio
3. Residencial Grande Rio
4. Hotel Residencial Rex
5. Tivoli Porto

RESTAURANTS
1. O Porto Tandoori
2. Suribachi

© ULYSSES

If you do decide to use public transport, there are several ways of paying. The most economical is the *Passe Turístico*, which allows an unlimited number of trips. The *Passe 1 Dia* is around 380 ESC, the *Passe 4 Dias* around 1,710 ESC, and the *Passe 7 Dias* is 2,250 ESC.

By Train

From Lisbon

Up to eight daily departures, with the last one at 7:50pm, leave Santa Apolónia station, on Avenida Infante Dom Henrique. Arrivals in Porto are at Campanhã station. From the station, two choices are available for reaching the city centre, either the suburban train, which goes straight to Estaçao São Bento, or bus #35 or #34, which leaves you downtown. The trip between Lisbon and Porto takes about 3.5hrs.
Fare: Alfa 2nd class, 3,150 ESC; Intercidades, 2,550 ESC

Caminhos de Ferro

Lisbon
☎*218 88 40 25*
☎*218 88 50 92*

Porto
☎*225 56 41 41*

Taxi

Taxis are convenient, cheap and easy to find in the city. Although metres are mandatory, they are sometimes hard to read or are already running when passengers are picked up, so be careful.

Night fares (*from 10pm to 6am*) as well as weekend and holiday fares are slightly higher than the regular daytime fares. The minimum charge is 250 ESC. There is an additional charge of 300 ESC for a second piece of luggage, and 150 ESC if you call for the taxi. It costs around 2,200 ESC to get to the airport.

Walking

When walking around Porto, be patient: At most intersections, you will only see one of the two street names. Sometimes the name is covered by a municipal street sign or is so rusted that it's illegible. The lack of good city maps indicating all the streets and street names also makes walking excursions more difficult.

Practical Information

Tourist Information

Porto

Câmara Municipal Porto
Rua Clube Fenianos 25
4000 Porto
Tourist information for the city only

Câmara Municipal Porto
Rua do Infante Dom Henrique no. 63 (in front of Praça do Infante Dom Henrique)
4000 Porto

ICEP
Palácio da Bolsa, corner Rua da Bolsa and Rua Ferreira Borges
Information on the region and city of Porto

Vila Nova de Gaia

For detailed information on the city and the wine storehouses:

Avenida Diogo Leita 242
4400 Vila Nova de Gaia

Magazines

A Agenda do Porto is an excellent magazine about shows and "happening" events in Porto and the surrounding area. It is published three times a year and is available at Porto's tourist office, most hotels, or on the internet at:
www.agendadoporto.pt

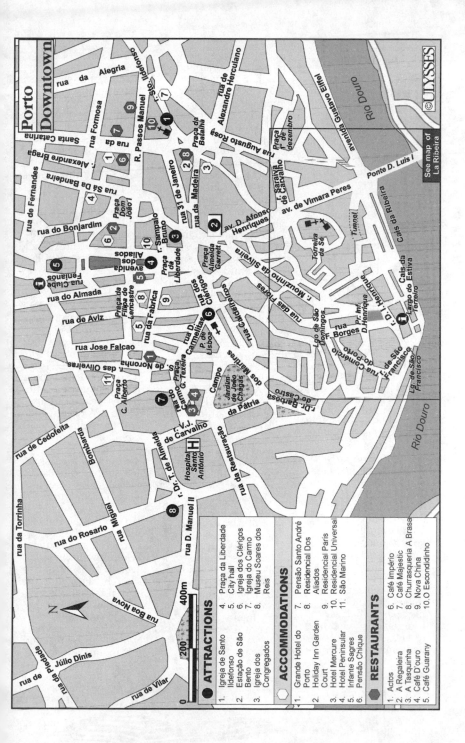

Porto Downtown

ATTRACTIONS

1. Igreja de Santo Ildefonso
2. Estação de São Bento
3. Igreja dos Congregados
4. Praça da Liberdade
5. City hall
6. Igreja dos Clérigos
7. Igreja do Carmo
8. Museu Soares dos Reis

ACCOMMODATIONS

1. Grande Hotel do Porto
2. Holiday Inn Garden Court
3. Hotel Mercure
4. Hotel Peninsular
5. Infante Sagres
6. Pensão Chique
7. Pensão Santo André
8. Residencial Dos Aliados
9. Residencial Paris
10. Residencial Universal
11. São Marino

RESTAURANTS

1. Actos
2. A Regaleira
3. A Tasquinha
4. Café D'ouro
5. Café Guarany
6. Café Império
7. Café Majestic
8. Churrasqueria A Brasa
9. Nova China
10. O Escondidinho

© ULYSSES

See map of La Ribeira

Post Office

Main office
Praça General Humberto
Delgado
*Mon to Fri, 8am to 9pm,
Sat and Sun, 9am to 6pm*

Emergencies

Emergency
(police and ambulance)
☎*112*

Exploring

A tour of the city starts atop Pena Ventosa hill, the spot where, in the 12th century, Count Henry of Burgundy, master of the county of Portucale, had a granite-fortified cathedral built on the site of a simple little chapel. The **Sé** (*9am to noon and 2:30pm to 5:45pm*) is one of the first largest Romanesque monuments erected in Portugal. Entirely rebuilt toward the end of the 13th century and largely remodelled during the 18th century, this fortified cathedral retains few of its original elements. Only the pillars of the central nave, as well as its foundations, remain today as reminders of its Roman past. Somewhat rough in appearance, it presents a motley architectural aspect, and styles as varied as the Romanesque, the Gothic (the rose window), the baroque (the portal and the interior, in part), are blended in a rather strange way. The general appearance is not very pleasing. Inside, attention will be drawn to the main altar, abundantly decorated with saints and golden angels (the work of Nicolo Nasoni, see p 293), and more particularly to the beautiful **silver retable** ★ above the altar in the Holy Sacrament chapel. This retable, conceived during the 17th century by several local silversmiths, is very precious. It escaped pillage by Napoleonic troops thanks to the clergy, who hid it behind a thick wall. At the entrance, you may also notice the beautiful marble holy-water basin. Also worth seeing is the austere 14th-century Cistercian **cloister** (*250 ESC; enter by the right transept*), its walls covered with gorgeous 18th-century *azulejos* ★ depicting Biblical scenes; vestiges of the ancient Romanesque cloister can also be seen.

In front of the Sé, a large esplanade called Torreiro da Sé, adorned by a **cabled pillory** dating from 1945, offers a very interesting vista of the city.

Pillory

A true sense of the complexity of the city, with its churches, houses and other buildings seemingly mixed together inextricably, is evident from here. On the south side of the square is the episcopal palace, built on the very site of the former castle; with its white facade, its pretty wrought-iron balconies and its baroque windows, it forms an elegant 18th-century building. The design of its facade is also the work of Nicolo Nasoni. On the left side of the cathedral, you can admire an equestrian statue representing Vimeira Peires, who freed the city from the brief Muslim occupation. From there, you can catch a distant glimpse of the pretty facade of the Igreja dos Congregados and the belfry of the city hall.

Those with a passion for the baroque can take a series of stairways leading down from the esplanade (found on the right side opposite the Sé) to reach a small square where the impressive facade of São Lorenço church can be admired; it is also called **Igreja dos Grilos**. Visiting the neighbourhoods located further down, which can be reached by an amazing tangle of alleyways in the process of restoration and by stairways that are often dark and dingy, is not particularly pleasant, but it does reveal a working-class facet of Porto. Visitors are strongly advised not to walk here at night or even in the early evening.

To continue the tour, head back up to the cathedral and take Calçada de Vandoma on your right farther down to Rua Saraiva de Carvalho. Praça 1 de Dezembro is further along to the right.

Situated within the Instituto Nacional de Saúde, at the end of a pretty little tree-shaded square, the **Convento y Igreja de Santa Clara** ★★★ (*Mon to Fri 9:30am to 11:30am and 3pm to 6pm, Sat 9am to noon, Larga 1° de Dezembro*) has one of the city's most intensely embellished church interiors. The church and the adjoining convent date from the 15th century but underwent substantial modifications in the 17th and 18th centuries. Before entering the church, you will pass through a superb **portal** ★ with a harmonious mixture of Gothic, Manueline and Renaissance styles. Inside, an incredible profusion of woodwork (*talhas douradas*) seems to brighten the semi-darkness of the place thanks solely to the shine of its gilding. It would seem the sculptors didn't miss a single inch! Unlike São Francisco church (see p 295), the overabundance of sculptures

makes the decor here seem almost grotesque. The only rest for the eyes is provided by the simplicity of the big grill separating the nave and the very beautiful portal leading to the convent. On display in the convent are several paintings and sculptures, mostly from the 18th century.

Leaving the church on the right side, you will see part of the city's ancient wall dating from the 14th century. Situated in the midst of a garden, it is called **Muralha Fernandina** ★ (*entrance at the Instituto Nacional de Saúdo*) in honour of King Dom Fernando I.

Built on the site of the ancient fortifications erected by the Swabians, it once entirely surrounded the city over a distance of 3km. Demolished bit by bit over the centuries, this is the only piece remaining, still adorned with its square towers. By strolling along its covered way, you can take in an interesting view over the Dom Luís I bridge and the Douro.

Go back to Rua de Saraiva de Carvalho and take Rua de Augusto Rosa to Praça da Batalha.

The very vivid Praça da Batalha is worth a visit especially to see the curious-looking facade of the **Igreja de Santo Ildefonso** (*Praça da Batalha*), covered in

pretty *azulejos*. It's all the more attractive at night when floodlights accentuate the contrast between the intense blue of the tiles and the coldness of the granite stones.

Continue on Rua 31 de Janeiro.

Along with Santa Catarina, a street reserved for pedestrians, Rua 31 de Janeiro is one of the best streets in Porto for shopping. Among its many shops, several are worth a visit for their rich decor – a sign of prosperous times. A good example of this can be seen at the very fashionable clothing store **Reis Filhos**, at the corner of Rua Santa Catarina (*Rua Santa Catarina no. 6*), which reveals a luxurious interior as well as an Art-Nouveau entrance. Further along Rua 31 Janeiro, at number 200, stop in at Joalheiro Machado to see the decor in which the jewellery is displayed. And finally, still further on, there's another clothing store to visit at number 174 for its rococo interior.

To continue the tour, head to the Praça de Almeida Garrett.

Occupying the site of a former convent, **Estação de São Bento** (the central railway station) is worth visiting just to see its elegant waiting room. There you can admire the beautiful *azulejo* scenes ★★

Talha Dourada

Talha dourada can be translated literally as "golden carving." It is an art form consisting mostly of wooden sculptures coated with golf leaf. Used individually (in statues, for instance) or in aggregate form (canopies, altars, retables, etc.) they are usually the work of several craftsmen, including sculptors, painters and even architects. *Talha dourada* workshops flourished in the cities of Porto, Braga and Lisbon; they were governed in corporatist and very hierarchical fashion. Broadly promoted by the Catholic church in the Iberian peninsula, the artform served to impress and dazzle the faithful, emphasizing the special nature of religious ceremonies. Widely promoted in Portugal between 1670 and 1770, it experienced a particularly intense period during the reign of João V (1706-1750). To this day, art historians distinguish three different periods: the mannerist period, the baroque period, itself divided into two styles (the national and the Joãonian), and the rococo period. The mannerist period is characterized by decoration described as "minor." *Talhas douradas* are not there only for aesthetic reasons. Mostly geometric, they provide frames for paintings and enrich the elements without really modifying them. The only existing figurative motifs are limited to statues and to a few meagre natural motifs such as leaves. The national baroque period is characterized by an abundance of symbolic themes (vines, children, flowers, bunches of grapes, birds, etc.) and especially by the presence of numerous wreathed columns. Also, and this is unique to Portugal, the monstrance (a type of receptacle) is placed atop a stairway-shaped pyramidal group. The Joãonian baroque develops a decidedly Italian influence with a predominance of lively, exuberant scenes as a main characteristic. A multitude of faces, cherubs, birds, Atlas-like figures and harvest motifs are intertwined. King João V, enriched by the discovery of gold mines in his Brazilian colony, was one of the main promoters, hence the name, Joãonian baroque. Finally, the rococo period corresponds to the familiar architectural style, with excessive curves and sinuous, flamboyant decoration as its most visible elements.

painted by Jorge Colaço in 1930. They relate several of Portugal's great historical events as well as the evolution of transport. Nearby, also facing the Praça de Almeida Garrett, the **Igreja dos Congregados** and its beautiful *azulejo*-covered facade also deserve a glance. The interior, however, is of no great interest.

The adjacent **Praça da Liberdade**, on which a statue of Pedro IV is enthroned, faces the majestic **Avenida dos Aliados**. This broad avenue, with many prestigious buildings scattered along it, is mostly bordered today by office buildings, hotels and banks, set on either side of a central passageway laid out as a garden. It is pleasant to stroll here and admire these big turn-of-the-century buildings, some of them set with domes and statues. At the top of the avenue, the **city hall** adorned with a Flemish-inspired **belfry**, dominates its surroundings. Inside are several murals and tapestries with the city of Porto as their theme.

Returning down toward the Praça da Liberdade, lovers of Art Deco will not want to miss stopping at the **Café Imperial** (*126 Praça da Liberdade, on the left side heading down*), which has recently been turned into a McDonald's of all things. Fortunately, a superb **stained-glass**

window ★ narrating the adventure of coffee, from its harvest to its shipment to its roasting has survived the transformation. Let's hope this little Art Deco treasure is preserved.

Continue your tour by taking Rua dos Clérigos, which will lead you, after a good climb, to the top of the square of the same name.

Built between 1732 and 1748, the **Igreja dos Clérigos** (*Praça de Lisboa*) is one of the finest examples of rococo-style baroque architecture to be found in the city. Once again, the architect was Nicolo Nasoni, an Italian. A master of this art form, Nasoni, who was of Tuscan origin, arrived in Porto in 1725 and worked for King João V until his death in 1773. Nasoni's remains may be found in the church crypt. The church is topped by a large cupola, making its exterior more conspicuous. Behind the church, the **Torre dos Clérigos** ★ (*100 ESC; Mon to Tue, Thu to Sat 10:30am to noon and 3:30pm to 5pm, Sun 10:30am to noon and 3pm to 5pm; Praça de Lisboa*), of the same style, was completed in 1763. Standing 75m high, it is to this day the tallest clock tower in Portugal. Climbing its 225 steps, you will discover a **magnificent panorama** ★ over Porto, the Douro and Vila Nova de Gaia. For a long time, the tower

served as a reference point for the many boats entering the port.

Take Rua Carmelitas to Praça Gomes Teixeira, the site of the university. On the way, stop for an instant at number 144 to see the superb neo-Gothic **facade** ★ of the **Lello & Irmão bookstore** (*Mon to Fri 10am to 7pm, Sat 10am to 7pm; Rua das Carmelitas no. 144*), dating back to the beginning of the century. On the second floor, there are two figures painted on either side of the windows: one represents art, the other science. Be sure to look inside, where they have superb **neo-Gothic wooden sculptures** ★, and a lovely little **staircase** ★ that is also entirely worked. Further along, on Rua do Carmo, the **Igreja do Carmo** ★ (*7:30am to noon and 2pm to 5pm*) has an enchanting 18th-century baroque facade and beautiful exterior *azulejos* dating back to 1912 (right side of the church). Inside, the *talha dourada* retable, worked in detailed rocaille style, is also worth seeing.

Further along the same square, on the west side, you will see the **Santo Antonio hospital** (*Rua Vicente José Carvalho*). This building constitutes a fine example of the English influence in Porto. The signing of the treaty of Methuen brought a sizable English colony

Porto

to Porto toward the end of the 18th century, and little by little they imposed some of their tastes and way of life on a portion of the local bourgeoisie. John Whitehead, the influential British consul, introduced the Palladian aesthetic, then very fashionable in Britain, to Portuguese architecture. Whitehead, a great friend of João de Almada e Melo, head of the city's public works council and a cousin of the Marquis of Pombal, managed to implement a series of building modifications by English architects. Santo Antonio hospital, erected starting in 1770 by English architect John Carr, is a fine example of the monumentality of the Palladian style. It was the first building of this style to be constructed in the city.

By going around the hospital by Rua Dr. Tiago de Almeida, you end up at Rua Dom Manuel II and the **Museu Soares dos Reis** ★ (*350 ESC; Tue-Sun 10am to 12:30pm and 2pm to 5:30pm*). Located in a former palace dating from the end of the 18th century, this museum is dedicated mostly to the sculptor Soares dos Reis (1847-1889), venerated in Portugal most of all for his famous *O Desterrado* ★★ (The Banished), symbolizing *saudade* (nostalgia). Besides these works, the museum also

houses paintings by Portuguese and foreign artists, mostly from the 19th and 20th centuries, as well as some antique furniture and oriental porcelain.

South of the Praça Gomes Teixeira are the Campo dos Martires de la Patria and the charming little *Jardim João Chagas*, a pleasant garden and a good spot to relax. Facing it, the beautifully restored **courthouse** displays its majestic facade.

Take Rua dos Clérigos again and, once you begin going downhill, take the first street on the right to Rua das Flores.

Rua das Flores merits a visit not only to admire its pretty baroque-style dwellings and its many silver shops but also to contemplate the very beautiful **baroque facade** ★ of **Igreja da Misericórdia** (*to the left heading toward and just before the Largo de São Domingos*), also the work of Nicolo Nasoni. Its interior is decorated with gorgeous *azulejos*. Right next door, the **Casa de Misericórdia** (*200 ESC; Mon to Fri 10am to noon and 2pm to 5pm; 15 Rua das Flores*) displays one of Porto's most beautiful and enigmatic paintings, *Fons Vitae* ★★★ (The Fountain of Life). The work portrays a crucified Christ in the middle of a fountain which is flowing with his blood. King Dom Manuel, his wife and

his two children face him on their knees while members of the clergy are praying all around. Executed around 1520, this painting is the work of an unknown artist. To this day, experts suggest it may be by Holbein or even Van der Weyden.

Continue down Rua das Flores until you reach the Largo do São Domingos.

The heavily sloped Largo de São Domingos is followed further down by the Praça do Infante Dom Henrique, a pretty square with a pleasant little park well suited for relaxing. By taking Rua Ferreira Borges, on the left side, you will see the old buildings that used to house a market. Following a tasteful restoration by the city, they now serve as an exhibition centre. This group of buildings, painted all in red, are truly charming.

On the Praça do Infante Dom Henrique itself is the **Palácio da Bolsa** ★ *(guided tours only, 700 ESC; Apr to Oct, Mon to Fri 9am to 6:40pm and Sat to Sun 9am to 12:30pm and 2pm to 6:30pm; Nov to Mar, Mon to Fri 9am to 12:30pm and 2pm to 5:30pm; Rua Ferreira Borges)*. This huge building, with its neoclassical facade used to house Porto's board of trade and ICEP. Today it is occupied by the chamber of commerce. Besides its beautiful marble and granite **stairway** and the rich **interior decoration of the listening room**, it is the **Arab Salon** ★ that draws the most attention. Its rich Moorish decoration is inspired by the Alhambra in Granada.

Perched next to the former board of trade and raised in relation to the street, the **Igreja de São Francisco** ★★★ is one of the most richly decorated churches in Portugal. For this reason, it merits an in-depth visit. After climbing the steps leading to an esplanade, you may start your visit at the small **museum of religious art** *(500 ESC including a visit to the church; Mon to Fri 9:30am to noon and 2:30pm to 5pm, Sat 9am to noon; entry through the monastery, left of the esplanade, Rua do Infante Dom Henriques)*, where several statues and religious items are displayed. In the basement, a crypt is also accessible to the public. You will notice numerous wooden hatches on the ground, beneath which lie the remains of monks who lived at the monastery. The museum also has an upstairs room with several religious paintings. After this brief tour of the museum, head over to the church, across from the entrance to the monastery. From the outside, São Francisco church is not really very exceptional and, like the monastery, it has undergone numerous modifications over the centuries. The most visible examples are the Romanesque-derived southern portal, the Gothic-style rose window and the main portal. The church is noteworthy mostly for its **interior decoration** ★★★. Visitors barely enter the vestibule when they are struck by the richness of the gilding. Whether in the central nave, in the side chapels, in the verge, in the transept or in the choir loft, *talhas douradas* (see box, p 292) are predominant. Starting from the top of the vaults, with a richness seeming to come from the sky, and running down the columns, this gilding surrounds the faithful in such oppressive fashion that the church ended up forbidding worship services here. Granted, this exuberant decoration, executed around 1753 with 210kg of gold, was perhaps not conducive to abnegation and deprivation! Among the outstanding pieces, do not miss the magnificent **Tree of Jesse** ★★, located in the left verge. The interior of São Francisco church is considered today as one of the most accomplished examples of the *talha dourada* technique. Unlike the interior decoration of Santa Clara church (see p 291), the presence of stone, still visible here, somewhat alleviates somewhat the overabundance of decor. This happy mixture gives the church its overall aesthetic quality.

Continue your tour by going east along the wide Rua Infante Dom Henriques; at the second street on the right, go down Rua Alfândega Velha to reach the piers on the Douro.

Shortly before arriving in front of the pier, on

Porto

the left side you will see an ancient residence (*the second-last house before arriving at the pier*) with its windows protected by metal grills and with a recess above the portal. This is the **Casa do Infante** (*Mon to Fri 9am to noon and 2pm to 5pm; Rua Alfândega Velha*). Having housed the customs office from the 14th to the 17th centuries, this house, according to some historians, may have been the birthplace of the infant Enriques, the famous Henry the Navigator in 1394. It was entirely rebuilt during the 17th century and used on and off as the headquarters of the board of trade. Largely restored today, it houses temporary exhibits.

Once in front of the piers, keep to the left while staying alongside them. Midway, in the middle of a pier, you will notice a very audacious building occupied by the **Café do Cais ★** (see p 305). Built entirely of glass and metal, and with long canopies over its broad terrace, it seems to symbolize modern-day *rabelos* (boats loaded with wine casks that used to go down the Douro). The view from this spot is charming with the river and the narrow little houses jumbled next to each other, seeming to reach chaotically toward the sky. Notice that several consulates are located here, showing that the

port wine trade is still important today. In the evening, a stroll along the narrow Rua Fonte Taurina, just behind the piers, enables visitors to see the big changes going on in this neighbourhood. A *movida* has only recently taken over, with many bars, restaurants, and nightclubs moving in here.

Next, head up to the **Praça da Ribeira ★**. Once the most important square within the city walls and a place of intense seafaring activity, today it is frequented mostly by residents of the neighbouring streets; they come to chat or simply to observe the comings and goings of tourists, who may be surprised by the dilapidation of the crumbling facades and the significant amount of laundry hanging from the windows. Despite the ambience, the square has plenty of charm and even a semblance of order. It was under the impetus of Whitehead, the British consul, that the square was entirely redone during the 18th century, yet another example of the English influence on the city. Unfortunately, nothing remains of the former medieval gate or the Palladian-style church that stood here until they were destroyed in the 19th century. Today, an amusing modern fountain with a cube on top is the focal point of the square.

Continuing your walk in the direction of the Dom Luís I bridge, you will soon come to the **Cais da Ribeira ★★**, where part of the ancient Fernandine wall still stands. With the many arcades along its entire length, it now houses many small shops. In small vaulted rooms, you are as likely to find tasty olives or aromatic cheeses as local handicrafts. Just in front, right by the piers, a small fruit and vegetable market is held every day, although Saturday and Sunday are the most important market days. Recently, just as with Rua Fonte Taurina, the Cais da Ribeira has seen several luxurious bistros and restaurants move in, contributing to a lively evening atmosphere.

Continuing alongside the wall, shortly before the bridge, you will notice a commemorative plaque, with flowers and lighted candles left in memory of the catastrophe of May 1809. In those days, a bridge formed by boats enabled people to cross by foot from one shore to the other. During the assault on the city by Napoleonic troops, some inhabitants who feared the worst fled along this bridge. Being too light, the bridge gave way, causing a great number of drownings. The city was freed two months later by English troops.

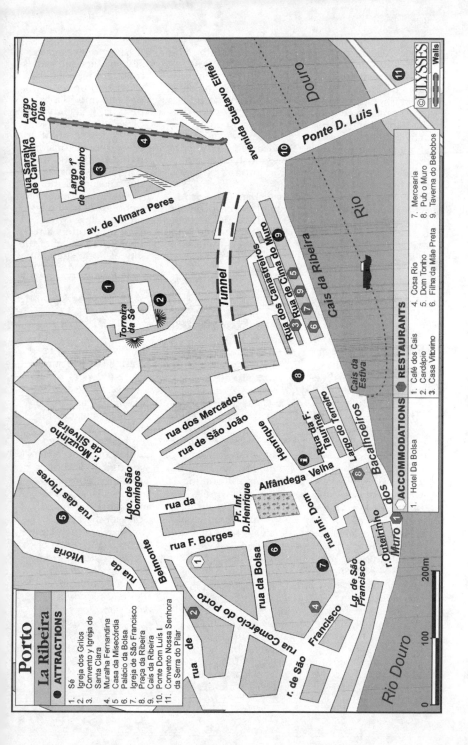

Porto

La Ribeira

● ATTRACTIONS

1. Sé
2. Igreja dos Grilos
3. Convento y Igreja de Santa Clara
4. Muralha Fernandina
5. Casa da Misecórdia
6. Palácio da Bolsa
7. Igreja de São Francisco
8. Praça da Ribeira
9. Cais da Ribeira
10. Ponte Dom Luis I
11. Convento Nossa Senhora da Serra do Pilar

○ ACCOMMODATIONS

1. Hotel Da Bolsa

⬡ RESTAURANTS

1. Café dos Cais
2. Cardápio
3. Casa Vitorino
4. Cosa Rio
5. Dom Toriño
6. Filha da Mãe Preta
7. Mercearia
8. Pub o Muro
9. Taverna do Bebobos

© ULYSSES ▬▬ Walls

Largo Actor Dias

rua Saraiva de Carvalho

Largo 1° de Dezembro

av. de Vimara Peres

avenida Gustavo Eiffel

Douro

Ponte D. Luis I

Rio

Cais da Ribeira

Rua de Cima do Muro

Rua dos Canastreiros

Rua de Cima do Muro

Tunnel

Cais da Estiva

Torreira da Sé

r. Mouzinho da Silveira

rua das Flores

rua da Vitória

rua da Belmonte

Lgo. de São Domingos

rua dos Mercados

rua de São João

rua da

rua F. Borges

Pr. Inf. D.Henrique

Alfândega Velha

rua Inf. Dom Henrique

Rua da F. Taurina

Largo do Terreiro

rua da Bolsa

rua Comércio do Porto

rua de São Francisco

Lg. de São Francisco

r. Outeirinho do Muro

rua dos Bacalhoeiros

Rio Douro

0   100   200m

For a pleasant end to a tour of this area, walk atop the wall, on Rua Cima do Muro. The street offers fine vantage points to contemplate the abundant activity taking place along the piers and also the Dom Luís I bridge, a very graceful metal structure. Across the river, Vila Nova de Gaia seems to arrogantly display its wine storehouses simply to prove that it is the guardian of the precious treasure that has made the Porto name famous. And finally, by making a quick stop at the small Largo Arcos da Ribeira, behind Rua Cimo do Muro, you can see a wonderful example of a revitalized area that had previously suffered from urban decay.

Ponte Dom Luís I ★★. Built between 1880 and 1886 by a Belgian company, this bridge is the work of Portuguese engineer Teófilo Seyrig. It has two levels accessible to cars and pedestrians, and it links the lower and upper towns of Porto and Vila Nova de Gaia. It is fairly unpleasant to cross the upper deck on foot, for it constitutes a major traffic artery, and the continuous noise spoils the pleasure of the views. It is a better option for those who are travelling by car; 60m up, it offers a **very impressive view ★** of the city of Porto stretching

Wine Storehouses

Just as there is for Douro Valley wines, there is a law that demarcates and regulates the storage of port wines. Already a traditional location for storage in the past, Vila Nova de Gaia was chosen officially in 1926 as the only place where port wine could be stocked. It was selected because of the quality of its climate, which is free of intense sunlight, and because of its ideal geographic location at the mouth of the Douro. Since then, several other storage places have been opened. Once the grape harvest and the first blending are over (see the description of port wine production, p 307), the wine is transported from the *quintas* to Vila Nova de Gaia, where it is placed in pipes. These pipes are big casks of Madeira wood that can hold up to 534 litres of wine and age it until it is ready for bottling. Since port wine is nearly always a mixture of several wines, it is also here that the blending is done. While some port wines are ready for consumption as early as their second year, others are stored for 20, 30 or even 40 years. The period of aging, whether in casks or bottles, will vary according to the type of wine desired.

Visiting a wine storehouse is an educational experience. Tours are free and well worthwhile as they nearly always include tastings of white and red port wines. The guides are generally well trained and offer tours in various languages. Tours last 20 to 25min on average. Some of the storehouses also keep table wines, but tastings of these are not offered *(winter: Mon to Fri every storehouse, Sat Porto Câlem only; summer: Mon to Sat every storehouse, Sun Porto Câlem, Sandeman, Vasconcelos and Graham only.)*

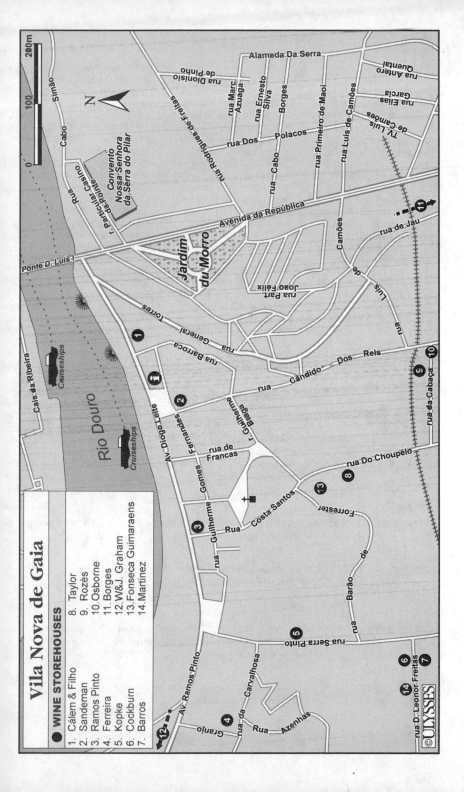

Vila Nova de Gaia

● WINE STOREHOUSES

1. Cálem & Filho
2. Sandeman
3. Ramos Pinto
4. Ferreira
5. Kopke
6. Cockburn
7. Barros
8. Taylor
9. Rozès
10. Osborne
11. Borges
12. W&J. Graham
13. Fonseca Guimaraens
14. Martinez

© ULYSSES

in the distance and, on the other side, of the Douro Valley and the beautiful **Dona Maria Pia railway bridge** ★. The famous Gustave Eiffel was put in charge of erecting the latter between 1875 and 1877. For a more pleasant tour on foot, we suggest taking the lower deck of the Ponte Dom Luís (be careful entering the bridge), from where a **magnificent view** ★ includes the piers on both shores, as well as the Douro Valley. Before you begin your crossing, take a good look at one of the entry pillars of the bridge, with its astonishing helix-shaped stairway, a genuine ·

little geometric and amusing piece of work. Once on the other side of the bridge, you will enter **Vila Nova de Gaia**, which stretches along the river bank across from Porto. This ancient city, formerly known as Cale, went through a prosperous period in the Roman era, becoming more important than its neighbour. Less well exposed, however, it lost its influence starting in the Visigoth period when Portus was chosen for the founding of the Visigoth's archbishopric. During the reign of Afonso III (1248-1279), it nonetheless enjoyed a brief period of development.

As it fell into oblivion, its inhabitants probably did not suspect that, much later, the signing of the Treaty of Methuen in 1703 would enable their city to become the world centre for the production and storage of port wine.

Today, the main attraction is a **visit to the wine storehouses** ★★, an absolute must. Established in great numbers on this side of the Douro, each one proudly displays the company name above the roof. Thus you can see great names such as Sandeman, Borges, Taylor's, Ferreira, Cálem and many others.

The main classifications of Portuguese wines

DOC (Denominação de Origem Controlado): this designation is reserved for Portugal's 19 best wine-growing regions. Wine produced in these regions undergo a number of quality controls.

IPR (Indicação de Proveniência Regulamentada): this appellation indicates from which of the country's 28 regions the wine originated.

VQPRD (Vinhos de Qualidade Produzidos em Regiões Determinadas): the European Union's designation for wines adhering to certain quality standards.

Vinho Regional: refers to wines from one of the eight major wine-growing regions designated in 1992-93 (see map p 31). Certain foreign grape varieties may be planted in these areas.

Vinho de Mesa: literally "table wine", they are produced in Portugal but the specific region is not indicated on the label.

Most wine storehouses offer guided tours of their facilities with free samplings. They also sell wine for better prices than you would pay elsewhere. Before beginning your tour of the wine storehouses, however, take the time to stroll along **Avenida Diogo Leite**, which runs alongside the Douro and provides a magnificent **view of Porto ★★★**, perhaps the most beautiful of all. The city and its piers are reflected in almost surreal fashion in the waters of the river. Moored along the bank, several *rabelos*, loaded with wine casks as in the past, add a further touch of romanticism to the scene.

Perched atop Vila Nova de Gaia, facing the upper deck of the Dom Luís I bridge, **Nossa Senhora da Serra do Pilar convent**, whose rotunda-shaped church is attached to a cloister, also circular in shape (*no visits allowed*), has a pleasant terrace offering a fine **panorama ★** of the Douro and its valley.

It was from this spot in 1809 that the English troops pounded the city to dislodge the Napoleonic troops. Although the site is stunning, visiting it should be left to the courageous. Accessing the site via the Dom Luís I bridge is long and not recommended for anyone who is afraid of heights.

Lovers of Romanesque art should visit the **Igreja Românica de Cedofeita ★** (*Rua da Cedofeita, near Avenida da Boavista*) to admire what some historians say may be the oldest Christian church in Portugal. Its foundations go back to 556, when it was erected by King Theodimir of Swabia. The current building dates back to the 12th century; despite its remodelled interior, it still has a superb portal in the purest early Roman style.

Located next to a pleasant park, the **Museu Romântico** (*100 ESC; Tue to Sun 10am to noon and 2pm to 5pm; 220 Rua de Entre Quintas*) exhibits antique European furniture in a setting redolent of the interior of a bourgeois house of the late 19th century.

Head west along Avenida da Boavista until you approach Avenida do Marechal Gomes da Costa and then take Rua de Serralves to admire the **Vila Serralves ★**. This 1930s ensemble will mostly interest those who like Art Deco. Built between 1925 and 1944 for a wealthy industrialist named Carlos Alberto Cabral, this is the work, both inside and outside, of several prestigious architects and designers including José Marques da Silva (for most of the structure), and Ruhlmann, Leleu, Lalique and Silva Bruhns (for the furniture and the interior decoration). Acquired by the Portuguese government in 1987, the estate is now managed by the Serralves Foundation, which uses the building as a centre for contemporary culture.

The foundation has recently opened the **Museu Serralves** (*800 ESC with access to the park, 500 ESC park only; Tue, Wed, Sat and Sun 10am to 7pm, Thu until 10pm; Rua de D. João de Castro, no. 210, ☎226 15 65 00*), Porto's first museum of modern art, in the beautiful **park ★** (*500 ESC; same schedule as the museum*) of the estate, one of the largest in the

Porto

Fundacao Serralves

city. The work of architect Alvaro Siza Vieira, the immaculate modern building is too massive in appearance and somewhat disappointing-looking. As for the excessively white interior, it is comprised of corridors and overly large rooms, devoid of any great originality. The new museum's goal is to assemble a permanent collection of contemporary art works from the 1960s to the present by both Portuguese and foreign artists.

★

The Douro Valley

The Douro Valley's contrasting weather, with harsh winters and hot summers, plays an important role in the production of Porto's famous wine; you can learn other secrets about this heavenly beverage at Vila Nova da Gaia (see box, p 298). While exploring the region, you will discover lovely steep valleys where terrace cultivation has shaped the landscape into fascinating undulations. However, due to the area's weak tourist infrastructure and the relative absence of historic attractions, the Douro Valley is primarily of interest to visitors in search of beautiful landscapes and scenic views. The Douro Valley extends across the Montanhas region, and the itinerary sug-

gested on p 357 will help you explore both the valley and the charming nearby town of Lamego.

Outdoor Activities

Cruises

Going up the Douro by boat is an unforgettable experience. During the high season, several companies offer outings for most budgets. For example, a cruise under the bridges that span the Douro lasts approximately an hour and costs about 1,500 ESC. An excursion up to the vineyards, lasting a full day and including breakfast and lunch, costs about 15,000 ESC. Several companies also offer night cruises, dinner included. Here are a few that offer these services:

Endouro
Rua da Reboleira no. 49-51
4050 Porto
☎ 223 32 42 36
⇌ 222 05 72 60

Douro Azul
Sociedade Marítimo Turística, LDA, Rua do São Francisco no. 4, 2nd floor, 4050 Porto
☎ 223 39 39 50
⇌ 222 08 34 07
Departures from Cais da Ribeira.

Turisdouro
For a *Rabelo* boat trip:
Rua Machado dos Santos no. 824, 4th floor, 4400 Vila Nova de Gaia
☎ 223 70 84 29
⇌ 223 70 63 89
Departures from Avenida Ramos Pinto, Cais da Gaia.

Via Douro
For a *Rabelo* boat trip:
Empreendimentos Turísticos, LDA, Edifício D. Nono, Praceta D. Nono, Álvares Pereira no. 20 3rd floor, 4450 Matosinhos
☎/⇌ 229 38 81 39
Departures from Cais da Estiva.

🛏

Accommodations

Pousada da Juventude do Porto
Rua Paulo da Gama 551
☎ 226 17 72 57

Pensão Residencial Santo André
$ no bkfst
pb
Rua Santo Ildefonso no. 112
4000 Porto
☎ 222 05 58 69
In a calm area on a street reserved for pedestrians, the Pensão Residencial Santo André has small rooms on three floors. The building has no particular allure and the decor in the rooms is rudimentary, but the property is well maintained, and you are greeted with a warm welcome. A good spot for travellers on restrictive budgets!

Hospedaria do Marquês
$
pb, tv
Praça do Marquês de
Pombal 181
☎*225 02 27 45*
A little away from the
city centre but in front
of a pleasant little park,
Hospedaria do Marquês
has 18 rooms with
modern furnishings;
most have views of the
park. Clean and quiet.

Residencial Santo Antonio
$ *no bkfst*
pb, tv
Rua Dom João IV no. 990
☎*225 07 02 01*
Located away from
downtown on a busy
street, the Residencial
Santo Antonio offers
well-maintained rooms
decorated with an odd
assortment of furniture.
The reception area,
attractively decorated
with *azulejos*, and the
many plants adorning
the other common ar-
eas make this a pleas-
ant, yet modest place to
stay.

Residencial Grande Rio
$
pb, tv
Rua do Bomjardim no. 77
4000 Porto
☎*225 09 40 32*
=*225 50 32 26*
Set on a quiet street,
Residencial Grande Rio
is a small hotel with 10
comfortably furnished
rooms. Mostly set at the
back of the building
and decorated in mod-
ern style, they consti-
tute an ideal spot for
people looking for
peace and quiet.

Pensão Chique
$
pb, tv
Avenida dos Aliados 206
2nd floor, 4000 Porto
☎*222 00 90 11*
=*223 32 29 63*
Occupying the first
floor up in a distinctive
building, Pensão
Chique is probably the
best pension in its cate-
gory. Well located in
the centre of town, it
has 23 comfortable
rooms, a few with
views of pretty Avenida
dos Aliados. This place
is well maintained, and
the decor is becoming.
Moreover, the friendly
staff welcome you with
a smile. Excellent
value.

**Pensão Residencial São
Marino**
$
pb, tv
Praça Carlos Alberto 59
4050 Porto
☎*223 32 54 99*
☎*222 05 43 80*
Set in an appealing
little house, Pensão
Residencial São Marino
faces an elegant tree-
shaded square, not far
from the main tourist
attractions. Among its
17 rooms, only a few
have views of the
square. This is a spot to
keep in mind.

Residencial Paris
$
pb
Rua da Fabrica no. 27-29
4050 Porto
☎*222 07 31 40*
☎*222 07 31 49*
=*222 08 22 65*
Well situated near the
Praça da Liberdade, the
Residencial Paris offers
around 40 rooms with

modest furnishings.
Visitors have a televi-
sion room at their dis-
posal and breakfast is
served in a room with
windows that open
onto a charming gar-
den.

Hotel Peninsular
$
pb, tv, ≈
Rua Sá da Bandeira 21
4000 Porto
☎*222 00 30 12*
=*222 08 49 84*
Located on a very busy
street, this 57-room
hotel is advantageously
located just a few steps
from São Bento railway
station and very near
the Sé. Its rooms,
though dark and fur-
nished in tasteless mod-
ern style, are well
equipped and main-
tained. Special prices
for students.

Residencial Dos Aliados
$$
pb, tv
Rua Elisio de Melo 27
4000 Porto
☎*222 00 48 53*
=*222 00 27 10*
Occupying a distinctive
building, this big hotel
offers rooms with old-
fashioned furnishings.
A bit antiquated but
very comfortable.

Residencial Universal
$$
pb and *ps, tv*
Avenida dos Aliados 38
1st floor, 4000 Porto
☎*222 00 67 58*
=*222 00 10 55*
This well-appointed 46-
room hotel has the
great advantage of of-
fering fine views over
the Praça Liberdade.
The lobby is well deco-

rated, but the rooms are plain. The efficient and friendly staff makes this a good spot.

Hotel Residencial Rex
$$
pb, tv
Praça da República no. 117
4050 Porto
☎222 00 45 48
Despite a particularly attractive reception area, this family *residencial*, in an old middle-class abode from the late 1800's, has only a few modestly furnished rooms. The property is well maintained and you can go for your morning jog in the small park across the street.

Hotel Residencial da Bolsa
$$$
pb, tv, ≡
Rua Ferreira Borges 101
4050 Porto
☎222 02 67 68
⇌222 05 88 88
This elegant hotel is one of the few located right near the Cais da Ribeira, a tourist area with a lively night scene. Tastefully decorated, it has a modern feel and offers very comfortable rooms. Ask for a room on one of the top three floors, where the views are pleasant. With its exceptional site and friendly staff, this is one of the best spots in Porto.

Grande Hotel do Porto
$$$
pb, tv
Rua de Santa Catarina no. 197
4000 Porto
☎222 00 81 76
☎222 00 57 41
⇌222 31 10 61
Located on Rua Santa Catarina, a pedestrian street with many shops, this hotel from the beginning of the century has managed to furnish its rooms comfortably while maintaining certain antique characteristics. The only drawback in this charming environment is that it offers a relatively poor quality for the high prices charged.

Hotel Mercure Batalha
$$$
pb, tv, ≡, ℜ
Praça da Batalha no. 116
4000 Porto
☎222 00 05 71
⇌222 00 24 68
In a large building across from the very colourful Praça da Batalha, the Hotel Mercure Batalha offers about 100 comfortably furnished rooms. The decor of both the rooms and the common areas is somewhat unoriginal and reminiscent of the 1970s. To get a pleasant view of the Sé, rent a room at the back of the building, on one of the upper floors.

Holiday Inn Garden Court
$$$
pb, tv
Praça da Batalha no. 127-130
4000 Porto
☎223 39 23 00
⇌222 00 60 09
Opened just recently, this Holiday Inn is particularly noteworthy for its convenient location, a stone's throw from the many shops on Rua Santa Catarina and 20min walking distance from the Ribeira district. Its 113 rooms are small, but appointed with appealing furnishings and matching fabrics. A pleasant little detail: thick stone walls adorn both the lobby and the breakfast room. Another perk: the hotel has non-smoking rooms.

Hotel Infante Sagres
$$$$
pb, tv, ≡, ℜ
Praça D. Filipa de Lencastre 62
4050 Porto
☎222 01 90 31
⇌222 31 49 37
Luxury and good taste meet in this charming hotel located right in the centre of town. In the rotunda of the lobby you will discover a superb stained glass window, and just next to it is a lounge furnished entirely with antiques and enhanced by a lovely fireplace, giving visitors a warm welcome. Outside, a pretty patio with plants and a fountain embellishes the setting. Rooms are comfortably appointed with modern furnishings. In this attractive hotel, the only blot is the reception,

which could be a bit friendlier.

Tivoli Porto
$$$$
pb, tv, ≈
Rua Afonso Lopes Vieira no. 66
4100-020 Porto
☎ *226 09 49 41*
≈ *226 06 74 52*
Away from the town centre and near major roads, this hotel is conveniently located near Porto's suburbs. Despite its dreary concrete exterior and surroundings, made up of residential buildings, the Tivoli Porto features a pleasant interior layout. Appointed with tasteful furnishings, its rooms and suites have a certain style. Comfort awaits, of course, and every room boasts a lovely, fully marbled bathroom. At the back of the building is a terrace as well as a large swimming pool surrounded by a garden, another considerable perk. Breakfast is served in a small room with a view of the garden.

Restaurants

Tripas à moda do Porto, containing a mixture of veal tripes, chicken, *chorço* and other sausages, ham and beans, is a Portuguese culinary specialty served in most restaurants. If you have a strong stomach, try "the thing".

If you're only a little bit hungry, the **Via Catarina** shopping centre (*every day; Rua de Santa Catarina no. 312-350, between Rua Fernandes Tomás and Rua Formosa*) is a good choice. On the fourth floor you will find a number of self-serve restaurants, the front of each modelled after the facade of a typical Porto house. Pleasant and fun!

Café Guarany
$
7am to 10pm, closed Sat
Avenida dos Aliados 89
Omelettes, hamburgers, meat or fish for under 1,200 ESC in a big room where Art Deco once reigned supreme. Service is slow and somewhat nonchalant.

Churrasqueria a Brasa
$
Praça da Batalha
You certainly wouldn't go to Churrasqueria a Brasa for its ambience, and plastic chairs and neon lighting don't help either, but rather to sample some of their famous grilled meat or chicken. For as little as 600 ESC, you can get tasty ribs accompanied by a refreshing beer (*180 ESC*), unless you prefer a grilled quarter-chicken (*480 ESC*). A good spot if you're on a tight budget.

Restaurante Nova China
$
Rua de Passos
Manuel no. 203 A-B
☎ *222 08 64 18*
The decor of the Restaurante Nova China

is devoid of charm and the food isn't highly original but the prices are very enticing for travellers on a tight budget!

Pub O Muro
$
every day 4pm to 2am
87-88 Muro dos Bacalhoeiros
☎ *222 08 34 26*
With its amusing burlap-covered ceiling, the many assorted decorative knick-knacks and magnificent little tables and chairs, Pub O Muro is quite charming. The food isn't outstanding, but the various *petiscos* and *feijoadas* provide sustenance. In season, there is a small terrace that allows you to contemplate the view of the Douro.

Café Império
$
Mon to Sat
Rua da Santa Catarina, across from Café Majestic
Whether it's for a small sandwich or a refreshing, inexpensive salad, Café Império is an interesting spot, all the more so considering the vast choice of exceptionally appetizing desserts offered here.

Café do Cais
$$
every day 10:30am to 2am
Casa da Estiva
☎ *222 08 83 85*
Built entirely of glass and metal (see p 296) and appointed with light-wood furniture, this modern restaurant and bistro is a very pleasant spot for a

drink or a light meal (hamburgers, salads, pastries, etc.). Its terrace, with long canopies, offers a superb view of the shores of Vila Nova de Gaia. The only disappointment in this design-oriented eatery is that the furnishings and the long canopies lining the garden have aged considerably. A spot not to be missed.

Casa Filha da Mãe Preta
$$
Mon to Sat
Cais da Ribeira no. 40
☎*222 05 55 15*
Wide exposed wooden beams and *azulejos* are the principal elements of decor in this inviting restaurant that offers good-quality standard Portuguese dishes. Tourist menu for 1,750 ESC.

A Regaleira
$$
noon to midnight, closed Sat
Rua do Bomjardin 87
Whether its for a quick snack (*snack menu starting at 550 ESC*) or a more copious meal, A Regaleira restaurant welcomes you in a big room with 1930s decor, set around an enormous counter. Classic cuisine.

Cardápio
$$
Rua Comercio do Porto no. 197
☎*222 08 84 53*
With high ceilings and a small mezzanine, Cardápio, decorated in pastel tones in a sparse and modern manner, offers a pleasant ambi-

ance. Here you can sample a good *frango estefado* or a *filete do pescado* for 700 ESC. Tourist menus for 2,200 ESC are also offered, but the choice tends to be limited and fairly unoriginal.

A Tasquinha
$$
9:30am to 9:30pm
Rua do Carmo 23
This restaurant, located in a charming little house with a rustic atmosphere, offers unpretentious Portuguese cuisine. Half-portions available.

🛥 **Restaurante Suribachi**
$$
Mon to Sat noon to 3pm
136 Rua do Bonfim
☎*225 10 67 00*
Vegetarians and others who appreciate the benefits of meatless fare should definitely investigate Restaurante Suribachi, located in the back of a health-food store. In this warm environment, you can enjoy delicious *seitan* and *tofu* dishes, salads and even a succulent fish *caldeirada* for the less strict. After making your choice at the self-serve counter, feel free to head upstairs, where you will find several small rooms and an amusing little, abundantly flowered winter garden. Although a bit cramped, it's very pleasant, and the tight quarters promote interaction with local residents.

Taverna do Bebobos
$$$
Tue to Sun noon to 3pm and 7:30pm to 11pm
Cais da Ribeira 24-25
☎*222 05 35 65*
This small restaurant is very popular with the Portuguese; it specializes in northern cuisine. Reservations advised.

Cosa Rio
$$$
Fri and Sat
Rua de São Francisco no. 8
☎*222 00 07 12*
Whether it's to quench your thirst at the bar on the ground floor, or to have a meal in the pleasant dining room upstairs, the Cosa Rio restaurant offers something for everyone. With both Portuguese and international cuisine, the menu is more varied than most, and there is a tourist menu starting at 2,700 ESC.

Casa Vitorino
$$$
Mon to Sat noon to 3pm and 7pm to 11pm
Rua Canastreiros 44-48
☎*222 08 06 68*
Here it is a true pleasure to enjoy excellent fish (salmon or trout) or *cabrito* (goat) grilled on site where stone walls and modern furnishings blend seamlessly. For dessert, try the coconut cake or the rum omelette.

Port Wine Production

Many people know this delightful beverage as an aperitif or digestif, but few know how it differs from most other wines in its production. Whether red or white, the grapes that go into these wines are grown in strictly demarcated areas and thus have a controlled designation (*appellation contrôlée*, or *região demarcada*). There are two important differences in the wine-making method compared to classical wines: the first is that in the middle of the fermentation process the grape skins are separated from their juice; the second is that high-alcohol grape liquor is added to stop the fermentation process. The wine thus obtained should have an alcohol content of about 20%. This sudden interruption of the fermentation allows the sugars contained in the grape to stay in their basic state, giving the wine a superior sweetness. Also, since the fermentation process lasts only two or three days, the grapes have to be crushed with bare feet to obtain enough tannin. This ancient method, formerly part of the production of all wines, is still widely used in the making of port wine.

For more information:
IVP
(Instituto do Vinho do Porto)
Rua de Ferreira Borges 27
4050 Porto
☎**222 07 16 00**
⇥*222 07 16 99*

Porto

🚢 Restaurant Mercearia
$$$
Mon to Sat noon to 3pm and 6:30pm to 11pm
Cais da Ribeira 32-33
☎*222 00 43 89*
As its name indicates in Portuguese, this restaurant used to be a little grocery store whose charm can still be appreciated. You can have your pre-dinner drink on the ground floor surrounded by the antique furnishings of the grocery. Upstairs, a pretty vaulted room welcomes visitors in a refined and warm setting. Those who are romantically inclined may ask for a table near the arched window: the view over the Douro is especially beautiful. On the menu: salmon soup, partridge *à la Mercearia*, Porto-style tripe, etc. Good food and friendly staff.

O Escondidinho
$$$
Mon to Sat
Rua de Passos Manuel no. 142-146
☎*222 00 10 79*
If you are interested in dining in a conventional setting with formal service, O Escondidinho offers just that. Their regional Portuguese cuisine is of good quality but not terribly original. Ideal for business dinners.

🚢 Restaurante e Bar Dom Tonho
$$$
every day 12:30pm to 3pm and 7:30pm to 11pm
Cais da Ribeira 13-15
☎*222 00 43 07*
⇥*222 01 30 93*
Restaurante e Bar Dom Tonho is Porto's most fashionable restaurant and bar. Founded by the famous Portuguese rock star Rui Veloso, it is spread over two levels. Downstairs, near the piers, is a futuristic bar (see p 309); up-

stairs, next to the Rua Cima do Muro, is the restaurant. Decorated in austere modern style with designer lighting, the restaurant was set up in such a way as to allow part of the ancient city wall to be exposed, the effect contrasting subtly with the inviting furnishings. During the restoration, workers discovered a small and ancient interior courtyard with a fountain, visible from the back of the restaurant. Also on view is a photo exhibition of old Porto and of the flooding of the Douro in 1962 and 1978. As for the menu, it leans to the classic, though the kitchen does create a few originals, and all dishes are carefully prepared.

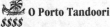 **O Porto Tandoori**
$$$$
Mon to Sun 7:30pm to 10:30pm
Largo do Priorado no. 104 opposite the Igreja Românica de Cedofeita
☎*222 08 53 91*
☎*222 00 06 97*
Set up on the second floor of a lovely house, this restaurant's dining room has a surprisingly Spartan character. Indeed, were it not for the delicious aromas emanating from the kitchen, the marvels of India would seem altogether absent. The usual Oriental paintings and tapestries are thus lacking and, with the exception of two impressive vases, the decor is confined to candle-lit tables and

wooden chairs. Fortunately, the food is a whole other matter. Tandoori chicken, beef with red curry, *murgh tikka masala*, *sheekh kebab* and many other specialties lend colour to the plates and delight the most demanding of palates. A few starters and vegetarian dishes are also available. Add to this the appealing selection of Indian music and jazz playing in the background, and you have the makings for a wonderful evening. The only hitch is the rather inelegant and tactless presence of the cash register in the very dining room.

Cafés and Tearooms

Café Majestic
Mon to Sat 8am to 1am
Rua Santa Catarina 112
Small marble tables, leather-covered chairs and booths, carvings of Madeira wood, objects of molten glass: such is the decor of this beautiful Art-Deco-inspired venue, popular with local artists and high society types. An economical *chá* (tea) service is offered for the modest sum of 1,000 ESC (1750 ESC for two people), including a choice of tea, hot chocolate or coffee with buttered toast, *petits fours* and a piece of pie. Despite its high prices, this remains a very pleasant spot for an afternoon break, and, with a bit of luck,

you can catch one of the small piano performances that are graciously offered on certain afternoons. Painting enthusiasts should have a look in the basement of the building where an art gallery has been set up.

Bica or Cimbalino?

You will often hear the word *cimbalino* in bistros and outdoor terraces. Keep in mind that it refers to a simple coffee. This term replaces *bica*, which is used more in Lisbon. This is just one of the many ways that Porto's residents distinguish themselves from their compatriots in the capital.

Pastelaria Império
Mon to Sat
Rua da Santa Catarina no. 149
A pastry shop with the most ordinary of interiors, but what a window display! They offer a wide assortment of pastries, each more appetizing than the last, and it's a good bet that after contemplating so many goodies, you won't be able to keep yourself from trying one! Enjoy!

Actos Casa de Chá
Tue to Sun 4pm to 2am
Rua Sá de Noronha 76, upstairs
ring to enter
Perhaps the most original tea house in Porto, the Actos Casa de Chá is well worth a visit. On the second floor of a private house, you can have tea or coffee in an intimate setting while seated on a comfortable sofa. Despite the limited choice of desserts, the *bolo de chocolate* is excellent. Light meals are also offered. Temporary exhibitions marvellously round out the charm of this spot, where intellectuals and people from Porto's wealthy families rub shoulders. A must see.

Café D'Ouro
Praça de Parada Leitão, behind the university
Those who prefer a more resolutely student atmosphere may want to head for the Café D'Ouro. Portuguese youth gather on the terrace here to contemplate their existence.

Entertainment

Fado

Mal Cozinhado
Mon to Sat 8:30pm to 3am
Rua do Outerinho 13
☎*222 02 63 84*
Although very touristy, this is an excellent spot to hear a *fado*, as good as any in Lisbon.

Drinks are rather expensive, though.

Bars and Nightclubs

Anikibóbó
Mon to Sat 9pm to 2am
Rua da Fonte Taurina 36-38
A wall covered with scaffolding, a sofa suspended on four steel cables, columns in glazed blue tones and a clientele of artists and trendy types: that's Anikibóbó. The club is named after the title of a Manuel de Oliveira film produced in the 1940s. In this attractive modern bar, blue, yellow and red blend harmoniously. Pleasant music and excellent Belgian beers are featured.

Porto Feio
Tue to Sam 10pm to 2am
Rua da Fonte Taurina 52
Porto Feio is the ideal spot to sip a delicious port wine in a room decorated with various old objects.

Cibercafé
Mon to Thu 10am to midnight, Fri and Sat 10am to 2am, Sun 2pm to 10pm
Rua Mártires da Liberdade no. 223-225
www.cibercafe.pt
As you've probably guessed, this is where "cybernauts" meet. In a modern and relaxed setting, you can explore the Net for 800 ESC per hour (*400 ESC, 30min*) or simply have a drink and chat with some Internet experts.

Bar Meia-Cave
Tue to Sat 10pm to 4am
Praça da Ribeira no. 6
In the heart of the old town, right on Praça da Ribeira, Bar Meia-Cave is one of the Porto's hip new nightclubs. After walking through their large modern red doors that are a bit out of place on the pretty Praça, you can quench your thirst to the sound of an eclectic assortment of music in an environment that is hypercharged on weekends.

Bar e Restaurante Dom Tonho
Mon to Thu 12:30pm to 3pm and 7:30pm to midnight, Fri and Sun until 2am
Cais da Ribeira 13-15
Steel is a key element in the decor of the futuristic bar of the Bar e Restaurante Dom Tonho, frequented by artists and a trendy crowd (see also p 307). Its owner, singer Rui Veloso, is known as the originator of Portuguese rock.

Bar Jam
Rua Comercio do Porto no. 155
Behind a huge window composed of many smaller ones, you will discover by surprise a large, almost theatrical room with imposing red velvet curtains and dramatic lighting. This lively (and smoky!) place is ideal for an evening of conversation.

Porto

Salão de Chá Aviz
every day 7am to midnight
Rua de Aviz no. 37
If you love billiards, make sure to drop by Salão de Chá Aviz, a virtual shrine to the game. On the ground floor you will find a large hall with an eclectic decor where customers come for refreshments (*petiscos* and pastries also available). In the basement, numerous pool tables are lined up just waiting to be used for a game.

Contra a Corrente
every day noon to 2am
Avenida Diego Leite 282, Vila Nova de Gaia
This pleasant little bar is interesting especially for its terrace with a view of Porto and its piers. Ideal for a drink or a *cimbalino*.

Pipa Velha Petisqueira
Rua das Oliveiras no. 75
With its stone walls and rustic furniture, Pipa Velha Petisqueira is great if you want to go for a drink in a warm setting. It's a small bar with a diverse clientele and alternating contemporary painting exhibitions.

Suave Café Bar
Rua do Dr. Barbosa de Castro no. 56
Popular among young people, the Portuguese Suave Café Bar is perfect if you're looking for a lively place. Interesting lighting and a pool table complement the moderately sparse decor.

Gay and Lesbian Bars

Moinho de Vento
every day 10pm to 2am
Rua de Sá de Noronha 76-78
ring to enter
The modern decor of this bar attracts a happening crowd that often includes a few transvestites. The finest gay bar in town. Guaranteed atmosphere.

Bar BZZZ
Rua da Reboleira no. 12
In a sparse modern setting, where bright colours and a counter made of glass blocks make up the electrifying decor, the small Bar BZZZ serves a mostly lesbian clientele comprised mostly of women. They offer light Portuguese dishes like the *caldo verde* (200 ESC) and various *petiscos*.

Cultural Activities and Festivals

Porto is rich in activities of all sorts almost year-round. Among the months with the most festivities, June comes up tops. The celebration of St. John (São João), the most popular of feast days, falls in the second half of the month, when the streets and back alleys are covered with all sorts of ornaments, including marionettes and aromatic plants. At nightfall, spontaneous parades are formed, and the real celebrations begin.

Shopping

Rua Santa Catarina, part of it a pedestrian mall, is the street with the most shops. It has everything to satisfy the intrepid shopper. On the left side of the street as you head north, the building occupied by the **C&A** store is another eye-catcher. Three giant statues that seem to hold up the cornices tower over the roof, while at the corner of the building a very pretty carillon clock chimes the hours.

Bookstores

Livaria Latina (*Mon to Sat 10am to noon and 2pm to 6pm; Rua Santa Catarina no. 2-10*). Books, newspapers and magazines in Portuguese, Spanish and English, and even a good selection of French novels: everything to satisfy booklovers.

The **Lello & Irmão** bookstore (*Mon to Fri 10am to 7pm, Sat 10am to 7pm; Rua das Carmelitas no. 144*) a little architectural gem (also see p 293), offers an extensive selection of fiction, maps, guides, and art books in various languages. You can even enjoy a *bica*, or *cimbalino* while comfortably seated at one of their tables on the second floor.

Crafts

Beneath the vaults of the wall, **Casa das Cestinhas** (*Casa da Ribeira 34*) offers various small and tasteful handicrafts items at reasonable prices.

Centro Regional de Artes Tradicionais (*Tue to Fri 10am to noon and 1pm to 6pm, Sat and Sun 1pm to 7pm; Rua da Riboleira no. 33-37 or Muro dos Bacalhoeiros no. 137*). As its name in Portuguese indicates, this centre is devoted to the promotion of traditional arts, particularly from the northern regions of Portugal. You can purchase various cultural objects or works by artisans from Porto and the Minho region.

Food

Garrafeira do Carmo (*Rua do Carmo 17-18, ☎222 00 32 85*). An appealing little shop with a big choice of port wines and other regional wines. You can also find dried cod.

On the Cais da Ribeira, the charming **Azeitoneira do Porto** boutique (*Mon to Sat 9am to 7:30pm, Sun 9am to 3:30pm; Cais da Ribeira 36*) is worth a visit on its own. Set under the vaults of the ancient Fernandine wall, this little shop

offers a fine choice of olives as well as cheeses, sausages and bread. The charming owner will be happy to have you sample her excellent olives. She will tell you that her family has run this shop for three generations. Among the curiosities, try the Boroa de Aveintas, a very rich-tasting multi-grain bread. Add a few olives and a chunk of cheese, and you have the fixings for an excellent picnic.

For eggs, bread, vegetables, spaghetti sauce and other produce, in other words, if you can choose by yourself, the **Pingo Doce** supermarket (*Rua Passos Manuel no. 221*) will meet all your needs.

Markets

Everything from clothing to footwear, kitchen items, cleaning products and all sorts of other accessories are sold at the **general market** (*Torreiro da Sé*), which is really busy every Saturday morning. Another market, located below the cathedral and busy every day, is in an

exceptional working-class district where you will discover an incredible assortment of products. Watch out for pick-pockets, however.

The **Numismatic market** (*Praça Dom João I; every Sunday morning*) sells coins, of course, but also medals, old postcards and a few antiques.

A very typically Portuguese atmosphere prevails at the **Animal market** (*Praça Almeida Garett at Rua da Madeira; every Sunday morning*), filled with birds, dogs, cats, hens, etc.

Flowers, fruits, vegetables, fish, meat and even a few prepared dishes that you can eat on the spot, all in a genuinely Portuguese ambience: this is what you will find at the **Mercado do Bolhão** (*corner of Rua Formosa and Rua Alexandre Braga*). Not far from there, at no. 279 Rua Formosa, don't miss seeing the charming facade of the **A Pérola do Bolhão** grocery store, which has superb *azulejos* ★ with Art-Nouveau-inspired designs.

Shopping Centres

With 98 stores and many restaurants, the **Via Catarina** shopping centre (*every day; Rua de Santa Catarina no. 312-350, between Rua Fernandes Tomás and*

Rua Formosa) is a good example of urban development. In addition to the entrance with an attractive neoclassical facade, the architects have ingeniously integrated this enormous commercial space by dividing its many shops lengthwise over five storeys, thus avoiding the construction of a huge building surrounded by parking areas, as is too often the case elsewhere.

Even if shopping centres generally don't interest you very much, it's worth a quick visit to the top floor to see the fronts of the restaurants. Each is a reproduction of one of the many styles of facades characteristic of the city. Amusing!

Costa Verde

Costa Verde lies at the edge of the country, squeezed between Porto, with its links to the British, and the Spanish border.

Make no mistake about it, however: this region is decidedly Portuguese – so much so, in fact, that it is home to the most backward-looking religious town in the country, Braga. Don't worry, though; Braga's rigid spirit hasn't spoiled everything. Visitors will be delighted to discover the medieval atmosphere of Guimarães, a fortress in Valença do Minho that also houses a bed and breakfast, and the outdated luxuriousness of the Pousada de Santa Luzia, which overlooks Viana do Castelo, a historic town and bustling seaside resort. Easily accessible from Porto, this region, the birthplace of Portugal's first king, boasts a number of historic sites and Peneda-Gerês national park. Staying in Guimarães or Viana do Castelo offers an opportunity to explore the

entire region and enjoy good food and the comforts of city living, while a night in the fortified village of Valença do Minho will give you an idea of what it was like to live under the threat of an invasion from Spain, which lies just across the Rio Minho; if you're lucky, you'll be able to see it from your room.

Finding Your Way Around

By Car from Porto

Amarante

Quick Route

Take the partly unfinished Highway A4-IP4 to the E82-N15, which leads straight to Amarante.

Scenic Route

Take the N108, which runs along the Rio Douro as far as the village of Entre-os-Rios. About 5km after the village, head left on the N210, which follows the Rio Tâmega straight to Amarante.

Braga and Bom Jesus do Monte

Quick Route

Highway A3-IP1 will take you as far as Braga. To reach Bom Jesus from the centre of town, take Avenida da Liberdade to Avenida João XXI and turn left. When you reach the N103, head towards Chaves. A few kilometres farther, turn right at the sign for Bom Jesus.

Scenic Route

Take the E82-N15 towards Amarante, then pick up the N101-IP9 in the direction of Guimarães, then Braga. To reach Bom Jesus, see directions above.

Guimarães

Quick Route

Take the A3-IP1 towards Braga. At the Vila Nova de Famalicão exit, pick up Highway A7, part of which is unfinished. A small road leads from the highway to Guimarães.

Scenic Route

Head towards Amarante on the E82-N15, then take the N101-IP9 to Guimarães.

Ponte de Lima

Take Highway A3IP1 to Braga, then the N201 to Ponte de Lima.

Valença do Minho

Take Highway A3-IP1 to Braga, then head north on the N201, and north again on the E1-N13 near the Spanish border.

Viana do Castelo and Santa Luzia

Quick Route

Take Highway A3-IP1 to Braga, then go west on the N103. When you reach the E1-N13, head north. To reach Santa Luzia from downtown Viana do Castelo, take Avenida dos Combatentes da Grande Guerra to the train station, then pick up Avenida Conde Carreira, to the left of the station. After passing the railroad tracks, located on the right, turn right on Avenida Humberto Delgado and continue until Avenida 25 de Abril, opposite which is the little road leading to the Basilica de Santa Luzia.

Scenic Route

Take the A3-IP1 to Braga, then the N201 towards Ponte de Lima.

From there, head west on the N202. To reach Santa Luzia, see directions above.

By Train

Although some of the places described below are accessible by rail, the train is not a very practical means of transportation. Except for the line to Braga, schedules are irregular and connections difficult. For Caminhos de Ferro departures and information, see p 69.

Braga

From Lisbon

on Avenida Infante Dom Henrique
Departure: several times a day from the Santa Apolónia station
Fare: Intercidades 2,700 ESC

From Porto

station on Rua da Estação (from Praça da Liberdade, take bus #34 or #35)
Departure: twice a day from the Campanhã
Travel time: approx. 1hr, 30min
Fare: Intercidades 1,100 ESC

By Bus from Lisbon

There are many departures daily with the **Rede Nacional de Expressos** and **Renex Expressos** bus companies, as well as with several other public transportation companies.

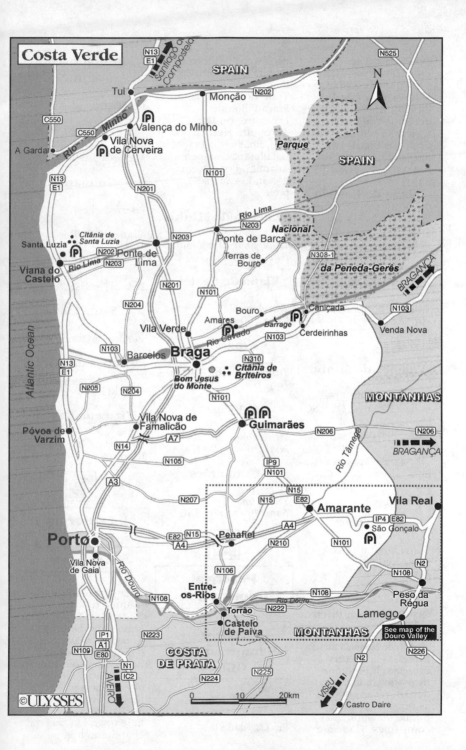

Rede Nacional de Expressos departures are from the terminal at no 18B Avenida Casal Ribeiro. **Renex Expressos** departures are from Cais das Cebolas, near Casa dos Bicos. For information in Lisbon, see p 69.

Viana do Castelo

Travel time: approx. 6hrs
Fare: 2,000 ESC to 2,200 ESC

Amarante

Travel time: approx. 7hrs
Fare: 2,200 ESC to 2,400 ESC

Valença do Minho

Travel time: 6hrs, 15min
Fare: 2,200 to 2,400 ESC

Braga

Travel time: approx. 6hrs
Fare: 2,100 ESC to 2,300 ESC

Guimarães

Travel time: approx. 5hrs, 30min
Fare: 2,100 ESC to 2,300 ESC

By Bus from Porto

The **Rede Nacional de Expressos** and **Renex Expressos** bus companies offer numerous departures every day, as do several other public transportation companies. There are no fewer than four bus terminals in Porto: on Rua Carmelitas, near Torre dos Clérigos; on Praça Filipa de Lencastre; on Rua Alexandre Herculano; and, finally, on Praça Batalha (at Garagem Atlantic). For information in Lisbon, see p 69.

Valença do Minho

Travel time: 2hrs, 45min
Fare: 1,000 to 1,200 ESC

Viana do Castelo

Travel time: 1hr, 35min
Fare: 750 to 950 ESC

Amarante

Travel time: 1hr, 15min
Fare: 650 to 750 ESC

Braga

Travel time: 1hr, 10min
Fare: 700 to 800 ESC

Guimarães

Travel time: 1hr
Fare: 700 to 800 ESC

Practical Information

Tourist Information Offices

Amarante

Rua Cândido dos Reis

Bom Jesus do Monte

(see Braga)

Braga

Avenida da Liberdade 1

Guimarães

Praça de Santiago
OR
Alameda do São Dâmaso

Ponte de Lima

Praça da República

Santa Luzia

(see Viana do Castelo)

Valença do Minho

on the N13

Viana do Castelo

Praça da Erva, near Rua Hospital Velho

Exploring

Amarante

Located on the border of three different regions (Tras-Os-Montes, Minho and Douro), Amarante was once an important crossing point, as its old Roman bridge, now greatly altered, attests. Although there are few attractions here, this little town has a certain charm about it.

Stretched alongside the Rio Tâmego, it lies tucked away in a pretty valley surrounded by verdant hills. Not only is Amarante reputed for its excellent pastries, but trout is a local specialty, adding to the pleasure of a brief, but worthwhile visit here.

The enchanting **Ponte São Gonçalo** is one of the first sights to greet visitors. Of Roman origin, it was completely reconstructed during the 18th century. Flanked by obelisks and adorned with baroque pinnacles, it has a great deal of character. Walking across it, visitors can admire the peaceful river below. The view ★ is extremely romantic.

Facing the bridge stands the **Igreja de São Gonçalo**, which with its big dome and bell tower, is somewhat crude-looking but nevertheless fits in well with the surroundings. Erected in the 16th century, the church houses the tomb of Saint Gonçalo and is the destination of an annual pilgrimage. On the first weekend of June, hordes of young couples arrive in Amarante. São Gonçalo, who lived here, earned the unusual reputation of making women fertile and favouring marriages. A large fair is held around the church each year at the same time. After taking a quick look at its Renais-

sance facade, enter the church and admire its rich **interior**, where you will find *talhas douradas* and polychrome columns topped by a nave adorned with *azulejos*. It is worth making a brief visit to the sacristy to see its interesting **coffered ceiling**. Right beside the church, the former monastery of the same name now houses the offices of the municipal government and the little **Museu de Albano Sardoeira** (*Tue to Sun 10am to 12:30pm and 2pm to 5pm; enter through the cloister*), which displays modern works by the great Cubist painter Amadeu de Sousa Cardoso, a friend of Modigliani's.

Finally, by all means don't leave Amarante without tasting one of the many local pastries. Take a stroll on the **Praça da República**, in front of the church, or along **Rua 5 de Outubro** and sample a few at one of the many outdoor cafés located there.

★★

Braga

If you had to sum up this city in a few words, "Braga the pious" would be appropriate. In fact, Braga has more churches per capita than any other city in Portugal. Despite its long history and impressive number of religious buildings,

however, the local architecture is conspicuously homogenous. The baroque style is most richly represented here; it could even be argued that the city is exclusively baroque. Admirers of the style will therefore be delighted to stroll through the streets seeking out the many baroque facades. As for other visitors, after a short stop at the cathedral and the former archbishop's palace, they will probably find Braga a bit monotonous, if not boring. Nevertheless, this city's ancient history lends it a certain grandeur.

By the time Braga fell under Roman control, in 250 BC, it was already known by the Gallo-Celtic name of Bracaros. Upon occupying the city, the Romans named it Bracarae Augusta in honour of Emperor Augustus. It wasn't until the 5th century, however, after the invasion of the Swabians, that the city began to stand out, becoming the capital and bishopric of their kingdom. After the Visigoths took over the city 100 years later, Braga answered its religious calling over the next three centuries. It was here that Theodoric II, king of the Visigoths, converted to Christianity. In AD 715, however, a Moorish invasion temporarily cast the city back into the shadows. Finally, around 1400,

Costa Verde

Braga was recaptured and once again assumed its role as a Christian city. The capital of the earldom under Henry of Burgundy, it became the seat of the country's first archbishopric soon after the creation of Portugal. From that point on, Braga's future was closely linked to that of the Church and its archbishops, who had direct control over the city. Proof of the church's influence on the city's development survives from two periods, the first being the reign of Archbishop Diogo de Sousa, in the 16th century, during which the city was traversed by wide, straight roads and studded with fountains and public squares. During the second period, in the 17th and 18th centuries, the archbishops literally covered the city with baroque buildings. The *talha dourada* art form, all the rage in the area at the time, flourished inside the churches. Since many people emigrated from here to the country's new territories, Braga's artistic influence extended as far as Brazil. Now a modern city, Braga is home to a university, numerous businesses, several textile mills, tanneries and a foundry.

Once plagued by constant traffic jams, downtown Braga's road system has recently been radically redesigned. After much impressive road work on Praça da República and around Avenida Central, where many terraces and lovely fountains confer a more elegant look to the place, the city appears to have endeavoured to make a good number of streets in the historic district more friendly to pedestrians. Evidence of this wise decision is the large, newly constructed underground parking lot beneath Praça Conde de Agrolongo. Today Braga has the most pedestrian streets of any city in Portugal, much appreciated by visitors who wish to stroll along them.

For an easy tour of the area, start off at the Praça da República, at the corner of Avenida da Liberdade. From this pleasant square, with its fountain and abundance of flowers, you will see the **Torre de Menagem**. Standing immediately behind an elegant building with an arcade, this tower is none other than the keep of the castle once connected to the city's fortifications. For a closer view of the building, head toward Rua dos Capelistas and take an immediate left onto Rua do Castelo. Keep walking until Rua do Souto, then turn right. Continue straight ahead, and you will end up on the city's main pedestrian street, **Rua Dom Diogo de Sousa**. This attractive street, named after the former archbishop of Braga, runs all the way across the historic centre, passing the city's main monuments on the way.

The first stop, on the right, is the **Largo do Paço ★**. The centre of this pretty square is graced with an unusual fountain in the shape of a small fortified tower surrounded by a crenellated wall. The harmonious series of buildings around the square serves as a fine example of 18th-century urban cohesion. These edifices replaced the **Antigo Paço Episcopal**, or former bishop's palace, built in the 16th century and almost completely destroyed by fire. Today, they house the municipal **library**, which boasts an extensive collection (as many as 300,000 titles, the oldest dating back to the 9th century!). To admire the only remaining wing of the former bishop's palace, head to the **Jardim de Santa Barbara**, located right behind the square (*enter via Rua Dom Diogo de Sousa, located opposite the Largo do Paço to the right*). This pleasant, flower-filled garden also contains some lovely archways, vestiges of a cloister that once stood here.

Across from the Largo do Paço, to the left of Rua Dom Diogo de Sousa, Braga's **Sé** seems to be hiding behind the Igreja da Misericórdia.

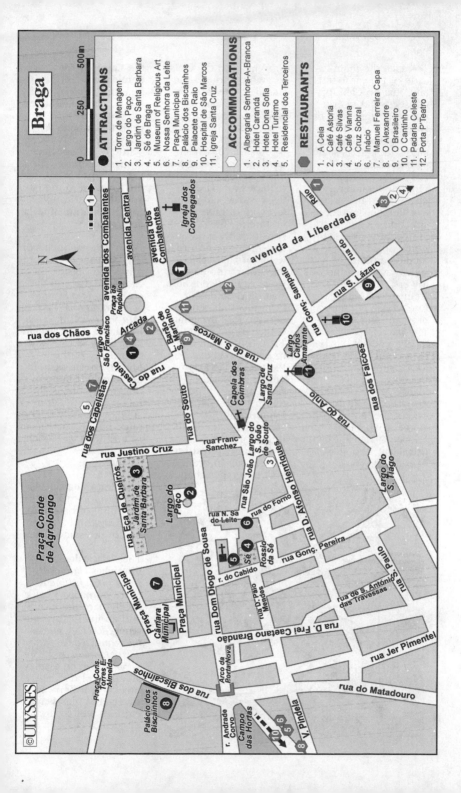

Braga

0 250 500 m

ATTRACTIONS

1. Torre de Menagem
2. Largo do Paço
3. Jardim de Santa Barbara
4. Sé de Braga
5. Museum of Religious Art
6. Nossa Senhora da Leite
7. Praça Municipal
8. Palácio dos Biscainhos
9. Palacete do Raio
10. Hospital de São Marcos
11. Igreja Santa Cruz

ACCOMMODATIONS

1. Albergaria Senhora-A-Branca
2. Hotel Carandá
3. Hotel Dona Sofia
4. Hotel Turismo
5. Residencial dos Terceiros

RESTAURANTS

1. A Ceia
2. Café Astoria
3. Café Silvas
4. Café Vianna
5. Cruz Sobral
6. Inácio
7. Manuel Ferreira Capa
8. O Alexandre
9. O Brasileiro
10. O Cantinho
11. Padaria Celeste
12. Porta P'Teatro

©ULYSSES

To reach the main facade of the cathedral, take Rua do Cabido, the second street on your left, right after the Largo do Paço. Before entering the building, take a look at its **south portal**, located on the Rossio da Sé. It is one of a few remaining elements of the primitive Romanesque construction, begun in the 9th century. The main portal, for its part, is a mediocre blend of styles, of which the bell towers, topped by a strange-looking structure, constitute the most striking example. The **interior** of the cathedral, which has been considerably altered, is also somewhat disappointing. A quick glance at the ornately decorated **choir** and one of the left-hand chapels, which contains a lovely **Manueline baptismal font**, should suffice.

Now head to the cloister, which houses the **Museu de Arte Sacra ★** (*300 ESC, obligatory guided tour including chapels; 8:30am to 12:30pm and 1:30pm to 5:30pm during winter, until 6:30pm during summer*), a museum of religious art. The first floor is devoted mainly to an assortment of vestments; the second, considerably more interesting, to a rich **collection of sacred objects**. Particularly noteworthy is the magnificent little **Moorish chest** dating from the 10th century and the rare **Byzantine cross** dating from the 11th. After visiting the museum, you can go to the **Capella dos Reis**, which houses the tomb of Henry of Burgundy and his wife, parents of Dom Afonso Henriques, the first king of Portugal. Next, cross the courtyard to the cloister in order to visit two other chapels,

the **Capela de São Geraldo**, covered with beautiful *azulejos*, and the **Capela da Glória ★**, which contains a superb **Gothic tomb ★** featuring a recumbent statue of Archbishop Gonçalo Pereira. The latter chapel is one of the loveliest in the city, and also merits a visit for its beautiful **Mudéjar decorations ★**.

For a lovely conclusion to your tour of the premises, go outside the cathedral, behind the choir (*on Rua Nossa Senhora da Leite, opposite Rua São João*), in order to admire **Nossa Senhora da Leite ★★** (literally, "Our Lady of the Milk"), an astonishing and elegant statue of the **Virgin** nursing the infant Saviour, set inside an ornately decorated niche. The piece is attributed to French artist Nicolas Chantereine.

The **Praça Municipal** is worth a look for its grouping of baroque buildings and a fountain in the same style.

The **Palácio dos Biscaínhos** (*Rua dos Biscaínhos, behind the Praça Municipal*) has a lovely baroque facade and an interesting **museum** (*400 ESC, guided tours only; Tue to Sun 10am to noon and 2pm to 5pm*), which displays a variety of decorative objects (earthenware, silver- and glassware, etc.), as well as archaeological relics.

The famous vineyards of the Douro Valley.
- *G. Sioen*

Magnificent Porto, a UNESCO World Heritage Site.
- *Marc Rigole*

The Atlantic Ocean forms a natural boundary around much of Portugal.
- *Marc Rigole*

A watchtower in Marvão, a fortified medieval village on the Spanish border.
- *Marc Rigole*

The lovely rocaille facade of the **Palacete do Raio** (*on Rua S. Lázaro, facing Rua do Raio, to the left of Avenida da Liberdade when heading towards Praça da República*) was designed by André Soares, a native of Braga and a past master of the baroque style.

Stroll along the Largo Carlos Amarante to view its **grouping of baroque buildings**, including the **Hospital de São Marcos** and the **Igreja Santa Cruz**.

Finally, for those still enchanted by baroque style, the **Alfaiate shoe store** (*754 Avenida da Liberdade*) is a real gem in purest rococo style. Mouldings, gilt mirrors, finely wrought ironwork and walls covered in rich damask fabrics await you here, the whole enhanced by magnificent chandeliers.

★

São Frutuoso de Montélios

(*4km from Braga*)

To reach São Frutuoso from downtown Braga, head south on Avenida da Liberdade, then turn right onto Avenida da Imaculada Conceição. At the next big intersection, at the Praça do Condestável, continue along the main road by keeping right, heading towards the train station. Once there, turn onto Rua Nova da Estação, which *then becomes Rua Costa Gomes. After the soccer field, located to the right, take a right onto Avenida São Frutuoso, which eventually leads to the church.*

Located in the heart of the former monastery of São Francisco and connected to the church of the same name, the **Capela da São Frutuoso** ★ (*Tue to Sun 10am to 5pm; entry on the right side of the nave of Igreja Matriz*) is one of only a few well-preserved Visigoth churches to have successfully survived 13 centuries of history. Built in 665 and probably reconstructed towards the 9th century, it still features typical Roman-Byzantine elements, such as its overall shape, in the form of a Greek cross, and its Corinthian columns. During your visit be sure not to miss the very beautiful *talhas douradas* that decorate the sacristy – a real gem!

Bom Jesus do Monte

(*7km from Braga*)

Located at an altitude of 400m, facing the Atlantic, Bom Jesus enjoys a mild climate that promotes the growth of luxuriant vegetation. The main attraction here, however, is the marvellous **baroque staircase** ★★, known as the **Via Sacra**, one of the most re- markable baroque structures in Europe. The stairway, like the church that towers over it, was erected in the 18th century by the archbishops of Braga for the sole purpose of flaunting their power. A dazzling white zigzag, it symbolizes the Stations of the Cross and abounds in allegorical decoration. Climbing it (*approx. 20min; parking lot next to the site; don't leave ANYTHING in your car*) is truly enjoyable, because it calls for some imagination. For example, the first part of the stairway relates to temptation, with divinities such as Jupiter and Saturn serving as reminders of our pagan origins. Next, the Escadório Dos Cinco Sentidos (Stairway of the Five Senses), preceded by two columns with a serpent wrapped around them, includes several fountains, reminding penitents of the dangers of sensual pleasures. These hazards are revealed by various streams of water (eg. water coming out of the ears, the mouth, the eyes, etc.). Lastly, the Escadório das Virtudes (Stairway of Virtues) is adorned with figures from the Old Testament, as well as fountains representing major Christian virtues, such as Faith and Charity. After completing this final stage, believers enter the sanctuary and are thus saved from temptation and are ready to be purified. As far as the

Costa Verde

church itself is concerned, its only exceptional feature is its lovely neoclassical facade. Upon reaching the esplanade, however, you don't have to be in a state of "purity" to enjoy the **magnificent view ★★** of both the city of Braga and the staircase. Those wishing to avoid stepping back into paganism by climbing back down the stairs can take the funicular (*50 ESC; every 15 min*), located on the right side of the staircase when facing the bottom. Although no miracle has ever taken place here, the site is frequented by a great many religious pilgrims.

Citânia de Briteiros

(*15km from Braga*)

From Bom Jesus, continue driving to Sobreposto, then follow the signs for Briteiros or Caldelas. The site lies about 8km from Bom Jesus.

Discovered in 1875 by archaeologist Martins Sarmento, this **castrum** (*200 ESC; 9am to 5pm*) is one of the largest Iron Age settlements in Portugal. The site, which was apparently occupied as early as 300 BC, includes the ruins of as many as 150 stone huts, two of which have been fully reconstructed. In addition to vestiges of three surrounding walls, visitors will also find several paved lanes and

stone conduits used to supply some of the streets with water. The numerous objects and Roman coins found here are now exhibited at the Museu Martins Sarmento in Guimarães (see p 325).

Guimarães

Like its neighbour Braga, Guimarães is one of the oldest cities in the country. It is the only one, however, that can pride itself on being the cradle of the nation, for it was here that Afonso Henriques, the first king of Portugal, was born. Although this illustrious figure took his first breath within its walls, the city was soon abandoned by the court. The kings opted instead for Coimbra and then Lisbon. Braga, for its part, became the favourite of Portugal's archbishops. Thus forsaken by the great and powerful, Guimarães' only consolation lay in conserving a large part of its original architecture. Precisely because it had fallen into obscurity, the city managed to escape the baroque excesses so widespread in this region. Both its charm and its architecture make Guimarães, like Viana do Castelo, farther north, a key destination in northern Portugal. Guimarães is also the native city of Gil Vicente, celebrated

author and father of the Portuguese theatre.

The historic centre is fairly small and the main monuments, other than the Castelo, lie on small streets and squares that are not easily accessible. Visitors are therefore strongly advised to explore the city on foot.

Appropriately, the tour begins at what could be called the birthplace of the nation, the **Castelo de Guimarães ★** (*Tue to Sun 9am to noon and 2pm to 5pm; Rua Conde D. Henrique*). Erected in the 10th century by order of Countess Mumadona (see "Nossa Senhora da Oliveira" box on p 325), it was enlarged and occupied in the 12th century by Henry of Burgundy and his wife Teresa (daughter of Alfonso VI of Castile and Léon), to whom Alfonso VI had allotted the region of Portucale. Although the castle was abandoned over the following centuries, much of it was restored between the two World Wars. In fact, a strong wave of nationalism in the 1930s and 1940s ultimately led to the restoration of many historical monuments reflecting the Portuguese identity. The Castelo was one of these. By climbing up onto the keep, you can enjoy a lovely **view ★** of the city and surrounding countryside.

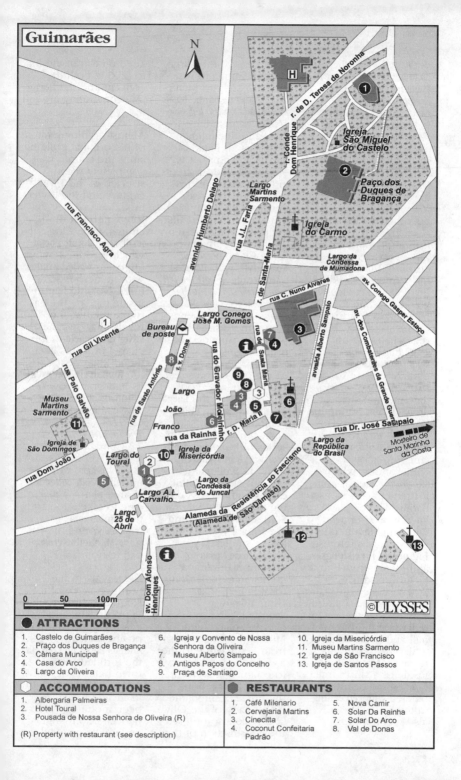

Guimarães

N

H

Igreja São Miguel do Castelo

Paço dos Duques de Bragança

Igreja do Carmo

Largo Martins Sarmento

Largo da Condessa de Mumadona

rua Francisco Agra

avenida Humberto Delago

rua J.L. Faria

r. Conde Dom Henrique

r. de D. Terosa de Noronha

r. de Santa-Maria

rua C. Nuno Álvares

avenida Alberto Sampaio

av. Conego Gaspar Estaço

av. dos Combatentes da Grande Guerra

rua Gil Vicente

Bureau de poste

Largo Conego José M. Gomes

rua do Gravador Molelrinho

r. V. Donas

rua de Santo António

rua da Santa Maria

Largo João Franco

rua da Rainha

r. D. Maria II

rua Dr. José Sampaio

Museu Martins Sarmento

rua Palo Galvão

Igreja de São Domingos

rua Dom João I

Largo do Toural

Igreja da Misericórdia

Largo da República do Brasil

Mosteiro de Santa Marinha da Costa

Largo A.L. Carvalho

Largo da Condessa do Juncal

Largo 25 de Abril

av. Dom Afonso Henriques

Alameda da Resistência ao Fascismo (Alameda de São Dâmaso)

0   50   100m

©ULYSSES

● ATTRACTIONS

1. Castelo de Guimarães
2. Praço dos Duques de Bragança
3. Câmara Municipal
4. Casa do Arco
5. Largo da Oliveira
6. Igreja y Convento de Nossa Senhora da Oliveira
7. Museu Alberto Sampaio
8. Antigos Paços do Concelho
9. Praça de Santiago
10. Igreja da Misericórdia
11. Museu Martins Sarmento
12. Igreja de São Francisco
13. Igreja de Santos Passos

▢ ACCOMMODATIONS

1. Albergaria Palmeiras
2. Hotel Toural
3. Pousada de Nossa Senhora de Oliveira (R)

(R) Property with restaurant (see description)

⬡ RESTAURANTS

1. Café Milenario
2. Cervejaria Martins
3. Cinecitta
4. Coconut Confeitaria Padrão
5. Nova Camir
6. Solar Da Rainha
7. Solar Do Arco
8. Val de Donas

Walking below the castle, you will spot the **Paço dos Duques de Bragança** ★ (*400 ESC, guided tour; every day 9:30am to 5pm, Jun to Sep until 9pm*), a former ducal palace. Constructed around 1420 for Dom Afonso, future Duke of Bragança and illegitimate son of King João I, the towering building reveals strong Norman and Burgundian influences. The permanent residence of the duke and his wife until she died in 1480, the palace was gradually abandoned; by the dawn of the 20th century it was in ruins. It wasn't until 1930 that the palace was restored and some parts of it were reconstructed to accommodate the president of the republic during his visits to the area. Despite its tiled roof and the numerous brick chimneys atop its crenellations, which sacrifice style for comfort, the palace is fascinating. The **interior** ★★, graced with an elegant courtyard, features interesting **period furnishings** and lovely French and Flemish **tapestries** ★. Equally noteworthy are the **Capela Gótica** and the extraordinary wooden **ceilings** of the banquet hall and ballroom, which bear a strange resemblance to the inside of a ship's hull. Finally, the beautiful painted **coffered ceiling** in the sitting room is also worth a look.

Now head to the Largo Martins Sarmento in order to pick up picturesque **Rua de Santa Maria** ★ (*on the left side of the square*). Mentioned in documents dating as far back as the 12th century, it is one of the oldest streets in Guimarães and features many old residences with pretty cast-iron gates. Of particular interest among these is the former convent of Santa Clara, now the **Town Hall**, with its elegant **facade** ★ (*on the left side of the street, on the Largo Conego José M. Gomes*), and, farther along, the **Casa do Arco**, with its suspended baroque loggia.

At the end of the street, on the left side, you will end up at the **Largo da Oliveira** ★★. This magnificent little square is graced with a lovely series of buildings with archways in front of them, as well as a curious but elegant **Gothic canopy** with a cross dating back to 1342. Somewhat dominating the square with its bell tower, the **Igreja y Convento de Nossa Senhora da Oliveira** ★ merits an explanation, for it is here that Guimarães was founded. After a miracle took place here, Mumadona, a countess from Léon, came to the area in the 9th century to establish a convent. In commemoration of the miracle, she named it Our Lady of the Olive Tree. She also ordered the construction of the

keep on top of the hill to protect both the convent and the fledgling community around it.

Almost nothing remains of the original building, since the church was completely reconstructed in the 14th century and the tower modified in 1513. Before entering the church, take a look at its lovely **Gothic portal**, which is topped by an imposing **walled window** with numerous sculptures. Notable features inside include the baroque retable, the lovely **altar** and the **silver tabernacle** in the chapel of Saint Sacrament. Right next door, the **Roman cloister**, with its handsome row of columns, houses the **Museu Alberto Sampaio** ★ (*250 ESC, guided tour; Tue to Sun 10am to 12:30pm and 2pm to 5:30pm*). On the second floor, visitors can admire a lavish **collection of silver plates**. Make sure to take a look at the **Aljubarrota triptych** ★ and the superb **Manueline cross**, dating from 1547.

Next, walk to the northwest side of the Largo and head to the Praça de Santiago by passing under the imposing archways of the **Antigos Paços do Concelho**, the fortified former town hall. It was built in the 14th century, but its facade has since been modified. The neoclassical triangular pediments were added

The Miracle of Nossa Senhora da Oliveira

The following two legends of the miracle of Guimarães attempt to explain the origin of the name of the convent of Nossa Senhora da Oliveira. Visitors might hear many other variations, however, since the popular imagination is fertile in these parts. The first story takes place in the seventh century. At the time, a Visigoth warrior named Wamba, who had taken up farming, suddenly learned that he had been named king by his peers. Unwilling to assume this heavy responsibility, he tried to trick his

way out of the situation. While publicly declaring himself unworthy of such a great honour, he took a dead olive branch, stuck it into the ground, and asserted that he would not take on the role of king until the branch came back to life. Only a sign from Heaven could justify his becoming king. It was then that the miracle occurred; the words had barely left his lips when the branch suddenly sprouted leaves.

According to the second, equally fabulous

version, an old olive tree was planted back in the 14th century on the exact spot now occupied by the Gothic canopy on the Largo da Oliveira. Unable to withstand being moved, the tree soon died. Later, a wealthy local merchant named Pero Esteves took a stone cross that he had brought back from a trip to Normandy and placed it alongside the dead tree. This is supposedly the same crucifix now found in the oratory. Several days later, the tree was miraculously covered with leaves.

Costa Verde

in the 17th century, along with a somewhat overly imposing war statue on the roof. The latter commemorates the conquest of Ceuta, Morocco, in 1415. Just next door, the Pousada da Nossa Senhora da Oliveira occupies an old mansion. Although the **Praça de Santiago** ★★ has no impressive buildings, it nevertheless merits a visit for its lovely **little houses**, with their granite bases and tiny wooden balconies. Its medieval air makes

this the most picturesque square in Guimarães.

Take Rua do Gravador Molarinho (*southwest side of the Praça de Santiago*) to **Rua da Rainha** and turn right. This street is lined with **sumptuous residences**, most dating back to the 18th century. At the end of the street, on the Largo João Franco, take a quick look at the elegant **portico** of the **Igreja da Misericórdia**, with its gemeled columns, then continue

straight ahead to the **Largo Toural**. This attractive square is to some extent the commercial centre of Guimarães, and many shops are located here. The east side of the square features a lovely row of houses with quarrelled windows.

The nearby **Museu Martins Sarmento** ★ (*300 ESC; Tue to Sun 9:30am to noon and 2pm to 5pm; Rua Paio Galvão, on the north and left side of the Largo do Toural*), set up partly in the cloister of the Igreja de São Domingos, is worth visiting. It contains a wonderful collection of objects discovered at the archaeological sites of the Citânia de Briteiros (see p 322) and Sabrosa. In addition to the many sculptures and pieces of jewellery from the pre- and post-Roman eras, visitors will also find an elegant **Gothic cloister** with lovely **geminated columns**.

By returning to the Largo do Toural and continuing eastward on Alameda de São Dâmaso (formerly called Alameda da Resistência ao Fascismo), you will reach the **Igreja de São Francisco** (*Sun 9:30am to 1pm and 3pm to 5pm; on the right side of the avenue*). After a brief look at the Gothic entryway, head **inside the church** ★ to admire its decor. Remarkable features include the lovely *azulejos* tracing the life of St. Francis and the ornate **Joanine altar piece** ★, one of the most lavish in the city. It is also worth making a quick visit to the sacristy to see its painted coffered ceiling.

Finally, by continuing eastward, you will end up at the top of the Largo da República do Brasil, which affords an interesting **view** of the highly baroque **Igreja de Santos Passos**. The long flowery path leading up to the building, with its two perfectly symmetri-

cal bell towers set against a backdrop of verdant hills, makes this scene picture-perfect.

The **Igreja do Carmo** (*Largo Martins Sarmento, on the left side of the square when facing south*) merits a visit, mainly for its splendid **altar piece** decorated with *talhas douradas*.

If you love gardens, make sure to visit the **Palácio Vila Flor** (*Avenida Dom Afonso Henriques*), an elegant 18th-century palace surrounded by terraces full of flowers, and the **Mosteiro de Santa Marinha da Costa**, a former monastery that has been converted into a *pousada* (see p 334).

To enjoy a **panoramic view** of Guimarães and the surrounding countryside, take the Teleférica da Penha (*500 ESC return; May to Sep, Mon to Fri 11am to 6:30pm, Sat and Sun, 10am to 9:30pm; Oct to Apr, Mon to Fri 11am to 5:30pm, Sat and Sun 10am to 6:30pm; near Largo São Gualter,* ☎51 50 85) up to the **Santuário da Penha**, at 400m in altitude.

Ponte de Lima

Although this site was apparently occupied as early as 150 BC, it was under the Romans that the community attained a certain level of im-

portance. At the point where the Roman road from Braga met the Rio Lima, they built an impressive bridge to make it easier to cross the often flooded river. Much later, around 1125, Ponte de Lima was granted a royal charter, which was then renewed in 1511. Over the course of its history, however, Ponte de Lima has always been a peaceful little rural village. To this day, the lives of local inhabitants still revolve around the **open-air market**. Every second Monday, the sandy riverbank becomes a showcase for local goods and livestock, as well as farming equipment. The atmosphere at this farmers' gathering is truly festive, and offers visitors an opportunity to sample some *vinho verde* accompanied by bread and sardines. Those wishing to soak up a positively enchanting, peaceful atmosphere are sure to find Ponte de Lima a vacation from their vacation. A large number of charming manor houses, recently converted to accommodate guests (see *Tourismo no Espaço Rural*, p 57), can also be found in this area.

Although there are few attractions here, it would be a shame to pass through Ponte de Lima without stopping. In addition to the lovely, peaceful river and surrounding hills, there are a few interesting sights well worth a look.

The first thing that will draw your attention here, of course, is the magnificent **bridge ★★**, remarkably long for the era in which it was built. Erected by the Romans at an undetermined date, it was partially reconstructed during the first half of the 14th century. Around the same time, the fortifications surrounding the town and the two towers at the beginning of the bridge were added; unfortunately, these structures have since disappeared. The few remaining traces of the original Roman bridge are visible in the arches on either end.

It is worth visiting the **Largo de Camões**, the village's central square, to see its elegant fountain and the lovely houses facing onto it.

Visit the **Igreja Matriz** (*10am to noon and 2pm to 5pm; Rua Cardeal Saraiva*), for its Roman portal.

The Manueline windows of the former palace of the Marquês de Ponte de Lima, now the **Câmara Municipal** (*Praça da República*), the town hall, are worth a look.

The **Torre de São Paulo** and the **Torre da Cadeia Velha** (*on Alameda Príncipe Real Dom Luís Filipe, the avenue that runs alongside the river*)

are two attractively restored towers that once formed part of the city's ramparts.

Valença do Minho

Located on the edge of Portugal, facing the Rio Minho and powerful Espanha across the way, Valença do Minho is a decidedly unusual town. The lower part of it is ugly and uninteresting, while the fortified city, perched atop a hill overlooking the river, is fascinating – the perfect place for a stroll. Renowned as a stronghold as early as the Middle Ages, the old city has equipped itself with imposing fortifications over the centuries. Most of those remaining were built in the 17th century. Perfectly conserved, these huge ramparts still encircle the old city, completely isolating it from the lower city. Even today, the area is only accessible by way of a single, heavily fortified door, which is so narrow that only one vehicle can pass through it at a time!

The main attractions here, of course, are the **fortresses ★** and the lovely views from their ramparts. Two Vaubanesque citadels, they are completely independent from one another, linked only by a small bridge over a moat. The entrance is particularly impressive,

giving visitors the sensation that they are infiltrating a highly guarded area. The first fortress is accessible through the narrow south door, known as the **Porta Coroada**. This citadel will appeal mainly to shoppers and people who love mingling with the crowd. Throughout the year, especially on weekends, Spaniards peacefully invade the little city in search of cloth, copper cookware, clothing and kitschy souvenirs. The streets, narrow to begin with, are almost entirely covered with stalls containing all sorts of merchandise intended to entice passers by. What with drivers looking for parking and tourists elbowing each other in front of the stalls, the traffic jams are unbelievable! It's a real free-for-all! The main street leads through the village to the second fortress. As of yet, this citadel is much less commercial than its neighbour, and therefore more pleasant, with its pretty little streets and houses free of shops and signs. If you go to the north end, near the Pousada do São Teotónio (see p 335), you will be able to enjoy a peaceful stroll and even scale the fortifications to admire the area's **splendid scenery ★** – a real treat after battling the crowds!

(see p 335)

Costa Verde

Viana do Castelo

Like almost all major cities in the northern part of the country, the city of Viana do Castelo was inhabited in ancient times by people of Celtic origin. Accordingly, visitors can still admire the vestiges of the former Citânia de Santa Luzia atop the hill overlooking the city. The Romans founded the actual town of Viana on the shores of the Rio Lima around the 2nd century BC. The city grew slowly during the Roman era, only to slip into oblivion during the Muslim occupation. It was finally revived around 1258, upon being granted a charter by Dom Afonso III. Originally geared towards fishing, the city came to play a role in the country's new colonial explorations in the 15th century. Many local sailors became famous, including Gonçalo Velho, who colonized the Azores, and João Alvares Fagundes, who drew a map of the shores of Newfoundland (Canada). Viana's golden age, however, did not actually take place until the 17th century. In those years, Brazil's gold mines and sugar made the city truly prosperous. Many luxurious residences and palaces were constructed; these buildings adorn the city to this day. In 1848, Viana's newfound importance earned it the status of a city. It was henceforth known as Viana do Castelo. At the dawn of the 20th century, after experiencing a long period of decline following Brazil's independence, the city launched a series of projects to revitalize its economy. The most marked of these were the construction of a bridge designed by Eiffel and the opening of Avenida dos Combatentes da Grande Guerra, a direct link between the pier and the train station. Today, Viana do Castelo is not only a fishing port, but also boasts a large shipyard. As far as tourism is concerned, Viana do Castelo can pride itself on being a very pleasant city and seaside resort of great architectural interest. While exploring the area, make sure not to miss the site of Santa Luzia and its magnificent panoramic view.

Because most of the city's many distinctive houses stand on small streets or around tiny squares that are inaccessible by car, exploring the city by foot is preferable.

To start your tour, head south on **Avenida dos Combatentes da Grande Guerra**, the busiest street in town. This wide commercial artery will delight both shopaholics and admirers of lovely houses. Once you reach the train station, head towards Rio Lima, then take the third street on the left, Rua da Picota. Immediately to the right lies the **Praça da Erva ★**, an attractive little square graced by the lovely **Hospital Velho** (*at the corner of Praça da Erva and Rua do Hospital Velho*), a must-see. Erected in the 15th century, this building once accommodated pilgrims passing through the area. It now houses the offices of the Região de Turismo do Alto Minho. Local crafts and various other products from the region can be found inside, as well.

From the square, pick up **Rua do Poço**, where you will find an old public fountain that once supplied the city with water. The street is also studded with beautiful Manueline residences. You will eventually end up at the **Sé**, whose most interesting features are its handsome **Roman portal** and **two crenelated towers** of the same style. The building is also adorned with beautiful **sculptures**. After a brief stop, continue your tour along Rua Sacadura Cabral, to the left of the cathedral, in order to reach the **Praça da Rebública ★**. This remarkable square is not only full of outdoor cafés where you will be tempted to while away the afternoon, but also boasts two of the loveliest historic buildings in town, the Paços do Concelho and the Casa da Misericórdia.

The **Paços do Concelho** ★ is none other than the former town hall. With its Gothic arches and facade topped by merlons, the building looks somewhat like its counterpart in Guimarães, although it is purer in style. Right next door, adjoining the former hospital of the same name, the **Casa da Misericórdia** ★ (16th century) has a magnificent **facade** ★★ of Italian inspiration. Atlantes and caryatids grace the two-story structure, supporting an elegant gallery. It is worth making a brief visit to the adjacent **Igreja da Misericórdia** (*entrance on the west side of the square*) to see the remarkable **altar piece** ★ decorated with a *talha dourada*.

Continue your tour by taking Rua Cândido dos Reis, located on the north side of the square, and go all the way to the end of the street.

According to some, the **Palácio dos Condes da Carreira** ★, at the corner of Rua dos Bombeiros and Rua Cândido dos Reis, is the most beautiful palace in Viana do Castelo. This former seigniorial residence was erected in the 16th century and remodelled in the 18th. It has a lovely **facade** ★ featuring a beautiful blend of Manueline and

classical ornamentation. The building now serves as the town hall.

The tour concludes at the **Museu Municipal** ★ (*200 ESC, guided tour; Tue to Sun 9:30am to noon and 2pm to 5pm; Largo de São Domingos*). A former seigneurial palace built in the 18th century, this museum is worth visiting for its splendid collection of **Portuguese earthenware** and its lavish **decor**, featuring remarkable **azulejos** ★ and **carved wooden ceilings**. In addition to some lovely Indo-Portuguese furniture, the museum houses examples of the traditional dress of this region.

Admirers of Manueline architecture won't want to miss the remarkable **facade** of the **Palácio Melo Avim** (*Avenida Conde Carreira*), located near the train station.

The **Rua da Bandeira** is a good place for a stroll, as it is lined with elegant mansions with richly decorated facades.

The **Pastelaria Dantas** (*at the corner of Rua Manuel*

Espregueira and Rua de Olivença) is a treat for its lovely **Art Deco** shop front.

Santa Luzia

(*2km from Viana do Castelo*)

Located at an altitude of 250m, the neo-Byzantine **Santuária de Santa Luzia** (*10am to noon and 2pm to 5pm*) overwhelms visitors with its massive dimensions. It was begun at the outset of the 20th century and took nearly 70 years to complete. Although Santa Luzia is of little architectural interest, make sure to visit its esplanade (which is unfortunately teeming with vendors selling kitschy souvenirs) in order to take in the **magnificent view** ★★. The road leading up to the building, moreover, is exceedingly pleasant, offering lovely panoramic views the entire way. Visitors who opt instead for the **funicular** (*70 ESC; Mon to Sun every hour from 9am to noon and 5pm to 7pm and every half-hour from 12:30pm to 5pm; after the train station, go past the railway tracks*) are treated to a spectacular view on their way up. Thrill-seekers will enjoy climbing up to the dome of the basilica (*50 ESC; not recommended for those who are afraid of heights*) by means of a narrow staircase that leads right

Costa Verde

to the top of the building. The view is guaranteed to take your breath away (in nice weather, at least!). Photographers can head to the terrace of the Pousada Monte de Santa Luzia (see p 336), located at an even higher altitude, for a **sweeping view** that encompasses both the basilica and the coast.

Citânia de Santa Luzia

(*2km from Viana do Castelo*)

Not far from the Pousada Monte de Santa Luzia, the Citânia de Santa Luzia (*150 ESC; Tue to Sun 9am to noon and 2pm to 5pm, closed on rainy days; entrance on the road leading to the Hotel de Santa Luzia*), like its counterpart in Briteiros, is an ancient Celtic settlement, whose fortifications, along with vestiges of a fair number of circular houses, are still intact. Visitors can tour the site on a footbridge overlooking the ruins.

Outdoor Activities

Pedal-Boating

Amarante

A large number of pedalos are available for rent on the banks of the Rio Tâmego.

Hiking

★ Parque Nacional da Peneda-Gerês

Hiking buffs will find all sorts of trails in this park, ranging in length from a few kilometres to long excursions requiring several days to complete. The mostly mountainous landscape is extremely beautiful, and it is not uncommon to come across mountain goats, eagles and even wild horses here. Several lakes in the park have been equipped with facilities for activities such as swimming, fishing, pedal-boating and motor-boating. While hiking, you will also have the opportunity to explore various archeological sites, mostly Celtic and Roman. Finally, several spas have been established here as well. For details on activities and hiking trails, contact the park's information office:

Parque Nacional da Peneda-Gerês
Quinta das Parretas-Rodovia,
4700 Braga
☎*253 61 31 66*

Guimarães

After reaching the **Santuário da Penha** by cable car, you can take one of several fairly short and easily accessible paved trails to the top of the Penha hill, at 617m in altitude. More gung-ho hikers can also take the small paved road (watch out for cars) that leads back down to Guimarães, zigzagging through vegetation and passing by the lovely Pousada de Santa Marinha. After taking a coffee break in the *pousada*'s beautiful gardens, continue on to the town centre. Unfortunately, this last stretch of road is less appealing, as it crosses several major thoroughfares with sometimes heavy traffic. The excursion takes an afternoon or so, though bolder hikers can always double back and make a day of it.

Cruises

Viana do Castelo

Several different companies offer delightful, romantic **excursions on the Rio Lima**. Contact one of the three travel agencies on Avenida dos Combatentes da Grande Guerra – Avic, Atlas or Turilis (*approx. 800 ESC for 1hr or 1,500 ESC for 3hrs*).

Much like the Algarve and the Costa de Lisboa, the Costa Verde has become a major golf destination, with no less than four courses to date.

Golf Courses

Name	Number of Holes	Par	Length (in metres)	Address
Golf Quinta	18	68	5,090	Quinta da Deveza, Louredo da Deveza 4600 Amarante ☎ *255 44 60 60* ≈ *255 44 62 02*
Golf Quinta	18	71	6,015	Quinta de Pias, Fornelos de Pias 4990 Ponte de Lima ☎ *258 74 34 14* ≈ *258 74 34 24*
Quinta da Barca	9	31	2,010	Barca do Logo 4740 Esposende ☎ *253 96 67 23* ≈ *253 96 90 68*
Golf Estela	18	72	6,020	Rio Alto Estela 4490 Póvoa de Varzim ☎ *252 60 18 14* ≈ *252 61 27 01*

Accommodations

Amarante

Campismo Municipal de Amarante
Quinta dos Frades, 4600 Amarante
☎ *255 43 21 33*
≈ *255 43 34 41*

São Gonçalo

(*18km from Amarante*)

Pousada de São Gonçalo
$$$
pb, ℜ
take the N15-IP4-E82 towards Vila Real; the *pousada* is about 18 km from the centre of Amarante, 4600 Amarante
☎ *255 46 11 13*
☎ *255 46 11 23*
≈ *255 46 13 53*
Set in the heart of the mountains, the Pousada de São Gonçalo is most suitable for visitors who enjoy peace and quiet and walks in the mountains. One of the oldest *pousadas* in operation, it has recently been remodeled but remains relatively modest.

The rooms offer unimpeded views of the Serra do Marão, compensating greatly for the building's lack of charm.

Braga

Câmara Municipal de Braga
Parque da Ponte, 4710 Braga
☎ *253 27 33 55*
≈ *253 61 33 87*

Pousada da Juventude
6 Rua de Santa Margarida
4710 Braga
☎/≈ *253 61 61 63*

Albergaria Senhora-A-Branca

$$

pb, tv

58 Largo da Senhora-a-Branca
4710 Braga
☎*253 26 99 38*
⇌*253 26 99 37*

Set in a lovely square planted with orange trees and surrounded by distinctive buildings, the Albergaria Senhora-A-Branca offers 20 modern, comfortably equipped rooms with austere furnishings. In addition to the ubiquitous brickwork and terracotta tiles, the decor of the common areas is composed of several antiques that help "warm up" the rather severe-looking surroundings. This inn is also one of the best bargains in town, and the reception is courteous and friendly.

Residencial dos Terceiros

$$

pb, tv

85 Rua dos Capelitas
4700 Braga
☎*253 27 04 66*
☎*253 27 04 78*
⇌*253 27 57 67*

Located on the ground floor of a building rather lacking in character, the rooms at the Residencial dos Terceiros have an antiquated decor recalling the 1950s but are clean and pleasantly lit nonetheless. Another asset is its ideal location, right next to the elegant Praça da República and a stone's throw from the historic district in the heart of the city and the Torre de Menagem.

Hotel Residencial Carandá

$$

pb, tv, ℝ

96 Avenida da Liberdade
4700 Braga
☎*253 26 14 50*
⇌*253 26 14 55*

A modern hotel lacking in charm but situated near the old city.

Hotel Residencial Dona Sofia

$$

pb, tv, ℝ

Largo S. João do Souto 131
4700 Braga
☎*253 26 31 60*
☎*253 27 18 54*
⇌*253 61 12 45*

Pleasantly located in the heart of the old city, this hotel offers well-equipped, tastefully decorated rooms.

Hotel Turismo

$$$

pb, tv, ≈, ≡, ℜ, ℝ

Praceta João XXI and Avenida da Liberdade, 4700 Braga
☎*253 26 12 20*
⇌*253 22 63 16*

This hotel has all of the modern conveniences, but lacks charm. Near, though not inside, the old city, it has the advantage of being located along one of the main roads leading into the city. Most of the rooms have balconies looking out onto a busy street.

Bom Jesus do Monte

(7km from Braga)

Hotel do Elevador

$$$

pb, tv, ≈, ℜ, ℝ

to the left of the sanctuary, Monte do Bom Jesus
4710 Braga
☎*253 60 34 00*
⇌*253 60 34 09*

This modern and tastefully decorated hotel offers rooms with lovely panoramic views of Braga. Some rooms have pretty handcrafted furniture. Ask for one looking out on the valley. Friendly service.

Castelo do Bom Jesus

$$$$
$$$$$ *with* ⊛

pb, tv, ≈

to the left of the road, just before the sanctuary, Monte do Bom Jesus, 4700 Braga
☎*253 67 65 66*
⇌*253 67 76 91*

A real 18th-century castle built on the ruins of a medieval castle, this hotel invites guests to a day in the life of member of the nobility. You will be ensconced, dear Counts and Countesses, in exceptional surroundings, complete with exotic wood floors, oriental carpets, lamps made of molten glass and a large reading room with a piano. The castle, with its turrets and *azulejos*, stands in the midst of superb multi-level garden including palm trees, fountains and a multitude of flowers. Expensive, maybe, but a dream come true!

Hotel do Parque
$$$
pb, tv, ≈, ℜ, ℝ
to the left of the sanctuary
Monte do Bom Jesus
4710 Braga
☎*253 67 65 48*
⇄*253 67 66 79*
This place has the same owner as the Hotel do Elevador, but its decor is considerably older. The rooms, however, are larger and more comfortable. As its name indicates, the hotel is surrounded by a beautiful flower garden.

Amares

(*17km from Braga*)

🌴 **Pousada Santa Maria do Bouro**
$$$$$
pb, tv, ≈, ℜ
4720 Amares
☎*253 37 19 70*
☎*253 37 19 71*
⇄*253 37 19 76*
Among the newest members of the Enatur network, the Pousada Santa Maria do Bouro certainly has no cause to be envious of its rivals, and architect Eduardo Souto de Moura can pride himself on having harmoniously blended past and present, to the great delight of travellers. A former Cistercian monastery dating back to the 13th century, the original structure underwent many changes throughout history, from being almost totally abandoned in the early 16th century to its full reconstruction during the 17th century and its occupation by

33 monks toward the end of that same century. The adjacent church was also rebuilt around this time. Now transformed into an opulent *pousada*, the monastery can once again welcome "pilgrims" passing through.

From the very entrance, visitors are amazed by the impressive size of the common areas. And, after taking the elevator with futurist designs to the rooms on the upper floor, guests will immediately understand the place's "recipe" for undeniable charm: the repeated use of metal, glass and stone in utterly ascetic surroundings. The only discernible features serving to relieve the monotony are a few rare antiques and religious curios, which stand out from the modern furnishings and large contemporary paintings gracing the stone walls. The long, wide granite corridors, the ceilings of which are adorned with strange, rust-coloured sheets of metal that are illuminated by rays of sun streaming through large windows, are but one example of the architect's ingenuity.

Beyond a heavy metallic door opening onto one of the 32 high-ceiling rooms (including two suites), guests will encounter a stunning open space whose only constraint is a wooden unit hous-

ing a modern bathroom. Guests can relax here amidst designer furniture with straight and simple designs while contemplating a virtually panoramic view of the lovely surrounding countryside through large windows. On a practical level, however, the lack of proper ventilation in the bathrooms, causing the rooms themselves to steam up, is deplorable.

Finally, no one should leave this enchanting place without visiting the *pousada*'s beautiful restaurant (see p 339) and its adjoining cloister. Once terribly damaged and missing its upper floor, the cloister has fortunately been restored, and guests can meditate here in peace, with only the lapping of the brook running through it to break the silence. For those who enjoy the great outdoors, a pleasant garden terrace with a swimming pool and tennis court is also accessible from a large esplanade planted with orange trees behind the building.

Costa Verde

Caniçada

(30km from Braga)

Pousada de São Bento
$$$$$
pb, tv, ℜ, ≈
from Braga, take the N103 for 28km; shortly after the village of Cerdeirinhas, turn left on the N304, heading north
4850 Vieira do Minho
☎*253 64 71 90*
☎*253 64 71 91*
⇌*253 64 78 67*
Located within the confines of the Parque Nacional da Peneda-Gerês (see p 330), the chalet-style Pousada de São Bento is best suited to visitors who enjoy the mountains and long walks in the wilderness. The rooms are not only attractively furnished but also offer a breathtaking view. On the restaurant level, guests will find a large terrace where they can admire the mountains, the valley of the Rio Cávado and the reservoir of the Caniçada dam. The scene is quite simply magnificent! As if the place weren't wonderful enough already, an outdoor pool beckons guests to enjoy a swim in this majestic setting. In short, if you go to Bragança, make sure to visit this perfectly idyllic spot.

Terras de Bouro

(31km from Braga)

Vilarinho das Furnas
Parque Nacional da Peneda Gerês, São João do Campo, 4840 Terras de Bouro
☎/⇌*253 35 13 39*

Campismo de Cerdeira
Campo do Gerês, 4840 Terras de Bouro
☎/⇌*253 35 10 05*

Guimarães

Campismo Municipal da Penha
Montanha da Pena
4800 Guimarães
☎*253 51 59 12*
⇌*253 53 65 69*

Albergaria Palmeiras
$$
pb, tv
Rua Gil Vicente, Centro Comercial Palmeiras
4800 Guimarães
☎*253 41 03 24*
⇌*253 41 72 61*
Not far from the historic centre, connected to a shopping centre, the Albergaria Palmeiras offers simple, practical modern rooms.

🌴 **Hotel Toural**
$$$
pb, tv, ℝ
behind the Largo do Toural, Largo A.L. de Carvalho
4800 Guimarães
☎*253 51 71 84*
⇌*253 51 71 49*
This is a pleasant modern hotel, very tastefully decorated with an attractive blend of modern and traditional elements. Most of the spacious rooms look out onto pretty Largo Toural. The excellent service and private parking make it a good place to keep in mind. Good quality-to-price ratio.

Pousada da Nossa Senhora da Oliveira
$$$$$
pb, tv, ℜ
Largo da Oliveira
4801 Guimarães
☎*253 51 41 57*
⇌*253 51 42 04*
Right in the heart of historic Guimarães, the extremely charming Pousada da Nossa Senhora da Oliveira is a former seigneurial residence. The rooms are small but very pretty, and some offer views of the splendid Largo da Oliveira and its lovely church.

🌴 **Pousada de Santa Marinha**
$$$$$
pb, tv, ℜ
once downtown, take Alameda do São Dâmaso to the Largo da República do Brasil, then turn right onto Rua Doutor José Sampaio, climbing straight up until the sign for the pousada Estrada da Penha
4800 Guimarães
☎*253 51 22 53*
⇌*253 51 44 59*
A few kilometres from downtown Guimarães, the Pousada de Santa Marinha occupies the former monastery of Santa Marinha da Costa. Upon arriving, visitors are sure to be impressed by the entrance of the *pousada*. The building stands alongside the pretty baroque facade of the Igreja de Santa Marinha da Costa. Erected in the 12th century, it was donated to the Augustinian order by the wife of Dom Afonso Henriques. Modified in the 16th and 17th centuries, it has belonged

to the state since 1951. After being beautifully remodeled, the monastery was converted into a *pousada* and equipped with a new wing, which fits in perfectly with the rest of the structure. The luckiest guests get to stay in the rooms with views of the cloister. Coffered ceilings, *azulejos*, lovely fountains and a pleasant garden make up the crowning features of this perfectly enchanting place.

Ponte de Lima

Residencial São João
$
pb, ℜ
Rua Rosario, corner of Largo de São João, 4990 Ponte de Lima
☎*258 94 12 88*
This guest house is attractively located near the Rio Lima, in the heart of the old quarter. Ask for a room facing the river.

Albergaria Império do Minho
$$
pb, tv, ≈
Rua Agostinho José Taveira 4990 Ponte de Lima
☎*258 74 15 10*
⇒*258 94 25 67*
Located alongside the Rio Lima, this hotel has 49 comfortable rooms.

Valença do Minho

🦐 Casa do Poço
$$$
$$$$ for a suite
pb, tv
at the far end of the fort, near the *pousada*, 4 Travessa de Gaviarra 4930 Valença do Minho
☎*251 82 52 35*
On the border of Spain, within the confines of the fortress, this place is a real little palace. A noble old residence, it has been entirely renovated, with splendid results. The furniture, both eclectic and sophisticated, has been chosen with care, and the place as a whole emanates a great deal of character. The hotel also happens to be located in the most interesting part of the old city, in the second fortress, away from the hordes of tourists. A number of the rooms offer exceptional views of the ramparts and the Minho, with the Spanish city of Tuy in the distance.

Pousada de São Teotónio
$$$$
pb
at the far end of the fort, near the Igreja Matriz; 4930 Valença do Minho
☎*251 82 40 20*
⇒*251 82 43 97*
Also in the second fortress, right alongside the fortifications, the Pousada de São Teotónio has the advantage of being located away from the flood of tourists. A few of the rooms also offer stunning panoramic

views, compensating for the rather impersonal lay-out of the building, which is not very appealing in itself.

Vila Nova de Cerveira

(*15km from Valença do Minho*)

Pousada da Juventude
21 Largo 16 de Fevereiro, 4920 Vila Nova de Cerveira
☎/⇒*251 79 61 13*

Pousada de Dom Diniz
$$$$
pb, tv, ℜ
from Valença do Minho, head 13km southwest on the E1-N13-IC; Praça da Liberdade
4920 Vila Nova de Cerveira
☎*251 70 81 20*
⇒*251 70 81 29*
Located in a little village founded by King Dom Dinis in 1321, this is arguably the most unusual *pousada* in Portugal. Tucked away behind the restored fortifications of Vila Nova de Cerveira, it occupies the entire walled portion of the village. Each little house has been completely or partially remodeled from the ruins and transformed into accommodations, a restaurant and other facilities necessary for the smooth operation of the *pousada*. Once inside the ramparts, guests will feel as if they are walking about in a private little village. The rooms are modern and spacious, and some have small patios. The ramparts offer truly romantic views of the Minho and

its valley. This place is simply marvellous!

Viana do Castelo

Campismomata do Cabedelo/Orbitur
4900 Viana do Castelo
☎258 32 21 67
≈258 32 19 46

Hotel Aliança
$$
pb, tv
at the corner of Avenida dos Combatentes da Grande Guerra and Largo 5 de Outubro
4900 Viana do Castelo
☎258 82 94 98
≈258 25 29 98
Clean, but a little old-fashioned, yet with a certain style about it, this place is located in a lively part of town, right next to the old city.

Casa dos Costa Barros
$$$
pb/ps
22-28 Rua de São Pedro
4900 Viana do Castelo
☎258 82 37 05
≈258 82 81 37
A member of the *Turismo de Habitação* association, the Casa dos Costa Barros offers a few rooms in an atmosphere of a bygone era. A lovely 16th-century residence graced with Manueline windows, this *habitaçao* features an unusually sophisticated decor, made up of antique furniture and bibelots. In addition to its splendid setting, the place has the advantage of being located in the historic quarter, right in the heart of the city. An unforgettable experience!

Estalagem Melo Alvim
$$$$
pb, tv, ℜ
Ave. Conde da Carreira no. 28
4900 Viana do Castelo
☎258 810 82 00
≈258 810 82 20
Boasting an elegant Manueline-inspired facade as well as thick stone walls and warm woodwork, the Estalagem Melo Alvim is sure to delight those in search of charming accommodations with a dream decor. Located right next to the train station, the 16th-century manor house offers 20-odd rooms with all the comforts worthy of major hotels. Beyond its impressive lobby and granite staircase are wonderful rooms individually decorated with tasteful furnishings and curios. Guests can thus relive, if only briefly, the period in which the nobility presided over the fate of the world.

Santa Luzia

(*2km from Viana do Castelo*)

Pousada Monte de Santa Luzia
$$$$$
pb, tv, ≈, ℜ
Bom Jesus do Monte,
4900 Viana do Castelo
☎258 82 88 89
≈258 82 88 92
This is a grand old luxury hotel, decorated with a great deal of taste in 1930s style. The furnishings of both the rooms and the common areas reveal various Scandinavian elements, in both style and materials – pale wood, leather and marble. The immense bathrooms are made entirely of marble. Ask for one of the rooms facing the sea, which are equipped with small balconies overlooking the sanctuary. There are numerous sitting rooms where guest can read or chat in a peaceful, hushed atmosphere. The exquisite dining room, with its large windows, offers a view of the entire valley and the Santuária de Santa Luzia. This *pousada* has a lot of style and is slightly more luxurious than the others.

Além do Rio

(*3km from Viana do Castelo*)

Quinta da Boa Viagem
$$$
$$$$ for 4 people
pb, tv, ≈, K
From Viana do Castelo, take the E1-N13-IC1 northwards to the village of Areosa, then take the road on the right under the railway tracks. At the next intersection, take the little road on the right, then, a little farther, the road on the left. The quinta lies about 200m away.
Alem do Rio, Areosa, 4900 Viana do Castelo
☎258 83 55 02
≈258 83 68 36
A splendid pastoral setting awaits you just 3km from Viana do Castelo, at the Quinta da Boa Viagem. Imagine a stately farm dating back to the 18th century, stained a lovely shade of ochre and

tucked away amidst verdant hills, with a view of the sea in the distance. What a setting! The farm has been divided into fully equipped apartments, all very tastefully decorated, some with rustic furnishings. Peacefulness and greenery abound in this enchanting place, where guests can enjoy some lovely outings.

Restaurants

Amarante

Zé da Calçada
$$$
Rua 31 de Janeiro
☎225 42 20 23
At this restaurant, you can dine on Portuguese cuisine while enjoying a magnificent view of the valley. The fish dishes are excellent. To avoid the television, opt for the terrace.

Cafés and Tearooms

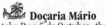 **Doçaria Mário**
take Rua 5 de Outubro, then veer to the left at the fork in the road; 135 Rua Cândido dos Reis
☎225 42 40 44
Slightly removed from the tourist activity, this pleasant café and pastry shop features local specialties. *Bolos de São Gonçalo, leiras, papos de anjo* and *foguetes* are but a few of the treats available. The recipes supposedly

come straight from the former convent of Amarante. On the terrace at the back, you can admire the lovely countryside, where the Rio Tâmega flows lazily between vine-covered hills and crops of vegetables.

São Gonçalo

(18km from Amarante)

Pousada de São Gonçalo
$$$
take the N15-IP4-E82 towards Vila Real; the *pousada* lies about 18km from downtown Amarante
☎225 46 11 13
▬225 46 11 23
After a nice walk in the mountains, what could be more enjoyable than dining at the Pousada de São Gonçalo. In the prestigious setting of the Serra do Marão, this restaurant serves such regional specialties as *Caldo Verde* (cabbage soup) and *Cabrito a Serrana* (mountain kid) in a dining room with a panoramic view. A pleasant spot to enjoy a meal or simply a good cup of coffee in a majestic setting (also see p 317).

Braga

Café Vianna
$
Praça da República, through the arcade facing Avenida Central
If turn-of-the-century interiors appeal to you, head to Café Vianna, where, in somewhat outdated surroundings (old seats and pink

marble decor), you can enjoy the daily special (classic Portuguese cuisine) for as little as 750 ESC.

Padaria Celeste
$
Ave. da Liberdade
on the left, just before Largo Barão de S. Martinho
Though hardly the height of luxury, this eatery is perfect for budget travellers seeking good but cheap sustenance. In fact, this unpretentious establishment not only serves *pão quente*, pizzas, sandwiches and burgers, but also sells bread and various kinds of cheese with which to prepare a simple picnic for your excursions. All this and a small, intriguing cake shop, too.

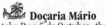 **Café Snack-Bar Silvas**
$$
Mon to Sat 11am to 11pm
Rua 25 de Abril, in the Granjinhos shopping centre
☎253 61 27 21
Given its name and location, you may well think this place is decidedly unoriginal. But make no mistake, for in the basement of this insignificant-looking shopping centre is a restaurant with a stunning designer decor. Drawing their inspiration from Japanese restaurants, the owners have created a space where patrons can sit around a large, U-shaped counter facing the kitchen. While only seven Portuguese dishes are offered daily,

Costa Verde

these vary throughout the week; though choice is limited, all dishes (*ranging from 900 to 1,000 ESC*) are of very good quality. A must-try if you get the chance to visit Braga.

Restaurante Café Astória
$$
Praça da República, through the arcade facing Avenida Central
Restaurante Café Astória also boasts a turn-of-the-century decor, featuring a profusion of ornamental mouldings along the ceilings and a floor charmingly decorated with mosaics, the whole accompanied by lovely woodwork and perfectly maintained furniture from this period. As for the cuisine, the proprietors also seem to have opted for continuity: classic Portuguese cuisine with the ubiquitous *bacalhau* on the menu, of course! Unfortunately, the television is always on and detracts a little bit from the friendly ambiance.

Restaurant A Ceia
$$
Tue to Sun noon to 3pm and 7pm to 10pm
331 Rua do Raio
☎253 26 39 32
Unpretentious, traditional local cuisine.

O Cantinho restaurant
$$
every day
Rua dos Petisco, southwest corner of Campo das Hortas
In modest but pleasant surroundings, the cook at the small O Cantinho restaurant will serve

you her lovingly prepared dishes from behind the bar in the dining room. Guests can thus savour one of the hearty house specialities (classic Portuguese cuisine) in a family atmosphere while enjoying refreshing *vinho verde*, a bottle of which is available for as little as 600 ESC. A real bargain! For those with smaller appetites, half-portions are also served, as are *petiscos*. Set menu at 1,600 ESC. Those seeking more opulent surroundings can eat in the warmly decorated dining room upstairs.

Cruz Sobral
$$$
Tue to Sun
7-8 Campo das Hortas
☎253 61 66 48
For a private evening in a refined setting, the Cruz Sobral restaurant is a good choice. Patrons can sample the great classics of Portuguese cuisine in a dining room where stone walls, terracotta-tiled floors, regional furnishings and attractively set tables make up the greater part of the decor. Guaranteed value, and no surprises. Set menu at 2,350 ESC.

Porta P'Teatro
$$$
Ave. da Liberdade no. 699, 2nd floor
☎253 26 36 97
Located on the second floor of a large bourgeois residence, right next to a theatre, the Porta P'Teatro restaurant, whose lovely business card aptly reflects its essence, features a particularly original layout. Indeed, its narrow dining room is very simply decorated with nothing more than a series of small tables arranged along an extensive white wall; simplicity and sparseness seem to be the restaurant's watchwords, as are the few flowers arranged on every table. Only the dull-chrome chair legs, the small modern wooden furnishings set out here and there and the cleverly designed lighting lend a little colour to the decor. As for the food, not only does the menu feature a vegetarian dish, but also more traditional offerings such as *linguado Argentino*, the house specialty. Overall, this delightful place is a must for those who appreciate sophisticated yet friendly surroundings.

Inácio
$$$
Wed to Mon
4 Campo das Hortas, near Praça Conde São Joaquim
☎253 61 32 35
At Inácio, you will find good regional cuisine served in a rustic setting. Try the *rillons* (a mixture of meats such as pork, kid, lamb, etc.) or venison, the house specialty, served in generous portions. The dessert list is limited, however. Ask for a table in the large room on the ground floor, which is attractively decorated with *azulejos*

depicting little animals. A set menu is available starting at 2,800 ESC.

O Alexandre
$$$$
Mon to Sat and Sun evening
Campo das Hortas no. 10, south side of the square
☎ *253 61 40 03*
A successful blend of old and new, the lovely decor of the O Alexandre restaurant is sure to please design enthusiasts. Despite these pleasant surroundings and the fine quality dishes served here, the lack of originality on the menu is regrettable. Appealing, but fairly expensive.

Cafés and Tearooms

Café Manuel Ferreira Capa
42 Rua dos Capelistas, near the Praça da República
The Café Manuel is a very pleasant place to enjoy a cup of coffee or a pastry in turn-of-the-century surroundings.

Café O Brasileiro
Mon to Sat 7am to midnight
corner of Rua de Sãomarcos and Rua do Barão de São Martinho
A charming place with a 1920's decor. Inside, interesting stucco bas-reliefs show the different phases of coffee-growing, while the outside is graced with lovely ironwork. Try the *bolo da senada*, one of a small assortment of pastries available here.

Bom Jesus do Monte
(7km from Braga)

Hotel do Elevador
$$
to the left of the sanctuary
☎ *253 60 34 00*
While dining at the hotel's restaurant, you can take in the entire valley at a single glance. Come sample regional specialties, such as *rojões* (pork, blood pudding and chestnuts; available in November), in an elegant atmosphere. The noon buffet on Sunday is a good bargain at 2,750 ESC and therefore very popular.

Amares
(17km from Braga)

Pousada Santa Maria do Bouro
$$$$
4720 Amares
☎ *253 37 19 70*
☎ *253 37 19 71*
Housed in the former kitchen of a monastery (see p 333), the Pousada Santa Maria do Bouro restaurant is a veritable marvel, and no one visiting Braga and its surrounding area can consciously miss out on dropping by. But before sitting down to eat, why not take the time to enjoy an aperitif in its lovely bar decorated with a few antique religious ornaments? Seated in plush leather armchairs, you can thus contemplate its imposing chimney while relaxing to the sounds of the lapping brook running through the cloister and branching off by the bar before reaching the gardens. Once used to supply the kitchen with drinking water, the brook, after ending up in a huge basin outside, flows freely through lovely gardens below the property. In the summer, tables face the gardens on an esplanade adjacent to the restaurant and bar.

From the bar, a long austere corridor that passes a series of small rooms, including a smoking room and a billiards room, leads to the restaurant. Two little fountains and skilful lighting heighten the place's monastic atmosphere all the more. As for the restaurant itself, you can partake of *arroz de cabrito* (rice and kid) or slices of *salmão com molho de camarões* (salmon with shrimp sauce) in the magnificent vaulted dining room, or opt for a table in its splendid chimney, covered by a huge pane of glass, allowing a generous amount of light to shine through. Finally, to top off the evening, be sure to try out the decadent Portuguese desserts (made with eggs, of course!), which are placed on a stone table that was once the cooks' work table, in the middle of the restaurant. The one slight drawback to this dream place is the annoying background noise from a fan in the chimney

Costa Verde

(nothing's perfect!).
Lastly, before going
back to the bar for a
bica and a comforting
after-dinner drink, be
sure to check out the
adjacent refectory. Con-
verted into a banquet
hall, it is graced with
three beautiful, modern
chandeliers that con-
trast wonderfully with
the austere monastic
decor, where a few old
frescoes and a small
chair built right into
one of its walls can still
be seen.

Bouro

(*20km from Braga*)

Restaurante Cruzeiro
$$
every day
on the N308 heading toward
Bouro, left of the highway, just
before the Pousada Santa Maria
do Bouro
☎*253 37 14 40*
Located in the central
square of the little
village of Bouro, right
next to the pillory, the
Restaurante Cruzeiro is
a good option for those
who want to enjoy a
few days' stay at the
Pousada Santa Maria do
Bouro. Here, guests can
sample regional dishes
such as *rejões* or a
cabrito assado in a
simple rural decor. Set
menu starting at
1,500 ESC.

Caniçada

(*30km from Braga*)

Pousada de São Bento
$$$
from Braga, take the N103 for
28km; shortly after the village of
Cerdeirinhas, turn left on the
N304 heading north
☎*253 64 71 90*
☎*253 64 71 91*
The chalet-style
Pousada de São Bento,
located in the Parque
Nacional de Peneda-
Gerês, is worthwhile
for visitors who enjoy
the mountains and long
walks in the wilder-
ness. The restaurant,
which features a large
terrace, offers views of
the mountains, the
valley of the Rio
Cávado and the reser-
voir of the Caniçada
dam. The whole thing
is quite simply magnifi-
cent! If you go to
Braga, make sure to
visit this perfectly idyllic spot.

Guimarães

Cinecitta
$
Praça de Santiago, under the
arches
Adorned with old
movie posters of the
great film classics, the
modest but charming
Cinecitta bar-restaurant
is just the place to have
a small sandwich with
a *cerveja* or a good
coffee. A few hot
dishes (spaghetti, lasa-
gna, toasted ham-and-
cheese sandwiches,
etc.) are also available
on request.

Cervejaria Martins
$
Largo do Toural
For a quick bite to eat
at a counter sur-
rounded by lovely
stone walls, head to the
small Piazza Martins
restaurant-bistro, where
a few simple dishes can
be had for less than
1,000 ESC. Pleasant and
unpretentious.

Solar da Rainha
$$
Tue to Sun
135 Rua da Rainha Dona
Maria II
The Solar da Rainha,
also known by locals as
the Casa da Corõa
(there is a small crown,
or *corõa*, on the fa-
cade), has an interest-
ing selection of re-
gional dishes starting at
2,500 ESC. Cozy decor
and friendly staff.

Solar do Arco
$$
48-50 Rua de Santa Maria, right
before the arch marking the
entrance of the old city
The Solar do Arco
serves good classic
cuisine with no sur-
prises. Modern decor.

Pousada da Nossa Senhora
da Oliveira
$$$
Largo da Oliveira
☎*253 51 41 57*
Right in the heart of
Guimarães, on the
splendid Largo da
Oliveira, the perfectly
charming Pousada da
Nossa Senhora da
Oliveira occupies a
former seigneurial resi-
dence. Its warmly deco-
rated dining room is a
treasure all in itself.

Vinho Verde

Produced in the Province of Minho, Vinho Verde was one of the first Portuguese wines to be exported. English merchants established a trading post in the port town of Viana do Castelo in the 14th century to export the wine to England.

This wine is usually white and slightly sparkling, and is traditionally drunk right after the wine-harvest. Vinho Verde's official demarcation came in 1929, and the wine was produced in six sub-regions. Most of the wine is produced in the south of the province, where a number of renowned grapes, including the *Loureiro, Trajadura* and *Pedernã* varieties, are cultivated.

Vinho Verde has a lower alcohol content (between 9 and 10%) than do most other white wines. Most Vinho Verdes are blends, but several are derived from a single grape, such as the *Loureiro*, with its hint of bayleaf, or the *Trajadura*, with a tropical fruity aroma.

In the north, two sub-regions, Monção and Melgaço, produce "green wine" with a slightly higher alcohol content (between 11 an 12%). The most widely used grape is the *Alvarinho*, which produces a wine similar to a Riesling. Several red Vinho Verde vintages are also available: these are slightly acidic and should be served at cool temperatures.

For more information on Vinho Verde, visit the Casa do Vinho Verde, located in the centre of Porto in an old building that has been completely restored (see address below). Here, visitors can sample various vintages on the marvellous terrace with a panoramic view of the romantic Douro and the *ribeira*.

A Casa do Vinho do Porto
Mon to Fri 9am to noon and 2pm to 5:30pm
Rua da Restauração No. 318
4050 Porto
☎*226 07 73 00*
226 07 73 20
www.cvrvv.pt

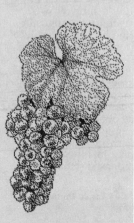

Aside from such local specialties as *Bacalhau à Vimaranense* and *Arroz de Frango Pica no Chão*, the menu consists mainly of meat and fish dishes. Saturday nights are Portuguese music nights after 9pm. Reservations are requested.

Pousada de Santa Marinha
$$$

once downtown, take Alameda do São Dâmaso to the Largo da República do Brasil, then turn right onto Rua Doutor José Sampaio, climbing straight up until the sign for the pousada; Estrada da Penha
☎*253 51 44 53*
Several kilometres from downtown Guimarães, the Pousada de Santa Marinha occupies the former monastery of Santa Marinha da Costa (see p 334). The entrance of the *pousada* is particularly striking. The building stands alongside the pretty baroque facade of the Igreja de Santa Marinha da Costa. Erected in the 12th century, it was given to the Augustinian order by the wife of Dom Afonso Henriques. Modified in the 16th and 17th centuries, it has belonged to the state since 1951. The dining room, with its period furniture and granite pillars, beckons guests to enjoy an evening in a thoroughly monastic setting.

 Val de Donas
$$$$
Rua Val de Donas no. 4
☎*253 51 14 11*
In a lovely, distinctive house, the Val de

Donas restaurant is one of Guimarães's finer local-cuisine establishments. Featuring a refined decor of elegantly set tables with regional crockery, the restaurant offers such treats as *arroz de feijão* served with a piece of breaded *bacalhau*, and *perna de porco assado* with pan-fried garlic potatoes. And why not wash down your meal with one of the famous regional wines, *vinho verde*, renowned for its lower alcohol content and for being more bubbly than its northern counterparts? Finally, should you have any room left after such a lavish meal, try one of the rich à-la-carte desserts: the abundance of eggs and sugar they contain will soon satisfy your appetite!

Cafés and Tearooms

Coconut Confeitaria Padrão
every day 7am to midnight
Largo da Oliveira
This friendly little café serves *francesas*, a type of grilled ham and cheese sandwich, as well as a few desserts. The Coconut Confeitaria is also a popular meeting place for the city's younger set. Its attractive little terrace, right on pretty Largo da Oliveira, makes this a decidedly pleasant spot.

Ponte de Lima

O Brasão
$$
Thu to Tue 8am to midnight
1 Rua Formosa
☎*258 94 18 90*
O Brasão is a beautiful restaurant in the old quarter. If only there were more places like this! For a change, there is no television, but rather soft traditional music. The vaults and candelabra make this a delightful ambience where you'll want to linger over dinner or lunch.

Restaurante São João
$$
every day noon to 3pm and 8pm to 10pm; Rua Rosario, corner Largo de São João
☎*258 94 12 88*
Good regional cuisine in a decor consisting mainly of small tables draped with cloth.

Restaurante Beco das Selas
$$
Sun to Fri
Beco das Selas
☎*258 94 35 16*
Frequented mainly by locals, the Restaurante Beco das Selas serves classic Portuguese cuisine in a large room decorated in a simple but attractive manner.

Cafés and Tearooms

S.A. Bar Galeria
Travessa B. Francisco Pacheco no. 5
This small, unpretentious bistro hosts painting exhibitions. Here

like everywhere, the curse of modern times called the TV is always on.

Valença do Minho

Restaurante Fortaleza
$$
5 Rua Apolinário da Fonseca right before the entrance to the second fort, on the left side of the street
☎251 82 31 46
The Restaurante Fortaleza boasts an attractive terrace, a modern decor and good regional dishes.

Pousada de São Teotónio
$$$
at the far end of the fort, near the Igreja Matriz
☎251 82 40 20
In the second fortress, right alongside the fortifications, the Pousada de São Teotónio has the advantage of being located away from the flood of tourists. The dining room offers a view of the lovely Rio Minho and the ramparts (also see p 327).

Vila Nova de Cerveira

(*15km from Valença do Minho*)

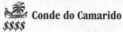 Pousada de Dom Dinis
$$$
from Valença do Minho, head 13km southwest on the E1-N13-IC; Praça da Liberdade
☎251 79 56 01
Located in a little village founded by King Dom Dinis in 1321, this is arguably the most

unusual *pousada* in Portugal. Tucked away behind the restored fortifications of Vila Nova de Cerveira, it occupies the entire walled portion of the village. Each little house has been completely or partially remodeled from the ruins and transformed into accommodations, a restaurant and other facilities necessary for the smooth operation of the *pousada*. Once inside the ramparts, visitors will feel as if they are walking about in a private little village. The restaurant is attractively decorated, with a large picture window looking out onto an inner court protected by ancient stone walls. After a good meal, you can take a stroll around the ramparts and enjoy the romantic view of the Minho and its valley.

Viana do Castelo

José Manuel Brito Portela
$
16 Rua da Boavontade
☎258 84 22 90
offers a buffet menu of local dishes for the modest sum of 1,300 ESC. Now that's a bargain!

Pastelaria Zê Natario-Café Sport
$$
Avenida dos Combatentes da Grande Guerra, corner Rua Manjovos
☎258 82 21 17
If you enjoy lively places, head to the Pastelaria Zê Natario-

Café Sport for a simple, inexpensive meal or even just to sample one of the delicious pastries. Tourist menu starting at 1,750 ESC.

Restaurante Náutico
$$-$$$
Praça da Galiza, at the foot of the Ponte de Viana
If you are looking for a verdant setting with an interesting view, the Restaurante Náutico will fit the bill. The building is attractive and the classic Portuguese cuisine unpretentious.

Conde do Camarido
$$$$
every day 12:30pm to 3pm and 7:30pm to 11pm
Ave. Conde da Carreira no. 28
☎258 81 08 20
In the grand Melo Alvim hotel, the Conde do Camarido restaurant offers several typical dishes from the Alto Minho region, such as delicious traditionally made duck with rice, specially prepared sole or, for those who prefer meat, a hearty dish of Minho-style diced fried pork. The particularly elegant dining room is perfect for either a romantic evening or a business lunch.

Cafés and Tearooms

Pastelaria Picotinha
Sun to Fri
36 Rua da Picota
For a good cup of coffee and a dessert at a reasonable price, head to the Pastelaria

Costa Verde

Picotinha. Good selection of pastries. Very popular with locals.

Café Girassol
in the little park known as the Jardim Marginal
The Café Girassol is a wonderful place to relax in a verdant setting. Light dishes and desserts.

Santa Luzia

(2km from Vania do Castelo)

Pousada Monte de Santa Luzia
$$$
see p 336 for address
☎ *258 82 88 89*
Guests enjoy carefully prepared cuisine in some of the most elegant surroundings imaginable. The menu occasionally includes a few alternatives to traditional Portuguese dishes. Friendly, professional service. Be warned, though, the desserts are enormous! The exquisite dining room, with its large windows, offers a view of the entire valley and the Santuária de Santa Luzia. This *pousada* is extremely stylish and slightly more luxurious than the others.
Excellent value.

Entertainment

Bars and Nightclubs

Braga

James Dean Café Bar
85 Rua de S. André
As its name suggests, the American actor is honoured here. The place boasts a designer decor worthy of the most prominent establishments in the capital. The long and narrow room is mostly adorned with woodwork enhanced by skilful lighting, with posters of the greatly missed celebrity. Patrons can enjoy a *bica* or a beer, as well as a few light dishes, all reasonably priced.

Club 84
Tue to Sun 11pm to 4am
basement of the Hotel Turismo
enter from outside
The discothèque Club 84 attracts a varied clientele. The decor is not quite kitschy enough to be interesting.

Bar Populum
Praça Conde Agrolongo
A lively weekend spot, the Populum bar features a particularly intriguing vaulted-cave setting make up of stone columns and walls. A fine place in which to drink until the wee hours of the

morning and meet Braga's young set.

Barbieri Café
Cover charge
Ave. Central or Ave. dos Combatentes
across from McDonald's
Weekends draw a young local crowd to the popular Barbieri bar-disco. While the main floor is decorated with funky barber chairs, the 2nd floor sports a long, modern-looking bar in a most designer-like setting where "party animals" can whoop it up till the break of dawn.

Latino Bar
Mon to Sat 9:30pm to 2am
56 Rua do Anjo
The Latino Bar attracts a mainly young, local clientele.

Viana do Castelo

Bar do Centro da Juventude
Rua do Poço
Young Viana hangs out at the Bar do Centro da Juventude, which features live music on Saturdays and Sundays, starting at 10pm.

Bar Jardim
every day 7:30pm to 11pm
Ave. Conde da Carreira no. 28
Those with an appreciation for elegant, charming decors should have an aperitif or a digestif at Bar Jardim, located in the beautiful Melo Alvim hotel, a grand 16th-century house.

Guimarães

Guimarães's many cafés are swamped with hordes of young people on weekends. But if you're looking for a bar, you should have no trouble finding one you like by strolling along the **Largo da Senhora da Oliveira** or hitting the **Praça de Santiago**.

Ponte de Lima

Rampinha
at Rua Formosa and Rua Inácio Perestrelo
Its walls covered with umpteen posters and photographs of everyone from Che Guevara to American celebrities, Café-Cervejaria Rampinha is a very pleasant place in which to sip a glass of port or cool off with a local *cerveja*.

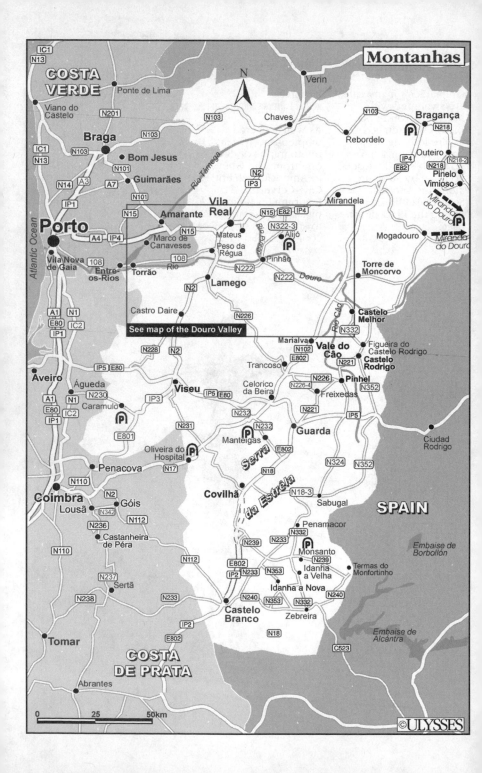

Montanhas

The end of the world...
as if there were no Spain beyond the mountains.

Well, no, it doesn't exist you say; yet you roll along toward Miranda do Douro, to the northeast, as if you were heading toward the edge of the known universe; you visit Monsanto, built in a great heap of stones, as if there could be no other human beings beyond this strange village; you wander around Marialva in search of a medieval past. You visit Guarda, as if it were the guardian of the civilized world; finally, you observe the thousand-year-old rock carvings in the Vale do Côa. In fact, you are carried away by this "upper" (Beira Alto) region "beyond the mountains" (Tras-os-Montes), and come to appreciate the pretensions of its fortresses and castles, the watchmen of Portugal, the holders of the keys to the country. It was Bragança that saw the birth of the dynasty

of dukes that gave Portugal its kings up to the beginning of the 20th century, and it is Bragança's fortress that cannot help but impress upon those that behold it. Travellers, art-lovers and gourmets alike, drawn to these distant sites must, without fail, stop over in Viseu, a pleasant little art town, and at Castelo Branco to dine at the Praça Velha.

Finding Your Way Around

By Car from Porto

Bragança

Quick Route

Follow Highway A4-IP4 toward Vila Real. Once there, continue by way of the N15-E82-IP4 until Bragança. The road alternates between a national highway (E82-N4) and a stretch of expressway that should be completed through to Bragança very soon.

Scenic Route

Take Highway A4-IP4 toward Vila Real and, from there, continue by way of the N2-IP3 as far as Chaves. Then take the N103, which crosses beautiful mountain scenery and leads the rest of the way to Bragança.

Castelo Branco

Take Highway A1-E80 south as far as Coimbra. Then take the N17 east and the N2 to the N112 further east, which will take you to Castelo Branco.

Guarda

Quick Route

Take Highway A1-E80 south and, at the junction with the E80-IP5, head toward Viseu and then Braga.

Scenic Route

If you have plenty of time, take the N108, with runs along the Rio Douro as far as the city of Peso da Régua, where you continue by taking the N2 southbound. At the junction with the N226, take the latter in a southwesterly direction. About 88km farther, at the village of Vila Franca das Naves, continue straight along the N226-N340 as far as the village of Freixeda. From there, turn right, continuing southwards on the N221, which will

take you straight to Guarda.

Lamego

Quick Route

Take Highway A4-IP4 toward Vila Real to the intersection of the N2, which will lead you directly to Lamego via the Douro Valley.

Scenic Route

Take Highway N108, which runs along the Rio Douro, to Peso da Régua, where the N2 runs through the Douro Valley and south to Lamego.

Miranda do Douro

Roads throughout the Miranda do Douro region are winding and are sometimes of only dirt and gravel, making it preferable to travel during the day for safety reasons. Because there are so few major arteries in this area, it is also important not to underestimate distances. With the many obstacles you may encounter (dogs sleeping on the road, herds of sheep, oxcarts, and so on), count on average speeds of 60kph on the medium-sized roads and 40kph on the smaller ones.

From Bragança, follow the N218 west for 32km as far as the village of Outeiro. Once there, continue along the N218 toward Vimioso or go left on the N218-2 toward Pinelo and

then toward Vimioso. This latter route, although very impressive because of its fine scenery, is also quite dangerous. For most of the way, it is very narrow and covered with gravel, making the curves perilous.

Mateus

Quick Route

Take Highway A4-IP4, part of which is not yet completed; you will reach the E82-N15, which goes directly to Amarante and then to Vila Real. Mateus is to the right of the E82-N15, a few kilometres past Vila Real.

Scenic Route

Take the N108, which runs alongside the Rio Douro, until the village of Entre-os-Rios. From there, cross the Rio Tâmega to continue along the N108 as far as Peso da Régua. Then follow the N2 north to Vila Real and then Mateus.

Viseu

Quick Route

Take Highway A1-E80 south and, at the junction with the E80-IP5, head in the direction of Viseu.

Scenic Route

Take Highway A1-E80 south and, at the junction with the E80-IP5, head toward Viseu. At the junction with the

N1-IC2, about 4km farther, turn off in a northerly direction and go 3kmuntil the fork with the N16, which goes directly to Viseu.

By Train

Though the towns listed below can be reached by train, using this means of transportation is not entirely practical. Indeed, with the exception of Castelo Branco and Guarda, only accessible from Lisbon, timetables prove irregular and connections difficult. For Caminhos de Ferro departures and information see p 69.

Castelo Branco

From Lisbon

Santa Apolónia station on Avenida Infante Dom Henrique
Departure: several times a day
Fare: Intercidades 1,950 ESC

Guarda

From Lisbon

Santa Apolónia station on Avenida Infante Dom Henrique
Departure: several times a day
Fare: Intercidades 2,250 ESC

By Bus from Lisbon

Rede Nacional de Expressos
terminal located at 18B Avenida Casal Ribeiro
Departure: numerous times every day
OR
Renex Expressos
Cais das Cebolas, near the Casa dos Bicos
Departure: numerous times every day

For information in Lisbon, see p 69.

Bragança

Travel time: approx. 9hrs
Fare: 2,200 to 2,400 ESC

Castelo Branco

Travel time: 4hrs
Fare: 1,200 to 1,400 ESC

Guarda

Travel time: approx. 6 hrs
Fare: 1,500 to 1,700 ESC

Viseu

Travel time: approx. 4hrs
Fare: 1,400 to 1,600 ESC

By Bus from Porto

Rede Nacional de Expressos and **Renex Expressos**
on Rua Carmelitas, near Torre dos Clérigos
OR
on Praça Filipa de Lencastre
OR
on Rua Alexandre Herculano
OR
on Praça Batalha (at Garagem Atlantic)
Departure: several times a day

For information in Porto, see p 286.

Bragança

Travel time: 3.5hrs
Fare: between 1,300 and 1,400 ESC

Castelo Branco

Travel time: 5.5hrs
Fare: Between 1,700 and 1,900 ESC

Guarda

Travel time: 2.5hrs
Fare: between 1,200 and 1,350 ESC

Viseu

Travel time: 2hrs
Fare: between 950 and 1,050 ESC

Montanhas

Practical Information

Tourist Information Offices

Bragança

at the corner of Avenida Cidade de Zamora and the Largo Principal

Castelo Branco

Avenida da Liberdade

Guarda

Praça Luís de Camões

Lamego

Avenida Visconde Guedes Teixeira

Miranda do Douro

Praça Mor

Viseu

Avenida Calouste Gulbenkian

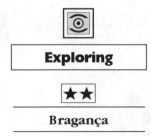

Exploring

★★

Bragança

If it can be said that Portugal has an impressive number of castles, the one in Bragança is among the most beautiful in the country. Although its name is famous throughout the country for its association with Portugal's last dynasty, (1640-1910), this small town suffered greatly from its geographic location. Lost in the northeastern edge of the country, in a relatively arid region, it was soon abandoned by its protectors. In fact, from the 15th century onward, less than a century after its promotion to the rank of duchy in 1442, the Brangances preferred Vila Viçosa, which was not as harsh or isolated. No matter, say Bragança's inhabitants, for the city, proud of its age-old communal freedoms, delights in recalling that it has the oldest town hall in Portugal. As for its isolation, this has helped preserve the town; today its fortifications and medieval quarter are in excellent condition. Only the 20th century changed the look of the place, with the discovery and exploitation of precious minerals leading to the creation of new urban areas outside the walls.

As you will have gathered, the major attraction here is the **old town** and its **fortifications**. Although the castle can be reached by car, we advise you to park your vehicle not far from the town's central square, the Praça da Sé. By doing this, you will avoid disrupting the quietness and the medieval charm of the place. From the cathedral square (Praça da Sé), take Rua dos Combatentes da Grande Guerra, a pleasant shopping street, which forms a sort of extension to the square. A pretty **plaza** named the Largo de São Vicente marks the end of this street. There stands the **Igreja de São Vicente** (*left side*), curiously forming the street corner. Some claim the secret wedding of Inês de Castro and Pedro I took place in this church. After this brief stop, continue climbing toward the castle, taking Rua Trindade Coelho, located on the right side of the Largo. Going up this little cobbled street constitutes a pleasant walk in itself, although it can be a bit strenuous. It will lead you directly to the fortified gate of the enclosure.

You will barely have gone past the gate of the **old town** ★★ when the calm and the almost medieval atmosphere that reign here suddenly take over. This singular sensation is equalled only by the experience of visiting the village of Ourém. Though Portugal is full of streets and squares with a medieval flavour, few of these can boast as genuine an age-old atmosphere as Bragança. Go along the main street to the end, where you will find the fortress. Before exploring it, notice the ancient *pelourinho* (pillory) on your left. Its base consists of a sculpture representing a wild boar caught in the pillory. Archaeologists believe the sculpture may date from prehistoric times.

Built in 1187 by Dom Sancho I, the **fortress** (*300 ESC; 9am to 11:45am and 2pm to 4:45pm, closed Thu*) has a fine **dungeon** called the Torre de Menagem. Turned into a palace in the 15th century, the dungeon now houses a small **military museum** (*150 ESC; same hours as the fortress*), which is more amusing than edifying to visit. Walking around the Torre de Menagem, you can reach the various towers, with **magnificent views** ★ over the old town and its surroundings. Be careful on the access stairs, which, besides being narrow, are also slippery in places. Going to the very foot of the dungeon, notice the bridge leading to the museum entrance; it forms a fine Gothic arch. Those looking for fine views in relative safety can go to the foot of the town walls, where a more secure circular road awaits.

Make your way to the front of the **Igreja Santa Maria**, located near the Torre de Menagem, to observe a beautiful **baroque portal**, adorned with two wreathed

columns. What really draws attention here, however, is the building located just next to the church, the **Domus Municipalis** ★. This is the oldest-known town hall in Portugal. Dating from the 12th century, it is the only example of a Romanesque civic building in the country. Walking alongside the building, be sure to notice its cornice, adorned with many sculptures.

Located in the former episcopal palace, the **Museu do Abade de Baçal** (*200 ESC; Tue to Sun 10am to noon and 2pm to 5pm; Rua do Consilheiro Abilio Beça 27*) is worth a visit for its small archaeological collection and its ethnographic section devoted to the region. Several paintings are also exhibited here.

Photographers in search of impressive scenery should take the road leading to the Pousada de São Bartolomeu (see p 364), south of the Rio Fervença, where an observatory (*300m from the pousada*) offers a fine **panorama** ★ of the castle, its setting, and the surrounding countryside.

Castelo Branco

A gateway to the Alentejo, in the eastern confines of the country, Castelo Branco could

be considered the most isolated town in Portugal. Unlike Bragança or Guarda, it is not linked to Spain by any major road. Founded in the 8th century by the Knights of Templar, it underwent several occupations, among them those by Spanish and Napoleonic troops. Little remains today of its distant past other than the ruins of its castle, which have been turned into an observation deck. Besides its role as administrative capital of Beira Baixa, Castelo Branco is best known for the production of excellent regional specialties such as honey, olive oil, cheese and sausages. In terms of handicrafts, the town is also esteemed for its bedspreads. Called *colchas*, these covers are embroidered in many colours and decorated with whimsical motifs. Even if the number of attractions is very limited in Castelo Branco, one should not miss the famous garden surrounding the former episcopal palace. Besides its medieval-looking historical centre, the town makes for a pleasant stop while discovering a region where two extraordinary little villages still slumber: Idanha-a-Velha and Monsanto da Beira.

To reach the gardens of the former episcopal palace, and to enjoy a pleasant walk at the same time, take the

Montanhas

following route: on Avenida da Liberdade, pass in front of the courthouse, the building located opposite the tourism office. Once there, go along the little street to the right of the building until it meets Rua da Santa Maria (*the fourth street on your right*). Going along Santa Maria, you will arrive at the pretty **Praça Luís de Camões**. There you can admire the fine **houses**, as well as the former **Câmara Municipal** (town hall), outfitted with arcades and an elegant **outdoor stairway**. Then take Rua dos Ferreiros, at the north side of the square to the right, which will lead you to the Largo de São João. An interesting **Manueline calvary** stands on this square.

garden **Jardim do Antigo Paço Episcopal** (*every day 9am to dusk; Rua de Frei Bartolomeu da Costa*). Besides the sculpted hedges, water basins decorated with *azulejos* and numerous flowerpots, the garden contains a multitude of baroque statues representing mythical and allegorical themes as well as religious personages. Among the curiosities, do not miss the stairway of the kings. Sculpted into the banister, royal figures follow in chronological order, thus recalling the various Portuguese dynasties. Note the amusing detail of the three effigies showing the Spanish kings who reigned over the country; they are portrayed as much smaller than the others.

From the Largo São João, Rua de Frei Bartolomeu da Costa, topped by an arcade-cum-stairway, will lead you straight to the entrance of the episcopal

Reducing them to the size of statuettes, the designers of this project wanted to show in what low esteem these kings were held.

Idanha-a-Velha and Monsanto da Beira

A pleasant tour allows for the discovery of Castelo Branco's surroundings, an area that includes two charming little villages that have remained isolated from the tourist throngs, Idanha-a-Velha and Monsanto da Beira.

From Castelo Branco, take the N233 north 23km to the junction with the N353, just after crossing the Ribeira de Alpreade. The road then goes straight to the village of Idanha-a-Nova. To get to Idanha-a-Velha, continue along the N353 for 1km and, after passing the Rio Ponsul, take the N354 west for 12km. At the junction with the N352, take the latter north. Idanha-a-Velha is about 7km from there, to the right of the road. For Monsanto da Beira, continue along the N352 until Medelim, where you turn right. The village is about 7km from this fork.

Idanha-a-Velha

(*52km from Castelo Branco*)

This sleepy little village has well-preserved Roman vestiges, which you will not want to miss. To respect the serenity of this place, avoid going through the village by car. You can leave your vehicle at the entrance to the village, at its northern gate, where a parking area has been set up.

Before entering the village, go along the enclosure heading left to admire one of the most impressive works in this spot, the beautiful **Roman bridge**. Although it dates from the 2nd century, it has been preserved perfectly and, despite its 18 centuries of existence, local peasants still cross it with their carts, just as the Romans used to do! Return now to the northern gate to reach the heart of the village. Although it has been entirely rebuilt, this **Roman gate** is no less impressive with its massive dimensions. After strolling through the village's picturesque alleyways, head to the main square to admire the **Visigoth basilica**. Recently restored, it contains a variety of stone objects and sculptures dating from the Roman and Visigoth periods (*with digging still going on, visiting hours are subject to frequent changes*). A **Paleochristian baptistry**, probably dating from the 3rd century, when the first church was built, can also be observed. Also, walking all around the village, you can see the ruins of the **Roman wall** that protected the site.

Monsanto da Beira

(*49km from Castelo Branco*)

To preserve the tranquillity of the village, and out of respect for its inhabitants, leave your car in the parking area at the entrance to the village.

This is perhaps the most impressive village in Beira Baixa. The inhabited area harmonizes perfectly here with the environment, blending in so completely that it almost forms a natural extension. Perched atop a hill, Monsanto da Beira is, in effect, "hidden" amidst an impressive scattering of often oval-shaped boulders. Walking along the village's cobbled alleyways, you can admire primitive-looking little houses, built entirely of local stone. Something truly astonishing is that while some of them are built of rock, others are hidden right beside or even beneath enormous boulders that seem ready to crush the little houses next to them. The effect is quite amazing. Climbing the alleyways, you can see the ruins of a **Romanesque chapel** and, atop the hill, those of the former **castle**. From the latter, a **breathtaking view** completes this visit to another century. Beneath a blazing sun, this can well be an exhausting and difficult

walk (watch out for the sometimes slippery ground), but it is also quite magical. And, with a bit of luck, you may have the chance to see elderly ladies seated on the ground, busy making the famous *rodilhas*. These are little ring-shaped cushions used by women to transport various objects (earthenware jars, bowls, pottery, etc.) on their heads. Made from many pieces of multi-coloured cloth, they make a pleasant little decorative souvenir. Moreover, by buying one, you are helping to preserve an age-old activity.

Guarda

Dubbed "the guardian", the town of Guarda sits atop all of Portugal from its altitude of 1,050m. It is the highest town in the country and forms the core of an impressive series of fortresses spread all along the Spanish border. Probably already inhabited in prehistoric times, the Guarda area was occupied successively by the Romans, the Visigoths and the Moors. Despite this rich past, it was not until the area was conquered by Dom Afonso Henriques that Guarda's site became permanently occupied. It owes its birth as a town to his successor,

Montanhas

Dom Sancho I. A charter was granted in 1197 and imposing fortifications were built. From this date onward, the town continued to play a strategic role. Considered by some as a cold-looking and charmless town, Guarda is worth a visit nonetheless. Despite an undeniable harshness, its old town possesses a certain aesthetic quality, and its beautiful cathedral is enough to justify the trip.

A visit should begin at the very heart of the town, on the Praça da Sé. After briefly admiring the pretty facade of the building housing the tourist office, head to the front of the **Sé ★★**. This imposing cathedral, whose severe grey granite countenance seems to stress a fortress-like appearance, is impressive. Its very extended period of construction, from 1390 to 1540, explains the presence of different styles, a mixture that comes across as quite harmonious. The grimacing gargoyles, the numerous pinnacles and the clover-shaped decorations of the balustrade roof may recall Batalha, its southern sister. These two cathedrals are the only ones in Portugal with flying buttresses. Before going inside the cathedral, take a look at its two portals, each of them imbued with character. While the **main portal**, framed by two crenellated towers, shows its

Manueline style, the elegant **north portal** is filled with Gothic decorations.

The **interior ★** features an imposing nave which reveals beautiful **wreathed columns** as well as thick-ribbed **vaults**. The most striking element, however, is the very fine main-altar **retable ★**, a work by Jean de Rouen, who also made the Batalha portal. Finely worked in soft Ança stone, used mostly in the Coimbra region, the retable's various tiers portray more than 100 personages! Another object of contemplation is the elegant **renaissance portal** to the fourth chapel on the lower left side. It marks the entrance to the Capela dos Pinas, where you can see a fine **Gothic recumbent statue**. Finally, if you appreciate good views, do not miss climbing atop the building by the stairway that winds around the angled column of the right transept (*150 ESC; Tue to Sun 10am to noon and 2pm to 5pm*). From its terrace, you can enjoy a **fine panorama** of the town and the nearby mountains.

Leaving the cathedral, head now (*on the right side*) to the top of the square and take the little Rua de Doutore Miguel Alarcão. At number 25-27 is the magnificent **Solar de Alarcão** (see p 365). Dating from 1686, this granite manor is

adorned with an elegant flagstone terrace facing a chapel, to which an attractive loggia is attached. After its restoration and conversion to tourist lodgings as part of the *Turismo de Habitação* program, it was inaugurated personally by Portuguese president Mário Soares.

On the east side of the cathedral, Rua da Torre leads across the **medieval quarter**, where you can admire the **Torre dos Ferreiros**, an ancient dungeon dating from the 13th century.

To discover the authentic Guarda, take **Rua Francisco dos Passos** (*located north of the Largo de Camões*) as far as the Largo São Vicente, and continue your walk along **Rua de São Vicente** until you reach the **Porta d'El-Rei**.

Lamego

Located near the Douro Valley, 13km from Peso da Régua, the small town of Lamego can take pride in boasting one of the most beautiful museums in the country, as well as a Way of the Cross, composed of a magnificent baroque staircase that rivals that of Bom Jesus (see p 321). In terms of gastronomy, the town is especially renowned for its sparkling wine and smoked ham.

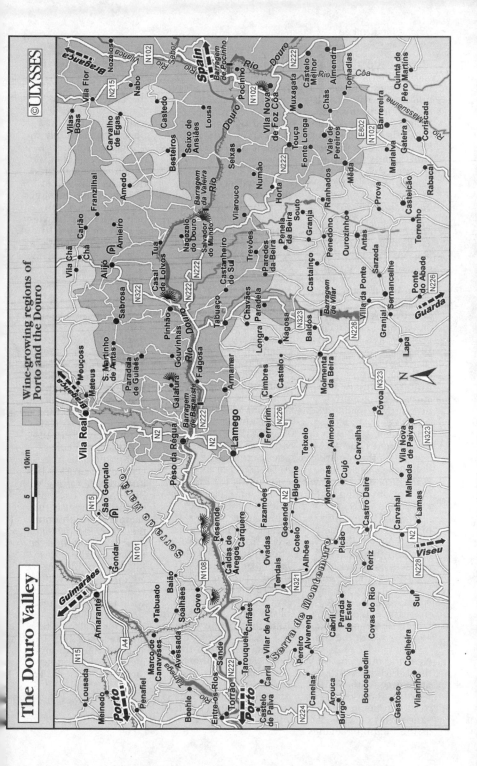

The Douro Valley

© ULYSSES

Wine-growing regions of Porto and the Douro

After passing through a series of neighbourhoods with prosaic buildings, visitors will end up in the historic heart of the city, on the Largo da Sé, extending from the Largo Camões. Here stands the exquisite **Museu de Lamego** ★★ (*250 ESC, free admission on Sun; Tue to Sat 10am to 12:30pm and 2pm to 5pm, Sun 10am to 12:30pm; Largo Camões*). Nestled in a former episcopal house dating back to 1750, this museum is a must for fans of **Flemish tapestries** ★★, who can admire six exceptional works from the Brussels School, most of which date back to the 16th century. Among the many treasures to be admired here are the paintings on wood by Vasco Fernandes, who was nicknamed *Grão Vasco*, as well as the remarkable **Capela de São João Evangelista** ★, a veritable riot of gilding with its set of *talhas douradas*. Lastly, the many *azulejos* dating back to the 17th century and the religious artifacts collected here are sure to please art lovers. Visiting the museum is all the more pleasant as the striking layout of the premises alone is worth the trip.

Near the museum, on the Largo da Sé, the **Sé de Lamego** (cathedral) is worth a short visit so as to admire its Renaissance cloister, as well as the beautiful ceilings gracing its nave. Upon leaving the cathedral, visitors can stroll along Avenida Visconde Guedes Teixeira, planted with numerous trees and bordered by elegant bourgeois residences.

Those who continue their stroll to Avenida Dr. Alfredo de Sousa, also abundantly planted with trees though less elegant, will end up at what constitutes the second pride of Lamego residents, the **Nossa Senhora dos Remédios** sanctuary, with its impressive **baroque staircase** ★★ that ascends up to close to 600m. Built in 1750, this monumental staircase rivals that of Bom Jesus; with its plethora of chapels, sometimes adorned with *azulejos*, it constitutes a veritable Way of the Cross, which many Portuguese continue to climb to this day. At its top end stands the church of the same name. Besides its impressive, immaculate white façade in the baroque style, however, this church has no particular charm. Moreover, though the esplanade before the church offers a panoramic view of the city and its surrounding countryside, the best perspective can be seen from the staircase itself; there is therefore no need to endure this long penance to admire what is truly a baroque masterpiece.

Finally, before leaving this charming little town, a short visit to the **Castelo** (*Rua do Castelo*) will end your tour of the area on a pleasant note. Only the dungeon remains of this old fortified castle, which was recaptured from the Muslims in 1057 and later modified several times. From here, a interesting view of the city is sure to delight photographers.

Mateus

Who has never heard of the famous Mateus wine, known for its fresh bouquet? Mateus is not only an esteemed wine area but also a very elegant **baroque palace** ★ built in the 18th century by Nicolo Nasoni. Besides the interior of the prestigious Solar, you can visit the wine cellars and participate in a tasting of Europe's best-known rosé (along with Provence's). The only disappointment is the shamefully high entry fee (*1000 ESC to visit the park, the palace and the cellars*) to take part in this form of hidden advertising. By way of comparison, the port wine tastings in the storehouses of Vila Nova da Gaia are free, and the entry fees to visit the finest monuments in the country rarely exceeds 600 ESC.

The Douro Valley ★

Schistose soil sheltered from the Atlantic's humid winds by two mountain chains (Serra do Marão and Serra de Montemuro) and a contrasting climate, with rough winters and sometimes sweltering summers, make up part of the recipe for Porto's famous wine; this nectar's other secrets lie in Vila Nova da Gaia (see box, p 298). From Peso da Régua, one of the first controlled vintage regions in Europe, the Douro region, regulated as early as 1757 on the initiative of the Marquis of Pombal, spreads over close to 100 km. Of the 250,000 ha it covers, only 40,000 are scattered with vineyards, stretching along the Rio Douro and around its tributaries. Upon exploring this region, visitors will encounter deep, lovely valleys where the omnipresent terrace cultivation moulds the landscape into amazing undulations, further accentuated by the meandering river. In addition to the impressive alignments of vine stocks, visitors will catch sight of a few parcels of land planted with olive and orange trees, and even a few almond trees, recalling the flora of the Mediterranean. Due to the area's weak tourist infrastructure and the relative lack of attractions (with the exception of Lamego, 13km away), the Douro Valley will primarily interest those with an appreciation for landscapes and beautiful views. Though visiting certain vineyards is feasible, most require appointments. This slight drawback, combined with the fact that *quintas* are sometimes very remote, makes visiting these plantations difficult. Despite these few inconveniences, however, those with time and vehicles (virtually indispensable in the region) will discover another facet of Portugal upon exploring this region: small isolated villages where certain inhabitants seem to have encountered the *estrangeiro(a)* (stranger) for the very first time. Surprising Portugal! Amazing Europe!

Suggested One-Day Itinerary

Though Highway N108 skirts a long stretch of the Rio Douro from the city of Porto, driving along the river only becomes truly pleasant from Torrão on, where travellers will also benefit from a lovely view of the Rio Tâmega, which, at this point, flows into the Douro. From Torrão, the N108 threads its way through Serra do Marão to Peso da Régua, offering many

Montanhas

panoramic views of the river's steep valleys. A real photographer's delight! However, because signs designating viewpoints only appear belatedly and are sometimes even altogether lacking, be cautious if you wish to stop at one of them, for local drivers are well acquainted with this road and travel at high speeds.

Once in Peso da Régua, after having covered close to 80km of particularly tortuous road, opt for a little detour to Lamego (around 13km), a pleasant place in which to stop before resuming your journey. Subsequently, the only way of prolonging your tour along the river is by taking the N222, which will lead you to the modest city of Pinhõa (25km farther). Though this latter section of the highway closely follows the river, the view it offers proves markedly less spectacular. Finally, to reach Pinhõa, you will have to cross a lovely narrow bridge overhanging the Douro, which flows freely from here toward the Spanish border and is followed only by the railway (see below). To end this tour on a high note, those who enjoy panoramas should head to the village of Casal de Loivos, located on a mountain top, where a *miradouro* offers a magnificent view *(to reach the vantage point, cross the village, heading toward the cemetery)*. Finally, if after this long journey a private evening in a quiet place sounds appealing, head to Alijó (16km from Pinhão), where a serene night at the comfortable Pousada Barão de Forrester (see p 363) awaits.

For those who wish to explore the Douro by boat, several companies based in Porto offer various package deals for all budgets (see p 302). For the more courageous, exploring the Douro Valley by train is also worthwhile (line 210). Though the railway pleasantly runs along the waterway for most of its course, thereby offering lovely scenery, travellers will have to exercise considerable patience while making this journey, for stops are frequent and timetables particularly inconvenient. Those who wish to do so nonetheless are advised to limit their trip to Pinhão; indeed, even though the train ventures to the Pocinho station near the Spanish border, there are no accommodations in the area and travellers will be obliged to spend long hours here (most likely until the next day) before going back, or will have to take a bus to reach one of the small surrounding villages. For further information, contact Caminhos de Ferro in Porto, at ☎225 36 41 41

Miranda do Douro

Even more than in Guarda, what most strikes anyone arriving at Miranda do Douro is the harshness of the setting. The scenery seems rougher and barer than elsewhere. Although it was raised to the rank of bishopric in 1545, the town lost this privilege to Bragança two centuries later and fell into oblivion. It took the building of a new highway providing a link to Spain and the construction of a dam in 1960 for the town to achieve something of a rebirth. Today Miranda do Douro draws Spanish tourists who are attracted by the austere charm of this spot and, more importantly, by the inexpensive goods they can find here. The country's most anachronistic folk dance, the **dance of the Pauliteiros**, takes place each year, on the third Sunday of August. On this occasion, men dressed in petticoats, long coloured stockings and flower-covered hats dance while simulating combat by means of rods or sticks. The jerky movements and the sound of the rods banging together, along with the music and shouts accompanying the dance, offer an unforgettable spectacle.

Another age-old particularity is the language. What is spoken here is, in effect, Mirandese, which comes directly from Latin. It is taught in the area's elementary schools, making this the only case in the whole country.

The **walled town** as a whole is worth a stroll for its charming little streets with their immaculately white houses. Before beginning your walk across the village, go to the right of the enclosed area, on a refurbished but ancient square, to observe the ruins of the Castelo. Dating from the 15th century, its **wrecked dungeon** is the only visible reminder of the terrible catastrophe of 1762. That year, during a military exercise, an explosion that probably came from a munitions dump destroyed nearly the entire castle as well as more than 200 houses in the village. Start your visit now on the main street crossing the village. You can observe lovely houses dating from the 17th and 18th centuries. Several other streets and squares are not to be missed: walk along **Rua da Costalinha** to admire its heraldry houses and on the **Praça Mor** to observe its fine Manueline and Renaissance dwellings. Finally, at the end of the village, the **Praça da Sé** ★ is worth a visit for its austere cathedral adorned with an impos-

ing facade. Going around the cathedral on the left side, you can enjoy a **fine panoramic view** ★ of the Douro valley and its surroundings. If you are spending the night in Miranda be sure to take a stroll through the walled town in the evening, when the small illuminated streets are even more picturesque.

The ethnographic museum, the **Museu da Terra de Miranda** (*200 ESC; Tue to Sun 10am to noon and 2pm to 4pm*), is worth a visit for its rich collection of local handicrafts.

Stroll among the restored ruins of the **former cloister of the episcopal palace** in the quiet and verdant little park behind the cathedral.

The concrete **vaulted dam**, built jointly with Spanish authorities, is worth the trip for its impressive setting, tucked into the flanks of the Douro Valley, which is especially steep at this spot. It is the first of a series of five dams shared by the two countries.

Vale do Côa

(*85km from Guarda*)

Were it not for the recent discovery of numerous **rock carvings** ★ along its valley, the Rio Côa

Montanhas

would have likely remained undiscovered by the outside world, merely pouring its tranquil waters into the famed Rio Douro, its tributary. Now classified as an archaeological park, the Do Côa valley boasts no less than 17km of numerous engravings, most dating back to the Upper Paleolithic Age. Though the approximate age of these artistic creations remains a heated subject of debate, they have led archaeologists to believe that humans have inhabited this valley as far back as 20,000 years ago.

Following its designation as a UNESCO World Heritage Site, and in order to prevent any defacement, a fence now protects the areas with the highest concentration of engravings. Visiting the area is therefore only possible with the authorization of one of the recently opened visitor centres, each of which organizes several guided tours (500 ESC) a day. Visitors are thus driven to the site, allowing them to see these stunning engravings in about an hour's time. Given the limited number of guides and the popularity of the site, however, it is strongly suggested that you reserve long in advance. Those staying in Guarda and heading to Bragança, or vice versa, will thus be treated to a particularly instructive experience,

provided they have reservations. At the moment, only three sites can be visited: Canada do Inferno, where the Parque Arqueológico's head office is located, close to Vila Nova de Foz Côa; Penascosa, right near the Castelo Melhor; and Ribeira de Piscos, next to the village of Muxagata. While the first two are located on the west side of the Rio Côa and are easily reached via the N102-E802, the latter requires that you cross the Rio to the east by taking the N222 toward Castelo Melhor or Figueira de Castelo Rodrigo. An interpretive centre together with a museum is slated to open its doors on the Canada do Inferno site (close to Vila Nova de Foz Côa) in late 2000. Because the average tour takes 1 to 2.5hrs, true enthusiasts can visit two sites in one day. Those short of time, however, should bear in mind that the Penascosa site, near the Castelo Melhor (see description, p 360), is of greater interest to neophytes.

If you do go, we highly recommend you take Route N221 from Guarda as it runs through Pinhel and Figueira de Castelo Rodrigo and crosses the **Serra da Marofa** ★★, where the **near-lunar setting** won't fail to amaze you. Indeed, atop the enormous hills of the Serra are thou-

sands of round, meteorlike rocks that seem to have fallen from space. Such is not the case, of course, as these are really granite formations moulded by the effects of erosion. A picture worth a thousand words, so have your cameras on hand! After visiting Penascosa, Canada do Inferno or Ribeira de Piscos, you can (literally) round out your tour by taking the southbound N102 (or E802) to the small village of Marialva (see p 361), then Guarda.

For all reservations:
Parque Arqueológico Vale do Côa
Tue to Sun 9am to 12:30pm and 2pm to 5:30pm
Av. Gago Coutinho no. 19
5150 Vila Nova de Foz Côa
☎*279 76 43 17*
⊟*279 76 52 57*
www.pavc-ipa.mincultura.pt
pavc@mail.telepac.pt

Castelo Melhor

(56km from Guarda)

In the heart of the humble village of Castelo Melhor is one of the **visitor centres** (*Tue to Sun, varying schedule, generally 12:45pm to 5pm;* ☎*279 73 43 44*) of the Parque Arqueológico Vale do Câo (see p 359). Housed in an old village dwelling, it is definitely worth visiting for its sparse interior layout, metal structures and elaborate lighting, all of which very commendably enhance the rusticity of its lovely stone walls. On the 2nd floor, a small computer room allows visitors to access the archaeological park's web site, which provides a great deal of information about the rock carvings. Competent and enthusiastic guides are also on hand to answer questions. Also on site are a small cafeteria (with sandwiches, pastries, coffee, etc.) and a very pleasant terrace.

After leaving the centre, take a little stroll through the village itself, a real trip back in time. But above all, take the time to climb the hamlet's steep alleys to the 13th-century **Castelo** ruins, enclosed within its medieval shale **ramparts ★**. The ramparts, which form an irregular polygon, afford beautiful views of the surrounding countryside.

★★★

Marialva

(59km from Guarda)

Almost beyond description, Marialva certainly won't leave anyone indifferent. Indeed, the mysterious atmosphere that prevails here is simply fascinating and seems to transport visitors right back to the Middle Ages – more so than anywhere else in Portugal. Perched atop a huge rock mass, Marialva, along with Monsanto da Beira, constitutes one of the country's most enchanting villages.

The tour begins with a stroll through the little village located outside the surrounding wall. The villagers have done everything to beautify their charming little houses, the granite, whitewashed walls and myriad flowers forming a lovely contrast sure to please photographers. Continue to the top of the rock for a trip back in time.

The ramparts not only encompass the remains of the 13th-century **Castelo**, but also the stunning ruins of myriad granite **cottages** lined up along equally time-worn alleys. The strange surroundings may well make you wonder what happened to this peaceful village. Was it suddenly cursed? Was it hit by the plague? Or again, was it put to fire and sword by invaders? In the heart of the main square is a well-preserved (15th-century) **pillory ★★** that seems to have proudly defied the ravages of time, while farther on is a rock-top church with an elegant Manueline portal. In fact, marvellous sights meet your eyes here at every turn and, as if this weren't enough, the **panoramic views ★★** of the plains below are quite simply breathtaking!

Viseu

Located in the heart of Dão-Lafões and surrounded by wooded hills, this commercial town makes for a pleasant stop on the way to Guarda. Although it boasts of being the homeland of Viriathe and the area that gave the country a great school of painting, Viseu remained a fairly modest town over the centuries. Forever in the shadow of neighbouring Coimbra, it suffered from this proximity. It was only in the 15th century that the town enjoyed a certain influence, especially because of its school of painting. Two great painters, Vasco Fernandes and Gaspar Vaz, effectively created the Viseu School, famous for its primitive paintings. Renowned for its Dão wine (see box p 370), Viseu today is a cheerful little town, pleasant for a stroll. Moreover, you may gain some insight into a troubling mystery: where do all these egg pastries come from when there are so few hens in the countryside? In fact, Viseu and its surroundings are famous for raising poultry, and the town supplies the whole north of the country with pastry. Portuguese hens, at least, have chosen Viseu as their favourite resort!

Montanhas

The tour starts at the end of Avenida 25 de Abril, on the little **Praça da República**, also called **Rossio**. On its eastern side you can admire a beautiful *azulejo* **panel** portraying rural scenes, attached to a hillock topped by a garden.

Go to the south side of the square, near the traffic circle, taking Rua da Victória to where it meets the post office, located on the left side. From there, continue your walk by taking Rua dos Andrades, which changes names to **Rua Direita**. This very lively little pedestrian street runs past some beautiful houses mostly dating from the 18th century, as well as many little shops. When you reach the end, on your left you will notice several boutiques "dug" into the rock, next to the cathedral. Head now in front of the Sé, on the **Praça da Sé**.

An ancient Romanesque church whose facade has been redone many times, the **Sé ★** is worth visiting for its **interior** in particular. There you can admire an elegant **Manueline vault ★**, decorated in a pattern of cords and knots. Coats of arms painted here form the keys to the vault. For a fine panorama, head to the **Coro Alto** (*access via the left transept*), where there are also some beautiful **stalls ★**. Made

of precious wood, they contain many sculptures presenting an epic of great discoveries. On the armrests you may notice many figures representing African and Native American heads. Finally, admirers of religious art will not want to miss visiting the small **museum of sacred art** (*Tue to Sun 10am to noon and 2pm to 5pm; access via the Coro Alto*), set upstairs in the cloister, from where there is a view of the lower cloister, decorated with fine *azulejos*. Before leaving the Sé, be certain to take a glance at the astonishing **main altar**; its very modern appearance, resembling an inverted pyramid, is sure to arrouse comments. Before leaving the Sé, go behind the cathedral, on the **Largo São Teotónio**, to get another look at the imposing blocks of granite that form the foundation of the building.

You simply cannot leave Viseu without seeing the **Museu Grão Vasco ★★** (*200 ESC; Tue to Sun 9:30am to 12:30pm and 4pm to 5pm; on the Praça da Sé, left of the cathedral*), occupying the former episcopal palace. Although sculptures and paintings by 20th-century Portuguese artists

are exhibited here, it is especially the second floor up that will draw your attention. Several magnificent paintings from the Viseu School are hung there, including works by the famous painters Vasco Fernandes (also called Grão Vasco, or "Great Vasco") and Gaspar Vaz. Among the masterpieces, the one portraying *São Pedro* and the more anecdotal *Adoration of the Three Wise Men*, with the black king replaced by a Brazilian Indian chief, are particularly noteworthy.

The **Igreja da Misericórdia** (*across from the cathedral, on the Praça da Sé*) has a rather pretty facade.

Perpendicular to the Rua Direita, two pleasant streets provide good glimpses of the medieval town. Heading north, the first of these is **Rua Dom Duarte**. There you can see an ancient dungeon. The second, a little further north, is **Rua da Senhora da Piedade**, skirted by pretty little dwellings dating from the 16th century.

Keen shoppers should check out **Rua Formosa** (*perpendicular to Rua Direita*), an elegant pedestrian street.

For those interested in dolmens or the Roman era, the Viseu tourist office (see p 350) provides an interesting brochure describing some 50 sites located in the tourist region of Dão-Lafões.

Finally, if you plan on visiting the area sometime between mid-August and mid-September, be sure to check out one of the biggest fairs in the region, the **Feira de São Mateus**, when furniture, clothing, handicrafts and more are on display.

Outdoor Activities

Cruises and Canoeing

Miranda do Douro

Turis Nautic S.L.
C/Amargura 2, Ent.
49013 Zamora
☎/≈*980-51 10 53 in Spain*
Turis Nautic S.L. organizes **river cruises**, as well as **canoe excursions**,

on the Douro. Several programs are offered:

One-hour river cruise on the Douro
Departure: Mon to Fri at 6:30pm, Sat, Sun and holidays at 11:30am, 4:30pm and 6:30pm
Fare: 1,500 ESC, children 500 ESC, minimum 6 people

Two-hour guided river cruise
Departure: Sat at 6:30pm
Fare: 3,000 ESC, children 1,000 ESC, minimum 6 people

Accompanied weekend expedition on the Douro by Canadian canoe
Departure: twice annually, both in mid-August
Fare: 14,500 ESC

Golf

Like the Alentejo, the tourist region of Montanhas does not have much in the way of golfing facilities, with only two courses in use to date.

See below for the addresses and main features of area golf courses.

Accommodations

Alijó

Pousada Barão de Forrester
$$$$$
pb, tv, ≈, ℜ
to the right of the main street crossing the village, heading toward Murça, 5070 Alijó
☎*259 95 92 15*
≈*259 95 93 04*
Nestled in the heart of the peaceful village of Alijó, the Pousada Barão de Forrester is an ideal stopping place for those who wish to see the Douro Valley. Housed in a stylish residence, the rooms and common areas have been entirely renovated, revealing a modern and comfortable interior. True to (tasteful) tradition, the decor consists of regionally inspired curios and furniture.

Montanhas

Golf Courses

Name	Number of Holes	Par	Length (in metres)	Address
Pavilhão do Golfe de Vidago	9	33	2360	5425 Vidago ☎*276 973 56* ≈*276 973 59*
Golfe Montobelo	18	72	6320	3510 Farminhão ☎*232 85 64 64* ≈*232 85 64 01*

For a pleasant view, opt for a room overlooking the *pousada*'s beautiful garden. In the summer, a large swimming pool and a tennis court are available to the clientele.

Bragança

Parque de Campismo Río Sabor Estrada Rabaçal
Câmara Municipal de Bragança, 5300 Bragança
☎273 33 15 35

Residencial São Roque
$
pb
Rua da Estacada 267
5300 Bragança
☎273 38 14 81
⇄273 32 69 37
Located near the historical centre, the Residencial São Roque offers 36 modern, well-appointed rooms. Several rooms offer fine views of the town and the castle.

Pousada de São Bartolomeu
$$$$$
pb, ℜ
Estrada do Turismo
5300 Bragança
☎273 33 14 93
⇄273 32 34 53
Perched on the Serra da Nogueira (Nut Mountain), the Pousada de São Bartolomeu has the advantage of offering superb views of the castle of the dukes of Bragance. Set up in 1959 in a relatively modern building, it has 16 comfortably appointed rooms with rustic decor. A pleasant terrace, literally on top of the Rio Fervença

valley, enhances this spot. The hotel and restaurant (see p 367) recently underwent major renovations.

Castelo Branco

Campismo Municipal de Castelo Branco
Câmara Municipal de Castelo Branco, 6000 Castelo Branco
☎272 34 16 15

Pensão-Residencial Arraiana
$$
pb, *tv*
Ave. 1° de Maio no. 18
6000 Castelo Branco
☎272 34 16 34
☎272 34 16 37
⇄272 33 18 84
Though located on a noisy avenue, the Arraiana boarding house offers clean and comfortable, if modest, rooms. The decor is definitely past its prime, a bit depressing even, but the reasonable prices make this a suitable place nonetheless. Moreover, it is conveniently located within walking distance of the old town.

Hotel Rainha Dona Amélia
$$$
pb, *tv*
Rua da Santiago 15
6000 Castelo Branco
☎272 32 63 15
⇄272 32 63 90
Hotel Rainha Dona Amélia, recently renovated, offers all the comforts of a top-rate hotel. Its setting near the old town and its private parking area make it a very good value in its category.

Idanha-a-Nova

(*36km from Castelo Branco*)

Campismo Baragem de Idanha-a-Nova Câmara Municipal de Idanha-a-Nova (camping)
6060 Idanha-a-Nova
☎277 20 27 93
⇄277 20 29 45

Monsanto da Beira

(*49km de Castelo Branco*)

Pousada da Monsanto
$$$
pb, *tv*, ℜ
6850 Medelim
☎277 31 44 71
⇄277 31 44 81
Located in the most picturesque village in Beira Baixa, the little Pousada da Monsanto blends modernism and comfort perfectly with a predominantly rugged environment, where the human presence seems to make itself as discreet as possible (see p 353). An unforgettable experience in another time and place!

Guarda

Campismo da Guarda/Orbitur (camping)
6300 Guarda
☎271 21 14 06
⇄271 22 19 11

Residencial Santos
$$
pb, tv
14 Rua Tenente Valadim, that is the continuation of Rua Camico Castelo Branco, which skirts the old city walls, 6300 Guarda
☎271 21 29 31
☎271 20 54 00
≈271 21 31 77
A stone's throw from the Largo João de Almeida, in the very heart of the old city, the Residencial Santos perfectly combines the pleasures of modernism with a medieval atmosphere, created by the building's architecture. Over and above the pleasant decor of the rooms, the establishment offers hearty breakfasts fit for the hungriest guests. Excellent value for your money!

Residência Filipe
$
ps and pb
Rua Vasco da Gama 9
6300 Guarda
☎271 22 36 58
☎271 22 36 59
≈271 22 14 02
This modern hotel has the advantage of being located at the foot of the old town, in a lively area.

Solar de Alarcão
$$$ no bkfst
pb
Rua de Doutore Miguel de Alarcão 25-27, 6300 Guarda
☎271 21 43 92
☎271 21 12 75
With only three rooms, the Solar de Alarcão is a private home that receives paying guests in a gorgeous old manor dating from

1686. The interior is tastefully decorated and has lovely fine furnishings. The *Solar*, with its adjoining chapel and flagstone terrace, forms a superb ensemble that well deserved its personal inauguration by President Mário Soares.

Manteigas

(46km from Guarda)

Pousada de São Lourenço
$$$$$
pb, ℜ
on Highway N232, about 60km from Guarda, 6260 Manteigas
☎275 98 24 50
≈275 98 24 53
Located in the heart of Serra da Estrela park, this *pousada*, built entirely of stone from the region, is an excellent choice for those who appreciate mountain hikes and peace and quiet. Pleasant, warm decor and a big terrace with a panoramic view help account for the charm of this establishment.

Lamego

Hotel Parque
$$
pb, tv
Parque Nossa Senhora dos Remédios, 5100 Lamego
☎254 60 91 40
≈254 61 52 03
Located at the top of the distinctly baroque Nossa Senhora dos Remédios staircase, next to the church, the Hotel Parque offers rooms that are small and modestly furnished, but well maintained. Given its dis-

tance from the downtown area, this establishment will especially suit those in search of peace and quiet.

Miranda do Douro

Campismo Parque Santa Luzia, Câmara Municipal de Miranda do Douro
Rua do Parque de Campismo
5210 Miranda do Douro
☎273 43 12 73
≈273 43 10 75

Residencial Flor do Douro
$
pb
Rua do Mercado Municipal 7
5210 Miranda do Douro
☎273 43 11 86
This modest pension can be a good choice for the price, especially the rooms facing the lake was created when the dam was built. Simple but adequate decor.

Pensão Restaurante Vista Bela
$
pb, tv, ℜ
Rua do Mercado Municipal 63
5210 Miranda do Douro
☎273 43 13 41
This pension offers pleasant decor and, from half of its rooms, views of the lake created by the dam. Reserve a room with a view in advance!

Pensão Restaurante Santa Cruz
$$$
pb and ps
Rua Abade de Baçal, near the Largo do Castelo, 5210 Miranda do Douro
☎273 43 13 74
During our visit, this spot provided the only

lodgings within the old town. Obviously, it has no views of the dam, but life in the old town largely compensates for this. Simple but adequate decor.

Pousada de Santa Catarina
$$$
pb, tv, ℜ
5210 Miranda do Douro
☎*273 43 10 05*
⇔*273 43 10 65*
Perched atop a steep hill, facing Spain the Pousada de Santa Catarina occupies the buildings that housed the engineers during construction of the dam. Although modern and not endowed with any special charm, its rooms offer extraordinary views of the lake and the dam. The classic decor is tasteful and the staff, like the inhabitants of Miranda do Douro, are very friendly.

Oliveira do Hospital

Pousada de Santa Bárbara
$$$$
pb, tv, ≈ ℜ
from the N17, take the road leading to Póvoa das Quartas, where the pousada is located
3400 Oliveira do Hospital
☎*238 60 96 52*
☎*238 60 96 53*
⇔*238 60 96 45*
Located halfway between Coimbra and Guarda, in a verdant setting where the fragrance of pine trees wafts over the region, the Pousada de Santa Bárbara is the ideal place from which to explore the Serra da

Estrêla national park. Built in 1971, this pousada, while certainly not the most attractive of its kind, does constitute a good choice for those wishing to enjoy both comfort and outdoor activities. Also, by reserving in advance, you can benefit from one of eight rooms with balconies and thus be favoured with a lovely view of the surrounding countryside. A swimming pool and tennis court are also available to guests.

Viseu

Campismo do Fontelo/Orbitur (camping)
3500 Viseu
☎*232 42 61 46*
⇔*232 42 61 20*

Residencial Duque de Viseu
$$ no bkfst
pb, tv
Rua das Ameias 22, 3500 Viseu
☎*232 42 12 86*
Well located in the centre of the old town, the Residencial Duque de Viseu has pleasant, well-maintained little rooms.

Hotel Grão Vasco
$$$
pb, tv, ≈
Rua Gaspar Berreiros
3500 Viseu
☎*232 42 35 11*
⇔*232 42 70 47*
Hotel Grão Vasco, with its dated but comfortable furnishings, boasts a pool and a location right next to the centre of the old town.

Caramulo
(32km from Viseu)

Pousada de São Jerónimo
$$$$
pb, ≈, ℜ
1km from the village of Caramulo, 3475 Caramulo
☎*232 86 12 91*
⇔*232 86 16 40*
Built just off the lovely N230 scenic highway, in the heart of the Serra do Caramulo, this modest six-room *pousada* is best suited to those who are looking for calm, though the major attractions are nearby (*Coimbra 80km, Viseu 42km and Aveiro 55km*). The *pousada* recently reopened after major renovations

Restaurants

Alijó

Pousada Barão de Forrester
$$$
in the heart of the small village of Alijó, to the right of the main street running through the village, heading toward Murça
☎*259 95 92 15*
Located in a stylish residence, the restaurant of the Pousada Barão de Forrester offers good regional cuisine in a lovely setting, where candelabras and tablecloths recall the proximity of the Douro Valley and its celebrated wines. Among the great classics of Portuguese

cuisine, do not miss the *Cabrito à Transmontana* (kid), a specialty in the region. But why not start your meal off with a port on the terrace facing the *pousada*'s lovely garden, or then again, accompany your wine with cheese, as tradition across the Channel demands?

Bragança

Restaurante Cervejaria O Açacio
$

Rua Calouste Gulbenkian 5
If you feel the urge for an *orelha de porco* (pork ear) or *rins de porco* (pork kidneys), or simply a good omelette, Restaurante Cervejaria O Açacio, across from a little park, is the ideal spot. This little family-run neighbourhood restaurant is probably the cheapest spot in town (*meals starting at 900 ESC*). The atmosphere is friendly.

Restaurante Bar Dom Fernando
$

every day 8am to midnight
Rua da Citadela no. 197; take the first street on the left after passing the entrance to the fortress
☎273 32 62 73
The only restaurant located within the old town, Restaurante Bar Dom Fernando has an adorable little upstairs dining room, where you can enjoy tasty regional dishes. The *Cordeiro na grelhac* and the *feijoada* are deli-

cious. The staff will make you feel welcome. The only jarring note is the unpleasant presence of the television. Good value.

Lá Em Casa
$$

Rua Marquês de Pombal 7
☎273 32 21 11
Located across from a pretty little park, this restaurant has attractive traditional decor in a big dining room. Meals starting at 1,950 ESC.

Solar Bragançano
$$$

Praça da Sé
☎273 32 38 75
Established in front of the Sé, upstairs in an 18th-century building, the Solar Bragançano restaurant is a great spot to sample regional specialties. Warm decor and a professional welcome. Good value.

Pousada de São Bartolomeu
$$$

Estrada do Turismo
☎273 33 14 93
The restaurant of the Pousada de São Bartolomeu has the advantage of offering a superb view of the castle of the Dukes of Bragança, as well as a pleasant terrace literally on top of the Rio Fervença valley. In this Serra da Nogueira (Nut Mountain) establishment, you will naturally find dishes accompanied by chestnuts and walnuts. The hotel and restaurant recently underwent major renovations.

Castelo Branco

A Muralha
$

Tue to Sun
Rua Santa Maria 13, 1st floor
☎272 32 89 21
Very well located, in a charming little inner courtyard, this restaurant offers an original specialty, *charbonada*. In an attractive upstairs dining room, smoke hoods have been installed above each table, so customers can grill their own food and enhance it with the sauce provided. Original and different. A friendly welcome.

Cervejaria Praça Velha
$$

Tue to Sun
Praça Luís de Camões
☎272 32 86 20
This is one of the best spots in the area, as much for the food as for the decor. In a group of old buildings, two especially pleasant rooms have been created, one for drinks and the other for meals. Lighting comes from enormous copper basins with golden wheat twigs arranged inside, illuminating the distinctive decor. Despite a few discreet 20th-century touches, the room retains a medieval character with granite columns and attractive exposed wooden beams. In the middle of the dining room lies a generous table of *acepipes* (appetizers) and desserts. This restaurant offers a

Montanhas

refined and more original cuisine than elsewhere: meat brochettes and Mexican-style fish are just some of the possibilities. Moreover, they serve delicious home-made French fries rather than the frozen ones that, unfortunately, seem to be found all over the place. The menu presents new dishes every day. Professional service and a very good quality-to-price ratio. Daily menu for 2,500 ESC.

Idanha-a-Nova

(36km from Castelo Branco)

Cafés and Tearooms

Café Bar Gelateria Egitânea
by Highway N353, at the entrance to the village coming from Oledo
Café Bar Gelateria Egitânea and its terrace make for a refreshing stop on your way to Idanha-a-Velha or Monsanto da Beira.

Monsanto da Beira

(49km from Castelo Branco)

Pousada da Monsanto
$$$
Monsanto
☎277 31 44 71
Located in Beira Baixa's most picturesque village, the restaurant of the Pousada da Monsanto allows you to dine in a modern setting in a unique environment (see p 364), in the heart of a village that seems frozen in time. An unforgettable trip through the ages!

Cafés and Tearooms

Monsantino
Rua Nossa Senhora do Castelo no. 4, before the ascent toward the castle
There are two establishments in this splendid and sleepy little village: the Monsantino, simple and friendly; and another one situated in front of the parking area (*the café is at number 21 but is not identified by name*), where a tiny terrace with two tables awaits you; light items such as sandwiches are served.

Guarda

Soda Cáustica
$
Rua Camilo Castelo Branco no. 19
☎271 22 40 60
Upon entering the lovely granite-fronted house built against the walls of the inner town, visitors may well be surprised to find a modern, decidedly designer decor consisting of metal structures and new woodwork. Those looking for a touch of authenticity, however, can head to the back room, where the old town walls can still be seen. The food here, though hardly fine cuisine, should please those seeking a change of pace from *bacalhau*, *açordas* and *borrego*. Lasagna, spit-roasted chicken, tuna salad and various sandwiches are offered at very humane prices, never exceeding 1,000 ESC. Moreover, for those craving North American fare, a meal that includes a burger, fries and a soft drink is offered for as little as 500 ESC. At that price, who can resist? Pleasant, friendly welcome.

A Floresta
$$
Rua Francisco Passos no. 40
☎271 21 23 14
A favourite with the locals, the A Floresta restaurant serves classic Portuguese fare. Among the noteworthy dishes featured on the menu are the fillet of veal and the escalope of kid. In addition to a worthwhile 1,400 ESC set menu, the establishment offers "student specials" for as little as 500 ESC. Family-style decor of mismatched kitsch objects and lovely *azulejos*.

Belo Horizonte
$$$
Largo São Vicente no. 2
☎271 21 14 54
Featuring a distinctly more refined setting, the Belo Horizonte restaurant specializes in regional cuisine. Try the *morcelas tostadas de Guarda*, roasted Guarda-style blood sausage, or the *feijoada de Javali*, bean stew with wild boar – a real treat! Located inside an elegant house, the main dining room is cozy and the tables carefully

set with lovely table-cloths (avoid the considerably less pleasant room on the right). What's more, miracle of miracles, the ubiquitous television set is nowhere to be seen!

Manteigas

(*46km from Guarda*)

Pousada de São Lourenço
$$$
by Highway N232, about 60km from Guarda
☎*271 98 24 50*
Located in the heart of Serra da Estrela national park, this restaurant is set in a pretty building made of local stone. The dining room, besides its rustic decor, offers a fine view of the nearby mountains. This restaurant is an excellent choice for anyone wishing to combine outdoor sports and a good meal. A big terrace with panoramic views is well suited for pre-dinner drinks in almost disconcerting tranquillity.

Lamego

Cafés and Tearooms

Café Buondi 4 Estações
corner of Avenida Dr. Alfredo de Sousa and Avenida 5 de Outubro
Whether for a *bica* or a refreshing drink, the modest little Café Buondi 4 Estações is a pleasant and unpretentious spot. Light meals (sandwiches, soup, garnished toast,

etc.) available at reasonable prices.

Miranda do Douro

Restaurante Pizzeria O Moinho
$
Rua do Mercado 47
☎*273 43 11 16*
For bouts of hunger or for limited budgets. Pizzas starting at 600 ESC and daily specials starting at 1,300 ESC.

Restaurante Buteko
$
Largo Dom João III, on Praça Mor, in the centre of the walled village
☎*273 43 12 31*
Local cuisine. Meals starting at 1,250 ESC. Ask for a table upstairs, where the decor is more refined. Pleasant terrace.

Pensão Restaurante Vista Bela
$$
Mon to Sat 8am to midnight
Rua do Mercado Municipal 63
☎*273 43 10 54*
Traditional cuisine served in a room with an extraordinary view of the lake created by the dam. Daily menu starting at 1,000 ESC.

Restaurant Balbina
$$
Rua Rainha Dona Catarina
☎*273 43 23 94*
Located in a charming area within the fortified town, Restaurant Balbina serves classical local cuisine. Warm, richly coloured decor.

Restaurante São Pedro
$$
Rua M. de Albuquerque 22
☎*273 43 13 21*
Unpretentious Portuguese meals, starting at 1,700 ESC.

Pousada de Santa Catarina
$$$
Miranda do Douro
☎*273 43 10 05*
Perched atop a steep hill facing Spain, the restaurant of the Pousada de Santa Catarina is located in buildings that housed the engineers during construction of the dam. From the dining room with its classical decor. You can enjoy a fine view of the lake created by the dam. Service with a smile.

Cafés and Tearooms

Bar Atalaia
5 Largo do Castelo, on the Praça Mor
Modern and equipped with a pool table, Bar Atalaia is a pleasant spot to quench your thirst among the local youth.

Café Panorama
every day 8am to 2am
Rua 25 de Abril
Café Panorama offers an impressive view of the dam, just as its name indicates. Ideal for a coffee break.

Montanhas

Wines from the Dão Region

Considered to be among the country's best, most wines produced in the Dão region are made from the *Touriga Nacional* grape, which is also used to make porto. The main characteristics of this grape variety are the relatively small size of the fruit and its bright colour, as well as its high tannin content. Meanwhile, the *Tinta Roriz* (a blackberry-mulberry aromatic wine) and the *Alfrosheiro Preto* (a spicy and slightly acidic wine) are the two other well-known varieties grown in the Dão region. Because of its rainy winters and hot, dry summers, this area is ideal for producing velvety wines with strong aromas. This is why most wines stemming from this region are red wines, although some white wine is also produced. The Dão region was created and gained its Denomination of Controlled Origin (DOC) in 1908. Today, the best vintages are labelled "Dão Nobre" (noble Dão). These are old wines and, of course, among the most expensive. Bottles simply marked "Dão" are grown in the region, and their quality is strictly controlled. Bottles labelled "Dão Clarete" are lighter than the "classic" Dão, while the younger "Dão Novo" is similar to a Beaujolais Nouveau.

Pinhão

Café Cais da Foz
by the docks, on the left, right after crossing the little bridge overhanging the Rio Pinhão
Set up by the Rio Pinhão, the modest Café Cais da Foz is a pleasant place to quench your thirst while admiring the river that meets the Rio Douro and its beautiful valley through large windows. Light meals, including sandwiches, soups, garnished toast and more, are served.

Torrão

Restaurante Tâmega a Vista-Tamis
$
on the N108, to the left, right after crossing the Rio Tâmega toward Peso da Régua
This modest restaurant, where the lack of decor and a ubiquitous television are almost enough to drive you right out of the place, does boast a terrace, which offers a pleasant view of the Tâmega Valley and is covered in clinging vines. The house specializes in grilled meats; those with smaller appetites can partake of a selection of light dishes such as sandwiches, garnished toast, soups, and more.

Viseu

Restaurante Casa Congolesa
$
8:30am to 10pm
Rua Direita 162-B
☎232 42 37 32
Classic meals, starting at 980 ESC, served throughout the day.

O Cortiço
$$$
Rua Augusto Hilário 47
☎232 42 38 53
Famous among Portuguese for its authentic regional cuisine, O Cortiço restaurant is not to be missed if you want a plentiful meal. Original decor in a warm setting.

Muralha da Sé
$$$
Tue to Sat
Adro da Sé no. 24
☎ *232 43 77 77*
In an elegant house adjacent to the lovely Igreja da Misericórdia, the Muralha da Sé res taurant serves up fish and grilled dishes (meat or fish) in a refined setting. However, to enjoy an evening with out television (the dreaded "boob tube" is downright omnipres ent!), opt for a table in the large dining room, where carefully set tables and lovely stone walls make up the better part of the decor. In addition to a dizzy ing array of regional (Dão) *vinhos*, the estab lishment also offers several French wines. A tad expensive, but suit ably elegant,

Caramulo

(32km from Viseu)

Pousada de São Jerónimo
$$$
1km from the village of Caramulo
☎ *232 86 12 91*
Located off the lovely and scenic N230, in the heart of the Serra do Caramulo, this restau rant makes for a pleas ant stop en route to Coimbra or Viseu. The *pousada* recently re opened after major renovations.

Entertainment

Castelo Branco

Patrímonio Bar
every day 2pm to 10pm
Largo Luís de Camões, to the right of the former Câmara Municipal, in the courtyard located next to the Praça Velha restaurant
Occupying a turn-of-the-century residence at the end of a lovely private courtyard facing Praça Luís de Camões, Patrímonio Bar is worth a visit for its sophisti cated decor. Modern furniture placed in an interior of gilding and stucco creates a stun ning and yet harmoni ous contrast. In this startling mixture, you will find a young, hip clientele that seems to come from throughout the surrounding area. An amazing place for a sleepy little town like Castelo Branco. Not to be missed!

Viseu

Café do Teatro
Mon to Sat
Rua Mestre Teotonio Pedro Albuquerque; Near Largo Mouzinho Albuquerque
Located right next to the Teatro, this huge café with large win dows is where the local youth gathers over a *bica* or a beer. A per fect and laid-back, if somewhat smoky, place to end (or kick off) the night. Sandwiches and

a few pastries are also available.

Café BláBlá
Ave. Emídio Navarro; in the Académico shopping centre
Located on the 2nd floor of a shopping centre, Café BláBlá is a small, unpretentious bistro with a very pleasant atmosphere. A very popular student hangout, the place is rather smoky and the decor limited to the view of the busy street, but drinks are dirt cheap. A glass of port, for example, costs a mere 120 ESC. What a deal!

Shopping

Monsanto da Beira

(49km from Castelo Branco)

During your visit to this marvellous village, you may come across el derly ladies seated on the ground making *rodilhas*. These are small ring-shaped cushions that women place on their heads to transport certain ob jects. Made from pieces of multi-coloured cloth, they make for a pleas ant little decorative souvenir, and by pur chasing one you will contribute to the pres ervation of an age-old tradition.

Guarda	Pinhão	Viseu

Artesanato da Catedral (*Largo Dr. Amândio Paúl 4, on the same side as the cathedral*). This is a very big shop offering a little of everything: ceramics, *solteiro* (carpets), clothing and even various wines. Despite the commercial feel and the somewhat mixed layout, you can find a number of tasteful items, and the prices are notably lower than in Viseu.

Cooperativa de Artesanato do Douro (*Mon to Sat 9:30am to noon and 2:30pm to 7pm, Sun 3pm to 7pm; Casa do Povo, heading toward Alijó, to the right of the main street running through the village, a little past the station*). As its Portuguese name suggests, this modest shop sells various local handicrafts. In addition to offering quality goods, this interesting co-op contributes to maintaining the traditional, rural way of life sadly neglected all too often these days.

Artesanato Viriato (*Rua Adro Sêno 21, to the left of the Igreja da Misericórdia, on the Largo da Misericórdia*). This shop sells carpets, porcelain and other tasteful items. Reasonable prices, although about 20% higher than in Guarda.

The Alentejo

Most see the
Alentejo simply as a region to be passed through on the way to the Algarve or Spain.

It would be a shame, though, to skip Évora, an elegant university town dating back to the 16th century, or to miss out on little jewels like Castelo de Vide, hemmed in by ramparts; Marvão, perched atop a promontory, with its unforgettable sunsets; or Estremoz, along the Spanish border, which boasts one of the most magnificent *pousadas* in the country. Though the Alentejo, or land "beyond the Tagus", appears harsh and poor at first sight, it supplies most of the country with wheat, olives and oil. Moreover, the countless cork oaks that speckle the plains provide us with the greater part of the world's cork output. The beauty of this region lies in its bare, vast landscape; you'll marvel at its people and the incredible towns they have managed to build in the

midst of so much emptiness.

Throughout the centuries, all these characteristics have given the inhabitants particular traits, starting with language. *Alentejanos* are actually known for speaking slower than their compatriots. They are also among the few citizens in Portugal to define themselves as *Alentejanos* first and Portuguese second. The Alentejo is also famous for its all-male choirs; indeed, the *vozes*

Alentejanos are considered the most beautiful in the country.

Aside from Évora, the area is not geared towards tourism, so be sure to plan your itinerary carefully, including accommodations and evening meals. Moreover, because of its geographical location, far from the coast, winters here are harsh and summers scorching hot.

Finding Your Way Around

By Car from Lisbon

Beja and Serpa

Take Highway A2-IP1-E1-E90 south past Setúbal, then continue heading south on the N5-E1-IP1. At Alcácer do Sal, take the N120-E1-IP1 to Grândola. Once there, head toward Ferreira do Alentejo on the N259-IP8, then to Beja on the N121-IP8.

To get to Serpa, drive east along the IP8-N260.

Castelo de Vide

Head north on Highway A1-E80-IP1 to the exit for Entroncemento, and pick up the N3-IP6. Continue driving until Abrantes, then take the N118 to Alpalhão. Once there, take the N246 to Castelo de Vide.

Elvas

Go to Estremoz (see below), then pick up the N4-E90-IC10, which leads to Elvas.

Estremoz

First, head south on Highway A2-IP1-E1-E90. After the junction for Setúbal, continue for 17km. When you reach the N10, head north to Cruzamento de Pegões, then pick up the N4-1C10, which leads straight to Montemor-o-Velho and then Estremoz. Highway A6 directly links Lisbon and Montemor-o-Velho. Then take the N4 to Estremoz.

Évora

Take Highway A2-IP1-E1-E90 south, in the direction of Setúbal. After the junction for Setúbal, continue driving for 17km to the N10. Head north to Cruzamento de Pegões, then take the N4-1C10 to Montemor-o-Velho. Once there, follow the N114-IP7 to Évora. Highway A6 directly links Lisbon and Montemor-o-Velho.

Marvão

First, head to Castelo de Vide (see above), and take the N246 to the N359, which leads to Marvão, about 5km farther.

By Train from Lisbon

Some of the towns described in this chapter are accessible by train. However, because of irregular schedules (with the exception of the Lisboa-Beja route) and difficult transfers, the train is an inconvenient means of transportation. Also, just to get to the Barreiro station, from which trains bound for the south of the country leave, you have to take the ferry (Estação Fluvial Sul e Sueste) from Praça do Comércio to a suburb of the capital across the river. For Caminhos de Ferro departures and information see p 69.

Évora

Departure: several times a day
Fare: Interciadades 900 ESC and 150 ESC to cross the River Tagus to the Barreiro station

Beja

Departure: several times a day
Fare: Intercidades 1,050 ESC, plus 150 ESC for the ferry across the Tagus to the Barreiro station

By Bus from Lisbon

The companies **Rede Nacional de Expressos** and **Renex Expressos** offer many departures daily, as do other transportation companies. **Rede Nacional de Expressos** departures are from the terminal at no 18B Avenida Casal Ribeiro. **Renex Expressos** departures are from Cais das Cebolas, near Casa dos Bicos. For information in Lisbon, see p 69.

Beja

Travel time: approx. 4hrs
Fare: 1,100 to 1,300 ESC

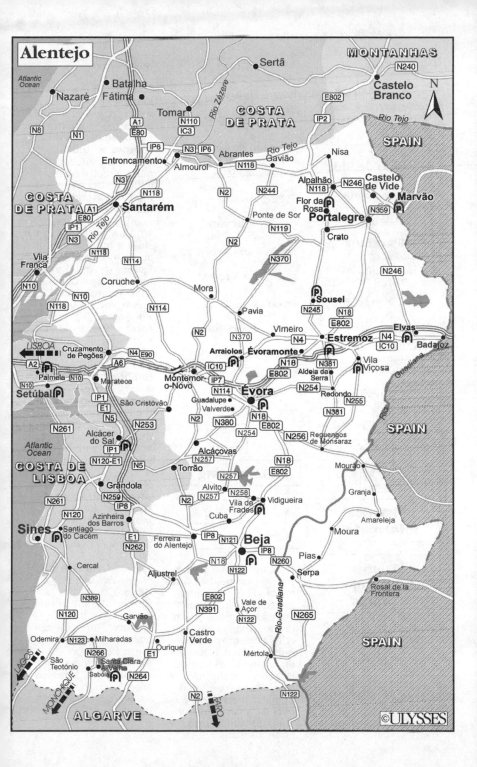

Elvas

Departure: up to four times a day
Travel time: approx. 4hrs, 30min
Fare: 1,200 to 1,500 ESC

Castelo de Vide

Travel time: approx. 5hrs
Fare: 1,450 to 1,650 ESC

Estremoz

Travel time: approx. 3hrs, 30min
Fare: 1,100 to 1,300 ESC

Évora

Travel time: approx. 2hrs, 30 min
Fare: 1,100 to 1,300 ESC

Marvão

Travel time: approx. 9hrs
Fare: 2,200 to 2,400 ESC

Practical Information

Tourist Information Offices

Beja

25 Rua Capitão João Francisco de Sousa

Castelo de Vide

81 Rua Bartolomeu Alvares da Santa

Elvas

Praça da República

Estremoz

28 Largo da República

Évora

71 Praça do Giraldo

Marvão

Rua Da Matos Magalhães

Vila Viçosa

Praça da República

Mértola

Largo Vasco da Gama

Serpa

Largo D. Jorge de Melo

Exploring

Beja

Beja, the capital of the Baixa Alentejo, has one major claim to fame: the celebrated *Lettres Portugaises*, a collection of love letters supposedly written by a local nun to a French nobleman. Due to its central location and the region's farm-based economic activity, Beja has become a fairly important agricultural hub, home to many businesses.

The tour of the town begins with the **Castelo**, which now lies in ruins but is worth the trip for its admirably restored **dungeon** ★ and adjacent crenellated ramparts. Erected in the 13th century over Roman and Moorish ruins, the Castelo is the pride and joy of *Bejanhecos*, who unabashedly consider it more beautiful and elegant than that of Estremoz. And higher too, it seems! Climbing to its summit (*100 ESC; Tue to Sun 9:30am to noon and 2:30pm to 6pm*) will provide you with a lovely panorama of the town and the remains of its ancient fortifications. Before setting off again, be sure to take a look at the remarkable **Roman arch**, right next to the dungeon. It was still walled up only a few years ago.

Now head down the street to the **Museu Visigótico** (*100 ESC, admission also valid for the Convento de Nossa Senhora da Conceição museum; 9:45am to 12:30pm and 2pm to 5pm; Largo de Santo Amaro*), housed in a former Visigoth church dating from the 6th century. Here you can admire a very interesting collection of columns from the same period, most of which are square-shaped and sometimes topped by a capital.

On the left side, be sure to look for the tombstone dedicated to a woman by the name of Moura. Those fortunate enough to read Portuguese will be privy to a splendid token of love that is as meaningful today as it was hundreds of years ago.

Take Rua Dom Manuel I, opposite the Castelo, to the **Praça República**, where a pillory as well as several lovely houses are worth a look. The most noteworthy attraction here, however, is the unusual **Igreja da Misericórdia**. Erected in the 16th century, this building was supposed to be a public market, but restoration work so beautified the building that it was later decided to turn it into a church. Today, centuries after the "merchants were chased from the temple", the structure has been restored to its original splendour, revealing its large covered entrance hall and beautiful columns. Could the merchants be coming back anytime soon?

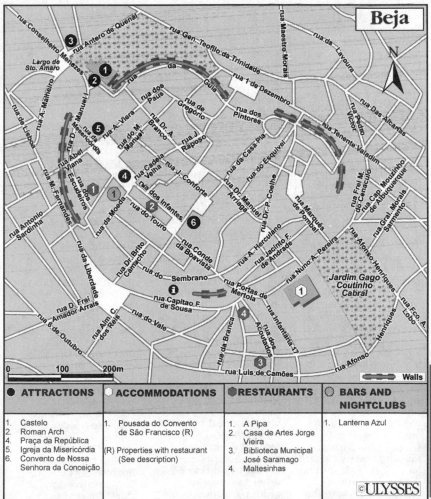

Beja

0   100   200m

⟨⟨⟨⟨ Walls

● ATTRACTIONS	○ ACCOMMODATIONS	● RESTAURANTS	○ BARS AND NIGHTCLUBS
1. Castelo 2. Roman Arch 4. Praça da República 5. Igreja da Misericórdia 6. Convento de Nossa Senhora da Conceição	1. Pousada do Convento de São Francisco (R) (R) Properties with restaurant (See description)	1. A Pipa 2. Casa de Artes Jorge Vieira 3. Biblioteca Municipal José Saramago 4. Maltesinhas	1. Lanterna Azul

©ULYSSES

The Alentejo

Finally, it would be sacrilege to leave Beja without visiting the **Convento de Nossa Senhora da Conceição** ★★ (*100 ESC, admission also valid for the Museu Visigótico; 9:45am to 12:30pm and 2pm to 5pm; Largo dos Duques de Beja*). Built in 1549 by the dukes of Beja, this convent long remained one of the most important in town for both its size and its many riches. Indeed, the attractive Gothic balustrade that crowns the entire convent still provides eloquent testimony to its splendour.

Today, the convent is home to the **Museu Regional Reina Dona Leonor**, which is worth the trip in itself. The museum can be reached via the chapel, where the opulence of *talhas douradas* seems positively overwhelming. Numerous treasures, both religious and archaeological, are exhibited here in a series of small rooms on two floors. Noteworthy among them are the stunning Flemish painting depicting the Virgin Mary breastfeeding baby Jesus and the very interesting exhibit devoted to the countless Roman-era oil lamps discovered in the Beja area.

Near the exit, a magnificent Chinese bowl bequeathed by a doctor with a passion for archaeology is also worth a look. Dating from the 16th century, it bears a few Portuguese inscriptions. Of course, romantics will also find the famous window from which a Portuguese nun was said to have conversed with her lover, the Count of Chamilly. Because the window is not in its original location, it is of little historical or architectural interest.

Finally, of the main rooms, the **cloister** ★★ is unquestionably the highlight of the Convento, its walls tiled with *azulejos* adorned with Arab-influenced motifs – a real little marvel! Upon closer inspection, you will notice that each of the panels is asymmetrical. An anecdote has it that the defect was intentional, only Allah having the right to create perfect things. Last but not least, end your tour on a high note by strolling along the two corridors by the cloister, respectively devoted to St. John the Baptist and St. John the Evangelist. Both saints were courted by the nuns, who quickly split into two camps of "staunch supporters". Trying to outdo each other in religious ardour and devotion toward their favourite, the nuns gradually glutted the two corridors with an excess of decorations, turning the place into a veritable little religious museum long before the town did so!

Serpa

(29km from Beja)

Known nationwide for its famous cheese, the town of Serpa looms up deep in the heart of the vast plains of the Alentejo region, teeming with olive trees and lovely fields of golden wheat in summer. Upon entering the village, visitors will soon understand why it is also known to residents as "Serpa the White"; so much do its countless gleaming whitewashed facades shine beneath the dazzling rays of the sun. Although these parts were inhabited as early as Roman times, the small town primarily developed under the Moorish occupation, which lasted here until the 13th century. After the Christian Reconquest that same century, King Dom Dinis had a fortified castle and mighty ramparts built so as to prevent any further invasions, Spain being only a few kilometres away. Despite this, during the War of the Spanish Succession, Serpa suffered under the yoke of the

Spanish occupation for some time and withstood the destruction of part of its castle during the retreat of its powerful neighbour.

Despite its terrible history, the small town still retains most of its imposing ramparts, which won't fail to impress visitors as they enter the historic heart of the town. Of course, doing so by car would be indecent, and in order to preserve the tranquillity of the place, we advise you to park your car outside the town walls.

If you're pressed for time and don't want to miss what constitutes the essence of Beja's charm, head to Rua dos Cavalos (right near the Praça da República),

from which you can stroll along **Rua dos Quartéis**, **Rua João Valente** and **Rua do Assento**. The small low houses, some of which are even devoid of windows, bear the Moorish stamp left on the town by its former occupants. Time seems to have stopped here, and the alleys lined with modest dwellings take us back to an Alentejo of a thousand years past, at once rich and poor. Those who wish to know more about the town's popular traditions should make a point of starting their tour with the beautiful **Museu Etnográfico ★** (*Largo do Corro*), which chronicles the life of local labourers through 12 trades (blacksmith, potter, mason, basket maker, carpenter, farmer, etc.).

On returning to the Praça da República and **Largo dos Santos Próculo e Hilarião**, you'll have covered several centuries in a few metres. Indeed, opposite the lovely square planted with trees stands the **Igreja de Santa Maria**, erected in the 17th century over the ruins of a former mosque. Inside the church, lovely *azulejos* partly adorn the walls. Farther on is the severe-looking **Castelo**, inside of which is a very modest **archaeological museum** (*Tue to Sun 9am to noon and 2pm to 5pm*).

Now head to Largo dos Condes de Ficalho, where you can admire the elegant facade of the **Palácio dos Melos**, the former residence of the Counts of Ficalho, a wealthy noble family of the Alentejo. Unfortunately, it is not open to the public.

The tour continues along Rua dos Arcos, reached by taking touristy **Rua das Portas de Beja**, which runs by the imposing door of the same name. This street also boasts a stunning **aqueduct** that, literally standing atop the ramparts, is a strange yet amusing sight to behold. Farther on, at the corner of Rua da Liberdade, you can also take a look at an old bucket waterwheel that seems to have seen better days.

The Songs of Alentejo

Male voice chants are one of the distinguishing characteristics of the city of Serpa, as well as other towns in the Alentejo, and are an integral part of that region's culture. People come together spontaneously after finishing their work in the fields or during popular festivals, forming choirs that sing songs about work or

the simple things in life. Called "*estilo*", most of the songs begin with a single voice, followed by another more powerful one, and finally the whole group joins in. The songs sung by their female counterparts are known as *moda*. The main instrument accompanying this type of performance is the guitar.

The Alentejo

Finally, those particularly interested in the Renaissance are sure to admire the **facade** ★ of the 16th-century manor house located right next to Largo de São Paulo – a stunning contrast to the houses visited at the beginning of the tour!

Last but not least, it would be utter sacrilege to leave Serpa without sampling its famous ewe's-milk cheese, whose recipe is jealously guarded by the locals.

Mértola

(*54km from Beja*)

Proudly perched on a tiered promontory hemmed in by the mighty Guadiana river on one side and the gentle Oeiras river on the other, Mértola is an interesting side-trip destination. Because of its proximity to these two waterways and its strategic location, close to both the copper mines of São Domingos and the road to Beja, which did a lively trade in olives and oil, Mértola experienced significant development as far back as Roman times.

Conquered by the Moors and later by the knights of the Order of St. James, the town retains many traces of its millennial past. Indeed, it has no less than four small the-matic museums, while major excavations currently under way should soon unearth yet more riches. Before going in search of all these little treasures, however, be sure to make a brief stop south of town, via Route N122 to Alcoutim, which affords a most picturesque view of the castle and its ramparts. You can also take in panoramic vistas from the north of town, on the east bank of the Rio Guadiana, though this vantage point is regrettably marred by the atrocious concrete bridge that spans the river.

These two short excursions can also be made after the tour of the historic heart of Mértola, still entirely surrounded by massive bulwarks, Once inside the town walls, another attraction draws us inexorably toward the summit: the **Igreja Nossa Senhora da Assunção** ★★, crowned with elegant pinnacles recalling the structure's Islamic origins. Erected under the Moorish occupation, this former mosque was converted into a church in the 13th century during the Christian Reconquest. A remarkable detail: despite the major modifications carried out in the 15th century, a few Moorish arches from the Muslim period can still be discerned, as can a *mihrab*, a niche cut into a wall that serves to guide the faithful to Mecca.

Just outside the church, a trail leads to the top of Mértola, within the very confines of the 13th-century **castle**, also built on ancient Moorish fortifications. From the *torre de menagem* (dungeon), you will be treated to a beautiful, sweeping **view** ★ of the village and the surrounding hills.

The tour continues with a leisurely stroll through the old town's narrow cobblestone alleys, lined with small houses whose whitewashed facades form a particularly romantic setting. By going down the south side to the edge of the ramparts, you'll end up at the **Museu Islâmico** (*10am to 12:30pm and 2pm to 5pm; Rua da República*), where a few Moorish-era ceramic vases are on exhibit.

Right nearby, at the foot of the high wall, the small Igreja da Misericórdia houses the **Museu de Arte Sacra** (*10am to 12:30pm and 2pm to 5:30pm; Largo da Misericórdia*), where a modest collection of religious artifacts is on display. Just next to it, outside the bulwarks and near the river bank, are the ruins of the **Torre do Rio**, ancient but relatively well-preserved Roman fortifications. Farther north, the **Museu Romano** (*Praça Luís Camões; guided tours only, see below*), located in the town-hall basement, contains the foundations of a Roman house and some objects from the same period.

Finally, outside the town walls, the **Museu Paleocristão** (*Ave. Prof. Luisa Sales; guided tours only, see below*), built on the very site of an old paleo-Christian basilica, exhibits many Roman-era pieces as well as some 30 tombstones in a particularly impressive modern space.

Those who understand Portuguese and wish to explore these sites in greater depth should go to the tourist office to take a guided tour (*Sat and Sun, varying schedule; Largo Vasco da Gama, ☎286 61 25 73*) organized by the municipality.

Castro Verde

(46km from Beja)

The village of Castro Verde, located near the main road leading to the capital of the Algarve, is a pleasant place to stop. Before setting out on the long, monotonous trip to Faro, you can visit the **Igreja de Nossa Senhora da Conceição.** Covered all the way up to the vault with elegant *azulejos*, it features some lovely panels commemorating the Battle of Ourique. Equally remarkable is the altar, decorated with *talha douradas.*

★★

Castelo de Vide

Évora may be the most elegant town in the Alentejo, and Estremoz, the most pastoral, but Castelo de Vide has the most charm. Located in the Serra de São Mamede, on the same side of the hill as São Paulo, Castelo de Vide is perfectly delightful. Its walled town and old Jewish quarter form one of those rare places where, as if by magic, the simplest of surroundings becomes a truly extraordinary setting. The steep alleyways, lined with little houses painted a dazzling white, are decorated with scores of flower pots, which residents hang from their windows or place on their doorsteps. The enchanting setting will soon make you forget the difficult climb up.

The medieval town is not accessible by car, so visitors are advised to leave their vehicle alongside the Jardim Central, a park located at the edge of town.

Castelo de Vide's main attraction consists of a stroll through its numerous streets and alleyways. Each of these has its own particular charm, so it would be very difficult for us to recommend a specific route. Perhaps the most interesting way to explore the area is to wander about every which way, allowing yourself to be drawn into those alleyways that seem to call out to you. That said, we have indicated some of the most charming spots below.

After passing the park in the centre of town, you will end up on **Rua Bartolomeu Alvares da Santa**, a pleasant commercial street. You will have no trouble finding an outdoor café here where you can quench your thirst. At the end of this street, there is a traditional *pelourinho* and, on the left side, a handsome 18th-century building containing the offices of the Câmara Municipal and the tourist bureau.

By walking underneath this building's arcade, you will come to **Praça Dom Pedro V.** Unfortunately, scores of parked cars detract somewhat from the appearance of this pleasant, open square. Most of the residences facing onto it date from the 17th and 18th centuries. An elegant white marble monument dedicated to Salgueiro Maio, one of the soldiers involved in the Revolution, stands in the middle.

The **Igreja Santa Maria**, flanked by two graceful bell towers, stands on the northeast side of the square.

Heading back down Rua Bartolomeu Alvares da Santa, turn onto Rua Nova in order to reach the **Praça Fonte da Vila** ★, in the heart of the old Jewish quarter. The centre of this lovely square is adorned with a peculiar fountain, supposedly the oldest in town, surrounded by six little Renaissance columns supporting a pyramidal roof. Its mineral-rich waters are renowned for their healing powers. At this point, if you've got the energy (and the courage), don't miss the opportunity to climb up picturesque **Rua de Fonte** ★ to the ramparts and the castle, which is flanked by Gothic doors and surrounded by flowers. Be careful on the uneven ground and slippery paving stones of this steep little alley. At the top, on the right side, at number 3, you can admire the **medieval synagogue** and a lovely view of the mountains.

To reach the **Castelo**, go through the archway that marks the entrance to the walled town and take an immediate left. From atop the **keep** (*10am to noon and 2pm to 5pm*), you can enjoy a **panoramic view** ★ of the town. Before heading back down to the lower part of town, make sure to take a stroll along **Rua Direita do Castelo**, another perfectly charming street abounding with flowers.

Marvão

(*13km from Castelo de Vide*)

Located just a few kilometres from Castelo de Vide, Marvão is a small medieval village perched atop a rocky peak at an altitude of 850m. Completely surrounded by fortifications, it is the most picturesque village in the province, a must for anyone with a taste for grandiose scenery. Just before the Santa Casa da Misericórdia hospital, on the left side of the road that zigzags up to the top of the village, is an imposing pile of granite blocks shaped into stunning rounded forms by the wind and rain. From atop this mass, you can enjoy an impressive **view** ★★ of the plains stretching endlessly in the distance – a thoroughly meditative sight! This impregnable village's **castle** and **ramparts** dominate its incredible setting. These ramparts were erected in the Roman era, expanded during the Moorish occupation and then remodeled shortly after the Portuguese regained control of the country. The walls you see today date mainly from the 17th century, when the castle and its keep, built in the 14th century, were enlarged. The village itself is peaceful, except during summer when tourists literally storm the fortress. Explore the back alleys of this area, by walking (or climbing!) up and down the narrow streets lined with charming little houses, some of which have pretty windows with Manueline decorations. To reach the castle and its ramparts, you must go through no less than five fortified doors. Shortly before the second, a small passage on the right leads up a steep stairway to the first rampart's impressive **cistern**, where there lies a body of water reflecting lovely arches. Heading back down, however, proves to be something of a challenge and is extremely inadvisable for those afraid of heights. If you appreciate grandiose landscapes, proceed to the second rampart on the **covered way**, or to the top of the **dungeon**, both of which offer breathtaking **panoramic views** ★★.

For an overview of the history of Marvão and its region, visit the small **Museu Municipal de Marvão** (*200 ESC; every day 2pm to 5:30pm; Largo de Santa Maria*), housed in the former Santa Maria church. Built in the 13th century, modified numerous times and later abandoned, the structure was restored in

1987 to accommodate the museum. Divided into five themes covering everything from archaeology and religion to ethnography, the museum features various objects from the town's past.

Farther on, in the small park opposite the Igreja de Santiago, is an interesting reconstruction of a castrum that was set up with the help of the European Community. The somewhat kitsch fountain, however, seems distinctly out of place in this idyllic setting.

Lastly, for a pleasant end to this trip back in time, be sure to have a meal or a little aperitif at the Marvão *pousada* (see p 396), a fine urban-development success story.

Elvas

Elvas is a small border town located opposite its larger Spanish sister city, Badajoz. Somewhat of a commercial centre, it is flooded each weekend with Spanish tourists seeking out bargains (jewellery, fabric, fruit, wine, olive oil, etc.), particularly on clothing, which is much cheaper here than in Spain. Besides enjoying a pleasant day of shopping, visitors can explore the pretty town centre, whose monuments alone are worth the trip. The excursion is made that much more pleasant by tak-

ing the road from Estremoz to Elvas, which passes through rolling fields studded with olive trees. For a hassle-free tour of the town, leave your car in the lot beside the aqueduct and the park.

Elvas' **Vaubanesque ramparts** are among the most impressive in Portugal. In fact, if you were to follow them, you'd have to walk no less than 5km to make a full circle. Dating back to the 17th century, they are fortified by two forts – Santa Luzia to the south, now a *pousada* (see p 397) and Nossa Senhora da Graça to the north. Both offer **panoramic views** of the town and its fortifications.

Equally impressive is the **Amoreira aqueduct ★**, which stretches about 7km, and rivals Lisbon's as the most beautiful in the country. Erected between 1498 and 1622, it stands four storeys and a total of 31m high, and includes nearly 800 arches. It was designed in part by Francisco de Arruda, the architect of Lisbon's Torre de Belém and many other religious and civic buildings in Portugal. The aqueduct still supplies part of the town with water.

Those with a taste for Manueline architecture should visit the **Igreja de Nossa Senhora da Assunçao** (*Praça da República*), formerly the

Sé. Particularly noteworthy features include the side portals and, inside, the **beautiful pillars** with Manueline ornamentation and the lovely 17th-century *azulejos*.

Behind the former Sé lies the Largo do Dr. Santa Clara and the **Igreja de Nossa Senhora da Consolaçao ★**, the most beautiful church in town, built in 1513. The inside of this octagonal building is entirely covered with **beautiful** *azulejos*. Its **cupola**, also adorned with ceramic tiles, is supported by **elegant painted and gilded columns**. The altar is richly decorated with gilding, as well.

Other interesting sights on the square include the amusing **decorated pillory** and the **Arcado do Mirandeiro**, a pretty arcade topped by an elegant gallery of Moorish inspiration. The road that passes under the arcade will take you straight to the **Castelo**, from which you can gaze down on the city.

Estremoz

The fortified city of Estremoz is divided into two centres of interest, each delimited by its defenses and geographical location. The medieval village, still completely surrounded by ramparts, is perched atop a hill,

The Alentejo

while the "new" city, now only partially fortified, lies below. The greatest attractions here are the **magnificent keep**, definitely the most beautiful one in Portugal, and the **picturesque village**. Although the old city takes precedence, the lower city is also very pleasant and not to be overlooked. The region is renowned for its marble, and visitors will notice the numerous marble staircases, portals and window frames adorning the city. Those with a taste for ceramics will also find a wide selection of pottery and terracotta dolls, a local specialty.

For a particularly impressive entrance into the old city, along a verdant, picturesque road, follow the signs for the pousada on the N4-IC10-E90. This will lead you straight to the west entrance of Estremoz, the Porta de Évora.

Pass through the gateway, and take the alley immediately to the right, which leads directly to the fortified gate of the medieval village that dominates Estremoz.

After passing through the **impressive fortified entrance** known as the Porta de Évora, you will find yourself inside the village that surrounds the castle. The small residences are modest, but for their dazzling whitewashed exteriors and Moorish-style chimneys. This is another world, seemingly untouched by time and the tumult of the modern world. Here and there, old Portuguese women dressed entirely in black chat together on their doorsteps, while a cat strolls nonchalantly across the street. By heading straight up to the top of the village, you can enjoy a **lovely view ★** of the countryside from the second fortified entrance.

Estremoz Dungeon

Rua Direita stretches forth before you, gradually blending into the verdant fields in the distance.

Now go to the medieval village itself, where you will find the *pousada*. The small, gently sloping road leading through the centre of town is studded with a handful of little houses bearing coats of arms. It will take you directly to the **Largo do Castelo**, in a setting straight out of a fairy tale. On this stately square paved like a checkerboard, you will find the castle's **keep ★★**, made entirely of white Estremoz marble. Topped by pyramidal battlements and equipped with extremely elegant machicolations, it is assuredly the most handsome structure of its kind in Portugal. Its construction, begun at the same time as the castle, around 1258, lasted three reigns, earning it the nickname Torre de Três Coroas (Tower of the Three Crowns). The castle now adjoining it dates from the 18th century, and has recently been converted into a luxurious *pousada*. Don't hesitate to go inside and admire the magnificent interior (see p 397).

Make sure to take a look at the pretty Renaissance-style façade of the **Igreja de Santa Maria do Castelo**, immediately to the right of the keep, and more importantly, the **Paço da Audiênca** ★, a bit farther along on the right. The latter building, also known as the Paço Real de Dom Dinis (since it was part of the former royal palace built for Dom Dinis), is graced with an **exquisite loggia**. The interior has been transformed into a small contemporary art museum of limited interest, but nonetheless merits a visit for its **beautiful star-studded vault**.

The **Capela Rainha Santa Isabel** (*opening hours vary, inquire at the pousada*) also stands on the Largo do Castelo, to the left of the keep. Its **remarkable interior** is decorated with *azulejos* illustrating the life of Dona Santa Isabel. The wife of King Dinis was particularly fond of Estremoz and spent the last years of her life here.

Before checking out the attractions in the lower town, take a brief tour of the **Museu Municipal de Estremoz** (*180 ESC; Tue to Sun 9am to 12:30pm and 2pm to 5:30pm; Largo Dom Dinis, ☎268 33 20 71*), where figurines, earthenware, regional furniture and *azulejos* offer a fine sampling of the local craft industry. A few archaeological pieces, as well as a modest collection of weapons, are also on display.

Lower Town

The pleasant **Rossio Marquês de Pombal**, in the lower town is also worth a stroll, in particular for the lovely residences there (especially along the south side of the square, where you will find the Câmara Municipal, with its pretty marble door- and window-frames). Make a brief stop at the **Câmara Municipal** to admire its elegant inner court and graceful flight of stairs, made entirely of marble and lined with *azulejos*.

Right beside the Rossio, at number 18 on the **Largo da República**, stands a former convent (*Soc. Recreativa P. Estremoncence*), which is worth visiting for its lovely inner court lined with little columns.

Ethnology buffs should head to the **Museu Rural** (*100 ESC; Tue to Sun 10am to 1pm and 3pm to 5:30pm; on the east side of Rossio Marquês de*

Pombal), which houses a collection of regional costumes and an exhibit on rural life.

Vila Viçosa

(17km from Estremoz)

Like Estremoz, Vila Viçosa is renowned for its white-marble quarries, and constitutes a pleasant excursion or stop for those in search of peace and quiet. Home to the Dukes of Bragança since the 15th century, the town was split into two parts: the old village crowned with a **Castelo**, dating from the 13th century and still entirely surrounded by a mighty wall, and the "new" town, which developed from the 16th century with the construction of the ducal palace, marking the apogee of Vila Viçosa. Paradoxically, the country's return to independence in 1640 (see p 20) instigated the town's lengthy decline, as its eighth duke was acclaimed King of Portugal, under the name of Dom João IV. The powerful Bragança family thereby moved to the nation's capital, only returning to Vila Viçosa for very short periods of time.

After a brief stroll along the castle's covered way, where lovely **panoramic views** ★ meet the eyes (or lens) of budding photographers, head to the vast **Terreiro do Paço** to admire the impressive marble facade of the

Paço Ducal, witness to a triumphant past. The ducal palace has now been converted into a **museum** ★ (*1,000 ESC; Tue to Sun 1hr guided tour 9:30am to 1pm and 2:30pm to 5pm*), devoted to the Bragança dynasty. In no less than 50 rooms, you can view Flemish tapestries, paintings, *azulejos*, weapons, period furniture and crockery in a setting pervaded with stucco and gilding, as well as pleasant gardens. Throughout this (overly long) guided tour, you will thus learn everything there is to know about the last ruling royal family of Portugal.

To digest this royal excess, head south of the square, where you can have a drink in the former Convento das Chagas, now converted into a magnificent *pousada* (see p 398).

Finally, before setting off for new horizons, be sure to take a look at the old city gate, the **Porta dos Nós** ("Door of Knots"), featured in countless tourist brochures.

Porta dos Nós

Évoramonte

(17km from Estremoz)

After passing through a romantic landscape made up of gentle hills studded with olive trees and cork oaks, you will suddenly spot the unusual **castle** (*200 ESC; Tue to Sun 10am to noon and 2pm to 5pm*) of Évoramonte, perched atop a steep hill. Partway through the "modern" village below, you can head up to the castle on a magnificent little serpentine road, which offers a **stunning view** ★ of the surrounding countryside. Upon arriving at the old village, park your car near the chapel, just after the castle, and continue your tour on foot. You can start by taking a quick look at the castle, an amusing three-storey structure whose facade, adorned with bows, is fit for an operetta.

Afterward, take the time to stroll through the village's **alleyways** ★. A sense of absolute tranquility prevails in this enchanting village, whose little white houses contrast sharply with the valley strewn with cork oaks. A trip not to be missed!

Évora

As the numerous megaliths in this region seem to indicate, Évora was probably inhabited in prehistoric times. However, the community did not really thrive until the Roman era. A remarkable temple bearing witness to this period of vitality still stands in the heart of Liveralitas Julia (Évora's Roman name). The Visigoths seized the town during the barbarian invasions, only to be followed by the Moors, who took over in 715. Although the Moors remained here for nearly 500 years, not a single building survives from that very prosperous era. Reconquered in 1165 by a knight named Geraldo Sem Pavor, Évora quickly won the favour of the royalty, particularly under the Aviz dynasty. The town thus reached its peak during the 16th century, under the reign of Dom João III. The king decided to take up residence here, bringing along a number of artists who, over the

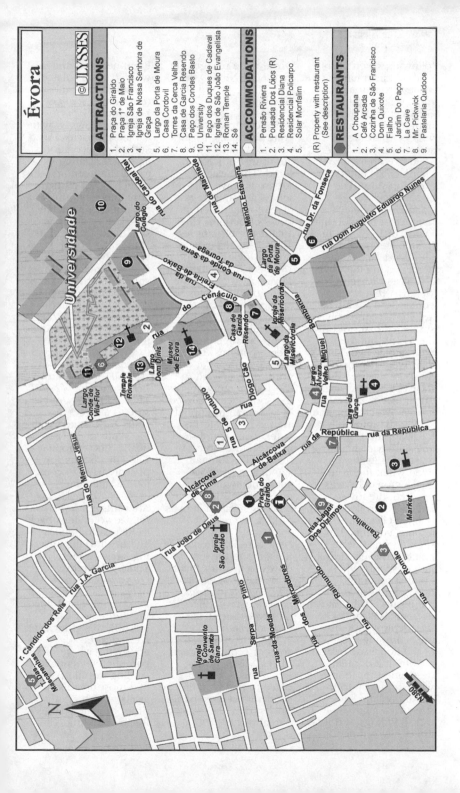

Évora

© ULYSSES

● ATTRACTIONS

1. Praça do Giraldo
2. Praça 1° de Maio
3. Igreja São Francisco
4. Igreja de Nossa Senhora de Graça
5. Largo da Porta de Moura
6. Casa Cordovil
7. Torres da Cerca Velha
8. Casa de Garcia Resendo
9. Paço dos Condes Basto
10. University
11. Paço dos Duques de Cadaval
12. Igreja de São João Evangelista
13. Roman Temple
14. Sé

○ ACCOMMODATIONS

1. Pensão Riviera
2. Pousada Dos Lóios (R)
3. Residencial Diana
4. Residencial Policarpo
5. Solar Monfalim

(R) Property with restaurant (See description)

⬡ RESTAURANTS

1. A Choupana
2. Café Arcada
3. Cozinha de São Francisco
4. Dom Quixote
5. Fialho
6. Jardim Do Paço
7. La Cave
8. Mr. Pickwick
9. Pastelaria Quidoce

following seven years, made Évora a familiar name throughout Europe. Celebrated poet Gil Vicente stayed here until his death, and writers André de Resende and Francisco de Melo lived here, providing entertainment for the royalty. The famous sculptor Chantereine created a number of his pieces in Évora. In 1559, Cardinal Infante Henrique I founded a university here, making the town a centre of learning, as well. However, when young King Sebastião arrived here, no one suspected that not only the town's but the entire country's golden days were numbered. After the disaster at el-Kasr el-Kebir (Alcázarquivir, see p 20), Évora lost its royal status, and slowly slid into oblivion, with the Jesuits and the Spanish as sole masters of its destiny. Even when the Portuguese monarchy was restored, the town, largely controlled by an ossified ecclesiastical regime, continued its slow decline. Évora finally fell even farther into obscurity when Pombal came into power and drove out the Jesuits. Today, it is not only the capital of the Alentejo, but also the "Portuguese capital of the Renaissance", making it a popular destination for tourists, who are drawn to its charming little back streets. Its many historic buildings, furthermore, have earned it

world-wide recognition. In 1986, UNESCO designated it a World Heritage Site.

Start your tour at the **Praça do Giraldo**, Évora's central square, where the tourist office is located. The busiest square in town, it serves as a meeting place for all different kinds of people. The arcades of elegant residences line its east side, bringing to mind a Mediterranean city. You can relax at one of the many outdoor cafés set up right on the patterned "carpet" of black and white paving stones arranged in geometric patterns. The marble fountain at the north end, erected in the 18th century, marks the spot once occupied by a Roman triumphal arch, which unfortunately was demolished in the 16th century. In front of the fountain stands the **Igreja São Antão**, noteworthy mainly for its lovely *azulejos*, as its interior is of little interest.

Now take Rua Romão Ramalho to the left down to the vast **Praça 1° de Maio** (*on the right hand side as you walk down the street*), the site of a weekly **craft fair** (*Tue to Fri 6am to 1:30pm*) featuring all sorts of ceramics (cups, plates, vases, bowls, etc.). This is a good place to find beautiful souvenirs at reasonable prices (don't hesitate to bargain).

Right nearby stand the whitewashed sides of the **Igreja São Francisco** (*every day 9:30am to noon and 2:30pm to 5:30pm*), crowned with cabled pinnacles. An arched portico adorns its facade. Dating back to the 16th century, this church is not particularly interesting from the outside. Nonetheless, before going inside, take a look at its Manueline portal, topped by a pelican and an armillary sphere, both royal emblems. Inside, after contemplating the impressive width of the vault, make sure to visit the **Capelados Ossos** (*150 ESC; same hours as the church; enter on the right side of the church; not for the faint of heart!*). This gloomy chapel is sure to impress; its walls are covered with the skulls and bones of nearly 5,000 people. The Franciscans supposedly used to come here to meditate!

After this macabre visit, retrace your steps back to Rua da Rebública and head to the amazing **Igreja de Nossa Senhora da Graça** (*Largo da Graça, on the right side as you head up the street*). Erected during the reign of João III, this church has a classical facade adorned with various baroque elements, including trophies, shells and most notably, four **giants**, which are disproportionately large for the building. The result is more comic than elegant.

Now take one of the little alleyways located immediately to the left of the church to reach Rua Miguel Bombarda. By continuing to the right, you will reach the **Largo da Porta de Moura ★**, made up of two successive squares. Picture-perfect views can be had from the lower one, with its pretty white marble fountain. This is surely the most picturesque square in Évora. If you stand near the fountain, facing north, you will see a cluster of gleaming white buildings elegantly crowned by the central spire and bell towers of the Sé. Charming Rua Dom Augusto Eduardo Nunes, also lined with dazzling white residences, runs along the south side of the square. Here, you will find the elegant **Casa Cordovil** (*on the left side of the square*). This mansion, with its **arched loggia** topped by a cone, is a fine example of Luso-Moorish architecture.

Head to the upper square, which is considerably busier. Walk straight across it into the alleyway of São Manços where the **Torres da Cerca Velha** are located. Set on either side of the street, these towers, remodeled in the Middle Ages, were part of the Roman fortifications that once surrounded the town.

Higher up, the alleyway ends opposite the **Casa de Garcia Resendo**, the former residence of humanist Garcia Resendo. It is worth making a brief stop here to examine the house's **lovely Manueline windows.** To the right, take Rua da Freira de Baixo until it ends at the Largo do Colégio, where the university is located. On the way, you will pass the **Paço dos Condes Basto**, the palace once occupied by the late lamented King Sebastião and the equally late but less lamented King Felipe III of Spain, who ruled over Portugal.

Although Renaissance in style, the **university** (*entrance on the Largo do Colégio*) reflects a definite classical influence. It is worth visiting for its **remarkable azulejos ★**, which can be found all over the interior, from the entry halls and long corridors to the staircases, making this, like Coimbra, one of the loveliest universities in the country. Make sure not to miss the beautiful Renaissance **cloister**, whose galleries are also covered with lovely ceramic decorations. If you have a chance, take a quick look at the *azulejos* adorning the classrooms alongside the cloister. Most depict themes related to the material taught there.

After exiting onto the Largo do Colégio, head northwest along the

path that leads through the little park opposite the university. This path runs alongside the former ramparts, then cuts across them, making for a pleasant walk. At the end, turn left to visit the Largo Conde de Vila-Flor, which has a little park in the middle and is bordered by the **Paço dos Duques de Cadaval**. King João I gave this palace to his adviser, Count Martim Afonso de Melo, Évora's first mayor. It has served as a temporary residence for several Portuguese monarchs, including João III. The palace is flanked by two crenellated towers and adjoined by an **attractive patio** (see p 406), which provides a pleasant place to relax in the shade of the orange trees. Visitors interested in the history of the world's luminaries won't want to miss the **Galería de Arte dos Duques de Cadaval** (*entrance fee; Tue to Sun 10am to 12:30pm and 2pm to 5pm; enter via the patio, on the right side of the palace*) located inside the palace itself, which displays various objects and documents related to the influential Cadaval line. The descendants of the de Melo family succeeded in "modestly" accumulating the titles of Marquis of Ferreira, Count of Olivença, Count of Tentúgal and finally Count of Cadaval – an impressive collection that was doubtless the

The Alentejo

The **Igreja de São João Evangelista** (*500 ESC*) stands alongside the palace's patio. This church, dating back to the 15th century, was part of the Convento dos Lóios and contains a beautiful altar decorated with *talha douradas*, as well as the tombs of the de Melo family. The *Convento dos Lóios*, alongside the church, was erected around 1485 by celebrated architect Francisco de Arruda, who designed Lisbon's Torré de Belém. It was converted into a *pousada* in 1965 (see p 400). The cloister, where the restaurant (see p 406, 407) is located, boasts a **magnificent double arcade ★★** supported by elegant cabled columns, a fine example of the Luso-Moorish style.

The **Roman temple ★★★**, which occupies the place of honour in the centre of the square, is not only Évora's most majestic monument, but also the most impressive Roman ruin in Portugal. Erected in the 2nd century, it was dedicated to Diana, the Roman goddess of hunting, and to the wilderness. Its columns are topped by **lovely Corinthian capitals** made of Estremoz marble. In the Middle Ages, the temple was transformed into a fortress, and stones were placed between its columns, creating a wall around the entire structure; this accounts for its excellent state of preservation. It served as the local slaughterhouse in the 14th century, and then as a market. It wasn't until 1870 that the temple was finally cleared out and restored. Surrounded by prestigious buildings, with the bell towers of the Sé off in the distance, this is Évora's stateliest square, the city's pride and joy. The Largo Conde de Vila-Flor would be idyllic if it weren't for the appalling water tower on the west side: like a blemish on the face of this otherwise beautiful spot.

Temple of Diana

Now head to the south side of the square, on the right, to admire the facade of the **cathedral ★**. Erected during the 12th and 13th centuries, it is a blend of several different styles, ranging from Roman to Gothic. The austere colour of this massive-looking granite structure contrasts dramatically, but nonetheless attractively, with the dazzling white of the adjacent buildings. The facade, with its unmatched pair of towers erected in the 16th century, is not exactly harmonious, however. The left tower is studded with windows and crowned by a cone covered with *azulejos*, while the right tower is equipped with a clock and topped by a roof similar to that of the lantern tower. From the outside, the cathedral's most impressive feature is its central spire, or **lantern tower ★**. A big cone surrounded by pinnacles of the same shape, it fits in well with the flat crenellated roofs. These last two elements clearly reveal a French, and more specifically Provençal, influence. On your way through the main portal, take a look at the elegant statues of the apostles. Aside from its impressive dimensions, the interior is worth visiting for its two **lovely Gothic rose windows** and unusual **pregnant Virgin**. The upper level of the **Gothic cloister** (*250 ESC including a tour of the*

Museu de Arte Sacra and the Coro Alto; Tue to Sun 10am to noon and 2pm to 4pm) offers an **attractive view** of the town.

Right beside the cathedral, in the former bishop's palace, the **Museu de Évora** (*250 ESC; Tue to Sun 10am to 12pm and 2pm to 5pm*) houses an **interesting archaeological collection** focussing mainly on the Roman and medieval periods. A number of pieces by celebrated sculptor Nicolas Chantereine are also displayed here,

along with a handful of Luso-Moorish architectural fragments from Évora's former palaces and churches. Various Portuguese and Flemish paintings from the 16th and 17th centuries are exhibited on the second floor, along with some furniture and antique earthenware.

Ermida de São Brás (*outside the fortifications, on Rua da República, on the left as you head toward the train station*). It is definitely worth making a trip to this unusual

15th-century church. Of Moorish inspiration, it is crowned by several conical domes. The result, however, is more amusing than beautiful.

Zambujeiro and Almendres

The Megaliths

The area around Évora is known for the many dolmens and menhirs scattered across its fields. As you travel

Dolmens, Menhirs and Cromlechs

The numerous megaliths–dolmens, menhirs and cromlechs–discovered in this region were made by tribes composed mainly of shepherds and farmers, who lived here around the fourth and third millennia B.C. The purpose of the dolmens indicates that these people were concerned with spirituality, while their structure proves the existence of actual communities. The dolmens are communal tombs, made up of huge stones standing on end and usually placed in a circle. Topped by a

large slab of rock, dolmens are sometimes preceded by a corridor leading to one or more chambers. Most have now been exposed, but they used to be covered by a heap of rocks and earth, known as a tumulus, forming a clearly visible mound. Anyone going to one of the funeral chambers thus had to do so in the dark. It is also interesting to consider that the very shape of the tumulus, rounded like a breast, might have been connected to ancient religious beliefs. Although unfounded, this theory suggests a

representation of the cycle of life and death, the nourishing earth welcoming back the being whose birth it witnessed, and whom it fed. One thing is for certain, though: the imposing mass of the monuments is proof of collective labour and therefore communal living. As for the menhirs (from the Breton word for "long stone") and cromlechs (a group of menhirs in a circle), their vertical position, according to studies still in progress, seems to be related to the stars.

The Alentejo

about, you will no doubt spot a few of these nestled between the area's numerous cork oaks. Below, we have included descriptions of two of the most noteworthy sites, both of which are easily accessible. If the subject fascinates you, obtain a copy of the excellent little *Évora Megalithism Guide* distributed by Évora's tourist office. It is very thorough, and outlines tours that will allow you to explore a number of different sites.

The **grand dolmen of Zambujeiro** ★ *(head south on the N380 for 10km, then take the road on the right towards Valverde. The path to the dolmen lies to the right shortly before Valverde.)* A national monument, this dolmen is the largest of its kind in Europe. Its funeral chamber is about 6m high; just imagine the tremendous weight of the stones and the effort required to move them! The dolmen used to be covered by a tumulus measuring about 50m in diameter, and was used as a place of both burial and worship. Numerous objects (pottery, pearls, stone arrows, etc.) were found there. Aside from the slab that used to lie across the top like an enormous hat, which was broken and has been removed, you can view the long gallery leading to the chamber.

The **Cromlech of Almendres** ★ *(Continue driving towards Valverde, then on to Guadelupe and Almendres, where you will find signs reading "Cromeleque de Almendres," leading directly to the site by via a dirt road.)*. This impressive site features 95 dolmens arranged in a circle. Today, it seems more and more evident that the position of the menhirs is directly related to that of the stars, suggesting the existence of an ancient astral cult, which has yet to be explained. The cromlech is an extremely impressive sight. If you look carefully at some of the dolmens, you can make out traces of engravings.

Vila de Frades

(26km from Beja)

In the middle of the fields about 2km from the sleepy little village of Vila Frades, lie the **Roman ruins of São Cucufate** *(From Vidigueira, take the N258 toward Vila Frades; which passes partially through the village, and continues on to Alvito, just after which you will see the signs for the ruins.)* These are the vestiges of a stately Roman residence, which was converted into a monastery, also in ruins. The charming site and beautiful surrounding countryside make for an extremely pleasant excursion.

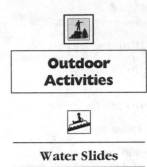

Outdoor Activities

Water Slides

The water slide at the **Parque Elxadai**, located on the N4-IC10-E90 *(4km from Elvas, on the right side of the road as you head toward Estremoz)*, is a pleasant place to escape from the extreme summer heat of this region.

Swimming

Estremoz

The large pool at the **Parque Desport Municipal**, at the western edge of town, is open to the public. The less courageous can simply soak up the sun. There is also an indoor pool, open only during winter.

Bicycling

Évora

For an energetic tour of the city (be careful on the uneven paving stones!), **Rent-A-Bike**

(☎ *266 76 14 53*) offers daily and weekly mountain-bike rentals (*approx. 1,500 ESC for a day, 3,500 ESC for three days and 7,000 ESC for a week*).

Golf

Marvão

Much like the tourist region of Montanhas, the Alentejo has a dearth of golf courses. Indeed, there is only one in the area to date, located near the marvellous little village of Marvão. Golf enthusiasts can thus play to their heart's content on the 6,156m-long, 18-hole (par-72) course amidst spectacular scenery, the impressive Serra de São Mamede crowned with the *Castelo de Marvão* ramparts looming in the distance. Reservations and information:

Quinta do Prado
São Salvador d'Aramenha
7330 Marvão
☎*245 99 37 55*
⇌*245 99 38 05*

Accommodations

Beja

Campismo Municipal de Beja (camping)
Avenida Vasco de Gama
7800 Beja
☎*284 32 43 28*
⇌*284 32 72 25*

Pensão-Residencial Coelho
$$ pb
tv
Praça da República no. 15
7800 Beja
☎*284 32 40 31*
☎*284 32 89 38*
⇌*284 32 89 39*
The small Coelho *residencial* is a decent choice for budget travellers seeking accommodations in the heart of Beja. Its 28 rooms are housed in a rather mundane building, but have comfortable beds and suitable, if somewhat worn, furnishings. For a relatively pleasant view, opt for one of the rooms overlooking the Praça da República.

Horta do Cano
$$$ pb
tv, K, ≈
Agroturismo Monte Horta do Cano, 2km from Beja on the N121; 7800 Beja
☎/⇌*284 32 61 56*
Do you enjoy waking to the sounds of cockcrow, neighing horses, clucking hens or gobbling turkeys? Do you appreciate the charms of the wide-open countryside and the benefits of its bracing air? Then this is the place for you! The Horta de Cano *quinta* offers two lodging options: a room in the main farmhouse, where guests also have the run of a common living room, or one of the small apartments in a house near the farm. The apartments come with a kitchenette as well as a living room with fireplace. Whatever your choice, the setting is quite simply magnificent. Decorated with farming tools and antique furnishings, each of the rooms reflects the place's rural character.

Breakfast is served in a charming little room decorated with sundry handmade dishes. And what a breakfast it is! Coffee or hot chocolate served with perfectly creamy milk, delicious-smelling farmhouse bread, scrumptious homemade jams, fragrant Alentejo cheese, freshly squeezed orange juice and, to top it all off, a slice of fruit cake. Now there's a breakfast you won't

The Alentejo

soon forget! After such a feast, more athletic types can cool off in the large swimming pool in the garden, enjoy a game of tennis on the adjacent court, explore the surrounding countryside by bike (available to guests), or go horseback riding (*10,000 ESC/hr*). And, for those still looking for something to do, a ping-pong table and a pool table are also on hand. Finally, the very courteous welcome and impeccably clean surroundings make this place an absolute must.

Pousada do Convento de São Francisco
$$$$$ pb
tv, ≈, ℜ
7800 Beja
☎ *284 32 84 41*
⇒ *284 32 91 43*
As may be gathered by its name, the Pousada do Convento de São Francisco is a former monastery which dates all the way back to 1268. Erected for the governor of Beja, it has been altered many times over the centuries, and still includes a church dating from the middle of the 16th century. The original Franciscan occupants gradually vacated the premises, and the buildings underwent major modifications, then were completely abandoned during the 20th century. This state of abandon can be seen in a series of photographs displayed in one of the galleries of the cloister; the photos were taken during the

extensive restorations carried out by Enatur. There is also a display case containing various objects from the Roman era, which were found on site, indicating that an imperial settlement was once located here. The restorations have led to the monastery's remarkable transformation into a *pousada*. The cloister has been entirely reconstructed, and its cells converted into rooms. The architect made an effort to retain as many of the building's original features as possible, thereby recreating a truly monastic atmosphere. An elegant Gothic chapel faces right onto one of the galleries of the cloister, while the chapter house, whose ceiling frescoes have been beautifully preserved, has been converted into a restaurant. The furnishings and colour schemes of the rooms and common areas have been chosen with great care. The resulting austerity of the surroundings seems not only appropriate, but inherently refined.

Serpa

(*29km from Beja*)

🏯 **Casa da Muralha**
$$ pb
tv, ⊗
Rua das Portas de Beja no. 43, 7830 Serpa
☎ *284 54 31 50*
⇒ *284 54 31 51*
Built on the massive bulwarks enclosing the historic heart of Serpa,

the Casa da Muralha has five pleasant rooms in a lovely 19th-century house. Guests can thus either stay in one of the particularly spacious, antique-furnished rooms in the house itself, or one inside an outbuilding facing the inner courtyard planted with beautiful orange trees. From the latter building, you can admire the stunning aqueduct that crowns the town's ramparts. During our visit, the owner, an ardent collector, was busy setting up a small farming-tool museum at the entrance to his house. Very warm welcome.

Alvito

(*45km from Beja*)

Pousada do Castelo de Alvito
$$$$$
pb, tv, ≈, ℜ
from Beja take the N18-E802 north for 23km, then the N258 to Alvito; 7920 Alvito
☎ *284 48 53 43*
⇒ *284 48 53 83*
The Pousada do Castelo de Alvito, in a fortress dating back to the end of the 15th century, will delight lovers of architecture. In fact, this large fortified building encompasses no fewer than three styles, from Mudéjar windows to Manueline decorations touching on the Gothic, whose traces are apparent throughout. As for the modern rooms, lovely regional furniture warms their rather cold atmosphere. This

spot is a perfect choice for those who want to avoid Évora's tourist influxes. In addition to being located half-way between the historic towns of Évora and Beja, this *pousada* is fewer than 20km from some lovely Roman ruins (see p 392). It also constitutes an excellent base from which to discover the marvellous back country of the Alentejo.

Castelo de Vide

Casa de Hospedes Xinxel
$
pb
Largo do Paço Novo 5
7320 Castelo de Vide
☎245 90 14 06
The rooms at the Casa de Hospedes Xinxel are somewhat small, but the place is clean and well kept and looks out onto an attractive little inner courtyard.

Residencial Isabelinha
$$
pb
Largo do Paço Novo,
7320 Castelo de Vide
☎245 90 18 96
The rooms at the Residencial Isabelinha, which belongs to the same owner as the Residencial Casa do Parque, are well maintained and reasonably comfortable. Some rooms are equipped with attractive regional furniture, which is somewhat kitch.

Residencial Casa do Parque
$$
pb
Aramenha corner Rua do Paço Novo, facing the central park
7320 Castelo de Vide
☎245 90 12 50
≈245 90 13 40
The Residencial Casa do Parque has the advantage of being located on a fairly quiet street, in front of a little park. Although their furnishings are slightly outmoded, the rooms are well kept. Ask for a room with a view.

🌴 Albergaria El Rei Dom Miguel
$$
pb, tv, ⊗, ≡
Rua Bartolomeu Alvares da Santa, 7320 Castelo de Vide
☎245 91 91 91
☎245 91 91 90
≈245 90 15 92
Though located on Castelo de Vide's noisy main street, this small inn boasts seven particularly comfortable rooms, set out in an old spotless manor house. What's more, despite the interior's modern refurbishment, the owners have managed to preserve all its charm by setting out antique curios and furniture here and there. Very warm welcome.

🌴 Garcia d'Orta
$$$
pb, tv, ℜ, ≈
Estrada de São Vicente, on the left side when heading toward Marvão, 7320 Castelo de Vide
☎245 90 11 00
≈245 90 12 00
The Garcia d'Orta, recently built just outside

of the village, is probably the loveliest hotel in the area. Very charming and tastefully decorated. Guests can also enjoy the swimming pool. To top it all off, there are conference rooms, a bar and tennis courts. Expensive but beautiful. The prices are more attractive on weekdays, when substantial discounts are available. Professional service.

Marvão

(13km from Castelo de Vide)

During the high season (from May to September), especially on weekends, both Portuguese and foreign visitors flock to Marvão. Although some residents rent out rooms at reasonable rates (about 4,000 to 7,000 ESC on average), it is wise to reserve ahead of time or visit the town on a weekday during this period. To reserve a room in a private home, contact the tourist office (see p 376).

Pensão Dom Dinis
$$
pb, tv, ℜ
Rua Dr. Matos Magalhães, in front of the tourist office
7330 Marvão
☎245 99 32 36
The little Pensão Dom Dinis has only eight rooms but is extremely well located alongside the ramparts, thus offering a view of the plains. The small rooms are simply but tastefully

decorated. Reservations recommended. Friendly service.

The Pousada de Santa Maria
$$$$
pb, tv, ℜ
private parking on Rua do Embique, below the pousada
7330 Marvão
☎*245 99 32 01*
⇄*245 99 34 40*
The Pousada de Santa Maria consists of a series of rustic little houses connected by a quaint arched passageway, and has the advantage of being located in the very heart of the picturesque village of Marvão. This clever setup enables guests to enjoy the comfort of a luxurious hotel in a pastoral setting. The cozy surroundings and tasteful decor compensate greatly for the small size of the rooms, some of which offer splendid views of the valley. This place is a real little jewel! Cheerful, welcoming staff.

Flor da Rosa

(*28km from Castelo de Vide*)

🏆 **Pousada Flor da Rosa**
$$$$$
pb, tv, ≈, ℜ
from Castelo de Vide take the N246 west for 16km and then the N245 to Crato; 7430 Crato
☎*245 99 72 10*
☎*245 99 72 11*
⇄*245 99 72 12*
Arriving in the little village of Flor da Rosa, Pousada Flor da Rosa is impossible to miss, set,

as it is, in the heart of an astonishing 14th-century monastery. Built for a chapter of the Knights Hospitallers, the order which later became the Knights of Malta, the monastery of Santa Maria da Flor resembles a forbidding fortress more than it does a peaceful monastery. Its peculiar architecture is the product of the nearby presence of the border, as well as of the quasi-warlike vocation of the order, demonstrated many times over in its history, especially in Portugal by the recapture of territory from the Moors. Heavily damaged by the earthquake of 1755, reconstructed soon after and then abandoned after the religious orders dissolved in 1834, the building has been subjected to numerous modifications. Despite its classification as a national monument in 1910, a fastidious phase of restoration was not begun until the 1940s. Transformed into a *pousada* by Enatur, the ancient monastery of Santa Maria da Flor da Rosa has finally returned to one of its first vocations, to welcoming and protecting pilgrims.

Once again, the architect chosen by Enatur, João Luís Carrilho da Graça, has found a particularly original approach to the design of this *pousada*. The purity of the lines of the modern buildings

annexed to the original construction contrast marvellously with the severity of the fortress. The noble colours of stone combine with the gleaming white of the new sections to create a magical union. Centuries, represented in these buildings, collide and seem to melt into each other with the help of a harmonious landscape, the secret for which only Alentejo seems to know.

The same formula appears to have been applied for the decor of the rooms in the new section. The simplicity of the few pieces of furniture found in the almost empty rooms, combined with the choice of warm-coloured fabrics, will greatly impress design aficionados. The rooms in the older section, in the monastery itself, are imbued with a more medieval atmosphere. The cloister, at the centre of which, on the floor, visitors can see a Maltese cross, and the former refectory, adorned with elegant wreathed columns and today transformed into a bar, are both admirable examples of a tremendously ingenious restoration. Even if you choose not to stay here, Pousada de Santa Maria da Flor da Rosa is worth the detour – it qualifies as a tourist attraction in itself!

Elvas

Varchotel
$$
pb, tv
Estrada Nacional N4
7350 Elvas, Varche
☎*268 62 88 72*
⇄*268 62 15 96*
On Highway N4-E90,
4km from Elvas,
Varchotel offers comfortable rooms decorated with modern furnishings. Ask for one of the rooms at the back of the building, which offer lovely views of the countryside.

Pousada da Santa Luzia
$$$$
pb, tv, ℜ
7350 Elvas
☎*268 62 21 94*
☎*268 62 21 28*
⇄*268 62 21 27*
The Pousada da Santa Luzia, located near the fortified gate on the south side of town, is a rather uninspiring modern building. Its main advantages are its proximity to the centre of town and the quality of its services.

Estremoz

Lower Town

Pensão-Restaurante Estremoz
$ no bkfst
Rossio Marquês de Pombal 14-15, 7100 Estremoz
☎*268 32 28 43*
The handful of rooms at the Pensão-Restaurante Estremoz, over the Café Alentejano, are pleasant enough, although their decor is somewhat outmoded. While amenities are limited to a sink in each room, the place is clean and well maintained. The handsome staircase on the second floor serves as a reminder that this region is a major producer of marble.

Residencial Carvalho
$ no pb or bkfst
$$ with pb
tv
Largo da Rebública 27
7100 Estremoz
☎*268 33 93 70*
⇄*68 32 23 70*
Located next to the Porto de Turismo, the Residencial Carvalho is a small, family run hotel with 18 cozy rooms and wooden floors. A lovely marble entryway adorned with *azulejos* tops off the decor of this modest but rather pleasant place.

Hospedaria Dom Dinis
$$$
pb, tv
Rua 31 de Janeiro 46
7100 Estremoz
☎*268 33 27 17*
☎*268 32 28 80*
⇄*268 32 26 10*
Located inside a completely renovated house, this little hotel has eight large modern but unremarkable rooms. Although the place is very comfortable, the services offered do not really justify the relatively high prices.

Upper Town

🐚 **Pousada Rainha Santa Isabel**
$$$$$
pb, tv, ≈, ℜ
Largo Dom Dinis, inside the castle in the old city
7101 Estremoz Codex
☎*268 33 20 75*
⇄*268 33 20 79*
Of all the *pousadas* that have been set up inside national monuments, the Pousada Rainha Santa Isabel is definitely one of the most remarkable. It has even been called the "jewel in the crown". After climbing up the hill to the castle, you will arrive right at the extraordinary entrance to the *pousada* and find yourself gazing up at a magnificent keep known as the Torre dos Três Coroas (Tower of the Three Crowns). The surrounding palace, built for Queen Dona Isabel, is now the *pousada*, which boasts a spectacular decor. As soon as you enter, your eye will immediately be drawn to the monumental but elegant stairway made of the marble so abundant in this region. The entry hall, sitting room and dining room, all furnished with lovely antiques, look out onto a garden-patio extending right to the foot of the keep. The guest rooms are located on two upper floors. To reach those on the second floor, guests must pass through a series of corridors separated by bays adorned with superb gilded-wood

frames. The rooms are all furnished with genuine antiques, including canopy beds. To top off this princely decor, the bathrooms are made entirely of marble in combinations of beige and white and pink and green. If you are staying with a group, check out the larger rooms, since each has a style of its own. All of the rooms on this floor offer magnificent views of either the surrounding countryside or the village.

The more modern-style rooms on the third floor are smaller but nonetheless very comfortable. Finally, the crowning touch to this heavenly place is a swimming pool set in the midst of a lovely little garden, where summer guests can sip aperitifs and nibble on *petiscos* (appetizers). What more could you ask for?

Aldeia da Serra

(15km from Estremoz)

Hotel Convento de São Paulo
$$$$$ pb
tv , ≈
from Estremoz, take the N381 toward Rodondo, Aldeia da Serra, 7170 Rodondo
☎266 98 91 60
≈266 99 91 04
A scenic but poorly maintained little road leads to the Hotel Convento de São Paulo. This luxurious hotel is a converted monastery built in 1376, and the owners have managed

to preserve its original charm. The cells of the cloister have been carefully transformed into guest rooms and equipped with all the modern comforts. In addition to its refined furnishings, the place features a large number of *azulejos* (as many as 50,000!), as well as remarkable works of art depicting religious and historical scenes. A stroll down the corridors of the cloister thus becomes a veritable feast for the eyes – a pleasure to be enjoyed every time you head to your room. Other highlights include an opulent dining room, a billiard room and a small swimming pool. The latter is located in the garden, which is surrounded by a vast property where guests can enjoy relaxing walks through the woods. The perfect place for visitors in search of peace and quiet.

Vila Viçosa

(17km from Estremoz)

Pousada de Dom João IV
$$$$$ pb
tv , ≈, ℜ
from Estremoz take the N4-E90 toward Spain to Borba, then take the N255 to Vila Viçosa 7160 Vila Viçosa
☎268 98 07 42
☎268 98 07 45
≈268 98 07 47
Just next to the imposing palace of the dukes of Bragança, Pousada de Dom João IV is among the youngest members of the large

family of *pousadas*. Laid out in the heart of a 16th-century convent, the *pousada* prides itself on its prestigious setting, in the Real Convento das Chagas de Cristo. Constructed on the orders of the second wife of sinister Jaime, Duke of Bragança, the convent was foremost dedicated to welcoming young girls of the nobility who wanted to devote their lives to the Church. The grounds also served to house the mausoleums of various duchesses of Bragança, the last of whom, Maria Francisca, was interred here in 1968. The name attributed to the *pousada*, Dom João IV, is that of the first duke of Bragança to have been granted the title of king of Portugal by the Cortés, thereby reinstating the independence of the country after 60 years of Spanish occupation.

Today, in addition to benefiting from luxuriously decorated, although classically furnished rooms, visitors can admire remarkable Italian Renaissance frescoes in the Capela do Senhor Jesus Ressuscitado and in the Capelinha do Evangelista. Lovely gardens and a pleasant pool also embellish the grounds. Its ideal location, just a few kilometres from Estremoz and a reasonable distance from Évora, make this *pousada* an ideal spot from which to explore the countryside.

Sousel

(18 km from Estremoz)

Pousada de São Miguel
$$$$
pb, tv, ℜ
from Estremoz take the N245 toward Sousel and Crato
7470 Sousel
☎ *268 55 00 50*
⇄ *268 55 11 55*
If the marvellous Estremoz *pousada* has no vacancies, Pousada de São Miguel is a good alternative. In addition to its location, just 18km from Estremoz, it offers a pleasant view of the countryside from its hilltop setting and a particularly calm environment. Its architecture, although modern and much less charming than that of its sister-establishment, is perfectly integrated into the gentle landscapes of the Alentejo, and its comfortable rooms are equipped with locally crafted furniture. The lack of a swimming pool is very disappointing, however, since this region is subjected to especially hot summers.

Évora

Campismo de Évora/Orbitur (camping)
7000 Évora, On the N380, in the direction of Alcáçova
☎ *266 70 51 90*
⇄ *266 70 98 30*

Pousada de Juventude
Rua Miguel Bombarda no. 40
7000 Évora
☎ *268 74 48 48*
⇄ *268 74 48 43*

🛏 **Residencial Policarpo**
$ sb
$$ pb
parking on the street parallel Rua Conde da Serra da Tourega; Rua da Feiria de Baixo 16, 7000 Évora
☎/⇄ *266 70 24 24*
Located in a Solar dating back to the 16th century, this former residence is decorated with pretty painted wood furniture typical of this region. Some of the rooms offer lovely views and – miracle of miracles – have no televisions. Although there are 22 rooms in all, it is best to reserve far in advance, since the place is very popular. Cheerful, obliging service. Unfortunately, the hotel does not accept credit cards.

Residencial Diana
$$$
pb, tv
Rua Diogo Cão 2-3, near the corner of Rua 5 de Outubro
7000 Évora
☎ *266 70 20 08*
⇄ *266 74 31 01*
This little hotel, located just steps away from the cathedral, has 20 rather charming rooms.

Pensão-Residencial Riviera
$$
pb, tv
Rua 5 de Outubro 49
7000 Évora
☎ *266 70 33 04*
⇄ *266 70 04 67*
The Pensão-Residencial Riviera, located on bus-

tling Rua 5 de Outubro, has 20 nondescript modern rooms. The double windows, however, are a real plus in this somewhat noisy area.

🛏 **Solar Monfalim**
$$$
pb, tv
Largo da Misericórdia 1
7000 Évora
☎ *266 75 00 00*
⇄ *266 74 23 67*
The Solar Monfalim rivals the *pousada* below as one of the most delightful hotels in town. Facing onto a peaceful, verdant little square, it has 25 rooms, each decorated differently with old-fashioned and sometimes slightly mismatched furniture. There is a certain charm about each of them, however. Finding your room can be a rather entertaining experience, involving a maze of corridors and stairways. The hotel also has a number of other noteworthy features, including a little bar with an oriental-style decor. Make sure to visit the pretty arched gallery and the terrace. Both are full of plants, making this a veritable oasis of greenery in the heart of the city. The staff is friendly, and the rates are reasonable for a hotel of this quality.

Pousada dos Lóios
$$$$$
pb, tv, ℜ, ≈
Largo do Conde de Vila Flor
7000 Évora
☎*266 70 40 51*
☎*266 70 40 52*
⇌*266 70 72 48*
In the very heart of the city, right next to the Évora's beautiful Roman temple, the Pousada dos Lóios is one of those rare places where the past blends perfectly with modern comfort. The former Gothic monastery of São João Evangelista, it has undergone numerous modifications, the most remarkable being the lovely decorations added during the Manueline era. The cloister is graced with a finely worked double arcade in the Manueline style, whose horseshoe arches reveal a distinctly Moorish influence. Although quite comfortable, the rooms are a little disappointing for such an elegant *pousada;*they are small (except for the suite) and somewhat noisy, with uninspiring views. The window in the bathroom, furthermore, looks right out onto the galleries of the cloister, limiting your sense of privacy. Finally, it is difficult, if not impossible, to park nearby during the high season. In spite of all these disadvantages, the *pousada* is worth visiting, if only to admire its cloister, which has been converted into a restaurant (see p 406, 407).

Arraiolos

(22km from Évora)

Pousada de Nossa Senhora da Assunção
$$$$$
pb, tv, ≈; ℜ
from Évora take the N114-4 north for 11km and then the N370 to Arraiolos; 7040 Arraiolos
☎*266 41 93 40*
⇌*266 41 92 80*
Nestled in a pleasant valley below the village of Arraiolos, the convent of Nossa Senhora da Assunção is now home to one of the most recently inaugurated members of the Enatur network, Pousada de Nossa Senhora da Assunção. Along with the *pousadas* at Flor da Rosa and Santa Maria do Bouro, it is among the three most innovative and audaciously designed *pousadas* in the network, boldly uniting modernism and traditional architecture. Formerly part of the order of Dos Lóios, dedicated to offering hospice to the ill, the religious community that resided here until 1834 was also known for the particularity of dressing exclusively in blue. Could this amusing contrast with the traditional white of convents have inspired architects Cristina Guedes and José Paulo dos Santos? The asceticism of this immaculate space is pleasantly broken up by only a few fragments painted a brilliant blue. As for the attractive furniture, modern and pure-lined, it discretely disappears under dominating vaults and ogives. Visible from many windows, the rolling hills surrounding the convent on a background of azure sky constitute the true decor here.

The church adjoining the convent, equipped with an elegant Manueline portal, is the only section of the site in where opulence is celebrated. Inside, in addition to mural panels entirely covered in 17th-century *azulejos,* there is an altar adorned with beautiful *talhas douradas* flanked by columns wreathed in vine- and grape-leaf motifs. Above the altar, a dome decorated with a beautiful set of frescoes and ornamented ogives richly completes the ensemble.

As for the comfortable rooms equipped with contemporary furniture, choose one in the modern section of the building; in addition to possessing a balcony, it will offer an unobstructed view of the lovely countryside. Services and facilities include a large swimming pool, and a tennis court is available for guests' enjoyment.

Santa Clara-a-Velha

Pousada de Santa Clara
$$$$$
pb, tv, ≈, ℜ
travelling north, take the N393
which leads to the Santa Clara
dam; 7665 Santa Clara-a-Velha
☎ *283 88 22 50*
≈ *283 88 24 03*
Pousada de Santa Clara,
a rural-style *pousada*,
constitutes above all a
pleasant stop for those
who want to travel to
the Algarve from Sines
on small byways.
Across from the impressive Santa Clara dam,
its rooms are comfortable and offer beautiful,
panoramic views of the
immense reservoir and
of the mountains that
border it. Rest and
relaxation guaranteed!

Restaurants

Beja

 A Pipa
$
Mon to Sat
Rua da Moeda no. 8
☎ *284 32 70 43*
Tucked away in a
picturesque alley a
stone's throw from the
Praça da República, the
A Pipa restaurant provides a pleasant setting
in which to try out the
regional specialties of
the Alentejo. Beyond
the large front doors is
a huge whitewashed
room whose simple
decor merely consists
of rustic wooden seats
and tables, as well as a
few farming tools hanging here and there. In
an unmistakably family
atmosphere, you can
sample the famous
açorda alentajana,
bread-and-garlic purée,
the *sopa de cação*, a
pleasing bread-and-dogfish soup, or the
ensopado de borrego,
mutton stew. Accompany this fine meal
with a glass of regional
red wine (the house
wine is excellent) and a
queijo, and you will see
why the inhabitants of
the Alentejo take so
much pride in their
cooking. And to top it
all off, be sure to sample one of the many
local egg-and-sugar-based desserts, as is
only right and proper!
A place not to be
missed.

**Pousada do Convento de
São Francisco**
$$$
in the former monastery of São
Francisco
☎ *284 32 84 41*
As its name suggests,
the restaurant of the
Pousada do Convento
de São Francisco is in a
former Franciscan monastery (see p 394). After
being abandoned for
many years, the building was converted into
a *pousada* and its cloister was completely
restored. The chapter
house, which has beautifully preserved frescoes on its vaults, now
houses the loveliest
restaurant in Beja.
Great care has been
taken with the design,
from the furniture to
the fabrics. Soft, innovative lighting enhances this sparse yet
refined decor. The cuisine is typical of the
pousada restaurants,
with the usual variety
of regional dishes.
Game is served during
hunting season but
must be ordered ahead
of time, which is not
very practical.

Cafés and
Tearooms

Maltesinhas
*Mon to Sat 8:30am to
8pm*
Rua dos Açoutados no. 35
☎ *284 32 15 00*
Nut pie, chocolate
cake, tea custard,
encharcada (egg-and-almond cake), cheesecake and many other
desserts await you at
this little tea shop. The
pleasant owner only
prepares traditional
regional pastries, some
of which originate from
convent kitchens. Don't
overdo it, though!

Casa das Artes Jorge Vieira
*Tue to Sun 1:30pm to
11pm*
Rua do Touro
☎ *284 31 19 20*
Located upstairs from
the Jorge Vieira Museum, this small,
charming café features
designer furniture and a
terrace on which you
can enjoy a *bica* while
musing about the sculptor's works.

The Alentejo

The Cork-Oak

Corks have been used to seal wine bottles since the 17th century, when people developed a taste for old wines. Cork comes from the *Quercus Super L,* more commonly referred to as a "cork-oak", a tree with a relatively short trunk and twisted branches. This tree only grows in certain Mediterranean regions, and has a thick, soft bark. This supple outer layer is made up of countless cells separated by air pockets that cannot be permeated by liquids or gasses. It is estimated that one cubic centimetre of cork contains 40 million cells. Portugal is the leading cork-exporting country in the world (more than 50%), followed by Spain,

Algeria and Italy.

Cork is harvested by stripping the tree of its bark. This is usually done every 10 years, and always in summer, when the bark has reached a thickness of 25cm or more. While a tree is usually 25 years old before the first cork can be harvested, a new species has been developed from which the cork may be harvested after 15 years. In both cases, the cork gathered during the first two harvests is not very pliable and can only be used for insulation. It is only as of the third harvest that a tree's cork can be used by the food industry. To prepare the bark for commercial use, it is first boiled to ensure

its elasticity. Only cork of the highest quality, with a homogenous texture, is used to make bottle corks. The cork is dried out until it only retains 8% of its moisture, so as to prevent mould from growing. The corks are then coated in paraffin and silicon before they are used to stop bottles.

The next time you open a bottle of wine, know that the cork in your hand is at least 10 years old. This might seem impressive, but it pales in comparison to the age of the tree from which it came, as they live an average of about 200 years.

Biblioteca Municipal José Saramago
Mon to Fri 9:30am to 12:30pm and 2:30pm to 11pm
Sat 2:30pm to 8pm
Rua Luís de Camões
☎*284 32 99 00*
What a marvellous idea it was to set up a café in Beja's brand-new municipal library, where bookworms can have something to

drink along with a pastry as they leaf through the many newspapers and magazines on hand. Located on the second floor, the place is all the more appealing for its particularly original main entrance and interior design, which are reason enough to visit. Pleasant, inexpensive, and surprisingly late

closing hours for a library – a stroke of genius!

Serpa

(*29km from Beja*)

Restaurante Cuiça
$$
Rua das Portas de Beja no. 18
☎*284 54 95 66*
Açordas, *migas* and *caldeirada*, not to men-

tion the "irresistible" *bacalhau*, are just a few of the typical dishes to be savoured in this quintessentially Portuguese restaurant, graced with a simple yet pleasant decor.

Mértola

(54km from Beja)

Café Restaurante Migas
$$
every day 11am to 4pm
Largo Vasco da Gama
Located right next to the small covered market, the Migas restaurant serves up good, quintessentially Portuguese fare. Notable selections include *migas com carne de cerdo, açorda de bacalhau* or *carne de cerdo com almejas*, all of which can be sampled in a rustic setting. As a starter, try the typical *jamón Pata Negra*, ham prepared according to a regional recipe, or the *queso tipo Serpa*, a delicious little cheese from the Serpa region. Good place for the family.

Castelo de Vide

Restaurante Goivo
$
Rua Bartolomeu Alvares da Santa, at the corner of Rua Santo Amaro
The modest Restaurante Goivo, which has only six tables, serves a daily special for 700 ESC. This place is very popular with locals. Tourist menu for 1,400 ESC.

Restaurante Dom Pedro V
$$
closed Mon
Praça Dom Pedro V
☎*245 90 12 36*
The unpretentious Restaurante Dom Pedro V serves traditional Portuguese cuisine in a pleasant room with a vaulted ceiling. Fixed price menu at 2,200 ESC.

Restaurante Casa do Parque
$$
Rua do Paço Novo
☎*245 90 12 50*
Adjoining the Residencial Casa do Parque, to which it belongs, the Restaurante Casa do Parque serves regional cuisine in a spruce setting.

A Castanha
$$$$
in the Hotel Garcia d'Orta
Estrada de San Vicente
☎*245 90 11 00*
At the sophisticated A Castanha, you can enjoy excellent regional and international cuisine in luxurious surroundings. Somewhat expensive, but very good.

Cafés and Tearooms

There are a great many cafés on Rua Bartolomeu Alvares da Santa; your only problem will be choosing which one to go to. If, however, you are looking for an inviting spot that is popular with the resident younger set, try the **Café Gelateria Mano a Mano** (*Rua*

Bartolomeu Alvares da Santa).

Flor da Rosa

(28km from Castelo de Vide)

Pousada Flor da Rosa
$$$
from Castelo de Vide take the N246 west for 16km, then the N245 to Crato
☎*245 99 72 10*
☎*245 99 72 11*
While passing through the little village of Flor da Rosa, visitors should not neglect stopping at Pousada Flor da Rosa, set in a 14th-century monastery that looks more like a fortress. Today a luxury hotel, the monastery of Santa Maria da Flor ranks as one of the most beautiful creations of Enatur, and design aficionados will not want to miss it (also see p 396). After an aperitif in the former refectory, where you can admire elegant wreathed columns, and before moving to the dinner table, do not hesitate to visit the cloister, the floor of which is emblazoned with a Maltese cross. This brief exploration of the site will reveal the amplitude and ingeniousness of the restoration work that was accomplished here. As for the food, regional dishes are featured. Gourmands of family fare will find satisfaction here, what with lamb stew and pig's feet in coriander sauce among the favourite dishes.

The Alentejo

Marvão

(13km from Castelo de Vide)

Veranda do Alentejo
$$
Praça do Pelorinho 1A
Regional dishes. Set menu starting at 1,600 ESC.

O Casa do Povo
$$
Travessa do Chabouco, at the corner of Rua da Cima
Conventional cuisine, a simple decor and a pleasant terrace with a good view. Set menu starting at 1,600 ESC.

Pousada de Santa Maria
$$$
private parking available on Rua do Embique, below the pousada
☎245 99 32 01
A charming, rustic little house, the restaurant of the Pousada de Santa Maria is well located right in the heart of the splendid village of Marvão. Its cozy, tastefully decorated dining room offers a lovely view of the valley. Welcoming, cheerful staff.

Cafés and Tearooms

Bar Marcelino
Rua da Cima 3
For a good cup of coffee, head to the Bar Marcelino, whose owner will welcome you with a smile. Simple, pleasant decor. Inexpensive meals available.

Café-Bar
Rua Dr. Matos Magalhães, opposite the Pensão Dom Dinis
Whether on its pleasant little terrace or under the watchful gaze of the wild-boar's head in its small, immaculate white-roughcast dining room, this modest bistro is a very pleasant place in which to have a *bica* or a *cerveja*.

Elvas

Pousada da Santa Luzia
$$$
near the south entrance of the city
☎268 62 21 94
☎268 62 21 28
Not far from the fortified entrance on the south side of town, the restaurant of the Pousada da Santa Luzia is a modern building with a nondescript, conventional decor. Nevertheless, its proximity to the centre of town and the quality of its cuisine make it a good place to keep in mind.

Estremoz

The Upper City

Besides the *pousada*, the old, or upper, city is home to only one restaurant and a little bistro (*on the left side of the village's main street*), where you can have a drink.

Restaurante São Rosas
$$
Tue to Sun 11am to 3pm and 7:30pm to 10:30pm
Largo Dom Dinis 11
☎268 33 33 45
Right beside the *pousada*, on pretty Largo Dom Dinis, the Restaurante São Rosas serves good regional cuisine in a cozy, antique setting. In season, guests can enjoy such dishes as woodcock, hare and a delicious partridge pie. For a lighter meal, the *açorda de bacalhau* or a simple salmon omelette will delight anyone with a taste for good food. The place hasn't been open for very long, and the staff seems a little inexperienced, but guests receive a friendly welcome.

Pousada Rainha Santa Isabel
$$$
Largo Dom Dinis, in the castle in the old city
☎268 33 20 75
Of all the restaurants in Estremoz, the one in the Pousada Rainha Santa Isabel is the most extraordinary. Located inside a national monument (see p 385), the former palace of Queen Dona Isabel, the dining room boasts an outstanding decor. As soon as you walk in, your eye will be drawn to the vaults high above, adorned with splendid gilded-wood chandeliers, and the massive stone pillars that support the ceiling. Guests dine in a refined setting, surrounded by

precious objects like antique tapestries, paintings and period furniture. A number of church decorations made with *talha douradas* have been placed here and there, creating a monastic atmosphere and enhancing the beauty of the place. For a good start to a summer meal, head out to the terrace, surrounded by a beautiful little garden and a swimming pool, and sip an aperitif while nibbling on *petiscos*. A dream come true!

The Lower City

Restaurante-Pensão Estremoz
$$
Rossio Marquês de Pombal 14-15, above the Café Alentejano
☎*268 32 28 43*
On the attractive Rossio, the Restaurante-Pensão Estremoz serves home-style cooking in a setting that is slightly outmoded but clean and pleasant overall. The set menu starts at 1,700 ESC.

Restaurante Aguias d'Ouro
$$
open every day
Rossio Marquês de Pombal 26
☎*268 33 33 27*
Also located above a café, the Restaurante Aguias d'Ouro features a set menu of Portuguese dishes starting at 2,200 ESC. The decor is a bit kitschy, but inviting. Friendly staff.

Cafés and Tearooms

Pastelaria Formosa
8am to 9pm
Largo da República 16B corner Rua Vasco da Gama
The Pastelaria Formosa is an excellent little pastry shop where you can also enjoy a *bica* (espresso).

Évoramonte

(17km from Estremoz)

A Convenção
$$
Tue to Sun
Rua de Santa Maria 26-30
☎*268 95 92 17*
In the rustic little village of Évoramonte, the restaurant A Convenção serves standard Portuguese cuisine. The highlight here is the terrace, which offers an extraordinary view of the region.

Vila Viçosa

Pousada de Dom João IV
$$$
from Estremoz take the N4-E90 toward Spain to Borba, then continue on the N255 to Vila Viçosa
☎*268 98 07 42*
☎*268 98 07 45*
The Pousada de Dom João IV constitutes an ideal break from exploring the Alentejo countryside. In a lovely vaulted room that was formerly the convent refectory, diners can savour an excellent *carne de porco à Alentejana* all the while admiring a superb fresco of the Last Sup-

per. Admirers of the Italian Renaissance style will not want to miss the chapels called Capela do Senhor Jesus Ressuscitado and Capelinha do Evangelista, in which several frescoes may be seen. Finally, before hitting the road, be sure to visit the convent's cloister and its pleasant gardens, veritable havens of peace.

Évora

Pastelaria Quidoce
$
open every day noon to 9pm
Lagar dos Dizimos 21, just off Praça 1° de Maio, facing Sapatoria Barbas
The tiny Pastelaria Quidoce is a sophisticated, modern restaurant where you can enjoy hot or cold dishes starting at 550 ESC. A real bargain!

Cozinha de São Francisco
$
open every day 9am to 11pm
Rua Romão Ramalho 56
☎*266 74 30 76*
For an inexpensive meal, head to Cozinha de São Francisco, which features a tourist menu starting at 1,500 ESC. Guests enjoy standard home-style Portuguese cuisine in a simple setting.

The Alentejo

Snack-Bar - Restaurante Dom Quixote
$
Mon to Sat noon to 3pm and 7pm to 10pm
Largo Álvaro Velho 31
☎ *266 70 82 42*
The Snack-Bar - Restaurante Dom Quixote offers typical Portuguese cuisine, with a set menu starting at 1,500 ESC. Half-portions available.

A Choupana
$$
Mon to Sat noon to 3pm and 7pm to 10pm
Rua dos Mercadores 20
☎ *266 70 44 27*
In addition to traditional fish dishes, A Choupana features a wide choice of meat dishes. The decor is warm and tasteful, and the food is served on lovely china. Set menu starting at 1,600 ESC.

La Cave
$$
Rua da República no. 26
☎ *239 11*
As its French name indicates, this restaurant really is housed in a cave. But don't expect French cuisine, for what this establishment offers is a Portuguese daily special, as well as a few other simple local dishes. The place's main asset is its decor, arches and lovely stone walls forming an elegant yet original setting.

Mr. Pickwick
$$
open every day noon to midnight
Alcárova de Cima 3
☎ *266 70 69 99*
If the thought of a reasonably priced, delicious little steak with mushrooms appeals to you, head to Mr. Pickwick, where you will find lovely brick vaults, an inviting decor and soft lighting.

⛵ Fialho
$$$
Tue to Sun 12:30pm to 11pm
Travessa das Mascarenhas 16
☎ *266 70 30 79*
Fialho just might be the best restaurant in Évora. Gabriel Fialho, who earned his diploma as a master chef in Belgium, offers guests mouth-watering cuisine (set menu) in a room decorated mainly with lovely earthenware and hunting trophies. While sipping a glass of port as an aperitif, make sure to sample one of the many house *acepipes*. As a snack or an appetizer, they are a treat for both the eyes and the palate. Those who prefer soup can try the famous *sopa de cação*. For a beautiful follow-up, the *borrego* (lamb), seasoned with fragrant herbs, or the *porco con amêijoas* (pork with clams) are epicurean delights. Other possibilities include the *ensopado de borrego* (lamb stew) and *cação de coentrada* (dogfish with coriander). Finally, as the perfect end to a

perfect meal, a *morgado* or *torrão de Évora* for dessert will satisfy even the most voracious appetite. The wine list is equally excellent (especially the white wines). If you only want a snack, opt for the *acepipas*, served any time. With its highly professional service and friendly staff, this restaurant is well worth a visit.

Jardim do Paço
$$$
Tue to Sun 12:30pm to 3pm and 7pm to 10pm
Largo Dom Dinis
☎ *266 74 43 00*
☎ *266 74 43 21*
Jardim do Paço, located near the *pousada* and the Roman temple, lies in the garden of the former palace of the Duke of Cadaval, who was the governor of Évora when the city was recaptured by the Portuguese. With its big bay windows, the restaurant offers an attractive view of rows of orange trees and the immaculately white Igreja de São João Evangelista. The restaurant serves classic regional dishes, such as *ensopado de borrego* and *açorda alentejana*. Various meal-size salads, starting at 700 ESC, are also available. The decor, for its part, is pleasant, but somewhat nondescript.

Pousada dos Lóios
$$$
Largo do Conde de Vila Flor
☎ *266 70 40 51*
In the heart of the city, right next to the lovely

Roman temple, the restaurant of the Pousada dos Lóios is one of those rare places where the past blends perfectly with the present. The dining room has been set up in the former cloister of the monastery of São João Evangelista, which has been modified many times over the centuries. Its most extraordinary feature is its ornamentation, added in the Manueline era. Particularly noteworthy is the finely worked double arcade, whose horseshoe arches reveal a distinctly Moorish influence. A splendid fountain adds to the charm of the place. The cuisine, although similar in quality to that of other *pousadas*, doesn't quite live up to the truly outstanding setting. Take note, furthermore, that parking near the restaurant is difficult, if not impossible, during the high season.

Cafés and Tearooms

Café Arcada
open every day 8am to midnight
Praça do Giraldo 7
The Café Arcada is probably the liveliest pastry shop in town. In a large, plainly decorated room, you can sample Évora's famous *pastéis*, whose sole ingredients are eggs, sugar, almonds and cream. Numerous other desserts are also available (mostly egg-based, of course), as well as

sandwiches to snack on. Perfect for those who like people-watching and, accordingly, noisy places. The café also has a terrace looking out onto Praça do Giraldo.

Arraiolos
(22km from Évora)

Pousada de Nossa Senhora da Assunção
$$$
from Évora take the N114-4 north for 11 km and then take the N370 to Arraiolos
☎ *266 41 93 40*
Tucked into the *vale* below the village of Arraiolos, Pousada de Nossa Senhora da Assunção is a member of the Enatur network and has an especially innovative and bold decor. A marvellous union of modern architecture and traditional construction, dominated by vaults and ogives, this building is worth the trip in itself (see p 400). After admiring its church, entirely covered in *azulejos* and adorned with a richly decorated altar, diners can savour regional specialties such as *lombo de porco asado com oregãos* – delicious pork chops grilled with estragon. This pleasant culinary excursion also reveals the beautiful landscape of the Alentejo.

Entertainment

Beja

Lanterna Azul
Rua da Moeda no. 11
Looking to meet Beja's young set? Then head to the Lanterna Azul rock nightclub on any given weekend, but expect to wait patiently in line before its green metal door to get in.

Shopping

Elvas

On Rua de Alcanim, there are a few lovely shops that sell decorative items and antiques.

Mértola
(54km from Beja)

Loja da Guida
every day 9:30am to 1pm and 3pm to 7:30pm
Rua M. Francisco Gomes
Located right next to the entrance to the old town, the Loja da Guida shop displays scores of little handicrafts, as well as a few regional products, such as homemade jams, in an imaginative setting. Just the place for a tasty and original little souvenir!

The Alentejo

Rossana
*every day 10am to 1pm
and 2pm to 7pm*
Rua M. Francisco Gomes
Also located near the
entrance to the old
town, this souvenir
shop offers a lovely
selection of hand-
painted dishes, blown-
glass items and some
jewellery.

Évora

Every week, vendors
selling reasonably
priced ceramics (cups,
plates, vases, bowls,
etc.) set up their stalls
on **Praça 1° de Maio**
(don't hesitate to bar-
gain). A covered mar-
ket, also on the square,
offers excellent prod-
ucts from local farms,
including delicious goat
cheese, at ridiculously
low prices. Add a few
olives and a little corn
bread, and you've got
the makings of an
excellent picnic.

Marvão

*(13km from Castelo de
Vide)*

Milflores Arte e Artesano
*(Rua Dr. Matos
Magalhães 1)* features a
good selection of crafts.

Inside the former **Igreja
de Santa Maria** *(every day
2pm to 5:30pm; Largo de
Santa Maria)*, now a
museum (see p 384), is
an interesting little
shop that not only sells
postcards, posters and
other souvenirs, but
reproductions of small
Roman oil lamps at
very reasonable prices.
Found in abundance
throughout the region,
these lamps are deco-
rated with erotic scenes
– a rather surprising
phenomenon in such a
"holy" place!

The Algarve

I n terms of sheer numbers, the Algarve is Portugal's premier tourist destination. Each year more and more tourists flock to the area, attracted by the year-round mild weather, sun and beaches.

Although the Algarve cannot boast the climatic splendours of the Mediterranean, its many beaches nestled in small inlets provide clement conditions for sunbathing even in winter. In fact, rare precipitation and pleasantly cool evenings make for a comfortable stay in the area and attract many older visitors. In summer, young Europeans take advantage of relatively affordable travel packages to gather at the seaside resorts, where the action is non-stop, day and night.

Like many sunny destinations, though, the Algarve has become a very popular – if not too popular – region. At some resorts it seems that not even a square inch has been spared by concrete, and many once-tranquil little fishing villages have been turned into large, contrived tourist attractions. Furthermore, a number of gigantic hotel complexes of dubious taste have literally disfigured the coastline. Sadly, the Algarve lacks the essence of the real Portugal – the imposing castles, marvellous Gothic cathedrals and Manueline monasteries that are quite rightly a source of pride for the country. Accordingly, history or architecture enthusiasts will not linger for long in this region.

In sum, the Algarve is more interesting for visitors who enjoy the crowds and entertainment of summer or the relaxation and mild temperatures of winter. To get the most out of this region, here are a few tips:

The most picturesque beaches – those which are sheltered by inlets or run along the base of handsome, reddish cliffs – are found mainly west of Faro.These beaches are some of the most popular with tourists in the Algarve. However, the beaches located east of the regional capital are much less frequented as they are surrounded by wilderness and sometimes don't have much in the way of facilities. To compensate for this, you can discover some of the most beautiful towns in the Algarve, such as Tavira and Cacelha Velha, which have miraculously preserved their magnificent residences and hotels that line the beach. Fine, golden sand and clean beaches can, however, be found along the entire Algarve coast. They offer a range of aquatic activities, such as diving, surfing, waterskiing or windsurfing. A number of companies specializing in equipment rentals for these sports operate from the more popular resorts.

This chapter also contains descriptions of a series of *praias* (beaches) chosen either for their beauty or for the quality of their services. And, as golf is a particularly popular sport in the region, a list of clubs, their addresses, and descriptions of their main features have been included in the "Outdoor Activities" section (see p 431).

As June, July, August, September and Easter weekend are peak tourist periods, visitors are strongly advised to reserve well in advance. During these months the temperature ranges from 25°C to 30°C and the water temperature is above 20°C. The rest of the year, despite fairly constant sun, temperatures vary between 12°C and 18°C; only the brave will want to swim in waters that only reach about 15°C. This period is ideal for touring and golfing.

During the high season (June to September), standard hotel rates tend to skyrocket. In some cases, a package purchased from a travel agency can prove to be more economical than a reservation made on the spot. Whatever the chosen formula, it is wiser to opt for the more luxurious establishments (both for accommodation and meals); the difference between the regular prices of "average category" hotels or restaurants and those reputed to be "deluxe" is well worth the extra cost, as the quality and services of the latter are far superior.

During the off season (October to May), rates are easier to negotiate as tourists are fewer and hotel managers are more willing to offer reductions, in some cases, slashing prices by as much as two-thirds! The month of February is probably the best time to visit the Algarve. Besides its particularly pleasant climate, the many almond trees that grow in the region (see p 423) blossom, contrasting marvellously with the fields covered with bright yellow *chelones*. Finally, an exploration of the less-travelled byways will reveal some of the charm of the more authentic Algarve.

The Algarve

Finding Your Way Around

By Car

From the Airport

The **Faro international airport** is 6km from Faro. The N125 leads directly to the capital of Algarve. To reach Quarteira (22km), Vilamoura (25km), Albufeira (39km), Portimão (65km), Lagos (80km) and Sagres (112km), take the same road (N125) eastward.

From Lisbon

There is still no highway that links the Algarve region directly with Lisbon. The best solution is to first take the highway to Sétubal and continue along the 1P1-N10-E1. As you continue south toward Grândola, the road often changes number (N5-E1, N120-E1, N259-E1, N262-E1, N261-E1) before finally becoming the N264-E1-1P1 until it reaches the Algarve.

To get to the towns or beaches of **Faro**, **Olhão**, **Tovira**, **Cacela**, **Velha**, **Quarteira**, **Vilhamoura**, **Almancil** and **Vila Real de Santo António**, you can take either Highway 1P1-E1, which follows the coast toward Spain, or National Highway N125, which runs all along the coast. To get

to Castro Marim from Vila Real de Santo António, take the N122 north for 4km. For **Almancil**, **Albufeira**, **Armação de Pêra**, **Lagos**, **Ponta da Piedade**, **Portimão**, **Praia da Rocha**, **Sagres** and **Silves**, **Almancil**, **Faro**, **Quarteira** and **Vilamoura**, take the N125. To get to Estói from Faro, take the N2 north for 10km, then the N2-6 east.

There are two ways to get to the **Ilha de Tavira**. The first way is to drive to the Quatro Águas docks, 2km from the centre of town, and take the ferry (year round, schedule varies, crossing takes 5 to 7min) to the island. The second way is to take one of the many boats (Jul to mid-Sep only, schedule varies, crossing takes 20min) from the docks in the centre of town (*Rua dos Cais*) to the island. Though the second option is more expensive, you will see more of the banks of the Rio Gilão and take in some lovely views.

By Train from Lisbon

Except for the Lisbon-Faro line, on which there is express service during the high season, and the Lisbon-Beja, Lisbon-Portimão and Lisbon-Lagos routes, the irregular schedules of the trains as well as difficult transfers make this mode of transportation impractical. Also,

just to get to the Barreiro station, from which trains bound for the south of the country leave, you have to take the ferry (Estação Fluvial Sul e Sueste) from Praça do Comércio to a suburb of the capital across the river. For Caminhos de Ferro information and departures, see p 69.

Olhão, Faro, Tavira and Vila Real de Santo António

From Lisbon

Departure: several times a day
Fare: Intercidades 2,000 ESC, plus 150 ESC for the ferry across the Tagus to the Barreiro station

Portimão and Lagos

From Lisbon

Departure: several times a day
Fare: Intercidades 1,900 ESC, plus 150 ESC for the ferry across the Tagus to the Barreiro station

By Bus from Lisbon

The companies **Rede Nacional de Expressos** and **Renex Expressos** offer many departures daily, as do other transportation companies.

Rede Nacional de Expressos departures are from the terminal at no.

18B Avenida Casal Ribeiro.

Renex Expressos departures are from Cais das Cebolas, near Casa dos Bicos. For information in Lisbon, see p 69.

Albufeira

Travel time: approx. 3hrs, 45min
Fare: 2,000 to 2,100 ESC

Almancil

Travel time: approx. 4hrs, 30min
Fare: 2,000 to 2,200 ESC

Armação de Pêra

Travel time: approx. 4hrs, 20min
Fare: 1,900 to 2,100 ESC

Faro

Travel time: approx. 4hrs, 50min
Fare: 2,100 to 2,300 ESC

Lagos

Travel time: approx. 4hrs, 30min
Fare: 2,200 to 2,400 ESC

Portimão

Travel time: approx. 4hrs, 10min
Fare: 2,200 to 2,400 ESC

Quarteira

Travel time: approx. 4hrs, 15min
Fare: 2,000 to 2,200 ESC

Sagres

Travel time: approx. 6hrs, 15min
Fare: 2,000 to 2,200 ESC

Silves

Travel time: approx. 3hrs, 50min
Fare: 1,900 to 2,100 ESC

Vilamoura

Travel time: approx. 4hrs 10min
Fare: between 2,000 and 2,200 ESC

Castro Marim

Travel time: approx. 5.5hrs
Fare: 1,900 to 2,100 ESC

Olhão

Travel time: approx. 5hrs.
Fare: 2,100 to 2,300 ESC

Tavira

Travel time: 5hrs 20min
Fare: 2,200 to 2,400 ESC

Vila Real de Santo António

Average travel time: 6hrs
Fare: 2,300 to 2,500 ESC

?

Practical Information

Tourist Information Offices

Albufeira

Rua 5 de Outubro

Castro Marim

2-4 Praça 1º de Maio

Faro

Rua da Misericórda 8-12

Lagos

Largo Marquês de Pombal

Olhão

6A Largo Sebastião Martins Mestre

Portimão

Largo 1° de Dezembro

Praia da Rocha

Rua Tomás Cabreira

Quarteira

Avenida Infante de Sagres

Sagres

Posto de Turismo do Promontório de Sagres, at Vila do Bispo

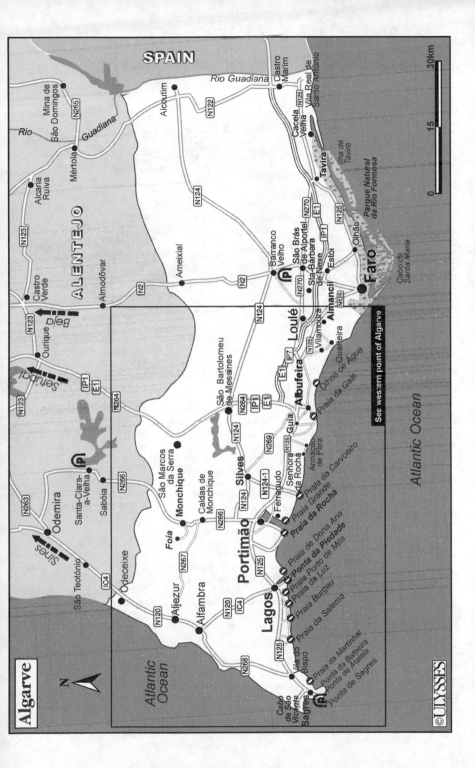

Armação de Pêra

Avenida Marginal

Silves

Rua 25 de Abril

Tavira

9 Rua da Galeria

Exploring

Albufeira

A former Phoenician trading post, Albufeira was named by the Moors, for whom the word meant "castle or fortification by the sea." It was mainly during this period of Arab occupation that the city enjoyed a certain prosperity, due mostly to steady trade with Morocco. Its siege by the Portuguese in 1250, shortly after that of Faro, made it the last of the country's cities to be reconquered. This date marked the beginning of a slow decline for Albufeira, a deterioration that became more pronounced after the defeat at the battle of el-Kasr el-Kebir (Alcázarquivir) in Morocco. In 1755, the great earthquake practically reduced the city to rubble and worse, in 1833 its fortified castle was destroyed by fire in the wake of the civil unrest that gripped the country. As a result,

almost all of the city's monuments have vanished.

It wasn't until the the emergence of mass tourism in the 1960s that Albufeira regained some of its stature. The peaceful little fishing village that it was gradually turned into one of the most popular beach resorts on the Algarve coast. Not a single square inch seems to have been left untouched by real estate developers, and the coast today is lined with buildings right up to the cliffs. Clean and dazzlingly white, Albufeira is a hive of activity during the high season.

Those who enjoy crowds will appreciate the downtown core (*Avenida 5 de Outubro and Largo Eng. Duart Pacheco*), where shops, restaurants, terraces,

bars, nightclubs, etc., attract a colourful, mainly youthful clientele. Here suntanning, parties, and shopping are the pursuits of choice. Visitors who prefer to indulge in such activities in quieter settings should head uptown to the Cerro Grande and Cerro da Piedade districts, where the setting is greener and more sophisticated.

Although it is a successful resort and has acquired a certain reputation, Albufeira has little of touristic interest to offer other than the beach and its entertainment. Nonetheless, here are a few attractions that are worth a quick visit.

For a glimpse at what the Albufeira of old might have resembled, stroll through the **Vila Vehla** (the old town)

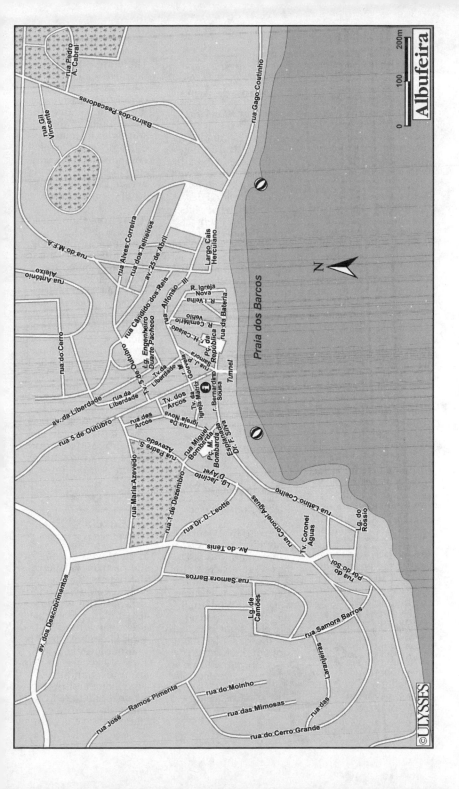

Albufeira

rua Pedro A. Cabral
rua Gil Vincente
Barro dos Pescadores
rua Gago Coutinho
rua António Aleixo
rua do M.F.A.
rua Alves Correira
rua dos Telheiros
av. 25 de Abril
Largo Cais Herculano
rua do Cerro
rua Cândido dos Reis
rua Engenheiro Duarte Pacheco
Tv. 5 de Outubro
rua Afonso III
R. Igreja Nova
R. I. Velha
R. Cemitério Velho
rua da Bateria
Pç. da República
r. H. Calado
av. da Liberdade
rua da Liberdade
Tv. da Liberdade
Tv. da Zamora
r. Bernardino Sousa
Tunnel
Praia dos Barcos
rua 5 de Outubro
rua dos Arcos
Tv. dos Arcos
rua da Igreja Matriz
rua da Governo
rua Nova
rua Miguel Bombarda
Pç. M. Bombarda
Esplanada Dr. F. Silva
rua Maria Azevedo
rua Padre S. Azevedo
rua 1.º de Dezembro
Lg. Jacinto D'Ayet
rua Dr. D. Leotte
av. dos Descobrimentos
rua Coronel Águas
Av. do Ténis
Tv. Coronel Águas
rua do Pôr do Sol
rua do Sol
Lg. do Rossio
rua Latino Coelho
rua Samora Barros
Lg. de Camões
rua Samora Barros
rua José Ramos Pimenta
rua do Moinho
rua das Mimosas
rua das Laranjeiras
rua do Cerro Grande

N

0   100   200m

© ULYSSES

along the **Rua da Bateria**, with detours through the steep alleyways. The city's soul can still be felt here and, along with lovely views of the coast, sightseers can observe the picturesque **Travessa da Igreja Velha**, with its charming arch.

Below the old town, the **Praia dos Barcos** (the boat beach) is better suited to whiling away the hours than the main beach; here, one can observe fishers at work and the small, brightly painted boats beached on the white sand.

At the end of bustling Rua 5 de Outubro is a **tunnel** that leads directly to the main beach. This rather odd and amusing structure was dug right out of the rock in 1935 to give residents direct access to the waterfront. Above the tunnel is the Sol é Mar hotel, not as inspiring a sight; in fact, it is an extreme example of how ruthless urban development can ruin the visual environment!

On the way to the west end of the beach, you will see an interesting rock formation right in the middle of the beach. From there, a staircase leads up the cliffs to Esplanada Dr. Frutuoso Silva, where you will be treated to lovely views of the coast.

★

Olhos de Água

(8km from Albufeira)

Several restaurants, a few colourful fishing boats, fishers and a fine white-sand beach with small twisted cliffs make up Olhos de Água. But what cliffs! Their magnificent brown shades, from shimmering rust to soft beige, which blend into each other marvelously, and the forest green of the several pine trees that grow on them, are quite a sight and worth the trip. To really enjoy the stunning scenery, go there just before sundown, when the sun's rays caress the cliffs and highlight their nicest features. What makes this place even more pleasant is its beach, which is less frequented than the one in Albufeira.

Armação de Pêra

(18km from Albufeira)

Armação de Pêra is not only less crowded than Albufeira, but it also has wide beaches along a rock-free coastline that makes swimming very safe. While night-life and commercial development are clearly on the rise, they have not yet encroached upon the town's tranquility.

There are only two negative aspects to mention: the village core is singularly lacking in appeal and the eastern part of the resort, with its many efficiency-apartment complexes under construction, is to be avoided if a peaceful stroll is on the agenda.

Apart from the remnants of its fortress – which are of little interest – this resort's attractions are limited to wide beaches and the **Capela de Nossa Senhora da Rocha** (*10am to 5pm; at Vila Senhora da Rocha*), located 3km to the west along the coast. This little chapel, erected near the edge of a cliff, contains fine examples of *azulejos*.

Boats are on hand to take passengers on a tour of pretty little marine grottos; excursions leave from the main beach (see p 431).

Cacela Velha

If there were a vote for the prettiest village in the region, Cacela Velha would win hands down. If you would like a glimpse of what the Algarve used to look like, a visit to this charming town is a must. However, to help keep this tranquil village intact and protect its unspoiled environment, do not drive there (vehicle access is

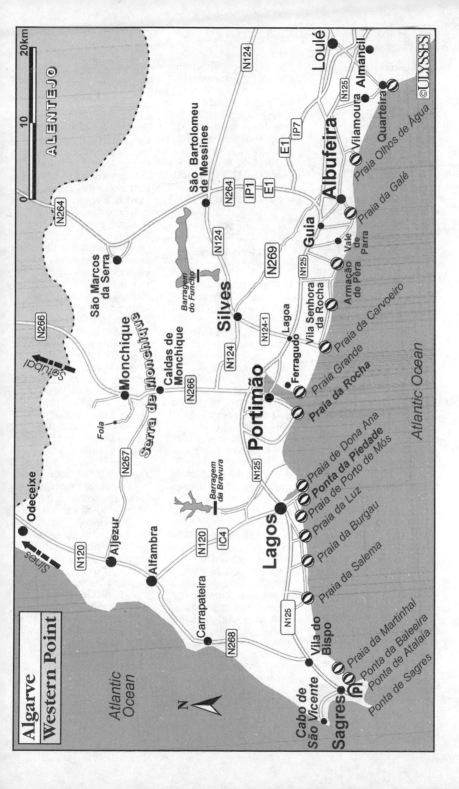

prohibited by the municipality for non-residents).

Strolling around town, it is hard to imagine that Cacela Velha was made a town by King Dom Dinis as early as 1283. A fort was built here, and thanks to the proximity of the ocean (before the port silted up), the village prospered and quickly developed. Cacela Velha was even the main town in the region until the 17th century, because the neighbouring town of Vila Real de Santo António was not founded until 1774. During the next few centuries, the coast slowly began to sand up, forming a lagoon between the town and the ocean, and the town's fishing industry slowly began to decline. The earthquake of 1755, which affected a large part of Portugal, completely destroyed the town, and it virtually ceased to exist. Despite the reconstruction of different buildings from the second half of the 18th century to the 19th century, Cacelha Velha would never regain its town status.

An old water pump still stands on the small lovely town square, and don't miss the 16th-century parish church, which has preserved its modest 18th-century side portal. Get your camera ready as you face the main portal because this spot provides an enchanting view of the sandbars and the ocean! From the patio, a small staircase leads down to the marsh where there is a short trail that goes through the Parque Natural da Ria Formosa (see p 431). Right next to the Igreja is a modest 18th-century fort.

Castro Marim

If you are travelling through Vila Real de Santo António, make a quick jaunt to the charming little city of Castro Marim, located right next to the Reserva Natural do Sapal de Castro Marim e Vila Real de Santo António. It is in this city that the Order of Christ was founded (see p 230), which replaced the Order of Temples. On top of its hill surrounded by modest gleaming-white houses is a 17th-century fortress, in the middle of which are well-preserved ruins of a 10th-century castle. Walking up the covered way (not for people with vertigo), you can get a panoramic view of the village, the reserves and its numerous salt mines, as well as the Rio Guadiana. Get your cameras ready and snap anything that suits your fancy!

Faro

Travellers arriving in the Algarve by plane touch down at Faro, the province's capital and a somewhat important port city. Though Faro is a coastal city, it is fronted by the Reserva Natural da Rio Formosa, a large nature reserve made up of a series of islets that effectively cut off the city from the sea. The exploitation of vast salt mines and tuna fishing are leading local industries. Another of the city's major resources is the cultivation of fig, almond, and cork-oak trees in the back country. After being completely razed by fire around the end of the 16th century and destroyed twice by earthquakes, Faro has almost no historic monuments left. Still, the inner-city old quarter has kept some of its old-world charm and is worth seeing. The capital of the Algarve can also pride itself on being the first city in Portugal to print a book, a Hebrew publication produced in 1487 by Samuel Gacon. On the outskirts of Faro are a number of shops that make the district quite animated and interesting for avid shoppers.

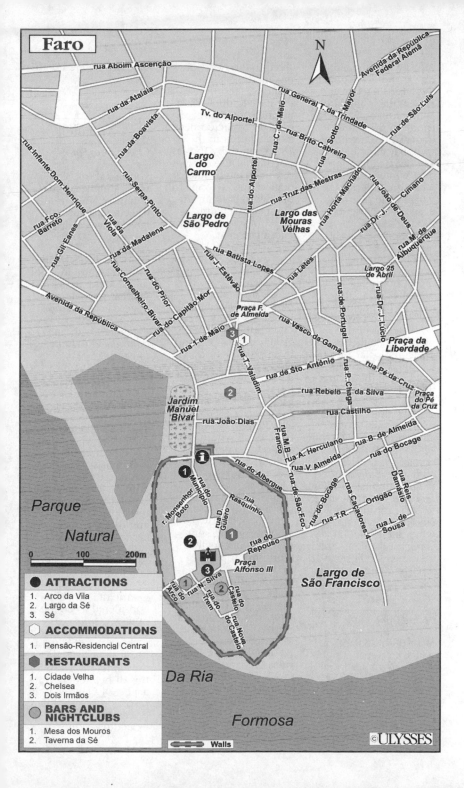

A foray into the **old city** ★ should begin at the imposing **Arco da Vila**, south of the Jardim Manuel Bivar. The Arco is one of the three doors in the medieval wall that girds the old city. Its façade, topped by a white marble niche and adorned with Italian-style pilasters, deserves a close look. Along the main street beyond it are lovely homes, most of which date back to the 18th century. A little farther on, a short alley branches off to the right of the main street and leads to **Largo da Sé**. To the right of the plaza stands the ancient episcopal palace; to the left, the Câmara Municipal; and in the centre, the **cathedral**. Except for the original Gothic steeple, the cathedral was entirely rebuilt after the earthquake of 1755. The cathedral contains a number of attractive *azulejos* as well as an altar of *talha dourada*. Don't hesitate to stroll through the old city in the evening, when the cathedral is especially striking and the lanes are lit by attractive lampposts.

Estói

(12km from Faro)

Most of the palaces for which Portugal is rightfully known are located north of Beja; almost none are located in the south. If you dream of castles, a visit to Estói, north of the Algarve capital, is a must. Located in the heart of this modest village with white-washed houses is the Palácio de Estói, a magnificent bourgeois residence erected next to the church in the 18th century by the last viscount of Estói. Today, it lies in a state of neglect and belongs to the City. There are rumours that Enatur might buy it and turn it into a **pousada**.

The building is appealing because of its lovely faded pink neo-classical facade with baroque elements. The interior is richly decorated but can only be visited in groups and by appointment only. Don't worry, you're not missing much, because the centerpiece is the **gardens** ★ *(Tue to Sat 9:30am to 12:30pm and 2pm to 5pm, in summer until 6pm)*, where many *azulejos* decorate the stair, low walls and recesses. Several small fountains, vases and statues enhance the site. Even though the place is overcrowded with tourists in summer, it is not really worth the trip.

Before returning to the coast and hoards of tourists, anyone who likes Roman ruins will want to make a short stop at Milreu, near Estói, where the **Roman ruins** *(Tue to Sun 9:30am to 12:30pm and 2pm to 5pm, summer until 6pm)* of an old first-century villa can be seen, as can thermal baths, some of which are still partially covered with mosaics.

Almancil

(13km from Faro)

Located about 3km from Almancil, left of Highway N125 in the direction of Faro, the **Igreja Paroquial de São Lourenço** *(200 ESC)* is worth a visit. This chapel is probably the most beautiful in all of the Algarve. Its **interior** ★ is entirely covered with *azulejos* and its **altar** is richly decorated with *talha dourada*. A definite must-see!

Quarteira

(21km from Faro)

This beach resort caters to visitors who enjoy both daytime and nighttime action and round-the-clock crowds. The waterfront is lined with an array of restaurants, hotels, bars and discotheques, attracting a non-stop, shifting stream of tourists looking for entertainment. On the urban development front, Quarteira is widely considered to be the outlaw of Algarve resorts; indeed, visitors will see the deplorable result of unplanned development. Despite this disheartening aspect of Quarteira, the resort's relatively low prices and very safe beach that slopes

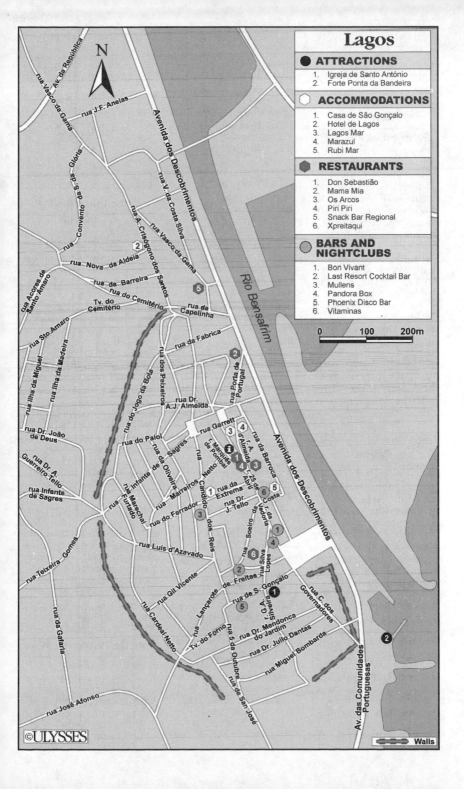

gently down to the sea appeal to many tourists, especially families.

Vilamoura

(21km from Faro)

Vilamoura, a suburb of Quarteira, is Portugal's largest seaside resort. It consists of a variety of hotels, efficiency-apartment complexes, and villas – tasteful, for the most part – grouped around a marina that can accommodate up to 1,000 boats. Surprisingly, the attraction here is not the beach, but rather the tennis courts, pools and, of course, the trio of world-famous golf courses (see p 433). Naturally, this resort's prices are in keeping with its reputation.

Lagos

Lagos, the former capital of the Algarve, is probably the prettiest city on the coast, despite the fact that it has very few actual attractions. It is a major port from which many expeditions were launched toward then-unexplored African coasts. On a darker note, Lagos is also notable for being the first European city to have a slave market fed by people shipped from Africa. Lagos was also the place from which the unfortunate Dom Sebastião embarked to meet his

destiny in Morocco. Partially enclosed by the medieval wall, the city covers the entire mouth of the Ribeira de Bensafrim up to the jagged peninsula that juts into the ocean.

Travellers on a quest for different *talhas douradas* must see the **Igreja de Santo António** *(3 ESC including musuem entry; corner of Rua General Alberto da Silveira and Rua de São Gonçalo)* for its magnificent, richly sculpted **altar** ★ and superb *azulejos*. Right next door, the **Museu Municipal** displays various ancient objects from the Algarve.

At the southernmost point of the city is the **Forte Ponta da Bandeira** *(3 ESC; Tue to Sat 10am to noon and 2pm to 6pm)*, an old fort which houses a small museum of "Great Discoveries," as well as a modest chapel adorned with *azulejos* and a restaurant with a terrace.

Praia Dona Ana

(1km from Lagos)

Located about 2km from Lagos, this pleasing beach attracts fair crowds in the summer and features wind-sculpted rocks that seem to surge up from the sand. Apart from a restaurant, there are few services here. The beach is reached by a set of stairs carved into

the rock. To the right of the parking lot, there is an enjoyable little trail that runs along the top of the cliff and provides a panoramic view of the coast (see p 432).

Ponta da Peidade

(2km from Lagos)

This is a series of stunning marine grottos that are reached by several staircases suspended from the cliff. The grottos are truly spectacular; the azure blue of the water contrasts beautifully with the vivid colours of the rocks sculpted by the sea and the wind. Visitors who travel here by car should leave NOTHING in their vehicles, as theft is common. The descent to the caves is fairly long, and the thieves undoubtedly wait patiently until tourists have made the trek down the cliff before breaking into cars. The stairs are located to the left of the lighthouse, near the cliffs. Anyone who's afraid of heights should take the boat instead (see p 431).

Praia Porto de Mós

(3km from Lagos)

This beach is probably the least frequented in the region, and, miracle of miracles, only one hotel complex and a few restaurants have opened up here so far. It has a lovely beach, and on the east side of it are cliffs, rocks and little sheltered coves that are full of fine sand but seldom frequented. Always check the level of the tide, because it can get quite high and engulf the entire beach in places.

Praia da Luz

(6km from Lagos)

Although Praia da Luz is busy and densely built up, its buildings are fairly elegant compared with those of Praia da Salema. The grounds of the villas are often bordered by pretty little gardens and flowers, and the town is fronted by an attractive, good-sized beach. The concrete building on the beach is an ugly sight and somewhat mars the beauty of the surrounding area. Naturally, you will also find shops of all kinds are established here, thus catering to visitors seeking food, souvenirs, and fun.

Burgau

(10km from Lagos)

Situated between the very popular Praia da Luz and Praia da Salema, Burgau has managed to preserve the picturesque tranquility of a small fishing village. Tucked away in the hollow of a bay, it

Legend of the Almond Trees

According to legend, almond trees came to this region as a result of a marriage between a Moorish prince and a Nordic princess. Just a few years after their wedding and arrival in the Algarve region, the princess grew sad because she missed the snow-covered landscapes of her childhood. The prince, head over heels in love with his bride and ready to do anything for her, ordered thousands of almond trees to secretly be planted throughout the province and their estate. When February arrived, the trees burst into bloom, their branches covered in tiny white blossoms that made the landscape outside the castle look as though it were covered in snow. When she saw this marvel, the princess was roused from her long melancholy, and a radiant smile lit up the face of the prince's beloved once more.

has a pretty, uncrowded beach with a number of services, such as food stores and a few simple restaurants. As the road through Burgau that leads to the beach is particularly steep and narrow, it is best to leave vehicles on the wider streets of the upper village.

Monchique

The peak of the Serra de Monchique may be 902m up, but it is worth the trip. Here, the vegetation is lush and varied: eucalyptus, chestnut, pine, olive, orange and even banana trees, as well as charming mimosas and rhododendrons. This wealth of plant life is made possible by the combination of two elements: fertile, volcanic soil and humid winds that sweep the sides of the Serra and trigger frequent rainfalls. After the extremely dry landscapes of the Algarve coast, a hike through this oasis is a refreshing change of scenery.

Starting at the coast by the N124 and then the N266, the highway winds slowly up the Serra to the thermal springs at **Caldas de Monchique** ★. Even among the Romans, the waters of this spa were renowned for their beneficial effects. The tiny village is nestled in a verdant valley and has a handful of venerable hotels and stately homes that make the area all the more delightful to explore. Numerous walking paths near the Albergaria Velha provide direct access to the village core.

The northbound N266 climbs up to the small town of Monchique, which sits at an altitude of 450m. Monchique is pleasant, but not interesting enough to be more than a mandatory stop on the way up to the top of the Serra. Partway through Monchique, follow the sign leading to **Fóia**. From here the road snakes between pines and eucalyptus trees and provides breathtaking **views** ★ of the valleys and hills below, where dense vegetation spreads a palette of shades ranging from deep, dark green to pale, soft greens.

This plant life becomes sparse around the summit's lookout point, which is marked by an obelisk. On clear days the panoramic view of the coast and various resorts is truly impressive. Even through light fog, observers can make out the tip of Sagres in the distance, jutting into the ocean.

Olhão

A modest fishing village with several wooden cabins dating from the early 18th century, Olhão was given the status of a town in 1808 as repayment from the Court for resisting Napoleon's troops. It was also from the port of Olhão that the ship *Bom Sucesso* sailed off for Rio de Janeiro, Brazil, to tell the Court-in-exile about Napoleon's withdrawal. Then at the dawn of the 19th century, Olhão grew rapidly and its port became one of the most important in the Algarve, its activity extending all the way to the Mediterranean.

Many fish and seafood processing plants were successively established, contributing to the town's growth. Today, these plants still process much of the fish and seafood consumed in the country. Many Portuguese families come to visit these sights and sample the delights of the sea.

Olhão is a bit different from other resort towns west of Faro. Though it is very developed touristically and has preserved its Portuguese character, the town's architecture is unique on the coast. While strolling along the very narrow and empty streets in the historic centre of town, you will discover modest square whitewashed houses with *açoteias* – flat roofs converted into terraces. The design of the houses was influenced by North African and Mediterranean styles brought back by sailors from their voyages along these coasts. Unfortunately, the white facades are dirty and decaying, giving the town a dull look.

A good place to start your tour of the city is on the oceanfront **Avenida 5 de Outubro**, where parking is also easy to find. Most of the town's restaurants are located here and are invaded by entire families who come for the fish and seafood, reportedly the freshest in the country.

Avenida 5 de Outubro is far from charming, but if you walk towards the ocean, you will come across two **covered markets** ★ (*Mon to Fri 7am to 2pm, Sat 6:30am to 3pm*), both worth a visit. They are located in two red brick buildings built at the beginning of the 20th century, and the sights around it are charming. There are many colourful fruit and vegetable stands in one building and all kinds fresh of fish and seafood from the morning catch in the other. Outside both buildings, there are several small cafés with terraces where you can have a drink while watching passersby and fishers attending to their business. Don't miss the **Jardim Pescador Ohanense**, a small park

The Algarve

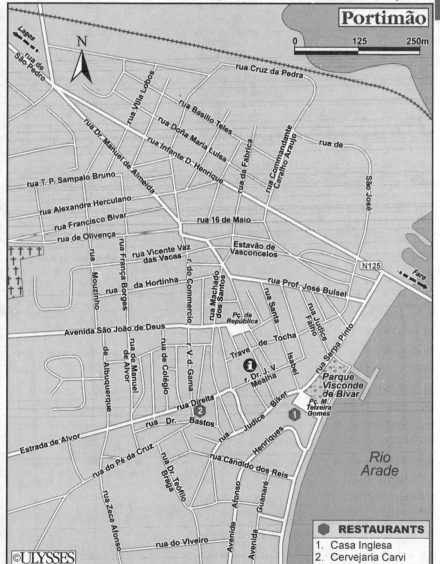

Portimão

Lagos

0   125   250m

N

rua de São Pedro

rua Cruz da Pedra

rua Dr. Manuel de Almeida

rua Vila Lobos

rua Basilio Teles

rua Doña Maria Luisa

rua Infante D. Henrique

rua da Fabrica

rua Commandante Caralho Araujo

rua de

São José

rua T. P. Sampalo Bruno

rua Alexandre Herculano

rua Francisco Bivar

rua de Olivença

rua Mouzinho

rua França Borges

rua Vicente Vaz das Vacas

da Hortinha

rua 16 de Maio

Estavão de Vasconcelos

r. do Commercio

rua Machado dos Santos

rua Prof. José Buisel

N125

Faro

rua Santa

rua Judice Falho

rua Serpa Pinto

Pç. da República

Avenida São João de Deus

de Albuquerque

rua de Manuel de Alvor

rua de Colégio

r.-V.-d.-Gama

Trave   de — Tocha

r. Dr. J. V. Mealha

Isabel

Biker

Judice

Henriques

Parque Visconde de Bivar

Pç. M. Teixeira Gomes

rua Direita

rua Dr. — Bastos

2

1

Estrada de Alvor

rua do Pé da Cruz

rua Dr. Teófilo Braga

rua Zeca Afonso

rua Cândido dos Reis

Afonso

Guanaré

Avenida

Avenida

Rio Arade

rua do Viveiro

©ULYSSES

RESTAURANTS
1. Casa Inglesa
2. Cervejaria Carvi

that is not well kept but has several benches covered with pretty *ajuelos* on the oceanfront, not far from the market. Next to the park is a cute little bandstand where musicians perform. Strolling along the seawall you can see the vast marshy stretches of the Ria Formosa in the distance; this area is part of the Parque Natural de la Ria Formosa (see p 431).

After this breath of fresh sea air, head to the **Praça da Restauração** ★ to see the shiny white baroque facade of the **Igreja Matriz**, built at the end of the 17th century. Except for its altar richly decorated with *talha douradas*, the inside of the church is simple and has nothing of much interest. Also on the Praça in front of the church is the modest chapel **Ermida de Nossa Senhora da Soledade**, built in the 17th century, and next to it the **Compromisso Marítimo**, which, despite its dome, is not a religious building but a social gathering place for fishers. Finally, before continuing to roam the many streets that wind through the historic centre of town, pay a short visit to the interesting chapel **Nossa Senhora dos Alfitos** (Notre Dame of the Afflicted), attached to the back of the Igreja Matriz but accessible via a separate entrance. Many people come here to

bring herbs and flowers, as well as dolls and various and sometimes bizarre *ex-voto* wax carvings representing body parts (heads, arms, legs, etc.).

Portimão

Despite its status as the biggest city in the Algarve, Portimão has almost nothing in the way of tourist attractions. Like most of its neighbours, the city was a victim of the earthquake of 1755, which reduced its churches and monasteries to rubble. A visit here will therefore be limited to a leisurely tour of its store-lined streets and to moments of relaxation at one of the many attractive beaches in the vicinity. A fine example of civil engineering can be found in the impressive suspended bridge that extends Highway N125 and spans the lagunas of the Rio Arade.

Praia do Carvoeiro

(13km from Portimão)

This modest beach, tucked into the hollow of a small cove at the foot of cliffs bordered entirely by little white cottages, has become a fairly popular vacation destination. Although the houses are crowded together on the coast, Carvoeiro has managed to keep a certain cachet, and oversized tourist facilities have been unable to gain a

foothold here. All of the several pleasant paths that run along its cliffs afford superb views of the ocean and this particularly jagged stretch of the coast. Commercial establishments here include restaurants, bars, and shops.

Praia da Rocha

(2km from Portimão)

Praia da Rocha is truly a jewel, interspersed by a network of inlets, washed by brilliant blue water, and rocks that have been intricately carved by the sea and wind. Wide, easy-to-access beaches, perfect for aquatic activities, add to its appeal. With so many natural assets, this idyllic setting would seem to be too good to be true. And it is. Along with Albufeira, Praia da Rocha is the most heavily frequented beach resort in the Algarve, and rates for accommodations are fairly steep. Add to this a waterfront that is becoming increasingly congested with modern hotels of debatable aesthetic value, and too many restaurants and hotels which fall short of value-for-your-dollar standards. These inconveniences aside, visitors with flexible budgets can find good lodgings in the 19th-century homes or older hotels. Apart from the beach, the main point of inter-

est for tourists is the **Fortaleza de Santa Catarina**. Built in 1620, this former fortress today houses a pleasant cafeteria and a belvedere.

Sagres

Henry the Navigator put Sagres in the history books by founding his navigation school here. Now, the city is neither a trendy beach resort nor an exotic destination with inviting turquoise waters. It is merely a rocky, wind-swept promontory that points like a finger into the Atlantic Ocean. Here, plant life is sparse and the shores evoke the landscapes of the Breton coast. At the very tip of this strip of rock is an ancient fort that once housed the famous School of Sagres, rebuilt after the calamity of 1755. Sagres is starkly beautiful but has little more to offer than a scattering of restaurants and hotels, including a lovely *pousada* (see p 442). In fact, it is best suited to those who seek isolation, quiet, and long walks through windy seascapes. For hardy types, there is an interesting hike to **Cabo de São Vicente**; the 6km trek leads to a lighthouse at the edge of a particularly sheer cliff, towering more than 80m above the ocean. Those looking for a nice, safe beach, should not miss Ponta da Baleeira, 3km from Sagres, where there is also a quaint little fishing port; thre is an outfitter on the site who rents diving equipment.

★

Silves

Silves was the prosperous capital of the Algarve during the Moorish occupation and at one time enjoyed a reputation that outshone even that of Lisbon. Located on the banks of the Rio Arade, it was an active port of call for trade ships from the high seas. After its recapture, decline set in; its diminishing status was hastened by the earthquake of 1755 and eventually, Silves became just another minor rural town. The road to this charming region takes motorists through picturesque landscapes of gently rolling hills dotted with orange groves.

At Silves, the eye is immediately drawn to the **fortress ★** constructed of reddish stone, silhouetted above the village against the blue Algarve sky. This stronghold was built

Water Dogs

While exploring the Rio Formosa region, visitors are likely to hear people speaking about "water dogs", which seems to have become one of the local attractions. This canine breed originated in the Algarve region, and the animals resemble large poodles. Reputed to be excellent swimmers, these dogs can spend up to a whole day in the water without getting tired. This is why they are often seen accompanying fishers, helping them with various tasks such as retrieving fishing nets or "delivering" messages between boats. Most Portuguese water dogs have black fur, although some are brown with white markings. The breed has been in danger of extinction since the 1930s, but efforts are now being made to breed it in special facilities throughout the province, and locals are discovering a new passion for their water dogs.

during the Moorish era and restored in 1940. The **rampart-walk** is of special interest for its **panoramic views** of the lower town, the Rio Arade, and the surrounding countryside. The elegant **Moorish door** near Praça do Município is worth a look: it admits visitors to the upper town. A little farther, next to the Sé in the cathedral square, is a **Manueline door** whose motifs include the head of a strange figure.

Near this fortress is the **Museu Municipal da Arqueologia** (*300 ESC; open every day from 10am to 5pm; Rua da Portas de Loulé 14*), which displays a collection of ceramics and various local objects. Through these, the exhibition chronicles the history of the region from the pre-Roman period to the second conquest.

The museum's interior layout – a walkway of metal – allows you to discover an old Moorish well dating from the 11th century and creates a very contemporary and successful ensemble that is worth the visit alone.

★★

Tavira

Although objects found during archeological digs indicate that the Tavira region has been inhabited since the neolithic period, it was only under Moorish occupation that the town gained any importance. It was conquered in 1242 by the Knights of Santiago, and later played a significant role in the capture of Ceuta (Morocco), when it was then the main port of registry for Portuguese troops.

After that, Tavira quickly prospered and received town status in 1520 during a royal visit. Unfortunately, the town's development was stunted by plagues during the 17th century and the 1755 earthquake, which destroyed many buildings and accelerated the silting up of its port. Nevertheless, Tavira managed to prosper from its tuna-fishing industry and many churches and cathedrals were built here.

For those who like religious architecture, this town is certainly blessed – it has no less than 32 churches and chapels for a population of only 7,000 inhabitants! Described below are the ones that stand out the most. There is also a small guide called *Roteiro das Igrejas de Tavira*, published in both English and Portuguese, that describes all of Tavira's religious buildings. It is available at the town's tourist office (see p 414). The tourist office also organizes free guided tours of Tavira (*tours leave at 10am and 3pm*) in English and Portuguese, depending on the availability of guides.

Whatever your interest in religious things may be, start your visit by strolling along the pier that runs along the Rio Gilão. Walk up palm-tree-lined **Rua do Cais ★** to the **roman bridge ★★** that crosses

the Rio. Rebuilt in the 17th century, these seven arches are the only remains of the Roman era. This bridge is particularily romantic and was once part of the route between Faro and Mérlota. Cross the bridge to reach the

Praça Dr. Padinha and the **Antigo Convento dos Ermitas de São Paulo** or Igreja de São Paulo. Once a convent, this church is worth the visit for its seven **carved wooden retables**. Don't miss the one depicting

the Last Supper – it is a real work of art!

Before you leave the building and head back to the Praça da República, take a walk on the nearby streets to observe the lovely facades of private homes.

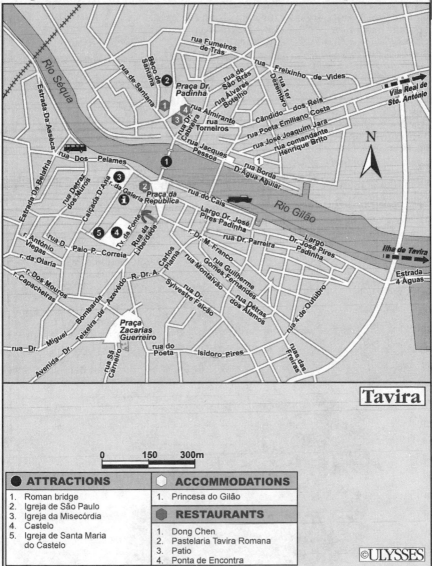

Tavira

0   150   300m

● ATTRACTIONS	⬡ ACCOMMODATIONS
1. Roman bridge	1. Princesa do Gilão
2. Igreja de São Paulo	
3. Igreja da Misecórdia	⬡ RESTAURANTS
4. Castelo	
5. Igreja de Santa Maria do Castelo	1. Dong Chen
	2. Pastelaria Tavira Romana
	3. Patio
	4. Ponta de Encontra

©ULYSSES

After walking up Rua da Galeria and past the tourist information office after the **Arco de la Misericórdia**, a small but elegant arc decorated with a coat of arms, you will come across a small alley that will lead you to the **Igreja de la Misericórdia**, famous for its Renaissance-style portal. Except for its lovely baroque *azulejos* and its altar with *talha douradas*, the church has nothing much of interest inside.

By taking the Travessa da Fonte, you will end up in front of the **Castelo** (*Mon to Fri 9am to 5:30pm, Sat and Sun 10am to 6pm*), built in the 18th century on top of a hill for King Don Dimis. Though only a few corners of the castle remain, if you climb to the top you will see some beautiful views of the lower town and the coast in the distance.

Next to the Castelo, the **Igreja de Santa Maria do Castelo**, built in the 18th century, has preserved its original portal, which blends harmoniously with the neo-Palladian facade built after the earthquake.

Tavira's other main attraction is **Ilha de Tavira**, 2km from dowtown, with its beaches of **Santa Luzia** and **Barril ★**. Forming an integral part of the Parque Natural da Ria Formosa (see p 431), this long (about 11km), sandy beach will delight swimmers and sunbathers. From May until late September, the island is frequented by many tourists, both locals and foreigners, and many restaurants and cafés open up for this part of the year.

On the western side of the island, after Barril, there are vast stretches of sand dunes and seemingly endless beaches that are less crowded and very pleasant to stroll along.

Vila Real de Santo António

Vila Real de Santo António is a strange town. Like *Baixa* in Lisbon, it also has an interesting architectural style called "Pombalian", and is the only town in Portugal built in this style. In 1773, for military reasons (relations were tense with Spain at the time), the Marquis of Pombal built Vila Real de Santo António as a fortified border town. The town's location, right next to the Rio Guadiana, was also strategic for controlling the large volume of merchandise shipped on the river between the ocean and the interior. Work began on building the town in March 1774, and it took less than five months to erect the main buildings.

Parks

Parque Natural da Ria Formosa

Covering 18,400ha, the Parque Natural da Ria Formosa will particularly interest those who enjoy vast expanses of wilderness. This enormous lagoon, which is over 60km long, has many islets and sandbanks, as well as a vast network of canals that run through the swamps.

The park has about 8,000 inhabitants who survive on fishing and extracting salt from the marshes. In the summer, the population of the park doubles when tourists flock to its beautiful sandy beaches and shallow lagoons.

Because of its location, the Ria Formosa is an ideal habitat for many birds that migrate to Northern Europe or Africa. An observation centre called **Quinta de Marim** (*9am to noon and 2pm to 5pm; 1km from Olhão, turn right on the N125 heading towards Tavira,* ☎*289 70 41 34,* ⇋*289 70 41 65*) was set up here with different

aquariums full of marine species found in the park. The staff will provide you with information about the area's rich flora and fauna. You can also admire one of the rare "**fish mills**" that were once common on the coast.

Various trails have been set up for those who want to explore the park further. Along the trails you will see some very interesting fauna; aside from birds, there are little mammals, turtles and chameleons. In order to spot the chameleons, visitors must be patient and look for them. Some of the birds that can be most easily seen are shovelers, teals, sandpipers, curlews, grey plovers, seagulls and white herons. With a little perseverance you might be able to see the rare purple gallinule, the park emblem.

Outdoor Activities

Cruises

Armação de Pêra

Several boats moored at the main beach can be hired for a tour of the **marine grottos at**

Furnas ★ (*2,200 ESC for a 2hr excursion*). The 18 grottos were carved out of the cliff by the sea and resemble strange sculptures that glimmer with the reflections of the azure water.

Ponta da Piedade

Many travel agencies offer cruises along the coast from Lagos to Ponta da Piedade, or to see the **underwater caverns** with amusing names like O Elefante (the elephant), Os Namorados (the lovers) and O Museu (the museum). Observing strange cavity formations shining from the reflections of the azur-blue water makes the excursion all the more pleasant. Even though the excursions leave from the towns of Sagres, Portimão and Quarteira, those that leave from Lagos are cheapter and more popular. Here are some travel agencies that offer cruises from Lagos:

Actividades Marítimos Bom Dia
Marina de Lagos (near the ferry docks), 8600 Lagos
☎*282 76 46 70*
2hr excursion for 3 000 ESC or 3 600 ESC including breakfast

Espadarte do Sul
at the fishing docks, quay no. 4
8600 Lagos
☎/⇋*282 76 18 20*
1hr 30min excursion for 2 500 ESC, including a glass of porto

Trigana
at the Lagos marina, opposite the Terra à Vista shop
8500 Lagos
☎ *282 76 19 61*
⇌ *282 76 39 69*
2hr excursion costs 2,700 ESC including a glass of porto
The only agency combining a cavern visit with a sea excursion on a traditional Portuguese sailboat.

Horseback Riding

Vilamoura

Just outside Vilamoura, on a charming country estate, is the **Estalagem de Cegonha**, which is reached by first following the directions to Quinta da Quarteira, Centro Hipico de Vilamoura
(☎ *289 30 25 77*). Horseback riding in this rural setting costs about 3,500 ESC per hour; lessons for beginners are 3,000 ESC per half-hour.

Lagos

For those whose passion is fishing, Lagos is one of the best places in the Algarve to practice this sport. Many outfitters offer excursions out to sea where seabream, tuna, swordfish and shark can be caught. Most of the agencies supply fishing equipment:

Imulgos
☎ *282 76 00 31*
☎ *282 76 00 32*
⇌ *282 76 00 35*
Deep-sea fishing: 6,000 ESC / 4hrs, 11,000 ESC/8hrs; shark fishing: 8,000 ESC/4 hrs

Espadarte do Sul
at the fishing docks, quay no. 4
8600 Lagos
☎/⇌ *282 76 18 20*
deep-sea fishing: 8,000 ESC/ 4hrs 30min, 11,000 ESC/7hrs

Golf

Golf is one of the most popular sports in the Algarve, and Portugal's reputation in this domain extends well beyond its borders. Each year, more enthusiasts choose Portugal both for the quality of its golf packages and the quantity of available services. In recent years, thanks in part to year-round mild weather, the number of golf courses in the Algarve has also multiplied. Today, the region has more courses than anywhere else in the country. The ones listed below were chosen either for their interesting courses or for the exceptional setting in which they are found.

Bicycling

Tavira

Rent A Bike (*Rua do Forno n° 22;*
☎ *281 32 19 73*)
This agency not only rents bikes for the day or week (*about 1,000 ESC/day or 4,200 ESC/week*) but also offers guided bicycling tours in and around the old city (*1,500 ESC/4hrs*) and bike in the Parque Natural da Ria Formosa.

Hiking

Praia Dona Ana

Around Lagos there is a **magnificent hiking trail** ★★ that runs along the coast westward to Ponta da Piedade and its striking marine grottos. The trail is located on the right side of the O Carnilo restaurant (when facing the building). It winds its way through fields of flowering grasses and offers excellent views of the deep ochre cliffs and sculpted rocks scattered on the beach or jutting from the sea. The contrast with the blue of the ocean is absolutely breathtaking.

Golf Courses

Name	Number of Holes	Par	Length (in metres)	Address
Alto Golf	18	72	6120	Hotal S.A Quinta do Alto do Poço 8500 Alvor ☎282 41 69 13 ⇌282 40 10 46
Carvoeiro Gramacho	18	72	5915	Pestana Golf & Resorts 8400 Carvoeiro ☎282 34 09 00 ⇌282 34 21 89
Carvoeiro Pinta	18	71	6150	Pestana Golf & Resorts 8400 Carvoeiro ☎282 34 09 00 ⇌282 34 21 89
Palmares	18	71	5960	Palmares Investimento Lda Meia Praia 8600 Lagos ☎282 76 29 53 ⇌282 76 25 34
Parque da Floresta	18	72	5870	Vigia Group Vale do Poço, Budens 8650 Vila do Bispo ☎282 69 53 33 ⇌282 69 51 57
Penina Champion	18	73	6340	Granada Group 8500 Portimão ☎282 41 54 15 ⇌282 41 50 00
Penina Resort	9	35	2990	Granada Group 8500 Portimão ☎282 41 54 15 ⇌282 41 50 00
Penina Academy	9	30	2030	Granada Group 8500 Portimão ☎282 41 54 15 ⇌282 41 50 00
Pinheiros Altos	18	72	5770	J.J Worldwide Ltd Quinta do Lago 8135 Almancil ☎289 3599 10 ⇌289 39 43 92

Quinta do Lago	18	72	6490	Golf da Quinta do Lago S.A. 8135 Almancil ☎*289 39 07 00* ⇌*289 39 40 13*
Quinta do Lago Ria Formosa	18	72	6200	Golf da Quinta do Lago S.A. 8135 Almancil ☎*289 39 07 00* ⇌*289 39 40 13*
Salgados	18	72	6050	Hersal S.A. Herdade dos Salgados Vale Rabelho 8200 Albufeira ☎*289 59 11 11* ⇌*289 59 11 12*
San Lorenzo	18	72	6240	Granada Group 8135 Almancil ☎*289 39 65 22* ⇌*289 39 69 08*
Sheraton Pine Cliffs	9	66	2280	United Investments Portugal Praia da Falésia 8200Albufeira ☎*289 50 01 00* ⇌*289 50 01 17*
Vale do Lobo Royal	18	72	6175	Vale do Lobo Lda Vale do Lobo 8135 Almancil ☎*289 39 39 39* ⇌*289 39 47 42*
Vale do Lobo Ocean	18	72	5495	Vale do Lobo Lda Vale do Lobo 8135 Almancil ☎*289 39 39 39* ⇌*289 39 47 42*
Vale de Milho	9	54	920	Multiger S.A. Praia do Carvoeiro 8400 Lagoa ☎*282 35 85 02* ⇌*282 35 84 97*
Vila Sol	18	72	6190	Imobiliária da Fonte Nova S.A. Morgadinhos Alto do Semino 8125 Vilamoura ☎*289 30 05 02* ⇌*289 30 05 91*

Vilamoura	18	73	6250	Lusotor Golf 8125 Vilamoura ☎289 31 03 41 ⇌289 31 03 21
Vilamoura Laguna	18	72	6133	Lusotor Golf 8125 Vilamoura ☎289 31 01 80 ⇌289 31 03 49
Vilamoura Pinhal	18	72	6300	Lusotur Golf 8125 Vilamoura ☎289 31 03 90 ⇌289 31 03 93

Amusement Park

Guia

Zoomarine (*Av. Tomás Cabreira, On Route N125; admission: adult 2,800 ESC, child (3 to 10 years old) 1,800 ESC Jan to Mar and Nov to Dec, Tue to Sun 10am to 5pm, Apr to Jun and Oct, every day 10am to 6pm, Jul to Sep, every day 10am to 10pm; ☎289 56 11 04; ⇌289 56 12 15; www.zoomarine.com*)
For those travelling with kids, Zoomarine is a pleasant change from the coastal beaches. This maritime theme park offers a variety of attractions. Besides the performances where dolphins and seals compete fervently and a parrot show where the birds clown around, there is a museum showcasing marine animals. There are also a pool, a merry-go-round and a Ferris wheel to delight children. Fast-food stands have been set up on site.

As you can imagine, during school vacation, this place really fills up!

Accommodations

Albufeira

Campismo Parque de Albufeira
Estrada das Ferreires
Albufeira 8200
☎289 58 76 29
☎289 57 76 30
⇌289 58 76 33

Residencial Vila Recife
$$
pb, K, ≈
Rua Miguel Bombarda 6
Albufeira 8200
☎289 58 67 47
☎289 58 77 82
Established in the upper town in a turn-of-the-century villa, the Residencial Vila Recife has small, comfortable and, for the most part, modern rooms, some with balconies. The residence is accessed by the bistro on the building's main floor. A

pretty garden with palm trees graces the grounds in front of the entrance.

La Residencia Boa Vista
$$-$$$
pb, tv, ≈
Rua Samora Barros 20
Albufeira 8200
☎289 58 91 75
⇌289 58 91 80
Perched atop a small hill, La Residencia Boa Vista has the added advantage of being removed from the hustle and bustle of the city centre. Its superb terrace – which has a large swimming pool – affords a sweeping view of Albufeira. The comfortable rooms each have a balcony with an ocean view and are equipped with standard furnishings.

Hotel California
$$-$$$
pb, tv, ≈
Rua Cândido dos Reis 10-16
Albufeira 8200
☎289 58 68 33
⇌289 58 68 50
This 55-room hotel, situated in central Albufeira, will suit travellers who like to be

close to the night-time action and summer festivities. Some of the rooms have their own little balconies with views of the city. Guests can use the pool. Because the establishment is completely booked by tourist groups in the high season, making reservations well in advance is a must. A comfortable place, but somewhat pricey considering the immediate surroundings.

Vale de Parra

(5km from Albufeira)

Quinta do Sol
$$-$$$/5 pers. Sep to Jun
$$$-$$$$/5 pers. Jul to Aug,
no bkfst
pb, tv, ≈
right off the highway from Albufeira to Pêra, near Vale de Parra, Albufeira 8200
☎289 59 15 14
≈289 59 13 32
When travelling with a group, the Quinta do Sol is the name to remember. This new tourist complex is composed of several houses designed to accommodate five to seven people. Each house is equipped with dishware and linens, and some have washing machines. Rooms are arranged on two floors and each has a bathroom or shower. A living room, kitchenette, and small terrace bordered by a flowering garden complete the amenities of the complex. The interior decoration is neat and tasteful. Guests can

swim in the pool (*free*) or rent the tennis court (*500 ESC/day*). An affordable solution for groups or families.

Praia da Galé

(7km from Albufeira)

Vila Joya
$$$$$
closed from mid-Nov to mid-Dec and from mid-Jan to mid-Feb
½b, pb, tv, ≈, ℜ
on the highway from Albufeira to Pêra, from Vale de Parra continue in the direction of Praia da Galé; Praia da Galé Albufeira 8200
if reserving less than 1 month in advance:
☎289 59 17 95
≈289 59 12 01
if reserving more than 1 month in advance: contact the office in Munich, Germany
☎49-89-649 33 37
≈49-89-649 26 36
If a dream could be named for an establishment, it would probably be that of the Vila Joya. This hotel has only 17 rooms and successfully combines cachet, luxury, and efficiency. After being greeted with a glass of champagne, guests are conducted to their rooms by the attentive staff garbed in North-African dress, through a maze of hushed hallways lined with fine objects. All of the rooms, save one, have private balconies with views of the gorgeous flowering garden that stretches down to the sea. While each room contains modern and antique *objets d'arts*,

each has been decorated differently and given its own character. Even the bathrooms are special: they are lined with superb *azulejos* with Moorish accents. A mini-bar, clock radio, satellite television, compact stereo system with CD player (and over 1,000 available musical choices)... not a single detail seems to have been overlooked!
Along with direct access to the seaside, visitors can enjoy the privacy of a heated pool surrounded by lush greenery. They will also want to partake of the best breakfasts Portugal has to offer on the delightful terrace adorned with arches. On the menu: fresh exotic fruits, croissants, muesli, German bread, cheeses and more. A real treat! Rounding out the amenities of this exceptional establishment is a restaurant (see p 444). Even without booking a room, it is worth sampling the creations of the restaurant's Austrian chef, Dieter Koschina – there's no better cuisine to be found in all of the Algarve! Only one inconvenience: credit cards are not accepted here. Expensive? Yes. But can we put a price on a dream?

Armação de Pêra

(18km from Albufeira)

Campismo Parque de Armação de Pêra
Armação de Pêra 8365
☎ 282 31 29 04
≈ 282 31 53 79

Hotel Garbe
$$$-$$$$ no view
$$$$-$$$$$ with view
pb, tv, ≈, ℜ
oceanfront
Avenida Marginal, Armação de Pêra 8365
☎ 282 31 51 87
≈ 282 31 50 87
≈ 282 31 51 02
hotelgarbe@mail.telepac.pt
www.nexus-pt.com/hotel garbe/index.htm
Located on a wonderfully large beach at the foot of a series of small cliffs, the Hotel Garbe is a modern establishment with 152 well-equipped rooms. Rooms with ocean views each have a pleasant private balcony. The decor is tasteful, if not overly original. Some of the rooms could use a bit of freshening up, and the bathrooms could be better equipped. A small pool overlooking the sea and a bar, game room and a cluster of shops round out the amenities. As the hotel often hosts groups of travellers, this is a good choice for those looking for animation.

Vilalara hotel
$$$$$
pb, tv, ≈, K, ℜ
from Armação de Pêra, take the N269-1 toward Porches; directions to the hotel on the left-hand side of the highway; Prai das Gaivotas, Armação de Pêra 8365
☎ 282 31 49 10
≈ 282 31 49 56
≈ 282 32 00 00
vilalara@ip.pt
www.vilalara.com
Those who seek the benefits of sea water therapy (thalassotherapy) might opt for the Vilalara hotel. This is an idyllic place to relax. Vast grounds, a private beach, superb apartments, an elegant decor and flowering gardens await visitors. Each set of living quarters has a generous terrace overlooking a pair of swimming pools (fresh and salt water) adorned with *azulejos*. Finally, the hotel boasts an oceanfront pool and several tennis courts. For 17,000 ESC, visitors can take the thalassic cure alone, albeit without accommodations.

Caldas de Monchique

(5km from Monchique)

Pensão Restaurants Central
$ no bkfst
heading north, shortly after the village of Montinho, take the road to the left of the N266 Caldas da Monchique Monchique 8550
☎ 282 91 22 03
Located 5km from the town of Monchique in a pretty little valley, Pensão Restaurants

Central is an old house, dating back to 1860. Its 10 rooms are rather rudimentary (sink in each room) but are furnished with period furniture and objects, giving them a rustic charm. Service is friendly and warm.

Nova Pensão Internacional
$ no bkfst
heading north, shortly after the village of Montinho, take the road to the left of the N266 Caldas da Monchique Monchique 8550
☎ 282 91 26 19
Just before the Pensão Central (see above), this small boarding house has bigger rooms – though less charming – than its neighbour. The rooms at the front of the building have a great view of the valley. The dining room is decorated with columns and mirrors in the Moorish style. The place is basic, but inexpensive.

Albergaria Velha
$-$$ Oct to Jun
$$ Jul to Sep
pb
heading north, shortly after Montinho, take the road to the left of the N266; Caldas da Monchique, Monchique 8550
☎ 282 91 22 04
≈ 282 91 39 20
At the very heart of the little village is the Albergaria Velha, offering modern-looking rooms that will suit visitors looking to combine comfort and outdoor activities. There are several hiking trails close by.

Faro

Campismo Municipal de Faro
Câmara Municipal de Faro
Praia da Faro, Faro 8000
☎ *289 81 78 76*
⇄ *289 80 23 26*

Pensão Residencial Central
$$ no bkfst
pb
Largo Terreiro do Bispo no. 12
☎ *289 80 72 91*
Though this city has no lack of hotels, most of them are extremely expensive and offer poor value for the money. Among the more decent properties, the Pensão Residencial Central offers rooms on the second floor of a small house. The rooms are not luxurious and are decorated minimally, but are exceptionally clean. Night owls are not welcome here because the curfew is at midnight. You'll have to get used to going to bed early in the capital of the Algarve, which should not be a problem since the city does not have much of a nightlife.

Santa Bárbara de Nexe

(13km from Faro)

Hotel La Réserve
$$$$$
pb, tv, K, ≈, ℜ
located on the road to Esteval at Santa Bárbara de Nexe
Faro 8000
☎ *289 99 94 94*
⇄ *289 99 04 02*
The Hotel La Réserve is the only establishment in Portugal affiliated

with the Relais et Châteaux chain. Situated in the heart of the countryside on an elegant 6ha estate, the hotel has 12 studio apartments and eight fully equipped duplexes, along with a pretty terrace adjoining a garden. Both the rooms and the common areas are tasteful, though the overall effect is a little old fashioned. A pool and tennis court (both free) are at the disposal of guests. Golf packages are also available. Surprisingly, the hotel does not accept credit cards! It is nonetheless a popular establishment that requires reservations at least one month in advance.

Quarteira

(21km from Faro)

Parque da Quarteira/Orbitur
Forte Novo, Quarteira 8125
☎ *289 30 28 26*
⇄ *289 30 28 22*

Vilamoura

(21km from Faro)

Estalagem de Cegonha
$$
pb, ℜ
closed Jan
Centro Hípico de Vilamoura
Vilamoura 8125
☎ *289 30 25 77*
⇄ *289 32 26 75*
Situated at the outskirts of Vilamoura (follow the signs to Quinta da Quarteira), this is a charming country estate surrounded by flowering gardens. It also

enjoys a reputation in the area for its equestrian centre. The 10 rooms have an old-fashioned appeal. Ideal for those seeking tranquil lodgings and plenty of fresh air.

Dom Pedro Golf
$$$ Nov to Mar
$$$-$$$$ Apr to Jun
$$$$$ Jul to Sep
pb, tv, ≈, ℜ
from the N125, follow the signs to Vilamoura and continue along the main road until signs for the hotel appear
Vilamoura 812
☎ *289 38 96 50*
⇄ *289 31 54 82*
In the new city of Vilamoura – a veritable suburb of Quarteira – is the hotel Dom Pedro Golf. As the name indicates, this place caters to golfers. It has 270 rooms, all comfortably appointed and each with a balcony. The hotel borders a major golf complex with three courses. The large nearby marina, with a capacity of up to 1,000 crafts, will be a magnet for boat-lovers.

São Brás de Alportel

(22km from Faro)

Pousada de São Brás
$$$$
pb, tv, ℜ, ≈
beside the N2, 2km north of São Brás de Alportel, 8150 São Brás de Alportel
☎ *289 84 23 05*
☎ *289 84 23 06*
⇄ *289 84 17 26*
Set in the heart of a beautiful, bright white villa, Pousada de São Brás is a pleasant alter-

The Algarve

native for those who want to escape the overcrowded, noisy resort towns of Algarve, but still have easy access to them. Actually located in the back country, fewer than 30km from the coast, this *pousada* offers tranquillity and comfort in the sort of refined environment for which the Enatur network is renowned. To profit fully from the beautiful surrounding countryside, rent one of the upper rooms with small balconies that offer lovely views of the mountains in the distance. As for the decoration, the clever use of small bamboo furniture pieces pleasantly tinges the rather rich-looking regional decor with exoticism. In addition to a large swimming pool that is much appreciated in the hot months of summer, a tennis court is at guests' disposal. The only little blemish is that the some of the bathroom furnishings are old and should be changed.

Lagos

Pousada de Juventude
50 Rua Lançarste de Freitas,
Lagos 8600
☎*282 76 19 70*
⇌*282 76 96-84*

Imulagos - Parque de Campismo de Lagos
Estrada de Porto de Mós
Apartado 105, Lagos
Codex 8601
☎*282 76-20-89*
⇌*282 76 00-35*
josebomba@mail.telepac.pt

Residencial Rubi Mar
$
Rua da Baroca 70, 2nd floor
Lagos 8600
☎*282 76 31 65*
The building's facade is not the most welcoming, but the rates are right for tight budgets. No frills.

Pensão - Residencial MarAzul
$$
pb
Rua 25 de Abril 13, Apt 338
Lagos 8600
☎*282 76 94 49*
⇌*282 76 99 60*
In the city-centre is the Pensão - Residencial MarAzul, an 18-room inn with adequate, though not luxurious, furnishings.

Pensão-Residencial Lagosmar
$$-$$$
pb, tv
Rua Dr. Faria e Silva no. 13
8600 Lagos
☎*282 76 37 22*
☎*282 76 35 23*
⇌*282 76 73 24*
This *pensão* offers about 40 rooms in several buildings that are interconnected by a series of hallways and stairs with nicely arranged woodwork and tiles. The rooms with lovely *azuelo*-decorated terraces overlooking the alley are more pleasant and afford a partial view of the port and the city. The furnishings and decor of the dwellings, though decent, are basic and outmoded.

The basement room where breakfast is served is dark and de-

pressing, and the orange juice made from concentrate and the artificial jams don't make things any better. The hotel's real advantage is its location on a small paved alley, far enough away from the noise of the downtown but close enough to all its services. Because getting to the *pensão* can be complicated, ask them to send you their brochure with directions.

Casa de São Gonçalo
$$$
pb/ps
Rua Cândido dos Reis 73
Lagos 8600
☎*282 76 21 71*
⇌*282 76 39 27*
Some travellers prefer old-world charm, antique objects, and period furniture; they will appreciate the Casa de São Gonçalo, at the very heart of the city. Each room is furnished differently, and some have their own small, wrought-iron balconies overlooking the street.

Hotel de Lagos
$$-$$$ Oct to May
$$$ Jun and Sep
$$$ Jul and Aug
pb, tv, ≈, ℜ
Rua Nova a Lobia corner Rua Antonio Christogono dos Santos
Lagos 8600
☎*282 76 99 67*
⇌*282 76 99 20*
hotel.lagos@mail.telepac.pt
This large, modern hotel has a slightly sterile lobby, but its 318 rooms are comfortable and elegant. It has two pools (one indoor and one outdoor) and numerous services, such

as a fitness room and a bar. A shuttle takes guests to the hotel's private beach, which also has a pool as well as a tennis court, a bar and a restaurant. Golfers can while away the hours on the one of Portugal's finest courses, the Golf Club Palmares (see p 433).

Praia da Luz

(6km from Lagos)

Hotel Belavista da Luz
$$$-$$$$
pb, tv, ≈, ⌂
Praia da Luz, Lagos 8600
☎282 78 86 55
≈282 78 86 56
hoteldaluz@mail.telepac.pt
www.belavistadaluz.com
Despite a somewhat kitschy exterior, the Hotel Belavista da Luz is pleasant enough. Forty-five large rooms have their own balconies and fridges, and there is a cafeteria on the premises. The decor is modern and tasteful. To enjoy a direct view of the ocean, ask for a room on the second floor in the middle of the building. A tennis court, exercise room, sauna and two pools round out the amenities.

Burgau

(10km from Lagos)

Casa Sequeira
$-$$
pb, tv, K
Travessa do Alecrim no. 7
8650 Vila do Bispo
☎282 69 72 88
In Burgau, a pleasant peaceful fishing village,

the residents rent rooms in their homes or apartments to tourists. Among the possible options, staying in the home of the Sequeira family is an excellent choice due to its location in the middle of the village, half - way up a hill. You can either rent the second-floor apartment, which can accommodate up to six people, or the third-floor apartment for two people. The second one has a large terrace with a stunning view of the ocean and the village. Both apartments are well equipped with a kitchen and an alcove living room. The place is as clean as can be and Mrs. Sequeira will welcome you with a smile. A choice place, so reserve well in advance!

Monchique

Estalagem Abrigo da Montanha
$$ Oct to Jun
$$$ Jul to Sep
pb, ≈, ℜ
Estrada da Fóia
Monchique 8550
☎282 91 21 31
≈282 91 36 60
Set among lush, green, well-tended gardens, this establishment has just six rooms, each with its own little terrace and a sweeping view of Serra de Monchique. Peaceful, and conducive to leisurely strolls.

Olhão

Parque de Campismo de Olhão
Apartado 300
8703 Olhão
☎289 700-13-00
≈289 700-13-90

Albergaria Nossa Senhora da Rocha
$$$
sb, tv
Praia Nossa Senhora da Rocha
Apartado 134
8365 Armação de Pêra
☎282 31 57 49
☎282 31 57 52
≈282 31 57 54
Located near the Nossa Senhora da Rocha beach and its stunning cliffs, this hotel offers 30 rooms inside a refined, shining-white building. However, there is a parking lot on the property instead of greenery. A garden would be welcome, but the owners prefer to offer their clientele places to park their polluting cars. To get a view of the ocean, ask for an upper room on the left side of the building. The decor, minus the *azulejos* adorning the walls of some of the common rooms, lacks originality. The room furnishings are rather cold but the hotel is extremely clean.

Portimão

Pousada de Juventude, Lugar de Coca
Maravilhas, Portimão 8500
☎282 49 18 04
≈282 49 18 04

Ferragudo

(*4km from Portimão*)

Clube de Campismo de Lisboa
Ferragudo 8400
☎282 46 11 21
≈282 46 13 55

Praia da Rocha

(*2km from Portimão*)

Solar Pinguim
$$
pb
just after Avenida D. Afonso
Henriques; Avenida Tomás
Cabreira, Praia da Rocha
Portimão 8500
☎282 42 43 08
This quaint-looking
establishment, a short
distance from the
beachfront, has 12 well-
appointed rooms. Ideal
for those seeking rest
and relaxation in a
genteel British atmo-
sphere.

🖥 **Residencial Praia do Vau**
$$-$$$ no bkfst
pb
closed mid-oct to Apr
Praia do Vau, on the west end of
l'Av. Tomás Cabreira, near the
Rotunda dos Três Castelos
Apartado 158
8502 Portimão
☎282 40 13 12
≈282 40 17 56
A little beyond the very
touristy Avenida Tomás
Cabreira, which is jam-
packed with establish-
ments, the Residencial
Praia do Vau is made
up of little houses
scattered about a pleas-
ant garden where palm
trees and bushes man-
age to hide the ugly
modern buildings a
little farther away. Each

unit has several rooms
with a bathroom and
dining room. Despite
the property's country
charm, the rooms and
furnishings need some
freshening up. Every
year, the warm Belgian
owners welcome a
regular clientele, so it is
strongly recommended
to reserve a room much
in advance. Pets are
allowed in this estab-
lishment, an unusual
thing in Portugal.

Hotel Bela Vista
$$$ Oct to Jun
$$$$ Jul to Sep
pb, tv
oceanfront
across from Rua Antonio Feu
Avenida Tomás Cabreira
Portimão 8500, Praia de Rocha
Portimão 8500
☎282 42 40 55
≈282 41 53 69
Hotel Bela Vista offers
16 comfortable rooms
decorated with *azulejos*.
Some of the rooms are
furnished with lovely
antique furniture and
have ocean views. The
majestic wood staircase,
also flanked by *azulejos*,
and an elegant lobby
with an ornate ceiling
are also noteworthy.
The charming atmo-
sphere and a good
location away from
other major hotels
make this place one the
best values for the
money in its category.
The only dark lining on
the silver cloud: the
open terrace may face
the ocean, but its ultra-
modern design and
garish furniture detract
from the hotel's bar and
lounge.

Hotel Oriental
$$$ Oct to May
$$$$-$$$$$ Jun to Sep
pb, tv, ⌂, ≈, K, ℜ
Avenida Tomás Cabreira, Praia
da Rocha, Portimão 8500
☎282 41 30 00
≈282 41 34 13
The big hotels along
the coast include Hotel
Oriental, with a cachet
all its own. The ochre
walls and loggia-
shaped balconies do
give it a slightly Orien-
tal appearance. The 85
studio apartments are
decorated with care
and have their own
balconies with views,
some directly overlook-
ing the ocean. The
common areas, inspired
by Moorish design, lack
harmony and border on
the kitschy. A pool and
flowering gardens
fronting the sea round
out the attractions of
this well-located but
unfortunately rather
expensive establish-
ment.

Praia Grande

(*5km from Portimão*)

Casabela hotel
$$$ Oct to mid-May
$$$$$ mid-May to Sep
pb, tv, ≈, ℜ
Praia Grande, Vale da Areia
Ferragudo, Lagoa 8400
☎282 46 15 80
≈282 46 15 81
Well away from the
touristy hustle and
bustle, and with the
added attraction of a
nearby beach, is the
Casabela hotel. This is
the place to go for
peace, quiet, and a
swim in the ocean far
from the madding
crowds. Ask for a room

with an ocean-view, since the ones at the front of the building look out over the parking lot. Classic and quite pleasing decor.

Praia do Carvoeiro

(13km from Portimão)

Casa Von Baselli
$-$$
at the top of the cliff skirting the left-hand side of the beach behind the Rampa de Nossa Senhora de Encarnação; Rua da Escola, Praia da Carvoeiro 8400
☎*282 35 71 59*
⁼*282 35 77 62*
Casa Von Baselli. This little inn has just five modestly equipped rooms, but a wonderful terrace overlooking the sea. Well-maintained.

Casa Brigitte
$$ or 55,000 ESC/wk no bkfst
pb/ps
at the top of the cliff to the left-hand side of the beach; Rampa de Nossa Senhora da Encarnação 27, Cerro dos Pios Lagoa 8400
☎*282 35 63 18*
Run by Canadians, this establishment has nine comfortable rooms, some with balconies and ocean-views. Guests can use the common kitchen, fully equipped with dishes, fridge, coffee machine and toaster. Three fully equipped efficiency apartments are also available for rent on a weekly basis. In the high season, reservations by the week are preferred.

Sagres

Campismo Parque de Sagres
Cerro das Moitas, Sagres 8650
☎*282 62 43 51*
⁼*282 62 44 45*

Fortaleza do Beliche
$$$
closed Dec and Jan
pb, ℜ
to the left of the highway from Sagres to Cabo de São Vicente Vila do Bispo 8650
☎*282 62 41 24*
⁼*282 62 42 25*
Located in a breathtaking setting at the edge of a cliff, inside an ancient fortress, the Fortaleza do Beliche hotel has just four comfortably and classically decorated rooms. Tranquility and salty sea air await visitors. Credit cards not accepted.

Hotel da Baleeira
$ Nov to Mar
$$$ Apr to Oct
pb, tv, ≈, ℜ
Ponta da Baleeira, Sagres, Vila do Bispo 8650
☎*282 62 42 12*
⁼*282 62 44 25*
hotel.baleeira@mail.telepac.pt
www.sagres.net/baleeira/index.htm
A stone's throw from the picturesque little fishing port at Baleeira, the large Hotel da Baleeira has 120 rooms, each with a balcony overlooking the ocean. Both the rooms and common areas are simple, with a classic touch. The grounds have a pool and tennis court. The staff is friendly and smiling.

Good value for the money.

Pousada do Infante
$$$$
pb, tv, ≈, ℜ
2 km from Sagres; Vila do Bispo 8650
☎*282 64 42 22*
⁼*282 62 42 25*
Near the tip of Sagres, where the illustrious Henry the Navigator established his famous school, is the Pousada do Infante. The building was built in the 1960s but looks very modern; it has 39 rooms, the majority with balconies and inspiring views of the ocean and cliffs. The furniture is outmoded and could use freshening up. The warm, all-wood bar gives you the impression of being inside a ship; the lounge has interesting period furniture and a beautiful wall tapestry. A large pool and a tennis court are at guests' disposal. A quiet, welcome respite from overcrowded resorts.

Martinhal

(7km from Sagres)

Os Gambozinos
$$-$$$ to 12,000 ESC
ps, K, ℜ
follow the signs to Quinta do Martinhal and drive to the end of the road; Praia da Martinhal Vila do Bispo 8650
☎*282 62 43 18*
⁼*282 62 42 48*
For blessed isolation there's nothing quite like the Os Gambozinos hotel, very close to the Martinhal beach, popular with

surfers. Because this area is quite isolated with few services nearby, a car is essential. Credit cards are not accepted.

Silves

Quinta do Rio
$$
pb
from the centre of Silves, take Hwy. N124 toward S. Bartolomeu de Messines and, then approx. 4km after the bridge, take the road to the left toward Santo Estevão; Sitio Santa Estevão, Apt. 217 Silves 8300
☎/⇆*282 44 55 28*
To enjoy of the great outdoors, travellers will opt for the Quinta do Rio. Orange trees abound in these particularly pretty surroundings. The charming Italian-born owners Luisa and Roberto warmly greet visitors to their establishment. Each of the six rooms is simply but tastefully decorated, and all have views of the surrounding countryside. On request, Luisa will prepare a delicious Italian dinner for around 3,000 ESC. The setting is quiet and rural, near the ocean, and close to several tourist centres. One of the region's best addresses!

Ilha de Tavira

Parque de Campismo da Ilha de Tavira
Ilha de Tavira
8800 Tavira
☎*281 32 44 55*
⇆*281 32 47 52*

Pensão Residencial Princesa do Gilão
$$
pb
Rua Borda de Água de Aguiar n° 10-12
☎*281 32 51 71*
☎*281 32 51 72*
Located inside the tallest building on the street, the *pension* Princesa do Gilão has small rooms that are modestly equipped, newly renovated and well kept. The decor of the rooms and the dining room where breakfast is served lacks charm. However, the front rooms have a lovely view of the Rio Gilão and the charming, palm-tree-lined Rua dos Cais.

Vila Real de Santo António

Pousada de Juventude
Rua Dr. Sousa Martins no. 40, 8900 Vila Real de Santo António
☎/⇆*281 54 45 65*

Hotel Guadiana
$$$
pb, tv, ℜ
Av. da República n°s 94-96
8900 Vila Real de Santo António
☎*281 51 14 82*
☎*281 51 14 92*
⇆*281 51 14 78*
Located inside a beautiful *belle-époque*-style building, Hotel Guadiana deserves mention mainly for its period architecture. The rooms are decent and relatively comfortable but not luxurious. The sumptuously decorated lobby is worth a look even if you are not staying at the hotel.

Restaurants

Albufeira

Rei do Petisco
$
Rua 5 de Outubre 84
A whimsical set of stairs leads patrons to O Rei do Petisco on the second floor of a winsome little house in the city core. The menu puts an emphasis on sardines, salads, and potatoes, starting at 1,200 ESC.

Restaurante Cave Vinho do Porto
$$$
Rua da Liberdade n° 23
☎*58 91 44*
Moussaka and spaghetti carbonara for 1,250 ESC or Hungarian goulash and tuna steak for 1,350 ESC? Now here's a good place for a little change! What's more, the portions are large and some vegetarian dishes are available. Whether you dine on the terrace on the pedestrian street or in the lovely vaulted dining room decorated with rustic wood and porto bottles, you will

be served by a friendly, smiling staff.

Restaurante Bizarro
$

Rua Latino Coelho 30
Somewhat off the beaten path, Restaurante Bizarro is ideal for a light meal or just a drink. On the menu: croque-monsieur, hamburgers, and other snacks at very reasonable prices. Wood banquettes and straw chairs add to the warm ambience. Guests can enjoy the view from the pretty terrace.

Il Bolero
$$

near the Praia dos Barcos, Cais Herculano 31
For a change of pace from traditional Portuguese fare, try Il Bolero, a Mexican restaurant located near the pleasant Dos Barcos beach. In a "Tex-Mex" setting, vegetarian tacos and burritos are served for 1,390 ESC.

O Dias
$$

closed Wed
12:30pm to 2:30pm and 6:30pm to 10:30pm
Praça Miguel Bombarda 2
☎289 51 52 46
O Dias, located in the middle of Albufeira, serves meat and fish (tuna steaks) either in the typically Portuguese-decorated dining room, or on the terrace with a wide view of the ocean.

Restaurante Atrium
$$
kitchen open from 6:30pm
Rua 5 de Outubro 20, 2nd floor
☎289 51 57 55
From its stuccoed, gilded quarters in what was once Albufeira's theatre, Restaurante Atrium specializes in traditional Portuguese cuisine but also offers such dishes as beef Stroganoff. Prices start at 2,600 ESC. Live bands perform some evenings.

Restaurante A Ruina
$$$
across from the Praia dos Barcos, Cais Herculano
☎289 51 20 94
For dinner in a rustic atmosphere complete with wood panelling, try the Restaurante A Ruina. Specialties: Portuguese fare with a preference for seafood and fish, everything served in an imposing stone house on the beach.

Praia da Galé

(7km from Albufeira)

Viveiros da Galé
$$
noon to 3pm and 7pm to 10pm
7km from Albufeira, on the left side of the road to Pêra; Estrada de Vale de Parra, Vale Rabelho Galé
☎249 59 18 27
Seafood and fish lovers will converge on the Viveiros da Galé, where a lovely terrace with a view of the fields and the sea await. A fish-tank in the establishment ensures a fresh

catch. A full meal with wine starts at 1,990 ESC.

Vila Joya
$$$$$
closed mid-Nov to mid-Dec and mid-Jan to mid-Feb
on the road from Albufeira to Pêra, from Vale de Parra head to Praia de Galé; Praia de Galé
☎249 59 17 95
Gourmet-food lovers should not miss the chance to dine at the restaurant at the Vila Joya hotel. With the Austrian chef Dieter Koschina at the helm, this restaurant might just be the best in the Algarve and rivals the finest Lisbon has to offer. A few mouth-watering examples: an entrée of shrimp accompanied by a ragoût of avocado and tomatoes; a chicken salad with lentils, or a creamy pumpkin soup. Main dishes include the fresh catch of the day – occasionally prepared in unusual ways, with horseradish or beets; a Knödeln-style fillet of beef with fine herbs; or a tender strip of veal served with fresh pasta. For dessert: scrumptious crepes filled with passion fruit, or house sherbets. A good selection of wines is on hand to wash down each unforgettable morsel. To ensure product quality and freshness, the restaurant changes its menu every day. A warm decor (see p 436) with brick archways, candlelight, classical music and impeccable service make this one

of the more pleasurable eating experiences on the coast. Reservations mandatory (minimum one day in advance); evening attire required. Credit cards are, unfortunately, not accepted.

Olhos de Água

(8km from Albufeira)

O Caixote
$$

Mon to Fri noon to 3pm and 6:30pm to 10:30pm
Praia Olho de Água
O Caixote serves reasonably priced sardines, tuna or swordfish either in its simply decorated dining room, or on its little terrace facing fishing boats. For smaller appetites, tuna salad and omelets are also available.

La Cigale
$$$$

Mon to Fri noon to 3pm and 6:30 to 10:30
Praia Olho de Água
☎50 16 37
Despite its French name, this restaurant does not serve French cuisine but rather fish and seafood. With its amusing facade covered with vibrantly coloured *azulejos*, La Cigale serves tuna, swordfish, crab, muscles, and other seafood dishes including the usual *bacalhau*. The dining room, with traditionally set tables, affords a view of the rocky oceanside.

Unfortunately, the excess of neon lighting detracts some charm from its warm ambiance. Despite this and time permitting, you can dine on its large, more tastefully decorated terrace, where you can get a view of the beach and its lovely cliffs in the distance. A little expensive but a good place for a formal, quality meal. Tourist menu for 4,2000 ESC.

Armação de Pêra

(18km from Albufeira)

A Fortaleza
$
oceanfront, to the left in the curve just after the fortress ruins
For a quick snack (salads, burgers, sandwiches) or a pizza with all the toppings, A Fortaleza proposes its pleasant, leafy terrace just a short walk from the ocean. Pizzas start at 650 ESC.

Grill-Hotel Garbe
$$
open from 1pm to 2:30pm and 7:30pm to 9:30pm
Avenida Beira Mar
☎282 31 51 87
The Grill-Hotel Garbe is an enjoyable restaurant inside a modern hotel facing a stretch of beach. The view from the dining room (sea and cliffs) is a feast for the eyes. Great atmosphere during the high season. No credit cards accepted.

Restaurante Santola
$$$
noon to 3pm and 6pm to 11pm
Largo da Fortaleza, oceanfront on Rua M. Gregorio, across from the fortress ruins; Largo da Fortaleza
☎282 31 23 32
If you like intimate settings with a view of the countryside, as well as a fireplace, Restaurante Santola serves seafood and fish prepared in the Portuguese style. And if you like to eat outdoors, this restaurant has a tiny terrace with several tables where you can dine facing the ocean.

Vilalara
$$$$
from Armação de Pêra, take the N269-1 toward Porches; directions to the hotel on the left-hand side of the highway
☎282 31 49 10
Set in a magnificent, lush estate (see p 437), the restaurant in the Vilalara hotel is an idyllic spot. Under the soft light of the dining room's molten glass chandeliers, patrons savour exquisite dishes complemented by various vegetables. For appetizers, a porto-laced terrine of partridge or a smoked swordfish de Sesimbra, followed by roasted *piri-piri* cockerel or tender fillet of bass flambéed in Pernod; to finish off these savoury suggestions is an excellent Black Forest cake with tropical fruit. Sublime! As long as they reserve in advance, waist-watchers can order a diet menu. The

establishment has direct access to the beach where, during the high season, guests can feast on grilled sardines or chicken while admiring the view of the cliff-lined coast. A terrace with a pool and an ocean-view is also an ideal spot for a pre-dinner drink.

Caldas de Monchique

(5km from Monchique)

Restaurante Pensão Central
$$
heading north, shortly after Montinho, take the road to the left of the N266
☎ *282 91 22 03*
Located in a scenic valley, Restaurante Pensão Central serves good, home-style Portuguese cooking in an undeniably rustic set-ting. A high, wood ceiling painted a pale green, a crystal chande-lier, antique furniture, flowers and candles on the table – a setting for hopeless romantics! The little outdoor ter-race is lush with green-ery and enjoys the shade of an imposing cork oak. With a little luck, the resident Siamese cat will come around and greet guests. All in all, a lovely, friendly place.

Faro

Cervejaria Baía
$
closed Sun
Largo Dr. Silva Nobre 7
☎ *289 82 28 45*
The Cervejaria Baía is located on an agreeable little plaza; it serves a selection of traditional Portuguese dishes at very affordable prices.

Café-Restaurante Pastelaria Chelsea
$
Rua D. Francisco Gomes 30
This contemporary, tasteful, and unpre-tentious café-restaurant boasts a wide choice of salads, along with pizzas, omelettes and a daily special starting at 900 ESC. For a more intimate dinner, eat in the dining room on the first floor, where the decor is warmer and the lighting dimmer.

Dois Irmãos
$$
every day 10am to 3:30pm and 6pm to 11pm
Largo Terreiro de Bispo 14
☎ *289 82 33 37*
A convivial atmosphere reigns at Dois Irmãos. Fish and meat-based Portuguese menu start-ing at 1,500 ESC.

Cidade Velha
$$$
closed Sun and Mon to Fri at noon
Rua Domingos Guieiro 19
☎ *289 82 71 45*
Located in the charm-ing inner city beside the Sé, the Cidade Velha restaurant spe-cializes in classic Portu-

guese cooking in a luxurious and very pleasant dining room.

Cafés and Tearooms

Pastelaria Gardy
Rua de Santo António 16
For a coffee or a good pastry, try Pastelaria Gardy, located on a very busy commercial street.

Délifrance
$
Av. 25 de Outobro
For baguette and crois-sant lovers, Délifrance has opened a café-pastry shop where you can have a French-style breakfast or just an excellent espresso with a small pastry. Sand-wiches and salads are also offered at reason-able prices.

Almancil

Pequeno Mundo
$$$$$
from Almancil, take the N125 west to the little village of Pereiras; Pereiras
☎ *289 39 98 66*
About one kilometre from Almancil, Pequeno Mundo is an elegant restaurant where fresh vegetables and herbs are given a place of honour. Partic-ular care is taken with the presentation of dishes. Along with a dining room painted in warm ochre shades to offset the handsome Portuguese furnishings, there is a lovely terrace with plenty of flower-ing plants – perfect for a romantic candlelight

dinner. The pre-dinner drink can be enjoyed in the bar, which was constructed around an old church altar! Reservations recommended. Appropriate attire expected. Excellent list of Portuguese wines. Good value for the money.

Pereiras

(2km from Almancil)

Restaurante Aquarelle
$$$$
Mon to Sat noon to 3pm and 7pm to 11pm
Estrada Vale do Lobo
Caminho Pereiras
☎ *289 39 79 73*
Located inside a stunning hexagon-shaped house with a modest but pleasant décor, Aquarelle will satisfy fine diners in search of French cuisine. Among the entrees, why not try the squab salad with pine nuts and honey, the marinated salmon with herbs or the country-style terrine with armagnac? Everything is prepared with love. For the main course, try the bass filet with candied lemon, the loin of lamb with fresh mint, or the doe filet with currant sauce. For dessert, the restaurant gives you sure value with the traditional Tatin pie and crepes Suzette. There is a terrace in a lovely adjoining garden open on sunny days. The only flaws are that the road is too close (but not that busy) and the prices are too high.

Santa Bárbara de Nexe

Hotel La Réserve
$$$$$
on the way from Esteval to Santa Bárbara de Nexe, right side of the road just before Santa Bárbara de Nexe
☎ *289 99 92 34*
Gourmets will make a beeline for the restaurant in Hotel La Réserve. Sauteed tarragon chicken, braised quail in sherry cream, and Atlantic *carabineiros* fish on a bed of saffron rice with truffles are just a few examples of what awaits guests. To tempt your sweet tooth, desserts run along the lines of crêpes Suzette, Sabayon, or a mousse. The only flaw in this gastronomic experience: no credit cards are accepted.

Quarteira

Natraj
$$
Mar to Dec, noon to 3pm and 6pm to midnight
near Quarteira on the left side of the road to Almancil, just after the Vilamoura exit, Estrada de Almancil
☎ *289 32 17 61*
Indian cuisine is featured at Natraj. This excellent little restaurant specializes in tandoori. Complete lunch menu, including a beverage, starting at 1,500 ESC. Avoid the desserts, however – they are too expensive and quite ordinary.

Vilamoura

Restaurante Estalagem de Cegonha
$$
closed Jan
Centro Hipico de Vilamoura
☎ *289 30 25 77*
Located on the outskirts of Vilamoura (follow the signs for Quinta da Quarteira), this restaurant is housed in a country home that is part of a reputed equestrian centre. Authentic Portuguese fare is served in this countrified setting; menu with wine starting at 2,700 ESC. A fine place to escape from the resort crowds!

São Brás de Alportel

Pousada de São Brás
$$$
at the side of the N2, 2 km north of São Brás de Alportel
8150 São Brás de Alportel
☎ *289 84 23 05*
☎ *289 84 23 06*
Set in the heart of a beautiful, gleaming white villa, the restaurant of the Pousada de São Brás is a pleasant alternative for those who want to escape the overcrowded, noisy resort towns of Algarve. Located in the back country, fewer than 30km from the coast, this establishment provides a peaceful, bucolic setting in which diners can replenish themselves. As for the decor, the shrewd use of small bamboo furniture pieces pleasantly tinges the rather opu-

The Algarve

lent regional decor with exoticism. Among the specialties offered, *cataplana de peixe com amêijoas* (a dish of clams and fish) and *trutas à Algarvia* (Algarve-style trout) deserve special mention.

Lagos

Piri-Piri
$-$$
Rua Agonso de Almeida 15, corner of Lima Leitão
☎282 76 38 03
For cheap eats, head to Piri-Piri, where a full meal – soup, omelette, fish or meat dish, dessert – is only 1,500 ESC. More fancier meals (at higher prices) are also served.

Snack Bar Regional
$
Rua Dom Vasco de Gama 15
☎282 76 37 08
The vegetarian menu, with a non-alcoholic beverage, starts at 1,300 ESC.

Pizzeria Mama Mia
$$
Rua Portas de Portugal nº 41
☎76 22 31
Mama Mia is not known for its very ordinary decor but for its excellent homemade pizzas. The menu is good, reasonably priced and extensive, and you will definitely find something you like, which you can enjoy with a glass of red wine. For a livelier ambiance, there is a large terrace facing the busy pedestrian street.

Os Arcos
$$
Rua 25 de Abril 32
Chicken, octopus and swordfish appear regularly on the menu at Os Arcos, in the large dining room decorated with wine bottles.

Don Sebastião
$$$$
noon to 3pm and 6:30pm to 10pm
Rua 25 de Abril nº 20-22
☎76-27-95
Drowned in a flood of restaurants on a commercial street, Don Sebastião serves classic Portuguese cuisine. Seated in the warmly decorated dining room with the most traditional of table settings, you can delight in fish and seafood dishes, also traditionally prepared. An excellent tuna steak with onion sauce, as well as shrimps, oysters, crabs, lobsters and scallops, make up the bulk of the extensive menu. Not the most original cuisine, but sure value for the money.

Cafés and Tearooms

Xpreitaqui
9am to 2am
Rua Silvas Lopes no. 14
☎76-27-58
Looking for a lively and relaxing place to have a *bica* or *cerveja*? Café Xpreitaqui is it. It has an original decor with small glass tables through which grains are visible and large jute coffee sacks

lying around. If your hunger is biting, you'll be glad to know that this place also serves cheap food: daily soup for 200 ESC, vegetarian quiche for 450 ESC and a salad for 500 ESC. What a deal! Friendly, smiling staff.

Praia Porto de Mós

(3km from Lagos)

O António
$$$
Praia Porto de Mós, west of the beach
☎282 76 35 60
After walking along the pleasant beach of Porto de Mós, why not give into temptation and try some of its succulent seafood? O António prepares cod, tuna, sardines, crab and other seafood dishes made from the catch of the day and served on the terrace or inside the long-windowed dining room where the decor is mostly provided by the wide view of the ocean. Everything is traditionally made and as fresh as can be. A good place to keep in mind!

Praia da Luz

(6km from Lagos)

Panini Pizzeria
$
Rua Direita 2
When budgets are tight and the urge for a pizza or a big plate of French fries strikes, Panini Pizzeria is the place to go. Pasta plates start at 780 ESC and pizzas at 650 ESC. The restau-

rant's tile-work and high ceiling give it an open, airy feeling.

Restaurante da Fortaleza
$$$
near the church
Rua da Igreja 3
☎ *282 78 99 26*
Set by the seaside, Restaurante da Fortaleza is housed in an old fortress with brick walls and arches. Swordfish, salmon, and prawns are just a few of the fish and seafood dishes prepared by the chef. Those who prefer meats can savour the excellent pepper steak. The delightful terrace is pleasant and a superb vantage point from which to admire the sea and sip a drink. Friendly service; good quality for the price.

Monchique

Estalagem Abrigo da Montanha
$$$
Estrada da Fóia, 2km from Monchique
☎ *282 91 21 31*
Set in a mountainous landscape with a panorama of the Serra de Monchique, the Estalagem Abrigo da Montanha restaurant serves excellent Portuguese cuisine in a warm atmosphere. Cork ceiling, authentic wood chandeliers, tiles and brick walls set the tone. Complete menu starts at 2,500 ESC. Ideal for a hearty meal after an invigorating walk in the fresh air. The terrace, encircled by lovingly tended

gardens, is a delightful spot for a drink.

Olhão

A Varanda
$
Rua do Comércio no. 121 or Praça da Restauração no. 19
☎ *70 51 82*
Located on the ground floor of a small shopping centre, the modest little A Varanda has two dining rooms back to back. One has a television and the other a kitchen, and each only has four or five tables. The restaurant is mostly frequented by locals. The specialty here, besides the obvious fish and seafood, including swordfish and shrimp and rice, is the *feijoada* with rib steak. The decor is a bit old, especially the smoky furniture, but the welcome is friendly and smiling. From the *açoteia* (small roof-terrace) overlooking the Praça da Restauração, you can have a glass of wine or dinner while admiring the baroque facade of Igreja Matriz.

Café Comercial
$
Rua do Comércio, between no. 104 and no. 114
For a change from the innumerable restaurants serving fish and seafood, the Café Comercial serves reasonably priced hamburgers, sandwiches and salads in a pleasant and resolutely modern decor.

Snack Bar Rio Formosa
$$
in the centre of the Jardim Pescador Olhanense
The Snack Bar Rio Formosa has two good things going for it: large portions of fish and seafood and a strategic location on the seawall, away from the succession of restaurants on Avenida 5 de Outubro. Though it is not attractive from the outside, the interior decor is relatively pleasant and mostly made up of *azulejos*, warm wood chairs and quaint tablesettings. There is also a large terrace beside the restaurant. For something different, try the good *Arroz de Pato* (rice and duck).

Portimão

Cervejaria Carvi
$$
Wed to Mon noon to midnight
Rua Direita 34 at Rua João Annes
☎ *282 41 79 12*
Quality Portuguese cooking is the leitmotif at the Cervejaria Carvi, where the clientele is mainly made up of locals. The delicious *açorda* of shrimp is a must. Menu starting at 1,700 ESC. Professional, attentive service.

Cafés and Tearooms

Casa Inglesa
every day from 11am to 9:30pm
Praça Manuel Teixeira Gomes
Casa Inglesa is located in a small square across

from a park. This shop displays a good selection of pastries that clients can eat inside (in the modern and very elegant dining room) or out on the terrace. There is also a daily menu starting at 1,600 ESC.

Praia da Rocha

(2km from Portimão)

Dona Barca
$
Av. Tomás Cabreira, opposite the Oriental hotel
By walking on the very touristy Avenida Tomás Cabreira, which is lined with numerous restaurants, you will probably be drawn to Dona Barca, a small restaurant and one of the few to have wooden tables and chairs instead of that despicable plastic furniture that seems to be on every terrace in the country. Beside this excellent example, the decor of the indoor dining room is most original with old pictures of the Praia da Rocha (Oh! The good old days!), as well as several old radios used as decorations. The place isn't known for its food, but it offers several simple dishes such as *bifana*, *prego*, or even a copious tuna salad. For small eaters, sandwhiches and toasted ham-and-cheese sandwiches are also on the menu. Last but not least, the service is friendly and Portuguese music is usually playing.

Restaurante Central
$$
near Rua Antonio Feu, facing the Bela Vista hotel; Avenida Tomás Cabreira
☎ *282 42 41 85*
Among the many restaurants at Praia da Rocha is Restaurante Central, worth a detour for its affordable prices and pleasant atmosphere. The Portuguese and international cuisine is fairly standard but quite good. Menu starting at 2,150 ESC; the spaghetti with shrimp, however, is just 950 ESC.

La Capanina-Chez Benny
$$
Av. Tomás Cabreira
☎ *282 48 32 24*
If you're craving a pizza, head to the pretty terrace at La Capanina-Chez Benny, where you can enjoy one with a glass of wine under a roof full of plants. There are also other Italian dishes on the menu.

Ao Mar
$$$
Rocha dos Castelos, Praia do Vau
at the western end of Tomás Cabreira
☎ *41 39 83*
Located inside a cute little house with small blue shutters that contrast well with the bright white walls, Ao Mar is worth the trip. Whether eating in its modern dining room or on its large terrace, you will get a superb view of Praia do Vau and the shimmering rocks strewn along the coast. The restaurant is even

more pleasant because, despite being frequented by tourists, it is located far from noisy Avenida Tomás Cabreira. The food is decent but isn't as original as the warm decor. The menu is limited to standard fish dishes or international dishes like spaghetti and steak. The food may be basic, but check out the view!

Falésia
$$$
closed Jan
Avenida Tomás Cabreira
☎ *282 42 35 24*
Situated at the western end of the beach, beside a cliff, the restaurant Falésia serves Portuguese dishes in a dining room with a predominently *azulejo* decor. An inviting terrace provides a superb view of the ocean and cliffs.

Fortaleza de Santa Catarina
$$$
east end of Av. Tomás Cabreira in the fortress
☎ *42 20 66*
To escape from the concrete buildings – but not the crowds – head to the large terrace at the Fortaleza de Santa Catarina de Ribamar, a fortress built in the 17th century to protect Portimão. The menu doesn't sparkle with originality nor does it offer anything other than classic Portuguese cuisine, but the tourist menu for 3,000 ESC is a decent choice, especially since the whole thrill of dining here is to admire

the fort and the magnificent view of the ocean.

Praia do Carvoiero

(13km from Portimão)

Restaurante Antonia-Bar Lanterna Velha
$$$
on the right side of the main road that goes to the beach
The menu of this restaurant should satisfy many because of its wide selection of dishes including chicken *piripiri* (a spicy red-pepper sauce), steak with Mexican sauce, German sausages and vegetarian dishes. The decor is as varied as the menu and you can dine in the bar-room, which is mostly decorated with large wooden objects, or on the terrace, located below the villa. Obviously, it is more pleasant to dine on the terrace sheltered from the sun and the heat by shady trees. Very popular with German tourists.

Sagres

A Tasca
$$
Praia da Baleeira, in the port itself
☎ *282 62 41 77*
Located in the picturesque little fishing port of Baleeira, A Tasca puts visitors in "down-by-the-sea" surroundings with its decorative shells and bottles. The cuisine is Portuguese, with an emphasis on fish and seafood.

Fortaleza do Beliche
$$$
closed Dec and Jan
located on the left of the highway from Sagres to Cabo de São Vicente
☎ *282 62 41 24*
Perched near the edge of a cliff in a former fortress, the hotel restaurant Fortaleza do Beliche serves good, if fairly predictable, Portuguese fare in a very pleasant dining room. The hotel itself is set in particularly beautiful surroundings.

Pousada do Infante
$$$
2km from Sagres
☎ *282 62 42 22*
⇆ *282 62 42 25*
Across from the Sagres point is Pousada do Infante, whose chef prepares good Portuguese cuisine. The interior design is accented by *azulejos*, while the inviting bar, warmly appointed with wood, resembles a ship's cabin. The lounge is done up in interesting period furniture and has an intriguing wall tapestry. Patrons can dine on the large terrace with an ocean-view in nice weather. Good value for the price.

Silves

Café Inglês
$
Sun to Fri 10am to midnight, winter until 5:30pm
behind the Sé; Escadas do Castelo
☎ *282 44 25 85*
A very enjoyable setting for a glass of freshly squeezed orange juice, a small dish of pasta with salad and bread (*600 ESC*), or a meal from the daily menu (*1,500 ESC*). Wood floors, gilded mirrors, plenty of plants and artfully sculpted shutters are just some elements of the attractive decor. A pretty little garden and a rooftop terrace add to the charm. In a departure from the traditional egg-based desserts, this restaurant serves English desserts such as cheesecake and brownies. A real find!

Casa Velha
$$
Mon to Sat noon to 4pm and 7pm to midnight
Rua 25 de Abril 11
☎ *282 44 54 91*
Simple but pleasant, Casa Velha specializes in fish dishes. And when the urge for red meat strikes, a Casa Velha steak will hit the spot.

Ú Monchiqueiro
$$
near the old bridge, facing the river, Mercado Municipal
☎ *282 44 21 42*
Grilled fish and meats are the products of choice at Ú

Monchiqueiro. The food is simple but the servings are generous enough to satisfy hearty appetites. From the terrace, you can admire the view of the Arade River and its old bridge.

Cafés and Tearooms

Café Rosa

on the Praça do Município under the arches below the Câmara Municipal
This charming little café is worth a detour for its rococo interior decor featuring *azulejos*, marble-topped tables, and stylish metal chairs. Light meals available.

Barragem do Arade

(10km from Silves)

Restaurante Coutada
$$
Mon to Sun 11am to 11pm
Barragem do Arade
3km from the intersection with the N124
☎ *282 33 22 92*
It is up on a hill next to the large Do Arade dam that you will find the beautiful Restaurante Coutada, located inside a villa. Its large shaded terrace with picnic tables not only welcomes tourists but also many animals. Parakeets, guinea pigs, quails and exotic parrots can be observed inside cages, safe from the cats and dogs that will also keep you company. Beside the presence of these adorable but noisy animals, you can get a pan-

oramic view of the lovely valley down below, or of the many orange trees. The interior decor is so eccentric that it is worth a look. Besides the plush red couches that look like they are from another century and a small room that serves as a dance floor, there is also a whole hodge-podge of other decorative objects, notably a collection of elephants of all sizes. The tourist menu goes for 1,900 ESC and the regular menu features *achega da barragem*, a fish from the reservoir (behind the dam), turkey or even simple ribs served with salad. Despite the slow service, this is a pleasant place, especially the road that winds its way there, on which you can take in some fantastic scenery.

Tavira

Pastelaria Tavira Romana
$
Praça da República no. 24 to no. 26
☎ *32 34 51*
Located near the roman bridge that spans the Rio Gilão, this modern pastry shop offers several daily specials *(600 to 800 ESC)*, as well as a wide choice of sandwiches *(400 ESC)* for less. Because the dining room is completely glassed-in, you can watch the passersby on the Praça da República while eating a *bacalhau* (cod) fritter, a good starter. Don't miss out on the

many Portuguese deserts available here.

Restaurante Patio
$$$
Rua Dr António Cabreira no. 30
☎ *281 32 30 08*
Located on the second floor of a cute house with a little terrace from which you can see the roofs of Tavira, the Patio is mostly frequented by tourists during the high season. Though its decor is a tad kitsch, the menu is in several languages and offers a variety of tempting dishes such as Périgourdine chicken or chicken with almonds. If, however, you prefer fish, make sure to try the fried calamari, or the local specialty, tuna steak with onions. The only downside is the price.

Ponto de Encontra
$$
Corner of Praça Dr. Padinha and Rua Almirante Cândido dos Reis
☎ *281 32 37 30*
Facing the lovely Praça Dr. Padinha, this restaurant serves reasonably priced classic Portuguese cuisine in an elegant decor. An ideal place for a romantic evening, or, as its name suggests ("meeting place") to meet someone!

Dong Cheng
$
everyday noon to 3pm and 6:30 to 11pm
Praça Dr. Padinha no. 14
Like most Chinese restaurants, Dong Cheng offers a wide choice of dishes from classic

sweet-and-sour chicken to the famous Peking duck, sautéed noodles and fried rice subtly flavoured with soya sauce. For tighter budgets, the restaurant makes a daily special including a drink for 895 ESC. Nothing special, but a good change from the local cuisine.

Entertainment

Albufeira

Taberna da Sangria
every day from 5pm to 2am
Rua Joaquim M. de Mendonça Gouveia 11
A pleasant place to relax with a cool drink. Mellow atmosphere with African music playing in the background.

Café Gémaux
Rua Coronel Aguas 20, or Rua Cândido dos Reis
A friendly little bar.

JC Bar
Avenida 25 de Abril
Cocktails, anyone? Be sure to stop in at JC Bar, where a wide array of cocktails is served in a cosy atmosphere.

Café Latino
Rua Latino Coelho 61
A modern style, friendly atmosphere, and great view of the sea await visitors at Café Latino for a drink or a cup of coffee. Light meals.

Bar Snoopy
Beco D. Cao, near Rua S. Gonçalo de Lagos
A hot spot for young people from Portugal and abroad.

Faro

Taverna da Sé
Praça Afonso III 26
Established in the charming inner city, Taverna da Sé is a good choice for refreshment and relaxation.

Mesa dos Mouros
$$
Largo da Sé, south side
☎289 87 88 73
Located inside a narrow room, this bar-restaurant only has a few tables facing a modern counter. Its location next to the cathedral, its warm decor and the owners' friendly reception make it a pleasant place to have a *cerveja* with tapas on the side or lights dishes (omelettes, hamburgers, ribs, etc.).

Vilamoura

(*21km from Faro*)

Disco Kadoc
6pm to 7am
near the Estalagem da Cegonha on the road to Albufeira
The immense Disco Kadoc has eight bars – five indoor, three outdoor – and has become the most popular dance club in the region. A colourful mix of trendy types, from gays to rockers, rub elbows until the wee hours in a pulsing, electrifying

atmosphere. Night owls, this is an address to remember!

Lagos

Bar Vitaminas
9:30pm to 2am
Rua 25 de Abril 103
For a quiet drink in a relaxed setting.

Bar Bon Vivant
closed winter
Rua 25 de Abril 105, corner Rua da Silva Lopes and Rua Soeiro de Costa
Inviting rooftop terrace.

Phoenix Disco Bar
Rua de São Gonçalo 29
To dance the night away until the wee hours, head to Phoenix Disco Bar. Energy-charged atmosphere and jam-packed dance floor.

Pandora Box
Rua da Vedoria no. 4
ou Rua Silva Lopes no. 5
With its dining room that is so long it has two entrances on two different streets, its wooden counter and several tables, this small bar is a friendly place where beer on tap costs only 150 ESC. A real deal! Most of the clientele is young. You can watch the latest North American and European TV shows here. "Happy Hour" from 6pm to 11pm.

Mullens
noon to 2am
Rua Cândido dos Reis no. 86
Located inside a former cellar with casks of wine, Mullens bar is worth a visit for its

rustic and original decor. You can sit at the large wooden tables with benches and have a beer or another drink while observing the large barrels of wine placed here and there for decoration. Chandeliers make the place even warmer; the dim lighting creates a convivial atmosphere.

Gay Bars

Last Resort Cocktail Bar
11pm to 2am
Rua Lançarote Freitas n° 30-A
Gay friends meet for a beer at the Last Resort Cocktail Bar, where, as its name suggests, they can try one of the many cocktails available in an atmosphere of good cheer.

Praia da Rocha

(*2km from Portimão*)

Pipa's Bar
Cheer's Pub
Pé-de-Vento
Av. Tomás Cabreira
All along the very touristy Avenida Tomás Cabreira, there are many different bars that will satisfy any taste. Among them, Pipa's Bar and nearby Cheer's Pub, are the most pleasant places for a drink in a casual atmosphere. Unfortunately, you may not hear any Portuguese tunes here since most of the music on this avenue is in English.

For those who want to get down to the latest tunes, there are two danceclubs on the same strip: **Pé-de-Vento** has an inviting terrace and **Katedral** welcomes the "beautiful people". Both are open until the wee hours of the morning.

Hotel Bela Vista
oceanfront, near Avenida Dom Afonso Henriques; Avenida Tomás Cabreira
Located by the sea in an appealing turn-of-the-century home, the bar of the Hotel Bela Vista is a very pleasant place for a pre-dinner drink or a coffee. Two features alone are worth a visit to this establishment: the superb staircase, with fine examples of *azulejos* on either side, which leads to the upstairs rooms; and the ceiling of the lobby, a study in elegance. On weekends during the high season, a pianist entertains guests. The only element that clashes is the too-modern, garishly furnished terrace; it mars the effect of the hotel's charming bar and lounge.

Olhão

Mastro Bar
every day 4pm to 4am
Av. 5 de Outubro, on the seawall side of the building housing the vegetable market
At this bar, which is decorated with old sea charts on its walls and elegant wood furniture, you can have a *cerveja* accompanied by several *acepipes* (snacks). You can also get a good view of the seawall and the ocean from the large windows, some of which are decorated with tarpaulins.

Shopping

Albufeira

The city has stores and boutiques selling every conceivable item, many of which are, unfortunately, very ugly. With the vast number of shops, however, visitors are sure to find whatever they need, from the most basic to the most luxurious products. Albufeira also has two big shopping malls. One store that deserves mention for its choice of interesting and tasteful objects is the **pottery boutique** (*Mon to Fri 9am to 7pm, Sat 9am to 1pm; Rua de 5 de Outubro 53*).

Glossary

Anyone with a smattering of Spanish or French should not have too much difficulty pronouncing Portuguese. This little pronunciation guide should help with some of the exceptions.

One of the major considerations in Portuguese is the use of the diphthong, which is two vowels pronounced as a single vowel sound. For example toy in English is an *o* with a weak *i* sound. In Portuguese *ai* is like fly, *au* is like bow; in other cases weak vowels combine and are occasionally pronounced nasally, for example informação which is pronounced "infourmasaong." Generally, however it is not easy to predict Portuguese diphthongs.

Consonants are pronounced as in English, except the following exceptions:

c	before *a*, *o*, *u*, is hard like *k* in king; *casa* is pronounced "kahza"
	before *i* and *e*, it is soft; *cebola* is pronounced "saybola"
ç	the use of the cedilla (˛) softens the *c*, like *s* in soft; *praça* is pronounced "prassa"
ch	is soft like *sh* in shout; *chamar* is pronounced "shamahr"
g	before *a*, *o*, *u* is hard like *g* in gut; *gata* is pronounced "gata"
	before *e* and *i*, it is soft like *s* in leisure; *giro* is pronounced "zheero"
h	is always silent; *hora* is pronounced "ora"
j	like *s* in leisure; *azulejo* is pronounced "azulezho"
lh	like *lli* in trillion; *olho* is pronounced "olliyoo"
n	when at the beginning or between vowels like *n* in not; *nove* is pronounced "novay"
	with other consonants or in a plural ending, the preceding vowel becomes nasal and the *n* softens; *branco* is pronounced "brahngkoo"
nh	like *ni* in onion; *vinho* is pronounced "vinyoo"
q	like *k* in king; *querer* is pronounced "kerrayr"
r	rolled like in French
s	when at the beginning or after a consonant, like *s* in soft
	at the end of a word or before *c*, *f*, *p*, *q* and *t* like *sh* in shout; *país* is pronounced "pahyish" and *pescador* is pronounced "peshcador"
x	generally like *sh* in shout; *baixa* is pronounced "bighsha"

z   at the end of a word or before c, f, p, q, s and t like sh in shout; *feliz* is pronounced "fehleesh"

elsewhere like s in leisure; *luz da* is pronounced "loozh dah"

Vowels are pronounced as in English, with the following exceptions:

a   like the second and third a in bazaar; *nado* is pronounced "nahdo"

e   when stressed and before a weak consonant, like e in get; *perto* is pronounced "pehrto"

when stressed and before a strong consonant, like a in cake; *cabelo* is pronounced "kahbaylo"

when unstressed like e in father; *pesado* is pronounced "pehzahdo"

é   like e in get; *café* is pronounced "cafeh"

ê   like a in cake; *pêra* is pronounced "payrah"

i   when stressed, like i in rice; *riso* is pronounced "reezo"

when unstressed like i in give; *final* is pronounced "finnahl"

u   like oo in soon; *número* is pronounced "noomerro"

silent in qu and gu before e and i; *aqui* is pronounced "ahkee"

GREETINGS

Good Morning	bom dia
How are you?	como está?
I am fine	muito bem
Good afternoon, good evening	boa tarde
Good night	boa noite
Goodbye (long term)	adeus
Goodbye (short term)	até logo
yes	sim
no	não
please	por favor, se faz favor
Thank you	obrigado (said by a man)
Thank you	obrigada (said by a woman)
Your welcome	de nada
Excuse-me	desculpe
I am a tourist	Sou um(a) turista
I am Canadian	Sou canadiano(a)
I am Belgian	Sou belga
I am Swiss	Sou suíço
I am American	Sou Americano
I am Australian	Sou Australiano
I am Italian	Sou Italiano
I am from Germany	Sou de Alemanha
I am from New Zealand	Sou de Nova Zelândia
I am from Great Britain	Sou de Grã-Bretanha

I am sorry, I do not speak Portuguese	*Desculpe, não falo portuguese*
Do you speak English	*fala Inglês?*
Slower, please	*mais lenta mente, por favor*
What is your name?	*como se chama o senhor, a senhora?*
My name is...	*o meu nome é...*
husband/wife	*esposo/esposa*
brother/sister	*irmão/irmã*
friend (m/f)	*amigo/a*
child	*criança*
father	*pai*
mother	*mãe*
single (m/f)	*solteiro(a)*
married (m/f)	*casado(a)*
divorced (m/f)	*divorciado(a)*
widow	*viúva*
widower	*viúvo*

DIRECTIONS

How do I get to ...?	*Como se ir até á...?*
Is there a tourist office here?	*há algum centro de turismo por aqui?*
There is no...	*não há...*
Where is ...?	*onde está... ?*
straight ahead	*sempre em frente*
to the right	*à direita*
to the left	*à esquerda*
next to	*ao lado de*
near the	*perto de*
here	*aqui*
there	*ali, além*
in	*em, dentro*
outside	*fora*
far from	*longe de*
between	*entre, no meio de*
in front of	*diante, frente*
behind	*atrás*

MONEY

exchange	*câmbio*
money	*dinheiro*
dollars	*dólares*
I don't have any money	*não tenho dinheiro*
credit card	*carta de crédito*
traveller's cheque	*cheque de viagem*
the bill, please	*a conta, por favor*
receipt	*recibo*

SHOPPING

open (m/f)	*aberto(a)*
closed (m/f)	*cerrado(a)*
How much is this?	*uanto custa isto?*
I would like...	*queri...*
I need...	*eu preciso...*

store	uma loja
market	mercado
salesperson (m/f)	vendedor(a)
customer (m/f)	cliente(a)
buy	comprar
sell	vender

batteries	pilha
blouse	uma blus
camera	máquina fotográfica
cosmetics and perfume	cosméticos e perfumes
cotton	algodão
crafts	artesanato
film	filme
gift	presente
gold	ouro
guidebook	guia
jacket	um casaco
jewellery	joía
leather	cabedal
magazines	revistas
map	mapa
newspaper	journal
pair of jeans	um par de jeans
pants	um par de calças
precious stones	pedras preciosas
shoes	uns sapatos
skirt	uma saia
shirt	uma camisa
silver	prata
records, cassettes	discos, casetes
watch	relógio
wool	lã

MISCELLANEOUS

new	novo
old	velho
expensive	caro
inexpensive	barato
beautiful	belo
ugly	feio
big, tall	grande
small	pequeno
short	curto
large	largo
narrow	estreito
dark (colour)	escuro
bright (colour)	claro
fat	gordo
skinny, thin	delgado
a little	poco
a lot	muito
something	algo
nothing	nada
good	bom
bad	mau
more	mais

less	*menos*
do not touch	*não tocar*
quickly, fast	*rápido*
slowly	*lento*
hot	*quente*
cold	*frio*
I am ill	*estou doente (doenta)*
I am hungry	*tenho fome*
I am thirsty	*tenho sede*
What is this?	*que e isto?*
when	*quando*
where	*onde...?*

WEATHER

rain	*chuva*
sun	*sol*
it is hot	*está calor*
it is cold	*está frio*

TIME

What time is it?	*que horas são?*
It is ...	*É... São*
minute	*minuto*
hour	*hora*
day	*día*
week	*semana*
month	*mês*
year	*anho*
yesterday	*ontem*
today	*hoje*
tomorrow	*amanha*
morning	*de manhã*
afternoon, evening	*tarde*
night	*noite*
now	*agora*
never	*jamais /nunca*

Sunday	*domingo*
Monday	*segunda-feira*
Tuesday	*terça-feira*
Wednesday	*quarta-feira*
Thursday	*quinta-feira*
Friday	*sexta-feira*
Saturday	*sábado*
January	*janeiro*
February	*fevereiro*
March	*março*
April	*abril*
May	*maio*
June	*junho*
July	*julho*
August	*agosto*
September	*septembro*
October	*outubro*
November	*novembro*
December	*dezembro*

COMMUNICATIONS

air mail	*correios por avião*
collect call	*chamada pagada pelo destinatário*
envelope	*envelope, sobrescrito*
fax machine	*telecópia*
long-distance	*larga distância*
phone book	*uma lista telefónica*
post and telegram office	*correios, telégrafos*
post office	*estação dos correios*
rate	*tarifa*
stamps	*selos*
telegram	*telegrama*

ACTIVITIES

beach	*praia*
museum or gallery	*museu*
mountain	*serra, montanha*
swimming	*banhar-se* or *nadar*
walking	*passear*

TRANSPORTATION

airport	*aeroporto*
arrival	*chegada*
avenue	*avenida*
boat	*barco*
bus	*autocarro*
bus stop	*a paragem dos autocarros*
bicycle	*bicicleta*
cancel	*anular, suspender*
car	*auto*
corner	*esquina*
departure	*partida*
luggage	*bagagem*
neighbourhood	*bairro*
one-way (ticket)	*ida*
plane	*avião*
railroad crossing	*passagem de caminho de ferro*
return (ticket)	*ida e volta*
safe, no danger	*seguro*
schedule	*horário*
station	*estação*
street	*rua*
train	*combóio*
north	*norte*
south	*sul*
east	*este*
west	*oeste*

DRIVING

caution	*cuidado*
gas station	*posto de gasolina*
gasoline	*gasolina*
do not enter	*proíbido a entrada*
highway	*auto-estrada*

no passing   proíbido de ultrapassar
no parking   estacionamento proíbido
pedestrians   peão
slow down   reduzir a velocidade
speed limit   limite de velocidade
stop   alto, parre
traffic light   semáforo
to rent   alugar

ACCOMMODATIONS
air conditioning   ar condicionado
accommodation   habitação
bed   cama
breakfast   pequeno almoço
double (room)   casal, para duas pessoas
elevator   elevador
fan   ventilador
floor   andar
hot water   água quente
high season   época alta
lobby   rés-do-chão
low season   época baixa
manager, boss   gerente, dono
mid season   época média
pool   piscína
room   quarto
single (room)   individual (de solteiro)
toilet   banho
with bathroom   com banho

GASTRONOMIC GLOSSARY
à bras   brazed
acepipe   appetizer
açorda   bread soup
alho   garlic
amêijoas   clams
arroz   rice
assada   toast
atum   tuna
azeitonas   olives
bacalhau   cod
bacalhau à brás   cod fried with eggs
batatas   potatoes
bife   veal, beef or pork steak
bolo   cake
caldeirada   fish chowder
camarão   shrimp
carne   meat
castanhas   chestnuts
cebolas   onions
cenouras   carrots
cerveja   beer
cheios (cheias)   dumplings
chouriço   sausage
cogumelos   mushrooms
copo   cup
cozida   cooked

cru	raw
de escabeche	marinated
doce	dessert
enguías	eel
entradas	hors-d'œvres
favas	large beans
feijão	dried beans
fígado	liver
frango	chicken
garaffa	bottle
gelado	ice cream
gelo	ice
grão	chick pea
grelhado	grilled
laranja	orange
lebre	hare
leitão	suckling pig
limão	lemon
linguado	sole
lulas	squid
meia garrafa	half-bottle
nata	cream
no forno	in the oven
ovo	egg
pato	duck
peixe	fish
perú	turkey
polvo	octopus
presunto	ham
pudim	caramel flan
queijo	cheese
rins	kidney
rojões	cubed, fried pork
salteado	sautéed
sardinhas	sardines
saúde!	cheers!
vinho branco	white wine
vinho verde	type of wine, usually white
vinho tinto	red wine

NUMBERS

0	zero	14	catorze	50	cinquenta
1	um ou uma	15	quinze	60	sessenta
2	dois, duas	16	dezasseis	70	setenta
3	três	17	dezassete	80	oitenta
4	quatro	18	dezoito	90	noventa
5	cinco	19	dezanove	100	cem
6	seis	20	vinte	101	cento e um
7	sete	21	vinte e um	200	duzentos
8	oito	22	vinte e dois	300	trezentos
9	nove	23	vinte e três	500	quinhentos
10	dez	30	trinta	1,000	mil
11	onze	31	trinta e um	10,000	dez mil
12	doze	32	treinta e dois	1,000 000	um milhão
13	treze	40	quarenta		

Index

Accommodations 55
Afonso I 15
Afonso II 15
Afonso III 16
Afonso IV 16
Afonso V 17
Águeda (Costa de Prata: the North)
   Accommodations 271
   Restaurants 276
Airports
   Faro 45
   Francisco da Sá Carneiro
     International (Lisbon) 45
   Portela de Sacavém (Lisbon) . . 45
Albufeira (Algarve) 414
   Accommodations 435
   Finding Your Way Around . . 412
   Practical Information 412
   Restaurants 443
Alcácer do Sal (Costa de Lisboa)
   Accommodations 200
Alcáçova Royal Palace (Lisbon) . . . 84
Alcântara (Lisbon) 114
   Accommodations 133
   Entertainment 156
   Restaurants 148
Alcazar (Leiria) 222
Alcobaça (Costa de Prata:
  the South) 216
   Accommodations 234
   Finding Your Way Around . . 215
   Restaurants 240
Aldeia da Serra (Alentejo)
   Accommodations 398
Alentejo 373
   Accommodations 393
   Entertainment 407
   Exploring 376
   Finding Your Way Around . . 374
   Outdoor Activities 392
   Practical Information 376
   Restaurants 401
   Shopping 407
Alfaiate Shoe Store (Braga) 321
Alfama (Lisbon) 84
   Accommodations 124
   Entertainment 150
   Restaurants 137
   Shopping 159
Alfeizerão (Costa de Prata: the South)
   Accommodations 235
Algarve 409
   Accommodations 435
   Entertainment 453
   Exploring 414
   Finding Your Way Around . . 411
   Outdoor Activities 431
   Parks 431
   Practical Information 412
   Restaurants 443
   Shopping 454
Alijó (Montanhas)
   Accommodations 363

Restaurants 366
Almancil (Algarve) 420
   Finding Your Way Around . . 412
   Restaurants 446
Almendres (Alentejo) 391
Almornos (Costa de Lisboa)
   Accommodations 196
Almourol (Costa de Prata:
  the South) 232
   Accommodations 240
   Finding Your Way Around . . 214
   Restaurants 241
Alvito (Alentejo)
   Accommodations 394
Amarante (Costa Verde) 316
   Accommodations 331
   Practical Information 316
   Restaurants 337
Amares (Costa Verde)
   Restaurants 339
Amoreira Aqueduct (Elvas) 383
Amoreiras (Lisbon) 98
   Accommodations 126
   Restaurants 143
   Shopping 161
Amusement Park
   Algarve 435
Antigo Convento dos Ermitas de São
  Paulo (Tavira) 429
Antigo Paço Episcopal (Braga) . . 318
Antigos Paços do Concelho
   (Guimarães) 324
Aqueduto de São Sebastião
   (Coimbra) 264
Aqueduto dos Pegões (Tomar) . . 229
Arab Salon (Porto) 295
Arcado do Mirandeiro (Elvas) . . . 383
Archaeological (Serpa) 379
Archaeological site (Conimbriga) . 267
Arco da Vila (Faro) 420
Arco de Almedina (Coimbra) . . . 260
Arco de la Misericórdia (Tavira) . 430
Armação de Pêra (Algarve) 416
   Accommodations 437
   Finding Your Way Around . . 412
   Practical Information 414
   Restaurants 445
Arraiolos (Alentejo)
   Accommodations 400
   Restaurants 407
Arts 32
   Architecture 32
Aveiro (Costa de Prata: the North) 252
   Accommodations 270
   Entertainment 280
   Finding Your Way Around . . 250
   Practical Information 252
   Restaurants 275
Avenida 5 de Outubro (Olhão) . . 424
Avenida da Liberdade (Lisbon) . . 104
Avenida Diogo Leite (Porto) 301
Avenida dos Aliados (Porto) 293

Index

Avenida dos Combatentes da Grande
    Guerra (Viana do Castelo) 328
Azenhas do Mar (Costa de Lisboa) 189
Azulejo (Viseu) 362
Bairro Alto (Lisbon) 92
    Accommodations 126
    Entertainment 150
    Restaurants 138
Bairro Sousa Pinto (Coimbra) . . . 264
Baixa (Lisbon) 80
    Accommodations 123
    Restaurants 135
    Shopping 158
Baluarte Redondo (Peniche) 226
Banco Totta & Açores (Lisbon) . . . 82
Banking 48
Baroque palace (Mateus) 356
Barril (Tavira) 430
Basilica (Mafra) 170
Basílica da Estrêla (Lisbon) 110
Batalha (Costa de Prata:
    the South) 219
    Accommodations 235
    Finding Your Way Around . . 214
    Restaurants 242
Beaches
    Azenhas do Mar
        (Costa de Lisboa) 189
    Costa da Caparica
        (Costa de Lisboa) 189
    Praia da Galé
        (Costa de Lisboa) 188
    Praia das Maçãs
        (Costa de Lisboa) 189
    Praia de Galapos
        (Costa de Lisboa) 189
    Praia do Guincho
        (Costa de Lisboa) 188
    Praia do Portinho da Arrábida
        (Costa de Lisboa) 190
    Praia dos Buizinhos
        (Costa de Lisboa) 190
    Praia Grande
        (Costa de Lisboa) 189
    Sintra Atlântico
        (Costa de Lisboa) 189
    Tamariz (Costa de Lisboa) . . . 188
Bed and Breakfasts 57
Beja (Alentejo) 376
    Accommodations 393
    Entertainment 407
    Finding Your Way Around . . 374
    Restaurants 401
Belém (Lisbon) 114
    Accommodations 133
    Entertainment 156
    Restaurants 148
Berlenga Island (Costa de Prata:
    the South) 232
Berlenga Island (Peniche) 228
Biblioteca Camões (Lisbon) 108
Bicycling
    Alentejo 392
    Algarve 432

Costa de Prata: the South . . . 233
Boca do Inferno (Cascais) 169
Bom Jesus do Monte (Costa Verde)321
    Accommodations 332
    Finding Your Way Around . . 314
    Practical Information 316
    Restaurants 339
Borralha (Costa de Prata: the North)
    Accommodations 271
Braga (Costa Verde) 317
    Accommodations 331
    Entertainment 344
    Finding Your Way Around . . 314
    Practical Information 316
    Restaurants 337
Bragança (Montanhas) . . . .· 350
    Accommodations 364
    Practical Information 350
    Restaurants 367
Buçaco (Costa de Prata:
    the North) 256
    Accommodations 271
    Finding Your Way Around . . 251
    Practical Information 252
    Restaurants 276
Burgau (Algarve) 423
Cabo da Roca (Costa de Lisboa) . 178
    Finding Your Way Around . . 164
Cabo de São Vicente (Sagres) . . . 427
Cabo Espichel (Costa de Lisboa) . 184
Cacela Velha (Algarve) 416
Cacilhas (Costa de Lisboa) 178
    Restaurants 205
Café do Cais (Porto) 296
Café Imperial (Porto) 293
Café Nicolas (Lisbon) 78
Cais da Ribeira (Porto) 296
Cais do Ginjal (Cacilhas) 178
Cais do Sodré (Lisbon) 108
    Accommodations 132
    Entertainment 154
    Restaurants 145
    Shopping 162
Calçada do Lavra (Lisbon) 107
Caldas da Rainha (Costa de Prata:
    the South)
    Finding Your Way Around . . 215
Caldas de Monchique (Algarve) . 424
    Accommodations 437
    Restaurants 446
Câmara Municipal (Cascais) 169
Câmara Municipal
    (Castelo Branco) 352
Câmara Municipal (Estremoz) . . . 385
Câmara Municipal (Palmela) 181
Câmara Municipal
    (Ponte de Lima) 327
Câmara Municipal (Sintra) 175
Camping 58
    Albufeira (Algarve) 435
    Amarante (Costa Verde) 331
    Armação de Pêra (Algarve) . . 437
    Braga (Costa Verde) 331
    Bragança (Montanhas) 364

Castelo Branco (Montanhas) . 364
Castelo do Bode (Costa de Prata:
  the South) 240
Coimbra (Costa de Prata:
  the North) 272
Évora (Alentejo) 399
Faro (Algarve) 438
Ferragudo (Algarve) 441
Figueira da Foz (Costa de Prata:
  the North) 275
Foz do Arelho (Costa de Prata:
  the South) 239
Guarda (Montanhas) 364
Guimarães (Costa Verde) . . . 334
Idanha-a-Nova (Montanhas) . 364
Lagos (Algarve) 439
Lisbon 123
Miranda do Douro
  (Montanhas) 365
Penacova (Costa de Prata:
  the North) 274
Peniche (Costa de Prata:
  the South) 239
Praia de Pedrógão (Costa de
  Lisboa: the South) 236
Quarteira (Algarve) 438
Sagres (Algarve) 442
São Jacinto (Costa Prata:
  the North) 271
Terras de Bouro (Costa Verde) 334
Tomar (Costa de Prata:
  the South) 239
Viana do Castelo
  (Costa Verde) 336
Viseu (Montanhas) 366
Campo de Santa Clara (Lisbon) . . . 88
Campo dos Mártires da Patria
  (Lisbon) 107
Canal Central (Aveiro) 254
Canoeing
  Montanhas 363
Capela da Glória (Braga) 320
Capela da Imaculada Conceicão
  (Tomar) 231
Capela da Memória (Nazaré) 224
Capela da São Frutuoso
  (São Frutuoso de Montélios) . . . 321
Capela de Memória
  (Cabo Espichel) 184
Capela de Nossa Senhora da Rocha
  (Armação de Pêra) 416
Capela de São Geraldo (Braga) . . 320
Capela de São Gonçalinho
  (Aveiro) 255
Capela de São João Baptista
  (Lisbon) 96
Capela de São João Evangelista
  (Lamego) 356
Capela do Fundador (Batalha) . 219
Capela Gótica (Guimarães) 324
Capela Imperfeitas (Batalha) 220
Capela Rainha Santa Isabel
  (Estremoz) 385
Capela São Miguel (Coimbra) . . . 263

Capelados Ossos (Évora) 388
Capella dos Reis (Braga) 320
Capuchos (Costa de Lisboa) 177
Car Rentals 48
Caramulo (Montanhas)
  Accommodations 366
  Restaurants 371
Carcavelos (Costa de Lisboa)
  Accommodations 194
  Restaurants 202
Carvalho, Mario de 36
Casa Cordovil (Évora) 389
Casa da Misericórdia (Viana do
  Castelo) 329
Casa de Garcia Resendo (Évora) . 389
Casa de Misericórdia (Porto) 294
Casa do Alentejo (Lisbon) 107
Casa do Arco (Guimarães) 324
Casa do Infante (Porto) 296
Casa do Paço (Figueira da Foz) . . 268
Casa dos Bicos (Lisbon) 82
Casa Visconde de Sacavém
  (Lisbon) 112
Casa-Museu Fernando Pessôa
  (Lisbon) 35
Cascais (Costa de Lisboa) 168
  Accommodations 195
  Practical Information 168
  Restaurants 202
  Shopping 210
Castelo (Castelo de Vide) 382
Castelo (Elvas) 383
Castelo (Lamego) 356
Castelo (Lisbon) 84
  Accommodations 124
  Entertainment 150
  Restaurants 137
  Shopping 159
Castelo (Óbidos) 225
Castelo (Sesimbra) 184
Castelo (Tavira) 430
Castelo Branco (Montanhas) 351
  Accommodations 364
  Entertainment 371
  Finding Your Way Around . . 348
  Practical Information 350
  Restaurants 367
Castelo de Guimarães
  (Guimarães) 322
Castelo de Leiria (Leiria) 221
Castelo de Ourém (Ourém) 222
Castelo de São Filipe (Setúbal) . . 181
Castelo de São Jorge (Lisbon) 84
Castelo de Vide (Alentejo) 381
  Accommodations 395
  Finding Your Way Around . . 374
  Restaurants 403
Castelo do Bode (Costa de Prata:
  the South) 231
  Accommodations 240
  Restaurants 241
Castelo dos Mouros
  (Palácio da Pena) 177
Castelo dos Templários (Tomar) . 228

Index

Castelo Melhor (Montanhas) 360
Castle (Évoramente) 386
Castle (Marvão) 382
Castle (Monsanto da Beira) 353
Castle of Almourol (Almourol) . . 232
Castro Marim (Algarve) 418
Castro Verde (Alentejo) 381
Cathedral (Évora) 390
Cathedral (Faro) 420
Caves of Mira de Aire
   (Mira de Aire) 221
Centro Comercial Amoreiras
   (Lisbon) 100
Centro Cultural de Belém (Lisbon) 118
Centro de Arte Moderna (Lisbon) 103
Chafariz del Rei (Lisbon) 87
Chapeleiro António Joaquim Carneiro
   (Lisbon) 92
Charola (Tomar) 229
Chiado (Lisbon) 92
   Accommodations 126
   Entertainment 150
   Restaurants 138
Church of São Pedro (Leiria) 222
Church of the Mosteiro de Santa
   Maria (Alcobaça) 217
Cinema 36
Cinématografo (Lisbon) 78
Citânia de Briteiros (Costa Verde) 322
Citânia de Santa Luzia
   (Costa Verde) 330
City Hall (Porto) 293
Claustro da Lavagens (Tomar) . . . 229
Claustro do Cemitério (Tomar) . . 229
Claustro do Silencio (Alcobaça) . . 217
Claustro dos Felipes (Tomar) . . . 229
Claustro Real (Batalha) 220
Climate 51
Cloister (Evora) 389
Cloister (Porto) 290
Cloister of Silence (Coimbra) . . . 265
Cloister of the Episcopal Palace
   (Miranda do Douro) 359
Coimbra (Costa de Prata:
   the North) 259
   Accommodations 272
   Entertainment 280
   Finding Your Way Around . . 250
   Practical Information 252
   Restaurants 277
   Shopping 282
Coliseu dos Recreios (Lisbon) . . . 107
Compromisso Marítimo (Olhão) . 426
Condeixa-a-Nova (Costa de Prata:
   the North)
   Accommodations 274
   Finding Your Way Around . . 250
   Restaurants 279
Conimbriga (Costa de Prata:
   the North) 267
   Finding Your Way Around . . 250
   Restaurants 280
Consulates 39
Convent of Jesus (Aveiro) 255

Convent of Santa Clara-a-Nova
   (Coimbra) 266
Convento da Arrábida
   (Portinho da Arrábida) 183
Convento da Madre de Deus
   (Lisbon) 91
Convento de Nossa Senhora da
   Conceição (Beja) 378
Convento do Cristo (Tomar) 228
Convento dos Capuchos
   (Capuchos) 177
Convento dos Capuchos
   (Costa da Caparica) 178
Convento dos Lóios (Évora) 390
Convento y Igreja de Santa Clara
   (Porto) 291
Cork 12
Coro Alto (Viseu) 362
Costa da Caparica
   (Costa de Lisboa) 178
Costa de Lisboa 163
   Accommodations 194
   Beaches 188
   Entertainment 209
   Exploring 168
   Finding Your Way Around . . 163
   Outdoor Activities 191
   Parks 190
   Practical Information 168
   Restaurants 201
   Shopping 210
Costa de Prata: the North 249
   Accommodations 270
   Entertainment 280
   Exploring 252
   Finding Your Way Around . . 250
   Outdoor Activities 269
   Practical Information 252
   Restaurants 275
   Shopping 282
Costa de Prata: the South 213
   Beaches 232
   Entertainment 246
   Exploring 216
   Finding Your Way Around . . 213
   Outdoor Activities 233
   Parks 232
   Practical Information 216
   Restaurants 240
   Shopping 246
Costa Verde 313
   Accommodations 331
   Entertainment 344
   Exploring 316
   Finding Your Way Around . . 313
   Outdoor Activities 330
   Practical Information 316
   Restaurants 337
Courthouse (Porto) 294
Crafts Fair (Évora) 388
Credit Cards 49
Cromlech of Almendres
   (Almendres) 392

Cruises
   Algarve 431
   Costa de Prata: the South   . . . 233
   Costa Verde 330
   Montanhas 363
   Porto 302
Cruz Alta (Buçaco) 258
Cupola (Elvas) 383
Curia (Costa de Prata: The North) 258
Curia Palace Hotel (Curia) 258
De Oliveira, Manoel 36
Dinis I 16
Dom Afonso V Cloister (Batalha) 220
Dom José I Equestrian Statue
   (Lisbon) 82
Domus Municipalis (Bragança) . . 351
Dona Maria Pia Railway Bridge
   (Porto) 300
Douro Valley (Porto) 302
Duarte I 17
Dungeon (Bragança) 351
Dungeon (Miranda do Douro) . . 359
East Lisbon (Lisbon) 87
   Accommodations 126
   Restaurants 138
Economy 29
Electricity 63
Elevador da Bica (Lisbon) 108
Elevador da Glória (Lisbon) 104
Elevador de Santa Justa (Lisbon) . . 81
Elvas (Alentejo) 383
   Accommodations 397
   Finding Your Way Around   . . 374
   Restaurants 404
   Shopping 407
Embassies 39
Emergencies 63
Entering the Country 44
Entertainment 61
Entrance Formalities 39
Ermida de Nossa Senhora da
   Soledade (Olhão) 426
Ermida de São Brás (Évora) 391
Escolas de Rendas de Bilros
   (Peniche) 227
Espace Oikos (Lisbon) 84
Estação de São Bento (Porto) . . . 291
Estação do Rossio (Lisbon) 80
Estalagem 58
Estói (Algarve) 420
Estoril (Costa de Lisboa) 168
   Accommodations 194
   Entertainment 209
   Finding Your Way Around . . 163
   Practical Information 168
   Restaurants 201
Estrêla (Lisbon) 110
   Accommodations 132
   Entertainment 154
   Restaurants 146
   Shopping 162
Estremoz (Alentejo) 383
   Accommodations 397
   Finding Your Way Around . . 374

Restaurants 404
Estufa Fria e Quente (Lisbon) . . . 102
Évora (Alentejo) 386
   Accommodations 399
   Finding Your Way Around   . . 374
   Restaurants 405
   Shopping 408
Évoramonte (Alentejo)
   Restaurants 405
Évoramonte (Estremoz) 386
Expo 98 (Lisbon) 120
Faro (Algarve) 418
   Accommodations 438
   Entertainment 453
   Finding Your Way Around   . . 411
   Practical Information 412
   Restaurants 446
Faro Airport 45
Fátima (Costa de Prata:
   the South) 223
   Finding Your Way Around   . . 215
Fauna 12
Feira de São Mateus (Viseu) 363
Fernando I 16
Ferrugado (Algarve)
   Accommodations 441
Fervença (Costa de Prata: the South)
   Accommodations 235
Figueira da Foz (Costa de Prata:
   the North) 268
   Accommodations 275
   Finding Your Way Around . . 250
   Practical Information 252
   Restaurants 280
First Aid Kit 52
Flemish Tapestries (Lamego) 356
Flor da Rosa (Alentejo)
   Restaurants 403
Flora 12
Fonte da Nogueira (Coimbra) . . . 264
Fortaleza de Peniche (Peniche) . . 226
Fortaleza de Santa Catarina
   (Praia da Rocha) 427
Fortaleza de São João Baptista
   (Berlenga Island) 232
Forte Ponta da Bandeira (Lagos) . 422
Fortifications (Bragança) 350
Fortified Castle (Penela) 268
Fortress (Bragança) 351
Fortress (Montemor-o-Velho) . . . 268
Foz do Arelho (Costa de Prata:
   the South)
   Accommodations 239
Francisco da Sá Carneiro International
   Airport (Porto) 45
Funicular (Nazaré) 224
Galería de Arte dos Duques de
   Cadaval (Évora) 389
Galeria Nacional do Chiado
   (Lisbon) 95
Garcia de Orta Gardens (Lisbon) . 123
Gays 61
Geography 12
Glossary 455

Index

Góis (Costa de Prata: the North) . 266
Golf
    Alentejo 393
    Algarve 432
    Costa de Lisboa 193
    Costa de Prata: the North ... 269
    Montanhas 363
Graça (Lisbon) 87
    Accommodations 126
    Restaurants 138
Grand Dolmen of Zambujeiro
    (Zambujeiro) 392
Gruta Lapa Santa Margarida
    (Portinho da Arrábida) 183
Guarda (Montanhas) 353
    Accommodations 364
    Finding Your Way Around .. 348
    Practical Information 350
    Restaurants 368
    Shopping 372
Guimarães (Costa Verde) 322
    Accommodations 334
    Finding Your Way Around .. 314
    Practical Information 316
    Restaurants 340
Health 52
Heraldry Houses (Lousã) 266
Hiking
    Algarve 432
    Costa de Lisboa 191
    Costa de Prata: the North ... 269
    Costa de Prata: the South ... 233
    Costa Verde 330
History 13
    Aviz Dynasty and Portuguese
        Expansion 16
    Birth of the Republic 22
    Bragança Dynasty 20
    Early Settlement 13
    Estado Novo 24
    Flower Revolution 26
    French Revolution 22
    From Republic to Dictatorship . 23
    House of Burgundy or Birth of
        Portugal 15
    Muslim Conquest 14
    O povo unido, jamais vencido:
        The Return of Democracy .. 25
    Origins of Lusitania 13
    Pombal Government 21
    Reconquest and Creation of the
        Kingdom of Portugal 15
    Roman Colonization 14
    Salazar Dictatorship 24
    Swabians and Visigoths 14
    Treaties of Westminster and
        Methuen 21
Hitchiking 48
Holidays 54
Horseback Riding
    Algarve 432
Hospital de São Marcos (Braga) . 321
Hospital Velho (Viana do Castelo) 328
Hotels 58

Iiana do Castelo
    Restaurants 343
Idanha-a-Nova (Montanhas)
    Accommodations 364
    Restaurants 368
Idanha-a-Velha (Montanhas) 352
Igreja da Graça (Lisbon) 90
Igreja da Madre de Deus (Lisbon) . 92
Igreja da Misericórdia (Aveiro) .. 254
Igreja da Misericórdia (Batalha) .. 221
Igreja da Misericórdia (Beja) ... 377
Igreja da Misericórdia (Guimarães) 325
Igreja da Misericórdia (Porto) ... 294
Igreja da Misericórdia (Viana do
    Castelo) 329
Igreja da Misericórdia (Viseu) ... 362
Igreja de la Conceição Velha
    (Lisbon) 82
Igreja de la Misericórdia (Tavira) . 430
Igreja de Lorvão (Lorvão) 266
Igreja de Nossa Senhora da Assunçao
    (Elvas) 383
Igreja de Nossa Senhora da Cabo
    (Cabo Espichel) 184
Igreja de Nossa Senhora da
    Conceicão (Castro Verde) 381
Igreja de Nossa Senhora da
    Consolaçao (Elvas) 383
Igreja de Nossa Senhora da Graça
    (Évora) 388
Igreja de Nossa Senhora da Nazaré
    (Nazaré) 224
Igreja de Nossa Senhora da Pena
    (Leiria) 222
Igreja de Santa Maria (Óbidos) .. 225
Igreja de Santa Maria (Serpa) ... 379
Igreja de Santa Maria do Castelo
    (Estremoz) 384
Igreja de Santa Maria do Castelo
    (Tavira) 430
Igreja de Santa Maria do Olival
    (Tomar) 231
Igreja de Santa Maria dos Alcáçova
    (Montemor-o-Velho) 269
Igreja de Santo António (Lagos) . 422
Igreja de Santo Ildefonso (Porto) . 291
Igreja de Santos Passos
    (Guimarães) 326
Igreja de São Francisco
    (Guimarães) 326
Igreja de São Francisco (Porto) .. 295
Igreja de São Gonçalo (Amarante) 317
Igreja de São João Evangelista
    (Évora) 390
Igreja de São Julião (Setúbal) ... 180
Igreja de São Pedro (Peniche) ... 227
Igreja de São Vicente (Bragança) . 350
Igreja do Carmo (Guimarães) ... 326
Igreja do Carmo (Lisbon) 94
Igreja do Carmo (Porto) 293
Igreja do Convento (Aveiro) 255
Igreja dos Clérigos (Porto) 293
Igreja dos Congregados (Porto) .. 293
Igreja dos Grilos (Porto) 290

Igreja e Mosteiro de São Vicente
da Fora (Lisbon) 88
Igreja Jésus (Setúbal) 180
Igreja Matriz (Olhão) 426
Igreja Matriz (Ponte de Lima) . . . 327
Igreja Matriz (Santiago do Cacém) 186
Igreja Nossa Senhora da Assunção
(Cascais) 169
Igreja Nossa Senhora da Assunção
(Mértola) 380
Igreja Paroquial de São Lourenço
(Almancil) 420
Igreja Românica de Cedofeita
(Porto) 301
Igreja Santa Cruz (Braga) 321
Igreja Santa Maria (Bragança) . . . 351
Igreja Santa Maria
(Castelo de Vide) 382
Igreja Santa Maria (Lisbon) 116
Igreja Santa Maria do Castelo
(Palmela) 182
Igreja São Antão (Évora) 388
Igreja São Francisco (Évora) 388
Igreja São Roque (Lisbon) 96
Igreja São Tiago (Óbidos) 225
Igreja y Convento de Nossa Senhora
da Oliveira (Guimarães) 324
Igreja-Panteão de Santa Engrácia
(Lisbon) 87
Ilha de Dentro
(Ilha do Pessegueiro) 187
Ilha de Tavira (Tavira) 430
Ilha do Pessegueiro
(Costa de Lisboa) 187
Accommodations 201
Restaurants 209
Instituto Nacional de Estatística
(Lisbon) 104
Insurance 52
Internet 50
Jardim Botânica (Coimbra) 264
Jardim Botânico (Lisbon) 98
Jardim da Estrêla (Lisbon) 110
Jardim de Santa Barbara (Braga) . 318
Jardim do Antigo Paço Episcopal
(Castelo Branco) 352
Jardim do Torel (Lisbon) 107
Jardim João Chagas (Porto) 294
João I 16
João II 17
João III 18
José Maria de Fonesca winery
(Portinho da Arrábida) 184
Kayaking
Costa de Prata: the North . . . 269
Keep (Castelo de Vide) 382
Keep (Estremoz) 384
Lago de Albufeira (Costa da
Caparica) 178
Lagoa de Santo André (Costa de
Lisboa)
Accommodations 201
Lagos (Algarve) 422
Accommodations 439

Entertainment 453
Finding Your Way Around . . 411
Practical Information 412
Restaurants 448
Laje dos Pargos (Peniche) 227
Lamego (Montanhas) 354
Accommodations 365
Finding Your Way Around . . 348
Practical Information 350
Restaurants 369
Language 50
Lantern tower (Évora) 390
Lapa (Lisbon) 110
Accommodations 132
Entertainment 154
Restaurants 146
Shopping 162
Largo Barão de Quintela (Lisbon) 108
Largo da Oliveira (Guimarães) . . 324
Largo da Porta de Moura (Évora) 389
Largo da Praça do Peixe (Aveiro) 255
Largo da República (Estremoz) . . 385
Largo da Sé (Faro) 420
Largo das Portas do Sol (Lisbon) . . 84
Largo de Camões (Ponte de Lima) 327
Largo do Carmo (Lisbon) 94
Largo do Castelo (Estremoz) 384
Largo do Chiado (Lisbon) 95
Largo do Marquês de Pombal
(Porto Covo) 187
Largo do Paço (Braga) 318
Largo do Rato (Lisbon) 98
Largo dos Santos Próculo e Hilariâo
(Serpa) 379
Largo São Teotónio (Viseu) 362
Largo Toural (Guimarães) 325
Leiria (Costa de Prata: the South) 221
Accommodations 236
Finding Your Way Around . . 214
Restaurants 242
Lello and Irmão Bookstore (Porto) 293
Lesbians 61
Liberdade (Lisbon) 104
Accommodations 129
Restaurants 144
Shopping 161
Library (Mafra) 170
Lisbon 65
Entertainment 150
Exploring 78
Finding Your Way Around . . 67
History of Lisbon 65
Practical Information 74
Restaurants 135
Shopping 158
Lisbon Today 67
Literature 34
Lorvão (Costa de Prata: the North) 266
Lousã (Costa de Prata: the North) 266
Accommodations 274
Finding Your Way Around . . 250
Practical Information 252
Restaurants 280
Luso (Costa de Prata: The North) 272

Index

Macau Pavilion (Lisbon) 122
MadreDeus 37
Mãe d'Água Reservoir (Lisbon) . . 100
Mafra (Costa de Lisboa) 169
    Restaurants 203
Mafra school (Mafra) 170
Mail 49
Manteigas (Montanhas)
    Accommodations 365
    Restaurants 369
Manuel I 18
Manueline portal (Lisbon) 82
Marialva (Montanhas) 361
Maritime Pine 12
Marquês de Pombal (Lisbon) . . . 100
    Accommodations 127
    Restaurants 143
    Shopping 161
Martinhal (Algarve)
    Accommodations 442
Marvão (Alentejo) 382
    Accommodations 395
    Finding Your Way Around . . 374
    Restaurants 404
    Shopping 408
Mateus (Montanhas) 356
    Finding Your Way Around . . 348
Medieval Synagogue
    (Castelo de Vide) 382
Megaliths (Almendres) 391
Megaliths (Zambujeiro) 391
Mértola (Alentejo) 380
Military Museum (Bragança) . . . 351
Mira (Costa de Prata: the North)
    Accommodations 270
Mira de Aire (Costa de Prata:
    the South) 221
Miradouro de Santa Catarina
    (Lisbon) 108
Miradouro de Santa Luzia
    (Lisbon) 86
Miradouro de São Pedro de Alcântara
    (Lisbon) 96
Miranda do Douro (Montanhas) . 359
    Accommodations 365
    Finding Your Way Around . . 348
    Practical Information 350
    Restaurants 369
Miróbriga (Costa de Lisboa) 187
    Restaurants 208
Monastery (Mafra) 170
Monastery-palace (Mafra) 169
Monchique (Algarve) 423
    Accommodations 440
    Restaurants 449
Money 48
Monsanto da Beira (Montanhas) . 353
    Accommodations 364
    Restaurants 368
    Shopping 371
Monserrate (Costa de Lisboa) . . . 176
    Accommodations 198
Montanhas 347
    Accommodations 363

Entertainment 371
Exploring 350
Finding Your Way Around . . 347
Outdoor Activities 363
Practical Information 350
Restaurants 366
Shopping 371
Montemor-o-Velho (Costa de Prata:
    the North) 268
    Finding Your Way Around . . 250
    Practical Information 252
Monumento à Batalha do Buçaco
    (Buçaco) 258
Mosteiro de Batalha (Batalha) . . . 219
Mosteiro de Santa Maria d'Alcobaça
    (Alcobaça) 217
Mosteiro de Santa Marinha da Costa
    (Guimarães) 326
Mosteiro dos Carmelitas descalços
    (Buçaco) 258
Mosteiro dos Jerónimos (Lisbon) 116
Mosteiro y Igreja de Santa Cruz
    (Coimbra) 264
Mountain Biking
    Costa de Prata: the North . . . 269
Muralha Fernandina (Porto) 291
Museo do Arroz (Península de
    Tróia) 186
Museu Alberto Sampaio
    (Guimarães) 324
Museu António (Lisbon) 83
Museu Arpad Szenes-Vieira da Silva
    (Lisbon) 100
Museu Arqueológico do Carmo
    (Lisbon) 94
Museu Calouste Gulbenkian
    (Lisbon) 102
Museu da Água Manuel da Maia
    (Lisbon) 90
Museu da Cidade (Lisbon) 104
Museu da Ciência (Lisbon) 98
Museu da Guerra Peninsular
    (Buçaco) 258
Museu da Marioneta (Lisbon) 90
Museu da Sociedade de Geografia
    de Lisboa (Lisbon) 107
Museu da Terra de Miranda
    (Miranda do Douro) 359
Museu de Albano Sardoeira
    (Amarante) 317
Museu de Arte Moderna (Sintra) . 175
Museu de Arte Popular (Lisbon) . 119
Museu de Arte Sacra (Braga) 320
Museu de Arte Sacra (Mértola) . . 380
Museu de Arte Sacra de São Roque
    (Lisbon) 96
Museu de Aveiro (Aveiro) 255
Museu de Évora (Évora) 391
Museu de Lamego (Lamego) 356
Museu de Marinha (Lisbon) 118
Museu de Peniche (Peniche) 226
Museu de Setúbal (Setúbal) 180
Museu de Vinho (Alcobaça) 218

Museu do Abade de Baçal
(Bragança) 351
Museu do Palácio Nacional da Ajuda
(Lisbon) 116
Museu Escola de Artes Decorativas
(Lisbon) 84
Museu Etnográfico (Serpa) 379
Museu Grão Vasco (Viseu) 362
Museu Islâmico (Mértola) 380
Museu Luso-Hebreu (Tomar) . . . 231
Museu Martins Sacramento
(Guimarães) 325
Museu Militar (Lisbon) 87
Museu Municipal (Lagos) 422
Museu Municipal (Viana do
Castelo) 329
Museu Municipal da Arqueologia
(Silves) 428
Museu Municipal de Estremoz
(Estremoz) 385
Museu Municipal de Marvão
(Marvão) 382
Museu Municipal Dr. Santos Rocha
(Figueira da Foz) 268
Museu Nacional de Arqueologia
(Lisbon) 118
Museu Nacional de Arte Antiga
(Lisbon) 112
Museu Nacional de Etnologia
(Lisbon) 120
Museu Nacional do Azulejo
(Lisbon) 91
Museu Nacional do Traje (Lisbon) 104
Museu Nacional dos Coches
(Lisbon) 123
Museu Nacional Machado de Castro
(Coimbra) 262
Museu Oceanográfico
(Portinho da Arrábida) 182
Museu Paleocristão (Mertola) . . . 381
Museu Regional Reina Dona Leonor
(Beja) 378
Museu Romano (Mértola) 380
Museu Romântico (Porto) 301
Museu Rural (Estremoz) 385
Museu Serralves (Porto) 301
Museu Soares dos Reis (Porto) . . 294
Museu Visigótico (Beja) 376
Museum (Conimbriga) 268
Museum of Religious Art (Porto) . 295
Museum of sacred art (Coimbra) . 263
Museum of Sacred Art (Viseu) . . . 362
Music 36
National palace (Mafra) 170
National Pantheon (Lisbon) 88
Nautical Exhibition (Lisbon) 123
Nazaré (Costa de Prata: the South) 223
Accommodations 236
Finding Your Way Around . . 214
Restaurants 242
Shopping 247
North Lisbon (Lisbon) 100
Accommodations 127
Restaurants 143

Shopping 161
Nossa Senhora da Leite (Braga) . . 320
Nossa Senhora da Misericórdia
(Ourém) 222
Nossa Senhora da Piedade Castle
(Lousã) 266
Nossa Senhora da Serra do Pilar
Convent (Porto) 301
Nossa Senhora de l'Encarnação
(Lisbon) 95
Nossa Senhora do Loreto (Lisbon) . 95
Nossa Senhora dos Alfitos (Olhão) 426
Nossa Senhora dos Remédios
(Lamego) 356
O Furado Grande
(Berlenga Island) 232
Óbidos (Costa de Prata:
the South) 224
Accommodations 237
Entertainment 246
Finding Your Way Around . . 215
Restaurants 243
Shopping 247
Oceanarium (Lisbon) 122
Oeiras (Costa de Lisboa)
Accommodations 194
Old Town (Bragança) 350
Olhão (Algarve) 424
Entertainment 454
Restaurants 449
Olhos de Água (Albufeira) 416
Olisipónia (Lisbon) 84
Oliveira do Hospital (Montanhas)
Accommodations 366
Ourém (Costa de Prata: the South) 222
Finding Your Way Around . . 216
Restaurants 244
Ovar (Costa de Prata: the North)
Restaurants 276
Packing 51
Paço da Audiênca (Estremoz) . . . 385
Paço dos Condes Basto (Évora) . 389
Paço dos Duques de Bragança
(Guimarães) 324
Paço dos Duques de Cadaval
(Évora) 389
Paço Ducal (Estremoz) 386
Paços do Concelho
(Viana do Castelo) 329
Padrão dos Descobrimentos
(Lisbon) 119
Painting 36
Palacete do Raio (Braga) 321
Palacete Ribeiro da Cunha (Lisbon) 98
Palácio da Assembleia Nacional
(Lisbon) 110
Palácio da Bolsa (Porto) 295
Palácio da Justiça (Coimbra) 265
Palácio da Pena (Costa de
Lisboa) 175
Palácio da Pena (Sintra) 171
Palácio das Necessidades (Lisbon) 114
Palácio de Monserrate
(Monserrate) 176

Palácio de Seteais (Seteais) 175
Palácio dos Biscaínhos (Braga) . . 320
Palácio dos Condes da Carreira
  (Viana do Castelo) 329
Palácio dos Melos (Serpa) 379
Palácio dos Valenças (Lisbon) . . . 110
Palácio Foz (Lisbon) 104
Palácio Melo Avim (Viana do
  Castelo) 329
Palácio Nacional (Sintra) 172
Palácio Nacional de Queluz
  (Queluz) 170
Palácio Nacional de Sintra (Sintra) 171
Palácio Valenças (Sintra) 175
Palácio Vila Flor (Guimarães) . . . 326
Palácio-Museu Condes Castro
  Guimarães (Cascais) 169
Paleochristian Baptistry
  (Idanha-a-Velha) 353
Palmela (Costa de Lisboa) 181
  Accommodations 200
  Finding Your Way Around . . 164
  Restaurants 207
Parks
  Parque da Pena
    (Costa de Lisboa) 190
  Parque de Monserrate (Costa de
    Lisboa) 190
  Parque do Buçaco (Costa de Prata:
    the North) 256
  Parque Eduardo VII (Lisbon) . 100
  Parque Mouchão (Costa de Prata:
    the South) 233
  Parque Nacional da Peneda-Gerês
    (Costa Verde) 330
  Parque Natural da Ria Formosa
    (Algarve) 431
  Parque Portugal dos Pequeninos
    (Coimbra) 265
  Parque Santa Cruz (Coimbra) 264
  Parque Urbano dos Moinhos 120
  Praça do Peixe (Aveiro) 255
  Reserva Natural do Estuário do
    Sado (Costa de Lisboa) . . . 191
  Serra da Arrábida (Costa de
    Lisboa) 193
Parque da Pena (Costa de Lisboa) 190
Parque das Nações (Lisbon)
  Accommodations 133
Parque de Monserrate
  (Costa de Lisboa) 190
Parque de Monserrate
  (Monserrate) 176
Parque do Buçaco (Costa de Prata:
  the North) 256
Parque Eduardo VII (Lisbon) . . . 100
Parque Nacional da Peneda-Gerês
  (Costa Verde) 330
Parque Natural da Ria Formosa
  (Algarve) 431
Parque Portugal dos Pequeninos
  (Coimbra) 265
Parque Santa Cruz (Coimbra) . . . 264
Parque Urbano dos Moinhos

(Lisbon) 120
Pastelaria Dantas
  (Viana do Castelo) 329
Pavilhão da Realidade Virtual
  (Lisbon) 122
Pavilhão dos Desportos (Lisbon) . 102
Pavilion of Knowledge (Lisbon) . 122
Pedal-Boating
  Costa de Prata: the North . . . 269
  Costa Verde 330
Pedernaira (Nazaré) 223
Pedro I 16
Pelhourino (Óbidos) 225
Pelourinho (Bragança) 351
Penacova (Costa de Prata:
  the North) 266
  Accommodations 274
  Finding Your Way Around . . 251
  Practical Information 252
  Restaurants 279
Penela (Costa de Prata: the North) 268
  Finding Your Way Around . . 250
Peniche (Costa de Prata:
  the South) 226
  Accommodations 239
  Finding Your Way Around . . 215
  Practical Information 216
  Restaurants 245
Península de Tróia
  (Costa de Lisboa) 184
Pensão 58
Pessõa, Fernando 35
Pillars (Elvas) 383
Pillory (Elvas) 383
Pinhão (Montanhas)
  Restaurants 370
  Shopping 372
Plane 44
Police 63
Politics 26
Ponta da Peidade (Algarve) 422
Ponte 25 de Abril (Lisbon) 114
Ponte de Lima (Costa Verde) . . . 326
  Accommodations 335
  Finding Your Way Around . . 314
  Practical Informatio n316
  Restaurants 342
Ponte Dom Luís I (Porto) 298
Ponte São Gonçalo (Amarante) . . 317
Population 26
Porta Coroada
  (Valença do Minho) 327
Porta d'El-Rei (Guarda) 354
Porta da Vila (Óbidos) 225
Porta dos Nós (Estremoz) 386
Porta Férrea (Coimbra) 263
Portela de Sacavém Airport
  (Lisbon) 45
Portimão (Algarve) 426
  Accommodations 440
  Finding Your Way Around . . 412
  Practical Information 412
  Restaurants 449

Portinho da Arrábida (Costa de
  Lisboa) 182
Porto 283
  Accommodations 302
  Entertainment 309
  Exploring 290
  Finding Your Way Around . . 285
  Outdoor Activities 302
  Practical Information 288
  Restaurants 305
  Shopping 310
Porto Covo (Costa de Lisboa) ... 187
  Accommodations 201
  Restaurants 208
Porto Covo (Lisbon) 110
Porto de Mós (Costa de Prata:
  the South) 221
Portrait of Portugal 11
Portuguese National Pavilion
  (Lisbon) 122
Posto de Turismo da Região de
  Setúbal (Setúbal) 180
Pousadas 55
Praça 14 de Julho (Aveiro) 255
Praça 1° de Maio (Évora) 388
Praça da Erva (Viana do Castelo) 328
Praça da Figueira (Lisbon) 80
Praça da Liberdade (Porto) 293
Praça da Rebública (Viana do
  Castelo) 328
Praça da República (Amarante) . . 317
Praça da República (Aveiro) 255
Praça da República (Tomar) 231
Praça da República (Viseu) 362
Praça da Restauração (Olhão) ... 426
Praça da Ribeira (Porto) 296
Praça da Sé (Miranda do Douro) . 359
Praça da Sé (Viseu) 362
Praça das Amoreiras (Lisbon) ... 100
Praça das Flores (Lisbon) 110
Praça de Bocage (Setúbal) 180
Praça de Santiago (Guimarães) . . 325
Praça de Touros (Lisbon) 104
Praça do Comercio (Coimbra) ... 265
Praça do Comércio (Lisbon) 81
Praça do Conde de Bracial (Santiago
  do Cacém) 187
Praça do Giraldo (Évora) 388
Praça do Municipio (Lisbon) 82
Praça do Peixe (Aveiro) 255
Praça do Príncipa Real (Lisbon) . . 98
Praça Dom Afonso Henriques
  (Alcobaça) 218
Praça Dom Pedro V
  (Castelo de Vide) 381
Praça dos Restauradores (Lisbon) 104
Praça Fonte da Vila
  (Castelo de Vide) 382
Praça Humberto Delgado (Aveiro) 254
Praça João da Câmara (Lisbon) ... 80
Praça Largo Contador-Mor (Lisbon) 84
Praça Luís de Camões (Castelo
  Branco) 352
Praça Luís de Camões (Lisbon) ... 95

Praça Marquês de Pombal
  (Lisbon) 102
Praça Mor (Miranda do Douro) . . 359
Praça Municipal (Braga) 320
Praça República (Beja) 377
Praça Rodrigues Lobo (Leiria) ... 222
Practical Information 39
Praia (Nazaré) 223
Praia da Carcavelos (Costa de
  Lisboa) 188
Praia da Galé (Algarve)
  Accommodations 436
  Restaurants 444
Praia da Galé (Costa de Lisboa) . 188
Praia da Luz (Algarve) 423
  Accommodations 440
  Restaurants 448
Praia da Rocha (Algarve) 426
  Accommodations 441
  Entertainment 454
  Restaurants 450
Praia das Maçãs (Costa de Lisboa) 189
Praia de Galapos
  (Costa de Lisboa) 189
Praia do Carvoeiro (Algarve) 426
  Accommodations 442
  Restaurants 451
Praia do Guincho
  (Costa de Lisboa) 188
  Accommodations 195
  Restaurants 203
Praia do Pedrogão (Costa de Lisboa:
  the South)
  Accommodations 236
Praia do Portinho da Arrábida (Costa
  de Lisboa) 190
Praia Dona Ana (Algarve) 422
Praia dos Barcos (Albufeira) 416
Praia dos Buizinhos
  (Costa de Lisboa) 190
Praia Grande (Algarve)
  Accommodations 441
Praia Grande (Costa de Lisboa) . . 189
  Accommodations 198
Praia Porto de Mós (Lagos) 422
Pronunciation Guide 454
Quarteira (Algarve) 420
  Accommodations 438
  Finding Your Way Around . . 412
  Practical Information 412
  Restaurants 447
Queluz (Costa de Lisboa) 170
  Accommodations 195
  Entertainment 209
  Finding Your Way Around . . 164
  Restaurants 204
Quinta da Regaleira (Seteais) ... 175
Quinta das Lágrimas Gardens
  (Coimbra) 265
Ramparts (Marvão) 382
Rato (Lisbon) 98
  Accommodations 126
  Restaurants 143
  Shopping 161

Reis Filhos (Porto) 291
Reserva Natural do Estuário do Sado
   (Costa de Lisboa) 191
Residencial 58
Restauradores (Lisbon) 104
   Accommodations 129
   Restaurants 144
   Shopping 161
Restaurants 59
Ria de Aveiro (Costa de Prata:
   the North) 256
Rio Grande 37
Rock Carvings (Vale do Côa) . . . 359
Rodrigues, Amália 36
Roman Bridge (Idanha-a-Velha) . 353
Roman Gate (Idanha-a-Velha) . . 353
Roman road (Conimbriga) 267
Roman Ruins (Conimbriga) 267
Roman ruins (Estói) 420
Roman Ruins of São Cucufate
   (Vila de Frades) 392
Roman Temple (Évora) 390
Romanesque Chapel
   (Monsanto da Beira) 353
Romanesque cloister (Lisbon) 83
Rossio (Lisbon) 78
   Accommodations 123
   Restaurants 135
   Shopping 158
Rossio (Viseu) 362
Rossio Marquês de Pombal
   (Estremoz) 385
Royal Hunting Palace (Buçaco) . . 258
Royal Tombs (Alcobaça) 217
Rua 5 de Outubro (Amarante) . . . 317
Rua Afonso Albuquerque (Leiria) 222
Rua Augusta (Lisbon) 81
Rua Bartolomeu Alvares da Santa
   (Castelo de Vide) 381
Rua Clube dos Galitos (Aveiro) . . 254
Rua da Bandeira
   (Viana do Castelo) 329
Rua da Costalinha
   (Miranda do Douro) 359
Rua da Rainha (Guimarães) 325
Rua da Senhora da Piedade
   (Viseu) 362
Rua das Flores (Porto) 294
Rua das Portas de Beja (Serpa) . . 379
Rua das Portas de Santo Antão
   (Lisbon) 107
Rua de Fonte (Castelo de Vide) . . 382
Rua de Santa Justa (Lisbon) 81
Rua de Santa Maria (Guimarães) . 324
Rua de São Vicente (Guarda) . . . 354
Rua Direita (Viseu) 362
Rua Direita do Castelo
   (Castelo de Vide) 382
Rua do Assento (Serpa) 379
Rua do Cais (Tavira) 428
Rua do Carmo (Lisbon) 92
Rua do Dr. Barbosa de Magalhães
   (Aveiro) 255
Rua do Poço (Viana do Castelo) . 328

Rua Dom Diogo de Sousa (Braga) 318
Rua Dom Duarte (Viseu) 362
Rua dos Quartéis (Serpa) 379
Rua Formosa (Viseu) 362
Rua Francisco dos Passos
   (Guarda) 354
Rua Garrett (Lisbon) 94
Rua João Valente (Serpa) 379
Rua São Bento (Lisbon) 110
Rua Viera-Portuense (Lisbon) . . . 116
Safety 53
Sagres (Algarve) 427
   Accommodations 442
   Finding Your Way Around . . 412
   Practical Information 412
   Restaurants 451
Sala dos Capelos (Coimbra) 263
Saldanha (Lisbon) 100
   Accommodations 127
   Restaurants 143
   Shopping 161
Sancho I 15
Sancho II 15
Santa Bárbara de Nexe (Algarve)
   Accommodations 438
   Restaurants 447
Santa Catarina (Lisbon) 108
   Accommodations 132
   Entertainment 154
   Restaurants 145
   Shopping 162
Santa Clara-a-Nova Convent
   (Coimbra) 266
Santa Clara-a-Velha (Alentejo)
   Accommodations 401
Santa Clara-a-Velha Convent
   (Coimbra) 265
Santa Cruz (Lisbon) 84
Santa Luzia (Costa Verde) 329
   Finding Your Way Around . . 314
   Practical Information 316
Santa Luzia (Tavira) 430
Santiago do Cacém (Costa de
   Lisboa) 186
   Accommodations 200
   Entertainment 210
   Finding Your Way Around . . 164
   Practical Information 168
   Restaurants 208
Santo Amaro (Lisbon) 114
   Accommodations 133
   Entertainment 156
   Restaurants 148
Santo Antonio Hospital (Porto) . . 293
Santuária de Santa Luzia
   (Santa Luzia) 329
Santuário da Penha (Guimarães) . 326
São Brás de Alportel (Algarve)
   Accommodations 438
   Restaurants 447
São Frutuoso de Montélios
   (Costa Verde) 321
São Gonçalo (Costa Verde)
   Accommodations 331

Restaurants 337
São Jacinto (Costa de Prata: the North)
    Accommodations 271
São Tiago Church (Coimbra) 265
Saramago, José 36
Scuba Diving
    Costa de Prata: the South . . . 233
Sé (Braga) 318
Sé (Guarda) 354
Sé (Porto) 290
Sé (Viana do Castelo) 328
Sé (Viseu) 362
Sé de Lamego (Lamego) 356
Sé Patriarcal (Lisbon) 83
Sé Velha (Coimbra) 260
Sebastião I 20
Second Defensive Wall
    (Conimbriga) 268
Security 53
Serpa (Alentejo) 378
Serra da Arrábida
    (Costa de Lisboa) 182
Serra da Marofa (Vale do Côa) . . 360
Sesimbra (Costa de Lisboa) 184
    Entertainment 210
    Restaurants 207
Seteais (Costa de Lisboa) 175
    Accommodations 197
    Restaurants 205
Setúbal (Costa de Lisboa) 178
    Accommodations 198
    Entertainment 209
    Finding Your Way Around . . 164
    Practical Informatio n168
    Restaurants 206
    Shopping 211
Shopping 62
Silva, Vieira da 36
Silves (Algarve) 427
    Accommodations 443
    Finding Your Way Around . . 412
    Practical Information 414
    Restaurants 451
Sintra (Costa de Lisboa) 171
    Accommodations 196
    Entertainment 209
    Finding Your Way Around . . 164
    Practical Information 168
    Restaurants 204
    Shopping 210
Sintra Atlântico (Costa de Lisboa) 189
Sítio (Nazaré) 223
Solar de Alarcão (Guarda) 354
Sousel (Alentejo)
    Accommodations 399
Sun 52
Swastika House (Conimbriga) . . . 267
Swimming
    Alentejo 392
Tabacaria Mónaco (Lisbon) 78
Tamariz (Costa de Lisboa) 188
Tancos (Costa de Prata:
    the South) 231
    Restaurants 241
Tavira (Algarve) 428
    Restaurants 452
Taxi 72
Teatro Eden (Lisbon) 104
Teatro Nacional de São Carlos
    (Lisbon) 95
Teatro Nacional Dona Maria II
    (Lisbon) 78
Telecommunications 49
Telephones 49
Terreiro do Paço (Estremoz) 385
Tetvocal 37
Theft in Cars 53
Time Zone 63
Tipping 61
Tomar (Costa de Prata: the South) 228
    Accommodations 239
    Finding Your Way Around . . 216
    Practical Information 216
    Restaurants 245
Tomb of Saint Joana (Aveiro) . . . 255
Torga, Miguel 35
Torrão (Montanhas)
    Restaurants 370
Torre da Cadeia Velha
    (Ponte de Lima) 327
Torre de Belém (Lisbon) 119
Torre de Menagem (Braga) 318
Torre de São Paulo (Ponte de
    Lima) 327
Torre de São Pedro (Lisbon) 87
Torre do Rio (Mértola) 380
Torre dos Clérigos (Porto) 293
Torre dos Ferreiros (Guarda) 354
Torre Vasco da Gama (Lisbon) . . 122
Torreira (Costa de Prata: the North)
    Accommodations 271
    Restaurants 276
Torres da Cerca Velha (Évora) . . 389
Tourist Information 41
Transportation 46
Travellers' Cheques 49
Travessa da Bateria (Albufeira) . . 416
Travessa da Igreja Velha
    (Albufeira) 416
Travessa da Laranjeira (Lisbon) . . 108
Travessa da Portuguesa (Lisbon) . 108
Tree of Jesse (Porto) 295
Truth Sculpture (Lisbon) 108
University (Coimbra) 262
University (Évora) 389
Vale de Parra (Algarve)
    Accommodations 436
Vale do Côa (Montanhas) 359
Valença do Minho (Costa Verde) . 327
    Accommodations 335
    Finding Your Way Around . . 314
    Practical Information 316
    Restaurants 343
Várzea de Sintra (Costa de Lisboa)
    Accommodations 198
Vasco da Gama (Lisbon) 122
Vaubanesque Ramparts (Elvas) . . 383
Via Latina (Coimbra) 263

Index

Via Sacra (Bom Jesus do Monte) . 321
Viana do Castelo (Costa Verde) . . 328
    Accommodations 336
    Entertainment 344
    Finding Your Way Around . . 314
    Practical Information 316
Vila de Frades (Alentejo) 392
Vila Nova de Cerveira (Costa Verde)
    Restaurants 343
Vila Nova de Gaia (Porto) 300
    Practical Information288 . . . .
Vila Real de Santo António
    (Algarve) 430
Vila Serralves (Porto) 301
Vila Vehla (Albufeira) 414
Vila Viçosa (Alentejo)
    Restaurants 405
Vila Viçosa (Estremoz) 385
Vilamoura (Algarve) 422
    Accommodations 438
    Entertainment 453
    Restaurants 447
Visconde Espinhal Manor (Lousã) 266
Viseu (Montanhas) 361
    Accommodations 366
    Entertainment 371
    Finding Your Way Around . . 348
    Practical Information 350

Restaurants 370
Shopping 372
Visigoth Basilica (Idanha-a-Velha) 353
Water Gardens (Lisbon) 123
Water Jet House (Conimbriga) . . 267
Water Slides
    Alentejo 392
Window of Tomar (Tomar) 229
Women Travellers 63
Youth Hostel
    Alfeizerão (Costa de Prata: the
        South) 235
    Braga (Costa Verde) 331
    Coimbra (Costa de Prata: the
        North) 272
    Lagos (Algarve) 439
    Leiria (Costa de Prata:
        the South) 236
    Mira (Costa de Prata:
        the North) 270
    Portimão (Algarve) 440
    Porto 302
    Terras de Bouro (Costa Verde) 334
    Vila Nova de Cerveira
        (Costa Verde) 335
Youth Hostels 58
Zambujeiro (Alentejo) 391

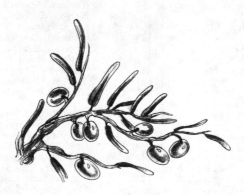

Travel Notes

Order Form

ULYSSES TRAVEL GUIDES

☐ Atlantic Canada .... $24.95 CAN / $17.95 US	☐ Martinique .... $24.95 CAN / $17.95 US
☐ Bahamas .... $24.95 CAN / $17.95 US	☐ Miami .... $9.95 CAN / $12.95 US
☐ Beaches of Maine .... $12.95 CAN / $9.95 US	☐ Montréal .... $19.95 CAN / $14.95 US
☐ Bed & Breakfasts .... $13.95 CAN / $10.95 US in Québec	☐ New Orleans .... $17.95 CAN / $12.95 US
☐ Belize .... $16.95 CAN / $12.95 US	☐ New York City .... $19.95 CAN / $14.95 US
☐ Calgary .... $17.95 CAN / $12.95 US	☐ Nicaragua .... $24.95 CAN / $17.95 US
☐ Canada .... $29.95 CAN / $21.95 US	☐ Ontario .... $27.95 CAN / $19.95US
☐ Chicago .... $19.95 CAN / $14.95 US	☐ Ottawa .... $17.95 CAN / $12.95 US
☐ Chile .... $27.95 CAN / $17.95 US	☐ Panamá .... $24.95 CAN / $17.95 US
☐ Colombia .... $29.95 CAN / $21.95 US	☐ Peru .... $27.95 CAN / $19.95 US
☐ Costa Rica .... $27.95 CAN / $19.95 US	☐ Portugal .... $24.95 CAN / $16.95 US
☐ Cuba .... $24.95 CAN / $17.95 US	☐ Puerto Rico .... $24.95 CAN / $17.95 US
☐ Dominican .... $24.95 CAN / $17.95 US Republic	☐ Provence - .... $29.95 CAN / $21.95US Côte d'Azur
☐ Ecuador and .... $24.95 CAN / $17.95 US Galapagos Islands	☐ Québec .... $29.95 CAN / $21.95 US
☐ El Salvador .... $22.95 CAN / $14.95 US	☐ Québec and Ontario .... $9.95 CAN / $7.95 US with Via
☐ Guadeloupe .... $24.95 CAN / $17.95 US	☐ Seattle .... $17.95 CAN / $12.95 US
☐ Guatemala .... $24.95 CAN / $17.95 US	☐ Toronto .... $18.95 CAN / $13.95 US
☐ Honduras .... $24.95 CAN / $17.95 US	☐ Vancouver .... $17.95 CAN / $12.95 US
☐ Jamaica .... $24.95 CAN / $17.95 US	☐ Washington D.C. .... $18.95 CAN / $13.95 US
☐ Lisbon .... $18.95 CAN / $13.95 US	☐ Western Canada .... $29.95 CAN / $21.95 US
☐ Louisiana .... $29.95 CAN / $21.95 US	

ULYSSES DUE SOUTH

☐ Acapulco .... $14.95 CAN / $9.95 US	☐ Huatulco - Oaxaca .... $17.95 CAN / $12.95 US Puerto Escondido
☐ Los Cabos .... $14.95 CAN / $10.95 US and La Paz	☐ Cartagena .... $12.95 CAN / $9.95 US (Colombia)
☐ Cancún & .... $19.95 CAN / $14.95 US Riviera Maya	☐ Belize .... $16.95 CAN / $12.95 US
☐ Cancun Cozumel .... $17.95 CAN / $12.95 US	☐ St. Martin and .... $16.95 CAN / $12.95 US St. Barts
☐ Puerto Vallarta .... $14.95 CAN / $9.95 US	☐ Guadalajara .... $17.95 CAN / $12.95 US

ULYSSES GREEN ESCAPES

☐ Cycling in France .... $22.95 CAN
$16.95 US
☐ Cycling in Ontario .... $22.95 CAN
$16.95 US
☐ Biking Montréal .... $3.95 CAN

☐ Hiking in the .... $19.95 CAN
Northeastern U.S. $13.95 US
☐ Hiking in Québec .... $19.95 CAN
$13.95 US

ULYSSES CONVERSATION GUIDES

☐ French for Better Travel .... $9.95 CAN
$6.95 US

☐ Spanish for Better Travel ... $9.95 CAN
$6.95 US

ULYSSES TRAVEL JOURNAL

☐ Ulysses Travel Journal .. $9.95 CAN
(Colours) $7.95 US

☐ Ulysses Travel Journal ... $14.95 CAN
80 Days $9.95 US

TITLE	QUANTITY	PRICE	TOTAL

Name	Sub-total	
Address	Postage & Handling	$4.00
....		
....	Sub-total	
Telephone		
Fax	G.S.T. in Canada 7%	
E-mail		
Payment : ☐ Money Order ☐ Visa ☐ MasterCard	TOTAL	
Card Number		
Expiry date		
Signature		

ULYSSES TRAVEL GUIDES
4176 St-Denis,
Montréal, Québec, H2W 2M5
(514) 843-9447 fax (514) 843-9448
Toll free: 1-877-542-7247
www.ulyssesguides.com
info@ulyssesguides.com